Crit Rudy Ruggles, Jr. 2004

WORKS ISSUED BY
THE HAKLUYT SOCIETY

———

THE MALASPINA EXPEDITION
1789–1794

VOLUME II
PANAMA TO THE PHILIPPINES

THIRD SERIES
NO. 11

THE HAKLUYT SOCIETY
Council and Officers 2003–2004

PRESIDENT
Professor Roy Bridges

VICE PRESIDENTS

Dr John Bockstoce
Stephen Easton
Mrs Ann Shirley

Sir Harold Smedley KCMG MBE
Mrs Sarah Tyacke CB
Professor Glyndwr Williams

COUNCIL (with date of election)

Captain M. K. Barritt RN (2003)
Dr Gloria C. Clifton (2002)
Dr Andrew S. Cook (2002)
Lt Cdr A. C. F. David RN (2002)
Professor Felipe Fernández-Armesto (2003)
Bruce Hunter (co-opted)
Dr James Kelly (2003)
Jonathan King (2003)
Professor Robin Law FBA (2003)
Professor Bruce P. Lenman (2001)

Mrs Margaret Makepeace (2003)
Carlos Novi (1999)
Anthony Payne (1999)
Michael J. Pollock (2001)
Paul Quarrie (1999)
Royal Geographical Society
   (Dr John H. Hemming CMG)
Dr Nigel Rigby (2002)
Dr Suzanne Schwarz (2001)
Dr John Smedley (co-opted)

TRUSTEES

Sir Geoffrey Ellerton CMG MBE
Dr John H. Hemming CMG

G. H. Webb CMG OBE
Professor Glyndwr Williams

HONORARY TREASURER
David Darbyshire FCA

HONORARY SECRETARIES AND SERIES EDITORS
Professor W. F. Ryan FBA
Warburg Institute, University of London, Woburn Square, London WC1H 0AB
Dr Michael Brennan
School of English, University of Leeds LS2 9JT

ADMINISTRATOR
Richard Bateman
(to whom queries and application for membership may be made)
Telephone: 0044 (0)1428 641 850   E-mail: office@hakluyt.com
Fax: 0044 (0)1428 641 933

Postal Address only
The Hakluyt Society, c/o Map Library, The British Library, 96 Euston Road,
London NW1 2DB
Web site: www.hakluyt.com

Registered Charity No. 313168   VAT No. GB 233 4481 77

INTERNATIONAL REPRESENTATIVES OF THE HAKLUYT SOCIETY

Australia:	Ms Maura O'Connor, Curator of Maps, National Library of Australia, Canberra, ACT 2601
Canada:	Dr Joyce Lorimer, Department of History, Wilfred Laurier University, Waterloo, Ontario, N2L 3C5
Germany:	Thomas Tack, Ziegelbergstr. 21, D-63739 Aschaffenburg
Japan:	Dr Derek Massarella, Faculty of Economics, Chuo University, Higashinakano 742–1, Hachioji-shi, Tokyo 192–03
New Zealand:	John C. Robson, Map Librarian, University of Waikato Library, Private Bag 3105, Hamilton
Portugal:	Dr Manuel Ramos, Av. Elias Garcia 187, 3Dt, 1050 Lisbon
Russia:	Professor Alexei V. Postnikov, Institute of the History of Science and Technology, Russian Academy of Sciences, 1/5 Staropanskii per., Moscow 103012
USA:	Dr Norman Fiering, The John Carter Brown Library, Box 1894, Providence, Rhode Island 02912 *and* Professor Norman Thrower, Department of Geography, UCLA, 405 Hilgard Avenue, Los Angeles, California 90024–1698

Plate 1. José Bustamante y Guerra in naval uniform. Anon. Museo Naval, Madrid

THE
MALASPINA EXPEDITION
1789-1794

Journal of the Voyage by
Alejandro Malaspina

VOLUME II
PANAMA TO THE PHILIPPINES

Edited by
ANDREW DAVID, FELIPE FERNANDEZ-ARMESTO,
CARLOS NOVI, GLYNDWR WILLIAMS

THE HAKLUYT SOCIETY, LONDON
in association with
THE MUSEO NAVAL, MADRID
2003

Published by The Hakluyt Society
c/o Map Library
The British Library, 96 Euston Road,
London NW1 2DB

SERIES EDITORS
W. F. RYAN
MICHAEL BRENNAN

© The Hakluyt Society 2003

ISBN 0 904180 81 6
ISSN 0072 9396

British Library Cataloguing-in-Publication Data
A catalogue record for this book is
available from the British Library

Typeset by Waveney Typesetters, Wymondham, Norfolk
Printed in Great Britain at
the University Press, Cambridge

MINISTERIO DE ASUNTOS EXTERIORES
DIRECCION GENERAL DE RELACIONES CULTURALES Y CIENTIFICAS

CONTRIBUTING EDITORS

W. R. P. Bourne
J. S. Cummins
Laurio Destéfani
Iris Engstrand
†Eduardo Estrella
Phyllis Herda
María Dolores Higueras Rodríguez

Robin Inglis
John Kendrick
Robert J. King
Manuel Lucena Giraldo
Jorge Ortiz Sotelo
Juan Pimentel Igea
Blanca Sáiz

CONTENTS

Illustrations and Maps	xi
Preface	xv
List of Equivalents and Abbreviations	xviii

Journal of the Voyage

BOOK FIVE
FROM CALLAO TO ACAPULCO *continued*

Chapter 5	From Panamá to Realejo	3
Chapter 6	At Realejo	25
Chapter 7	From Realejo to Acapulco	32
Chapter 8	At Acapulco	51

BOOK SIX
FROM ACAPULCO TO PORT MULGRAVE AND NOOTKA SOUND

Chapter 1	From Acapulco to Port Mulgrave	79
Chapter 2	At Port Mulgrave	107
Chapter 3	Port Mulgrave to Nootka Sound	138
Chapter 4	At Nootka Sound	169

BOOK SEVEN
FROM NOOTKA SOUND TO ACAPULCO

Chapter 1	From Nootka Sound to Monterey	191
Chapter 2	At Monterey	205
Chapter 3	From Monterey to Acapulco and visit by *Descubierta* to Isla Guadalupe and San Blas	213
Chapter 4	Return to Acapulco and preparations for crossing the Pacific	228

BOOK EIGHT
FROM ACAPULCO TO MANILA

Chapter 1	Acapulco to Guam	249

Chapter 2	At Guam	260
Chapter 3	From Guam to Port Palapag in the Philippines	269
Chapter 4	At Port Palapag	273
Chapter 5	From Port Palapag to Manila and at Sorsogon	281

BOOK NINE
AT MANILA AND THE SEPARATION OF THE CORVETTES

| Chapter 1 | Events in Manila Bay | 299 |

BOOK TEN
THE ISLAND OF LUZON AND *ATREVIDA*'S VISIT TO MACAU

Chapter 1	Survey of the coast of Ilocos by *Descubierta* and her return to Manila Bay	307
Chapter 2	Laying up *Descubierta* in Cavite and the survey of Manila Bay	315
Chapter 3	Bustamante's account of *Atrevida*'s visit to Macau and her return to Manila	328
Chapter 4	Viana's account of his survey of the coasts of Pangasinan, Ilocos and Cagayan	360
Chapter 5	The survey of the eastern coast of Luzon from Cape San Ildefonso to Rapu Rapu Island	373
Chapter 6	Neé's account of his journey from Sorsogon through the provinces of Albay, Camarines, Tayabas and Manila	389
Chapter 7	Haenke's account of his journey from Manila to Bangui, near Cape Bojeador	399
Chapter 8	An account of Pineda's journey to various provinces east and north of Manila and his death in Badoc	403
Appendix 1	The Malaspina–Valdés correspondence	417
Appendix 2	The Ferrer Maldonado fantasy	427
Appendix 3	Tova's account of his survey of the south coast of Luzon	487
Works Cited		501

ILLUSTRATIONS AND MAPS

1. José Bustamante y Guerra in naval uniform. Anon. Museo Naval, Madrid — *Frontispiece*

Text
2. View of Realejo and Volcán del Viejo, by José Cardero. Museo de América, Madrid — 24
3. Women of Realejo, by Felipe Bauzá. Museo de América, Madrid — 28
4. View of Acapulco, by Fernando Brambila. Museo Naval, Madrid — 50
5. Cock Fight in Acapulco, by Tomás de Suria. Museo Naval, Madrid — 58
6. Main Square, Mexico City, by Fernando Brambila. Museo Naval, Madrid — 60
7. Mexican Indians, by Felipe Bauzá. Museo de América, Madrid — 64
8. The state of the corvette's ships' companies in Acapulco, signed by Alejandro Malaspina, 30 April 1791. Courtesy of the Oregon Historical Society, Malaspina Papers, MS 2814/201 — 73
9. Port Mulgrave and the Indian (Tlingit) village, by José Cardero. Museo de América, Madrid — 108
10. Tlingit man and the Chief at Port Mulgrave, by José Cardero. Museo Naval, Madrid — 111
11. Tlingit woman and child, Port Mulgrave, by José Cardero. Museo de América, Madrid — 116
12. Tlingit Burial Ground at Port Mulgrave, by José Cardero. Museo Naval, Madrid — 120
13. Disenchantment Bay, by Juan Ravenet. Museo Naval, Madrid — 127
14. 'Plano del P^{to} del Desengaño trabajado a bordo de las corbetas de la Marina Real *Descubierta* y *Atrevida*, año 1791.' Museo Naval, Madrid. The line A–B depicts the edge of the fast ice. — 129
15. Confrontation at Port Mulgrave, by Tomás de Suria. Museo Naval, Madrid — 134
16. The Chief at Port Mulgrave making peace overtures. Anon. Museo de América, Madrid — 136
17. *Descubierta* and *Atrevida* at anchor off Mount St Elias, by Felipe Bauzá. Museo de América, Madrid — 157
18. View of the Spanish Establishment in Friendly Cove, by Fernando Brambila. Museo de América, Madrid — 168

19. 'Plano del Puerto de la Sta Cruz de Nutka llamado por los naturales de Yucuat, levantado por orden del rey en 1791.' Museo Naval, Madrid — 170
20. Maquinna, by Tomás de Suria. Museo Naval, Madrid — 173
21. Nootka Chief and his Wife, by José Cardero. Museo de América, Madrid — 177
22. Dance on the beach in Friendly Cove, Nootka, by Tomás de Suria. Museo Naval, Madrid — 181
23. 'Plano de los Canales interiores del Puerto de Nutzca examinado en los años de 90 y 91 por Dⁿ Francisco Eliza y Dⁿ Alexandro Malaspina.' Courtesy of H. P. Kraus, Inc. — 182
24. Presidio of Monterey, by José Cardero. Museo Naval, Madrid — 204
25. Misión del Carmelo at Monterey, by José Cardero. Museo Naval, Madrid — 207
26. Indian of Monterey, by Tomás de Suria? Museo Naval, Madrid — 210
27. 'The Port of Acapulco, on the coast of Mexico, from a Spanish Survey in 1791.' British Admiralty chart based on Malaspina's survey. Private collection — 229
28. The Waterfall at Querétaro (120 miles NW of Mexico City), by José Gutiérrez. Museo Naval, Madrid — 235
29. The anchorage of Umatac in the island of Guam, by Fernando Brambila. Museo Naval, Madrid — 261
30. Man of the Caroline Islands, by Juan Ravenet. Museo Naval, Madrid — 267
31. View of the port of Palapag in the island of Samar, by Fernando Brambila. Museo de América, Madrid — 277
32. 'Carta general del archipielago de Filipinas' (northern sheet, detail), showing the corvettes' track from San Bernardino Strait to Manila. UKHO, E939. Reproduced by permission of the Controller of Her Majesty's Stationery Office and the UK Hydrographic Office. — 282/3
33. View of Sorsogon in the island of Luzon, by Fernando Brambila. Museo Naval, Madrid — 285
34. View of Cavite and the city of Manila, by Fernando Brambila. Museo Naval, Madrid — 313
35. 'Plano del puerto de Cavite.' UKHO, E932. Reproduced by permission of the Controller of Her Majesty's Stationery Office and the UK Hydrographic Office. — 317
36. Manila Cathedral, by Fernando Brambila. Museo Naval, Madrid — 320
37. The *Descubierta* careened in the port of Cavite, detail from View of the port of Cavite and Manila Bay by Fernando Brambila. Whereabouts unknown — 321
38. Dwellings in the outskirts of Manila, by Fernando Brambila. Museo de América, Madrid — 322
39. *Negrillos* from the mountainous area around Manila Bay, by Juan Ravenet. Museo de América, Madrid — 324
40. View of Macau, by Fernando Brambila. Museo Naval, Madrid — 346
41. The death of Antonio Pineda, by Juan Ravenet. Museo Naval, Madrid — 411

Appendixes

42. Map of the world showing in the northern hemisphere Ferrer Maldonado's voyage, and in the southern hemisphere the shadowy outlines (T) of Quiros's discoveries of 1606. [1609/1781]   443
43. (a) Perspective view of the Strait of Anian from the north. [1609/1781]
    (b) Perspective view of the Strait of Anian from the south. [1609/1781]   445
44. Plan for fortifying the Strait. [1609/1781]   447

SKETCH MAPS

1. Panamá to Cabo San Lucas, December 1790 to May 1791, and Cabo San Lucas to Acapulco, October 1791   2
2. Cabo San Lucas to Vancouver Island, May to June 1791, and Vancouver Island to Cabo San Lucas, August to October 1791   78
3. Vancouver Island to Prince William Sound and return to Vancouver Island, June to August 1791   95
4. The Philippine Islands, March to December 1792   274
5. Luzon and the Visayan Islands, March to November 1792   306
6. The approaches to Macau, April 1792   335
7. Central Luzon, March to November 1792   486

PREFACE

This second volume of Alejandro Malaspina's journal covers the middle part of the voyage from 15 December 1790 to 15 November 1792. During the first months of this period Malaspina in the *Descubierta* and José Bustamante in the *Atrevida* continued to survey and investigate Spain's American territories as they sailed from Panama north along the Pacific coast of Central America. For the third time on the voyage they operated independently of each other, for Bustamante sailed ahead of Malaspina to San Blas, Spain's main naval base on the Mexican coast, while Malaspina called at Acapulco. From there he travelled to Mexico City to report to the Viceroy of New Spain, the Conde de Revillagigedo. This marked the end of the first stage of the voyage, in which the corvettes sailed along coasts ruled and settled by Spain. From the Mexican coast onwards the expedition would be venturing into little-known waters.

The original plan of the voyage (see Volume I of this edition, pp. 312–15) had rather optimistically envisaged the vessels sailing west from Acapulco across the Pacific to the Hawaiian Islands before exploring the Northwest Coast of America. After going as far as conditions would allow in those ice-bound waters, the corvettes would make for Kamchatka, and then call at Guangzhou [Canton] before turning south to the Philippines. All this was to be accomplished in nine months. By the time he reached Callao in September 1790, Malaspina had proposed a more realistic timetable in which the visit to Hawaii was to be postponed in favour of a voyage north to Alaska from San Blas, which the ships would leave in February 1791 (see Volume I of this edition, pp. 320–21). This, it was hoped, would determine whether the Strait of Anian allegedly found by Lorenzo Ferrer Maldonado in 1588, and described in a memorial of 1609 which was given to Malaspina shortly before his departure from Cádiz, actually existed. The order of events had been left to Malaspina's discretion, and the lateness of the *Descubierta*'s arrival at Acapulco in March, and the necessity of visiting the Viceroy in Mexico City, prompted yet another change of plan when Malaspina decided that his survey of the Hawaiian Islands should take precedence over exploration along the Alaskan coast. It was at this point that matters were taken out of his hands. On 22 December 1790 Antonio Valdés, Ministro de Marina, sent orders to Malaspina for the expedition to sail north to 'verify' the existence of the strait reported by Ferrer Maldonado. Enclosed with his letter was a copy of a memoir by the French geographer, Buache de la Neuville, in support of the supposed discovery of 1588 that had taken Ferrer Maldonado from the Atlantic to the Pacific, and back again.

There was a considerably irony in the fact that an expedition which consciously sought to represent Enlightenment science and scepticism should be sent on a wild-goose chase based on Ferrer Maldonado's preposterous claims. Malaspina's journal entries describing his unsuccessful search along the Alaskan coast for a passage, and the expedition's encounters with native peoples virtually unknown to Europeans, are supplemented by a series of documents printed in Appendix I and Appendix II. Appendix I contains the correspondence between Valdés and Malaspina about Ferrer Maldonado's alleged discovery. Appendix II contains the text of Ferrer Maldonado's 'Relation' of 1609, Buache de la Neuville's supportive memoir of 1790, and the critical responses of Bustamante, Malaspina and Juan Bautista Muñoz. Some of these documents appear here in print for the first time; none except the text of the 'Relation' of 1609 has been published in English before. Together they form the concluding chapter in the long Spanish search for the rumoured strait north of New Spain, and will be of particular interest to readers familiar with the British quest for a strait between the Atlantic and Pacific oceans, the Northwest Passage.

From Alaska the corvettes sailed south to Nootka Sound, flashpoint of the diplomatic crisis the previous year that had almost led to war between Spain and Britain, and from there to Monterey, San Blas and Acapulco. In late December 1791 the vessels left Acapulco and headed out into the Pacific for the long oceanic crossing to the Philippines by way of Guam. Malaspina spent nine months in the Philippines, while Bustamante in the *Atrevida* visited Macau to carry out gravitational observations. Malaspina's time was spent in making coastal surveys, while his naturalists – Pineda, Haenke, and Neé – left on inland excursions to make observations and collect specimens. Malaspina incorporated their reports into his journal, and they are printed here. Tova Arredondo also journeyed into the interior of Luzon, and although Malaspina did not include his report in his journal, its interest is such that we have printed it as Appendix III. The expedition's stay at Mindanao, its track across the South Pacific, with visits to Port Jackson and Vava'u, and the return voyage along the coasts of South America, will be covered in the final volume of this edition. That will also contain a full bibliography and a cumulative index.

Our debt, financial and otherwise, to those who helped us both with this edition in general and with Volume I in particular was acknowledged in the Foreword and Preface to that volume (pp. xvi, xviii–xix). Here we would both like to repeat our thanks to the individuals and institutions listed there, and to mention those who have given us special assistance with Volume II. We are grateful for a generous donation from Elizabeth Crownhart-Vaughan and Thomas Vaughan CBE, which they have made in memory of Helen Wallis OBE and Admiral Sir Charles Madden Bt, GCB. The translation of Malaspina's text was undertaken by Sylvia Jamieson, with Philip Grundy's help. As in the first volume of this edition the translation has been of Malaspina's holograph journal, published under the editorship of Ricardo Cerezo Martínez, *La expedición Malaspina 1789–1794. Tomo II: Diario general del viaje por Alejandro Malaspina*, Madrid, 1990, although the printed text has again been checked against the manuscript originals in the Museo Naval, Madrid: AMN MS 610, 423, 92. For the difficulties involved in translating Malaspina, which have not lessened as this edition has progressed, we would refer new readers to Carlos Novi's essay in Volume I of this edition, pp. xxiii–xxviii. Our Contributing Editors have continued to lend assistance both with the annotations and in other ways, but among them we should like to pay particular tribute to Robin Inglis, who, with help from Iris Engstrand and Donald C. Cutter (who wrote the Introduction to this edition in Volume I, pp. xxix–lxxvii), provided many of the annotations to the Northwest Coast section; and to J. S. Cummins, who undertook many of the annotations for the long section on the Philippines. The Oregon Historical Society kindly supplied a print of the crew list drawn up and signed by Malaspina at Acapulco in April 1791. We are grateful to Sir James Watt for solving problems concerning the fevers encountered in Acapulco, and to Adrian Webb and Sharon Nichol of the United Kingdom Hydrographic Office for help with charts. As before, the many annotations on hydrography and astronomy have been the responsibility of Andrew David.

In Spain archivists and librarians have continued to help us at every stage. The Real Academia de la Historia, Madrid, through its Librarian, María Victoria Alberola, gave permission to use two important documents, included here in translation as Documents 1 and 5 of Appendix II. The staff of the Biblioteca del Palacio Real (Director María Luisa López Vidriero), helped our searches for documents in the Ayala Colección. Francisco Gallo at the Sección Nobleza of the Archivo Histórico Nacional, Toledo, where the archives of the Casa Ducal del Infantado are now kept, confirmed that the original manuscript of Ferrer Maldonado's account was no longer in the ducal library when its holdings were purchased by the Spanish state. At the Archivo General de Indias, Seville, the Deputy Director, María Antonia Colomar Albajar, and the Head of Reference, Pilar Lázaro, gave much personal guidance on the puzzling matter of the location of the ministerial archives of the Indies Department at the time of the Malaspina expedition, and on the creation of the Archivo General de Indias. At the Museo de América, Madrid (Director Paz Cabello), we are indebted to Luisa Ferrer Garcés for supplying reproductions of paintings and drawings from the museum's superb collection. Finally, we should like once more to express our appreciation of the collaboration of the Museo Naval, Madrid (Director Almirante Fernando Riaño Lozano), where María Dolores Higueras Rodríguez (Directora Técnica), and her staff have responded generously to our many demands on their time and patience. We are especially grateful for reproductions of the many paintings, drawings and charts held at the Museo Naval which appear in this volume. Together with those from the Museo de América, they have enabled us once again to illustrate the work of the fine artists who sailed on the Malaspina expedition.

Andrew David
Felipe Fernández-Armesto
Carlos Novi
Glyndwr Williams

EQUIVALENTS AND ABBREVIATIONS

SPANISH NAVAL RANKS

Ranks in the *Real Armada* correspond with those in the eighteenth-century British Royal Navy as follows:

Capitán General	Admiral
Teniente General	Vice Admiral
Jefe de Escuadra	Rear Admiral
Brigadier de Real Armada	Commodore
Capitán de navío	Post Captain
Capitán de fragata	Commander
Teniente de navío	Senior Lieutenant
Teniente de fragata	Junior Lieutenant
Alférez de navío	No exact equivalent
Alférez de fragata	No exact equivalent
Contador de fragata	Junior Paymaster and Purser
Capellán	Chaplain
Cirujano	Surgeon
Guardiamarina	Midshipman
Práctico	Pilot
Cartógrafo	Cartographer
Piloto	Master
Segundo piloto	Second master
Pilotín	Master's mate
Director de historia natural	Director of natural history
Botánico	Botanist
Pintor	Artist
Dibujante	Draughtsman
Guardián	Quartermaster

EQUIVALENTS AND ABBREVIATIONS

ABBREVIATIONS

AGI	Archivo General de Indias, Sevilla
AMN	Archivo del Museo Naval, Madrid
AMNCN	Archivo del Museo Nacional de Ciencias Naturales, Madrid
ARJB	Archivo del Real Jardín Botánico, Madrid
UKHO	United Kingdom Hydrographic Office, Taunton

WEIGHTS AND MEASURES

Spanish terms which have a direct English equivalent have been translated into English; terms for which there does not appear to be a direct equivalent have not been translated.

Spanish terms which have been translated into English

braza	5·48 feet = one fathom
cable	one-tenth of a sea mile = one cable
cuartillo	0·9 pints = one pint
legua	three sea miles = one league
milla	the internationally accepted unit of distance at sea, one-sixtieth of a degree of latitude = one [sea or nautical] mile
nudo	the internationally accepted unit of speed at sea of one sea mile an hour = one knot
pie	0·91 feet = one foot
pulgada	0·91 of an inch = one inch
línea	one-twelfth of a *pulgada* = one line (an obsolete English term for one-twelfth of an inch)

Spanish terms which have not been translated

arroba	approximately 25 lbs
codo	18 to 22 inches
toesa	approximately 6·4 feet – the French *toise*
quintal	approximately 102 lbs
vara	approximately 3 feet

18TH-CENTURY SPANISH COMPASS DIRECTIONS AND ENGLISH EQUIVALENTS

Spanish	English	Spanish	English
N¼NE	NbyE	S¼SW	SbyW
NE¼N	NEbyN	SW¼S	SWbyS
NE¼E	NEbyE	SW¼W	SWbyW
E¼NE	EbyN	W¼SW	WbyS
E¼SE	EbyS	W¼NW	WbyN
SE¼E	SEbyE	NW¼W	NWbyW
SE¼S	SEbyS	NW¼N	NWbyN
S¼SE	SbyE	N¼NW	NbyW

SPANISH-ENGLISH GLOSSARY OF GEOGRAPHICAL TERMS USED IN THIS WORK

Spanish word	English meaning	Spanish word	English meaning
alto(s)	height/heights	golfo	gulf
archipiélago	archipelago	isla	island
arena	sand	islote/islita	small island, islet
arrecife	reef	lengua	tongue
arroyo	stream	monte	mountain
bahía	bay	morro	headland, bluff
bajo	shoal	morrito	small headland
banco	bank	pájaro	bird
batería	battery	nuevo/a	new
boca	mouth	pan de azúcar	sugar loaf
bodega	warehouse	piedra	rock, stone
cabo	cape	playa	beach
caleta	cove	península	peninsula
camino	road	promontorio	promontory, headland
canal	channel	pueblo	town, village
casa	house	puerto	port
castillo	castle	punta	point
cerro	hill	quebrada	gorge, ravine
cerrillo, cerrito	small hill, hillock	río	river
cordillera	mountain range, especially the Andes	roca	rock
		sierra	mountain range
ciudad	city	silla	saddle
ciudadela	citadel	teta	nipple, pap, breast
ensenada	bay	tierra	land
estrecho	strait	torre	tower
estero	creek, inlet	vigía	lookout
farallón	small needle-shaped rock	volcán	volcano

BOOK FIVE

From Callao to Acapulco

continued

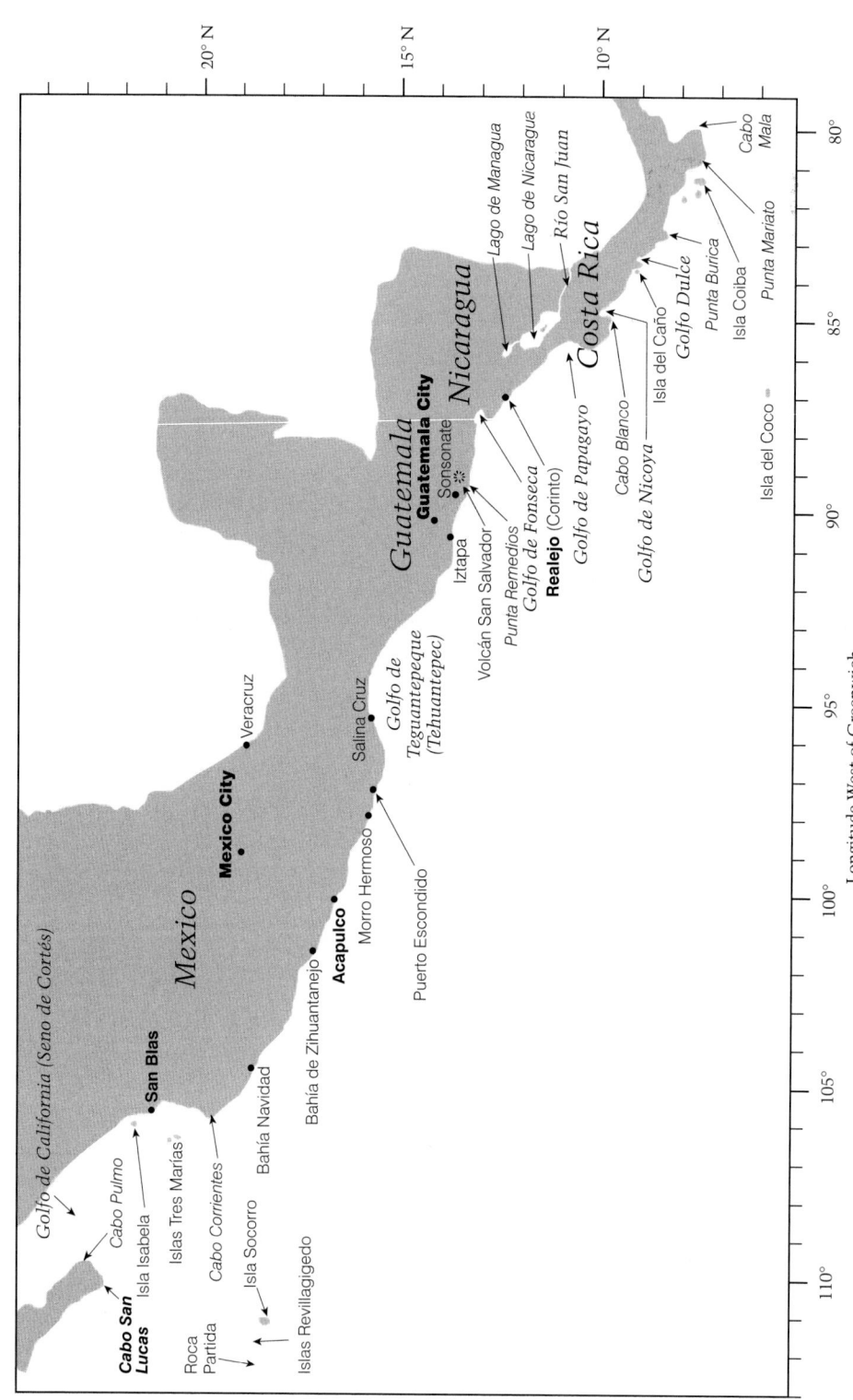

Fig. 1. Panamá to Cabo San Lucas, December 1790 to May 1791, and Cabo San Lucas to Acapulco, October 1791

CHAPTER 5

From Panamá to Realejo

15 December 1790
At dawn, the following day, we set to work with a will to hoist the boats, a task prolonged by the considerable weight of the launch. Finally, towards seven o'clock, we set sail for Islas Otoque[1] under topsails and topgallants and later under full sail. At first we sounded twenty and twenty-five fathoms, ooze, but we soon obtained greater depths of forty fathoms when, with the aim of avoiding the shoal surveyed on the previous days, we set a course to pass three cables off the [eastern] extremity of Isla Urava.[2] Our observed longitude at ten-thirty, on the meridian of Islote de Otoque,[3] was [blank] and the latitude by meridian altitudes of the Sun was [blank].[4]

As the weather remained very clear with a fresh breeze from NW and WNW, we were assured of good progress in our survey, which would enable us to extend it from Punta Chamé,[5] by way of the inner part of the bay[6] to the vicinity of Punta [Cabo] Mala. At sunset this point bore approximately SW[7] and our soundings, some two or three leagues offshore, having remained all afternoon at eighteen to twenty fathoms, black sand, had increased to twenty-nine and thirty-five fathoms. At the end of the day, having finished our work, we steered ESE so as to give ourselves more sea room for our run the following day. Twice during this afternoon we had taken the precaution of observing longitudes at suitable places and intervals.

The bay, lying between Punta Chamé and Punta Mala, is named Parita on our national charts, but it extends much further inland than these indicate. On the other hand, it is considerably less deeply indented than shown on Jefferys's English chart under the name Golfo de Natá.[8] Its coastline is undulating rather than flat and there are several lofty ranges inland of which the westernmost is easily distinguished by four

---

[1] A group of islands consisting of Isla Otoque, Isla Estiva, Isla Boná and Roca Redonda.
[2] A small island close SE of Isla Taboga.
[3] Possibly Isla Boná, the southern island of the group.
[4] For Malaspina's survey methods see Vol. I of this edition, pp. 325-7.
[5] Situated 6 miles WNW of Isla de Otoque.
[6] Bahía Parita on the western side of Golfo de Panamá.
[7] SE in the MS journal, which is clearly in error.
[8] Thomas Jefferys (d. 1771) publisher of numerous charts and maps. The chart was possibly 'An Accurate Map of North America ... by Eman Bowen Geog^r to His Majesty and John Gibson Engraver' in 2 sheets. Printed for Robert Sayer ... 2^d June 1775, in Robert Sayer and John Bennett, *The American Atlas ... by the Late Thomas Jefferys*, London, 1776, on which Bahía Parita is named Nata Bay.

fairly high peaks. Islote de Chirú is in the middle of the bay[1] and, if our soundings and what we could see are to be believed, there is no danger extending far enough offshore to be feared.

But when we examined the above mentioned charts we were unable to reconcile them with the extremities we had in sight. We were therefore apprehensive of a considerable discrepancy both in our survey the following day and in our run that night. Accordingly we thought it wiser to sail only as far east as was necessary to give ourselves sea room and then to close the coast the following day to examine it in safety. Therefore, at ten o'clock at night, in a depth of thirty-five fathoms, we hove-to on the port tack under topsails, with the breeze continuing strong from NNW and with a fairly choppy sea.

16 December

As dawn approached the wind began to drop and at first light we could see Isla Iguana[2] and Punta Mala very close. We made a short tack to the east and then immediately bore away under full sail to make as much use as possible of the breeze, which was still fresh from the north, first passing Isla Iguana at a distance of one-and-a-half leagues, and then passing two leagues off Punta Mala. At that distance it was not easy to identify those dreaded shoals said to extend two or three leagues offshore in our sailing directions, apart from what we could see extending three or four cables either side of the point.

As the Sun rose above the horizon the breeze became still more favourable and, in depths of thirty and thirty-five fathoms, black sand, we continued surveying Punta de la Higuera[3] and the two islets commonly known as Los Frailes.[4] These islets are treeless, and lie some three leagues offshore. The coast, everywhere thickly forested, rises considerably towards Punta de la Higuera, terminating at a much greater height at Morro Puercos[5] and its adjacent coast to the west, which finally joins the moderately elevated Punta Mariato, near the much praised Islas Quibo.[6]

At noon Morro Puercos, probably the southernmost point that we would encounter on our passage to Realejo, bore WbyN by compass distant four leagues, when our latitude was 7°9′21″. Morro Puercos, or Punta de la Higuera, may be considered the western extremity of the great bight of Panamá, the eastern extremity

---

[1] Farallón de Chirú, about 1 mile offshore, on the north side of Bahía Parita.
[2] Situated 9 miles north of Punta Mala.
[3] Not identified.
[4] Frailes del Norte and Frailes del Sur, 10 miles SW of Punta Mala.
[5] About midway between Punta Mala and Punta Mariato.
[6] An alternative name for Isla Coiba, 46 miles WNW of Punta Mariato; Malaspina uses both names indiscriminately. It is not certain whose praise Malaspina had in mind. It was a favoured wooding and watering place of the buccaneers. Dampier, who visited the island in June and July 1685, described it as being 'all over plentifully stored with great tall flourishing Trees of many sorts; and there is good Water on the East and North East sides of the Island.': John Masefield, ed., *The Voyages of Captain William Dampier*, 2 vols, New York, 1906, I, p. 232. Anson (who is mentioned by Malaspina in his next day's journal entry), spent nine days at Quibo in December 1741. The official account of his voyage described it as 'extremely convenient for wooding and watering … the soil to be extremely rich … [with] prodigious quantity of turtle.': Glyndwr Williams, *A Voyage round the World in the Years MDCCXL, I, II, II, IV by George Anson*, Oxford, 1974, pp. 201–5.

being Cabo Corrientes, whose shores and face had appeared to be as steep as those now in view. At a distance of two or three leagues we obtained no bottom on either side [of the headland] with one hundred fathoms of line.

At three in the afternoon, when we were just abreast of Morro Puercos, the favourable northerly breeze abandoned us and was followed by light, variable airs from west and WSW, obliging us to haul our wind on the starboard tack. At nightfall these gave way to such a complete calm that we lost all steerage way for many hours.

17 December

The following morning in particular we had several fairly strong gusts from north and NE, but each time our hopes were immediately dashed, so that noon found us in almost the same position as at nightfall on the previous day. We did, however, make use of the extremely clear and pleasant weather to repeat our observations to determine variation, which usually gave a result of 7° or 8°NE by both azimuths and amplitudes.

During this day we compared our chronometers with those of the *Atrevida* by means of pistol shots. The only discrepancy was of 5″ in number 10, our chronometers having already been corrected by the daily equations.

It was not until nightfall that the strong northerly breeze set in again, when we immediately altered course to WNW, close hauled, to close Punta Mariato and the nearby islands, the survey of which had to be considered of the greatest importance. Having been a stopping place for many freebooters and later for Commodore Anson,[1] they had become the subject of constant plans for settlement by rival nations and the cause of a certain apprehension in our own when war or private interests brought other nations to the Pacific Ocean.

With this in mind, and with the breeze freshening still further towards eight in the evening, we furled the small sails. At eleven we also had to strike the topsails, with the object of making as little leeway as possible from our present position, which seemed the most suitable spot from which to begin our survey the following day. The sacrifice of so clear a night and of a favourable and splendid strong breeze after a fairly lengthy calm could not but cause a certain surprise and perhaps gratitude in those who, knowing the sailor's lot and the fact that our circumstances did not allow for any delay, were also aware of the frequency of calms and the scarcity of favourable winds.

18 December

At dawn the next day – as clear and pleasant as the previous ones – a truly pleasing prospect was spread before our gaze. In the distance, to the west, we could see the high sierras near Morro Puercos. Puntas Mariato and Las Filipinas[2] showed as well, as

---

[1] Anson passed Punta Mariato, without stopping, two days before anchoring off Quibo. George Anson (1697-1762) led a British expedition to the Pacific Ocean, 1740-44, during the war of Jenkins's Ear to harry Spanish shipping and ports on the west coasts of South America and in the Philippines, where he successfully intercepted a galleon from Acapulco. Although his voyage was ravaged by scurvy and resulted in no new geographical discoveries, it did suggest that Spain could be successfully challenged in the Pacific and that in this ocean lay the enticing prospect of future expansion for Britain's imperial and commercial interests.

[2] Punta Jabalí, the eastern entrance point of Bahía Honda, 48 miles NW of Punta Mariato.

did Ensenada del Montijo[1] and some islands lying half way across its mouth.[2] Islas Coiba and Quicara,[3] stretching out to the NW and WSW, added to the beauty of the scene and, lastly, the breeze, still steady and strong, promised a rapid and accurate performance of this day's work.

We immediately hoisted all sail and steering NWbyW, close hauled, began to measure bases, which we later linked to our longitude observations when the Sun was higher. We set a course for the southern[4] extremity of Coiba and, at about nine o'clock, when very close to the anchorage off the island, we bore away to examine it closely, altering course to SSW to pass barely a league from the SE extremity of the island, where we sounded thirty-five fathoms, fine sand, observing that the shoal indicated by Anson[5] is much closer to the coast than previous accounts appeared to indicate.

At first sight it seemed better to take the channel between the mainland and the NW extremity of Quibo [Coiba], both because it would make the survey of the following stretch of coast much easier and because the weather and our position seemed to encourage us to take that passage, which, furthermore, appeared clear and free of dangers. However, considering that Islas Coiba and Quicara had been, and would be again, a lure for those who might visit these waters under flags other than ours, and somewhat apprehensive of the calms that might leave us at the mercy of the currents, setting us onto the coast and adjacent islets, we chose, in the end, to coast Isla Quicara and the nearby islet[6] at close range and pass to the south of all the islands.

The breeze continued fair throughout the morning as we steered SSW with the wind astern. Very soon, having passed the SE point of Quibo [Coiba], we found ourselves out of soundings, obtaining no bottom with sixty fathoms of line. At noon the southernmost islet bore N74°W, two miles distant, in latitude 7°10′, when we obtained no bottom with one hundred fathoms of line.

Soon after the Sun had passed the meridian the breeze fell, causing us some anxiety just when we were only a mile south of the islet. We tried to make use of a few light airs, seeing fortunately, while we were losing steerage way, the swell was setting us somewhat to the SE. This, however, was also bringing the *Atrevida* too close to us, so at half past four we had to resort to taking a tow from the pinnaces to separate us a little. At sunset [Isla] Montuosa[7] was in sight bearing N58°W, six leagues distant. At the same time we were about a league off the southern islet, while the extremities of Quicara and Quibo [Coiba] bore NbyW to NNE.

19 December

The night was calm, and as clear as the previous ones. We steered west to make use of a few light puffs of air from the east, and at dawn Montuosa bore N40°W, three or

---

[1] Bahía Montijo.
[2] The largest being Isla Cebaco, 24 miles NW of Punta Mariato.
[3] Isla Jicarón, 3½ miles SW of Isla Coiba.
[4] N in the MS journal, which is clearly in error.
[5] 'a shoal which stretches off about two miles from the South point of the Island': Williams, *Anson's Voyage round the World*, p. 199.
[6] Isla Jicarita off the southern extremity of Isla Jicarón.
[7] Situated 21 miles west of Isla Coiba.

four leagues distant. Even under full sail to make use of the light airs from the NE, we made very little progress during the morning, and by noon we had hardly made more than two-and-a-half leagues towards the island. At two o'clock in the afternoon, however, a moderate sea breeze set in from south, with which we did not hesitate to alter course to the north, passing east of Montuosa with the intention of examining that stretch of the mainland coast and making better use of the land breeze which we were almost sure of having during the coming night.

At eight o'clock that night Montuosa bore west, one league distant, and as the wind had dropped considerably we attempted to steer a westerly[1] course to make use of the land breeze, but we were thwarted by a flat calm, in which we were set to the east by the current. Dawn found us scarcely two leagues from the NW tip of Quibo [Coiba], [20th] from which the corvettes managed to get clear, using every breath of air, although hardly perceptible and generally very variable. Nonetheless, we could not consider our time entirely wasted, because the great clarity of the horizon gave us a background view of more features of the mainland coast, which seemed to be low and scattered with hummocks and a few islands. We were also able to make a more detailed survey of the western coast of Quibo [Coiba] and observe a meridian altitude precisely on the parallel of Montuosa, obtaining a latitude of 7°27′.

The light sea breeze was not noticeable until two in the afternoon, when we immediately altered course to WNW, passing to the north of Montuosa again. As we approached it (the sea breeze towards the late afternoon giving us a speed of three knots), we saw that it was luxuriantly forested. A league NNE of its centre we obtained no bottom with seventy fathoms of line. In approximately this position the breeze dropped and the current began to set us towards the east, but fortunately at eleven at night a fresh land breeze set in from the north and, close hauled under the courses and topsails, making five or six knots, we finally got well clear of the island.

At half past three in the morning we saw, by the brilliant light of the Moon, the two Islas Ladrones[2] to the north, three leagues distant. These gave us a mark for the accurate plotting of the islets adjacent to Punta Burica which were too important for us to consider passing. Accordingly, although the breeze continued fair and fresh, we lay to on the NW tack with the courses and topsails lowered, waiting eagerly for the dawn to reveal to us a most interesting scene.

21 December
Indeed, our hopes were not in vain, as apart from the two islets mentioned above, we saw other islands further inshore, Punta Burica, the entrance points of Golfo Dulce, Isla del Caño[3] and Volcán Barú,[4] not usually to be seen clearly because of thick cloud cover (according to the pilots). At the same time we could see the summits of Montuosa, Quibo[Coiba] and Burica, and hence it was easy to link together with some certainty all of this somewhat complicated stretch of coast.

However, as if to ensure that we were to suffer the same vexations today as on

---

[1] E = east in the MS journal, which is clearly an error for O = west.
[2] Situated 26 miles ESE of Punta Burica.
[3] A steep-to wooded island, 10 miles offshore and 70 miles NW of Punta Burica.
[4] Situated about 50 miles NE of Punta Burica.

previous ones, the wind dropped almost as soon as the Sun rose and once again we were left to the mercy of the calms and currents. Our latitude at noon was 7°45′.

Towards two in the afternoon light airs from SW began to get up and with these we steered WNW, close hauled. By sunset, as we had the advantage at the time of a fairly strong current setting NW, we were only some five leagues from Isla del Caño, whose southern extremity bore N70°W.

In order to make some way against the current during the following night we thought it best to alter course to the south at nightfall, particularly as the heavy cloud cover we could see inshore and the proximity of the full Moon led us to hope for a land breeze during the night, even though it could bring squalls.

This proved to be correct. At ten o'clock that night, during a heavy downpour, the wind shifted to the NW with a few gusts, which, while obliging us to shorten sail, seemed to promise better conditions in the coming hours. Despite this, and the fact that it continued drizzling until midnight, this hope was to be thwarted. We had to continue close hauled to the SW and SSW with very light airs from west and WNW and, with the current setting so hard against us, we found ourselves at dawn much closer to Montuosa, bearing east four leagues distant. Isla del Caño was only just visible to the NW and the Ladrones to the north, and it was not easy to make out the land behind Golfo Dulce and Punta Burica.

22 December

From this day until the 24th it might be said that we were in a state of continuous inactivity, although we worked ceaselessly, day and night, to profit from any breath of wind in the third or fourth quadrant. Dusk and dawn found us still within sight of Montuosa, a few hours of calm and a contrary SE current, especially at night, being enough to undo all that we had gained in as many hours. The extremely clear and beautiful skies by day and by night, and the delightful brilliance of the Moon itself, seemed almost to mock our eagerness to make too early use of the season. Variation remained constant at 8°NE and our latitude was 7°21′.

To some extent, however, to offset the considerable delays caused by this inactivity, new and curious objects of interest to our natural history research were found among the almost countless schools of fish that surrounded the corvette. These at times presented an agreeable spectacle with the fish suddenly leaping, startled, from the sea, which appeared to be boiling. Various dorado,[1] tuna and bonito were caught, either with fizgigs or hooks. We also saw a manta ray with three fish,[2] each a *codo* in length, clinging to it. A fight between a blue shark and a turtle and the instant destruction by two blue sharks of a bonito wounded by our fizgigs, offered new and interesting sights. Finally we managed to catch a striped fish which our naturalists found to be of an amphibious class of the Balistes,[3] similar to the Guapervas of Brazil described by Linnaeus.

[1] Also known as the dolphin, a strong, speedy and predatory fish, with a marked preference for flying fish.
[2] Presumably remoras or sucking fish.
[3] Generally known as file-fish on account of the strong first spine of the dorsal fin, which is roughed in front like a file.

The different and multiple combinations of the molluscs had also been an object worthy of new and repeated study for Don Antonio Pineda, and among the birds we caught alive two boobies and a species of tern or sea-swallow.[1]

24 December

At last, on the morning of the 24th with a few hours of a gentle NE breeze we lost sight of Montuosa and in the afternoon, despite our low latitude, we sighted Isla del Caño again and the nearby coast leading to Ensenada [Golfo] de Nicoya. The lack of breeze prevented us from getting to within five leagues of it [the coast] during the rest of the day's run. [25th] At noon the following day the island bore N18°[W] and the extremities of the land in sight from N15°[W] to N30°[E] by compass, distant six or eight leagues, our latitude at the time being 7°38′ and our longitude 3°26′ west of Panamá by the chronometers.

At noon we compared these for the third time with those of the *Atrevida* and it was with great satisfaction that we saw the differences to be scarcely perceptible. In consequence the longitudes of various points on the coast, which we assigned each day, were all the more certain.

For a proper celebration of Christmas for our officers, seamen and marines, we did not forget that it was usually marked ashore with some extra provisions at table. So we took care not only to include some pickled cabbage and a pint and a half of wine to the daily rations, but also to add some flour, sugar and fresh meat from our stores to give some semblance of tradition and provide variety and pleasure to the palate and, of course, to raise their spirits and encourage their affection for the Service.

We now considered our passage along this stretch of the coast as to be almost complete, expecting to have either a few hours of moderate sea breeze or the land breeze with us for a time early the next morning. In the afternoon we had, as well, some recompense for our recent delays with the sight of Isla del Caño at closer range and the next stretch of mainland coast running westward, which was generally quite high in the middle and ending further on in a fairly low, wooded point, which appeared to extend towards Farallones de Quipo.[2] Before nightfall, however, we were left in no doubt that our hopes were not to be fulfilled so soon, although they had seemed to be founded on a high degree of probability. As the breeze slackened still further and shifted to the west, bearings taken to the coast and the comparison of longitude by the chronometers with that of the morning indicated a current setting east at about one-and-a-half knots. We immediately altered course to the south to see if we might overcome its effects, entirely or partially, by standing offshore.[3] A calm during the night rendered this precaution almost useless, so that at dawn on the following day Isla del Caño and the adjacent coast could hardly be seen from the

---

[1] Brown Boobies (*Sula leucogaster*), Masked Boobies (*Sula dactylatra*), Red-footed Boobies (*Sula sula*), Sooty Terns (*Sterna fuscata*) and Brown-winged Terns (*Sterna anaethetus*) are encountered in these waters.

[2] Charted 19 miles NNW of Isla del Caño on 'Carta esférica desde el Golfo Dulce … hasta Sⁿ Blas … construida con las observaciones executadas en las corvetas Descubierta y Atrevida', Madrid, 1822.

[3] Between Punta Mariato and Punta Burica an easterly set will usually be experienced within 20 miles of the coast due to the influence of the Equatorial Counter-Current.

masthead, while not far off, bearing EbyN by compass, was the all too familiar sight of Isla Montuosa.

26 December
Once again we set to work to overcome the almost imperceptible and continually varying airs, or rather, to use them to struggle against the contrary current. At times we made progress and at others we lost much ground, but every day at dawn the first and usually the only object in sight was Isla Montuosa, which we saw from NE to the ENE according to the southerly set of the current. Fortunately the fish did not abandon us and at times their numbers, either as hunters or prey, or their usefulness for food or their novelty to natural history, soothed or distracted the natural irritation at finding ourselves in the same position for so many days.

The dorado and sharks were easily taken by hook. We had to lie in wait with the fizgigs to catch the bonito, one of which Don Antonio Pineda examined in great anatomical detail. We also saw some turtles, a few whales and flying fish, a swordfish and an infinite number of small fish which followed the corvette at a short distance.

28 December
Only at dawn on the 28th, helped by a SE squall with fairly heavy rain, were we able to lose sight of Montuosa and approach Isla del Caño, which at noon bore N20°W, eight leagues distant. We would now have preferred to steer a more westerly course so as to stand further offshore and lessen the effect of the adverse currents. The calms and the very light sea breezes at noon did not allow us to make any progress on this day or the following one, so that at dawn on the 30th we thought Montuosa would be in sight for the third time, as, due to a flat calm throughout the previous night, we were without steerage way and entirely at the mercy of the currents.

30 December
However, we had not lost as much ground as we had feared, even though a point on the coast which bore NNW at nightfall now bore N30°W and we had lost some three or four leagues to the south. When a moderate breeze set in at nine o'clock from NW and WNW, enabling us to steer close hauled under full sail in the third quadrant in company with the *Atrevida*, these losses seemed of little importance and easily to be made up, should we enjoy the alternating land and sea breezes that this favourable change seemed to promise.

During this period we had taken care to protect the crews of both corvettes from the direct and very harmful Sun, spreading awnings above the deck from sunrise to sunset, washing the decks with vinegar and allowing nobody to stand still in the Sun, even for fishing, and adding half a pint of wine to the daily rations. With these precautions, particularly the good fortune that the calms were not accompanied by frequent downpours, as often happens, we were able not only to prevent the spread of fevers, already affecting both crews because of the excessive heat of Panamá, but even to eradicate them entirely. The number of sick had reached thirteen on board one corvette and fourteen on board the other. One of the seamen on board the *Atrevida*, suffering from complications to this illness with a rupture of blood vessels caused by the violent recoil of a musket onto his chest, which he had concealed from the surgeon until the last moment, was unfortunately beyond reach of our remedies and on the afternoon of the 28th he made the final sacrifice to Nature.

Don Francisco Flores knew from the start that the illness from which various men on board the *Descubierta* (and among others Alferez de Fragata Don Felipe Bauzá) were suffering were synochal fevers,[1] either simple or putrid, all marked by an excess of blood and a bilious humour, the former no doubt arising from the effects of the Sun and the latter from eating too much, particularly bananas and other unripe fruit. In some cases this was complicated by malignancy, but, when treated with quinine and, usually, with bleeding, antimonials and vegetable acids, these were soon completely eliminated, although followed by a considerable weakness during convalescence, which was difficult to treat at sea. Particular mention should be made here of the antimonial mixture to bring on vomiting and the expulsion of bilious matter, and the use of rosella[2] for the convalescents, both proposed by Doctor Masdevall[3] and now used with great success by Dr Francisco Flores. The Fahrenheit thermometer, which was now set up on deck in the shade, frequently reached 90°.

31 December

Although the calm continued throughout the next day, we did not lose ground according to the bearings taken on Isla del Caño and the westernmost part of the coast. As the set of the current was at this time to the south rather than to the east, we did, however, lose much of the estimated latitude that we had been able to gain by dint of constant work, and thus we found ourselves once again in latitude 7°28′.

The last day of the year finally saw an end to the greater part, at least, of the trials of a fortnight's calm, which doubtless would have deserved a description by the eloquent narrator of Lord Anson's voyage, who had most vividly depicted the difficulties of a successful passage to Acapulco with a delay of just five days in sight of Isla del Coco.

At nightfall light airs from ESE and ENE began to set in, with a fairly heavy sea from the same quarter, and as the currents were now in our favour rather than against us, steering WNW we could make use of the favourable short swell. In the morning, at last, Punta Burica bore N20°E and we were in sight of the new stretch of the coast that we had so long desired to see.

1 January 1791

This was, to the best of our knowledge (given that it seemed impossible to reconcile what we saw with [what was depicted on] the charts with any probability), the stretch of coast on Jefferys' chart that runs from Isla del Caño and Punta Mala[4] towards

---

[1] Unremitting fevers.
[2] The Red or Indian Sorell (*Hibiscus sabdariffa*), the seeds of which are used medicinally; also the Catalan name for a species of poppy (*Papaver rhoeas*), from which Masdevall, as a Catalan, may have derived a medicine.
[3] See Vol. I of this edition, p. 25, n. 1.
[4] Charted 20 miles NW of the western entrance to Golfo Dulce on 'Carta esférica desde el Golfo Dulce ... hasta Sⁿ Blas ...', probably Punta Llorona, charted 28 miles WNW of the same point on British Admiralty chart 2145.

Puerto del Inglés.[1] The land was generally quite high and opened into a bay of considerable size, the extremities of which were barely visible, not so much because of the distance that it receded,[2] but because it was surrounded by low ground, with higher land behind that was hard to make out.

To these sights, most delightful in themselves, and to the very calm and sunny day was added a new and pleasing spectacle with the capture of a large number of excellent dorado. Lured by the flesh of some tuna caught beforehand and remaining gathered around the stern with a constancy uncommon in this species, they fell easily to one or another of the many hooks before them. Being so easily caught, there was a risk of their very weight breaking the hook, as frequently happened, or of them freeing themselves by their violent struggles before they could be landed on deck, so this struggle sometimes ended in escape, making the fishing more entertaining and interesting.

We continued to make progress during the afternoon and night, although very slowly. The wind was light from SW, giving us hope of soon approaching Golfo de Nicoya. However, at one in the morning, fairly close to the coast and suspecting that the current might turn against us, we altered course to the south with a light breeze from WSW accompanied by a few passing showers.

2 January

The following morning, although we did not have a land breeze, we were able to come about onto the port tack once again and continue our survey, when not prevented by the flat calm still prevailing. We were some five leagues offshore, but as there were considerable differences between what we now saw and its appearance the previous afternoon, we began to fear that the *Atrevida* had been right when she called over to us last night, that this coast appeared to be the part running from Punta Burica around Golfo Dulce towards Punta Mala and Isla del Caño.

From the low ground that we had always thought to be Isla del Caño, and the higher ground nearby that during the recent days of calms we had plotted as the westernmost point of the mainland, the coast begins to descend gradually, finishing in a low point which is the eastern extremity of Golfo Dulce.[3] The western entrance point[4] is also low, but the coast soon rises steeply and continues in this fashion for some four or five leagues to the WNW, before turning north and descending again to Punta Mala, which is about this distance from the former point. Far off, beyond the head of the gulf, we could see various irregular ranges, and the entire coast appeared to be uniformly bold and thickly forested.

At noon Punta Gorda[5] bore true north, some five leagues distant, and at the same time the two entrance points of Golfo Dulce bore N59°[E] and [N]57°E and Punta

[1] Charted 25 miles NNW of the western entrance to Golfo Dulce on 'Carta esférica desde el Golfo Dulce ... hasta Sⁿ Blas', probably Bahía Guajamal, charted 33 miles NNW of the same point on British Admiralty chart 2145.
[2] Golfo Dulce.
[3] Punta Banco.
[4] Punta Matapalo.
[5] Not charted on 'Carta esférica desde el Golfo Dulce ... hasta Sⁿ Blas', but probably Punta Salsipuedes, 18 miles WNW of Punta Matapalo.

Mala N30°W by compass. Our latitude was then 8°15′ and our longitude, by the chronometers, 4°16′ west of the Panamá observatory.

The breeze, which had been very light and contrary all morning, dropped still more in the afternoon. At half past two, as we were threatened with an imminent calm and the swell and current were setting us onto the coast, we thought it best to go about onto the starboard tack and steer to the south. We were indeed becalmed all night and at times hardly had steerage way, but we found in the morning that the current had carried us considerably to the south, so that at noon on the 3rd our latitude was 7°50′, while bearings taken to the same points as the previous day showed that we had also fallen off to the east.

From eleven o'clock, with the moderate SW breeze, we steered close hauled in the fourth quadrant. At half past ten [that night], now able to steer SW and SW5°W, we tacked offshore again. These small gains were, however, of no advantage to us, as once again they were cancelled out by the current and the lack of breeze. At noon on the 4th, in latitude 7°54′, we had hardly gained a compass point on the bearing of Punta Gorda, although from the masthead we could sight an island lying approximately NW which we believed to be Isla del Caño.

We could no longer ignore that our position since the 1st was little different from that which had kept us in sight of Isla Montuosa for so many days. In three days we had gained barely 16′ of longitude, our latitude had not changed, and the weather promised nothing but a flat calm, all the more to be feared in that the proximity of the new Moon confirmed rather than dispelled this suspicion. It would have been wrong, therefore, to waste precious time in persevering with our intention of keeping to the coast, when the passage of Lord Anson from Coiba to Acapulco, at about the same time of year, led us to believe that we would probably find more favourable winds in latitude 5° or 6°.

With these doubts we continued during the afternoon, close hauled on the starboard tack, with extremely light airs from WSW and SW, which veered to the west again at sunset. As the current continued to set to the south and the coast was somewhat hidden [by haze], the furthest extremities in sight were now limited to the arc between N5°W and N10°E. The island which still seemed to lie to the NW was now visible only from the masthead.

During this time the dorado and other species of fish remained with us. We continued the allowance of half a pint of wine and took the greatest care to keep the ship clean. To our great pleasure not only did our convalescents return rapidly to their original state of good health, but also no one else had fallen ill for some time, despite the constant labour and the temperature frequently reaching 90°, as measured by the Fahrenheit thermometer placed in the open air.

5 January
Although we had continued close hauled on the starboard tack, we found our position at noon the following day to be latitude 7°10′ and longitude 4°11′, due more to the current than the breeze. The weather remained very calm but squalls began to show on the horizon, particularly in the second and third quadrants, promising an imminent change in the weather which must surely be favourable.

6 January

There was no change in the weather conditions during the following day. A flat calm, or light airs from NW to WSW, reigned supreme and seemed to have established its dominance in these parts. At the same time the current cancelled out all the gains of our continuous labours; we lost the little ground we had made in longitude and increased our latitude, so that at noon that day we were in 6°46′, having gained nothing in longitude since the 4th. However, as the squally appearance of the horizon in all four quadrants continued and even increased, with a few flashes of lightning to the south and SE during the night, we had some relief from the excessive heat of so many days of unbroken sunshine, and the prospect of the long-awaited change in the weather seemed closer.

This expectation could in itself delay the execution of a new plan of operations adapted to these unfavourable circumstances, which I had been considering for some time, in order to prevent the present delay, already harmful enough, from affecting our programme for the whole of the year.

When the only indications of the much-desired change in the weather on the following night were a few heavy downpours and a freshening breeze from WNW with a fairly heavy sea and some indication that it might last, I did not hesitate for a moment at dawn the next day in sending orders to the commanding officer of the *Atrevida* regarding the new plan that I proposed. Before giving the details of this, it will be worth considering our original plan, and the present circumstances which made the alteration necessary.

At the time of our departure from Panamá the information in the sailing directions agreed unanimously with the pilots' reports on the prevailing winds after the end of November and assured us that the northerly winds were now fully established.[1] We set sail from Taboga on the morning of 15 December, and on this and the following day we were fortunate enough to complete the survey of the coast as far as Morro Puercos, which was as much as we had hoped to achieve. During the days of calm weather that followed until the 21st, we had two nights of the strong North-east Trade Wind, which, while generally confirming our first assumption, only led us to believe that it would not set in completely until the next new Moon, but it did continue favourably for our course, interrupted only by an occasional calm. In view of this it was not rash to hope that we might reach Realejo by the end of the year, surveying the coast and measuring bases as we had done so far, although without entering Golfos de Nicoya and Papagayo; then to complete our survey at the said port in a week, including a survey by land of Golfo de Fonseca or Amapala; finally, in the time remaining until mid-February, to continue along the coast as far as Acapulco either in company with the *Atrevida* or separately, as circumstances required, to rendezvous there or at San Blas[2] at a suitable season, according to the sovereign's orders, to sail to the north.

With the timber from Realejo and the workmen in San Blas, we could complete,

---

[1] The *papagayos*, north or NE winds which are frequent and persistent in January and February between Costa Rica and Guatemala.

[2] The principal Spanish 18th-century naval base in New Spain some 400 miles NW of Acapulco: see Michael E. Thurman, *The Naval Department of San Blas*, Glendale, Calif., 1967.

if necessary, the work of strengthening and reconstructing the *Atrevida*'s launch. The Acapulco galleon,[1] given the usual lack of manpower in San Blas, would provide the voluntary crew that we needed. Finally, before embarking upon new dangers, we would see the completion of an essential part of our mission, namely the hydrographic charts of our Pacific coasts. We could never have believed that, contrary to all the information we acquired, there would be a fairly strong and constant current setting to ESE.

One may imagine, therefore, my fears at the time of total failure of the plan described. From 18 December to 6 January, that is in twenty days' of sailing, we had made thirty leagues to the west and lost a little less than this to the south. During this period the currents had caused an error in our dead reckoning of ninety-seven leagues to the east and forty-five to the south, with an average set of sixteen and one-fifth miles to the ESE for each day's run, a distance which we were unable to make up in the flat calms or extremely light and variable breezes.

Although we had stood offshore from the 4th, following the route of Admiral Anson from Coiba to Acapulco, and now were more than forty leagues from the coast, our luck had not changed. The currents were now setting even more strongly against us and the westerlies had freshened with a heavy sea, which increased our leeway. In the last three days the only result of our manoeuvres was two degrees of latitude lost without having gained more than eight or ten minutes of longitude.

With these considerations in mind, and with the imminent change in the weather giving me no time to discuss them with the commanding officer of the *Atrevida*, whom I assumed in any case to share my opinion, I urged him, when sending him my orders for the rest of the passage, to use this corvette's pinnace and his own boats to transfer the baggage and family of the Regente de Guatemala [to the *Descubierta*], and that when we had compared our chronometers he should consider himself as independent of this corvette for the immediate future. The instructions principally directed the *Atrevida* to make for Acapulco with all possible dispatch, where her commanding officer was to inform himself, through the official letters of His Excellency the Ministro de Marina[2] or from any orders of the Viceroy of New Spain,[3] about the King's intentions regarding our northern cruise next summer.[4] If we were

---

[1] A reference to the *nao*, the galleon that regularly made the round trip between Acapulco and Manila, although by this time the trade was in decline. The Acapulco-Manila galleon route was established in 1565. The galleon left Acapulco in February-March to arrive in Manila in May. The more time consuming return voyage took advantage of the Kuro Shio and North Pacific Currents and, leaving in the summer, reached Acapulco in January.

[2] Antonio Valdés y Bazán.

[3] Juan Vicente de Güemes Pacheco de Padilla Horcasitas y Aguayo, Conde de Revillagigedo (1740-99) was born in Havana, but spent his early years in Mexico where his father was viceroy. In 1755 he moved to Spain where he joined the army. In 1766 he assumed the title of second Conde de Revillagigedo. In 1789 he was appointed viceroy of New Spain, an office he held until 1794, the most able person to do so. Officially Mexico was the area of jurisdiction of what is now central and northern Mexico, but the term was also used loosely to cover anything north of Istmo de Panamá. Virrey de Nueva España included everything north of the isthmus, while the phrase Virrey de Mexico was also used loosely to apply to the same area. But Malaspina also used the term 'Mexico' to apply to the capital of New Spain. In this case and elsewhere it has been rendered as Mexico City.

[4] A reference to Malaspina's request for instructions as to whether he should sail to Alaska to search for the strait of Ferrer Maldonado: see his letter of 15 September 1790 printed in Vol. 1 of this edition, pp. 319-23.

to carry it out, he was to leave the supplies of victuals or equipment considered useful or necessary in Acapulco for me, so that I could collect them on my way. He was then to set sail immediately for Puerto de San Blas, where, with the assistance of Capitán de Navío Juan de la Bodega y Quadra,[1] he was to begin the construction of a new launch fitted out for long independent passages. Meanwhile, if he found the Manila galleon in Acapulco, he was to recruit some twenty carefully chosen seamen, while avoiding any kind of trade. He was also to inform the Ministro de Marina of the unexpected reasons which had disrupted our original plan and prompted the present separation. If we had not rejoined him by the end of March or there was no word from us, he was to sail for whatever destination seemed wisest and best with regard to the King's orders, his present circumstances and, above all, the opinion of Capitán de Navío Bodega y Quadra. I suggested that he choose Anson's route, while paying attention to the effect of the currents, which would doubtless carry him towards Los Galapagos. I recommended that he should pass within sight of Isla del Coco, but without letting it delay his passage. Finally I was officially transmitting to His Excellency the Viceroy of New Spain[2] a summary of these measures and, above all, my insistent request that all the orders directed to me should be passed on to the commanding officer of the *Atrevida* and that I should receive in Acapulco the ten thousand *pesos* that I had requested in advance, with any other orders that His Excellency might have seen fit to convey to me.[3]

[7 January]

It was half past seven in the morning when the baggage and servants had been brought over, the chronometers compared and the pinnaces of both corvettes hoisted. The *Atrevida* took her departure, setting a course to the SW under full sail. We put about onto the port tack with the intention of closing the coast again to make, if possible, a landfall near Cabo Blanco, at the western entrance to Golfo de

---

[1] Juan Francisco de la Bodega y Quadra was born in Lima in 1744. He enrolled as a *guardiamarina* in Cádiz in 1762. In 1775 he commanded the *Sonora* during the Second Bucareli Expedition, under the overall command of Bruno de Hezeta (see p. 58, n.3 below) in the *Santiago*, to assert Spanish rights north of Alta California. When the two ships became separated, Bodega y Quadra continued to the north as far as Bucareli Sound in present day Alaska before returning to Monterey. In 1779 he commanded the *Favorita* during Ignacio de Arteaga's expedition to Alaska in a vain attempt to intercept Cook; Arteaga turning back in the vicinity of Kodiak Island. Bodega y Quadra served in the Naval Department in Cádiz in 1785-8 and on being promoted to *capitan de navío* in 1789 he returned to New Spain as Comandante del Departamento de San Blas. In April 1792 he arrived in Nootka Sound as the Spanish Commissioner to carry out the terms of the Nootka Convention, but finding it impossible to reach agreement with Captain George Vancouver, the British representative, returned to Monterey later that year. He died in Mexico City on 26 March 1794.

[2] Presumably to Revillagigedo via the *Atrevida*.

[3] In his journal entry of 10 January 1791 Bustamante confirms the receipt of these instructions, adding that one of the objectives was to test the accuracy of Anson's latitude of 5°20′N for Isla del Coco, which differed from those of other surveys of 5°43′ or 5°45′N, but which commanded respect as Anson had spent five days in the vicinity of the island. Between 12 and 14 January Bustamante obtained observations from which he concluded that the island should be assigned a latitude of 5°33′10″N and longitude 80°47′31″ west of Cádiz: María Dolores Higueras Rodríguez, ed., *La Expedición Malaspina 1789–1794*. Tomo IX: *Diario general del viaje corbeta Atrevida por José Bustamante y Guerra*, Madrid, 1999, pp. 188-92. Isla del Coco is in fact in latitude 5°32′N.

Nicoya. In so doing we [i.e. Malaspina and Bustamante] would be able to divide our fortunes in finding favourable winds as quickly as possible and give us more freedom and independence in our navigation.

Before noon we had lost sight of each other, although the wind was little more than a gentle breeze. We then altered course to NNW, with the weather still looking squally, and with the breeze and choppy sea from WNW to west. We were no longer surprised to find, when making our observations, that the current had caused us to lose much ground. Our latitude was 6°29' and our longitude 4°26' west of Panamá. With either no wind at all or a contrary one we did not have the least idea of the probable length of the passage or which measures to take for the best use of the weather, as was our desire.

The next night we believed that the weather had finally turned in our favour, when, having had a light NW breeze until midnight, with some rain, pitch darkness and lightning, there was a sudden easterly shift with a violent downpour which was certainly heavier than any we had seen so far on this passage. However, the wind soon backed to NW and WNW, very light with continuous rain, so that we found ourselves once more in the same situation and uncertainty as on the previous days.

8 January

Nonetheless, at noon on the 8th we believed that we had made some progress as the variable and sometimes fresh breezes during this day's run had allowed us, by tacking first in one direction and then another, to make good a more direct and faster course. Our surprise may be imagined when our observations showed that we had not made even a minute to the north or west, although our dead reckoning, carefully calculated, indicated that we had made twenty-two miles to the north and eighteen to the west.

Fortunately there had been no lack of fish during this period, with abundant daily catches of dorado and bonito, to which we could now add another entertainment in the form of the catch of small fish, which followed at the stern in vast numbers and were very easily hooked. According to Pineda and Haenke these were of the Gasterosteos species or pilot fish;[1] they were good eating and so numerous that from the ports of the gunroom we caught seventy or eighty within an hour.

As well as this species, interesting enough in itself, Don Antonio Pineda had many others on which to exercise his scientific curiosity in the variety found in a careful examination of the stomachs of the larger fish. Several balistes[2] were found, among them one of a copper colour, a new species of swordfish, some marlin and with the fizgig we were able to take a turtle of excellent flavour and some three *arrobas* in weight, no doubt the same species that was so useful to Admiral Anson. All these provided the natural historians with new subjects for consideration.

9 and 10 January

During the next two days the weather looked more promising, although the constant

---

[1] A striking fish with broad vertical bands of deep blue – the *Gasterosteus ductor* of Linnaeus, now *Naucrates ductor*.
[2] See page 8, n. 3 above.

rain and heavy cloud cover continued, making it impossible for us to take observations to calculate how long we might remain at the mercy of the currents. With the exception of a few hours of light breezes from north and NNE, the wind was fairly fresh from SW to south, enabling us to steer NWbyW by compass, under full sail, with the intention of sighting Cabo Blanco and putting ourselves in a better position to use the trade winds rather than the *vendavales*.[1] Indeed, we could no longer doubt that this year the trade winds were setting in a couple of months later than usual. However, as the season was now well advanced and the weather conditions and the frequent wind shifts to the north seemed to indicate that they [the trade winds] were now approaching, it seemed wiser to plan our course so as to encounter them, particularly as in this way we could continue with our essential hydrographic work.

The following night the south and SW breeze died down once more, being followed by several hours of calms and light airs, with the horizon so beautifully clear that at last we were able to take observations for latitude and longitude. [11th] At noon our latitude was 7°57′ and our longitude 5°15′, with Cabo Blanco therefore bearing N38°W and our position thirty-five leagues from Isla del Caño according to Jefferys's chart. We calculated that the currents had carried us some twenty leagues ESE since noon on the 8th.

With fairly clear skies in the afternoon we were able to observe thirty sets of lunar distances to the Sun. These were highly consistent and their mean was only 5′48″ east of number 72, the chronometer which we considered at the time as our standard one, the accuracy of its rate being used for the daily comparisons.

12 January

With little breeze, and under threat of new calms, we continued the next day steering towards Cabo Blanco, but as our latitude at noon was only 8°27′ and our longitude 5°30′, the coast was not in sight, despite the clarity of the horizon. During the afternoon, when we repeated the observations of the distance from the Moon to the Sun, the results, however, were almost the same as those of the previous day.

We now found, to our great pleasure, that the currents had entirely ceased, and accordingly we could flatter ourselves with the hope of an earlier arrival at Realejo, particularly as all the signs promised that we would soon have fresh land breezes from NE and north.

13 January

Indeed we finally sighted land at dawn the next day, when our position was even better than we had hoped. We were off Golfo de Nicoya, and we could clearly see at a great distance the entire coast from north to NE and from Punta Herradura[2] to Farallones de Quipo. We also had in sight what appeared to be an island bearing NWbyN, a sure sign that it was Cabo Blanco.[3]

Our progress was rather slow all day, with no more than light airs from SSW.

---

[1] I.e. the North-east Trade Wind rather than *vendavales*, which are from the SW.

[2] The eastern entrance point of Golfo de Nicoya.

[3] Isla Cabo Blanco, a high rocky island which has the appearance of a white sail at a distance, lies off Cabo Blanco.

Nevertheless, at sunset we could see, seven or eight leagues distant, the coast running westward from Cabo Blanco, looking like a string of islands or an irregular coastline.[1]

This chance confirmation of the positions determined by His Excellency Ulloa,[2] contrary to all the indications of Jefferys's English chart regarding the entrance points of Golfo de Nicoya, gave us unexpected confidence in our own chart. From Punta Herradura to Isla del Caño the coast, according to all the sailing directions, was fairly straight. So that once we had established the positions of both entrance points by bearings we had no fear of mistakes of any importance, unless we had made an error in the position given in the sailing directions for Farallones de Quipo, which we had not sighted, which in any case would be only a small one.

After nightfall the wind dropped to almost a flat calm, then gradually backed to west and WNW; from midnight we sailed close hauled on the starboard tack, with the weather continuing extremely clear and pleasant. At first light our situation improved even further when we had a pleasing view of the coast. At the same time the breeze set in fair and fresh, which the season and the appearance of the weather led us to believe was now settled in from NE and would remain so.

14 January
However contradictory were the various sailing directions and charts we had regarding both the latitudes, the trend of this coast and its distinguishing features, there seemed little doubt that the stretch of coast now in sight was that which runs from Cabo Blanco to Punta Guiones[3] and then to Morro Hermoso,[4] although we could not see, perhaps because of the distance, a few islets which might have allowed us a more reliable identification. We took two sets of hour angles and these, with the bearings and the sight of land the previous afternoon, confirmed the existence of a contrary current which, without having the least effect on our latitude, had set us back by some eighteen leagues in longitude on this and the previous day's run. At noon our longitude was 6°10′ and our latitude 9°3′. Variation remained 8½° to 9°NW. Later, when we had closed the coast again, we found ourselves among a shoal of excellent fish as large as those seen from both corvettes between Punta Burica and Isla Montuosa. While fleeing from the larger fish, an almost infinite number of jack mackerel came close to the ship, while the bonito and dorado supplied a new and more interesting sport, either for the hook or the fizgig.

The crew was served two meals of fresh fish every day. There was much left over to be salted, while we still had some agreeable variety supplied by a few turtles. These were of a new species, not noted by Admiral Anson, which Don Antonio Pineda found a subject for anatomical research.

The almost uninterrupted calm during the afternoon and following night made us fear that the bearings we would take at dawn on the 15th, would show a considerable loss of ground, given the many tide rips that we could see, in combination with

---
[1] The coast actually turns sharply NNW and then NW at Cabo Blanco.
[2] For Antonio de Ulloa see Vol. 1 of this edition, p. xciv, n. 1.
[3] Situated 38 miles NW of Cabo Blanco.
[4] Standing above Cabo Velas, 63 miles NW of Cabo Blanco.

the current setting to the east and south that had held us back in recent days. Fortunately, however, we found that our fears had been needless when we sighted Morro Hermoso bearing N11°E and the coast beyond it running towards Punta Santa Catalina.[1] At noon our position was further confirmed by our latitude and the sight of a current setting quite strongly to the north, which had already put us 17′ ahead of our dead reckoning.

With the very little time we had left, it would have been unwise to attempt a more detailed survey of the coast, which, being fairly high and having well marked points, already gave us the means of obtaining reliable latitudes and longitudes, particularly as the old sailing directions offered a clear and specific description of this stretch of the coast.

With this in mind we set a course as closely as possible for our destination, making use of the light and variable breezes in the afternoon, which, after midnight, then settled in to NNW, north and NNE with some consistency, allowing us to steer a much better course, so that at dawn on the 16th, with the help of a clear horizon, we could see plainly the land near Punta Santa Catalina and even thought we could sight the islets, bearing NEbyN, which serve to identify that point. At noon our longitude was 7°24′ and our latitude 10°20′N, once again very different from our dead reckoning position.

This position, the fact that the coast was lost from sight beyond the point which we believed to be Punta Santa Catalina, the landmarks mentioned in the sailing directions, all combined to persuade us that we were off Golfo de Papagayo, from where the communication with [Lago de] Nicaragua, and from there by Río San Juan to the Atlantic Ocean, has always been considered a point of major importance as much for the general geography of the globe as for Spanish interests. However, the charts of Jefferys and His Excellency Ulloa and the sailing directions for this coast differed among themselves as to the trend of the following stretch of coast as far as Realejo.

By happy chance we sighted land at sunset, bearing NbyW, which we immediately assumed to be Volcán de Santa Juana[2] at the northern end of the gulf, particularly as it stood out in the far distance, somewhat in the shape of a table – a landmark shown in the sailing directions for this coast. Not imagining that we would see it during the afternoon, since at four o'clock the land near Punta Santa Catalina was still in sight, we had neglected to take observations for longitude in the latter part of the day, which would have avoided any danger of an error in longitude since noon. Consequently, at about a quarter past seven in the evening, we ventured to obtain longitude by absolute altitudes of Sirius, in which we were promised more than average accuracy not only by the size and brilliance of the star and its rapid movement, but also by the wonderful clarity of the horizon, much assisted by the extraordinary radiance of the Moon. The results were most satisfactory, and to these we added, for greater accuracy, the meridian altitudes of Aldebaran and α Persei[3] in the early hours of the night

---

[1] Situated 110 miles NW of Cabo Blanco.
[2] Possibly Volcán Concepción on Isla de Ometepe in Lago de Nicaragua.
[3] Mirfak.

and those of β Centauri¹ in the half-light of dawn the next day, as we feared considerable errors in latitude.

During the night we had noticed the effects, admittedly very slight, of the proximity of Golfo de Papagayo on our navigation, with gusts of wind from north and NE, about which our sailing directions gave us dire warnings, although Dampier describes them as only of medium strength.² We continued for some time with an eye to the topgallants as it seemed that the gusts, now from NE, might indeed strengthen, but later we made use of them under full sail on a NNW tack, so that although the wind fell almost completely at dawn we had made good progress in latitude. [17th] A hill that we thought we had seen on the previous afternoon bore NEbyN and two prominent hills lay to the north and NNW, but because of the distance and, to a greater extent, the haze, these bearings had to be taken from the masthead as it was not possible to do so from on deck until noon, when our latitude was 11°30′ and our longitude 8°20′ west of Panamá.

We obtained no bottom with eighty-five fathoms of line. The wind, which had been very light all morning, now began to set in as a weak sea breeze, while the fish which had accompanied us in almost infinite numbers, particularly during the previous night, now appeared to have left us.

As the sea breeze remained light all afternoon, by sunset we had learnt nothing more of the sierras, still shrouded in haze, in sight from N5°W to NEbyN, although we no longer doubted that the coast continued its northerly trend after Punta Santa Catalina, despite indications to the contrary in the charts and sailing directions. The light breezes remained constant from NNW during the afternoon and night and therefore had to be used to make an easterly rather than a northerly course to close the coast, the survey of which, without fear of errors, was now very important to us. At three in the morning we could see all the coast clearly in the moonlight and as a fresh NE breeze had come up by then we altered course under full sail, close hauled on the starboard tack, so as to be as close inshore as possible by dawn.

At dawn the sight of the coast was very grand and impressive. From Volcán León to that of Telica and Viejo,³ various mountains raise their sharp peaks, some higher, some lower. To the NW, after an area of fairly flat terrain, there follow the Sierras de Cosivina, the Mesa de Roldan and Montes de Peltacarpe, near [Volcán] Conchagua.⁴ To give greater variety to the scene there was smoke, which we thought to be from the volcanoes, although we later found that it came from burning stubble. The pleasant day, indicating the arrival of the sea breeze, promised that soon our troubles would be over and we would reach our long-desired destination.

---

¹ Hadar.
² '... between Cape Blanco ... and Realeja ... there are Winds which blow only in the Months of May, June, and July, call'd by the Spaniards Popogalos. They blow Night and Day without intermission, sometimes 3 or 4 Days or a Week together. They are very brisk Winds, but not violent.': Masefield, *Dampier's Voyages*, II, p. 268.
³ Volcán Viejo, the highest mountain in Nicaragua, now Volcán San Cristóbal, is situated 15 miles NW, Volcán Telica, 22 miles east and Volcán León, now Volcán Momotombo, 35 miles ESE, respectively of Realejo.
⁴ A double-peaked summit, 7 miles north of Punta de Amapala, the western entrance point of Golfo de Fonseca.

In truth, we had been under several misapprehensions earlier in the day regarding the true nature of this coast, largely arising from the highly confused information received so far and also from the considerable increase in latitude caused by the currents. Our doubts were soon dispelled, however, with the realization that it was Volcán Viejo which reached the greatest height and particularly when our noon latitude of 12°19′ agreed exactly with the observations made by Piloto Mestre[1] in these waters, which he had communicated to us in Lima with much other information concerning the anchorage as accurate as it was important to us.

The first puffs of the sea breeze did not come up until two in the afternoon, when we made use of them immediately, steering NE5°N under full sail, a course on which the Volcán Viejo was the only sure landmark for identifying the river or the entrance to the port. At five in the afternoon, although we were only a bare two leagues off the low shore at the foot of the volcano, we could not yet make out the smallest opening to indicate an entrance, even from the masthead, but finally at sunset we saw the false or blind entrance[2] and at seven o'clock, with the help of the Moon and a few light airs which had continued after sunset, we sighted the real entrance,[3] masked by the length of Isla del Cardón,[4] while the summit of Volcán Viejo bore NEbyN by compass.

After sunset, both because the wind had dropped almost entirely and because the reports I had of the anchorage were somewhat confused, I decided to anchor and wait for dawn. As the great clarity of the night invited an accurate examination of the river mouth and entrance, all the better in that it would not expose the crew to the dreadful Sun, Piloto Sánchez was ordered to make the examination in the pinnace. Finally, a little before eight, we anchored in fourteen fathoms, ooze, less than two miles from the entrance, the current having already set us considerably to the south. This current, which remained constant at one to one-and-a-half knots throughout the night, appears to set to the SSE by the island and towards the false entrance, independently of the tide which began to flood later, running ENE and east a short distance off the NW end of Isla del Cardón. The swell was still heavy from the west and broke with a roar on the coast, and so we paid out some cable to counteract it.

19 January

At daybreak we saw the pinnace returning. Piloto Sánchez reported to us that they had entered the false mouth, wandered about the blind channels to the east for a time and, having finally come upon the real channel, they made their way up it with the help of the tide. They saw a large vessel[5] which they approached, finding on board a local pilot who was willing to come to the corvette at first light (as their lookouts had sighted us the previous afternoon), so he took him on board and brought him back immediately in the pinnace, consequently omitting to sound the real river mouth by which we were to enter.

---

[1] Don Esteban Ventura Mestre, master of the merchant vessel *Galga*: see Vol. 1 of this edition, p. 228.
[2] Between Isla del Cardón and Peninsuls Castañones.
[3] Between Isla del Cardón and Isla de Aserradores, a narrow island which extends some distance along the coast north of the entrance.
[4] Fronting the entrance channel to Realejo.
[5] The *Belén*: see p. 23 below.

When the sea breeze began to blow lightly and favourably and the ebbing tide reached slack water, which was to last until half past nine, Cardero, the draughtsman,[1] occupied himself with a maritime view of the coastline and, having ascertained the names of the various points in sight with the help of the local pilot, we took detailed bearings of them, so that this port should serve, with two or three reliable bearings and the determination of longitude by means of the chronometers, as a new centre for our work if lack of time or some other obstacle should prevent us from repeating the bearings taken to high points in the distance. Meanwhile, Teniente de Navío Valdés, Señores Pineda and Haenke made their way to Realejo in the pinnace, the former for various naval purposes and the others to make up, to some degree, for the length of the last passage with new scientific excursions. The numbers of volcanoes in sight, a country not yet frequented by scientists, even our lack of time, were further incentives which increasingly stimulated their keen love of natural history.

We thought that the sea breeze would not set in until the early hours of the afternoon, as we had noticed the day before, but we had better luck on this occasion as the breeze started with the flood tide and, having lowered the boats beforehand, we set sail at ten o'clock for the mouth of the port. We sounded fourteen, ten and eight fathoms, ooze, giving a good berth to a reef which runs out for half a cable to the north from the end of Isla del Cardón, and then luffed up to the east to approach to within less than half a cable of the inshore side of the island so as to avoid the shoals which extend from the mainland and narrow the channel to little more than a cable's width. Here the depth increases suddenly from four to ten fathoms, sand and ooze, a depth which continued until the yardarms could almost touch the [nearby] point. When we had passed this point, the wind and current now becoming more favourable, we continued in mid-channel, leaving various dangers at a safe distance and generally in depths of eight, seven, six and five fathoms, until eleven o'clock when we reached the Xagués anchorage and, at high water, dropped an anchor in five fathoms astern of the merchant vessel *Belén* of Lima, the only other ship in port, with the summit of the volcano bearing N25°E and Punta Icacos[2] S10°W by compass. As this, evidently, was a very safe port, our moorings were, naturally, laid according to the set of the tide and consisted, for the sake of economy, of half of a very worn cable to the south and a fairly heavy hawser to the north.

---

[1] By this time José Cardero, who had joined the expedition as a cabin boy, had become a valued addition to the scientific corps as an artist: see Carmen Sotos Serrano, *Los pintores de la expedición de Alejandro Malaspina*, 2 vols, Madrid, 1982, I, pp. 40-46.

[2] An unidentified point inside the harbour.

Plate 2. View of Realejo and Volcán del Viejo, by José Cardero. Museo de América, Madrid

CHAPTER 6

At Realejo[1]

[19 January]
As it was my intention not to stay in this port beyond the last days of the month and as there was a great deal of work to be done in such a short period, we would have been very remiss to lose any time unless unavoidable. At first sight the land around the anchorage, being both thick with mangroves and most of it flooded, did not offer a convenient spot for setting up the observatory. Upon careful examination in the yawl, however, Don Dionisio Galiano and I found on the shore to the east, close enough to be within range of a speaking-trumpet, a small area of open ground which seemed to be above the level of the tide, where it would be easy to remove the surrounding trees which obscured the greater part of the horizon. By nightfall, therefore, the tent, the astronomical clock and quadrant had been mounted so as to be able to take equal altitudes the following day to rate the chronometers, while being ready for the many important observations to be made during succeeding days.[2]

Teniente de Navío Valdés returned before nightfall, having learnt about the possibility of gathering some timber and the distances to surrounding areas, so that our intended tasks could be adapted to fit the time fixed for our stay. Consequently I was very pleased to find that there would be enough time to achieve most of our purposes [20th] and accordingly Valdés set off without delay for León[3] to find out about the administration of the province, particularly in the field of construction, with regard to labour, costs and supplies. The chief carpenter saw to the collection of timber, particularly of pieces which were to be sawn. I undertook the geodetic work, while Galiano and Vernacci continued with an uninterrupted series of observations. The few remaining officers took charge of duties on board and the examination of the inner channels.

The fishing, led by Don Fernando Quintano, resulted in a good catch on the first afternoon, both in quantity and in the variety of species for new scientific research in natural history. A detachment of marines and marine gunners under the orders of the Sergeant of Marines was sent to cut firewood near the observatory. A well close to

---

[1] Founded in 1534 by Pedro de Alvarado at the mouth of Río Realejo; its original name has fallen into disuse; it is the present day Corinto.

[2] These included lunar distances, magnetic variation and inclination and tidal observations: for details see José Espinosa y Tello, *Memorias sobre las observaciones astronómicas, hechas por los navegantes españoles en distintos lugares del globo*, 2 vols, Madrid, 1809, 2nd memoir, pp. 103, 116, 123.

[3] Founded in 1523 by Francisco Hernández; at the time of Malaspina's visit it was the capital of the province of Nicaragua in the Kingdom of Guatemala.

Xagués[1] was cleaned out and the empty barrels were sent at once to be filled. While attending to these secondary tasks, we took heed of the lesson we had learnt at Panamá and worked only the hours from dawn to ten o'clock in the morning, renouncing work for the rest of the day until the late afternoon, because of the excessive risk of tertian fevers, from which a few seamen were already suffering.

21 January
The next morning, accompanied by Teniente de Navío Novales and Piloto Sánchez, I myself began our intended tasks, taking the pinnace and the *bombo*, with two men who had local knowledge of these estuaries. At Los Aserradores[2] chronometer 71 was to check the longitude as determined by the geodetic work, while a meridian altitude of the Sun was to do the same for latitude. A marine skilled in hunting and a great deal of fishing gear were to be usefully employed, whenever the occasion arose, in providing either for our sustenance or for the purposes of natural history. With these preparations it was my intention to reach Los Aserradores by way of the inner channels,[3] where I would measure a base and observe latitudes and longitudes. Afterwards I would return by the outer route taking soundings as far as [Isla del] Cardón, then examine the entrance channel, carefully sounding and taking bearings with two theodolites, and finally link all the above points to the observatory with good bearings by means of signal flags placed at appropriate places between the anchorage and [Isla del] Cardón.

The inner channel, which follows a fairly winding course, runs from Punta Icacos near the anchorage to the southern end of Los Aserradores, passing between an island of little width,[4] particularly at various points, and the adjacent coast to which it is joined by a sandy spit which is difficult to distinguish from a distance, contrary to appearances and what, up to now, was shown on charts. The channel, particularly in the vicinity of Los Aserradores, then joins many others leading to the cedar forests, enabling rafts carrying timber for construction or other purposes, with the aid of marks, to reach the port promptly and in safety. The tides enter at Los Aserradores and Xagués simultaneously, meet about halfway between them at a spot known as *las dos aguas*[5] and from there, united again, they flood rapidly towards Estero de [blank].[6] A very dense and almost impenetrable growth of mangroves lines all the inner channels. The icacos,[7] (a bush bearing a fruit of excellent taste and quality) produces the greenery along the seashore, which ends in a strip of sand very easily crossed at half tide. The jaguars may justly be considered the only inhabitants of this flood-prone terrain.

About three leagues distant a cordillera of volcanoes, running from WNW to ESE, rises majestically, among which Viejo[8] towers over the rest. The extremely clear skies

---

[1] The anchorage at the head of the harbour; see p. 23 above.
[2] An area depicted at the northern end of Isla de Aserradores [the island of sawmills] on Malaspina's MS survey: AMN; Sig. Borradores. Carp. IX. C-13 (48).
[3] The narrow channel between Isla de Aserradores and the coast.
[4] Isla de Aserradores.
[5] Literally 'the two waters'.
[6] Unidentified.
[7] Common local name for *Chrysobalanus icacos*.
[8] Volcán San Cristóbal: see p. 21, n. 3 above.

of the dry season of the North-east Trade Wind give added splendour to the prospect, already most pleasing in any case.

With the ebb and flood of the tide and the many bends we did not reach Los Aserradores until sunset. The pinnaces[1] were beached and a hut was set up on shore. While attempting to catch some of the turtles which came onto the beach we found, at about ten o'clock at night, that a most redoubtable band of rival hunters had preceded us by an hour. They were a large number of jaguars, one of which, although we shouted at it, would not abandon its prey and skillfully fled into the trees with the turtle. We could still see them on the beach at dawn the next day, within gunshot range of our hut, but our huntsman was out in pursuit of deer at the time and very soon they went back into the trees again.

As soon as dawn had broken Don Manuel Novales and I occupied ourselves measuring a base nearly a mile long on the beach, its western end being very close to Los Aserradores. We then observed for latitude and longitude, and when the Sun had passed the meridian all the implements and instruments were embarked and the same inner channel was chosen for our return, rather than the outer route, shortening the passage considerably without delaying our work and enabling us to sleep on board the corvette, which we reached at seven in the evening.

After an expedition of two days, which was both tiring and instructive, Pineda and Haenke had already returned from the summit of Volcán Viejo. The examination of a double crater at the summit, some deposits of sulphur, various other branches of lithology and, particularly, a magnificent view from the summit itself, had made up for the discomforts of excessive heat and exhaustion and the danger to Don Tadeo [Haenke], who narrowly escaped being bitten by a rattlesnake.

With the same efficiency and success the astronomers had observed the immersion of the second and third satellites of Jupiter on the nights of the 20th and 21st and had determined the latitude of the observatory. Meanwhile Don Juan Vernacci took the opportunity to measure the height of Volcán Viejo from the beach by the observatory. Those in charge of collecting water and firewood had also carried out their duties and had replenished at least half of both commodities, the good conduct and energy of the marines and seamen aiding our work considerably.

23 January

To complete our geodetic tasks we still had, on the one hand, to link the area around Isla del Cardón to the anchorage and the observatory and on the other to the bearings taken at Los Aserradores. We also thought it necessary to tie in the soundings at the entrance with bearings taken by theodolites. With these aims I went to the entrance to the port myself on Sunday the 23rd, with Don Manuel Novales. At the same time I sent a pinnace to sound the entrance on our bearings and another to examine the depths over the bar and then to go round to seaward of Isla Icacos. Bearings were taken on this island and on two places on Isla del Cardón. Finally, at the end of the day, we made use of the short time remaining to set out the nets, with which

---

[1] The pinnace and the *bombo*.

Plate 3. Women of Realejo, by Felipe Bauzá. Museo de América, Madrid

we made a fairly good catch, with a variety of species which were very useful and pleasing to Don Antonio Pineda.

This tireless naturalist and the surgeon, Don Francisco Flores, had accompanied me since early in the morning towards Isla del Cardón, where, taking advantage of low tide, they had made a large collection of shells. Among these the murex, the dye-yielding shellfish, so serviceable, beautiful, abundant and beneficial on these shores, deserved particular attention.

Despite the fact that we now had enough information to calculate the longitude of the observatory with the chronometers, we were obliged to defer this task as the first set of observations to obtain their rates indicated an unusual gain in all three chronometers. As a result we were able to obtain only a very approximate result while anxiously waiting observations of the first satellite of Jupiter. An immersion observed at dawn on the 25th by Galiano and Vernacci, in very good conditions, apart from the Sun being rather too close to the horizon, was confirmation enough of this gain, but we thought it wiser to wait for an observation of the same type, expected for midnight on the 27th, which would be all the more advantageous in that it could be compared with those of the European observatories.

27 January

It was indeed most successfully observed, and the following day at dawn, the astronomers and I also observed eighteen sets of lunar distances. The rates of the chronometers were adopted according to the results of the satellite observations, so as not to make too abrupt a change, and to agree with number 10 from the *Atrevida* until we could make comparisons with her results. Finally, the longitude of the observatory, or the anchorage, was determined as follows:

	Number 72	Number 61	Number 71
Difference west of Panamá	30 11 28	31 35 36	29 51 12
Equation to conform to number 10	+ 20 56	−1 6 00	+ 38 44
Distance expressed in time	30 37 24	30 29 36	30 29 56
Idem in degrees	7 39 21	7 37 24	7 37 29

	Day	Number of sets	Lunar Distances — Difference from chronometers	Resulting longitude
Under sail Referred to the chronometers	11	30	E 10′ 38″	7 48 27
	12	36	7′ 34″	
At the observatory	27	18	W 20′ 30″	7 19 21
Result		84		7° 33′ 54″

Leaving aside the still dubious observations of the second, third and fourth satellite, we could therefore bring together for this calculation the following information:

Chronometer 72, or the good set of longitudes (west of Panamá)	7° 39′ 21″
The first satellite at dawn on the 25th (somewhat dubious)	7 40 15
That of the night of the 27th (very reliable)	7 39 45

At this time we made two short excursions to measure another two bases to link still further the various intermediate points between Isla del Cardón and the observatory and, when the wooding and watering had been completed, we were able to grant a full day of rest and recreation for the greater part of the crew. Meanwhile, in order to combine work and pleasure as far as possible, Don Dionisio Galiano, Don Juan Vernacci and I, succeeded in determining the positions of Realejo, Chinandega[1] and El Viejo[2] by means of bearings taken during an excursion on horseback, made with the aim of inspecting these parts while taking leave of the Regente de Guatemala and Coronel Hodgson who, having set up camp at El Viejo on arrival, were preparing to make their way very soon to Guatemala [City] overland – I was unable to offer them a passage to Sonsonate[3] as I could not risk any delay to our arrival in Acapulco and San Blas.

29 January
By the 29th Pineda and Haenke had also rejoined us on board, bringing a vast amount of useful information and many specimens for the three branches of natural history. The intended collection of timber had been made. Teniente de Navío Valdés had also returned from León having, in the short space of seven days, informed himself of a great many matters relative to our mission and having also made an excursion to Volcán Telica, where he collected specimens and information of the greatest importance for our natural history collection. These were all the more to his credit for the considerable dangers and labour involved in obtaining them. From this volcano he had plotted accurately various points and from the city of León he had taken bearings to its summit and to that of Viejo, so that we could consider the geographical position of that city to be fairly precisely determined, as it resulted directly from our work in the port.

Volcán Telica can be considered far more active at present than Viejo. It is not as high, but its caldera is no smaller, neither being less than about a thousand *varas* in diameter. Don Cayetano Valdés remarked that there could be no more beautiful a sight than the inner coating or layer of the walls of the caldera, which were entirely of the very brilliant yellow of the sulphur which covers them. There was smoke almost everywhere, not only inside, but outside the volcano as well. The ground yielded underfoot as one approached the summit. A stone cast into the opening sent back after a long interval a distant murmur, proof of the depth to which it fell. The conversations of those at the peak could be heard at a considerable distance by those on the lower slopes. The vegetation was extremely sparse; in short, everything indicated a cavity of great depth, from which a thick moist vapour issued and in which the liquidation of a great deal of matter, particularly various small piles of stones which could be seen scattered about in the interior as if with deliberate uniformity, seemed a work of ceaseless occupation for the provident hand of Nature. It was not long since the last time this volcano caused destruction. In the year 1765 a hail of ash and sand covered the lower stretches of land as far as the town of El Viejo, some ten leagues away. The shaking, or tremors, lasted from fifteen to twenty days. At times it was accompanied by roaring from the mountain itself. Even in these convulsions the grandeur of nature

[1] A town about midway between Realejo and Volcán San Cristóbal.
[2] A town about 3 miles NW of Chinandega.
[3] A town 8 miles inland, 160 miles WNW of Realejo.

was displayed at the same time, and more powerfully, in Volcán de Rincón de la Vieja[1] near Golfo de Papagayo. The eruptions of Momotombo[2] had, by 1610, already forced the residents of León to move away and they had again become dangerous by 1636. The eruptions of Nindirí[3] on 16 March 1772 were even more fearsome, the molten lava that issued from it fortunately separated at the same time into four streams, one of which ran towards Laguna de Masaya,[4] another, two *cuadras*[5] wide and about six *varas* high towards the Nindirí highroad, a third to Sierra de Managua and the fourth towards the south coast. This range of maritime volcanoes appears to run approximately WNW to ESE. A strip of low land extends seaward from its foothills, watered partly by the rivers and partly by the tides. Words hardly suffice to describe its great fertility and the excellent timber which grows all along the shore encourages construction, particularly as it is quickly and cheaply transported and worked.

In a land where the admirable works of Nature are displayed with the greatest vitality and variety, the survey and detailed description of whose shores should be considered as of the highest importance for navigation and national prosperity, particularly as the inlets are of such vast extension and Golfos de Amapala and Papagayo of such interest, the former for its shipyards and the latter because of its vicinity to [Lago de] Nicaragua and the excellence of its marine products, one may imagine how much we felt the delay caused by the recent calms and the need to reach Acapulco as soon as possible. However, we could now no longer afford the loss of even a single day, since such an investigation would take several months.

Thus, having rated the chronometers by equal altitudes on the 29th and, having brought on board that afternoon the astronomical instruments and the forge, which had been set up ashore for various purposes, by nightfall we were entirely ready to set sail, only missing one marine from the men we had allowed to go to the town of Realejo during the past two days.

---

[1] Volcán Miravalles in Rincón de la Vieja National Park.
[2] Previously referred to by Malaspina as Volcán León: see p. 21, n. 3.
[3] Midway between Lago de Managua and Lago de Nicaragua.
[4] A small lake close NW of Lago de Nicaragua.
[5] A measure varying from about a quarter of a *milla* to 83·5 metres; the latter seems a much more likely width for a lava stream than the former.

CHAPTER 7

From Realejo to Acapulco

30 January
At three o'clock the following morning, having hoisted our launch and after using the launch of a nearby merchant vessel from Lima[1] to weigh the kedge, we prepared to set sail, intending to make use of the light land breeze that usually blows at dawn, before the tide set against us. However, as there was no breeze at all and as the tide began to flood at six in the morning, our progress, under tow, was extremely slow. Shortly before seven we had to drop a kedge in four fathoms, almost abeam of the sandy flats by the watering place and about two cables ahead of the merchant vessel *Belencito*.[2]

Since we would have to remain there for several hours, either until the turn of the tide or until a favourable breeze set in, we accordingly occupied ourselves taking azimuths for variation with the Gilbert compass, substituting times by number 61 for altitudes of the Sun because of the lack of a good horizon, an operation we considered important as the theodolite indicated a variation of only 6°NE,[3] while all our observations before approaching the port had consistently shown 8° to 9°. The compass confirmed the theodolite results on this occasion, indicating a variation of not more than 5°30′NE.

At ten o'clock in the morning a fresh breeze began to get up from the north, with which we immediately set sail under topsails and topgallants, steering to keep to the channel that passes Punta Icacos and then leads towards [Isla] Cardón, while avoiding the sandy shoals which restrict the entrance to less than one cable in width and, despite the tide still being against us, the breeze was so favourable, that by eleven o'clock we were already some thirty *varas*[4] off Piedras del Cardón and a good mile off by half past eleven, when the wind fell to a flat calm or alternated between NE and a sea breeze. For this reason we were able to confirm with bearings the position of various significant points in sight and at noon we took the opportunity of observing the latitude, which was 12°28′50″.

By two in the afternoon, with the sea breeze now set in from the south, we were able to steer WbyN under full sail, which allowed us to give Bajos de Los Aserradores a wide berth and then to make a detailed examination of the entire low mangrove

---

[1] The *Belén*: see p. 23 above.
[2] The diminutive of *Belén*.
[3] Presumably taken on shore some time before sailing.
[4] Malaspina is unlikely to have passed so close to these rocks – probably an error for three hundred *varas*.

coast leading towards the entrance to Golfo de Amapala.[1] The view of all the mountains from [Volcán] León[2] to [Volcán de] San Miguel[3] and the various bends in the low shore provided sufficient material for our hydrographic tasks. The day was beautifully fine and, furthermore, in the evening the breeze backed slowly to the east, thus increasing our speed. It then shifted towards a strong land breeze from NNE and NE.

At this time, with the mutual assistance of the skill of our surgeon, Don Francisco Flores and the efficacy of the quinine, selected among the best from Loja,[4] which the Regente de Guatemala[5] had given us upon taking our leave, we had the satisfaction of seeing the marines and seamen almost entirely free of the fevers caught in Panamá. Almost all the convalescents were now fit for service and Don Fernando Quintano, whose health, owing to a disorder of the stomach, had deteriorated rather than improved since leaving Lima, now seemed as if he was about to overcome a malady as much to be feared as it is common in the tropics. We continued distributing clothing and tobacco at intervals to those who most needed or wanted them and we settled into a routine of washing down the decks every third day, allowing half a *cuartillo* of wine as a reward for this cleanliness. Finally, with encouragement on our part of anything which might influence the marines and seamen with regard to their health, discipline and respect for the officers, little by little we laid the foundations for the orderly routine we considered so necessary for the more complicated tasks of the coming summer.

In a season as favourable as this for surveying the coast as far as Acapulco, we would have been remiss to sacrifice, for the sake of speed, much of the accuracy we had been able to achieve so far. The chain of volcanoes which runs in almost the same direction as the coast, at some distance from the sea, did indeed excite our curiosity, as several peaks, clearly and easily distinguished at a distance of up to thirty leagues, would provide the bearings necessary to link our surveys together, even if we were to continue under full sail during the nights, which were still very long. However, as well as the fact that at times the low-lying coast of sand and mangroves extends eight or ten leagues further out to sea than the line of the volcanoes, they were also difficult to survey because of their general uniformity. We therefore considered it very important to make a detailed examination of the depths and measure as carefully as possible the elevation of each volcano above sea level.

These objects did not seem incompatible with the time fixed for our arrival at Acapulco, if the alternating land and sea breezes that we enjoyed at present were to allow us to survey some twenty leagues of coast a day.

Accordingly, although the fresh breeze from NNE and NE strengthened in the evening until we could no longer use the small sails, we were still making eight or nine knots. Soon we were under half-reefed topsails alone and before midnight we hove-to on the shoreward tack in depths of forty-five, forty-eight and forty-nine

---

[1] Golfo de Fonseca, although both names were in use at the time of Malaspina's voyage.
[2] Volcán Momotombo, a name Malaspina has used earlier: see p. 31, n. 2.
[3] The most prominent peak in its vicinity, visible at a long distance to seaward, 28 miles NW of the western entrance point of Golfo de Fonseca.
[4] A town about 120 miles SSE of Guayaquil.
[5] Don José Villalengua: see Vol. 1 of this edition, p. 261, where his first name is given erroneously as Juan.

fathoms, sand, having made not more than twelve leagues from the early hours of the night until dawn the following day.

31 January
The weather continued extremely clear, the breeze having dropped considerably. Variation deduced by eastern amplitude was closer to the results determined by the theodolite at El Viejo and Chinandega than those reached at the observatory. It now returned to the 8° or 9°NE obtained when we were approaching the anchorage.

Volcán Viejo now bore E4°S, true, while Volcán Cosivina[1] and Volcán San Miguel had now come much further into view. Monte de Amapala, close to the coast at the western entrance point[2] of the gulf [Golfo de Fonseca], Entrada del Cantadillo,[3] Ríos San Miguel[4] and Lempa,[5] and the successive volcanoes of Sacatecoluca,[6] San Salvador[7] and Los Isalcos,[8] as far as the vicinity of Sonsonate, presented, in their variety, magnificence and size, a series of features, the sight of which could not fail to delight man's untiring curiosity.

Our survey, therefore, continued with much repetition until noon, during which we were able to run good base lines with the log, measuring the height of the mountains, observing two sets of hour angles and, finally, linking to the different points the latitude deduced from the meridian altitude of the Sun. Light airs from SE continued until three in the afternoon, when they gave way to the westerly sea breeze. Soon after nightfall this in turn was replaced by the northerly land breeze which, with very strong gusts and a fairly choppy sea, obliged us to proceed with some caution, the fore topgallant yard having broken across the middle. Our soundings, which had shown a depth of thirty-five fathoms, mud, in the afternoon, three leagues offshore, had increased to fifty fathoms, so we could then set a course parallel to the coast under reefed topsails until, at one o'clock, we had made the distance necessary to bring into view the coast sighted the previous evening, when we hove-to again on the landward tack in depths of fifty-eight to fifty fathoms, mud.

1 February
The strong NE gusts abated at first light the next day when the many bonfires of stubble burning along the coast as far as Sonsonate were lost to sight, having made a very beautiful and pleasing spectacle for us the previous night. We made use of what little breeze remained to close the coast, when the volcanoes of Cosivina, San Miguel, Sacatecoluca, Isalcos, Sonsonate[9] and those of Guatemala now came into view. These

---

[1] Volcán Cosigüina, 8 miles NE of Punta Cosigüina, the eastern entrance point of Golfo de Fonseca.
[2] Formerly Punta del Cantadillo, now Punta de Amapala.
[3] Probably the entrance to the river, which enters Golfo de Fonseca just north of Punta de Amapala.
[4] Río Grande de San Miguel, which enters the sea 28 miles west of Punta de Amapala.
[5] Río Lempa, which enters the sea 50 miles west of Punta de Amapala.
[6] Volcán San Vicente, 19 miles ESE of the city of San Salvador, with the town of Zacatecoluca on its southern slopes.
[7] Volcán de San Salvador, 6 miles WNW of the city of San Salvador.
[8] Volcán de Izalco, 25 miles WNW of the city of San Salvador together with Volcán de Santa Ana, the highest volcanic peak in San Salvador, 2 miles north.
[9] The only volcanoes close to Sonsonate are Volcán de Izalco and Volcán de Santa Ana; perhaps Malaspina is referring to the latter.

lay abreast of us behind Costa del Bálsamo, which runs from Islote Bernalillo,[1] sighted the previous afternoon, to Punta Remedios, the eastern end of Rada de Sonsonate. Only the haze hindered, to some extent, the fairly detailed survey of these parts. The sea breeze set in rather late, delaying us considerably in our attempt to close the coast before nightfall.

Fortunately, at noon, in an observed latitude of [blank], the breeze got up from SWbyS, when we made use of it immediately under full sail steering NWbyN until barely two leagues off the sandy beaches. We then hauled the wind again to run along the coast and acquaint ourselves thoroughly with this locality. At half past three we were still doubtful as to the true position of Punta Remedios because two large rocks could be seen in different places, only one of which marked this point, apart from the bearing of the volcano given in the sailing directions. All our doubts were dispelled, however, when the sky over the coast cleared and we could see, all at once, a brigantine at anchor, the wine vaults of the town and the stream at the watering place, all of which gave us a good opportunity to plot this roadstead accurately.

Sonsonate, despite its extremely uncomfortable anchorage, is the place from which almost all the products of the Kingdom of Guatemala are sent to Peru and Mexico. The dyes for American factories in both kingdoms, with pitch, tar, cotton and a large quantity of valuable timber, form the majority of these exports, while the major imports are wines, spirits and some dried foods from Peru and Chile and sugar from the Kingdom of Mexico, the difference being made up by a payment in money from these countries. The need to shorten the land route to the capital of the kingdom has no doubt been the reason for ships gathering in this roadstead, which is made very uncomfortable by its complete lack of shelter from onshore winds. Other inconveniences are the very heavy swell from SW which breaks violently on the beach, obliging the continuous use of a life-line for the launches, the bottom itself being scattered with sharp stones which put the cables constantly at risk.

When we had observed hour angles on its meridian and Don Felipe Bauzá had taken views of the surrounding parts so that the mariner need no longer have the least difficulty in identifying it, we stood offshore somewhat and struck the national ensigns which we had kept flying while passing the anchorage. The depth of thirty-six and thirty-seven fathoms now increased to forty-three and fifty fathoms, mud, and as we had only light airs from the north during the night, we made use of them under full sail, steering west and WbyN, having noted this to be the approximate direction of the coast.

2 February

At dawn we could still see the coast from Punta Remedios to Monte Esclavos,[2] which bore N17°E, and beyond it the low, mangrove coast which stretches for a long distance to the navigable river and bar of Iztapa.[3] Some way inland the volcanoes of Guatemala soared to a majestic height, the easternmost of which, easily distinguished

---

[1] Not identified from contemporary Spanish charts, but probably in the vicinity of La Libertad, which modern sailing directions describe as the eastern limit of Costa del Bálsamo.

[2] Situated 28 miles NNW of Punta Remedios.

[3] At the mouth of Río Michatoya, 56 miles WNW of Punta Remedios.

by its single peak at the summit, bore N20°W,[1] while the westernmost had two peaks, perhaps belonging to two separate mountains close together.[2]

At ten o'clock in the morning we still had the light NE breeze that had set in at about seven, but this then began to abate. Finally, the moderate sea breeze having got up after midday, we continued close hauled in the fourth quadrant until four in the afternoon. The breeze then shifted to WSW and WNW, obliging us to steer south and SW, although we tacked back to a northerly course at ten o'clock at night so as not to stand too far offshore in order not to miss any of the land breeze if it were to blow at dawn the following morning.

3 February
Our assumptions, however, were very much mistaken on this occasion, as on this and the following days, with no breeze at all, we were becalmed for much of the night and all morning. At two o'clock in the afternoon, when a weak and irregular sea breeze set in, we were unable to tack properly. Even when we managed to do so, we made little progress as we had to stand close inshore, which was low and overgrown with mangroves, in order to be able to determine its limits with some probability, independently of the volcanoes inland.

The height of the Guatemalan volcanoes and that of Atitlán or Sacatepéquez,[3] which were in sight every day was, therefore, one of the essential objects that we had decided upon at this time, during which, although there was an abundance of different species of fish to be seen and some enormous whales, we caught nothing except a dorado and a turtle with a fizgig.

The bar at Iztapa, which in previous times had been the principal port of Guatemala, was not the least of our interests. It was, however, difficult to find among the mangroves, although we tried to extend our tacks to within two leagues of the coast, in depths of fifteen to eighteen fathoms, at times mud and at others sand, while carefully following lines of bearing of NE and NNE by compass on the Guatemalan volcanoes, as indicated by the sailing directions. In the end we were only able to determine its location with some degree of probability at the position where the coast turns rather abruptly from running west to NWbyW.

8 February
At noon on the 8th, therefore, our latitude was only 13°40′ and our longitude 4°30′ west of Realejo, although the further volcanoes of Sapoticlan[4] and possibly of Amilpas[5] were now coming into view for the first time. Both the appearance of the weather and a somewhat fresher sea breeze promised an imminent favourable change which might bring back the land breezes, even if only at night. We continued on the

---

[1] Volcán Agua, which rises to a perfect cone, 15 miles SW of Guatemala City.
[2] Volcán de Fuego and Volcán de Acatenango, two conical peaks of similar appearance, 1½ miles apart, 22 miles WSW of Guatemala City.
[3] Volcán Atitlán, 34 miles west of Guatemala City.
[4] Probably Volcán Santa Maria, 57 miles WNW of Guatemala City.
[5] Probably Volcán Tajamulco, 82 miles WNW of Guatemala City which, with an elevation of 4,220 metres, is the highest in Central America.

shoreward tack with the sea breeze until seven o'clock in the evening, when we were only a league and half offshore in seventeen fathoms, mud. Later in the night we stood off and on in soundings of thirty to forty fathoms, as the sea breeze remained fresh until the Moon had set. [9th] At dawn, with light airs from the NE, we steered NWbyW, keeping the same distance offshore so as to be ready to take advantage of the sea breeze some distance from the coast, to be able to continue close hauled in the fourth quadrant.

The haze that had gathered every day so far either over the coast or the mountains, which we took as clear proof of the absence of a land breeze, appeared even thicker at dawn, denying us a chance of taking any useful or reliable bearings and frustrating our hopes of the previous afternoon of soon having fresh and fair breezes.

Truly our situation at present was not favourable, both because the sacrifice of a single day was a loss of much consequence if we were to effect our departure from Puerto de San Blas, at least before the middle of March and also because, even with the doubtful possibility of accomplishing this, we would be obliged to abandon a detailed survey of the following stretch of coast as far as Acapulco, a survey which, furthermore, should be considered as of the greatest importance for the ports of Ventosa,[1] Aquatulco[2] and Los Angeles,[3] these being useful for mercantile and defensive connections between the kingdoms of Peru and Mexico and for the forthcoming and necessary presence of ships of the royal navy on coasts that enemies of the crown would undoubtedly consider easily and profitably invaded.

Our prospects did not change until the 14th. In fact the sea breeze having been even weaker and less lasting and the land breeze almost imperceptible, we were losing ground rather than making any progress. We were also disabused of any hopes we might have formed by the unanimous evidence of the soundings, the view of the volcanoes and, almost daily, that of the low coast, where we could distinguish each tree that stood out above the dense growth of mangroves. Among these our attention was particularly drawn on the last afternoon, near the beach, by two dry trunks that we could see standing out well above the other trees, looking very much like watchtowers. We might have thought these to be the *Anabacas*,[4] dried by the passage of time, but it was not easy to make the sailing directions agree in regard to transit lines with the nearby mountains, which were generally covered by dense haze from sunrise onwards. We could now see that the trend of the coast, now no more than two leagues abeam of us, was very much more northerly, the extremities in view not extending beyond NWbyN, although we could sight them from the masthead at eight or nine leagues.

Although in some ways the lesson we had learnt from the calms off [Isla] Montuosa and Golfo Dulce on the passage to Realejo made our position less trying, our unease was now heightened by the lack of even the slightest sign of improvement in the weather, although the proximity of the full Moon gave us some grounds to hope

---

[1] Now Bahía Ventosa, a slight indentation in the coastline at the head of Golfo de Tehuantepec and close east of the artificial harbour of Salina Cruz, for which it provides an additional anchorage.
[2] Puerto de Huatulco, 58 miles WSW of Salina Cruz.
[3] Puerto Ángel, 80 miles WSW of Salina Cruz.
[4] Possibly an unidentified common name for a Central American tree.

for it. Every day was a very significant loss for our proposed plan, and now either the least inactivity on our part or continuation of the weather conditions would make it impossible to carry it out during the coming summer. We were still 120 leagues from Acapulco, taking its position as given by Piloto Mestre[1] in latitude 16°49′N and, according to the observations made by Don Vicente Doz in San José in [Baja] California,[2] as shown on the chart of Piloto Mendizábal,[3] in longitude 10°46′ west of Realejo.

The current had set against us and the dull sound of a heavy swell from west and NW gave some indication of prevailing winds from that quarter. Each day convinced us further of the inadequacy of the sailing directions, which referred to fearsome northerly gales where we encountered nothing but calms and sea breezes. Our very desire for accuracy, among so much inadequacy or conflicting detail, increased our doubts and delayed our decision. Eventually it was necessary to take the opportunity of changing our procedure. We therefore decided to stand some thirty or forty leagues offshore, to see if we could find the trade wind and make some longitude and then gradually return towards the coast to take advantage of the sea breezes. This course of action had been so effective for Admiral Anson that in the space of a few days he had been able to approach Acapulco from the same latitude as ours and in the same season. Several reports that I had heard, by chance and not very clearly, of the passage of the Manila galleon on its return to Acapulco, jointly persuaded me that the coast as far as Acapulco was subject to calms and that the northerlies would be stormy but infrequent.

14 February
From dawn on the 14th, therefore, we continued steering to the SSW, at which time we were obtaining soundings of thirty fathoms, with the volcanoes of Guatemala bearing NE5°E by compass. The swell remained high from the west; several boobies and a species of frigatebird[4] fluttered around us; several turtles, dorado and bonito were speared and several blue sharks were hooked, among which were one or two of enormous size.

The absence of sea and land breezes for almost all of the following twenty-four hours left us without steerage way, while the rolling was very violent, causing damage of some significance to the sails and rigging. At dawn on the 15th we had made very little progress in latitude and had to replace with new two of the topgallants sails which had split during the previous night. However, a very low swell from the east

---

[1] Don Esteban Ventura Mestre, master of the merchant vessel *Galga*: see Vol. I of this edition, p. 228.

[2] In 1769, Don Vicente Doz, a Spanish naval officer, took part in the French expedition under Abbé Jean Baptiste Chappe d'Auteroche, a French astronomer sent by the Académie Royale des Sciences in Paris to lead a combined Franco-Spanish expedition to observe the Transit of Venus at San José del Cabo in Baja California in June 1769. For a translation of the observations of Vicente Doz see Doyce Nunes, ed., *The Transit of Venus*, Los Angeles, 1982.

[3] A chart covering the coasts of California and China by Mendizábal was one of a number of charts copied by Vernacci in Cádiz for the expedition,

[4] For the three species of boobies Malaspina may have encountered in these waters see p. 9, n. 1 above. Both the Magnificent Frigatebird (*Fregata magnificens*) and the Great Frigatebird (*Fregata minor*) occur off the west coast of Mexico.

and cloud approaching from the same quarter seemed to indicate that the weather might soon change for the better.

Light airs did indeed begin to get up from NE during the night, enabling us to steer to the SW, both to lessen the rolling to some extent and so as not to get too far off course, altering course the following day [16th] to WSW and W5°S. The westerly swell having dropped considerably and a gentle breeze having set in from the east, we then believed the weather prospects to have changed; our observed latitude was 12°40′.

During the night the falling breeze, although freshening somewhat as dawn renewed the day's energy, had backed to the north after continuing in the east for some time. We sailed close hauled under full sail at three or four knots, so that the distance of one degree westward made on this day's run seemed a victory for which we had longed for without success for a fortnight. Our surprise may be imagined, therefore, when we calculated the observed longitude with the chronometers, and found that it was 40′ east of our dead reckoning.

17 February

We were no luckier on the following days, during which we continued close hauled with very light breezes from NNW, north and NNE. Despite this we saw each day at noon that our position had hardly changed, as the currents[1] cancelled out any small progress made with the breeze, our vigilance, the corvette's good sailing qualities and favourable high sea from NE and east, which had taken the place of the westerly swell that had hindered us so far. We did, however, observe a little northerly progress.

19 February

Thus, at noon on the 19th, in latitude 13°16′, we found ourselves to be only 5°35′ west of Realejo and in no doubt, furthermore, that both the set of the currents against us and the backing of the breeze, however slight, to the north, indicated that a coastal passage would be preferable to the offshore course that we had taken on the 14th.

That evening, towards sunset, the light breeze conveniently backed to WNW and west, allowing us to keep a northerly heading all night, close hauled, but fearing that the currents might cause a new deviation from our course and reveal at dawn a view of the same volcanoes of Guatemala and Sacatepéquez[2] that we had left behind on the 15th. Towards midnight we were somewhat reassured by obtaining no bottom with eighty fathoms of line, which indicated (assuming some progress in latitude) that we were west of our position on the 14th, a supposition which was indeed borne out at dawn the next day, when we saw the coast in the distance bearing NEbyE to NNW5°W; [20th] our latitude at noon being 13°41′ and our longitude 5°52′ [west] of Realejo. The breeze had veered to the north again, obliging us to sail close hauled on the starboard tack from the early hours of the day, but this was of no great consequence to us, for we founded our hopes on soon completing this passage with the aid of the northerlies alone.

During all this period we had been accompanied by various species of birds and

---

[1] Malaspina may have encountered the Mexico Current which, in winter, sets SE along the coast as far as 95°W, but on occasions may extend as far east as Honduras, with rates between half and one knot.
[2] Volcán Atitlán: see p. 36, n. 3 above.

fish, boobies, frigatebirds and a tropicbird[1] standing out among the former and among the latter, dorado, tuna, bonito, whales, turtles and various fish of very small size. Meanwhile, Don Antonio Pineda was very successful in his favourite study of molluscs, having found many of these which displayed a new and delightful aspect of nature in their variety, movements and habits.

As we no longer had any current against us, having found at noon on the previous day an error in our favour of 15' to the west, we had no hesitation in choosing to make a coastal passage. Accordingly we followed the same tack on this day's run as on the one before, hauling the breeze in the third quadrant by day and setting a course in the fourth quadrant by night, which, at the time, seemed to be when the sea and land breezes blew. [21st] Our observations agreed pretty well with our dead reckoning, giving our position at noon as latitude 13°44' and longitude 6°40' [west of Realejo]. Variation, observed daily as 8° to 9°NE, continued unchanged. The sight of the coast that we had at dawn, although very uncertain, seemed to bear out the belief of His Excellency Ulloa[2] that Golfo de Teguantepeque[3] and Puerto Ventosa did not run nearly as far inland as shown on the modern chart by the English geographer, Jeffreys.

22 and 23 February

Very soon, however, the weather and currents having thought better of giving us even fleeting grounds for a new and favourable opinion of this passage, turned against us once again. The strength of the southerly current, accompanied by noisy tide-rips until midday, increased, making it impossible to disregard and at the same time lessening the strength and regularity of the breeze, which we could no longer classify as either a land or sea breeze. As far as possible we steered to north and west. Our dead reckoning showed some progress, but the noon observations on the 23rd still placed us in latitude 13°39' and longitude 8°0' [west] of Realejo. This small progress in longitude being due to the breeze from NNE which had got up a few hours before, with a very promising outlook.

This was, at last, the wind from Golfo de Teguantepeque which instilled such fear of coastal passages in the sailing directions,[4] and which we had so earnestly desired. We welcomed it, therefore, with corresponding pleasure, and made the most of it under full sail, following a NW course which, it appeared, would take us directly, though somewhat offshore, to Acapulco. The wind and sea got up strongly in the afternoon, gusting heavily and allowing us to make six to seven knots, while the cloud cover, position and season seemed to indicate that we would be able to maintain this speed. With darkness the wind did slacken considerably, it is true, but as it continued favourably until noon the next day. At the same time the sea gradually calmed, greatly lessening the rolling. This day's run was unusually successful, [24th] our latitude at noon being 14°30' and our longitude 9°12' west of Realejo. We thought it of little importance at the time that the currents had set us back by 20' of latitude.

[1] The Red-billed Tropicbird (*Phaethon aethereus*), the only species found off this coast.
[2] Antonio de Ulloa: see p. 19 and n. 2 above, also Vol. I of this edition, p. xciv, n. 1.
[3] Golfo de Tehuantepec.
[4] 'In Golfo de Tehuantepec strong N winds, known as *Tehuantepecanos*, are often encountered during the cooler months.': *Pacific Coasts of Central America and United States Pilot*, 9th edn, Taunton, 1995, p. 131.

This, however, was the last progress we were to make in the month of February, as the currents were constantly against us for the next four days, although sometimes setting south and at others, east. They daily cancelled out any ground we made on either tack. Indeed, even the most apathetic spirit could hardly remain tranquil in the face of such a lengthy period of calms making us almost a plaything of the elements, when, given the class of our ship and the strength of our crew, we believed we had no reason to fear, even in their worst combination. Many fish and molluscs were caught every day, but by now neither the pleasant taste of the former nor the almost inexhaustible variety of the latter could do anything to mitigate such an unpleasant situation.

28 February
At noon on the 28th, in latitude 15°19′ and longitude 8°56′, we caught sight of a long stretch of the coast. It was the part running WNW from Puerto Escondido towards Las Barrancas[1] and Pesquerías.[2] Even through the haze we thought we could make out Morro Hermoso and El Cerillo,[3] so that we cannot have been more than forty leagues from the entrance to Acapulco.[4] As we then had a moderate SW sea breeze, which abated in the evening, and we were also only six or seven leagues from the coast, we thought it all the more likely that the land breeze would get up, as lightning, the direction of the cloud movement, the dull sound of a low swell from NE and occasional puffs of wind, seemed to indicate.

1 March
However, we had nothing but light variable airs, not only during the night, but all the following day as well, adding to our natural frustration at our lack of progress in spite of making constant fruitless manoeuvres, reminding us that our entire progress during the past month of February had been six degrees of longitude and a mere two degrees of latitude.

These inconveniences were naturally compounded by the extreme heat and probably eating too much fish, the consequence being attacks of indigestion, recently accompanied by fevers, which affected three or four of the seamen. The rest remained in good health and spirits and we took all possible care to keep them in good condition. The sail lockers and all the stores kept in them were ventilated. Cleaning and other work below decks did much to promote a healthy and moderate perspiration. Our faces and our example dispelled the boredom that these distractions could not overcome in a few of the more sensitive and observant seamen.

2 March
The next day, the 2nd, revealed that our troubles were not yet at an end, circumstances

---

[1] Literally the ravines.
[2] Literally fishing ground.
[3] Not identified.
[4] According to 'Carta esférica desde el Golfo Dulce ... hasta S^n Blas', on which the tracks of the *Descubierta* and *Atrevida* are shown, Malaspina was off Puerto de Huatulco at noon on the 28th, some 53 miles east of Puerto Escondido, making it difficult to identify the other points Malaspina thought he had sighted. In this position Malaspina was some 80 leagues from Acapulco. Clearly the chart he was using was unreliable.

still conspiring to make our situation as irksome and tedious as possible. To the calm and the contrary currents were added the heat of the Sun. A fairly high sea from NE, which caused a violent and ceaseless rolling as tiring as it was uncomfortable, rolled in from Golfo de Teguantepeque, reminding us at the same time that, however close the favourable breezes were, they were deliberately tantalizing us, aware of our unfortunate situation but showing no pity.

By then we had fallen off course to a latitude of 15°3', while chronometer 72 gave a longitude of 9°21'; but as the atmosphere on this and the previous afternoon had cleared considerably we could see the land in greater detail, particularly some high mountains inland, and if our expectations were to be guided by what we had learnt from our vexatious experience off Guatemala, we could assume that, when the haze over the coast had dissipated, the land and sea breezes would be more regular and lasting.

The sea breeze did indeed drop almost entirely soon after nightfall and the sea calmed. We continued tacking to the north, although not making good progress, in the pleasing hope that the land breeze would allow us to make some westing at dawn the following morning, according to our position. In these hopes we were sadly deceived once again. At three o'clock in the morning we put about onto the starboard tack under full sail, but made hardly a mile to the SSW and SWbyS. The breeze then dropped completely, the promise of fair breezes from the east receded and at last, towards eleven o'clock, we felt the first puffs of the sea breeze, with which we continued close-hauled to WNW.

3 March

The view of the nearby coast had never been as clear as it was throughout this morning. We measured some bases and, being only two or three leagues offshore in the afternoon, we were able to confirm our original belief that we were off Morro Hermoso and to extended our survey from Las Pesquerías to Puerto Escondido. The shore looked extremely arid, apart from a few small cultivated areas near Las Barrancas, from where we saw the glow of a fire during the night, definite proof of habitation nearby.[1]

With the new Moon the breeze had set in lightly from the west and as this continued during the night, veering a little at times into the third or fourth quadrant, we allowed ourselves to hope that, making the best of our tacks and the corvette's speed, we might soon reach Acapulco, from which we now believed ourselves to be no more than thirty-five leagues, our latitude being 15°13' at noon on the 4th and our longitude 9°22' west of Realejo. Soon this hope too had to be abandoned, a mortification all the greater for being continually in sight of the same points, disabusing us at every moment of any illusion of progress provided by our dead reckoning. The current at the time was setting more to the east than to the south and at times we found a difference in the former direction of half a degree, within a single day, between our dead reckoning and our observed position.

Finding ourselves at dawn on the 6th in precisely the same position as in the afternoon of the 3rd and knowing these handicaps to be insuperable, we thought it best to

---

[1] Malaspina was once again off Puerto de Huatulco in almost exactly the same position he was in on 28 February.

change our plan by standing offshore and abandoning the very short tacks that we had made during the previous days. During the night, on a NW tack with a very light breeze, we had to navigate with some caution believing ourselves to be only one league off the reefs that the sailing directions warned as extending for some distance offshore along Costa de las Barrancas.

It cannot be denied that our situation at this time was extremely strange and disagreeable. Although almost in sight of the port that we longed to reach, in the best season for the passage, with an excellent vessel and certainly not wasting the slightest breath of wind, nevertheless we found our efforts thwarted every day and our forthcoming plan of operations disrupted, even had we been able to combine them with this somewhat unusual chain of events. Finally we had to sacrifice the survey of a considerable part of the coast between Guatemala and Puerto Escondido in our desire to reach the port for which we now yearned as strongly as we had at the beginning of February.

Meanwhile, the heat was excessive, affecting not only our general health, but also exacerbating the damage to the rigging, decks and boats. Not a single cloud appeared in the sky to moderate the Sun's heat and give a sign of a fair breeze. Various species of birds and fish remained our constant companions, regarding us almost as fellow-inhabitants of these waters. Finally we feared that the excessively passionate disposition of the Spanish seaman might soon disturb to some degree the agreeable harmony and peace that we had enjoyed so far under the influence of the calm, which perhaps would not have been possible among the extreme dangers of high latitudes.

Surrounded by so many uncertainties and, in particular, with no way of judging the weather and currents to come, wherever we might find them, it was inevitable that we would waver in our first decision, (particularly in having ignominiously yielded to a calm) with regard to the necessity of combining our coming movements with those of the *Atrevida* and with the instructions of either His Excellency the Viceroy of Mexico or the Ministro de Marina. These would indicate whether it was better to continue towards Acapulco, considering the short distance and the fact that various provisions and Teniente de Navío Espinosa[1] would be there or, on the other hand, if the weather, the constancy of the currents, and the little time remaining of the dry season on this coast, suggested that it would be more appropriate to alter course to the east to survey the coast as far as Puerto Ventosa and work on a section of the chart which could not be overlooked without leaving us open to criticism of being less than exacting in fulfilling His Majesty's intentions for the greater good of the nation. Any letters and instructions directed to Acapulco could easily be sent on to us in that port. Perhaps we would also be able to obtain scientific information relating to the natural history of the nearby range of mountains and the hydrography of the connecting system and navigation of Río Guazahualcos[2] as well as making an additional extension of our longitudes into the Atlantic, as we had already carried out from Panamá to Chagres.

---

[1] Malaspina had received several letters from the Ministro de Marina informing him that Tenientes de Navío José de Espinosa y Tello and Ciriaco Cevallos y Bustillo would join the expedition in Acapulco: AMN, MS 1,826, ff. 104-13, letters dated between 6 April and 26 November 1790.

[2] Río Coatzacoalcos which rises in the sierras at the head of Golfo de Tehuantepec and flows north before entering the Gulf of Mexico in Bahía de Campeche.

Faced with contradictory possibilities we were more inclined to the latter, although perhaps, before undertaking it, we might make another attempt to reach Acapulco, taking an offshore tack for twenty leagues, which the moderate westerly breezes after the new Moon seemed to lend themselves to, as did the probability of some moderation of the currents setting against us. If the following inshore tack did not bring any advantage, we would leave ourselves to the will of the wind and current to survey the coast to the east, having lost only one or two days. We therefore put about onto the starboard tack, and by noon, although the WSW wind was abating, we lost sight of the coast, partially because of the haze and partially because of the strong southerly set of the current; our latitude at the time being 14°59′.

Very soon the calms persuaded us that the attempt was useless, and as we were afraid of being set off course by the current, we waited only until eight o'clock that night to alter course to sail close hauled in the fourth quadrant, with very light airs from the third.

7 March

At noon the following day, however, far from having made the progress promised by our dead reckoning, we found ourselves 27′ further south; the longitude of 9°11′ showed no easterly error.

The constant calms of the 8th and 9th were succeeded by gentle breezes in the second quadrant, which we attempted to use, steering WbyN by compass, to make, if possible, the small remaining distance in longitude to reach the meridian of Acapulco, still hopeful that our somewhat less laborious progress in latitude would finally carry us, by means of the sea breezes, to the port we so longed to reach.

The currents had never before set so strongly and constantly against us as they did during these days. We soon found ourselves set back to latitude of 13°15′ and longitude 10°23′, where we were at noon on the 12th, or that of 10°38′ which we reached on the 13th. The resulting small progress of a single degree, could hardly make up for the two degrees of latitude that we had lost, despite the fact that our dead reckoning showed a daily advance of 8′, 10′ and even 15′.

13 March

Not until too late did we discover how mistaken we had been to leave the coast, even for a few hours. Our present situation led us almost inevitably to consider the early days of this month, which had seemed almost unbearable at the time, to be happy in comparison. Regrets were useless, however, and no remedy was within reach, so we thought it best to prepare ourselves for future events, in case the weather were to remain contrary. To this end a moderate limit on the daily consumption of water was imposed, even though we believed we still had enough for about two and a half months, the four hours of the morning, when the coppers were available, were used to distill salt water, the weed was cleaned from both sides of the hull, the boatswain's spare stores were aired and great care was taken with cleanliness and ventilation below decks. Finally, having almost used up the fresh foods and provisions for the sick, we applied ourselves more assiduously to fishing, particularly for the turtles which we saw every day and which we could catch easily and in abundance by harpooning them either from the ship or, when it was calm, from the yawl.

14 March

Both at noon on the 13th and on the following day we were no further to the south, raising brief hopes of a change of fortune. On reaching latitude 13°51′ once again and wishing to return, if possible, to the vicinity of Morro Hermoso and Puerto Escondido, we considered the loss of 20′ in longitude of little importance, taking into account what we must have made according to dead reckoning. For this reason we decided to set courses either in the first or the fourth quadrant, which would allow us to make some progress in latitude. It already seemed more probable, according to the weather conditions, that either in Puerto de Aquatulco or in Ventosa we should soon be able to make some use of the last two months of the favourable season and avoid the monotonous inactivity, which would be the most unhappy of our misfortunes, should we be forced to abandon hope of continuing our expedition further north or of joining the *Atrevida* before too long.

Soon even these hopes seemed impossible to realize. From the 15th until the 18th the currents set so strongly to the south and east that at noon on the 18th, in latitude 13°14′ once again, we had hardly made the longitude of 9°10′ that we had reached on 24 February and 6 March. This we considered extremely poor progress so much so that the last fortnight's sailing since leaving the coast had served only to increase our doubts about whether we would complete this passage and extend its duration to a period equal to that of our voyage from Cádiz to Montevideo.

Fortunately the approach of the full Moon, and perhaps of the equinox, combined to give new strength to the northerly and NE breezes from Golfo de Teguantepeque. After several days of seeing the horizon dark with cloud and the Sun pallid and opaque when rising and setting, and with the appearance of some *pamperillos*,[1] the wind got up strongly on the morning of the 19th. This allowed us to steer NW by compass under courses, topsails, jib, and main topmast staysail, leaving us somewhat over-canvassed for the heavy gusts and rolling that we experienced from noon onwards, which increased greatly during the afternoon and evening. We had to make frequent repairs to the sails and rigging, which were particularly affected after midnight by the rolling, the breeze having dropped considerably. As [the breeze] had fallen completely by noon the next day [20th], [the rolling] continued with unusual intensity and constancy. In consequence we were hardly able to enjoy the good progress we had made in the previous twenty-four hours, because of the great discomfort we were suffering, particularly because of the slackness of the main shrouds, since both masts had become unchocked[2] due to the violent rolling. Our noon position, therefore, of latitude 15°11′ and longitude 10°24′ seemed excellent and unexpected progress, although the contrary currents had lessened it considerably. The breeze dropped almost completely at nightfall, to be followed at midnight by a light northerly land breeze, leading us to fear that noon the next day would find us having gone backwards rather than forwards.

21 March

However, at first light next morning we were pleasantly surprised by the sight,

---

[1] The diminutive of *pampero*, the name for Wilson's Storm Petrel (*Oceanites oceanicus*) in Spanish speaking South America. Several species of storm petrels may be encountered off the west coast of Mexico.

[2] I.e. the softwood wedges inserted at the heel of the mast had become loose.

although at some distance, of a long length of the coast, stretching from NNW to NE and not only was our noon position better in both latitude and longitude than our dead reckoning, but we also felt the first puffs of a sea breeze which promised more regular and favourable breezes to come.

If, as we believed at dawn, our distance offshore was at least twenty leagues, our observed latitude of 15°52′ would put us on the meridian of the port. We did, however, find from the longitude of 11°9′ calculated with number 72 that the difference of 10°47′ that we had assumed between Realejo and Acapulco fell short of the truth,[1] particularly as the daily comparisons of the chronometers showed that a gain of 26′44″ was very probable compared with the results according to number 72, whose rate had several times been disturbed during the last season's work, with number 71 standing out among the three for the regularity and uniformity of its rate.

Having reached the coast again after so many misfortunes and having made some forty leagues westing in fifteen days of constant difficulties, it now seems a suitable moment to examine the extent of the effect of the contrary currents, combined with persistent calms and contrary winds which, if frequent on this coast, even though this seems improbable, would lead us to advise any merchant vessel to avoid it. The following table begins at noon on the 6th, and includes, as has been seen, an area from the parallels of 13°15′ to 15°15′, and from the meridians of 9° to 11° west of Realejo, that is, the coast from approximately Morro Hermoso to Acapulco.

Day's run	Latitude				Longitude			
	Difference by dead reckoning			Observed difference referred to dead reckoning	Difference by dead reckoning			Observed difference referred to dead reckoning
7............N	1′	30″	S	28′ 30″	W	7′ 00″	E	6′ 00″
8............	12	15		22 15		8 00		7 00
9............	11	15		37 15		32 00		9 00
10............	9	00		29 00		25 45		7 45
11............	9	30		31 30		11 00		9 00
12............	17	45		16 45		19 00	W	9 00
13............	12	30	N	9 30		20 45	E	5 45
14............	17	00		0 30		13 00		32 00
15............	8	15	S	16 15		16 00		29 00
16............	7	00		22 00		20 30		30 30
17............	15	15		28 15		6 00		25 00
18............	44	15		24 15		0 30		29 30
19............	50	45		26 45		29 00		17 00
20............	1° 29	15		17 15		1° 16 30		12 30
21............	28	00	N	13 00		36 45	W	8 19[2]

It may be seen from this table that our losses due to the effect of the currents in these fifteen days were 4°37′ to the south and 3°23′ to the east; that is, approximately sixty-eight leagues.

---

[1] The difference in longitude between Realejo and Acapulco is in fact 12°42′.
[2] A transcription error for 8 00.

The short distance that we made to close the coast during the afternoon disillusioned us in our belief that we were on the meridian of Acapulco, especially as we could see no land of any great height, only a hummocky coast on which a headland rising vertically from the sea was particularly conspicuous. We believed this to be the promontory noted in the sailing directions as lying to the west of Puerto Escondido,[1] leading us to suspect that we were still some twenty leagues from Acapulco.[2]

We continued on the shoreward tack until nightfall, when we were only two leagues offshore, in twenty-four fathoms, sandy mud. As it was now a likely moment for the land breeze to set in, the sea breeze having dropped completely, we expected to make good progress to the west next morning. This belief was also mistaken as a flat calm left us without steerage way almost all night, keeping us in depths of thirty-eight to forty-five fathoms. It was only at dawn could we make one or two knots to the west, with excessively light airs from north and NNW.

22 March

At noon these too gave way to the sea breeze, which was finally replaced by a gentle land breeze, so that we made fair progress along the coast, which we surveyed in detail, tacking onshore and offshore as required by either the land or sea breeze.

It is hard to convey how far from the truth were the sailing directions, regarding both the landmarks and the trend of the coast. Everything we saw gave us new cause for doubt; only latitudes were data that we could cling to as being likely to be reliable, but we had to depend very much on the results of Piloto Mestre's observations, as the only ones that we could consider trustworthy at the time.

The various fires that we saw at different points along the coast left us in no doubt that it was populated. The very heavy dew that fell during the night seemed to promise that the land breeze would continue, the sea shone beautifully with vast numbers of molluscs which Don Antonio Pineda took care to examine, while the turtles that we caught from the yawl during the hours of calm contributed pleasantly, either with their flesh or their eggs, to make up for our complete lack of fresh meat.

23 March

Dawn on the 23rd found us some four leagues from the coast with high sierras in front of us which, according to a Filipino seaman who had made three voyages in the galleon,[3] were those of Acapulco. He identified them confidently one by one to our satisfaction, as the haze prevented us from examining them in detail. This persuaded me to send the launch under the orders of Teniente de Navío Don Cayetano Valdés with Piloto Sánchez and four days of rations, either to go ahead of us and meet us with the letters, reports and other papers being kept for us in Acapulco, if that was the port we could see, or if, as appeared possible, it still lay seven or eight leagues to the west, to make for it, keeping well inshore. The latitude of 16°33′ that we observed at noon did not yet disillusion us, our distance offshore being somewhat mistaken,

---

[1] Probably Morro Hermoso, 28 miles WNW of Puerto Escondido.
[2] According to *Descubierta*'s position on 21 March on 'Carta esférica desde el Golfo Dulce ... hasta S^n Blas', Malaspina was 25 leagues from Acapulco.
[3] See p. 15, n.1 above.

but as the sea breeze cleared the sky and horizon shortly afterwards, our error became clear to us before one o'clock. Accordingly we hauled the breeze to the west and fired a cannon to inform the launch, which was sailing about two miles ahead of us.

In these parts the coast runs approximately WNW/ESE and here the sandy flats with mangroves begin, extending towards the vicinity of the small port, with several beautifully forested ridges visible in the foreground and many mountains further inland. The numerous fires to be seen at night indicate that it is populated, although thinly.

By three in the afternoon the sea breeze had, as usual, veered from south to SW and WSW. As we had fallen off considerably towards the coast, we had to tack, being then only a league offshore in fifty-three fathoms, sand. We tacked towards the land again at half past four and finally, at six o'clock, we came about again onto the starboard tack, observing that the launch was rapidly gaining on us inshore, while we were falling off to the east, no doubt because the currents had set against us once again.

24 March
The light land breeze was very weak during the night and the following morning and even before midday it had shifted considerably towards the east. According to our bearings we had made a little progress, but we were some six leagues offshore, this also being indicated by the latitude of 16°26' that we observed at noon. A fresh sea breeze having set in by then, we hauled the wind under full sail, although it was a little light. At five o'clock we were able to tack when four miles from Playas de Naguala[1] and three or four leagues to leeward of the hills that surround the port. We had already seen various landmarks which confirmed this identification and meanwhile we could see the beaches so clearly that we were left in no doubt that the launch had reached its destination.

Our progress was no better the following morning. Far from dropping, the westerly breeze freshened in the evening. [26th] At moonrise and at dawn we made short tacks, close hauled, making for the shore, in case the breeze should draw towards the land. Our efforts were in vain. Daylight revealed, although indistinctly (the various points on the coast being veiled in haze as usual) that although we had made some ground to the west we had lost much more to the south.

At last, however, this was the end of our passage. At noon a fresh breeze set in quite suddenly from WSW, with which we came about onto the port tack, close hauled. Therefore as we could identify the coast clearly by nightfall and the breeze continued, we were able to remain on the same tack until ten o'clock at night when we were barely a league off the steeply rising shore at Puerto del Marqués.[2] The two further tacks that we made during the night allowed us to make better progress [27th] and at dawn we were almost at the mouth of the port, although a little to leeward of it.

We put about to the SW again and stayed on this heading until nine in the morning when the breeze backed a little to the south, enabling us to came about onto the

---

[1] The beaches to the east of Acapulco.
[2] Bahía de Puerto de Marqués, a small sheltered inlet near the SE entrance to Bahía de Acapulco.

port tack again and make good a course of NNW, which brought us to windward of the port.

By ten o'clock we could see the launch to windward, which altered course towards us. It joined us at about eleven, when Don Cayetano Valdés handed over the official letters for me from His Excellency the Ministro de Marina, the Viceroy of Mexico, and the commanding officer of the *Atrevida*. These letters and our circumstances in general required much more time to arrange our future movements, particularly that from the commanding officer of the *Atrevida*, who advised me not to count on less than a month for the passage to San Blas. Thus I thought it not only prudent, but necessary, to enter the port and so we made for it under full sail, dropping anchor at last at two o'clock in the afternoon and by evening, with the aid of warps, we were moored with three lines – one secured ashore to a tree near the quay, and two hawsers laid out to seaward.

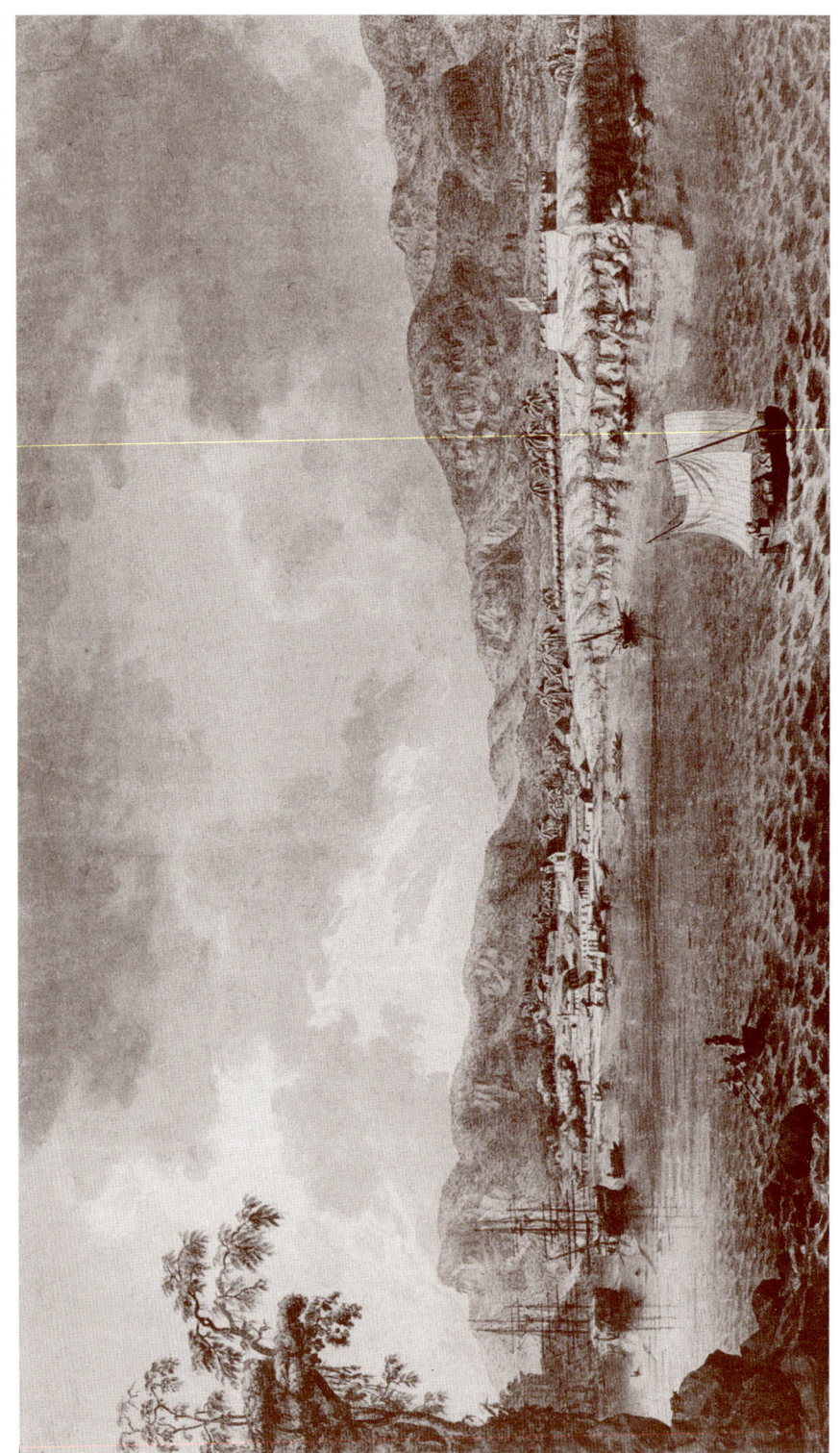

Plate 4. View of Acapulco, by Fernando Brambila. Museo Naval, Madrid

CHAPTER 8

At Acapulco[1]

[27 March]
As stated in the previous chapter the corvette *Atrevida* had already sailed for San Blas in accordance with her instructions, leaving in Acapulco the sealed letters from their Excellencies the Ministro de Marina and the Viceroy of Mexico[2] and also a summary of the tasks she had carried out subsequent to our separation off Costa Rica. Don José Bustamante had, with industry and unusual good fortune, sighted and fixed the latitude and longitude of Isla del Coco,[3] then after a few days of calm, interspersed with stormy squalls within sight of the island, he had encountered the trade winds and, steering a direct course, managed to anchor in this port on 30 January.

He had not wasted any of the time that he was obliged to remain here – contrary to our initial plan – because the Viceroy's orders required that he should await the arrival of Tenientes de Navío Don José Espinosa and Don Ciriaco Cevallos who, by Royal command, were to join the expedition. In addition, the desertion of thirteen seamen, no doubt fearful of the imminent northern cruise, required him to take effective steps either to apprehend them or to find replacements for them, at least in part. They were, however, apprehended. With a well executed series of astronomical observations and geodetic tasks he determined the position of the port and made a plan of it. On the morning of 26 February Espinosa and Cevallos joined the ship. On the 27th he sailed for San Blas, preferring an offshore passage to a coastal one in accordance with the guidance provided from Mexico City by Teniente de Fragata Mourelle[4] who, nevertheless, warned him that, due to the strength of the

---

[1] The fullest treatment of the expedition's visits to Acapulco can be found in Virginia González Claverán, *Malaspina en Acapulco*, Madrid, 1989.
[2] For Conde de Revillagigedo see p. 15, n. 3 above. These instructions were received by Bustamante on 2 February and read by him in case they contained revisions relating to his route. At the same time he learnt from the acting governor of Acapulco, Diego Carrillo, that although Spain and England were both continuing to make preparations for war, the optimistic expectations of peace which the expedition had encountered in Panamá still prevailed: Bustamante, *Diario general del viaje*, p. 197.
[3] For Bustamante's position for Isla del Coco see p. 16, n. 3 above.
[4] The Galician mariner Francisco Antonio Mourelle de la Rúa (1750-1820) had extensive knowledge of navigation of the NW Coast of America. After being posted to San Blas in 1775 as a *primer piloto*, he served under Juan Francisco de la Bodega y Quadra that year in the *Sonora* in a voyage to Alaska (see p. 16, n. 1 above). Mourelle's 'Journal of a Voyage in 1775' was published by Daines Barrington in his *Miscellanies*. London, 1781. In 1779 he again sailed to Alaska with Bodega in the *Favorita*. In 1780 he sailed for Manila in the *Princesa* under Bruno Hezeta, returning to San Blas in 1780-81 in

currents and contrary winds, his passage would not take less than thirty or forty days.[1]

Tenientes de Navío Espinosa and Cevallos advised me in their letters that fear of an imminent break with England had delayed the departure of merchant vessels for New Spain for several months. As a result they had only been able to begin their voyage towards the end of November the previous year although His Majesty had intended them to set out on 6 April. They had made their landfall at Cabo Francés[2] on 31 December and finally reached Veracruz[3] on 19 January. On this occasion two Arnold pocket chronometers, referred to the longitude of Cabo Francés (as determined by Señores Verdun, Borda and Pingré[4]), gave the longitude of Veracruz as:

Number 344 . . . . .98° 39′ 00″
Number 351 . . . . .99° 04′ 00″ } . . . . .98° 51′ 30″

And the mean of fifteen sets of lunar distances taken under the best conditions on 14 January and their differences carried forward by the chronometers } . . . . .98° 48′ 35″

The latitude observed by sextants was 19°13′40″N and, in Mexico City (near the cathedral), using one of the sextants and a good artificial horizon, they obtained a latitude of 19°25′25″.

They had scarcely arrived in Mexico City when dispatches from the commanding officer of the *Atrevida* expressing his wish to rejoin the expedition forced them to journey quickly to Acapulco, leaving their luggage, instruments and books to be forwarded directly to San Blas, where the *Atrevida*'s stay would have to be extended for the purpose of providing themselves with a large launch like the one that had been reconstructed for the *Descubierta* in Guayaquil. Both officers, already well known in the navy for their ability, energy and zeal, were too valuable an acquisition for this not to be the cause of celebration among the other officers. His Majesty, of course, had demonstrated through this very appointment that not only our past work,

---

command of the *Princesa*, during which he made some discoveries in the South Pacific. In his later years Mourelle returned to Spain, crowning a distinguished career by being promoted *jefe de escuadra*: see Amancio Landín Carrasco, 'Mourelle de la Rúa in the South Sea', in *Spanish Pacific from Magellan to Malaspina*, Madrid, 1988, pp. 133-44; Donald C. Cutter 'California, Training ground for Spanish Naval Heroes', *California Historical Society Quarterly*, 40, June 1961, pp. 109-22 and Warren Cook, *Flood Tide of Empire: Spain and the Pacific Northwest*, New Haven and London, 1973, p. 303, which also contains much useful information on Spanish voyages to the NW Coast.

[1] In March the current sets to the SE at about 13 miles a day, while the trade wind blows from NW parallel to the coast.

[2] Probably Cabo Francés Viejo on the north coast of the Dominican Republic.

[3] At that time a major port on the east coast of Mexico and contact point for ships to and from Spain.

[4] In 1771-2 Jean-René-Antoine de Verdun de la Crenne, Jean-Charles de Borda and Alexandre-Gui Pingré (1711-96), three French scientists, took part in a voyage in the North Atlantic at the instigation of the Académie Royale des Sciences in the *La Flore* to test the performance of chronometers by Pierre Le Roy and Ferdinand Berthoud, during which the longitude of Cabo Francés Viejo was obtained: see Verdun de la Crenne, *Voyage fait … par Verdun de la Crenne, Borda et Pingré*. 2 vols. Paris, 1778. For Borda see also Vol. I of this edition, p. 7, n. 1 and p. 240, n. 6.

but also our desire to carry this on as far as possible, particularly in pursuit of progress in navigation and geography, had merited his royal approval.

The official letters from His Excellency the Ministro de Marina, which in due course had reached Acapulco, stated only His Majesty's approval of the progress of the tasks we had carried out from the coasts of Chile to Lima but gave no indication as to what our future steps should be. The replies from His Excellency Conde de Revillagigedo, the current Viceroy of New Spain,[1] to various official letters I had written to him from Lima, Guayaquil, Panamá and the coasts of Nicaragua, while indicating that His Excellency had taken the most active measures to ensure that our activities did not meet with the slightest obstacle, did not in any way resolve my uncertainty as to the best course of action for the corvettes in future.

If one examined the most recent surveys carried out along the northern coasts of California, whether by our own continuing surveys expeditions between 1775 and 1790, or by the English under Captains Meares,[2] Guise,[3] Hanna,[4] Portlock,[5] Barkley[6] and Dixon[7] and published by the latter in 1788 [1789], or finally by Mr Etches,[8] also

---

[1] Viceroy of Mexico: see p. 15, n. 3 above.

[2] John Meares (1756-1809), after forming a company in Calcutta to trade for furs on the NW Coast of America, reached Unalaska in August 1786 in command of the *Nootka*. After calling at Nootka Sound and Hawaii, Meares left for Macau where he sold the *Nootka* and fitted out a new expedition, sailing directly for Nootka Sound in the *Felice Adventurer*, which he reached in May 1788. The seizure of three British vessels together with a memorial by Meares, dated 30 April 1790, which was laid before the British parliament on 13 May 1790, brought Britain and Spain to the brink of war, which was only averted by the signing of the Nootka Sound Convention on 28 October 1790. For an account of Meares's voyages see J. Richard Nokes, *Almost a Hero: The Voyages of John Meares R.N., to China, Hawaii and the Northwest Coast*, Pullman, Wash., 1998, and John Meares, *Voyages made in the Years 1788 and 1789 from China to the North-West Coast of America*, London, 1790. A copy of Meares's book was one of a number held for the expedition in Ferrol 16 February 1791 for forwarding to Acapulco: Oregon Historical Society, Malaspina papers, MS 2814/183.

[3] Captain John Guise, who traded for furs on the NW Coast in 1786 in the British snow *Experiment*.

[4] James Hanna was the first of the fur traders, arriving on the NW Coast in 1785 in the 60-ton brig *Harmon*, returning the following year in the 120-ton snow *Sea Otter*: see Cook, *Flood Tide of Empire*, p. 101 and W. Kaye Lamb and Tomás Bartroli, 'James Hanna and John Henry Cox; the first Maritime Trader and his Sponsor', *B.C. Studies*, #84, Winter 1989-90, pp. 3-36.

[5] Nathaniel Portlock (1748?-1817) first visited the NW Coast while serving under Cook during the latter's third voyage. He returned to the NW Coast in command of the trading vessel *King George* in 1786 and 1787: see Nathaniel Portlock, *A Voyage round the World; and more particularly to the North-West Coast of America*, London, 1789: see also Barry Gough, 'Nathaniel Portlock', *Dictionary of Canadian Biography*, V, Toronto, 1983, pp. 686-7.

[6] Charles William Barkley, who traded on the NW Coast in 1787 under Austrian colours in the *Imperial Eagle*. In June 1788 Barkley sighted a large opening near Cape Flattery which, in the words of his wife, Frances, who was on board the *Imperial Eagle*, he 'immediately recognized as the long lost Strait of Juan de Fuca, and to which he gave the name of the original discoverer'. See W. Kaye Lamb, 'The Mystery of Mrs Barkley's Diary', *British Columbia Historical Quarterly*, VI (1942), p. 43.

[7] George Dixon first visited the NW Coast while serving under Cook during the latter's third voyage. He returned to the NW Coast in command of the trading vessel *Queen Charlotte* in 1786 and 1787. For his account of the voyage see [William Beresford], *A Voyage round the World 1785–1788 by Captain George Dixon*, London, 1789; see also Barry Gough, 'George Dixon', *Dictionary of Canadian Biography*, IV, Toronto, 1979, pp. 217-19.

[8] Richard Cadman Etches, who set up the King George's Company with other London traders in 1785 to sponsor the voyages of Portlock and Dixon (see notes 5 and 7 above). Malaspina was mistaken, Etches never visited the NW Coast, nor did he sail in the *Princess Royal*.

THE MALASPINA EXPEDITION 1789-1794

English, in 1789 on board the merchant ship *Princesa Real*,[1] it seemed all the more inopportune for us to make a voyage to the north. This would mean sacrificing six or eight months, since our ships at San Blas, under the command of Capitán de Navío Don Juan de la Bodega y Quadra,[2] were obliged as a result of the latest dispute to pay an annual visit to the settlement at Nootka,[3] and at the same time to spend the greater part of the useful summer months exploring thoroughly and with much benefit to geography, various stretches of that immense coast. Thus, the previous year [1790] Teniente de Navío Don Salvador Fidalgo[4] had surveyed the entrances to Prince William Sound and Cook River [Inlet] along the latitude of 60° in the snow *Filipino*[5] and Teniente de Fragata Quimper[6] with Piloto Martínez[7] in a schooner had penetrated a very deep sound in 48°, where some had rashly imagined they had discovered Almirante Fonte's celebrated passage.[8] In addition to this, we could not ignore that the season was well advanced, especially, as seemed natural, our priority was to ensure the rendezvous of the corvettes. Nor could we forget that the same coastline had been surveyed by Messieurs La Pérouse and Langle, doubtless with the same steadfastness,

---

[1] The *Princess Royal*. Commanded by Thomas Hudson, she was one of the ships impounded by Esteban José Martínez in July 1789, an event that sparked the Nootka Sound Crisis. As the *Princesa Real* she served as a Spanish supply ship.

[2] For Bodega y Quadra see p. 16, n.1 above.

[3] A Spanish *establecimiento*, Santa Cruz de Nutka was built in Friendly Cove, Nootka Sound, in 1789 under the command of Esteban José Martínez to protect Spanish interests in the area: see Thurman, *The Naval Department of San Blas*.

[4] Salvador Fidalgo (1756-1803) was one of a group of young officers sent to San Blas in 1789 after training and service in Spain to strengthen the base at San Blas and maritime initiatives aimed at California. The following year, on promotion to *teniente de navío*, he was part of Francisco de Eliza's expedition to occupy Nootka Sound from where, in the same year, he commanded an expedition to Prince William Sound and Cook Inlet in the *San Carlos*. For the most comprehensive account of this voyage see Elizabeth Nelson Patrick, 'The Salvador Fidalgo Expedition, 1790: the last Spanish Exploration of the Far North Pacific Ocean', unpublished doctoral thesis, University of New Mexico, 1981. In 1791 Fidalgo was temporarily in command of the Naval Department of San Blas in Bodega y Quadra's absence. In 1792 he was sent from Nootka Sound in the *Princesa* by Bodega to occupy Núñez Gaona, or Neah Bay on the south shore of Juan de Fuca Strait, but the settlement was abandoned later that year. On Bodega's departure for Monterey, Fidalgo took temporary command in Nootka Sound.

[5] Also known as *San Carlos el Filipino*, but more usually as *San Carlos*.

[6] Manuel Quimper was appointed to the Naval Department of San Blas in 1789, taking passage from Spain with Bodega y Quadra and Fidalgo. He was part of Francisco de Eliza's expedition to occupy Nootka Sound in 1790. Later that year he was sent by Eliza to explore the entrance and Strait of Juan de Fuca in the *Princesa Real*: see Freeman Tovell, 'Manuel Quimper and the Exploration of the Strait of Juan de Fuca', in *Resolution* (Maritime Museum of British Columbia), #14, 1990, pp. 14-21.

[7] Esteban José Martínez Fernández was born in Seville on 9 December 1742. He was serving as *segundo piloto* in the Naval Department of San Blas by 1773. He served under Juan Pérez in 1774 in the *Santiago* on the expedition which discovered, but did not enter, Nootka Sound and became commandant of the Spanish garrison at Nootka Sound in 1789. His arrest of Captain James Colnett later that year precipitated the Nootka Sound Crisis: see Roberto Barreiro-Meiro, ed., *Colección de diarios y relaciones para la historia de los viajes y descubrimientos*. VI: *Esteban José Martínez (1742–1789)*, and Christon Archer, 'Esteban José Martínez', *Dictionary of Canadian Biography*, IV, Toronto, 1979, pp. 519-21.

[8] A reference to the apocryphal voyage of Admiral Bartholomew de Fonte to the NW Coast in 1640, when he allegedly sailed through an entrance in latitude 53°N to within easy distance of Hudson Bay. On this and the supposed voyages of Juan de Fuca and Lorenzo Ferrer Maldonado to the same region see Henry R. Wagner, 'Apocryphal Voyages to the Northwest Coast of America', *Proceedings of the American Antiquarian Society*, n.s., XLI, 1931, pp. 179-234, and Appendix 2 in this volume.

zeal and intelligence as directed the first passages of the corvettes *Boussole* and *Astrolabe*.[1]

However, these considerations, while of great importance in themselves, were, on reflection, counterbalanced to a large extent by the objectives we would have to face in the coming months. Since we would have to leave the coasts of New Spain, Guatemala and Costa Rica during the rainy season, where our hydrographic tasks were still far short of the state of completeness which our national shipping demands, we would as a consequence have to resume our surveys as soon as the favourable season set in during the months of October and November.

Beset by these doubts and not forgetting how important our rendezvous was if we were to visit coasts that were highly hazardous to Europeans, I had in the end to choose, as the course preferable to all others, to await our rendezvous with the *Atrevida* in Acapulco, where we could, while attending to the overhaul of the corvette and the much delayed completion of the launch, also take on water and firewood. The *Atrevida* would be able to sail from San Blas to Acapulco in seven or eight days while we could not hope to reach San Blas for at least another month.

28 March
My first action was therefore to advise the commanding officer of the *Atrevida* of this decision by special courier through the good services of the Viceroy. I asked him to take charge of the launch and after any necessary work had been done on the hull, he should not lose a moment in returning to Acapulco unless Capitán de Navío Bodega y Quadra, bearing in mind the seasonal weather in Seno de Cortés,[2] the assistance he could make available to us and the value of the work and the time it would take, should be inclined to use the *Atrevida*'s officers and instruments in a survey of that gulf. At the same time the *Descubierta* would visit the Sandwich Islands[3] and make a thorough exploration of our coastline from Cape Mendocino[4] to Cabo San Lucas[5] and San Blas, where we would rejoin company the following October.

Meanwhile, a new set of astronomical observations was undertaken under the supervision of Galiano and Vernacci; Pineda and Haenke started to organize their collections and explore the surrounding area; Don Felipe Bauzá was to put in order the charts produced since Lima; and Don Cayetano Valdés was to be responsible for the completion of the launch and the supervision of our work on board and later to undertake an excursion to Puerto del Marqués[6] where the *Atrevida*'s officers and *pilotos* had not had time to carry out any work.

---

[1] Jean François Galaup de la Pérouse and P. A. Fleuriot de Langle had been on the Alaskan coast in *La Boussole* and *L'Astrolabe* in 1786. There they investigated Lituya Bay in search of an entrance to the Northwest Passage before sailing south to California.

[2] The Gulf of California.

[3] The Hawaiian Islands.

[4] A prominent cape 185 miles NNW of the entrance to San Francisco Bay, which was a famous landmark for Spanish navigators. The name can be traced back to an Ortelius map of 1587. For a full discussion of the naming and discovery of this cape which is shrouded in obscurity see Henry R. Wagner, *The Cartography of the Northwest Coast of America to the Year 1800*, 2 vols, Berkeley, 1937, pp. 396-7.

[5] The southern tip of Baja California. On almost all early maps this cape was named Puerto or Playa Ballenas or Punta de la California: ibid., pp. 410-11.

[6] See p. 48, n. 2 above.

It is not easy to express in a few lines how useful to all these activities were the positive measures taken by the Viceroy and the executive orders issued by the *coronel* and warden of the castle Don José Manuel de Alava.¹ Very soon afterwards the warden's house itself became the home for our observatory, dissections, chemical experiments and hydrographic tasks, and even the storehouse for many of our provisions. The most effective measures were taken to control disorder and particularly desertion. Timber was cut in the vicinity in order to complete the fitting out of the launch and men with some skill in carpentry and caulking were brought in. The proximity of the corvette to the beach enabled us without confusion or excessive effort to attend to our tasks and the care of our people, somewhat wearied by the extreme heat and the length of our last passage, who now expected to remain in a climate which was among the worst encountered in America up to this point.

Since one of the most important aims which we next had to attend was to reduce as far as possible, if not eliminate, the cockroaches which had multiplied excessively since leaving Guayaquil and Panamá. At the same time we sought to relieve ourselves as far as possible of stores, landing gun carriages, spare timber and so on, and also to paint the interior of the living quarters. These measures, as well as the favourable situation of the onshore hospital and the certainty that it would follow the regime prescribed by our surgeon, led me to have four patients transferred there. Among them the one causing us the greatest concern and distress was Liborio Rodriguez, a corporal of the marines who had been suffering for a long time from a suppuration of the liver which now threatened to spread to the chest. The Hippolitan Fathers² who were in charge of the hospital at once displayed the greatest degree of care, gentleness and cleanliness so that we were able to set our minds at rest with regard to that most essential part of good order. Tenientes de Navío Don Fernando Quintano and Don Manuel Novales, whom we saw at the time, to our inexpressible sorrow, to be racked by a tropical dysentery, also went to live ashore. It was found not only that the peace, exercise and relaxation would be more advantageous in making up for the differences in climate, but also that in this way they would not be deprived at all hours of the companionship and relaxation provided by their fellow officers, among whom the qualities of friendship and high morale were increasing day by day.

29 March

The astronomical clock and quadrant having been set up on shore, our first aim was to measure the longitude of Acapulco by the chronometers in order to compare it

---

¹ Brigadier José Manuel de Alava succeeded Bodega y Quadra as Comandante del Departamento de San Blas and Spanish commissioner to carry out the terms of the Nootka Convention. He sailed for Nootka with Fildago on 16 June 1794 in the *Princesa*, where he met Vancouver. Their discussions were friendly but unsuccessful, since neither had received the necessary instructions from their respective governments. It was left to Lieutenant Thomas Pierce of the Marines, who had been appointed British Commissioner in place of Vancouver, together with Alava to officiate at the ceremony of restoration and mutual abandonment on 28 March 1795.

² These were the Brothers Hospitallers of Christian Charity of San Hipolito, a religious congregation founded in Mexico in 1585. They ran hospitals in Latin America and were later merged with the Brothers Hospitallers of St John of God.

both to the results obtained by the *Atrevida* and to our own calculated from observations of the first satellite of Jupiter, as well as to obtain fresh rates for our chronometers.

Before long everything combined to confirm the suspicion that the rates of chronometers 61 and 71 had increased considerably, as the daily comparisons had already indicated, although we could attribute this neither to changes in temperature nor to the rolling sustained over the recent period of fifty-eight days. These then were the calculations for longitude:

	Number 72	Number 61	Number 71
Slow on mean time at Acapulco	$1^h\ 16^m\ 44^s\ 37$	$4^h\ 48^m\ 30^s\ 7$	$0^h\ 34^m\ 55^s\ 37$
Same with regard to that of Realejo	$2^h\ \ 6^m\ 24^s\ 59$	$5^h\ 41^m\ 44^s\ 13$	$1^h\ 27^m\ 41^s\ 50$
Difference between meridians...........	$49^m\ 40^s\ 22$	$53^m\ 14^s\ 6$	$52^h\ 46^m\ 13$
Equation to conform	$2^m\ 00^s\ 32$	$1^m\ 36^s\ 23$	$1^m\ 9^s\ 6$
Corrected time difference	$51^m\ 40^s\ 54$	$51^m\ 37^s\ 43$	$51^m\ 37^s\ 7$
Therefore Acapulco west of Realejo	$12°\ 56'\ 14''$	$12°\ 54'\ 26''$	$12°\ 54'\ 16''$
From which (using our series of longitudes deduced from satellites) the mean longitude west of Paris can be deduced			$102°\ 27'\ 39''$
The longitudes obtained by the *Atrevida* with her chronometers (assuming a uniform rate)			102 22 00
From an observation of the first satellite, of the utmost reliability, but using a weaker telescope and excluding observations that gave.......... a greater longitude			102 20 38
From lunar distances...			102 29 00
And from our own observations of the first satellite, carried out on the 7th of the following month and without doubt completely reliable,........ given the circumstances..			102 26 45
Latitude of the observatory			16 50 30
Variation by theodolite			[blank][1]

29 March

Very soon afterwards we experienced one of the scourges with which nature counterbalances her otherwise prodigious generosity in these regions. At around half past one in the morning of the 30th a very strong tremor was noticed even on board. It had been preceded for several hours by signs of a storm not far off and, a few minutes before, by a loud subterranean noise and the usual howling of the dogs as well as the natural urge of a great mass of fish to rise to the surface of the sea, coming up from the deepest parts in an instant. This earthquake lasted for about twenty seconds with a shaking movement that caused not a little damage to several houses and yet no perceptible effect on the astronomical clock in the observatory whose oscillations and movement we found the following morning to be much the same as we had observed before.

[1] 7°12′NE in AMN, MS 753.

Plate 5. Cock Fight in Acapulco, by Tomás de Suria. Museo Naval, Madrid

All the relevant activities thus having been set in place and having taken steps to avoid an increased consumption of stores by supplying the crew's daily rations in cash and having arranged two months payment to all classes for the middle of April, I found there could be no better way of employing the twenty or thirty days remaining before the rendezvous with the *Atrevida* than by making an excursion to Mexico City. Here I would be able to confer with the Viceroy on the most useful arrangements for the expedition in the future and at the same time to extend and perfect my knowledge of these kingdoms when compared with South America and perhaps to contribute to the progress of geography with some astronomical observations.

I was to be spurred on, particularly in this latter purpose, by the happy coincidence that the occultation by the Moon of α Cancri[1] was to occur on the night of 12 April and would be visible simultaneously from Mexico City, Acapulco and San Blas. The meridians of these places relative to one another would therefore be very accurately determined, the *Atrevida* probably being in San Blas while I was to travel to Mexico City. Nor would I consider the impossibility of carrying with me the appropriate instruments by this long and stony road in the very short time I could be away from Acapulco to be an insurmountable obstacle for, in addition to the fact that the astronomical instruments with which the Abbé Chappe[2] and Don Bruno de Hezeta[3] had travelled to the coast of California had not been sent back to Europe, there might also

---

[1] The principal star in the constellation Cancer, but only of the fourth magnitude.
[2] For Abbé Jean Baptiste Chappe d'Auteroche see p. 38, n. 2.
[3] Teniente de Navío Bruno de Hezeta y Dudagoitia (1751–1807) led the second expedition to the NW Coast ordered by Viceroy Antonio Bucareli in 1775 in the corvette *Santiago* during which he

be in the possession of the many distinguished people in that capital, other instruments, chronometers and average-sized telescopes that could be of use for the observation.

30 March
With these reflections and having handed over command of the corvette to Don Dionisio Galiano, at daybreak on the 30th I began the planned journey to Mexico City on horseback with all possible speed and succeeded in reaching that delightful capital not long after midday on 5 April. That very afternoon I had the pleasure of presenting myself to His Excellency the Viceroy and finding out at the same time how the planned observation could best be carried out. The following morning, accompanied by Teniente Coronel de Ingenieros Don Miguel Constansó[1] and Teniente de Fragata Don Francisco Mourelle, I first examined the instruments belonging to the Real Observatorio at Cádiz which consisted of a good Ellicott astronomical clock,[2] an Adams astronomical quadrant,[3] both of which had been very little used for a long period and then Abbé Chappe's instruments which were then in the possession of Don Antonio de Gama,[4] in whom a natural love of astronomy and many years experience were united with a wealth of study.

Already my conception both of the state of the sciences in Mexico City and its geographical position were much changed by my conversations with the three people mentioned. For, leaving aside the observations performed by Doctor Alzate[5] (whom I met later) and which, in spite of the approval of the Academia de Ciencias, appeared to leave much room for perfection, Señores Velázquez[6] and Gama had worked for many years to determine it with the greatest accuracy and, as a result of their diligent

---

examined parts of the coast from the vicinity of Vancouver Island to Cabo San Lucas and was the first European navigator to sight the entrance to the Columbia River. For an account of Hezeta's voyage see Herbert K. Beals, transl. and ed., *For Honor and Country: The Diary of Bruno De Hezeta*, Oregon Historical Society, Portland, Oreg., 1985.

[1] Miguel Constansó arrived in New Spain in 1764 with Juan de Villalba's expedition. He served as engineer and cartographer with José de Gálvez at San Blas and La Paz. He accompanied the Gaspar de Portolá expedition to settle Alta California in 1769 and prepared some of the earliest and best maps of Alta California in 1769 and 1770. He continued his cartographic works and taught mathematics at the University of Mexico: see Janet R. Fireman, *The Spanish Royal Corps of Engineers in the Western Borderlands*. Glendale, Calif., 1977, pp. 93–136.

[2] John Ellicott (1706?–1772), a London clockmaker, who made a number of astronomical or regulator clocks. For an illustration of an Ellicott astronomical clock see Derek Howse and Beresford Hutchinson, *The Clocks and Watches of Captain James Cook* (reprinted from the four quarterly issues, 1969, of *Antiquarian Horology*), p. 280.

[3] George Adams (1750–95), a London instrument maker.

[4] Antonio León de Gama (1735–1802), born and died in Mexico City; Professor of Mechanical Engineering at the College of Mines, was distinguished as an astronomer, physicist and archeologist.

[5] José Antonio de Alzate, born in Mexico in 1737, was educated in theology in Mexico City and was ordained in 1756. His major interest, however, lay in natural science: see Francisco de las Barras y de Aragón, 'Noticia de la vida y obras de D. José Antonio Alzate y Ramírez', *Boletín de la Real Sociedad Española de la Historia Natural*, sección biológica 48, 1950, pp. 339–53: see also Virginia González Claverán, *La expedición científica de Malaspina en Nueva España, 1789–1794*, Mexico, D.F.: El Colegio de Mexico, 1988, pp. 109–28.

[6] Joaquín Velázquez Cárdenas de León (1732–86), a Mexican-born astronomer who helped set up the observatory for the Transit of Venus observations by the Abbé Chappe d'Auteroche in Baja California in June 1769: see Iris Wilson Engstrand, *Royal Officer in Baja California: Joaquín Velázquez Cárdenas de León*, Los Angeles, 1976.

Plate 6. Main Square, Mexico City, by Fernando Brambila. Museo Naval, Madrid

activity, had arrived at figures for both latitude and longitude which can scarcely have differed in the least from the true ones.

Nevertheless, Don Antonio Gama's offers and the quality of the planned observation were too oportune for me to give up the idea of carrying it out. From that very day Gama undertook to check the rate of the astronomical clock using equal altitudes. The astronomical clock and astronomical quadrant were brought to the observatory in case they might be of use, especially since Don N. Guadalajara, a skilled craftsman and current Master of Mathematics, had offered to assist with anything within his capabilities. We searched for an achromatic telescope, not without success, so that when the moment arrived, Gama would not have to relinquish the one he had.

Unhappily, the Mexican climate is so given to squalls during the months of April and May, before the onset of the rainy season, that an afternoon during which it does not rain may be considered a fortunate occurrence. This inconvenience, which rendered useless the hours from noon until almost midnight and, on occasion, until two or three the following morning, consistently upset our earliest hopes, forcing us to make use of absolute altitudes in the morning to adjust the rate of the astronomical clock and causing us to fail in our observation of the emergence of Jupiter's first satellite on the night of the 7th, which Galiano, Vernacci, Concha and Cevallos had observed (as I found out later) in Acapulco under the most favourable circumstances.

[12th April]

On the morning of the 12th we observed two sets of equal altitudes, although they were too close to noon. Soon after nightfall, once the gloomy weather had cleared somewhat and broken clouds were beginning to blow over, we were able to entertain some hopes of fulfilling our wishes, which were encouraged much further when the time for the observation drew close and the sky was in parts very clear. However, only a few minutes before the observation the sky clouded over and finally (having missed the occultation), we had to consider ourselves fortunate to be able to catch the emergence, which both Don Antonio Gama and I observed with considerable agreement and accuracy, through a break in the clouds lasting a few minutes. The equal altitudes of the 13th were satisfactory and through them we could tell that the emergence had taken place at 10h 32m 6s apparent time.

During the days that had elapsed since the 5th, I had lost no opportunity in learning, not only more of the current state of that flourishing kingdom, but also anything that might have any bearings on the corvette's future employment or the surveys which we had just carried out. His Excellency the Viceroy, whom I had previously informed which books and papers I regarded as essential to the continuation of our method of work, saw fit to let me have both the relevant instructions, including an account of the current state of affairs in Europe and various pieces of news to which I attached the greatest value and importance since they affected our ability to carry out our mission. The History of California,[1] the Treatise of Botarini,[2] a comparative

---

[1] Andrés Marcos Burriel, *Noticia de la California*, 3 vols, Madrid, 1757.
[2] Lorenzo Boturini Benaduci (1702-55), an Italian historian and one of the first great collectors of American antiquities, who went to Mexico in 1736 and gathered a large collection of aboriginal writings and other records. In 1745, on his return to Spain he was appointed Historiographer for the Indies.

vocabulary of a great many words from Mexico, Sandwich [Hawaiian Islands] and Nootka, another small vocabulary from Cook River and Prince William Sound,[1] a summary from the journal of Teniente de Navío Don Salvador Fidalgo,[2] the reports of Padre Consag,[3] part of the coast of California by Padre Kino,[4] a copy of the very chart of the Seno de Cortés [Golfo de California] that was made at the time of the Conquest.[5] These acquisitions were as useful as they were opportune; and their number was increased by other individuals who, either as a result of His Excellency's influence or of their natural love of the sciences, contributed further to the stock of learning. I was indebted to Don Francisco Mourelle for the voyages of Dampier,[6] a sextant five inches in radius on a stand and a geodetic graphometer;[7] to Dr Alzate for the Cartas [de Relación] of Hernán Cortés,[8] a plan of Mexico City and some basic products of the colony; to Don Gama for many of his astronomical and meteorological observations, some printed, others handwritten; to Don Pablo Santelices[9] for an opportunity to examine his precious manuscripts and colllections; to Don Felix Cepeda[10] for his compilation of a number of useful works by Velázquez;[11] to Don

---

He included a valuable catalogue of his collections in his only published work, *Idea de una nueva historia de America*, 1746. This was presumably the treatise to which Malaspina was referring.

[1] Possibly collected during various Spanish voyages, including Fidalgo's voyage: see n. 2 below.

[2] Fidalgo's account of his 1790 voyage is held in the Archivo General de la Nación, Historia 68, Mexico City.

[3] Fernando Consag, a native of Hungary and a Jesuit priest, arrived in Baja California in 1732 and served at Mission San Ignacio, about 40 miles inland from Santa Rosalia. In 1746 he skirted the coast of Baja California and reached the mouth of the Colorado River, finally dispelling all doubts that California was an island. He explored the western coast of Baja California in 1753 in the company of Captain Fernando de Rivera y Moncada. Consag's map of 1751 was engraved and printed in Rome by the Jesuits in 1754 to show the locations of the missions of that order: see Wagner, *Cartography*, p. 147.

[4] Eusebio Francisco Kino (1645-1711), a Tyrolean and a Jesuit priest with a reputation as a mathematician and astronomer, came to Mexico in 1681 believing that California was a peninsula. As a result of an expedition he made in 1701 he apparently drew a map which was published in 1705 in *Lettres édifiantes*, V, Paris, 1705, which proved that California was not an island: see Herbert E. Bolton, *Rim of Christendom: A Biography of Eusebio Francisco Kino*, New York, 1936.

[5] A reference to the time of the conquest under Hernán Cortés from 1521 up to 1533-4 with the first landings on Baja California.

[6] Probably a reference to Dampier's best-known book, *A New Voyage Round the World*, London, 1697.

[7] A graphometer was a surveying instrument which was popular in France. It was introduced by Philippe Danfrie in 1597. It consisted of a graduated semicircle with a pair of sight vanes at either end, and a movable alidade with another pair of sights. Some later graphometers had telescopic rather than open sights. Graphometers were also known as semicircles or semicircumferentors. On these instruments see J. A. Bennett, *The Divided Circle*, Oxford, 1987, pp. 49-50.

[8] Hernando Cortés, *Cartas de relación*, Seville, 1522. The five letters of Cortés to Carlos V, following the conquest of Mexico in 1521, have been edited and translated by A. R. Pagden, *Hernán Cortés: Letters from Mexico*, New Haven, 1986.

[9] Juan Eugenio Santelices Pablo, a mine owner and linguistic expert who, at the request of the Viceroy, prepared a small dictionary containing the Mexican (Nahuatl), Nootkan and Sandwich (Hawaiian) languages for the use of Malaspina, which is held in the British Library, Add MS 17,631: see González Claverán, *Malaspina en Nueva España*, pp. 103-4.

[10] Felix Cepeda, a junior Spanish naval officer who had come to New Spain in 1789; he served in the *Santa Gertrudis*, and was at Nootka with Bodega during the Limits Expedition of 1792.

[11] Probably Don Domingo Velázquez, whose knowledge of the coast from Chiloé to Acapulco was unequalled: see Vol. I of this edition, p. 179.

Miguel Constansó for the useful work carried out by other engineers in Teguantepeque [Tehuantepec]. To Señores Don Ciriaco González,[1] Dr José Fernández Córdova, Super Intendente de la Casa de Moneda,[2] and Don N. Buenavía, Corregidor[3] of the City, I was indebted for such constant attention and instructive information that it would be as remiss of me to forget them for an instant as it would be to deny them to the nation precisely when, given the flourishing state of her colonies, tribute is owed to those worthy subjects for the important part they have played. Even the vaguest sketch of Mexico City would require many pages and an elegant turn of phrase: I will therefore confine myself to stating here that, in that illustrious capital, Nature with all her gifts, the Monarch with his wise rule and those who govern her with a diligence, selflessness and intelligence hitherto not well known, seem to vie with one another in their determination to adorn her and bring her wealth.

13 April
I had barely fulfilled the main objects of my journey to Mexico City and was preparing on the morning of the 16th to undertake the return to Acapulco, when a special courier arrived from San Blas with sealed letters, dated 7 April, from the commanding officer of the *Atrevida* to the Viceroy and myself. He advised of his happy return to that Department on 29 March, stating that fitting out was proceeding with dispatch and that orders from the King addressed to me from his Excellency the Ministro de Marina had arrived at San Blas the previous day and prescribed for the following summer a survey of the coasts of northern America at around the parallel of 60° so as to ascertain whether there was any possible truth in the obscure report of Ferrer Maldonado about a channel to the Atlantic.[4] We had been forwarded a memorial read to the Académie des Sciences in Paris by M. de Buache[5] on the likelihood of the existence of such a channel, and Don José Bustamante, unaware as yet of the arrival of the *Descubierta* in Acapulco, proposed to carry out the command, either with the one corvette or in the company of a schooner from San Blas, should His Excellency see fit to approve.[6]

I could not hesitate an instant, therefore, either in hastening my return as soon as

---

[1] Ciriaco González Carvajal, Judge of the Real Audiencia de Mexico who, according to Malaspina, supplied the expedition with all necessary written accounts, assisted officers who were ill and provided them with persons informed in natural history: see Iris H. W. Engstrand, *Spanish Scientists in the New World*, Seattle and London, 1981, p. 102.

[2] José Francisco Fernández de Córdova, Superintendent of the Mint: see González Claverán, *Malaspina in Nueva España*, p. 376.

[3] Chief Magistrate.

[4] For a full discussion of the apocryphal voyage of Ferrer Maldonado see Appendix 2 below. For the new instructions see p. 417 below.

[5] The noted French geographer Jean-Nicolas Buache de la Neuville, who gave credence to the mythical voyage of Ferrer Maldonado in 1588: see Appendix 2 below.

[6] It was on 5 April and not 6 April that Bustamante recorded receipt of these documents and the dispatch of his proposal to conduct without Malaspina the exploration of the region of the supposed strait. He intended, by his own account to wait until 24 April for the Viceroy's reply. Meanwhile, however, on 11 April he received Malaspina's dispatch ordering a reunion of the corvettes at Acapulco prior to an expedition to the Hawaiian Islands. Although these orders had been written in ignorance of the most recent instructions relating to the strait of Lorenzo Ferrer Maldonado, Bustamante submitted to them partly because, in any case, he considered the season too far advanced to begin a voyage to the far north: Bustamante, *Diario general del viaje*, pp. 211-12.

possible or in sending warning to Bustamante that very afternoon, to say that he should only ensure in the shortest possible time the rendezvous of the two corvettes in Acapulco, from where we would set out at once to fulfill His Majesty's orders. His Excellency the Viceroy added to the original small amount of funds I had requested the further amount which I now stated as necessary. He also agreed to allow a few men from each corvette (should it seem useful to subdivide the tasks) to occupy themselves at different localities within the kingdom, with matters of either geography, hydrography or the natural sciences. At last, at midnight on the 15th, I was able to set out once more on the road to Acapulco and soon after nightfall on the 19th I rejoined the corvette.

19 April
All the preparations I had ordered had been carried out by Don Dionisio Galiano and the other officers with the greatest zeal, energy and intelligence. The repairs and general overhaul of the ship were complete, the launch was almost ready and good discipline had prevailed. Don Cayetano Valdés, Don Felipe Bauzá and Don Tadeo Haenke had carried out the excursion to Puerto del Marqués and related tasks. The natural history collections, especially in regard to fish, had been much enlarged by Don Antonio Pineda; Haenke had made botanical excursions to all areas in the vicinity and draughtsman Cardero had added to the collection of views. Finally Galiano and

Plate 7. Mexican Indians, by Felipe Bauzá. Museo de América, Madrid

Vernacci had performed such a useful and flawless set of observations, both of the Moon and the satellites of Jupiter, that we could not wish for better information with which to determine the geographic position of Acapulco. Galiano informed me at the same time that Able Seaman Bernardo Martínez was under arrest at the castle and had already been tried. On the very day that I had left for Mexico City, he had wounded, though only slightly, Marine Francisco Vázquez, who had appeared with Iglesia, a seaman deserter from the *Atrevida*. The various patients at present in the hospital with very slight ailments, where they were being looked after by the Hippolitan Fathers with as much care as they were being treated by Don Francisco Flores, would all be in a fit state to embark, except for Marine Corporal Rodríguez, for although they had operated on him with much skill, he nevertheless appeared at that moment to be near his end. Tenientes de Navío Quintano and Novales were somewhat improved and the former was particularly determined to continue with the forthcoming cruise.

20 April
The esteem, friendship and gratitude I felt for a body of officers so deserving the higherst praise had allowed me to sacrifice a few hours to sleep and rest when I had the pleasure of seeing the *Atrevida* appear, already just a short distance from the port. Our separation had lasted almost four months and since the season was now well advanced for the forthcoming cruise, this timely reunion would contribute greatly to its success. These were powerful reasons to prevent us from mutually succumbing to a friendly complacency. By midday, after a few tacks, she was able to anchor and moor near us and not a moment was lost in making the necessary arrangements and preparations in both ships.

That same day Don José Bustamante advised me officially that the highly effective assistance of Capitán de Navío Don Juan de la Bodega y Quadra and the timely orders issued by His Excellency the Viceroy had enabled him to take delivery of the new launch, overhaul the hull, decks, sails and boats and to acquire ample provisions as planned with such speed that the day after receiving my letters from Acapulco he had been able to set sail and reach this port in a passage of seven days. He had produced a plan of the port and its surroundings as far as Cabo Corrientes and searched in vain for a shoal near that cape which had been mentioned to him by a merchant captain who happened to be in San Blas. The astronomical position of that Department had been determined using very good observations by Concha and Cevallos and stretches of the coast between there and Acapulco had been plotted as far as this passage would permit, since he had thought it advisable to avoid even a moment's delay on this occasion.

The results of the astronomical observations for the Plaza Mayor [in San Blas] were as follows:

	Longitude west of Acapulco
By number 10 from Alcapulco (over a period of thirty-one days)	5° 12' 6"
By the corresponding observation of the emergence of the first satellite of Jupiter on the night of the 7th using a weaker telescope but made under very favourable circumstances	5° 15' 40"
By numbers 10 and 105 in agreement (over a period of ten days)	5° 20' 27"
Latitude of the observatory	21° 32' 46"

The last longitude reading given by number 10 seemed the more reliable, especially since it was confirmed by an error of a few minutes in the corresponding observation of the first satellite, attributable to the inferior strength of the achromatic telescopes which Concha and Cevallos were using.

At the same time Capitán de Navío Bodega y Quadra, with much zeal and eagerness, had provided him [Bustamante] with a number of charts giving all the information about our most recent discoveries and also those which he hoped would be carried out in the course of this year in accordance with the instructions passed to the corvettes lying at Nootka. Bustamante, in agreement with Bodega y Quadra, had in addition informed himself in detail about the Department as well as the local advantages and disadvantages when compared with Puerto de Acapulco, where, as I had already hinted to Bustamante, I believed it preferable to establish the base for the naval forces assigned to the defence of this coast.

21 April

On the following day, the 21st, Tenientes de Navío Don José Espinosa and Don Ciriaco Cevallos handed over to me the books and instruments they had been entrusted to bring. The former were four copies each of the English *Nautical Almanac* up to and including 1794 and the latter the two Arnold pocket chronometers numbers 344 and 351, which had been sent from England with chronometers 71 and 72, together with a pendulum, also constructed in London. This was to be used, as I was informed in an official letter from his Excellency the Ministro de Marina, to repeat as far as was possible the experiments with gravity at different parallels of the Earth, not only to arrive at an agreement on measurements based on consistent observations which would eventually be checked in Europe precisely on the 45th parallel, but also in order to continue the investigations as to the true shape of the Earth which was suspected, not without foundation, of showing some discrepancies between one hemisphere and the other. Since these officers had joined the corvette *Atrevida* at such short notice after arriving in Mexico City, their luggage could only reach them at San Blas, whither it was taken in great haste by mule. During this journey the steel leaf or spring which joins the wooden shaft [of the pendulum] to the suspension was broken. Although it was immediately replaced by a skilled craftsman in San Blas, the replacement being so like the original, in dimensions if not in temper, that when one was placed beside the other and examined beneath a lens they showed not the slightest difference.

The method agreed upon for these experiments (assuming the astronomical clock to have been adjusted perfectly beforehand) was normally to carry them out over a space of one or two hours in the calmest possible conditions with an officer responsible for counting on the pendulum and another on the astronomical clock. The officer in charge of the pendulum was to make a note every sixty oscillations and again each time these reached five or the oscillations reached three hundred. He was to call out so loud so that at the same time the officer in charge of the astronomical clock could indicate the second or fraction of a second to which it corresponded. These would both be noted down immediately by the *pilotín* acting as observatory assistant. A final comparison of the total number of oscillations with the mean time elapsed according to the astronomical clock would determine the gain or loss of the pendulum compared to the astronomical clock over the period of the observation.

22 April

Meanwhile preparations for the forthcoming cruise were continuing with all possible speed, for our wish was to make our departure on the morning of 1 May. The *Descubierta* took on half the bread and salt pork which the *Atrevida* had embarked in San Blas and handed over to her thirty quintals of much better bread which had been made in Acapulco and Tiscla.[1] Similar arrangements were made for pitch and timber. Both ships left a considerable part of their spare masts and spars as well as gunner's stores in the King's warehouses and the *Decubierta* left in addition some ten bundles of warm clothing and some trade goods. Supplies of water and wood were replenished and the ships were cleaned on the outside and, since we managed at the same time to come close to finishing the charts, manuscripts and natural history collections that had to be sent to Madrid, it seemed our agreed plan could not fail to be implemented.

This was not, however, as simple as had first been imagined, since a mature examination of the circumstances surrounding the expedition at the time had led us to subdivide certain missions so that they would hasten the completion of the work undertaken and would bring possible scientific advantages to the nation. Our circumstances (now that the northern cruise had been decided upon) could not fail to bring home to us that the recent adverse weather encountered between Realejo and Acapulco, as well as the *Atrevida*'s hasty return from San Blas, had resulted in many imperfections in the charts concerning those localities. This could not be put right, or at least not without a long delay and considerable deviation from our route, if some event, whether very fortunate or calamitous,[2] were to prevent the return of the corvettes to Acapulco the following October. After a careful look at the nature of the surveys mentioned and the importance of surveying with precision not just the coast but also the important ports of Zihuatanejo,[3] Aquatulco,[4] Los Angeles[5] and Teguantepeque,[6] it appeared that a smaller vessel, which would be easy to obtain in San Blas, could perform this task more exactly and doubtless with greater economy of time and resources.

Reflections of this nature led us directly to others no less useful, namely that the same officers who carried out that programme could afterwards occupy themselves with the surveys of Golfos de Amapala[7] and Nicoya which the corvettes had not been able to enter and, having explored thoroughly the isthmus which lies beween the Pacific Ocean and Golfo de Nicaragua, could then enter that gulf, plot its shores exactly and reach the Atlantic by Río San Juan. Nor were we guided solely by our hydrographic aims in relation to the charts, although these were of no small account, in addition to the benefits described, a new correlation of our longitudes to the other

---

[1] Tixtla de Guerrero near Chilpancingo in the state of Guerrero.
[2] I.e. the discovery and subsequent passage to the Atlantic through Maldonado's strait or the loss of both vessels such as happened to La Pérouse.
[3] Bahía de Zihuatanejo, a small but excellent harbour, 108 miles WNW of Acapulco.
[4] See p. 37, n. 2 above.
[5] See p. 37, n. 3 above.
[6] Golfo de Tehuantepec.
[7] Now Golfo de Fonseca.

sea by means of our chronometers should not be disregarded.[1] The areas adjacent to the river and Golfo de Nicaragua were at the time a most compelling attraction for our rival nations, and an incentive for an invasion. Therefore a good and accurate survey of these areas had to be seen as important to national maritime defence. Moreover, the former was the only convenient departure point for forwarding to Europe a considerable quantity of valuable commodities which up to now had failed to materialize, which are produced in that fertile province without our ships having even tried to obtain them, either because of the frequent hostilities with the Mosquito Indians[2] or lack of navigational knowledge in the river.

The desire to extend our longitudes to the opposite coast and to examine any points of interest to national shipping and defence as far as was possible with the officers, instruments and time at the expedition's disposal, naturally also inclined us to look at the region of the continent between the mouth of the Guazahualcos[3] in the Sea of the North[4] and the port of Ventosa[5] in the Sea of the South.[6] It was not only the convenience of sailing up the rivers, the short extent of flat land which lay between them, and the passable bar of the Guazahualcos that had attracted the attention of the first conquistadors to that area. It had also been seen as an easy point for the invasion of the Kingdom of Mexico and perhaps the only one which should be feared because of its sheltered access to the sea, because the land is intersected by many channels and largely unpopulated and because of the distance from Mexico City, which would be the source of assistance not only for that area but also for the Kingdom of Guatemala, if invaded.

In addition to the reflections mentioned above, the nature of our imminent northern cruise, which would be restricted to a few outings with the launches, nearly always under the corvettes' guns, meant that a considerable part of the fine officers and instruments that were to be found in the two corvettes would without any doubt remain idle, with their professional skills frustrated. These scruples were the worthier of consideration insofar as they related to natural history, the investigation of which would be as tentative and limited on the extremely dangerous shores that we were intending to visit as it would be extensive and useful in New Spain, where Don Antonio Pineda, with his unwavering devotion to his work, could make a very useful fresh comparison of all its products with those of South America where he had so recently visited so many localities.

Finally, these same ideas came to be confirmed both by economic considerations, since at that time these tasks could be combined without the slightest extra burden on our finances, and scientific considerations, since the ordering of much as yet disorganized material and the completion of certain individuals's many excellent ideas would proceed with the energy and method that could only be expected with peace and uninterrupted study.

---

[1] I.e. to obtain the difference in longitude between the Pacific and the Caribbean at this point.
[2] The indigenous inhabitants of Nicaragua's Mosquito coast.
[3] Río Coatzacoalcos: *see* p. 43, n.2 above.
[4] I.e. the Atlantic.
[5] Now Bahía Ventosa: *see* p. 37, n. 1 above.
[6] I.e. the Pacific.

The commanding officer of the *Atrevida* agreed on the usefulness of these steps and by the next day the equipment was allocated in such a way as to enable the following individuals to be assigned work outside the corvettes.

	Individuals		Astronomical and geodetic instruments	
	Descubierta	*Atrevida*	*Descubierta*	*Atrevida*
Senior Officers	D. Alejandro Malaspina	D. José Bustamante	Chronometers 61, 71, 72	Berthoud No 10
	D. José Espinosa	D. Antonio Tova	Astronomical quadrant by Sisson	Arnold pocket chronometers Nos 105 and 351
	D. Cayetano Valdés	D. Juan de la Concha	Astronomical clock	Astronomical quadrant by Ramsden
	D. Fernando Quintano	D. José Robredo	Simple pendulum	
	D. Juan Vernacci	D. Ciriaco Cevallos	Three large achromatic telescopes	A medium size achromatic telescope
	D. Secundino Salamanca	D. Francisco Viana		
	D. Felipe Bauzá	D. Fabio Ali Ponzoni	A smaller one	A smaller one
			A barometer by Magallanes	A marine barometer by Nairne
			A magnetic inclinometer	
Pilotos	D. Juan Maqueda	D. Jacobo Murphy	Two theodolites	A similar one by Magallanes
	D. José Sánchez	D. Juan Inciarte	An equatorial by Dollond	A magnetic inclinometer
	D. Juan Delgado	D. José Hurtado	A eudiometer by Fontana[1]	Two theodolites
Naturalist	D. Tadeo Haenke		Various natural history instruments	A eudiometer by Fontana
Paymaster	D. Rafael de Arias	D. José Ezquerra		
Chaplain	D. José de Mesa	D. Pedro Añino		
Surgeon	D. Francisco Flores	D. Pedro González		
Figure	D. Tomás Suria	draughtsman		

Specialized Branches

For Geography and Astronomy		For Natural History	
Individuals	Instruments	Individuals	Instruments
D. Dionisio Galiano	A large achromatic telescope	D. Antonio Pineda	A large microscope
D. Arcadio Pineda	Pocket chronometer 344 for longitude	Botanist D. Luis Neé	Two eudiometers by Volta[2]
D. Martin de Olavide		Artist D. José Guío	The Parker apparatus
D. Manuel Novales (at present sick)	Another silver one from the collection	Clerk D. Juan del Villar[3]	Various instruments for physics, chemistry and dissection
	Reflecting circle by M. Borda		
	Three officers' sextants		
	The astronomical clock } From the royal collection in Mexico City		
	The astronomical quadrant }		
	A theodolite) From the mines in Mexico City		

[1] Félix Fontana (1730-1805), Italian naturalist, chemist and physicist, who contributed to the study of eudiometry as a means of testing air purity.

[2] Alessandro Volta (1745-1827), Italian physicist, who studied electricity and electro-magnetism and who also invented a eudiometer.

[3] Julián del Villar y Pardo joined the expedition as a servant (Pablo Antón Solé, 'Los padrones de cumplimiento pascual de la expedición Malaspina: 1790-1794', in *La expedición Malaspina (1789-1794): bicentario de la salida de Cádiz*, Cádiz, 1991, p. 199. In April 1791 he was appointed to Pineda's expedition to Mexico as Pineda's clerk, during which he acted at times as an artist. He remained in Mexico on account of ill health, during which he took part in further expeditions: Engstrand, *Spanish Scientists*, pp. 100, 147.

In this way, while still retaining quite a large number of officers in the corvettes, we were likely to increase considerably the fruits of the expedition without any increase in expenditure. The instructions given to Don Dionisio Galiano required that he proceed to Mexico City with his officers without delay, taking advantage of the next rainy season to work up and put in order our astronomical and nautical material, which, having been the fruit of uncommon talent and industry, would undoubtedly enhance the reputation of our national shipping and be of great value to it. He would at the same time set about making a thorough series of astronomical observations which in the same season he could perhaps extend as far as Veracruz with no great difficulty. Then, the following October, when the dry season came round once more, he was to travel to Guazahualcos and Teguantepeque unless, having received no news from the corvettes, he found it necessary in November, over and above everything else, to attend to the completion of the hydrographic charts between Acapulco and Sonsonate, a task that would nevertheless be the responsibility of two other officers if our return took place as we planned. It was suggested to Galiano that he could make use of Don Arcadio Pineda's abilities in gathering together the useful unedited material relating to different areas of enquiry covered by the expedition. He was advised to take every care to ensure that Don Manuel Novales, whose health was in a very poor state, should attend solely to his own recovery, in calm and comfort, whether this should take him to Europe or detain him in Mexico City, and he was assigned the funds needed to ensure that neither the individuals attached to him nor those with Don Antonio Pineda would lack any of the necessary resources. Finally, all our original documents were handed over to him and he was charged, always subject to the orders of His Excellency the Viceroy, to try to combine any possible scientific benefits to be gained in that kingdom with his arrival in Spain around the beginning of 1793 so as to attend immediately to the final stages of the hydrographic work on our coasts.

As regards Don Antonio Pineda, he was merely told to seek the advice of certain people in Mexico City with local knowledge so as to draw up the programme of his investigations with success. These should, nevertheless, concern themselves more with lithology and a comparison of the majestic works of nature in South America with those of this locality than with the other areas of natural history, bearing in mind that already for several years past His Majesty had commissioned a number of people, as skilful as they were zealous, for this purpose throughout the realm. If some unforeseen event should prevent the corvettes returning to Acapulco within the time agreed, he was instructed to set out in the Manila galleon directly to those islands and that he should stay there, continuing his work until we managed to reach those seas in the corvettes and so be reunited.

I reported these arrangements both to His Excellency the Ministro de Marina and to the Viceroy of Mexico. To the latter I suggested in more detail not so much the assistance these two valuable detached parties of the expedition might need but the benefits that would arise from them.

Don Tomás Suria, an individual of great skill both in drawing and engraving in the service of the Real Casa de Moneda de Mexico, was included in the present ship's complement as a draughtsman. His Excellency the Viceroy had seen fit to appoint him for this purpose after I had told him in my letter from Guayaquil how useful a person with the skills to perform this function would be.[1] We were also indebted to the goodness of that authority for the prompt arrival in Acapulco of all the provisions we had either requested from Mexico City or that had been sent to us from Spain.

Unfortunately an apparent error in the markings made us wish once more that we had the box of physics instruments collected in Paris which had been missing in Lima. In its place we found a little box of mineralogical instruments which we returned immediately to Mexico City, consoling ourselves with the idea that on our return at least we would be able to take them to expand our investigations into physics as far as we desired.

Now all that remained to be done to complete the preparation of both crews (double wages having also been granted to the *Atrevida*'s crew) was the punishment of the seaman assailant from the *Descubierta*, the embarkation of the sick and the issuing of the instructions for the coming cruise. The trial of the seaman had left no doubt as to his crime nor the barbarous manner in which it had been commited, so he undoubtedly deserved to be court-martialled. But since the delinquent had succeeded in obtaining ecclesiastical immunity[2] and because the complete recovery of the wounded marine suggested that the penalty should be much lighter, it was to be feared that the imposition of a sentence of imprisonment, far from correcting the assailant, or serving as a warning to the others, would merely deprive me of a good seaman who, moreover, would thereby be rewarded rather than punished. Bearing these thoughts in mind, I decided it would be preferable to punish him on board, taking good care first with all available formalities, such as assembling the crews and having the marines from both corvettes fall in with an officer at their head. He was publicly sentenced to six months detention, reduced to cabin boy and to complete the voyage at our discretion in chains at every port we might visit. The others were warned and the reasons why this crime was not being judged by court-martial, in spite of its gravity, were explained to them. Finally the proceedings were referred to His Excellency the Viceroy and his approval sought for the arbitrary sentence imposed, since lack of time and our other circumstances had not permitted us to request it beforehand.

25 April
At about this time we had the misfortune to lose in the hospital Corporal Liborio Rodríguez, a marine whose service and courage made him worthy of a better fate; so much so that to the last he maintained a truly enviable degree of constancy and resignation in the face of immeasurable suffering. The ships' complements were now short of five marines, including this man. Nor was the *Descubierta*'s crew complete and on board the *Atrevida* three Filipino sailors, recently admitted to the service and trusting no doubt to their familiarity with the area around Acapulco, though it was known to be the least favourable for desertion, had dared to desert once more. In view of these developments I requested replacements from the troops at the castle, if there were any

[1] For an account of Suria's life see Arsenio Rey Tejerina, ed., *Tomás de Suria a l'expedició Malaspina Alaska 1791*, Valencia, 1995.
[2] Presumably by taking refuge in a church.

who would volunteer. As there were many, in fact, who were also of good conduct and robust disposition, the warden granted my written request. Soldiers from the artillery company and two from the fusiliers joined the corvettes as auxiliaries for the coming voyage. In addition a lance corporal, also from the artillery, a deserter from the Royal Marine Artillery on board the *San Ramón*, had given himself up and so rejoined his former colours on board the *Atrevida*. In addition, numerous and energetic measures were taken to apprehend the three deserters. Two of them were in fact caught, together with another absentee, and brought on board the *Atrevida* immediately. Our complements for the next cruise were therefore as set out below, after all the measures described had been taken.

	Descubierta	*Atrevida*
Commissioned and senior officers, naturalist and artist	15	13
Warrant officers	16	16
Able seamen, seamen and landsmen	42	45
Marines	12	15
Marine gunners	4	4
Auxiliary troops from Acapulco	4	1
Servants	7	6
Totals	100	100

In addition, we had stores of provisions in quantities as set out in the victualling book.

	Descubierta		*Atrevida*	
	Quantity	For No. of months	Quantity	For No. of months
Quintales of bread	392	10⅔	251	9½
Quintales of salt pork	67	11	67	11
Quintales of dried vegetables fine and ordinary	60	7	70	8
Arrobas of wine	864	18	862	24
Arrobas of vinegar	100	24	108	24
Arrobas of olive oil	175	24	203	30
Barrels of pickled cabbage	16	–		
Casks of water	120	4		
Quintales of firewood	300	6		

At this point I also thought it would be opportune to examine all the losses from the two crews since our departure from Cádiz. The state of the crews at that point should not only serve as a warning to any other ships frequenting the ports of the Pacific Ocean, with larger and less carefully chosen crews than ours, but also to justify in our case the present state of the crews, the regular distribution of clothes and refreshments, a certain relaxation of military discipline and last of all our reserving until Manila the wine ration issued on ships of the royal navy to everyone entitled to the full sea-going daily allowance. Thus a considered examination of the books gave the following results to both paymasters.

Classes	Deserters	Died on board or in hospital	Left in hospital	Transferred for unruliness or other actions	Discharges for other reasons	
		Descubierta				
Warrant officers	2				1	
Seamen	28	1	1	6	4	
Marines	8	1		2	0	
Marine gunners	2	1			0	
Servants					3	
Artist					1	
Total	40	3	1	8	9	61
		Atrevida				
Warrant officers	5	0	1	1		
Seamen	39	3	5	4	4	
Marines	4	1	2	1	0	
Seamen gunners	3		1	3	0	
Servants	2				3	
Totals	53	4	9	9	7	82
Total losses in both corvettes						143[1]

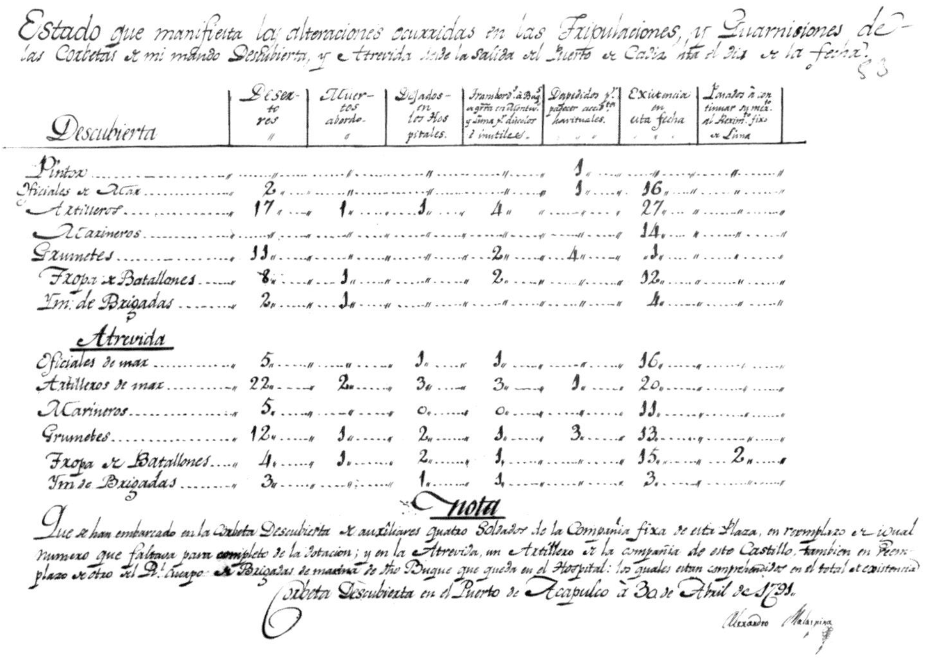

Plate 8. The state of the corvette's ships' companies in Acapulco, signed by Alejandro Malaspina, 30 April 1791. Courtesy of the Oregon Historical Society, Malaspina Papers, MS 2814/201

[1] For a slightly different version of this table, signed by Malaspina, see plate 8 above.

On the 29th, all the plans, paintings and boxes of natural history specimens that made up the latest shipment of the results of our work were ready. Not as methodically as we had managed in Lima, but at least with the dispatch, efficiency and versatility required by our desire to earn our Sovereign's approval. At this time I informed His Excellency the Ministro de Marina that Don Dionisio Galiano would be charged with completing all astronomical, meteorological, chronometer, magnetic variation and tidal logs which were not being sent on this occasion. In order that these very results should reach the Throne with the greatest possible speed and acceptability, I begged the Viceroy to take charge of the whole consignment which I sent him, partly by courier and partly by ordinary means, in the following manner.

By Courier

Items	Contents	
Tin tubes numbers 1 and 2	Navigation	Two Mercator charts covering the coast from Lima to Golfo Dulce on Costa Rica. Five draft plans of the ports of Perico,[1] Chagres, Realejo, Aserradores and Acapulco.
	Natural History	74 botanical paintings by José Guio. 58 zoological paintings, 46 by José Cardero and 12 by Tomás Suria.
	Perspective	16 views taken and drawn by José Cardero.
Packet No. 1		The journal of occurrences on board the corvettes from Lima to Acapulco. The astronomical journal as far as Acapulco. Part of Don Tadeo Haenke's botanical treatise and the account of his journeys.
Packet No. 2		The journal of occurrences on board the *Atrevida* following her separation off Nicaragua and her rendezvous with the *Descubierta* in Acapulco. Continuation of Don Pineda's zoology.
Packet No. 3		Three notebooks with sketches of the views of the entire coast from Montevideo to Acapulco.

With the muleteers

Item	Marking	Contents
1 box	Above: D.A. No. 1 Beneath; T.H.	Continuation of Don Tadeo Haenke's botanical collection.
1 idem	Above: D.A. No. 2 Beneath: L.N.	Continuation of Don Luis Neé's botanical collection.
2 idem	Above: D.A. Nos 3 & 4 Beneath: A.P.	Continuation of Don Antonio Pineda's collections relating to zoology, lithology and minerals.

The only thing left to do before we made our departure was to draw up the plan for the coming cruise and to inform the commanding officer of the *Atrevida* of the instructions and the corresponding places of rendezvous. The plan had to take into

---

[1] The anchorage off Panamá.

account not just the orders and instructions I had just received regarding the verification of the passage of one Ferrer Maldonado from the Atlantic to the Pacific Ocean and then from there to the Atlantic, but also the considerably advanced season, any work previous to our own so as to combine possible hydrographic advantages, and finally the attention due to our Californian coast south of 37° called for by our national interests and with regard to the present political situation in Europe. A summary of the present state of geographical and nautical knowledge of the northern coasts of California and the north-west of America, however general, seemed to be of some use and will try to justify the plan of the operations that resulted from it.

BOOK SIX

From Acapulco to Port Mulgrave and Nootka Sound

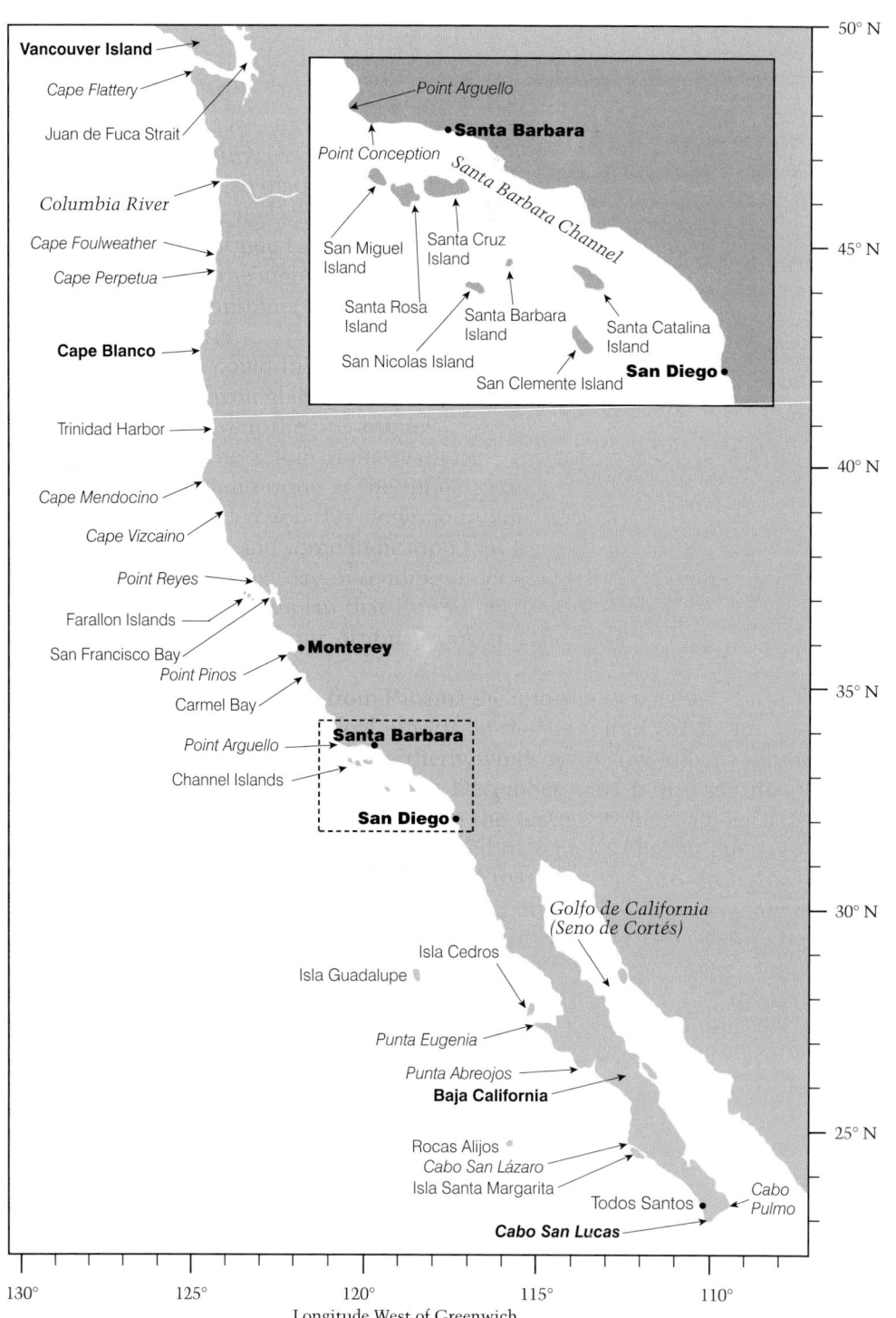

Fig. 2. Cabo San Lucas to Vancouver Island, May to June 1791, and Vancouver Island to Cabo San Lucas, August to October 1791

CHAPTER 1

From Acapulco to Port Mulgrave

1 May
At dawn, following the measures taken during the previous day and night, both corvettes were completely ready to set sail. The mail from Mexico City, which arrived before eight in the morning, brought nothing to oppose our intentions. At half past nine, with the first light airs from NW, we were able to cast off the last mooring line and, having hoisted the pinnace, set a course without delay to clear the harbour mouth under full sail.

Unexpectedly the breeze backed to SSW and remained there, very light, while the tide was not in our favour, except very close to the coast to the south. Accordingly we had to continue tacking until two in the afternoon. When the light breeze at last veered to west, we were able, on the starboard tack, to pass one-and-a-half cables off Punta de la Bruja and half a mile from Punta del Diamante.[1] Finally, at four in the afternoon, we no longer felt any need to [prepare to] anchor.[2]

If one considered only the tracks followed by the Manila galleons, Commodore Anson's experience at about the beginning of May and the common hearsay along these coasts, it would not be very easy to reach the trade winds; even to achieve this we would have to lose much ground to the south. But recent passages made by our own corvettes seemed to belie the infallibility of these rules. The *Descubierta*, in latitude 13° and some seventy leagues offshore, had found only calms and light variable breezes, while the *Atrevida*, on her first passage, had had the good fortune to encounter the trade winds to within sight of the port. She also encountered strong trade winds on her passage to San Blas, when some 6° or 7° west of Acapulco she had been able to attain latitudes of 15° and 16°. As for the choice between an offshore route and a coastal passage, which both the NW breezes and the strong currents would make very difficult, there could be no hesitation, particularly as any route, if it were to take us rapidly to high latitudes, must make us stand well off the coast of California to avoid the northerlies and have the NE[3] winds at a better angle.

With these considerations in mind, whenever the winds would tend to be a land

---

[1] The NW and SW entrance points, respectively, of Bahía de Puerto del Marqués.
[2] As a seamanlike precaution, Malaspina would have kept an anchor ready to drop until clear of all dangers.
[3] In the original MS NE (i.e. the North-east Trade Wind) has been erroneously altered to NO [NW]: AMN, MS 753 confirms that NE is the correct direction.

breeze, particularly in the early morning, a westerly course was steered, close hauled, so as to make the best possible speed. However, whenever they were sea breezes from west or WSW, southerly courses were preferred.[1] Since we were bound to fall off too far to the south due to the effects of winds and currents, we were not readily going to contribute to this by choosing courses likely to delay us.

5 May
At first, however, there were few opportunities for us to depart from the conventional route. At noon on the 5th, four days after our departure, with the weather still giving no sign of the proximity of the trade wind, we had hardly made a degree to the west, while losing two degrees of latitude. [6th] On the following day, however, when the breeze set in a little fresher and more constant from NNW and north, we began to make good progress, with signs that the trade wind was not far off. At the time, and even the day after losing the coast from sight, we could see few birds on the horizon, which were mostly limited to the two species of *Pelecanus* and *Larus*.[2] So far we had caught only a very small bonito.

The clarity of the sky and horizon, and the calmness of the sea and wind, reminded us that we were in the Pacific Ocean.

Variation which we observed daily, either by azimuths or by amplitudes, remained almost constant at 6°30′NE, and the second comparison of our chronometers with those of the *Atrevida*, made on the following day, gave very little difference between them, the daily equation of corrections showing that this was due more to a loss in number 72, rather than to a gain in number 10.

8 May
On the evening of the 8th we observed some lunar distances in quite favourable conditions. The results were 12′ west of the chronometers, which would have been only 7′ with number 10, thereby bringing it very close to the longitude assigned to Acapulco by the satellites of Jupiter and much closer by our chronometers than the lunar distances taken on board the *Atrevida*. On this day our latitude was 13°13′ and our longitude 3°40′ west of Acapulco.

Variation had decreased and remained constant at 5°30′[NE]. It seemed that the differences to south and east, very common near the coast, were coming to an end, having been caused by an error in our dead reckoning of 50′ in latitude and 1°6′ in longitude.

Until now the essential purpose of our arrangements for maintaining discipline had dealt with two problems only, desertion and absence from work. It would have been unwise to apply a harsher or more irksome discipline either to impress upon the crews the idea of imminent danger, requiring the use of arms, or to impose an unyielding regime to guard against the risks to health to be encountered at any time in the various ports we had visited so far. In this way we had been able to prepare them gradually for our objective by instilling in them two other qualities which we

---

[1] A northerly course would take the corvettes back towards the land.
[2] Probably Brown Pelicans (*Pelecanus occidentalis*) and members of the Gull family.

could not do without, namely, good health and a certain feeling of trust and affection towards us, so that they would consider us as friends rather than superiors on all occasions not directly connected with military service. At this time, however, the need for military discipline could not be overlooked in order to avoid taking any chances concerning either our intentions or those of the natives we were about to encounter, without prejudicing the friendly contacts upon which progress in our planned scientific investigations had to be founded. Nor could we fail to do anything likely to assist in the preservation of health given the rapid change of climate we were to encounter, and the cramped conditions in which we would have to live for the next six months.[1]

To this end the measures for good order and cleanliness on board were increased. The officers of the watch were strictly instructed to attend tactfully to both matters daily so as not to jeopardize, even for a moment, our mutual trust and affection. Some warm clothing was distributed. Any idea of danger in the coming cruise was dispelled. Finally a plan of engagement was drawn up on the basis of lessons learnt by those who had preceded us on voyages of this type, which could at the same time be adapted to allow for all our purposes and for any other coasts that we might visit in the future. We took care to prepare various implements for the most convenient and rapid use of our offensive weapons.[2]

[10 May]

Then, on the afternoon of the 10th, the pinnaces of both corvettes were lowered to communicate these measures to the *Atrevida*. At the same time there was an opportunity for the officers of each ship to meet, those of the *Atrevida* thus being able to see for themselves these preparations, which were difficult and troublesome to communicate in writing, but which needed to be established uniformly on board both corvettes, particularly with regard to the launches, which might have to be sent to work for some time at a distance from the corvettes. All those who know the character of our seamen, [on the one hand] heedless of any restraint other than reason and the example of the officers, whom they respect, and, on the other hand, so much given to excessive passions, and opposed to direct coercion, will not be surprised that our measures in this regard always entail a system almost diametrically opposed to that followed by the English under Captain Cook. However, in the memorials concerning the preservation of health, these reasons will be discussed at greater length so as to

---

[1] Malaspina clearly realized that, after 18 months visiting Spanish possessions in the Americas, the expedition's diversion to the NW Coast represented a major shift not only in focus (exploration) but also in potential danger (climate, native peoples and foreign ships). In a series of instructions (AMN, MS 427, ff. 80-81ᵛ and 83-89), Malaspina prepared the ships and men for their new obligations and opportunities: see Donald C. Cutter, *Malaspina and Galiano: Spanish Voyages to the Northwest Coast in 1791 and 1792*, Vancouver, 1991, pp. 8-17.

[2] Bustamante provides further details. Malaspina's concerns were with security in case of conflict with native peoples, whose respect he hoped to command by vigilance and preparedness. Bustamante adopted Malaspina's measures in order to ensure the maximum collaboration between the launches. Bustamante ascribes to his own initiative the 'particular attention' to hygiene he had instituted on board the *Atrevida* since leaving Acapulco in anticipation of sickness induced by the abrupt change of climate and as a precaution against scurvy: Bustamante, *Diario general del viaje*, p. 231.

show to what extent in dealing with Spanish seamen one has to consider the sensibility, reasoning and lively passions so different from those of northern seamen.[1]

On encountering the trade wind, which had remained in the NE since the previous day, we found ourselves at noon in latitude 14°27′ and longitude 6°43′ west of Acapulco, with a favourable outlook. We then had the choice of starting to make our way northward, sailing close to the wind with which at present we were sailing free, or continuing to the west, so as to stand well offshore. The following considerations decided us in favour of the latter. First, if we made too much northing we would undoubtedly approach Isla Socorro and Roca Partida,[2] near which Comandantes Hezeta and Bodega y Quadra[3] had found only variable breezes and calms; second, that we would immediately lose the north and NW breezes that blow along the coast of California; third, that all previous passages had found that at latitudes of 28° and 30° the northerlies veered to east and SE, but only a considerable distance offshore; and finally, that if we reached the meridian of the places we were to examine on the north coast of America, the NW winds would allow us to tack to NNE, when the west and SW winds would be abaft the beam on our course. As for the latter, our only object at the time was our speed and, having made a careful study of Ferrer Maldonado's account[4] and those of previous voyages, its direction could only be towards Cross Sound[5] and Captain Cook's Cape Fairweather.[6] From here we would begin surveying to the west, with particular attention to Bahía de Behring,[7] immediately

---

[1] From the moment he and Bustamante proposed an expedition to rival that of Cook and La Pérouse, Malaspina liked to consider the voyage as a great enterprise in which a collegiality of interest and enthusiasm and sense of obligation infused all its participants. Unfortunately the facts betray this view of the noble endeavour. By the time the ships had reached Acapulco and were preparing for the NW Coast campaign, a high percentage of the original crews had deserted or had been replaced for some reason such as poor health or inadequate performance: see plate 8. Thus a major replacement of personnel took place in Acapulco and this included a number of Filipino sailors recently arrived on the Manila galleon: see Cutter, *Malaspina and Galiano*, pp. 15-16.

[2] A steep-to barren rock, 62 miles WNW of Isla Socorro, which when seen from a distance resembles a jury-rigged vessel.

[3] This is a reference to the experience of Bruno de Hezeta and Juan Francisco de la Bodega y Quadra when they set out on their voyage to the NW Coast in March 1775: see p. 16, n. 1 above. Bodega had assisted the preparations for Malaspina's northern voyage with lengthy advice on the route to be taken to catch the most favourable winds: see AMN, MS, 332.

[4] See Appendix 2 below.

[5] Passage that separates continental Alaska from Alexander Archipelago off the Alaska 'Panhandle'. Named by Captain Cook on Holy Cross Day, 3 May 1778. In this instance Malaspina has not translated this name into Spanish.

[6] Promontory in the shadow of Mount Fairweather, the highest peak (4,670 metres) in the range of the same name in Glacier Bay National Park, north of Cross Sound.

[7] The supposed anchorage of Vitus Bering was placed on Cook's chart between Cape Fairweather and Yakutat Bay - a location repeated in the charts of George Dixon and Malaspina. In 1786 La Pérouse thought it more likely to be the mouth of a river than a bay, but retained the name 'Bhering.' Bering appears to have actually anchored off Kayak Island, where Georg Wilhelm Steller, the natural historian, landed to make a collection. For a discussion of the various problems surrounding 'Bering's Bay' see J. C. Beaglehole (ed.), *The Journals of Captain James Cook on His Voyages of Discovery*. III. *The Voyage of the* Resolution *and* Discovery, *1776–1780*, 2 vols, Hakluyt Society, extra ser. 36a–36b, Cambridge, 1967, p. 338, n. 4. Cook found the description and chart of Bering's visit to Alaska in Gerhard Friedrich Müller's *Voyages from Asia to America for Completing the Discoveries of the North West Coast of America*, London, 1761, so confusing that he never satisfactorily resolved the issue for himself.

behind which the Captain had noted a stretch of low coast, with no backing hills, leaving him in some doubt as to whether there might be a body of water to the north.[1] Having referred the position of these places to the longitude of Cabo San Lucas, as determined by Don Vicente Doz,[2] it finally followed that our investigations would begin at latitude 58°30′ and [longitude] 28° west of Cabo San Lucas, which, according to our observations, lay 9°38′ west of Acapulco and 4°18′ from San Blas. The routes taken by Captain Cook and Teniente de Navío Don Salvador Fidalgo[3] seemed to leave no doubt as to the ease of sailing westward along this stretch of the coast. Thus, after dispelling in a short time all suspicion regarding the existence of the above-mentioned passage to the Atlantic, we could be able to make good use of the months of August and September to rectify the conclusions of Captain Dixon[4] and those of Mr Coxe,[5] and, lastly, confirm with good observations of latitude and longitude the positions of our *presidios* and the other ports on the coast of California.

Given these considerations and the fact that the season was now well advanced, we had to give up all thoughts of surveying any or all of the islands lying between the mainland and the Sandwich [Hawaiian] Islands. Furthermore, Comandantes Hezeta and Bodega y Quadra had sighted Isla Socorro, Piloto Mourelle had sighted Roca Partida and Comte de la La Pérouse, when running along the parallel of Las Ulua and Los Majos[6] had identified these as the Sandwich Islands, with only the usual error in longitude made by the galleons crossing from Acapulco to the Marianas Islands. We therefore steered WbyN and the wind, although shifting somewhat between NNE and ENE, was so favourable that by noon on the 13th we had reached latitude 16°25′ and longitude 14°22′ west of Acapulco, with Isla Santa Rosa[7] (or perhaps Nublada)[8] bearing almost due north, according to the position shown on the San Blas charts.

On the afternoon of this day the sky became even more overcast than on previous

---

[1] 'Behind the bay ... or rather to the South of it, the chain of mountains before mentioned, is interrupted by a plain of a few leagues extent; beyond which the sight was unlimited; so that there is either a level country or water behind it.': James Cook and James King, *A Voyage to the Pacific Ocean ... for making Discoveries in the Northern Hemisphere*, 3 vols, London, 1784, II, pp. 347–8.

[2] See p. 38, n. 2 above.

[3] See p. 54, n. 4 above.

[4] See p. 53, notes 2 and 7 above.

[5] William Coxe (1747–1828), cleric, traveller, and first British historian of Russian voyages in the North Pacific, whose 'later Russian discoveryes' were among a number of books purchased for the expedition in Paris in 1789: AMN, MS 3435. The work referred to would have been either Coxe's *Account of the Russian Discoveries between Asia and America*, London, 1780, or his *A Comparative View of the Russian Discoveries with those made by Captains Cook and Clerke*, London, 1787, or possibly both.

[6] In May 1786, when on passage from Easter Island to the Hawaiian Islands and the NW Coast, La Pérouse, 'Wishing to render an important service to geography by deleting from the charts these pointless names which apply to non-existent islands and merely serve to perpetuate errors that are harmful to navigation', made for the latitude of Hawaii far to the east and then sailed west to prove that various islands that had appeared on early Spanish charts were in fact the Hawaiian Islands wrongly located and that there were no islands between the latter and Islas Revillagigedo: see John Dunmore, ed., *The Journal of Jean-François de Galaup de la Pérouse, 1785–1788*, 2 vols, Hakluyt Society, 2nd ser. 179–180, London, 1994, pp. 79–80. La Pérouse passed through the charted positions of Isla Disgraciada and Los Majos without the slightest indication of land. He makes no mention of Las Ulua in his journal.

[7] A volcanic island in Islas Revillagigedo, now called Isla Clarion.

[8] A volcanic island in Islas Revillagigedo, now called Isla San Benedicto.

days. The wind, now strong, veered rapidly from north to east. We saw a few flocks of gulls, all signs confirming the position of Isla Rosa as being approximately on the same meridian as shown on the San Blas charts. During the following night the sea was fairly high and choppy and towards midnight there were several strong gusts from between north and SE, obliging us to steer west for a time. The wind finally settled to a moderate northerly which cleared the sky considerably and allowed us to steer WbyN once more, under full sail.

14 May
Nothing could be more beautiful and peaceful than the conditions we had at dawn on the 14th. The heavy swell of the previous night had dropped. The atmosphere was now pleasantly relieved of the heavy haze and the breeze, now moderate again from NE, gave us a speed of six to seven knots, which did not lessen even though we steered NW by compass from noon, when our latitude was already 17°5' and our longitude 17°0' from Acapulco.

Variation had decreased to 2° and 3°NE by this time, according to several azimuth observations since the misty weather usually prevented the observation of eastern and western amplitudes. We now saw very few birds, these being mostly frigatebirds, and although there were a great many flying fish, no fish were to be caught by fizgig or hook.

15 and 16 May
Once again we were able to reach and quickly cross the parallel attained by the Sun at this time.[1] The light NE breeze persisted, enabling us to continue to steer NW, although, on the morning of the 16th, it fell to very light airs for a few hours with overcast skies and misty weather. At noon that day our latitude was 20°4', our longitude 20°21' and variation about 5°30'NE. We gradually altered course to north, but not so much as to take us too close inshore; the Sandwich Islands bore some 700 leagues to the west on this parallel.

Daily observations still showed a current setting to the west, although tending more to the south than to the north. In spite of repeated changes in our stowage, the *Atrevida* retained a clear advantage in speed, which we could only attribute to the fact that her draught was a foot deeper than ours, except for the small or virtually non-existent difference [in length] from bow to stern, which we knew conferred a particular advantage with regard to steering, the balance of advantages must be considered to be equal in other respects between the two corvettes.

18 May
As far as latitude of 22°18', which we reached at noon on the 18th on the meridian of 22°40', our passage had been almost more satisfactory than we had dared to hope when setting sail from Acapulco, since we had not only reached, in far less time, the

---

[1] On 15 May the Sun's declination would be about 19°N.

same position as our expeditions from San Blas in the years 1775 and 79,[1] but we also had a considerable advantage in the type of vessel and it seemed probable that, as expressed in many journals, the wind would more often tend to the east and SE as the summer wore on and the distance offshore increased.

On the night of the 18th, however, our hopes were somewhat dashed by several hours of calm and by the gentle northerly breeze that followed some light showers accompanied by moderate cloud cover from the NW, which seemed to promise an imminent favourable change. A little earlier we had seen various whales and tuna, and from time to time we caught one or two bonito. The sea remained very smooth, and variation appeared to increase rapidly, as two sets of azimuths observed on that day agreed in putting it at 7°15′NE.

19 May

Next day the weather improved markedly and we were often able to steer NW and NNW, which is unusual in these parallels, making good speed which allowed us, on this and the following day's run, to make approximately 3° progress to the north. The sky and horizon were generally bright and cloudless, at least from nine or ten o'clock in the morning until sunset. During the night and early morning it was fairly overcast, but with no sign of change or foul weather.

By this time we had completed a very large plotting sheet of the stretch of coast on which our surveys were to be mostly concentrated, almost from the northern extremity of Bucareli Bay[2] to the eastern side of Kodiak Island,[3] that is between the parallels of 57° and 62°.[4] For this purpose we had with us the surveys of the English Captains Cook and Portlock, and the Spanish ones made by Tenientes de Navío Bodega y Quadra, Arteaga and Fidalgo and by Pilotos Martínez and Haro,[5] adopting as the prime point of reference for longitude that which Captain Cook had determined at Cape Edgecumbe.[6] Tribute would be paid to each of these men by giving

---

[1] Malaspina is referring to the voyage of Bodega y Quadra in 1775 and that of Arteaga and Bodega y Quadra in 1779: see p. 16, n. 1 above.

[2] Where Bodega y Quadra anchored in the *Sonora* during his first voyage to Alaska in 1775 and named by him on 24 August 'Puerto y Entrada de Bucareli' after Antonio María Bucareli de Ursúa, Viceroy of New Spain. It is a large body of water in the Alexander Archipelago in 55°13′N, 133°32′W, separating Baker Island and Suemez Island and leading NE to the west coast of Prince of Wales Island.

[3] Malaspina's 'Isla de Codio' is not today's Kodiak Island, but rather Nagai Island in the Shumagin Islands.

[4] Bucareli Bay would have fallen outside the the southern border of Malaspina's plotting sheet according to Bodega's latitude: see n. 2 above.

[5] Malaspina is referring here to the previous Spanish voyages into the Gulf of Alaska of Bodega y Quadra and Arteaga in 1779, Martínez and Gonzalo López de Haro in 1788 and Fidalgo in 1790.

[6] Its longitude according to Cook was 224°07′ east of Greenwich; the cape is backed by Mount Edgecumbe, a striking volcanic peak, at the southern end of Kruzof Island at the entrance to Sitka Sound. Named 'Cabo de Engaño' and 'Montaña de San Jacinto' respectively by Bodega y Quadra in August, 1775: see Wagner, *Cartography*, pp. 176 and 450. The name Edgecumbe, which has survived, was given by Cook. His artist John Webber produced a fine drawing of Mount Edgecumbe: see Andrew David et al., eds, *Charts and Coastal Views of Captain Cook's Voyages*. III. *The Voyage of the* Resolution *and* Discovery, *1776–1780*, Hakluyt Society, 2nd ser. 179-180, London, 1997, item 3.118, p. 165. See also 'A View of Mount Edgecombe from the ship at anchor in Norfolk Sound' in [Beresford], *Voyage ... by Captain George Dixon*, f.p. 192.

names according to the first discoverer, whether Spanish or foreign, so as to avoid, from now on, any confusion or injustice on our part.[1]

21 May
We thought it best, and necessary, to inform the *Atrevida* of this at once, together with other plans and details of our findings. To this end we hove to for a short time, and lowered the pinnaces of both ships, so that friendly meetings among ourselves as well as recreation and change for the junior ranks could agreeably break the monotony of the voyage and help to preserve the solid foundation of mutual trust and good humour. These were not the only documents that I had to pass to the commanding officer of the *Atrevida*. Indeed, a careful study of the voyages which had preceded our own had shown me that it was better and much quicker to survey the coast from east to west, given that the prevailing winds in those latitudes were from NE to SE and south. With this in mind I had to change our rendezvous at the cape where we were to separate and accordingly it was Port Mulgrave[2] that I gave as the meeting place. At he same time I informed him that it was my intention (having surveyed the coast from Cabo de Engaño [Cape Edgecumbe] to [Prince] William Sound,[3] as instructed by royal orders) to employ the remainder of the summer preferably in surveying the coast between 50° and 40°, about which we only had dubious and very confused information. Among which was that Mr Etches, an English shipowner,[4] had passed through Entrada de Hezeta and found a vast inland sea, which incautious European writers extending as far as the vicinity of Hudson Bay, reviving memories of the

---

[1] Bustamante, on the other hand, states that Malaspina decided to adopt English toponyms, where already assigned, in order to reduce confusion, irrespective of international disputes over priority of discovery: Bustamante, *Diario general del viaje*, p. 234.

[2] This anchorage, in the SE side of Yakutat Bay, was named by the fur trader George Dixon (see p. 53, n. 7 above) after Constantine John Phipps, noted for his voyage towards the North Pole in 1773, who succeeded to the title Baron Mulgrave in 1775. Port Mulgrave was to be the site of Malaspina's Alaskan stopover, the base for his search for the Strait of Ferrer Maldonado and the location of his expedition's encounters with the Tlingit Indians. Dixon anchored in what is today the Yakutat Roadstead at 59°33′N, 139°46′W on 23 May 1787, staying there until 4 June. His journal contains a fine chart of the port: see [Beresford], *A Voyage ... by Captain George Dixon*, f.p. 170. The area had been reconnoitred by members of the La Pérouse expedition on 27 June 1786 when the French navigator named Yakutat Bay 'Baie de Monti' after the officer in charge of the longboats that undertook a short excursion into the entrance to the bay. Although the Frenchman missed finding the Mulgrave anchorage, he is still remembered by 'Monti Bay', the entrance into Yakutat Harbour.

[3] A large gulf 70 miles wide, stretching north from the Gulf of Alaska in the shadow of the Chugach Mountains and bounded to the west by the Kenai Peninsula. Originally named Sandwich Sound by Cook on 20 May 1778, but changed to Prince William's Sound prior to the publication of Cook's journal and charts in 1784: see Beaglehole, *Cook's Journals: Voyage of the Resolution and Discovery*, p. 356, n. 1. Unusually Malaspina used the English rendering of the name, whereas earlier he had used the Spanish *Entrada de Principe Guillermo*.

[4] Richard Cadman Etches was a London merchant who, with others, set up the King George's Company to trade for furs on the NW Coast of America: see p. 53, n. 8 above. Malaspina's reference to dubious and very confused information probably refers to the purely speculative chart produced by the fur trader John Meares who was on the coast in the summer of 1788: see Meares, *Voyages*, f.p. 1, whose chart supposedly shows the track of the American sloop *Washington* entering an inland sea through Juan de Fuca Strait and regaining the open sea north of Queen Charlotte Islands. Malaspina here adds to the confusion by his reference to Entrada de Hezeta, the mouth of the Columbia River, sighted by Bruno de Hezeta in August 1775.

imaginary voyages of Admiral Fonte.[1] Finally, in the same instructions, I invited the commanding officer of the *Atrevida* to consider the importance of determining, upon his return, the exact positions of Cape Mendocino, Monterey Bay, Isla Guadalupe[2] and Cabo San Lucas, all essential features for merchant shipping coming from Manila. He was to take as long as necessary in carrying out these tasks and those previously mentioned, without running any risk of wintering in high latitudes, so as to reach Acapulco, which was to be considered our final rendezvous, by the end of the year.

Neither corvette had any sick men on board at the time and the instructions regarding discipline and cleanliness, lately prescribed, were applied with equal firmness, both crews now being dressed in the clothes recently distributed, the alterations and sewing of which had occupied them constantly during the last fortnight. The cold was beginning to become noticeable, particularly for men who had been living in very hot climates for a year; the Fahrenheit thermometer that we had in the open air now reached 64° at night, when it had not been uncommon to see it at the same time at 82° and 84° in the waters where we had [recently] been sailing.

At noon on this day our latitude was 25°43′, our longitude 25°22′ and variation, according to various observations, was 7°15′NE. Nearly all the birds and fish had by now left us and the sea was somewhat higher from the NW, this having only become perceptible on the previous morning.

22 and 23 May

We were not so lucky with progress on the following two days. As the state of the sea and the parallels in which we were had led us to suspect, the wind shifted further north and began to become very variable in strength, so much so that in distance as well as in course and leeway we gained much less in latitude. We had some threats of rain and at times the horizon was considerably overcast, leaving us to hope that there would soon be a change, which would allow us to reach the variables at a latitude of about 30°, where at last we would be able to use the SW and SE winds that we expected in higher latitudes. At noon we were in latitude 27°22′, longitude 28°20′, variation then being 8°40′NE.

Until now I had thought that to undertake eudiometer experiments, if not superfluous, would be at least premature in showing accurately the salubrity of the air we breathed and the progress of the septic infections, as the length of the voyage, the food, the cold and any other causes, worked together to cause them. However, being now twenty-two days out, with weather conditions very different to those we had

---

[1] Malaspina overestimated the capacity of his northern campaign to explore the coast of Alaska, visit Nootka Sound and examine the coast between latitudes 50° and 40°N. He was, however, correct in his assessment that the lack of any definitive survey of this part of the coast perpetuated doubts and confusion about a passage through the continent. This was particularly the case with respect to the supposed voyage of Bartholomew de Fonte, 'Admiral of New Spain and Peru and Prince of Chile' who was said to have sailed from Callao in 1640 and entered a deep inlet in latitude 53°N in which he met a Boston merchant on his way from the east. The story first emerged in London in 1708, and in 1752 the French geographers Joseph-Nicolas Delisle and Philippe Buache gave credence to the fiction by publishing a number of fanciful charts of the central NW Coast. See also p. 466, n. 1 below.

[2] A small mountainous island of volcanic origin, 1,295 metres in height, about 140 miles off the west coast of Baja California and one of the landmarks for the California supply ships from San Blas.

experienced in Acapulco, the cold or the fairly high seas having obliged us to close the ports on the weather side, we would have been remiss not to start the experiments again with all the accuracy required by the novelty and importance of this field of study.

Don Francisco Flores and Don Tadeo Haenke took charge of examining, with a Fontana eudiometer, the quality of the air that I wished to have tested. The results, which I had ordered them set out in a report to ensure consistency and uniformity with subsequent studies, set our minds at ease. We found that there was much salubrity in the atmospheric air, with a considerable similarity among all the other samples that were examined, including the hold and the entrance to the bilges. However, the air in the steward's room differed by a factor of sixty-four to ninety-five, that being the place where provisions are distributed daily and casks, particularly those containing food in brine, are opened, giving off foul and unhealthy fumes.

Shortly after noon the *Atrevida* signalled that she wished to speak to us. When she was within speaking distance, her commanding officer informed me that chronometer number 10, by M. Ferdinand Berthoud, had stopped the night before because it had not been wound and it could not be set going again, although it had been wound up as far as possible and given the horizontal shaking that seemed necessary. He asked for the printed instructions by this famous maker, which we had on board and, having sent his pinnace over with one of his officers, he asked my advice about this difficult situation. I sent the instructions to him immediately and said that for the time being, the fairly heavy rolling would prevent an internal inspection, and that I would attend such an operation myself. However, if the difficulty arose, as seemed probable, from condensation or thickening of the oil caused by the cold weather which we experienced again during the past days, one could warm it up to a good temperature, which that might solve the problem.

This was attempted in vain, as he informed me on the following day. Although we could be reassured by the probability that no part of it was broken, there had to be some concern at the fact that, having wound it as far as possible, the tension on the spring might, as time passed, cause it to break. [24th] Meanwhile new comparisons of chronometer 72 were made with number 105. The daily comparisons between the three chronometers showed many irregularities in chronometer 61, although 71 and 72 kept a fairly regular rate, the latter having been the same as number 10, until the moment that it stopped.

Apart from this mishap, we ought to consider this day's run as one of the best we had had, for, with a fresh breeze from the NE and ENE, we had reached latitude 28°36′, longitude 29°17′, despite the somewhat high sea from the NW; variation being 9°30′NE. At the same time the appearance of the sky indicated a favourable change in the near future and the warmth once more to be felt gave us hope of a southerly breeze, which might carry us up to a considerable latitude in a few days.

Neither the calms nor the generally clear skies of the next three days [26th and 27th] discouraged these hopes. We made good use of the time to measure lunar distances, drill the marines and seamen and to communicate with the *Atrevida*, using the pinnaces. I took the opportunity to go on board her with Don José Espinosa in order to examine the condition of number 10. Having taken the instrument out of its drum, or case, we could not see any damage at all, but as we did not dare to take any step which might have unfortunate consequences, neither the shaking we gave it nor the heating, once again, to a considerable warmth, were enough to set it going again. We contented ourselves, therefore, with gently securing the plane of weights in place with small wooden wedges between the copper ones,[1] and put it away again in exactly the same condition in which we had found it, leaving another attempt to set it going for a better occasion, after we had studied the instrument more closely. The eighty-two sets of lunar distances observed on board the *Descubierta* on the mornings of the 24th and 26th had given a longitude 35′ further east than those taken with number 72. The observations made on board the *Atrevida* showed 40′, which we thought was due largely to an error in the lunar tables rather than by the chronometers.[2]

At this time, particularly during periods of calm, we sighted several blue sharks and dorados, which looked exactly like those we had already seen off Costa Rica and Guatemala, one of which was successfuly speared with a fizgig by the *Atrevida*.

At noon on the 27th we were in latitude 29°6′, longitude 31°38′, with variation approximately 10° NE. The weather continued very clear and calm, except for a few light airs from SE and south which seemed to promise good progress on our course.

28 and 29 May
These hopes, however, were very misleading and harmful in that they led to considerable errors in our dead reckoning or in the direction of a current setting to the south. At noon on the 29th our position was almost unchanged. On the two preceding mornings we had drilled the marines and seamen with cannon, muskets and pistols, ensuring that each seaman was instructed in the loading and firing of the latter two weapons.

30 and 31 May
At last, contrary to our expectations, the breeze began to show some strength in the first quadrant, enabling us to steer NW, close hauled, making good progress on our route. Thus by noon our latitude was 30°48′, longitude 33°55′ [west] of Acapulco and variation, according to many observations (which did not entirely agree), was between 9° and 11° NE.

So far, if we compared ourselves to other navigators, particularly our own, we could only consider ourselves truly fortunate, although the last seven days had largely destroyed the hopes we had formed before the 25th. Indeed, since the journals of those who had sailed in high latitudes on the American coast stated that winds from east to SE and south to be the most prevalent in summer, in our imagination we had

---

[1] This appears to be one of a number of early chronometers by Ferdinand Berthoud driven by weights instead of a balance spring: see R. T. Gould, *The Marine Chronometer*, London, 1923, pp. 94–8.

[2] The position of the Moon given in the lunar tables, being predicted, was liable to be slightly in error. Such errors were of little consequence to the ordinary navigator, but could produce errors of some consequence to surveyors. Thus Matthew Flinders, on his return to England in 1810, following his Australian surveys, found that he had to recalculate all his lunar distances using the actual position of the Moon as observed at Greenwich and other observatories.

expected to encounter them very close to the parallels of 29° and 30°. We were thus given new impetus to our wishes to extend our hydrographic work, next summer, as far as required by the present state of physical and navigational sciences.

There was still almost no signs of marine life in the waters in which we were now sailing. With the exception of a few dorados that we saw briefly during periods of calm and one or two small black birds that Don Tadeo Haenke thought to be the pelagic *procellaria* mentioned by Linnaeus,[1] the solitude around us could not have been greater, impressing on us the belief that, in these latitudes, our chances of paying much of a tribute to the wealth of geography were slim.

Although, having already experienced a considerable variation in temperature after a month's sailing, we were fortunate in seeing a great improvement in the only two sick men we had brought with us from Acapulco. We thought a renewal of the eudiometer experiments would lead to a more orderly arrangement of tasks. It was with considerable pleasure that we saw not only the confirmation of our original experiments, with a salubrity of ninety-five in the atmospheric air, but also that the air taken below showed a quality very close to this, including in the steward's storeroom. Here it was realized that the lack of salubrity noted in previous experiments was caused almost entirely by a large open cask of pickled sauerkraut, somewhat spoilt. Another result of these second experiments was the discovery that by substituting in the eudiometer tests sea water for fresh water from our supplies, a greater rather than a lesser degree of salubrity was recorded, so that there was now no reason not to repeat all the experiments with sea water, and to hope for even greater accuracy.

We continued to compare the rates of the chronometers every four days. If the observed irregularities were attributable to number 105 in the *Atrevida* rather than to the other chronometers, among which number 72 still seemed to hold first place, the latter's total error in longitude, according to daily comparisons, did not exceed approximately 4′ to the west.

1 June

On the following day the moderate breezes continued from NNE and NE, with a threatening sky and a fairly high swell from NW, but we made excellent progress. As the new Moon fell precisely on this day and the weather cleared at last, we thought the easterlies would set in once again, enabling us to make good use of them under full sail, so by noon on the 2nd our latitude by obervation was 33°7′ and longitude 35°53′00″. This was, however, another period of damaging delays for our passage. Very soon the NW swell increased, with the atmosphere thick with clouds and passing showers. The wind backed through north to the fourth quadrant, occasionally shifting to NNW and increasingly to NW, with gusts and some rain, so that a westerly tack was as difficult for us as a NE one for making any progress in latitude without sacrificing longitude, which we feared might set us too close inshore.

Accordingly, we thought it wiser to change tack frequently, preferring always a

---

[1] Storm Petrels, several species of which may have been encountered by Malaspina; originally they were placed in the family Procellaria by Linnaeus, but are now placed in the family Hydrobatidae.

westerly to an easterly course, and to either of these any course which allowed us to make better progress in latitude. The evening and early hours of the night of the 3rd were indeed more favourable for this attempt, the wind, now almost from the west, allowing us to steer NbyW, close hauled, at better than moderate speed. At nine in the evening, however, the wind began to veer to NW, with strong gusts, accompanied by rain and threatening weather, so that we had to furl the topgallants and signal this to the *Atrevida*.

The threat of heavy weather not having materialized, after midnight we hoisted all sail, setting courses in the first quadrant the following morning and afternoon, which were fairly calm and clear. However, the heavy swell from the NW persisted, with passing showers and gusts of little strength. At noon on the 4th we were in latitude 34°2' and longitude 35°9', variation 11°NE. At midnight we went about onto the starboard tack, trusting that the wind would shift into that quarter, as indicated by several showers which had obliged us to shorten sail.

5 June
At ten o'clock in the morning we had to tack to the NE again, though this time with more success, since soon after midday the wind, although accompanied by fairly heavy rain, began to back through west to SW, promising us good progress in latitude. Our hopes, however, were to be dashed once again. At three o'clock the wind fell suddenly and, in the heavy NW swell, a roll caused the fore topsail, the two topgallants and the jib to split all at once. We substituted new sails for the jib and the fore topgallant, the others were repaired immediately, when with light breezes from NNW and north we set a course in the first quadrant until midnight, then altering course to west and NNW. By noon on the following day [6th] our latitude and longitude were 34°38'.[1]

By this time, the NW breeze had dropped almost entirely, with occasionally a few light airs from the SE and south, with a very clear sky. With much less of a swell, we believed that a change to fair weather was approaching. Indeed, after a flat calm until nearly midnight, which left us almost without steerage way, a moderate breeze sprang up at last from WSW, with the appearance of fair weather, enabling us to steer NWbyN. Our position at noon on the 7th by observation was latitude 35°12' and longitude 35°3'.

Our hopes for progress in natural history were also answered to a greater extent on this day. For as well as sighting an albatross[2] and several storm petrels, we found various molluscs which Don Tadeo Haenke examined in great detail, finding them to be the *Medusa velella*[3] and *Lepas anatifera*[4] described by Linnaeus, which, furthermore,

---

[1] There is no blank space in Malaspina's MS after latitude so it is possible that he meant that latitude and longitude were both 34°38'.

[2] 'pájaro carñero' in the original MS, a term used by Malaspina for the Wandering Albatross he encountered in southern waters, but not found in the North Pacific, where three species of albatross are found.

[3] The jellyfish *Velella velella*.

[4] The Goose Barnacle, so-called on account of the medieval belief that Barnacle Geese did not procreate in the usual way but sprang from these organisms. For this reason these birds were considered as a class apart from other animals and so could be eaten on fish days.

had several snails stuck to its different globules (*Helix janthina*,[1] described by the same author), that gave off a beautiful purple dye.

On the following two days the winds in the third quadrant continued moderate, tending rather to the west, generally accompanied by damp weather, a lot of haze on the horizon and fairly clear skies. We continued steering NNW and NWbyN, according to whichever gave us better speed and less leeway, so that by making the most of these conditions under full sail, by noon on the 9th we were in latitude 37°13′ and longitude 35°13′, with variation, as shown by several fairly consistent azimuth and amplitude observations, 14°0′NE. By then, however, the fair winds had left us and we were even obliged to put about onto the starboard tack, to a westerly course, for at nine o'clock the wind had shifted suddenly to NNW and north and increased to storm force, accompanied by a heavy shower, which obliged us for a while to lower or furl the topgallant sails.

With this wind from north and NNW, we were pleased with the gain of 2° in longitude we were able to make, without any sacrifice in latitude. The wind, however, dropped completely soon after noon on the 10th to be replaced at eight in the evening by variable breezes in the fourth quadrant with which we thought it best to steer north and NNE under full sail, particularly as the somewhat overcast sky and horizon seemed to indicate an imminent change.

11 June

Thus at noon on the 11th our latitude was 37°46′ and longitude 36°49′, with no errors of any consequence apparently so far in our dead reckoning, except that there appeared to be an easterly set with a slight northerly tendency.

The Sun had no sooner passed the meridian when the breeze, until now very light to moderate, began to back to the third quadrant and freshen rapidly. At sunset, with the horizon still clear and the sea smooth, our speed was six knots and, at one in the morning, when we were still able to carry full sail, with the wind just abaft the beam, it reached eleven knots. However, when the Moon was close to setting, shortly before two o'clock, we were obliged to shorten sail in some haste, for as well as strong gusts, shifting towards the bows, the sea was now fairly high and so confused, that we could only just hold our course under foresail and topsails.

At sunrise while appearances seemed to threaten an imminent wind shift to NW, the wind, still from WSW, continued very strong, while the sea had risen considerably. In such conditions it seemed best to take in two reefs in the topsails (the operation being undertaken by the *Atrevida* at the same time), so as to continue under these and the foresail for a time, waiting to let the weather reveal what should be done. Before ten o'clock the wind finally settled in the west, so we immediately hauled the main tack inboard, although the wind and sea were then really high and the conditions very uncomfortable.

12 June

Since dawn when the wind, now stronger, had backed from SW towards west, we

[1] Now *Janthina janthina*.

decided to sail fairly free to avoid making a great deal of leeway and letting our speed drop below six or seven knots. Having taken this precaution, our day's run was very good, and at noon our latitude by observation was 40°00' and our longitude 36°33', Cape Mendocino bearing approximately east, 198 leagues.

In the early hours of the afternoon, with the sea even higher, we had to reduce the rolling to some extent by sending down the yards and striking the topgallant masts. Both corvettes were riding too high in the water at the time, and this caused them not only to roll excessively and continuously, but also to make considerable leeway, with most unfortunate consequences for our course. However, despite the increasing strength of the gusts, we did not have to shorten sail all afternoon, continuing under the four principal sails, with the topsails double-reefed. At times we steered NNW and NbyW and at others NbyE and NNE. The sky remained fairly clear, and at about eight o'clock the wind and sea finally abated.

13 June
We took the opportunity to make good use of these conditions, swaying up the topgallant masts again at four in the morning, then continuing under topsails and staysails, with all reefs shaken out, although there was still a risk of slight damage to the rigging from the fairly high sea. The courses we steered on this day's run had been too open in the first quadrant for us not to fear a considerable sacrifice of longitude. The chronometers did indeed show a longitude at noon of 35°6', our latitude calculated by meridian altitude being 41°38'.

The sky and horizon continued fine and clear almost throughout day, the sea and wind having fallen very much calmer. Even when sailing close hauled we could scarcely maintain a northerly course. The wind eased still further after nightfall and finally, at midnight, we had an almost flat calm. However, this could not last long in our present latitude.

14 June
Before four o'clock the following morning light airs began to get up from SW, soon freshening and promising a favourable change in the weather, all the more likely as the full Moon was approaching. As this was accompanied by a calm and peaceful morning we made the most of it, not only by cleaning and ventilating below decks, but also by airing all the boatswain's gear, whose storeroom we feared might have become damp. At noon we again compared our chronometers with those of the *Atrevida* and had the pleasure of finding the rate of number 105 to be as regular as that of chronometers 71 and 72 appeared to be. This was also confirmed by many observations of the distance between the Sun and the Moon made on both corvettes on the 6th, 7th and 10th, some 180 in number, the mean of which was only 10' or 12' to the east of chronometer 72, without applying the equation to compensate for its minor irregularities. As for chronometer 61, we intended to put it on gimbals again, although the last examination in Acapulco led us to believe that the present irregularities of 8" and 10" seconds a day could in no way be attributed to the rolling or to the temperature, which, furthermore, we attempted to maintain as even as possible.

From this time onwards the weather appeared to wish to favour us with even more constancy than we could hope for. The breezes from NW and north were moderate and did not last long, and the skies were clear enough for us to take Sun sights which allowed daily confirmation of our position with good observations. These pleasant breezes were followed either by brief calms or fresh breezes in the second and third quadrants, which, although accompanied by heavy cloud cover and drizzle, neither caused us difficulty in keeping company nor prevented us from maintaining a speed, under full sail, of seven, eight and nine knots, from which we profited in approaching longitude 40° west of Acapulco, enabling us to stand well offshore to reach stronger and less variable winds. Since, at the same time, we were able to keep the ports open, the work was easy and the cold only moderate, we saw the whole crew in such a fine state of health and strength that the eudiometers showed, on the morning of the 15th, no difference at all between the air below decks and that of the atmosphere.

18 June
Thus, at noon on the 18th, our latitude was 48°37′ and longitude 38°17′ from Acapulco; Nootka Sound therefore bore E9°N, 160 leagues. Variation, according to several fairly satisfactory observations, was then 21°NE.

Despite all our vigilance, we had not yet been able to sight the famous signs which serve to mark the distance of 200 leagues from the adjacent coast for the Manila galleon on its passage to New Spain, which are therefore regarded as indicating the end of hardships and the point of reaching milder climates.[1] Finally, this morning, we sighted a tree-trunk and at almost the same moment a considerable number of small whales and two or three species of sea birds, other than the storm petrels which had been our only companions so far, almost since leaving Acapulco.

Until the following midnight the weather was extremely calm but changeable, varying between drizzle and clear skies, at times from the east and at times from NW and west. At about this time, however, a moderate and steady breeze set in from west to SW, towards which we sailed close-hauled under full sail and by noon the next day our latitude was 49°45′ and longitude 38°54′.

19 June
We were only one hundred leagues from Queen Charlotte Islands,[2] therefore, and 125 from Bucareli Bay,[3] when we sighted greater numbers of birds and small whales and even a seal. Accordingly I thought it wise to have the cable bent on to two other anchors and I signalled the *Atrevida* to do likewise, as the very flat sea and pleasant weather encouraged us to undertake tasks of this nature, which are often fraught with danger. We had to continue steering NW to reach a longitude of 40° to 41°, but the breeze was somewhat light and we could only steer NNW until dawn on the following day. We were then able to luff up to NW and NWbyW with a moderate breeze in the third quadrant, the sea still very smooth, and the wind at times dropping suddenly, with a slightly overcast sky.

[1] For a detailed discussion on the signs of land see W. L. Schurz, *The Manila Galleon*, New York, [1939] 1959, pp. 238-9.
[2] A group of islands off the northern coast of British Columbia, named by George Dixon in 1787.
[3] See p. 85, n. 2 above.

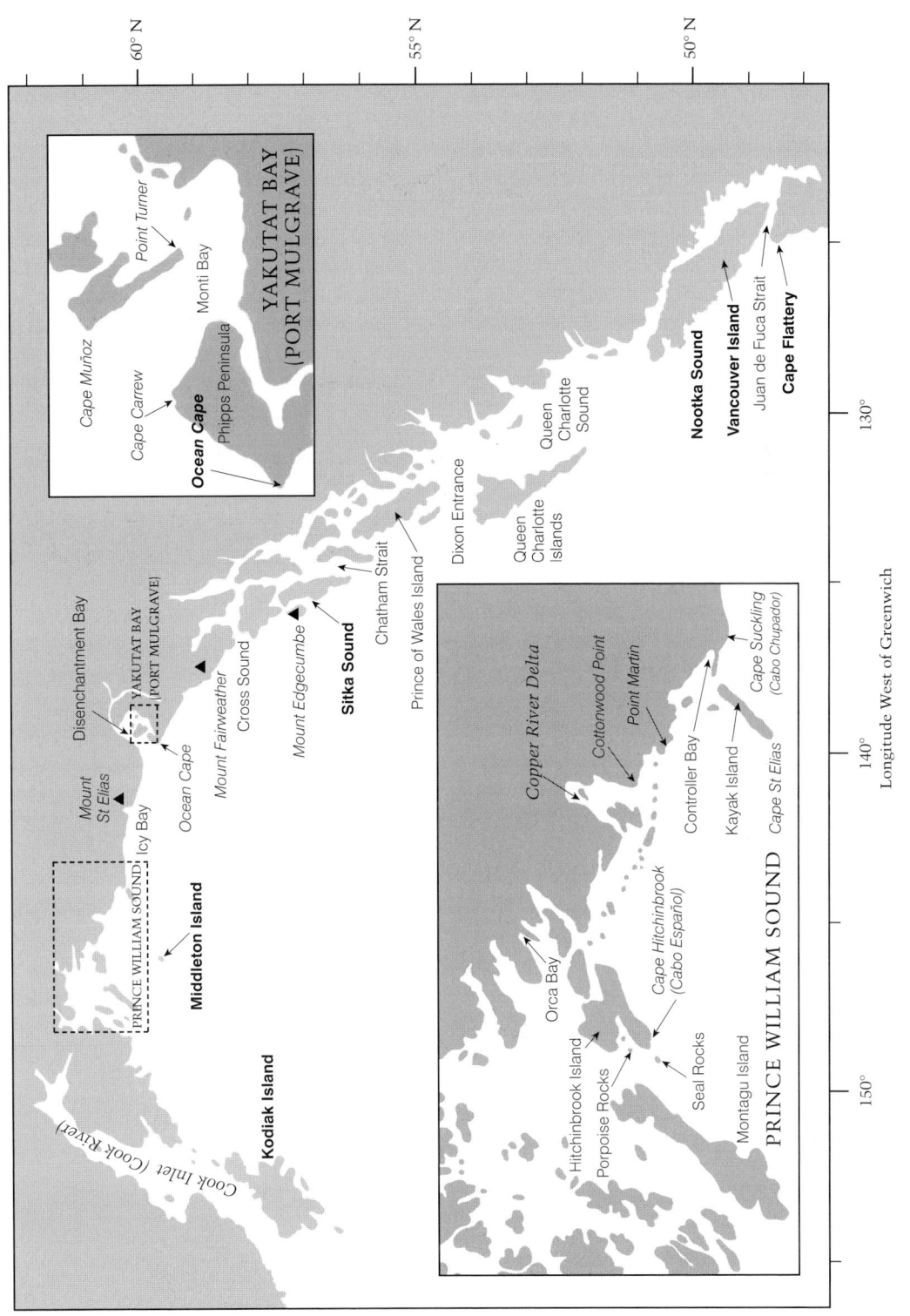

Fig. 3. Vancouver Island to Prince William Sound and return to Vancouver Island, June to August 1791

21 June

The precaution of steering these courses, which brought us to latitude 53°15' and longitude 39°30' by noon on the 21st, was all the more beneficial as, shortly afterwards, light breezes from NW, WNW and west got up, and we were able to tack to the north, the sooner to reach the latitude of 60° that we so earnestly desired. However, on this occasion we could not be indifferent to the considerable sacrifice of 2° or 3° of longitude. Nor could we help being set towards the coast faster than suited us. At noon on the 22nd we were only sixty leagues from the entrance to Bucareli Bay. Although there was no signs of our approach to land either from greater numbers or different species of birds and small whales, or in a wind shift to north and NE, we suspected it because of the extraordinarily calm conditions and also because the commanding officer of the *Atrevida* called over to us that he had calculated, by several sets of lunar distances observed on board that morning, a longitude one degree further east than that given by the chronomters.[1]

The weather became even calmer during the following afternoon and night. At last, at dawn on the 23rd, we saw the sky beautifully clear, the beneficent rays of the Sun giving us a feeling of spring on these coasts, even although they were so arid and mountainous. The sea took on a change in colour, showing that we were in soundings; many whales swam about us, and the breeze, although moderate, promised a fair change in the near future, fulfilling our hopes more and more.

23 June

On board both corvettes we continued to observe a large number of distances between the Sun and Moon, these being all the more important in that we would soon be able to relate them to sightings of land. Furthermore, they would confirm or deny the error in the chronometers indicated on the previous day by the *Atrevida*'s observations. Indeed, at ten o'clock in the morning, even before we had finished our observations, a considerable stretch of the coast came plainly into view. At first it was a little blurred by distance and the heavy cloud cover, but at noon, when our latitude by observation was 56°17' and the sky less overcast, we could see it clearly.

It was the stretch of coast between Cabo Engaño [Cape Edgecumbe] and the islands lying to the north of Cape St Bartholome,[2] surveyed by Teniente de Fragata Don Juan (Francisco de la Bodega y) Quadra in 1775, by Captain Cook in 1778, and by Captain Dixon in 1786. We soon made out Mount Edgecumbe, named by Bodega

---

[1] For the MS chart showing Malaspina's progress northward up the coast and then west following the sweep of the Gulf of Alaska see 'Carta esférica de los reconocimientos hechos en la costa NO de América entre los paralelos 57° y 60°30', lat.N., por las corbetas *Descubierta* y *Atrevida* de la Marina Real, año de 1791': AMN, Sig. II. B. (7) (María Dolores Higueras Rodríguez, *Catálogo crítico de los documentos de la expedición Malaspina (1789–1794) del Museo Naval*, 3 vols, Madrid, 1985-94,no. 1723). For an engraved chart showing the tracks of Malaspina and other Spanish navigators see chart no. 3 in the atlas accompanying *Relación del viage hecho por las goletas Sutil y Mexicana en el año 1792 para reconocer el Estrecho de Fuca*, Madrid, 1802. Along with the cartographic surveys, a number of finely drawn *vistas de costa* (coastal views) were executed on the voyage north (or on the return south) by or under the supervision of Felipe Bauzá: see AMN, Sig. Vistas. Carp. II, 51–6, Sig. Vistas. Carp. IV, 84–88, Sig. Vistas. Carp. VII, 251–267 (Higueras, *Catálogo crítico*, nos 2535–2540, 2568–2572 and 2744–2760).

[2] The southern extremity of Baker Island in the Alexander Archipelago, marking the northern entrance to Bucareli Bay, named by Bodega y Quadra on that Saint's day, 24 August 1775.

y Quadra as [Monte] de San Jacinto, the large bay that he called Susto,[1] and soon afterwards we saw the inlet at Cape Lauder[2] and Port Banks,[3] visited by Captain Dixon. Cabo Engaño was then bearing N14°30′W by compass, the southern point of Ensenada del Susto,[4] which we called Serena because of the calmness of the day, N5°30′E, and what seemed to be a bluff at its eastern end,[5] not far from a fairly large island,[6] bore N77°30′E. The very detailed description of this stretch of coast by Captain Cook was just what we would expect of the accuracy of that illustrious mariner. A considerable number of low hillocks, probably islands, indicated an almost equal number of good harbours.

Between the island and the bluff to the east, we could clearly see an opening or strait of considerable size;[7] it was also evident that Mount Edgecumbe and the land around it formed another island. The magnificent height of this mountain made it stand out from the rest and it is therefore a very useful guide for the uncertain mariner in these waters when, as often happens, a latitude observation cannot be taken. The views we give of this mountain[8] possibly show it as lower than may be inferred from the account of the voyage of the English navigator. We were able to measure its height very accurately and, as the difference in latitude allowed the distance to be determined very reliably, we could believe our results to be very close to the truth. Don Juan de la Bodega y Quadra had already calculated a latitude of 57°2′ for Punta or Cabo Engaño, only one minute more than that assigned to it by Captain Cook. Accordingly we had complete faith in the distance of [blank] leagues to the mountain and, lastly, of a height of [blank] *toesas* above sea level.[9] We could see little snow on the peak. In fact, it seemed that other sierras inland from Ensenada del Susto and Punta Serena had retained a lower and heavier snow cover.

We obtained no bottom with 120 fathoms of line, variation, according to both a meridian azimuth[10] and several other azimuth observations, was 24° to 25°NE, and our dead reckoning at noon this day differed from the longitude given by chronometer 72 by [blank].

---

[1] Sitka Sound between Baronoff and Kruzof Islands – the 'Norfolk Sound' of George Dixon. Ensenada del Susto, named by Bodega y Quadra in 1775, means the 'Bay of Alarm', which artist Tomás Suria suggested referred to 'the many shoals which it contains': Donald Cutter, ed., *Journal of Tomás de Suria of his Voyage with Malaspina to the North-West Coast of America*, Fairfield, Wash., 1980, p. 33. Bodega, however, gave no reason for this particular name.

[2] The southern point of the entrance into Whale Bay on the SW coast of Baronoff Island; named by Dixon after William Lauder, the surgeon of the *Queen Charlotte*.

[3] An inlet on the south side of Whale Bay on the SW coast of Baronoff Island, 26 miles NNW of Cape Ommaney; charted and named by George Dixon on 23 June 1787 in honour of Sir Joseph Banks, President of the Royal Society: see [Beresford], *Voyage ... by Captain George Dixon*, p. 195 and chart f.p. 193.

[4] Povorotni Point in the shadow of Mount Kinkaid.

[5] One of a number of points of land visible at this time in the Necker Islands.

[6] Biorka Island.

[7] The opening into Sitka Sound: see also p. 161, n. 3 below.

[8] Several coastal views by Felipe Bauzá include Mount Edgecumbe, which is named Monte del Engaño on them: see AMN, Sig. Vistas. Carp. IV, 84–88 (Higueras, *Catálogo crítico*, nos 2568–72).

[9] Mount Edgecumbe is 997 metres high.

[10] When time is known, variation can be obtained by observing a heavenly body as it crosses the meridian, when its true bearing will be north or south.

The comparison of our longitudes with those of the English navigator was too important a matter to be overlooked. The present occasion being all the more suitable in that Cape Edgecumbe or [Cabo] Engaño was one of the landmarks whose position he had fixed with great accuracy, situated as it was, on a passage of only a few days from Nootka, after finding close agreement between the results of lunar distances and an observation of the first satellite of Jupiter, and having made a very careful adjustment to his chronometers. To these reasons for supporting the determination of this position was added the notable fact that the longitude of the harbour of St Peter and St Paul [Petropavlovsk] in Kamchatka[1] on the English chart accorded with the results of observations of a satellite of Jupiter made in the same port by Señor Krissinlinkov,[2] and so astutely examined by Mr Coxe.[3] Thus the fact that these most widely separated longitudes were accurate tended to suggest that those in between should also be considered reliable.

The longitude of Cape Edgecumbe, according to Captain Cook, was thus 138°15′30″ west of Paris and ours, calculated with chronometers 72 and 71 and dependent on the observations made in Acapulco, was 138°50′43″, that is 35′13′ further west than the former. We would not have been the least surprised by this difference, particularly as it was supported by almost all the lunar distances, if the excellent rates of the chronometers since Acapulco, as shown by daily comparisons, did not incline us toward the other conclusion. That is, that the longitude of Acapulco determined by so many observations of the first satellite of Jupiter would make such an error most improbable. This seemed to be confirmed both by the nature of observations of this type and by the first lunar distances observed on 8 May, which gave a longitude even further west than that of the chronometers. That six chronometers, almost all of excellent construction, could at the same time, in a temperate climate, and without rolling, change their rates in the same direction, seemed to us all the more unlikely given that the frequent comparisons of the chronometers with number 10 until 20 May, compensated for even the slightest variations of chronometer 72, to which we had chosen to refer our longitudes since leaving Acapulco. However, eighty-two sets of lunar distances observed on board this corvette on 24 and 26 May in the best of conditions gave a longitude 34′ further east than that of the chronometers, which was confirmed at the same time by the observations made by the *Atrevida*. In the following quarter,[4] that is, over 6 and 7 June, having repeated the distance observations in very good conditions, although not with complete consistency, the mean of a hundred sets was a difference of 17′ to the east of chronometer 72. Finally ninety-seven sets observed by us on the morning of this day, which agreed exactly with

---

[1] Petropavlovsk-Kamchatskii in Avachinskaia Guba (Avacha Bay), where Vitus Bering began his last voyage on 5 June 1741. Visited by Charles Clerke in 1779, following the death of Cook, and by La Pérouse in 1787.

[2] Andrei Dmitrievich Krasil'nikov, Russian astronomer and geodesist, who spent several years studying astronomical observations in St Petersburg Observatory and later in Kamchatka in the early 1740s, at the time of Bering's second voyage, to work on 'the important question concerning the longitude of the extreme parts of Asia': see Coxe, *Account of the Russian Discoveries*, pp. 267–76.

[3] For Cook's confirmation of the accuracy of Krasil'nikov's observations see Coxe, *Comparative View of the Russian Discoveries*, pp. 9–10.

[4] The Moon's first quarter, following the new Moon on 1 June.

those of the *Atrevida* for the same period and the previous day, showed, much to our surprise, a longitude 1°18′ greater than that of number 72. It was fortunate that the excess of 35′ noted in the longitudes of Captain Cook had been due entirely to an error in the distances, and that we had preferred the results of chronometers 61 and 105, which gave a longitude 10′ further east than chronometers 71 and 72. There would remain, unaccounted, a difference of 25′, which we could not explain at present unless, having recalculated another observation of the first satellite of Jupiter made in very good conditions by Messrs Cook and King in Nootka, we found that the Captain had omitted it, because it did not agree with the results of his distances, from which any deficiency in the determination of longitude would have to come. Meanwhile, for the continuation of our tasks until we could obtain better data we had thought best to adopt for Cape Edgecumbe the mean of the longitudes determined with the four chronometers. The results of the lunar distances and those determined by Captain Cook, which at present we note here without adopting them, will be given their due weight in this matter when, having collected new material for this comparison, we shall come to the final drafting of the Mercator chart of these coasts.

	Western longitudes for Cape Edgecumbe by the chronometers		Idem by lunar distances	Idem by Captain Cook
Chronometer 72	138° 49′ 13″	115 sets observed)		
Chronometer 71	138 48 28	on 6, 7 and 10 June)	138° 31′ 38″	138° 15′ 30″
Chronometer 61	138 38 30			
Chronometer 105	138 42 10	Idem on 23 June)	137 31 00	
Means	138 44 37		138 1 19	138 15 30

Today Señor Haenke, somewhat more successful than us in his studies of natural history, succeeded in examining several species of molluscs, including a completely new one, to which he gave the name *Speciosa*. This deserved attention not only for its size and rapid undulating movement, but also for its mixed colouring of pearl and purple, presenting in different parts a most vivid and pleasing contrast. It was not surprising that the other species, previously known by the names of *Medusa equorea*, *cruciatae* and *aurita*, should be exactly the same as those found in the Baltic Sea. A great harmony in the products of nature is revealed at every step when they are examined and compared over the entire globe.

I did not intend to sacrifice a single day of the present favourable season for the detailed survey of the coast now in view. Indeed, with the desire to reach the vicinity of latitude 60° as soon as possible, towards which our investigations must be directed,[1] I could not overlook the fact that making the land in such low latitudes was the result of the recent light winds and the fact that being only a short distance offshore would itself be a new obstacle to finding strong and favourable winds.

24 June
Accordingly, at dawn on the 24th, after several hours of calm, a moderate breeze set in from ENE and east, enabling us to stand somewhat offshore, which, however, we

---

[1] Malaspina is here referring to the fact that the Pacific entrance to Ferrer Maldonado's supposed strait was located in 60°N.

managed to keep in sight with the help of the very clear and pleasant weather. At three in the morning Mount Edgecumbe bore north by compass, and at noon it bore N72°30′E. The snow covered peak of Mount Fairweather or [Monte]Buen Tiempo could be seen bearing N25°30′W. At that point our latitude was 57°10′, our longitude by chronometer 72 was 37°56′30″ west of Acapulco and variation approximately 25°[NE].

At the distance we were from the coast we attempted in vain to determine the true position of Puertos de Guadalupe[1] and de los Remedios,[2] which had been visited in the year '75 by Teniente de Navío Bodega y Quadra. Several low hills, which were becoming visible at various points to the NW of de Cabo de Engaño, were easily confused with one another, with openings seeming to appear at times, which we soon found to be, in fact, the effect of the terrain, parts of which were snow covered and other parts clear. However, we could not fail to see Cape Cross, so named by Captain Cook,[3] from which runs the range ending at Mount Fairweather. We measured its height and that of this latter conspicuous peak, which even in this mild season was still covered in snow down to its foot.

Until four in the afternoon we had enjoyed a fair breeze in the first quadrant, although it was falling to calm, but soon afterwards it backed to NNW and NW, obliging us to continue steering WSW, close hauled, with a somewhat high sea which, in our unfavourable condition of trim, caused us to make considerable leeway. We remained on the same tack until four in the morning, when Cape Fairweather bore N15°E by compass. We then went about onto the port tack, flattering ourselves with the hope that the wind, still in the NW, would shift closer to a sea breeze at dawn. The weather at the time could not have been more serene and delightful. At half past one Don Felipe Bauzá managed to draw a view of Cape Fairweather,[4] although it was at some distance, and at sunrise [25th] a reliable bearing to its central point indicated a variation of 24°15′ NE.

On the same morning 105 sets of very consistent lunar distances were taken in very good conditions, giving a longitude even further east than that of the 23rd, being 1°32′ from that of chronometer 72, whose rate continued as regular and uniform as we had found so far.

At noon our longitude was 39°35′ and latitude 57°59′, Cape Fairweather then bearing N3°E by compass and the mountain N11°E, so that we could now continue on our tack towards Bahía de Behring without any apprehension, particularly as our daily dead reckoning indicated that there was almost certainly a favourable current setting to the north.

Indeed, by eight o'clock in the evening Mount Fairweather bore N33°E at about seven leagues, and at the same time we could see part of the coast trending to the

---

[1] Shelikof Bay on the west coast of Kruzof Island; explored and named by Bodega y Quadra and Mourelle on 17 August 1775.

[2] Sea Lion Cove, a small bay on the NW coast of Kruzof Island, which was the initial Alaskan landfall of the first Bodega y Quadra expedition on 18 August 1775: see Wagner, *Cartography*, p. 490.

[3] Now Cape Cross: 'The South East point of this Sound is a high promontory, which obtained the name of *Cross Cape*.': James Cook and James King, *A Voyage to the Pacific Ocean for making Discoveries in the Northern Hemisphere*, 3 vols, London, 1784, 2, p. 346.

[4] See p. 97, n. 8 above.

west, on which our imagination and our expectations placed several large inlets, which at times we suspected to be that of Behring, and at others those of a longer and more useful entrance.[1]

In fact, however, many of the conjectures of M. de Buache about the existence of a passage were limited to the parallel of 60°. After careful consideration, I could not disregard either the relative inaccuracy of nautical instruments in the year 1588, which may very well have given a latitude with an error of one degree, or the warnings of Captain Cook, who had noticed, towards Bahía de Behring, a stretch of flat ground which logically had to be surveyed with all possible precision. However, fearing that the haze or contrary winds might prevent the corvettes from making this examination, I thought it better to do it with the launches, while the corvette took on water, wood and ballast in Port Mulgrave.

With these considerations in mind, I felt at least it would be wise to take a look at the nature of these coasts, so that the launches could venture inshore with better knowledge and make for places where it would be easier to find shelter in contrary winds. For this reason only I stood inshore during the evening until we were very close to the coast. Only at eleven o'clock was it necessary to tack offshore, when the weather closed in with squalls and variable breezes, generally very light and at times dropping completely, setting us too close inshore without offering any gain in latitude or longitude. No bottom was obtained with 120 fathoms of line.

At two in the morning a fresh SW breeze set in, which cleared the sky to some extent and allowed us to steer NW under courses and topsails. There was still heavy cloud over the coast, however, so that we did not sight land until three, and then only dimly, although we were not more than four or five leagues off at the time, finding ourselves to be halfway between the two bays sighted on the previous afternoon.[2] We believed we could see an island which we thought to be that shown on the English charts[3] while the mountains in the distance were all snow-covered down to their foot. [26th] At five o'clock we were only four miles offshore, particularly from a number of large rounded rocks, which we thought at first to be islets, but then saw to be joined to the mainland by a sandy spit. The breeze was still very light and falling and the swell was fairly high. Consequently we were obliged to tack offshore, tacking again towards the shore at seven in the morning, from which we were now some three or four leagues distant.

By eight the sky had cleared, and we could enjoy the most delightful view one could desire in these latitudes. Close to the shore and in front of the whole snow-capped cordillera running from Cape Fairweather, there is a long strip of low-lying land, so thickly covered with magnificently luxuriant pine trees, that if the snow which dominates the view could be hidden for a while, it would doubtless give the

---

[1] As Malaspina viewed the coast sweeping north and west, he would have considered the indentation north of Cape Fairweather to have enclosed 'Bahía de Behring' and have glimpsed the significantly more pronounced opening of Yakutat Bay.

[2] See n. 1 above.

[3] Probably the small island depicted off the SE entrance of 'Bherings Bay' on Cook's 'Chart of the NW Coast of America and NE Coast of Asia': see David, *Charts and Coastal Views*, III, 3.95A and Dixon's chart, [Beresford], *Voyage ... by Captain George Dixon*, frontispiece.

impression of an equatorial latitude, rather than one not far from the Arctic Circle. To this splendid scene were added various patches of snow on the prominent escarpments, which either reflected with greater brilliance the beneficial rays of the Sun or, with the play of shadow, seemed to the imagination now a broad road and now fields of perfect smoothness. Many flocks of plovers flew about.[1] The water had become much greener in colour and much less salty than most sea water. As the haze or cloud dissipated, the forests that set off the scene so beautifully seemed to stretch further and further to the west.

Several sets of hour angles were taken, while bases were being constantly measured. At noon our latitude was 59°0′, our longitude by dead reckoning 39°18′ and variation by meridian azimuth 34°[NE], which, although unusual when compared to the others, could no doubt be attributed to the remarkably strong attraction of the nearby mountains.

As the Sun approached the meridian the wind gave signs of shifting soon to SSW and south, which would be against us if we came too close inshore, as the low coast runs for a long stretch to the west, without anywhere to shelter in case of a calm. Furthermore, the fairly heavy westerly swell, which must be almost constant, tends to drive one onshore. With this in mind, we had tacked to SSE and SE by half past ten in the morning, so that soon after midday, the wind having indeed shifted as we had suspected it would, we were able to tack back to west, then luffing up to WSW and SW, as it was too light to allow us to get any distance offshore. Finally, towards four in the afternoon, the *Atrevida* obtained a depth of fifty fathoms about three leagues from the coast.

For the present survey of the coast, any ideas regarding the existence of a passage, or even an inlet, having been dispelled, our investigations were now directed towards accounting for what Captain Cook had seen. Since the island that he places at the entrance to Bahía de Behring does not exist, we wished to ascertain which part of the coast had caused this error, which was hardly surprising when he was sailing seven leagues offshore. What had appeared to us to be an island early in the morning was a long way off to the east of the end of the cordillera which runs from Mount Fairweather, and from there to the beginning of another cordillera which continues towards Mount St Elías.[2] There was not an isolated hill visible on the flat ground that we could see stretching inland beyond the first range. If Comandante Bering (as Captain Cook suspected) made the land on this part of the coast, which cannot be called anything but wild, it is hardly surprising that he was unable to remain at anchor for any length of time, although he had landed his men on an island, and the very fact

---

[1] Probably any of a number of species of the auk family found in numbers off the SE coast of Alaska, including auklets, murrelets, puffins and pigeon guillemots.

[2] The sighting of this 5,489-metre mountain, by Vitus Bering on 16 July 1741 traditionally marks the beginning of European exploration of the upper NW Coast of America. Although many authorities give Bering credit for naming the mountain, it appears more likely that the name was borrowed by 18th-century map-makers from Cape Elias (the SW point of the Russian explorer's Kayak Island, named on the Saint's Day on 20 July 1741) and applied to the 'high volcano' left unnamed by its discoverer: see Donald J. Orth, *Dictionary of Alaska Place Names*, Geological Professional Paper 567, Department of the Interior, Washington, D.C., 1967, p. 825. Bauzá's sketch of this mountain accurately presents its huge size: see plate 17. It is fronted to the SW by the largest icefield in the world that has been named the Malaspina Glacier.

that this lay in latitude 58°28′ leads one to believe that his landfall must have been near Cross Sound.¹

The longitude observations made at six in the evening indicated a moderate current setting to the east and, indeed, despite all our efforts to make use of every puff of wind, we had hardly made 10′ of longitude since noon, when we were no more than seven or eight leagues offshore. The breeze, from south, was light and falling and the sky and horizon very clear and tranquil, but soon were shrouded in haze. When the breeze began to shift to the east after sunset, we immediately made use of it to get clear of the coast a little. At midnight we could see it about five leagues distant, when in a depth of seventy fathoms, sand.

27 June

With a favourable breeze from SE and east, now settled at least for a few hours, we took the opportunity to take up our detailed survey again, altering course first to NW and then to north under topsails, so that at three o'clock the following morning we were barely two miles offshore in twenty-two fathoms, fine black sand. Before reaching this position the fortunate chance of having a clear horizon in the first quadrant had allowed us a view of the mountains behind Bahía de Behring, snow-covered and regular in height, forming a second range and thus dispelling any idea of the existence of a sea to the north, as Captain Cook appeared to indicate.² At the same time we saw what was undoubtedly the isolated hill that could be taken for an island from a distance,³ although if we took into account the latitude of 59°15′ determined by the English captain, our suspicions would have fallen, instead, on a stretch of flat ground continuing to WNW.

From a distance of one to two leagues offshore we continued our survey of the coast towards Captain Dixon's Point Carrew.⁴ By six in the morning, still enjoying a fair breeze, we had already cleared that point and had examined in great detail the entrance to Port Mulgrave. We then saw at the furthest point of Admiralty Bay,⁵ among the cordillera whose lower slopes are washed by the sea, an inlet⁶ whose mouth and course seemed to tally with the coast described by Ferrer Maldonado. At once

---

¹ Malaspina was off the long stretch of low coastal plain lying between Cape Fairweather and Yakutat Bay, broken only by the descent of the Grand Plateau Glacier from Mount Fairweather. He rightly doubted Cook's suggestion that Bering ever landed there, finding no island or shelter for a safe anchorage. The results of his survey, reflected in the expedition's chart of the coast (see p. 96, n. 1 above), however perpetuated the erroneous location of 'Behring's Bay.' The only bay on this part of the coast is Dry Bay, the delta of Alsek River which, as its name indicates, cannot be entered by ships. Bering actually anchored not 'near Cross Sound' but off Kayak Island some 130 miles west of Yakutat Bay.

² Malaspina appears to be referring to Cook's 'Chart of the NW Coast of America and NE Coast of Asia' (David, *Charts and Coastal Views*, III, 3.95A), in which there is no indication of an inland sea north of Bherings Bay.

³ Probably Chamberlain Peak.

⁴ This point, named by Dixon after his first mate, John Ewen Carew, is the northern extremity of Phipps Peninsula, which shelters Monti Bay and Port Mulgrave, the modern-day Yakutat Roadstead: see [Beresford], *Voyage ... by Captain George Dixon*, chart f.p. 170.

⁵ So named by Dixon and Portlock in 1787, modern Yakutat Bay from the Tlingit Indian name 'Jacootat' or 'Yacootat' reported by the Russian explorer Iurii Lisianskii in 1805: see Orth, *Dictionary of Alaska Place Names*, p. 1063.

⁶ Disenchantment Bay at the head of Yakutat Bay, Malaspina's Puerto del Desengaño actually means 'undeceived' or 'disillusioned' in the sense of a deceit or illusion being shattered by reality.

imagination soon supplied a thousand reasons in support of hope. We considered everything that might agree with the description of the passage. As we rejected or attempted to justify what did not accord with the terrain described, each of us in the end, according to his own fantasy, either increased the length of the narrows to the north, or put down to distance and eyesight the absence of any features which could not yet be found to dispel any remaining doubts.[1]

As may be imagined, we did not hesitate for a moment in altering course towards that inlet for, although it was not my intention to risk the corvettes on the account of Ferrer Maldonado alone, it was most important to examine closely the possibility of its continuation to the north. If this were found to be entirely false, we would continue on our passage towards Prince William Sound. I had informed the commanding officer of the *Atrevida* of this by voice, and he was in complete agreement, given the circumstances.[2]

In fact, a pleasant breeze from east and ESE, rather than obscuring the coast, had allowed us to observe several sets of hour angles and promised a latitude observation at noon. This was too much of an incentive to induce us not to abandon instantly the idea of anchoring in Port Mulgrave.

The entire coast running from Bahía de Behring towards Punta Muñoz[3] consists of the same strip of sand, gravel and then wooded ground, which we had noticed the day before, beautifully forested with majestic pines. It may be assumed that at a distance of one or two miles offshore the depth of twenty to twenty-two fathoms, sand, remains the same, but there is no shelter at all to encourage mariners to approach it. Near the above-mentioned point the depth increases rapidly to fifty and sixty fathoms, gravel, and there is no lesser depth to be found anywhere in the outer bay at a distance of only a mile from the shore or the reefs.

From Punta Muñoz [Ocean Cape] the coast runs to the north, turning more sharply after the next point, Punta Phipps,[4] and then trends to the west.[5] As various islands, which face the coast, lie spread out close inshore, they naturally form anchorages which are as comfortable in the safety and shelter they offer as they are agreeable

---

[1] Tomás Suria confirmed this sense of excitement in his journal when he wrote 'Great was the joy of the commander and of all the officers because they believed, and with some foundation, that this might be the so much desired and sought-for strait ...': Cutter, *Journal of Suria*, p. 35

[2] Bustamante reports this communication on the previous day, adding that from the *Atrevida* coastal fires, a sure sign of human settlement, had been observed on shore: Bustamante, *Diaro general del viaje*, p. 241.

[3] Today's Ocean Cape, but on Malaspina's 'Plano del Puerto de Mulgrave', AMN, Sig. II. B. (10) (6) (Higueras, *Catálogo crítico*, no. 1725), the name 'Cabo Muñoz' designates the western point of Phipps Peninsula at the Yakutat end of the Malaspina Coastal Plain. However, by the time the 'Plano' was published in 1802 as chart no. 8 in the atlas accompanying *Relación del viage hecho por las goletas Sutil y Mexicana*, it was realized that this cape had been named earlier by Dixon after Phipps: see p. 86, n. 2 above. In consequence the name 'Cabo Muñoz' was transferred to the NW tip of Khantaak Island which, NE of Phipps Peninsula, encloses Port Mulgrave. The name 'Muñoz' was given in recognition of the contribution to the expedition of Tomás Muñoz, the engineer who had supervised the building of the corvettes *Descubierta* and *Atrevida* at La Carraca shipyard in Cádiz during 1788-9: see p. 136 below.

[4] Point Carrew: see p. 103, n. 4 above and n. 5 below.

[5] It is impossible to reconcile Malaspina's description with names and the trend of the coastline on his chart of Port Mulgrave (Chart 8 in the atlas accompanying *Relación del viage hecho por las goletas Sutil y Mexica*) and on the charts in [Beresford], *Voyage ... by Captain George Dixon*, frontispiece and f.p. 170,

in the lushness of their vegetation. These islands and the low ground extend about three leagues to seaward from the nearby cordillera, which approaches the coast again, towards the above-mentioned inlet and the head of the bay, and then turns inland once more, giving way to another equally luxuriant strip of low ground which, after a few gullies, runs westward to the foot of Mount St Elías.

Steering towards the entrance to the inlet, we now began sounding as a precaution, particularly as we had found eleven fathoms, gravel, one-and-a-half miles from the outer point of the southernmost island, and the reefs extending offshore looked somewhat ominous. We soon found that the bay, even around the inner islands, was inconveniently deep, rather than dangerously shallow. We were unable to obtain bottom with forty or fifty fathoms of line, while at times the *Atrevida* was unable to do so with less than eighty fathoms of line. Our attention was also drawn to the fact that both sides of the entrance were so steep-to that they left us in little doubt that off them the bottom would be extremely deep and rocky.

At 9 o'clock in the morning we were a league and a half from the suspected entrance, with a falling easterly breeze, showers on the horizon and a fine drizzle. Although the extremely weak tidal stream tended to support the belief I formed by observation that the channel penetrated only a short distance inland we could not really be sure of this without fear of error such as could easily arise in judging the depth of the inlet. In consequence it seemed our duty to make for the nearby Port Mulgrave to undertake a detailed survey with the launches while the ships took on water and wood. We therefore put about and set a course towards the channel, which leads from Punta Phipps[1] to the harbour already surveyed by Captain Dixon. By then the moderate breeze had settled in from east and ESE, with an overcast sky, drizzle and a few gusts of no great strength.

We were aware from Captain Dixon's account that these islands were inhabited by a small number of people, and this was borne out by two large canoes and a small one, a short distance from one another, that came out from a channel between the islands and seemed to be making for the *Atrevida*, which was just astern of us. From a considerable distance a harmonious hymn of peace rang out, which was then accompanied by the unmistakable sign of their arms held open to show that they came unarmed, desiring only our peace and friendship.[2]

As we had just decided to go about and make for the anchorage, both the large canoes were soon able to come alongside the corvettes and take a line, not without some signs of fear, while closely following the commands and warnings of a venerable old man who paddled the small canoe back and forth, and giving every indication of being the chief of this little tribe.[3] At first preceded on both sides by easily-misunderstood signs of social contact, in which each gesture and expression was interpreted

---

which Malaspina consulted. It seems likely that he meant to write 'From Punta Phipps the coast runs to the north as far at Punta Carrew where it turns sharply to the east', which then makes sense with the rest of Malaspina's description.

[1] Point Carrew: see p. 103, n. 4 and p. 104, notes 4 and 5.

[2] Natives with their arms open and raised appear in two of the NW Coast drawings from the Malaspina Expedition by José Cardero. For one of these see plate 16.

[3] The Tlingit, considered by explorers and traders of the period to be one of the more warlike tribes on the NW Coast.

as if suggested, as was natural, by the dictates of imagination rather than reason. We made efforts to encourage the natives to come on board, first with generous offerings of biscuit, salt pork and tallow, and then acceding to their requests that an equal number of our crew should get into their canoes as hostages as their men came on board. In this way they were soon convinced of our peaceful intentions. As we then took care to present a few trifles to the first who came up, within half an hour we neither needed to leave hostages with them for those who came on board nor did we urge them to do so, particularly as it was clear that almost all of them had a strong inclination to slip below decks, no doubt with the aim of getting hold of a few little objects from among those that came to hand.

They stayed on board until past midday, showing a lively and cheerful disposition in all their actions. As for our marines and seamen, it was not long before they parted with a portion of their rations or some of their clothing. On our part much persuasion was needed to convince them to disembark and move away in their canoes, which could have been at risk with the strong breeze then blowing from ENE and the repeated long tacks that we would have to make.

In the afternoon the weather closed in much more, so that we could hardly see the two shores which limited our tacks. We therefore had to put about with greater care because of several fairly long ledges running out to the SE from Punta Carrew. The tide was constantly against us, the breeze dropped almost completely, our tacks were necessarily short. Thus it was seven o'clock in the evening when, having rounded Point Turner,[1] we were able to drop anchor in twelve fathoms, ooze, opposite the Indian settlement on the islet, not more than a cable off the beach.

From the moment we passed Punta Carrew and had begun to approach the shelter of the anchorage, many canoes came out to meet us, sometimes repeating the hymn of peace and at others with a general and harmonious chant which seemed to indicate invitation or admiration and offering to trade some salmon and wooden artifacts, while attempting to obtain a much greater value on their sea otter skins.[2] In great silence, and perhaps in some apprehension, they watched in wonder as we lowered the boats, particularly the launch. Finally, as it was now nine o'clock at night and both corvettes had to lay out a kedge to the NW as a second mooring, we made our farewells with reciprocal signs of friendship, to enjoy a reasonable rest.

---

[1] The southern end of Khantaak Island, named by Dixon after James Turner, his mate in the *Queen Charlotte*.
[2] The Tlingit were clearly aware of the value Europeans placed on sea otter skins following Dixon's visit.

CHAPTER 2

At Port Mulgrave

[27 June]
Our position in Port Mulgrave, and the pleasant surroundings will be better shown by the views which accompany this journal than by any description, however detailed and carefully studied for the purpose.[1] Despite the rainy and overcast weather everything indicated a period of fair weather. The harbour was more like a basin, with the natives living nearby in numbers large enough to be studied without fear of disturbing their customs.[2] Finally, water, wood, ballast, fishing and edible plants, all of which we needed, were so close to hand that it would be very little trouble to bring them on board.

28 June
Water and ballast had, in fact, to be brought from the island or beach to the east of the anchorage. It would not have been easy for us to find a suitable spot for the former so soon if one of the more alert of the Indians who had gathered on board since dawn

---

[1] Among a number of drawings of scenes and events relating to Malaspina's visit to Port Mulgrave, only one general view of the anchorage has survived. By José Cardero, it shows the corvettes at anchor in front of a village on Khantaak Island surrounded by canoes full of Indians. In the foreground sailors from one of the corvette's boats can be seen trading with the natives: see plate 9. This drawing is clearly taken from the shore trading station set up by Malaspina on Point Turner (see p. 112 below) to avoid uncontrolled trading activity on and around the ships. In his journal Suria described the bay as 'very beautiful, all surrounded with various rocky islands, covered with big pine forests, which present a beautiful view': Cutter, *Journal of Suria*, p. 37. Colnett, who anchored at the eastern end of Khantaak Island in 1788, described the place as 'on the whole its the pleasantest place I had met with on the coast. The shores in every part were full of Currents, Gooseberries, Strawberries, Rasberries, apple Trees and wild peas all in bloom, & the natives ... brought salmon & Halibut.': Public Record Office, London, ADM 55/146, f. 210v.

[2] The Indians encountered are now identified as the Yakutat Tlingit who lived traditionally by fishing and hunting marine animals. By the time of European contact in the 18th century the distinctive elements of Tlingit, and indeed NW Coast, native culture were easily apparent - relatively permanent settlements, large plank houses, social stratification, primary dependence on the salmon fishery, ocean-going dugout canoes and established art forms, which included totem poles, developed from skilled woodworking abilities that were immediately stimulated by the acquisition of iron tools and wealth from trade. For further information see Frederica de Laguna, 'Tlingit: People of the Wolf and Raven' in William Fitzhugh and Aron Crowell, *Crossroads of Continents: Cultures of Siberia and Alaska*, Smithsonian Institution Press, Washington, D.C., 1988, pp. 58-63, Steve J. Langdon, *The Native People of Alaska*, Anchorage, 1993, pp. 70-85 and Frederica de Laguna, 'Tlingit', in *Handbook of North American Indians*, 7, Smithsonian Institution, Washington, D.C., 1990, pp. 203-28). The most detailed analysis of the people encountered by the Malapina Expedition is in the exhaustive study of Frederica de Laguna, *Under Mount Saint Elias: The History and Culture of the Yakutat Tlingit*, Smithsonian Contributions to Anthropology, 7, pt 1, Washington D.C., 1972.

Plate 9. Port Mulgrave and the Indian (Tlingit) village, by José Cardero. Museo de América, Madrid

had not accompanied us to look for it. The constant calmness of the sea, the weakness of the tidal stream and the length of the day were of such assistance in these tasks that we could regard them as pleasure rather than labour.

From early in the morning the natives had assembled in some numbers on board both corvettes, beginning to offer some skins, many fresh salmon and a few wooden tools, in exchange for clothes and iron, the only things they really seemed to desire. Nevertheless they accepted any kind of buttons, several nails and various other items of the many that could be included under the heading of hardware and so succeeded in establishing a closer relationship with the crew. As caprice or fancy outweigh necessity in the seaman's character, particularly in that of the Spanish seaman, to a degree difficult to comprehend, during the first exchanges the natives realized immediately that dealings of this type would be highly advantageous for them. If we were to judge by the eagerness of the parties we would have to infer that it was our seamen who could not live without acquiring everything they saw rather than the natives, who lacked the clothing and iron that they so understandably craved.[1] The tricks used by the natives in their exchanges or dealings have been very well described by Captain Dixon.[2] Not only do they keep hidden the goods they wish to barter, but they also present them with the greatest indifference when they intend to make any exchange. After a long period, sometimes over an hour, during which they remain quite unconcerned before the many objects shown to them, they finally produce a strip of fur, a doll, a spoon, or some other trifle, and propose exchanging it for all they can see. They dwell on the size and symmetry when they cannot make much of the quality. When the deal has finally been agreed upon, they withdraw from it again. At last, if among the things they have brought, there is a skin of real value, they show it with such an air of mystery, putting it away in no time and bringing it out again, that they incite in the most placid mind a singular mixture of annoyance and desire, which the call of interest alone can hardly control. There is not the slightest competition to be seen among them, either in the acquisition or disposal of goods. They show, indeed, a remarkable unanimity of interest and either consult each other about completing the exchange or, if it is carried out, they applaud it with one, two or three exclamations in chorus, according to the advantage or otherwise of the deal.

At nine o'clock in the morning the two pinnaces, carrying most of the officers, set out to look for the best place to obtain water. One of the natives, making himself understood by signs with the admirable speed of understanding which they all possess, guided the officers first to a spot not far away, but with very little depth. He then took them to a beach opposite or to the SE, where within a musket shot of this

---

[1] Tova's commentary on the NW Coast section of the voyage is, like Suria's, an especially interesting complement to Malaspina's journal. In this particular context of trade he noted 'the anxiousness with which our people bought the vilest objects for the single reason of it [sic] having belonged to the natives.': Enrique J. Porrúa, ed., *The Diary of Antonio de Tova on the Malaspina Expedition (1789–1794)*, Lewiston, Queenston and Lampeter, 2001, p. 378. An interpretation of the various texts available for the study of the expedition's NW Coast campaign can be found in Catherine Poupeney Hart, *Relations de l'expédition Malaspina aux confins de l'empire espagnol*, Longueil, Quebec, 1987.

[2] In particular Dixon was frustrated by the tedious delay he encountered in trading with the Tlingit 'occasioned by the slow, deliberate manner in which these people conduct their traffic.': [Beresford], *Voyage ... by Captain George Dixon*, p. 169.

very well sheltered beach several springs were found, which would indeed supply all the water necessary when some wells were dug. On this occasion the officers visited a hut not far from the watering place which the Indian, who was leading them, seemed to indicate belonged to his family and in which two women and several children lived in filth and poverty. Having duly shown their natural curiosity and admiration at the decorations, clothing, food and utensils that were to be seen in it, the officers returned on board at midday, during a heavy rainstorm which hid from view all but nearby objects. After examining the beach near the anchorage for a site for measuring a base, I thought it best, however, to continue with our daily tasks, while endeavouring to form a closer friendship with the natives, to familiarize myself as far as possible with the words of most immediate necessity and to study carefully their customs and propensities. We had, of course, made every effort not to cloud a friendly relationship. Our constant vigilance and the precaution of giving the password at night from one corvette to the other, must have dispelled any idea of taking us by surprise. On board various firearms, ready for use, were placed where they could be seen on board, which should have caused them some fear. The lower ranks were forbidden any contact with the women and children in their huts. Finally, in an attempt to put aside from their minds any thoughts of hostilities, our gifts were constant and generous, particularly on the part of the seamen.[1]

The repeated signs that had been made to us, beginning the previous day, to allow us the use of the women while in port, although fairly clear, still seemed ambiguous and perhaps wrongly interpreted, considering the few visits made to these parts by European ships and the strangeness of such an offer, which was prompted neither by veneration nor affection towards us, nor by customs debased by luxury, self-interest or example. Finding myself not far from the huts at the time and importuned by proposals of this nature, I wished to ascertain their real meaning, particularly because if this were a genuine offer, as we assumed it to be, it would be most important for the sake of good order to watch the first movements of the crew very carefully, and if it were not, to dispel this unfortunate idea of the natives' character and customs. Guided, therefore, by two young natives who, with an air of mystery, repeated the well-understood word *Jhoüt*,[2] I approached some trees by the huts, where all my doubts vanished at once. Indeed, at the foot of a tree were four or five women, partially clad in seal skins and, of course, obedient to the will of almost the entire tribe, which seemed unanimous in its intention of prostituting them. If neither morality nor example had sufficed to discourage any such thoughts, it would certainly be achieved by their ugly appearance and the quantity of grease and filth that covers them, giving off a smell so unpleasant that it can hardly be described.[3]

---

[1] In addition to the general instructions issued in Acapulco prior to the northern campaign, Malaspina drew up very specific instructions for his officers to ensure that the Spaniards could replenish their supplies and maintain harmonious relations with the natives which he rightly regarded as a prerequisite to carrying out successfully on land the expedition's scientific activities: see Cutter, *Malaspina and Galiano*, p. 27.

[2] The spelling in the original MS is difficult to decipher. It could be *shoüt* or possibly *choüt*. According to Suria, who spelled it *chouut*, its meaning is woman: Cutter, *Journal of Suria*, p. 48. This seems to correspond to the modern Yakutat Tlingit word *shawt* for woman.

[3] According to Malaspina the offer of women 'caused much surprise'. He concluded, however, that the women involved were slaves: see Pedro Novo y Colson, ed., *Viaje político-científico alrededor del mundo*

Plate 10. Tlingit man and the Chief at Port Mulgrave, by José Cardero. Museo Naval,

The old chief, who had been entertained on board the *Atrevida* the previous morning, then came over to the *Descubierta* at the instigation of Bustamante, with whom he seemed to have established a firm friendship. We soon instructed Don Tomás Suria to take a very accurate likeness of him,[1] while the chief allowed one of his sons to attend to the bartering, in which he preferred clothing to anything else. Finally he struck up a long conversation with us, the aim of which, as far as we could gather, was to describe some fights with his neighbours that had taken place not long before. He was a man of truly impressive bearing, either because of his age, his stature, or the vigour revealed in all his actions. Every part of the fight was represented to us most vividly. We understood that his enemies had up to six muskets, that there had been some deaths on both sides, and that in they end they had asked for peace, which was soon granted, but what was to cause us the greatest difficulty in reaching a full understanding of this story was his claim that there was a horseman among the

---

por las Corbetas Descubierta y Atrevida, al mando de los capitanes de navio D. Alejandro Malaspina y D. José Bustamante y Guerra desde 1789 a 1794, Madrid, 1885, p. 347. Tova, however, commented that even members of the chief's family seemed prepared to sell themselves for very little: Porrúa, *Diary of Tova*, p. 377.

[1] Suria's 'accurate likeness' is reproduced in Sotos, *Los pintores*, II, fig. 586, titled 'Jefe del Puerto de Mulgrave nombrado Ankaiui' ('Chief of Puerto Mulgrave called Ankaiui'); for a portrait of the chief and a Tlingit man by Cardero see plate 10. In his journal the artist described his subject as 'an old, venerable and ferocious looking man with a very long gray beard, in a pyramidal form, his hair flaccid and loose on his shoulders. False hair over it in various locks, without any order or arrangement, made him look like a monster.': Cutter, *Journal of Suria*, pp. 37-8. Cardero also sketched the chief and his son, but his depiction of the chief lacks the flourish of Suria's fine portrait: see Sotos, *Los pintores*, II, fig. 589.

enemy. His desire to convey this to us being strong enough to have him call his son and have him get down on all fours, then showing how the enemy rode astride. By then his portrait had been finished. He was highly pleased at the sight of it, eagerly requesting not only a drawing of the headgear (which he showed us) of the enemy chief, defeated in the conflict, but also that it should be specifically indicated that it was the prize and token of the victory.[1] At last, as the day was now well advanced, having offered the chief all possible flattery that might strengthen trust and friendship, we saw him ashore, enabling us to dine in peace.

29 June
At dawn the following day there were signs that the weather would continue from SE, with overcast skies and drizzle. We therefore had to abandon all thoughts of hydrographic and astronomical work, but started on the tasks of taking on water and ballast with the two armed launches under the orders of Teniente de Navío Tova of the *Atrevida*. In the vicinity of the spot where we were to obtain these supplies there were only a few sparsely scattered huts, but as I intended to avoid even the slightest cause of discord, I not only manned the boats with an officer and some armed marines, but also endeavoured to encourage respect for us from the natives, and direct to us any complaints against the crew, by having all the officers wear a red hat-band, as a mark among us of leadership and the bearers of authority.

The natural inclination towards theft[2] that these Indians had shown at the beginning became more confident when, under cover of the variety of goods exchanged or their very number, they thought they could continue with impunity. An iron padlock had been stolen from the *Atrevida* the previous morning, but by chance Alférez de Fragata Murphy noticed it in such good time that after detaining the culprit, although threatened by him with a dagger, he managed to persuade the same chief, then present, to insist that the stolen article be returned immediately. This was not the case on board the same corvette this morning with two iron fids,[3] whose return we failed to achieve, although we brought much pressure to bear upon the chief, who was eager to oblige us. We had to accept his assurances that the offenders had been of another and distant family. Meanwhile, however, new precautions were taken to avoid recurrence of this problem, not only by forbidding the natives from coming on board, but also by assigning a place for bartering on the shore near the corvettes. As this was covered by our guns, while being at some distance from their settlement and

---

[1] It is possible that this Tlingit war trophy was acquired by the expedition. Suria describes the helmet as being 'of a figure, and an extraordinary construction of wood, copper and of straw cloth [probably woven spruce root], and with a mask in front which appeared to be a wolf.': Cutter, *Journal of Suria*, p. 38. In the collection of the Museo de América in Madrid there is a remarkable wolf's head war helmet: see Araceli Sánchez Carrido, *Indios de América del Norte*, Madrid, 1991 p. 92, #55.

[2] Explorers and traders on the NW Coast regularly complained about what they considered the natives' penchant for theft. Like Malaspina, La Pérouse found the Tlingit, whom he encountered at Lituya Bay in 1786, particularly aggressive, finding that they 'were great thieves [who] ... spent every night watching for the appropriate occasion to rob us ... .': Dunmore, *Journal of La Pérouse*, I, p. 108.

[3] Square bars of wood or iron, with a shoulder at one end, used to support the weight of the topmasts.

completely free of any hiding place, stand of trees or other shelter, I thought it the best place to set up the observatory.[1]

The idea of having the bartering take place at this spot, to which the chief had agreed, thereby attracted the greater part of the natives. This necessarily gave me, with the sacrifice on my part of a couple of hours to arrange the first negotiations, the opportunity to propose erecting the observatory tent on the pretext of providing some shelter and comfort for both sides, as we were exposed to much cold and rain. They naturally had the same desire and, indeed, as soon as it was erected, with the rain still falling, they gathered around it in some numbers and continued trading with greater energy. These dealings were limited to the acquisition of the tools, arms and products that I had to assemble for the Real Gabinete in Madrid,[2] rather than to barter for otter skins, of which they usually brought very few. A new and essential advantage of this first contract was the establishment of a fixed price for fresh salmon, which I wanted to give the crews every day. This was fixed at a nail of three to three and a half inches for each salmon, the average weight of which was about seven to eight and a half pounds, which we succeeded in keeping unchanged until the last day, although at times the inevitable inequality in their numbers tempted either one side or the other to alter it.[3]

By midday the weather seemed to be improving greatly. As soon as the rain stopped Don Felipe Bauzá was able to measure a base from the observatory to Point Turner, taking as many bearings at each end as the indistinctness of distant objects allowed. At three o'clock in the afternoon the Sun began to break through the clouds. Finally, at about five o'clock, we saw that erecting the tent and landing the Ramsden astronomical quadrant had not been a fruitless undertaking. We observed absolute altitudes, which when referred to the chronometers by means of signals, determined the first period for the comparisons of their rates to our great satisfaction.

The numbers of natives gathering around our tent increased at every moment. At one time they wanted to look through the telescopes and at another to come to the chests and examine their contents. Since the experience of two days left us in no doubt of their considerable propensity to theft, I eventually thought it safer to bring all the instruments and the tent itself on board rather than tire the marines with

---

[1] Cardero was on this beach facing the ships at anchor when he sketched his general view of Port Mulgrave: see plate 9 above. From the position of the observatory noted on 'Plano del Puerto de Mulgrave' (AMN, Sig. II. B. (10) (6) (Higueras, *Catálogo crítico*, no. 1725) we know that the site was on Point Turner.

[2] The collections of the Malaspina voyage and the other Spanish voyages to the NW Coast at the end of the 18th century are discussed in Paz Cabello, 'The Ethnographic Collections: A Special Legacy of the Spanish Presence on the Northwest Coast, 1774-1792' in Robin Inglis, ed., *Spain and the North Pacific Coast: Essays in Recognition of the Bicentennial of the Malaspina Expedition, 1791-1792*, Vancouver, 1992, pp. 137-54. See also Bill Holm, 'Cultural Exchange across the Gulf of Alaska: Eighteenth Century Tlingit and Pacific Eskimo Art in Spain', in José Luis Peset, ed., *Culturas de la costa noroeste de América*, Madrid, 1989, pp. 105-13. In one of his reports, Malaspina discussed in greater detail the 'market' and 'every kind of article the natives had made either from necessity or by ingenuity': Novo y Colson, *Viaje político-científico*, p. 348. An idea of the articles involved is also provided in the illustrations in the study of the Yakutat Tlingit in de Laguna, *Under Mount Saint Elias*, part III, plates 105-39.

[3] Suria reported differently suggesting that the rate of exchange was a salmon for a button. He noted that 'This fish in the north is the most delicate thing which can be imagined. We could never satisfy ourselves with it notwithstanding that we ate an abundance of it.': Cutter, *Journal of Suria*, p. 37.

continual night watches or to let these articles become the cause of a breach which in the inevitable confusion might be misunderstood and unjust. Our relations with the natives at present could not have seemed more promising. We had acquainted ourselves with the most useful words of their language and freely visited their huts. Don Tomás Suria was able to take the likeness of several of the women,[1] and draw a small number of domestic utensils.[2] The bartering had become more active on both sides and we had also been given permission to cut as much firewood as necessary in the vicinity of the huts, without any preliminary contract, to which, however, I would have acceded immediately.

Near the observatory (as the natives showed us) was buried the body of a man killed in the most recent fight. The place was marked by a small pole stuck in the ground among the grass. It had a rush mat to cover it, held down by a few stones. The natives showed some reluctance to approach the spot, and even insisted that we should not do so, accompanying their demands by the signs and silence which indicate the fear of disturbing a peaceful rest.

Among the many things that by then the natives had brought to the market we often saw traces of Captain Dixon's visit to this harbour in the brig *Queen Charlotte*.[3] We saw axes, cooking pots, a silver spoon, two or three books and a few articles of clothing. Often the younger men repeated the chants used when working the ships and one or two English words. As for the scraps of iron, we knew that they would soon be converted, with the aid of fire and stones, into the knives or daggers that each of them always carried under the left arm, hidden by a wolf, otter or bear skin. Equally clear, as a sign of this visit, was the insistent offering of their women. Today I was obliged to reprimand the old chief severely when he brought a woman towards the observatory, where I was at the time. I also had to repeat the order that no one but the officers of both corvettes might approach the huts. At this the women increased their cajolery and at about six in the evening we saw near the stern of the *Descubierta* a canoe carrying three women, two of whom would not have been more than eighteen or twenty years old. After repeating a few English words and talking with their natural loquacity for a long period, they sang quite a melodious song, which Don Tadeo Haenke transcribed with his innate accuracy and musical knowledge.[4]

---

[1] The ethnographical importance of Suria's drawings at Port Mulgrave (and indeed those of Cardero) cannot be overestimated particularly when combined with the comments in his journal. Some of his sketches, of both men and women, appear in the original manuscript of his journal; others were worked up into more finished drawings. The extant results are both described and presented in Sotos, *Los pintores*. Malaspina himself wrote to his friend Paolo Greppi that without these visual aids 'the descriptions of the voyage would be entirely weak', which is quoted in an appreciation of Suria's important contribution to the record of the voyage in Catherine Poupeney Hart, 'A Personal View of the Northwest Coast: the Journal of Tomas de Suria', *To the Totem Shore: The Spanish Presence on the Northwest Coast*, Madrid, 1986, p. 183.

[2] No drawing of utensils has survived, but in the collection of the Museo de América a basket and two spoons are likely to have been collected by the expedition in Port Mulgrave: see Sánchez, *Indios de América*, pp. 91 (#53) and 112 (#81 and #82).

[3] Malaspina's *La Reyna Carlota*.

[4] Although Haenke busied himself recording the songs and music of the Indians, only one transcription of the 'Canto de la Paz' from Port Mulgrave seems to have survived: AMN, MS 425, ff. 158-159. Tova commented 'I do not know if one is able to judge a work of music without great understanding of the art, but it is possible to attest that the Mulgrave songs were agreeable to everyone.': Porrúa, *Diary of*

As the evening progressed, however, the weather now being completely clear, the scene which lay before us was far more novel and impressive than those previously described. Like a theatre curtain being suddenly raised, instantly revealing to the wondering spectator a great number of objects as new as they were varied and pleasing, the cloud and gloom, which had until now concealed distant objects, vanished to unveil the entire majestic cordillera running from Mount Fairweather to Mount St Elias. The ice which covered them from their summits to their lowest slopes reflected the Sun's rays with added brilliance. The latter peak, unmistakable by its height, bore N38°49′W by compass. We could see, stretching out in front of the higher ground for several leagues, the whole pine forest growing with a rich luxuriance hard to describe. The exceptional clarity of the air, with a gentle breeze from NW, extended the daylight hours considerably with the greater length of twilight, so that even at midnight we were not deprived of this delightful and majestic sight. Don Felipe Bauzá immediately took the theodolite to one end of the base line, to observe further bearings and correct those previously measured. As it was already ten o'clock in the evening when he returned on board, we retired for a few hours of rest, the better to be able to make use of the fine day that was expected to follow.

30 June
Before four o'clock in the morning Don José Espinosa, whose watch it was, set out with the armed launches and *bombos* to continue collecting water and firewood. Don Felipe Bauzá took a pinnace, also armed, to continue his work from the entrance channel to Punta Phipps,[1] Piloto Maqueda, in another pinnace, checked the soundings inside the harbour, while the astronomers began preparations for all possible manner of observations.[2] First among these was to measure the oscillations of the pendulum, which was accordingly set up in the tent in the same place as the day before, chronometer 71 being substituted for the astronomical clock to time [the oscillations], as it would have been unwise to depend upon its [the astronomical clock] results almost at the same time as it was set going.[3] With the Sisson astronomical quadrant we then observed equal altitudes of the Sun and determined the latitude by the meridian altitude of the same heavenly body. Finally we measured the height of Mount St Elias above sea level from the end of the base line.[4]

At about six in the morning, as we continued with our preparations for these operations, with only a small number of natives gathered near the observatory, we suddenly saw the old *Ankau*[5] coming towards us, accompanied by another person,

---

Tova, p. 380. Bustamante explained that friendly relations were established without verbal exchanges. The Spaniards signified peaceful intentions by firing into the air; the song reported by Malaspina is reported by Bustamante as a 'song of peace': Bustamante, *Diario general del viaje*, p. 247.

[1] Probably Point Carrew: see p. 104, notes 4 and 5 above.

[2] These included observations to determine the force of gravity, observations for magnetic variation and inclination: see Espinosa, *Memorias* (1809), 2nd memoir, pp. 117-8 and 190-212.

[3] The astronomical clock would take some time to settle down after being set going, whereas the chronometer was kept going continuously.

[4] For Malaspina's calculation of the height of Mount St Elias see p. 156, n. 2 below.

[5] The principal chief of the tribe.

Plate 11. Tlingit woman and child, Port Mulgrave, by José Cardero. Museo de América, Madrid

whose precedence over the others was obvious, although we were never able to determine his privileges or function in the tribe. Both of them eagerly, and not without signs of considerable fear, announced to me the arrival of two large canoes that they had just spotted and whose intentions, either peaceful or hostile, were still unknown. When the canoes were only one or two miles from the harbour, they anxiously begged us to go to the outer shore[1] and fire a musket shot, so as to force them to show their intentions. Meanwhile they ordered the whole tribe to take up arms, the women to withdraw and the two large canoes drawn up on the beach to be launched. I immediately decided to do as they asked and, crossing to the beach opposite with Don Ciriaco Cevallos, who was with me at the time, I asked him to fire his musket into the air as soon as we were in a position visible to the people in the canoes. At this signal all those manning the canoes, about forty men, immediately broke into the hymn of peace, continuing the song as they approached the inner shore, not without new suspicions and precautions on the part of our *Ankau*, who did not stop calling out to them that they should consider carefully what they did as we were their allies.[2]

Almost all fear of a breach having now been dispelled, the inhabitants of the harbour, although not yet laying down their arms, approached the canoes and took the chiefs of both canoes in their arms to be carried ashore without getting wet. These were then presented to me by our *Ankau* and in the same fashion I was presented to both of them. This ceremony was followed by a general peace-making. Very soon both sides, among embraces, merriment and tales, went off to the vicinity of huts, except for the place where the skins were drying, and prepared a meal, where they all seemed more like members of a single tribe than people who had been ready for mutual destruction an hour before.

I did not know whether any of the many natives who approached the observatory understood the religious ideas concerning the Sun by which I attempted to give some colour to our astronomical observations or, even if they did understand them, whether this would secure the tranquillity that we needed. However, it is certain that in this regard we must consider ourselves extremely fortunate, as we were not disturbed in the least during the period of about twelve hours during which the astronomical instruments were in their sight. The pendulum was compared to the chronometer three times and, since each comparison took not less than an hour, we were able to make them correspond to within a quarter of a second, taking care, furthermore, for the definite determination of mean time, to tie in chronometer 71 to the other chronometers of both corvettes by means of repeated comparison signals.[3]

---

[1] The seaward side of the peninsula ending in Point Turner.

[2] Although Malaspina was convinced that the Port Mulgrave natives had feared an attack by the visitors, an interpretation shared by both Suria and Tova, the anthropologist de Laguna, citing also the work of other colleagues, maintains that the Spanish had witnessed not a near hostile encounter but a ceremonial reception that arose from a complex relationship between potlaches, peace ceremonies and warfare: see de Laguna, *Under Mount Saint Elias*, p. 147.

[3] Malaspina's explanation of these observations is somewhat obtuse. For a clearer explanation see pp. 66-7 above.

As for the other conditions which had to be considered at the time of making this delicate observation, we may flatter ourselves that they will be found to be satisfactory by the scientists when we assure them that the pendulum was fixed very firmly in place, that the Fahrenheit thermometer remained between 67° and 68°, that the location, at a considerable distance from any mountain, was clear and consisted, for the most part, of shingle, that the experiments were made close to midday and that the chronometer used for comparisons gave the same time, to the second, according to the observations of the previous and following days. Having examined the quality of the air in the tent where the experiments were carried out, the Fontana eudiometer gave a measurement of salubrity of 0·92. Don José Espinosa had taken care to observe the meridian altitude of the Sun near the watering place with an excellent Stancliffe sextant, which came with a stand and an artificial horizon. His results, when referred to the observatory on our plan, confirmed the latitude calculated with the astronomical quadrant on this and the following day and, having determined apparent noon by equal altitudes, we could also calculate the longitude of the observatory, by means of both lunar distances and the chronometers.[1]

At four o'clock in the afternoon all the instruments and the tent were packed away, and at the same time Señores Espinosa, Bauzá, Haenke and Piloto Maqueda returned from their respective professional missions. We were then able to dine in peace and spend the remaining hours of the afternoon in the physiological examination of the inhabitants of these parts.[2]

Don Tomás Suria took this opportunity to make drawings from life from the information gathered during the previous days. Don Cayetano Valdés and Don Fernando Quintano examined the weapons and utensils and found many worthy of acquisition for the Real Gabinete. Furthermore, many of the women were diligently occupied in making cooking baskets, as were the men in making dolls, spoons, and other wooden tools, which the officers and even the seamen had eagerly purchased.[3] Finally some

---

[1] For full details of the astronomical observations at Port Mulgrave see Espinosa, *Memorias* (1809), 2nd memoir, pp. 58–60 and José Espinosa y Tello, *Memoria sobre las observaciones astronómicas, que han servido de fundamento á las cartas de la costa NO de América*, Madrid, 1805, pp. 4–5. This 20-page leaflet was intended as an appendix to the already published *Relación del viage hecho por las goletas Sutil y Mexicana*.

[2] The accounts of Malaspina, Suria and Tova all provide detailed descriptions of the Tlingit natives whom they referred to as *tejunés* – subjects of Ankau Juné: see Novo y Colson, *Viaje político-científico*, pp. 342–9; Cutter, *Journal of Suria*, pp. 42–7 and Porrúa, *Diary of Tova*, pp. 394–7.

[3] Complementary to the official collection, Haenke made a personal collection that now resides in the Náprstek Museum in Prague. Some of these items are clearly Tlingit in origin: see Joseph Kandert, 'Catalogue of Ethnographic Collections of Tadéus Haenke', *Annals of the Náprstek Museum*, 13, Prague, 1985, pp. 201–15. At some time after he left the expedition in Lima in 1793, Haenke sent his collection to Europe through the good offices of the Bohemian glass-trading firm of Hieke, Rautenstrauch und Zinke [HRZ] which operated in both Spain and America. In 1819, some three years after Haenke had died in Bolivia, Count Kaspar von Sternberg, representing the Bohemian National Museum, bought thirty-one Indian artifacts from California and the NW Coast which the HRZ Company had carefully kept in their warehouse in Cádiz, along with Haenke's personal herbarium (now in the Přírodovědecké Muzeum in Prague). They were shipped to Northern Europe via the port of Hamburg: see María Victoria Ibáñez Montoya, *La expedición Malaspina, 1789–1794. Tomo IV: Trabajos científicos y correspondencia de Tadeo Haenke*, Madrid, 1992, p. 95.

[of the officers] in learning new words¹ and others in studying the local domestic customs, had shown that constant love of science and study that had borne such fruits for the expedition.

This was also a very timely occasion for the commanding officer and officers of the *Atrevida* to apply themselves to target practice. As they were trying their best to hit the target, with a large number of natives watching, this exercise could not but have a salutary influence on the continuation of a relationship which was as peaceful as we could wish. Among the spectators was a particularly observant one who, to the general approval or rather amazement of the rest, thought he had found a way of making his clothing impervious to bullets. He moistened thoroughly the skin that covered him, then proudly set it up as a target at the required distance and was so convinced that it was impenetrable that when Don Ciriaco Cevallos pierced it with a bullet he grew bitterly angry and withdrew.

Everything had gone smoothly in obtaining water, although a few more natives appeared than on the day before. Indeed, Don José Espinosa had been able to inform himself from a family living nearby about various domestic customs and to acquire one or two pieces from the women's clothing and adornments. What happened this day on board the *Atrevida* to a servant born in the Philippines was to cause us particular surprise as to the character of these natives. From the first day of visiting that corvette they had taken him for one of themselves, carefully examining his skin and hair, his facial features and even his limbs. They now asked him to stay with the tribe and tried to find out how he came to be among us and whether he had been sold or captured. Finally they were about to take him with them when fortunately the officers arrived in time to make them let him go and give up the attempt.

As was to be expected the new arrivals had brought some good otter skins, which during the afternoon began to appear in the market held from canoes under the gangway of each corvette. As their interests were now linked to those of the old tribe, they were always accompanied by one of them, not only did they not lower their demands in view of the competition, but raised them little by little to such a point, particularly when bartering for clothing, that several of our seamen made a not insignificant loss in the exchanges, even taking the value of the skins as that of the Canton market.² It was, nonetheless, a most remarkable and curious spectacle to see at some point a good half of the old tribe and some of the new so strangely clad in old marines' uniforms, seamen's jackets, caps, neckcloths, shirts, breeches etc. Summer and winter clothing were worn indiscriminately, which doubtless would have caused the

---

¹ A number of the officers, assisted by Haenke, compiled a limited vocabulary of Tlingit numbers and words (AMN, MS 633, ff. 82-83ᵛ) which was published in Novo y Colson, *Viaje político-científico*, pp. 349-51 and by María Dolores Higueras and Juan Pimentel Igea, eds, *La expedición Malaspina, 1789-94. Tomo V: Antropología y noticias etnográficas*, Madrid, 1993, pp. 108-11. Suria described the language as 'very harsh. It abounds greatly in KK's and HH's'. He noted six words, one of which, *chouut*, he said meant woman: Cutter, *Journal of Suria*, pp. 48-9. See also p. 110, n. 2 above.

² Refers to the successful trade of Cook's men in exchanging furs collected at Nootka in 1778 for high prices in Canton [Guangzhou]. The thick pelt of the sea otter (*Enhydra lutris*) quickly became highly valued, but the intensity of the fur trade caused prices to fluctuate wildly and almost wiped out the otter. Malaspina never went to Canton, but Bustamante visited Macau during the expedition's long stopover in the Philippines.

Plate 12. Tlingit Burial Ground at Port Mulgrave, by José Cardero. Museo Naval, Madrid

greatest surprise on any vessel they might have boarded, probably leading to the suspicion that the crew of a Spanish ship had been murdered in these waters.

As Don Felipe Bauzá informed me, the stretch of coast from the watering place to [blank][1] was very heavily forested, and the adjoining country had such an abundance of a very good species of wild strawberry, that his party, which included some five seamen, would have tried in vain to exhaust them. Furthermore, they had gone some way up the nearby river and inspected, with wonder, the burial ground mentioned by Captain Dixon.[2] What they saw there was so curious and may shed so much light on the religious principles of these peoples, that it would have been wrong not to visit it myself. [1 July] Accordingly, on the following morning, accompanied by Don Tomás Suria and Don José Espinosa, I took the pinnace to the river and shortly after nine o'clock I was there. Four or five natives conveniently appeared, wandering in the fields nearby, picking strawberries to eat. They did in fact seem to be of the lowest class and therefore unlikely to be able to satisfy my curiosity, but as it was my intention to take one or two objects from these graves for the Real Gabinete, their

---

[1] This refers to the NW extremity of Khantaak Island, for which Malaspina had not yet decided on a name, but which was subsequently named Punta Muñoz on chart no. 8 in the atlas accompanying *Relación del viage hecho por las goletas Sutil y Mexicana* and in Palau et al., *Diario de viaje de Malaspina*, p. 248. For an earlier use of this name by Malaspina see p. 104, notes 3–5 above.

[2] On his entry into Port Mulgrave Dixon's attention 'was a good deal engaged by the sight of a number of white rails, on a level piece of ground, not far from the creek' which when he visited the spot 'to his great surprise found it to be a kind of burying-place': [Beresford], *Voyage ... by Captain George*

company suited me better at the time than any other of people from the anchorage. These, indeed, through either fear or veneration, might not have allowed me to carry out my intentions. First we measured, while Don Tomás Suria drew a perspective view of the posts and beams that enclosed a long dwelling, apparently arranged for the winter season.[1] We then spent some time doing the same with the old grave and after that with the new one which, with its collection of decorations and good state of preservation, could not fail to arouse our astonishment and admiration. Finally, without any objections from the natives, whom I had prepared with several gifts, I removed and sent to the pinnace one of the boxes from the old grave.

This was lightly decorated on the outside with the usual shells. It enclosed a smaller casket in which we found, wrapped in a sort of basket, only a few bones, reduced to ashes and mostly powder. The view of these graves which accompanies our report will give a better idea of their different aspects and proportions than a description, which would be difficult and tiring.[2] We will only specify here that these graves, as we understood from the natives, were those of the *Ankaus* or ruling family, alone, and it was clear that the bodies were cremated around the great carved figure.[3] Indeed as the natives indicated this to us and we also saw three or four small pits, the length of a man's body on which the coals or wood that had served for the funeral pyre were covered by boards and stones. In the following chapter we will describe at greater length this interesting aspect of the natives' customs and we will venture our conjectures as to the interpretation of what we were able to observe.

Meanwhile the armed launches and the *bombos*, under the command of Teniente de Navío Concha of the *Atrevida*, had again collected an abundant supply of water. Also, with the fine weather continuing with the same clarity as the day before, Don Juan Vernacci had been able to take another latitude observation and, in the middle of the day, a satisfactory set of equal altitudes which confirmed the rate of chronometer 71, as determined in Acapulco, and which showed a not insignificant gain in chronometers 61 and 72.

As the collection of water and ballast, for which the launches were necessary, was

---

Dixon, p. 175. The location was on Phipps Peninsula; the modern chart still identifies the place as a cemetery: see de Laguna, *Under Mount Saint Elias*, part III, plate 32.

[1] The only surviving drawing of the winter house is one by Cardero: see Sotos, *Los pintores*, II, fig. 561. Because Suria was the senior artist he is often referred to as the author of the work done at Port Mulgrave. However, from the extant material it is clear that Cardero made as important a contribution to the record of the northern campaign as the Mexican: see Donald Cutter, 'José Cardero: Proto artist of the Pacific Coast'; paper given at the Vancouver Conference on Exploration and Discovery, Simon Fraser University, 1992, in Special Collections, The Library, University of British Columbia, Spam 22863. See also John Frazier Henry, *Early Maritime Artists of the Pacific Northwest Coast, 1741–1841*, Seattle, 1984, pp. 149–70.

[2] Cardero certainly seems to have been on this excursion. Malaspina mentions his drawings of the burial monuments 'sketched with much accuracy by the painter Cardero' (Novo y Colson, *Viaje político-científico*, p. 346) and his presence is further supported by the fact that the two original drawings of the site that have survived are by him: see plate 12 and Sotos, *Los pintores*, II, figs 562 and 563. Fernando Brambila, who joined the expedition as an official artist on its return to Mexico, produced an 'improved' (i.e. 'finished') version of the latter drawing (Sotos, *Los pintores*, II, fig. 564); in so doing he introduced a number of new elements and gave the overall scene a much more sinister quality. Malaspina discusses elsewhere in some detail this burial ground and another found later by Tova on Knight Island: Novo y Colson, *Viaje político-científico*, p. 346.

[3] The giant bear-like figure that dominates the scene of the Cardero and Brambila drawings is clearly a clan symbol.

now complete, I did not delay for an instant in starting on the survey of the inlet which had led us to the harbour where we were now anchored. It was my intention, if the passage we wished for existed, to make for it with the corvettes. I wanted to examine the locality myself and resolve beyond any doubt this important geographical question. To this end I had the launches well armed and manned, with provisions for a fortnight and an adequate supply of water and firewood. Don Felipe Bauzá accompanied me in the *Descubierta*'s launch, while that of the *Atrevida* was under the command of Teniente de Navío Don Antonio Tova. We also took with us pocket chronometer 351, the Ramsden astronomical quadrant, a caulker and a carpenter, with all the necessary instruments.

2 July

Having left the corvettes, therefore, in the care of Don José Bustamante, and having sent the *bombos* to collect firewood, we set sail early on the following morning, choosing to run between the islands, both because the gusty SE breeze then blowing would be more favourable and so as to study the true position of the channels again. At first we had to proceed under oars for a long time, but as we began to come out from among the islands we began to get a light southerly breeze, which soon brought us close to the inlet.[1] There were loose ice floes floating near the western side, while on the eastern side one could see near the shore a stretch of flat ground, well sheltered to the north by the nearby hills. Smoke rising at various spots showed that it was the dwelling place of some Indians.[2] Only within a musket-shot of the coast could we find a depth of twenty or thirty fathoms. Further offshore we could not obtain bottom even with sixty fathoms of line. When we had passed the flat ground and were approaching the entrance, the depth increased so much that the *Atrevida*'s launch, only a boat's length from the shore, could not obtain bottom with 120 fathoms of line. By then the southerly breeze had dropped. At times we had a flat calm and at others a contrary breeze from NE, with rain, which obliged us to take to the oars again, although the men were tired and the launches somewhat overladen.

No sooner had we come abeam of the huts than we saw a canoe approaching us with a single Indian, whose dress we could not make out although we scrutinized it carefully. It was indeed impossible to distinguish what it was until the canoe came up to our launch when we saw not only that his clothing consisted of a cap, shirt, breeches and uniform jacket, but that the new arrival in the canoe was a son of the *Ankau* of the harbour, who had visited us repeatedly on board. With the new clothing his manners seemed much improved, as I had on various occasions found him to be the most arrogant and provoking of the tribe, but I now noted a meekness and subservience in his conduct for which it was difficult to find the cause. He came on board the *Descubierta*'s launch, indicating to us that he was the chief of the small settlement nearby, and that his wives and children, whom he named with great fondness,

---

[1] Leaving the shelter of the islands surrounding Port Mulgrave, the little expedition to find the Strait of Ferrer Maldonado had headed out into the main body of water forming Yakutat Bay.

[2] The flat land bordering Yakutat Bay to the SE is the end of the southern portion of the Malaspina Coastal Plain. It stands in strong contrast to the ice field leading up to Mount St Elias on the opposite NW side of the bay.

were there. At length he agreed to accompany us, after the gift of a few trifles and a good meal, of which he appeared to be in much need.

The weakness of the tidal stream and the answers of the new *Ankau* were already convincing us not only that the desired passage did not exist in these parts, but that the inlet was very short, and that we were almost at the end of this channel. We saw, furthermore, that all the inner shore to the west was permanently ice-bound, which could not have happened if the current at any time of the year had been of a speed consistent with either a communicating passage with another sea or the bends assumed to exist by Ferrer Maldonado. However, the heavily overcast sky and the contrary wind left us with our hopes for another couple of hours, only supported, as I have said, by the great depth off both shores and by a certain similarity in the breadth, steepness and bends of the entrance.

At last, guided by the Indian, we reached the anchorage at the far end of the bay at about one o'clock in the afternoon. The beach, mostly covered with gravel, was opposite a ravine, running down between two fairly high hills, which were watered by a stream. A small area of flat ground on the beach presented a most pleasing growth of vegetation to the eye.[1] However, with the exception of these small areas, which might properly be called green patches, the whole area surrounding the bay was ice-covered rock. This ice was so permanent that on the many ice floes floating near us, which we heard from time to time calving from the nearby mountains with a thunderous clamour, we could see above the old ice the recent layers of new ice that had accumulated on top. Not even the few places where vegetation was to be seen were free of enormous blocks of ice, so firmly consolidated that it seemed impossible that they could melt in the short space of summer that remained.

Despite the continuing rain and cold, we did not lose the chance, while both crews prepared their meal, to improve our knowledge of these parts. Don Felipe Bauzá measured a base and took bearings, although these were limited, both at its extremities and on a small hill close to the anchorage.[2] Don Antonio Tova attended to the hunting, while I undertook the collection of everything relating to natural history, which I would later see subjected to scientific examination by Don Tadeo Haenke. As the *Ankau* insisted on returning to his hut before nightfall, we sent him off with a few presents, and he promised to return the next morning with the fresh salmon we had requested.

Our desire to make good use of the time and the fear that the cloud cover, rain and cold might continue or even increase, prevented me from allowing the crews any

---

[1] In the collection of the Museo Naval there is a water-colour painting of this scene (where Yakutat Bay narrows into a fiord at its northern end) with a group of Spaniards from one of the launches on the beach with the Indians who had accompanied them up the bay: see plate 13. It is attributed to Juan Ravenet in Sotos, *Los pintores*, II, fig. 580. As Ravenet did not join the expedition until after the corvettes had returned to Acapulco and because Suria indicates in his journal that he did not take part in this particular excursion (Cutter, *Journal of Suria*, pp. 38 and 40), the original was probably drawn *in situ* by Bauzá as the view was from the observatory where he was in charge. Ravenet must have worked from this original to produce his 'improved' version.

[2] Bauzá's survey survives in 'Plano del Puerto de Desengaño': AMN, MS Sig. II. B. (3), (Higueras, *Catálogo crítico*, no. 1722): see plate 14. It was reproduced in the atlas accompanying *Relación del viage hecho por las goletas Sutil y Mexicana* as plate 9.

more rest than the time allowed by the tides, which we had already noted to be regular and almost simultaneous with those at Port Mulgrave.

At about nine in the evening, therefore, we began to make our way up the inlet under oars, examining the ends of the adjacent inlets, the permanent ice limit and the channel which appeared to run between the mainland and a small island that we had seen opposite the anchorage.[1] A great many circumstances made this examination extremely irksome and, above all, tiring for the seamen, due to the difficulty of rowing between the many ice floes that surrounded us and the necessity of constantly altering course to avoid them. In addition it was difficult to obtain soundings which Don Antonio Tova, who was much closer inshore to our right, could not obtain with 120 fathoms of line. Finally, at half past eleven that night, even before reaching the island, we reached the permanent ice limit and had to return to the old anchorage where, having anchored soon after midnight, the men were allowed the rest they needed.[2]

3 July

The weather, until now overcast with rain, had not allowed us to get as clear an idea of the cordillera behind this bay as I really wished for the accuracy of our operations. Nor had we been able to fix the true extremity of an entrance that we could see to the NW, because it was situated within the limits of the permanent ice. Furthermore, as our astronomical instruments remained useless[3] the geographical position of this harbour remained poorly determined, although indeed fixing its position would be more useful for future mariners to avoid it rather than to look for it. Luck was with us, however, dispelling our worry and unease at dawn on the following day. A light NW breeze cleared the cloud and haze and allowed us eagerly to continue all our operations. To this good fortune was added the appearance of several canoes from the settlement near the entrance, who generously supplied us with an excellent fresh salmon and thus the seamen could have a complete rest and we could finish all our operations soon after midday. We managed to take an excellent perspective view which will show the full desolation of these parts and the latitude of $59°50'30''$ was observed with the astronomical quadrant. Six azimuths to the Sun agreed in showing variation to be a very unusual $32°49'$. The bearings taken the day before were confirmed and augmented by others. We would also have been able to calculate the longitude directly if either the irregularity of the chronometer or some mistake in the observations had not caused the failure of this part of our work, as it was impossible to link the bearings to the anchorage where the corvettes lay.

In the early hours of the afternoon, as the tide was turning in our favour and all the tools and instruments had been stowed on board, we were preparing for the return trip when it was noticed that Able Seaman Manuel Fernández was missing from among the seamen of the *Atrevida*. His companions declared that they did not know

---

[1] The party was faced by what is now known as the Hubbard Glacier. The little island was later named in honour of Tadeo Haenke. A comparison between the modern chart and the *plano* shows the extent to which the glacier has retreated. In 1791 Haenke Island, as indicated later in the text, was still ice-bound.

[2] For Malaspina's later 'Dissertation' on Ferrer Maldonado's supposed voyage and strait see pp. 468-80 below.

[3] Presumably because the weather conditions prevented observations.

where he was. He had left the others at about eight o'clock without saying where he was going, his absence not being noticed until meal time. This seaman, who had been treated with moderate severity on board his corvette since he had been apprehended with the other deserters in Acapulco, had keenly requested to be among the launch party, so as to prove by his conduct his repentance for this involuntary lapse. Accordingly it was difficult to make his actions tally with this, believing as we did that punctuality and close attention to his work were the only way in which he could redeem himself. Fortunately we knew that he had gone along the right-hand shore towards the island and the end of the bay. With this information we immediately sent out another seaman, who was to follow his tracks, call out to him, and bring him back.

Our confusion may thus be imagined when we found this measure also to be fruitless, although the seaman went a considerable distance from the launches and shouted with all his might from the top of some extremely steep crags, from which he could almost see the bottom of the bay. Don Antonio Tova then took the *Atrevida*'s launch to make another search. I told him to go as far up the bay as he could, firing a musket shot from time to time and searching the shore carefully, in case some illness or fall was preventing him from calling out and returning on board. As the launch moved up the bay and neared the ice, Don Antonio Tova's fears for the fate of this wretched man grew stronger. As there was no trace of him to be found and no response to the musket shots, he could only fear that he had either taken his own life or had fallen prey to one of the bears which, according to the natives, roamed these parts in large numbers. These fears were finally dispelled by the sight of him a long distance off. When Tova got him back to the launch, he even had to repress his natural annoyance and desire to reprimand him until the seaman satisfied him by explaining that he had intended to look for the strait that we so eagerly sought to find.

In fact, his desire to distinguish himself, after overhearing our conversation about not having surveyed the end of the right-hand inlet, had persuaded him to try and reach it overland. Fearing that others might want to share his glory, he had not only hidden his intention from everyone, but had also carried it out with corresponding tenacity, making his way for six hours through crags and ice of a ruggedness truly difficult to imagine. I hardly knew whether we should have been more amused by the failure of this plan or have marvelled at the honourable sentiments which inspired it. The seaman was forgiven his misunderstood absence and also, at my request, Don José Bustamante returned him to his old position of main top-man.[1] The account of this event will be seen as neither frivolous nor idle if we consider the purpose of recording it – either to demonstrate the noble sense of honour of the national character or to show how mistaken are those who regard the seaman as a mere brute, barely able to feel or think for themselves.[2]

Before leaving this bay I buried a bottle containing a record of our survey, the date on which it was made, and the possession taken in the name of His Majesty,

---

[1] A specially selected seaman, stationed in the maintop to attend to the taking in or setting of the upper sails.

[2] In his account of this incident, Tova suggested that while the unauthorized excursion would normally have merited punishment he agreed with Malaspina's leniency towards the sailor because of the 'honourable intention' of his quest for glory: Porrúa, *Diary of Tova*, pp. 386-7. Suria provides a

confirmed by a coin buried beside the bottle.[1] The harbour was given the name of Desengaño,[2] the outer entrance that of Ferrer, after the ancient mariner, who was the cause of our investigations, and the inner island was named after Haenke, in honour of the botanist who shared with us on this voyage all the dangers and discomforts of sea voyages.[3]

With the help of the tide and a gentle NE breeze, we hoped to make good progress the next afternoon, but both soon dropped away. So we had to take to the oars and continue under them without a pause, although the excessive heat was very trying for the crews of both launches. The natives had gone ahead of us in their canoes and came out to meet us when we closed the shore near the settlement for Don Felipe Bauzá to take some bearings with the theodolite, including one to Mount St Elias, now in view. The young *Ankau* continued to show the same affability as on the previous day. He even brought to me in a canoe two of his very young children, whom he treated with the greatest tenderness and to whom, therefore, I did not fail to give a few trifles. The little stretch of flat ground where the huts stood was indeed well sheltered from northerly winds tending sufficiently towards the south, so that it did seem a better spot to live in On the other hand, however, offshore it was extremely deep and doubtless so exposed to the heavy swell in the passage that often, particularly in winter, it would be impossible to fish. The fishing must be very productive in these waters, considering the many salmon with which they supplied us on this day and the next.

While proceeding for the rest of the afternoon at about two musket shots off the shore, in depths of twenty-five and thirty fathoms, at times rock and at others gravel, we were able to survey it in detail and look for reasonable shelter in which to pass the night. It was ten o'clock when we dropped anchor, yet Don Felipe Bauzá did not fail to take the necessary bearings with the theodolite, tying them in once again to Mount St Elias, which was still in sight.

The locality reached by the launches was a channel between the mainland and an island of moderate height,[4] which would have made an excellent anchorage if the

---

second-hand account of the event suggesting that Fernández's trip was one of the talking points when the launches returned to Port Mulgrave. However, he identifies the sailor as 'José Berelo, a native of Coruña in the kingdom of Galicia': Cutter, *Journal of Suria*, p. 41. As he was not with the launches, his account must be considered suspect on this point. Frederica de Laguna, *Under Mount Saint Elias*, p. 149, referring to Suria's statement that the sailor had been to the farthest point of the bay where he saw 'that it ended in a copious river which ran between those mountains and was lost to view winding about like a snake' (Cutter, *Journal of Suria*, pp. 40–41), speculates that Fernández had actually reached the head of Russell Fiord which leads south from Disenchantment Bay, with an arm going off east into Nunatak Fiord. Although what is today the junction of Russell Fiord with Disenchantment Bay would at the time of Malaspina's visit have been filled with ice, there would very likely have been open water in the two fiords beyond. Whatever the sailor had seen, Malaspina obviously did not consider the 'copious river' to be the much-desired passage and thus worthy of further exploration.

[1] The first of two Acts of Possession carried out by Malaspina during the voyage: for details see Vol. 1 of this edition, p. lix and Cutter, *Malaspina and Galiano*, pp. 38–9.

[2] Disenchantment Bay.

[3] Three of the names bestowed by the Spaniards in this part of Yakutat Bay still remain on the modern chart: Haenke Island, named in honour of Tadeo Haenke who took part in this excursion; Bancas Point on the northern side of the inlet; and Disenchantment Bay.

[4] Knight Island.

Plate 13. Disenchantment Bay, by Juan Ravenet. Museo Naval, Madrid

depths off both shores had not dropped rapidly to forty and fifty fathoms and if they were not fringed with rocks, making them very inconvenient for boats. [4th] A swarm of mosquitoes hastened our departure on the following morning, but before that we had measured a short base to survey this harbour. Then with the occasional shower and a moderate westerly breeze, falling at times to calm, we got under way to continue our investigations into this small archipelago, and ultimately, to rejoin the corvettes.

The island that we were surveying, which we named Pineda in honour of Don Antonio Pineda, one of our number who had remained in New Spain, is thickly wooded and parts of it are rich in shellfish. Furthermore, on its southern shore, there are other graves visible, exactly like those I had visited near the harbour [of Port Mulgrave]. We saw very few native settlements, these being either scattered on the islands or nearby on the mainland and, if we were to judge by the considerable number of thirty or forty salmon sold to the launches from only two canoes, the fishing must be very productive in these channels, providing an easy subsistence for their inhabitants.

The breeze continued favourable, although accompanied by rain, enabling us to make use of it under full sail. Having been thwarted in our attempt to make our way towards another inner channel, which we found to be a dead-end forming only a fairly wide bay, we finally sighted the corvettes at five o'clock and soon afterwards we were on board.[1]

Don José Bustamante informed me that, during these last days, our relationship with the natives had changed considerably. Even though no harm had been done by either side, there had been some very awkward moments, obliging us to take greater care on all occasions. The day the launches departed for Puerto del Desengaño the woodcutting parties went to an area not far from the huts, led by Don Cayetano Valdés, whose turn it was to take them, accompanied by Alférez de Fragata Ali Ponzoni, for his instruction. All arrangements for safety, the work and the conveyance had, of course, been made with the greatest care. Indeed, although many natives gathered at the spot, there was no break in either the diligence of the work or in our friendly relations. However, when a seaman from the *Descubierta* forgot to put his jacket with those of the other men, which were wisely left with a sentinel to guard them, inevitably a native swiftly made off with it. When the seaman missed it he told the officer in charge. One of those present soon told him who had done it and he informed the *Ankau*, pressing him either to insist on its return or to punish the offender, as we would have done ourselves with anyone who had violated the law of ownership. His authority, however, was weak or (as is probable) the Chief himself was party to these offences, although always with the appearance of great friendship towards us, and so the jacket was not returned. Don José Bustamante, on the advice of the *Ankau* himself on board the *Descubierta*, prohibited any bartering on the following day and insisted on the return of the jacket.[2]

---

[1] Malaspina's expedition to Disenchantment Bay had lasted three days.

[2] Bustamante's account of the beginning of deteriorating relations is slightly different. The theft of the seaman's jacket and a cap, and the refusal of the natives or their evasion when asked to make restitution, followed Bustamante's order to discontinue exchanges which, he believed, were dangerous, time-wasting and costly in terms of the hospitality given to the natives. He later recorded the resentment this caused the natives: Bustamante, *Diario general del viaje*, p. 250.

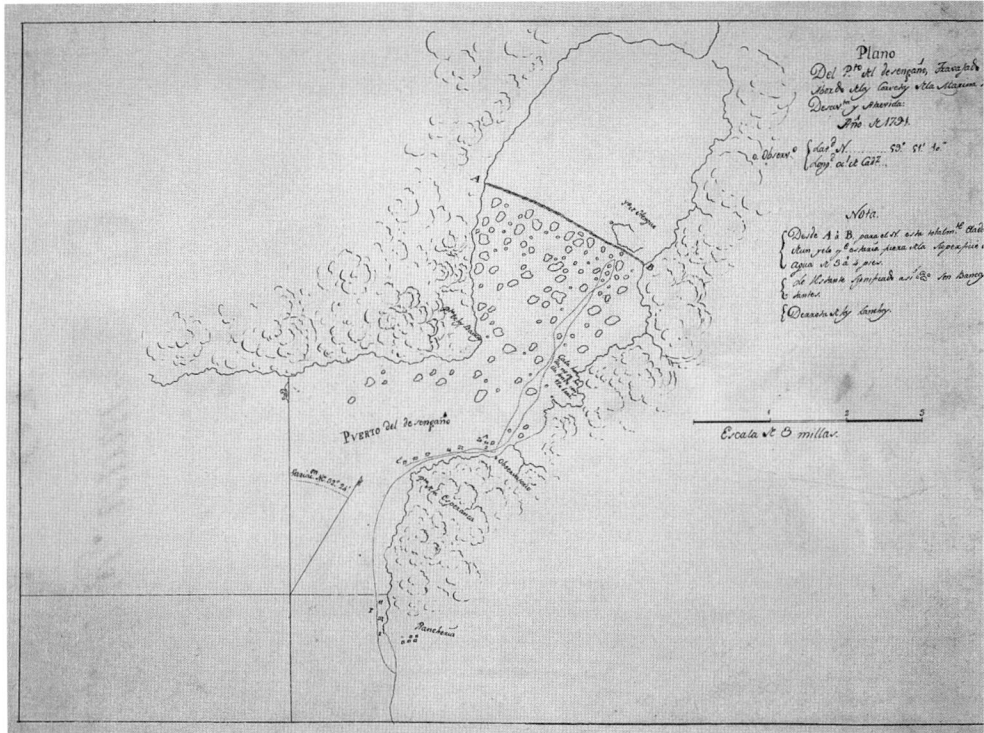

Plate 14. 'Plano del P.^{to} del Desengaño trabajado a bordo de las corbetas de la Marina Real *Descubierta* y *Atrevida*, año 1791.' Museo Naval, Madrid. The line A–B depicts the edge of the fast ice.

The natives were soon angered by this measure and accordingly, when Don José Robredo set out with the usual parties to cut firewood, he not only noted provocation and insolence in their behaviour, but he also had to threaten with his musket one who insulted the sentinel who had been appointed to guard the jackets. At the slightest reprimand he turned on the officer with his dagger unsheathed. At the same time they came alongside both corvettes, telling us arrogantly to leave at once if we did not wish to continue with the bartering. In short, in all their actions they made it clear that only the lack of a suitable opportunity prevented a bloody and destructive rupture.

The officers of the *Atrevida*, most opportunely, then began amusing themselves again with target practice on the beach. Their continued skill in hitting the tree trunk, the dampened hide having been previously perforated, convinced the natives once more that the superiority of our weapons would quickly decide any encounter in our favour.[1] These being the circumstances, the officers and the wood cutting parties

---

[1] The Spaniards were under no illusion that, despite the outward signs of friendship because it suited the natives' trading interests, their relationship with the Yakutat Tlingit was essentially a tense and fragile one. Indians challenged in any way were quick to flash a knife. While the exploring party had been away, the balance of power had shifted and, although Bustamante's men had their firearms, the absence of a large group of the visitors, their chief among them, obviously emboldened the natives. Tova considered that it was essential for Bustamante to act as he did because respect for the Spaniards' power was

having returned on board, the natives continued to appeal now and again for the resumption of the bartering. However, they showed no immediate anger, nor did we have any fears after the warning had been given and following the assurances of the commanding officer of the *Atrevida* that bartering would start again the next day. At the time it was difficult to guess the true intentions of the *Ankau*. On board the corvettes he seemed to wish to help with our intentions of recovering the jacket. Among his own people, he either expostulated weakly or showed, by the mildness of his conduct, that he did not disapprove of the theft. Although he so frequently put himself in our power and assured us that we should never doubt the constancy of his friendship, we did not suspect any unfortunate consequences, particularly as each of our own men was always on guard with suitable weapons for his own safety.

Towards four in the afternoon Don José Bustamante decided to land on the beach opposite the *Descubierta*, with the intention of taking steps towards peace and to continue with target practice as a recreation, now almost a necessity. The natives were crowded around their huts and some of them set off to the very beach where the pinnace was about to land. This having been left in charge of two seamen, who were to keep it afloat, the rest began to make their way towards the huts preceded, at a distance, by the commanding officer of the *Atrevida*, with a few seamen between him and Tenientes de Navío Cevallos, Concha and Viana, who had stopped to load their muskets. This opportunity seemed too good to be missed by one of the natives who was considering taking hostage one of our seamen, whom he saw were unarmed, possibly to impose on us for his ransom a resumption of the bartering or any other measure they cared to request. He therefore seized him from behind and ran as fast as he could towards his own people. The seaman was a young American[1] who, either believing that it was one of his own companions who was carrying him off, or overcome by fear, did not even try to call out to the officers. These fortunately could not fail to see what was happening and immediately informed Don José Bustamante, who quickly threatened the native to make him release the seaman. This he succeeded in doing, but at the same time Don José saw the native in this struggle coming at him with his dagger unsheathed. The man stopped for a moment, when very close, to shout to his own people, who moved rapidly towards him, the *Ankau* himself among them.

The encounter was now looking fairly serious. Bustamante's musket was not loaded and its bayonet was not fixed, while the enraged native was now threatening

---

crucial in allowing the expedition to replenish its supplies, to undertake its astronomical observations and various other 'scientific' investigations, and to avoid the sort of disaster that had befallen Captain Cook in Hawaii. He also describes the demonstration of firepower: Porrúa, *Diary of Tova*, pp. 390-92.

[1] *Americano* in the original MS, which in Spanish means a person born in America, that is in the New World (the Americas). Suria records that at this time of tension he also was captured and was sufficiently scared by the experience that he complained to the officers for abandoning him: Cutter, *Journal of Suria*, p. 39. However, de Laguna suggests that the Suria's capture was a peace-hostage incident, in which the hostage or 'deer' is cleansed by a ceremony that includes dancing and a series of 'tests'. Perhaps this was the young American's intended fate. A similar event occurred when a sailor on Bodega y Quadra's stopover at Bucareli Bay in 1779 was captured by Tlingit natives: see Walter Thornton, 'An Account of a Voyage made by Fr John Riobo as Chaplain of His Majesty's Frigates the *Princesa* and *Favorita*', *Catholic Historical Review*, 4, 1918, p. 225.

him at very short range.[1] On the one hand the number of armed natives was growing rapidly and on the other the three officers already named, the purser, Ezquerra and a couple of seamen, who had armed themselves with sabres, were preparing to defend their commanding officer, particularly as they saw the adversary making as if to take him cunningly from behind. At this critical juncture Bustamante did not forget the principles of humanity, nor those of his own safety. He shouldered his musket as if it were loaded, postponing for the moment telling his men to do the same so as to suspend hostilities, and boldly called out to the *Ankau* to hold back his subjects. The *Ankau* hesitated for a time, but then decided to speak to the most aggressive one, although not in his customary tone of command. The latter, perhaps persuaded or scared by this, quickly held out his arms and chanted the hymn of peace. This step, however, did not yet appear to gain the approval of the rest, who remained armed in the vicinity of their huts and, having sent their women away, called out anxiously to the few canoes alongside the corvettes. The officers noticed these events, but did not think it wise to embark so soon and thus show signs of inferiority, nor did they think it right to ask for reinforcements from the corvettes, which might be misinterpreted and prevented by the natives. Therefore they remained on the beach for some time, looking scornfully at their adversaries, before finally returning on board in the pinnace.

Such a successful combination of firmness and kindness could not fail to throw a new light on these unpleasant events and to convince the natives of both our strength and our truly peaceful intentions. The *Ankau* soon explained this to his people in a long and emphatic harangue, which we could see from the corvettes. Finally he appealed to them to ask unanimously for peace when the jacket, the origin of all discord, had been returned. He then went on board the *Atrevida* with it, accompanied by the most solemn demonstrations of genuine peace and begged Don José Bustamante to have the hymn of peace sung on board both corvettes by our men, as his would do on the shore opposite. Soon afterwards this agreeable and somewhat harmonious clamour from both ships and on shore, with the expressive gesture of open arms, presented to our gaze a very different spectacle from that which we had feared a short time before. Our crew, forgetting the anger roused by hearing of the threat to their officers, revived those thoughts of compassion and humanity which we so eagerly desired to inspire in them on every occasion.

Peace now being well established, the natives wished to ratify it after sunset with a greater solemnity. With this intention they lit some fires on the shore near the corvettes and began dancing and celebrating to the accompaniment of tuneful and joyful songs (which Señor Haenke immediately transcribed), often mingling with them the words 'Atrevida' and 'Descubierta', while facing towards the ships and imitating our way of calling to each other.

The following day, which was rainy, Don José Bustamante thought it best to stop work, as a considerable amount of firewood had already been collected, the men needed a rest and thereby we were able to study the nature and intentions of the natives at some

---

[1] Bustamante and his colleagues were clearly in a very exposed and dangerous situation. As Tova pointed out in his journal, firearms were of limited use at close quarters because 'once fired it would not have been possible to reload them before being trampled by the crowd.': Porrúa, *Diary of Tova*, p. 391.

leisure. The officers of the *Descubierta*, accompanied by the *Ankau*, visited the graveyard, and on this occasion learned a great deal about their customs and the language. The bartering was revived, under the original system of not allowing the natives on board. A large quantity of salmon was brought to the market, without altering its price and a new tribe, led by a son of our *Ankau*, which had just arrived had joined the others. At the time of my arrival everything was peaceful and orderly, the chief repeating to me his assurances of sincere friendship and his pleasure at the return of the launches.

5 July

Having achieved both purposes which had brought me to this harbour, it was my intention to leave as soon as possible to make use of the favourable season in surveying the next stretch of coast to the west. The weather, however, was overcast and rainy and, furthermore, another load of water would be very useful for our trim. I therefore decided that early the next morning the launches and *bombos*, well armed and under the charge of Teniente de Navío Cevallos, should undertake this task, while other preparations on board should be hastened for a prompt departure. Later, as the day improved somewhat and even promised that the Sun would put in the odd appearance, Piloto Maqueda was sent with an armed pinnace to obtain some soundings that we did not yet have. At the same time Teniente de Fragata Don Juan Vernacci with the Ramsden astronomical quadrant, pocket chronometer 351, a *pilotín*[1] and two armed marines had orders to wait on the nearby beach for breaks in the clouds, in case we could obtain a new and final period for rating our chronometers.[2]

Very early next morning the *Ankau* came on board the *Atrevida* to attend to the bartering, in which he always had the great advantage over the rest of being allowed on board, a privilege only granted to him. Many canoes also attended, but at the spot where the astronomical quadrant had been set up to take equal altitudes after noon only a few natives were to be seen, as relaxed observers of any operations of this kind.

Shortly before noon, however, inspired either by idle curiosity or by a new urge to abuse our patience, the natives began first to gather in greater numbers around the astronomical quadrant, then to try to touch one or other of the instruments and finally to surround the marines who were attempting to keep them back, even demanding their muskets with some insolence. Don Juan Vernacci, who was within hailing distance of the *Atrevida*, quickly informed her commanding officer of these developments. He immediately passed the word to me, advising me that he had the *Ankau* on board, and asking me to tell him of my intentions so that we could work in unison. The weakness of our forces on shore at present, the risk of losing any part of the astronomical quadrant, which would be difficult to replace and, above all, the desire to avoid any discord which might be disastrous for either side, left me no choice as to the best measure to take. I told him to detain the *Ankau* and to instruct him to warn his people to move away from the quadrant and, finally, to have his guns ready for use if necessary. Meanwhile I set out in the *Atrevida*'s pinnace with Don Juan de la Concha, preceded at a short distance by Don Cayetano Valdés with four armed marines.

[1] The name of the *pilotín*, Jerónimo Delgado, has been deleted in the original MS.
[2] Vernacci was to obtain a set of equal altitudes to complete the rating of the chronometers, the first set having been observed on 29 June (see p. 113 above). The period between the observations should not exceed ten days, nor be less than five days.

On this occasion it would have been unwise to attempt to remain in this position until the time of the afternoon observations, making the astronomical quadrant a palladium[1] and a cause of bloodshed. Accordingly the first action taken by Tenientes de Navío Valdés and Vernacci, and then by Don Juan de la Concha and myself, was to call on the marines to protect the quadrant and to move aside those who were standing too close, persuading them (taking charge of this ourselves) of the necessity of this measure, expressing ourselves as peacefully and gently as possible. Meanwhile I told the *pilotín* to put the quadrant into its case and ordered the seamen to carry all the instruments to the pinnace. The natives were unwilling to withdraw; their postures and faces, now well known to us, showed that they would resort to their daggers if the opportunity arose. All the canoes had now left the corvettes and simultaneously we could see other people approaching from the lagoon, almost under cover of some trees. At the same time I received word from the *Atrevida* that the whole tribe was in arms and making its way towards us. I then turned commandingly to one of the boldest of the natives and, showing him my musket, told him to stand back, but he moved only two or three paces away and unsheathed his dagger to show that he also was armed and fearless. In vain the *Ankau*, held against his will on board the *Atrevida*, called out to his people to fall back, warning them that the guns were ready to fire and in vain did we, united and strong, tell them to withdraw. They pressed forward and even redoubled their blind rage, to the point of a native even coming face to face against Don Cayetano Valdés, who had his musket and bayonet ready. At this juncture I thought it best to have the astronomical quadrant taken to the pinnace at once, without waiting for it to be put in its case and to tell Bustamante to fire a blank from a gun, while we, gradually and in an orderly fashion, approached the shore. At the loud report everyone turned to see what damage had been done. The *Ankau* begged us not to aim at the huts. Some [of the natives] seemed to have decided to withdraw, but they very soon took heart again and one of them, following close behind us, seized a weapon with fine audacity and called out to the *Ankau* to take cover as he was ready to attack.

With the quadrant embarked, and all our party near the pinnaces, now reinforced by the arrival of the one that had been sounding, our efforts were now directed to our own safety rather than preventing one or another of the natives seeking to meet his end at our muskets and bayonets. I therefore had several marines to embark and then, covered by them, I ordered Señores Concha and Vernacci do the same, thinking myself fortunate to have avoided the shedding of any human blood at a moment when such an outcome had been so close.[2]

---

[1] A reference to the image of the goddess Pallas, in the citadel of Troy, on which the safety of the city was supposed to depend. It seems that Malaspina felt that the success of his voyage depended on the safety of the astronomical quadrant.

[2] Three drawings of this incident on 5 July have survived. One is attributed to Suria from a position on the beach showing a native brandishing a knife at a Spanish officer: Sotos, *Los pintores*, II, fig. 566. In his journal Suria notes 'in spite of the voice of the chief whom they saw a prisoner, they came very near to attacking us, having collected a considerable body of the Indians of this island': Cutter, *Journal of Suria*, p. 41. The other drawings, one each by Cardero and Suria, are similar and would appear to be from the vantage point of *Descubierta* looking towards the beach. They show the guns of the *Atrevida* firing, keeping the natives at bay from the Spaniards, some of whom are pointing their muskets at the Indians while others get the astronomical quadrant into the pinnace: plate 15, see also Sotos, *Los pintores*, II, figs 565 and 568.

Plate 15. Confrontation at Port Mulgrave, by Tomás de Suria. Museo Naval, Madrid

With the withdrawal of our pinnaces there was a marked change in the circumstances of the confrontation. The natives were now deprived of any immediate object for their scheming and revenge while we could see their chief and another Indian held on board the *Atrevida*, which gave us the same advantage that they had hoped to gain by holding our seaman. To this were added the repeated calls from the *Ankau* himself and the suspension of bartering, facts that brought about the early resumption of peace. Our even-handed conduct, aimed at encouraging the renewal of friendly contacts with neither fear of insult nor the lure and self-interest of trade, also paid off. Thus it was not long before many of the natives came to the shore and called out to the *Ankau* that they were ready to make peace. However, as the launches sent to obtain water, had not yet rejoined the corvettes, I advised Don José Bustamante that it would be best to keep the *Ankau* on board, under various pretexts, until Don Ciriaco Cevallos had returned on board with his little convoy.

It was not long before Cevallos returned when, at three in the afternoon, as the natives repeated their appeals for the return of their chief, even offering to give back a pair of breeches that they had skilfully taken from a seaman on the second day of woodcutting, we finally agreed to allow him to return ashore in a canoe which came out to fetch him, with the usual signs of peace. Very soon we saw him appear again, chanting the hymn and holding up the breeches with great solemnity to confirm the peace, asking us to give the customary words and signs from the gangway, as his people repeated them from the beach.[1] After this formality, all mistrust disappeared again, and not half an hour had passed before the same people who were willing to risk their lives at midday for the sole pleasure of insulting or attacking us, were back alongside to offer a skin or some other trifle.

At five in the afternoon a moderate breeze set in from the west, instantly clearing the sky and horizon. The tide was to continue in our favour until ten o'clock, so I did not hesitate to start weighing anchor and, after the launch was hoisted, of setting sail.

The natives did not lose the chance for as many exchanges as possible during these last hours, bringing us everything that they thought might please us, lowering their claims considerably, which until now had been excessive, particularly for the hatchets and clothing. When we set sail most of the canoes withdrew, but even as the *Descubierta* was making for the harbour mouth she was followed by a woman in a canoe, who not only wished to wipe from our memory, with a good deed, the unfortunate impression that we had gained from her people, but also to remind us that not even these harsh climates could destroy the sweet and affectionate character which has always been the true nature of her sex. The surgeon of the *Descubierta*, Don Francisco Flores, noticing that this woman had a baby with her, still almost at the breast, threw from the stern a few little bells and beads, telling her to use them as adornments for the child. He then went up to the quarter-deck and, nearing the gangway, found the

---

[1] A unfinished drawing by José Cardero in the Museo de América captures this remarkable scene: Sotos, *Los pintores*, II, fig. 567. A 19th-century painting of the incident (plate 16), signed by José Cardano, not Cardero, is also in the Museum's collection: ibid., fig. 569. Suria recorded the scene: 'The Chief believed we were angered about some trousers which an Indian had stolen and which he ordered him [the Indian] to bring [back]. It was something to laugh at to see him in his canoe giving the sign of peace while hoisting high the trousers after Bustamante had turned him loose.': Cutter, *Journal of Suria*, p. 41.

Plate 16. The Chief at Port Mulgrave making peace overtures. Anon. Museo de América, Madrid

canoe now alongside, when he was moved by compassion to make her a second present of the same kind.

The woman could no longer restrain her gratitude and quickly cutting in half a skin that she had with her, she put it on the child's head and then gave it to Don Francisco Flores, as if in the child's name. Such an act required a show of grateful approbation on our part. Those present did not hesitate to give her a few trinkets from those that came to hand. The woman, however, far from giving way to the constraints of poverty or her natural liking for adornments, preferred to compete with us in generosity, giving us now one thing and now another in the child's name as our presents were received, continuing with determination until she was entirely divested of the skins that covered her. As may be imagined, we eventually had the upper hand in this contest, although without lessening the admiration that the woman's behaviour rightly aroused in us.

It was already nine in the evening when, after passing Point Turner, we encountered the breeze, then very light from SW, allowing us to tack out of the channel formed by Isla Dixon[1] and Point Muñoz,[2] as it is named on our charts in proper appreciation and recognition of the chief engineer who directed the construction of the corvettes in the naval dockyard at La Carraca. On one of these tacks, towards the mouth of a river off whose [northern entrance] point there was little depth at low water, as was now the case, the *Descubierta* grounded at the bow when going about,

---

[1] Phipps Peninsula where the burial monuments were located is here referred to as Isla Dixon. The channel is named Bahía de Monti (see p. 86, n. 2 above) on chart no. 8 in the atlas accompanying *Relación del viage hecho por las goletas Sutil y Mexicana*, which also shows the site of the burials.

[2] See p. 120, n. 1 above.

although she had no less than three to five fathoms on both sides and at the stern.[1] Manoeuvres were immediately begun to make her back off under sail, but as this did not answer, we laid out a kedge with the *bombo*. Then by hauling on the hawsers from the stern we were afloat again by eleven o'clock in ten fathoms, without having suffered any damage other than the loss of a false timber keel, which, lightly fixed to the scarfs of the keel[2] at the bow and projecting further than the rest of the keel, served precisely for protecting the protruding parts of the ship when running aground.

The corvette *Atrevida* had already sent her pinnace under the orders of Don Francisco Viana to help us, while she then bore away to anchor nearby, as I had told her commanding officer of my intention of remaining at anchor until the next ebb tide, which would not begin until four o'clock.

Piloto Maqueda sounded around the corvette in the pinnace, obtaining depths of five fathoms until a cable from the ship towards the point named Varada,[3] after the grounding, rising rapidly to twenty, thirty and forty fathoms, ooze, in the direction of the channel. A kedge was then laid out to the NW, on which to set sail the following morning. When these tasks were completed we could allow some rest for the men, who had been working for twenty-four hours.

---

[1] The river is clearly 'Estrecho del Ancau' on chart no. 8 in the above atlas.
[2] The joints, when a keel is made of several pieces.
[3] Marked 'Placer de la Barada' on chart no. 8 in the above atlas.

CHAPTER 3

Port Mulgrave to Nootka Sound

6 July
Soon after sunrise, in bright sunlight and with a light breeze from WNW, the tide started to turn in our favour, enabling us to begin to get under way. This took the *Descubierta* some time and effort, not so much because of the difficulty in weighing the kedges, as for that of coming off the wind before being able to set the sails. However we managed to do it by towing her with the pinnace, as well as by the usual manoeuvres. We had to make repeated tacks towards both shores before being able to consider ourselves clear of Punta Muñoz, from where shoals extend some four or five cables offshore.[1] At nine o'clock, however, the breeze having veered to the fourth quadrant, we managed to leave them half a mile [to port] and finally to alter course to SW under full sail, with a light breeze from WNW, a fairly smooth sea and the weather fine and calm.

The latitude of 59° 24′ observed at noon and bearings taken to all points in sight, allowed us to make a detailed comparison of all our work since leaving harbour, which we could now link to the area of Cape Fairweather, the head of Entrada or Abra de Ferrer[2] and the coast running westward from this inlet towards the foot of Mount St Elias.

The cruise that we were now undertaking was the real object of the voyage,[3] as we

---

[1] Malaspina surely means Carrew Point, the southern entrance point of Monti Bay [Bahía de Monti], from which shoal ground extends about 5 or 6 cables offshore and the point he would round once clear of the channel and not Muñoz Point, the northern entrance point of the bay, which was subsequently named Punta Muñoz. See 'Plano del Puerto de Mulgrave', chart no. 8 in the atlas accompanying *Relación del viage hecho por las goletas Sutil y Mexicana* and also p. 104, n. 3 above.

[2] The entrance to Disenchantment Bay.

[3] During the extension of the voyage into the Gulf of Alaska Malaspina was obviously ambivalent in his enthusiasm for the task at hand. Viewing the unbroken cordillera as they proceeded, he could have had very little faith in the existence of Ferrer Maldonado's passage after the experience in Disenchantment Bay; yet it was important to carry out his orders to sail further north, to 60° N and, as artist Suria noted in his diary, 'to reconnoiter the great piece of coast from Cabo Hinchinbrook to the Cabo and Monte Buen Tiempo, a reconnaissance which was indispensable not only to dispel once [and] for all the scrupulous doubts which might remain about the desired passage … but because this was a piece of coast which, except the great mountain of San Elias, marked and situated by Captain Cook, is not known to have been seen [i.e. explored in detail] by any traveler.': Cutter, *Journal of Suria*, p. 54. For the chart that resulted from Malaspina's exploration of this coast see AMN, MS Sig. II. B. (7) (Higueras, *Catálogo crítico*, no. 1723). It was incorporated with the results of the other Spanish voyages to Alaska into chart no. 3 in the Atlas accompanying *Relación del viage hecho por las goletas Sutil y Mexicana*.

were making for the stretch of coast below the 60th parallel, just where the supposed passage of Ferrer Maldonado was to be found according to the speculations of M. de Buache.

On our part, indeed, we no longer had even the slightest hope of the veracity of that memorial, since to all the considerations specified at the time of examining it, which, for the sake of a clearer exposition will be include in a separate chapter,[1] there was now the added certainty not only that the whole cordillera from Cape Fairweather to Mount St Elias is continuously unbroken, but also that a strip of low land lies before it, extending to the coast, which was never mentioned by the navigator Maldonado. To the west of Mount St Elias it was never possible to confirm his narrative since it was particularly notable that, of the land bordering the passage, all the western coast was extremely high and inaccessible, while the eastern coast was very fertile and suitable for cultivation. However, up to now this stretch of the coast had not yet been surveyed in detail by our navigators nor by Captain Cook or by Captains Porlock and Dixon. Consequently our work would be of considerable benefit to hydrography, even if we did not succeed in the original intention of finding a passage from this ocean to the Atlantic. Therefore I thought it right to set about it with all possible accuracy, however much of the remaining months of the summer it might take.

The explorations made prior to ours and the observations that we had been able to make since our landfall, all contributed to persuade me that no survey could be made with the wind in the first, second and, at times, the third quadrant, since NW and west winds were the only ones which cleared the atmosphere, allowing a good view of all the points along the coast and the corresponding observations to determine their latitude and longitude. Urged by these considerations, I had hastened our departure from Port Mulgrave on the previous afternoon when the first light airs from NW got up and, with these in mind, I now decided on the course that we were to follow.

There was no doubt of the nature or position of the coast from Entrada de Ferrer to Punta Barrientos.[2] We had seen it on various occasions, first rather bleak and steep-to, and then extending in luxuriant forests beyond the point, with no other entrance to be seen apart from an estuary or narrow channel, very similar to many of these formed by the islands recently surveyed. Furthermore, the coast in these part would be some four leagues from the foot of the cordillera and had the same lush growth that we had seen at Port Mulgrave. It was consequently not only unnecessary to close the coast here, but if we were to do so we would lose the clear and moderate weather that we were presently enjoying.

In these circumstances we chose to make a long tack to the SSW, the wind now being settled in the west. At eight o'clock in the evening we went about and during the following morning [7th] we had to tack twice more, both to make as much westing as possible with the light and variable breezes, while waiting for a better occasion

---

[1] For Malaspina's subsequent 'Disertación' see pp. 468–80 below.

[2] The western entrance point of Yakutat Bay, probably named by Malaspina after Capitán de Fragata Don José Barrientos y Rato, acting Comandante de la Compañía de Guardias Marinas at Isla de León, with whom Malaspina was in correspondence concerning chronometers, books and instruments prior to the expedition's departure from Cádiz. Malaspina's name has not survived being replaced by Point Manby, named by Vancouver in June 1794 after Thomas Manby, Master of the *Chatham* at the time.

to survey the coast, which became shrouded in haze and drizzle when the breeze backed into the third quadrant. We took advantage of every break in the cloud that the weather allowed, even remaining in a position where the land would not be hidden from us towards midday or the early hours of the afternoon. Accordingly, at six in the morning we had taken bearings to Mount Fairweather and the land around the old anchorage. We had then taken two sets of hour angles and, having observed the meridian altitude of the Sun at noon, we could then extend our surveys somewhat and consider them securely established. Our latitude was then 59°30' and our longitude 55' west of Port Mulgrave, the meridian of which we adopted to leave subsequent charts free of any doubts regarding the true longitude of that port. Punta Barrientos was then bearing NNE and the western extremity of Abra de Ferrer NE, true.

After midday the haze covering the land cleared to some extent, but at the same time the breeze began to die away in the fourth quadrant, obliging us to set a course in the first so as to close the coast as we wished. At two o'clock, when we were only two leagues offshore, the *Atrevida* signalled to us that the depth was sixty-eight fathoms. We were able to make a detailed survey of the coast as far as Punta Novales,[1] which, although we had sighted it with our theodolite from the cape,[2] was at too oblique an angle for us to be able to determine properly what lay between the various bends of the coast. It was not easy to take reliable bearings to the higher points of land, including Mount St Elias. As for the lower ground which was now in sight, we were in no doubt that it was completely joined to the mainland, since we could see that where the forest stopped shortly beyond Punta Barrientos, the land continued in a series of reddish gullies, with low hillocks extending inland towards the foot of the same mountain. In this position we went about and, almost at the same moment, the breeze, which had for a short time been very light in the third and fourth quadrants, now set in from WSW again, quickly covering the whole of the coast in haze.

8 July

Thus it remained throughout the following day and since our intention was solely to make some westing before turning back towards the coast already surveyed, we only tacked to suit this purpose, disregarding any tack that would take us towards the coast which we could only see indistinctly in the morning, running from NNW to NW. Despite having no more than a very superficial knowledge of the weather signs on these coasts, the appearances left us in no doubt that there would soon be a change to the SE, particularly as the cloud cover was increasing rapidly, preventing us from observing even an altitude of the Sun. Indeed, by midnight, the wind had already backed to SW and south, with drizzle and heavy overcast, allowing us to make good a westerly course, which we immediately did under full sail.

---

[1] Cape Sitkagi at the NW end of Sitkagi Bluffs, about 35 miles WNW of Ocean Cape, named by Malaspina after Manuel Novales, one of his officers in the *Descubierta*. Malaspina's name has not survived, being replaced by the Russian name Sitkagi: see Orth, *Dictionary of Alaska Place Names*, p. 880. Malaspina Glacier, the largest glacier in Alaska, nearly reaches the sea behind Sitkagi Bluffs.
[2] Identified as Muñoz Point in Palau *et al.*, *Diario de viaje de Malaspina*, p. 265.

9 July

As we expected, the wind backed quickly from south to SE and east, fairly fresh, but with such haze that any attempts to survey would have failed. Accordingly we had no doubt as to the course we should take, which was to continue under full sail to the entrance to Prince William Sound,[1] there to wait for a favourable change in the weather, and then to retrace our steps to make a careful survey of the coast. I hailed the commanding officer of the *Atrevida* to advise him of this and, so as to conserve our hydrographic work, I informed him that from midday onwards we would sail in company, one vessel a league directly north of the other, to ascertain the existence of a shoal seen in these waters by our corvettes *Princesa* and *Favorita* in 1779.[2]

At the time I was convinced by our dead reckoning that we were in the right area for this purpose, based on the original journals of Teniente de Navío Arteaga and Piloto Mourelle and the chart of that expedition from the Archivo de Indias in la Corte.[3] Later, however, we were able to observe a fairly accurate meridian altitude of the Sun around noon with the aid of some breaks in the cloud. When the breeze, on the other hand, backed to ENE, clearing the coast to some extent, I thought it better to omit this undertaking and make straight for Captain Cook's Cape Suckling,[4] then on the following morning to stand either to the east or the west, according to the wind.

Until six in the evening the breeze continued fresh from ENE to east, without clearing the cloud and drizzle, although we could see the land indistinctly from north to WNW. Later, however, the weather improved considerably and as the coast became visible at the same time we were able to make out the whole of Kaye's Island[5] clearly, Cape Suckling itself, and some three leagues of the coast to the east of this cape, which I took care to survey immediately. Soundings had been the charge of the *Atrevida* all afternoon, but no bottom was obtained with one hundred fathoms of line,

---

[1] Entered and surveyed by Cook in May 1778, its entrance is guarded by Hinchinbrook and Montague Islands. It was also surveyed by the Salvador Fidalgo expedition in the summer of 1790 (see Wagner *Cartography*, p. 220) and by Vancouver in 1794. See also p. 86, n. 3 above.

[2] This shoal, Roca Pamplona, was allegedly discovered by José Cañizares, *primer piloto* in the *Favorita*, who stated it was 'a half-league around, twelve leagues from the coast in 59°02′ and 40°34′ W of San Blas'. Arteaga thought that it was 'only white wood floating on the sea': Wagner, *Cartography*, p. 194. The Russians also reported a shoal in the same vicinity, but no such reef exists. The name, however, has been perpetuated in Pamplona Spur, with depths of less than 100 fathoms over it and a least depth of 68 fathoms, which juts out some 35 miles from the coast in this vicinity.

[3] Malaspina refers here to the ministerial archive of the Secretaría de Indias in Madrid, i.e. at Court. At that time the now famous Archivo General de Indias in Seville, which began to be set up in 1790 by Juan Bautista Muñoz, was still in its infancy. It was thus the archive of the Secretaría de Indias in Madrid which was visited by officers of the expedition prior to the expedition's departure and not the Archivo General de Indias in Seville, as stated in Vol. 1 of this edition, p. lv.

[4] Named by Cook after Captain Maurice Suckling, Comptroller of the Royal Navy, at the time his expedition left England in 1776. Curiously Malaspina later referred to this cape in Spanish as Cabo Chupador.

[5] An island off Cape Suckling, known today by its Russian-derived name Kayak Island. Named St Elias Island by Bering, it fronts Controller Bay. It is the island on which Bering's naturalist Georg Wilhelm Steller is presumed to have landed on St Elias Day, 20 July 1741. It was named Kaye's Island by Cook in 1778 in honour of Sir Richard Kaye, Chaplain to the King. Arteaga named it Isla del Carmen in 1779 to honour the feast day of Our Lady of Carmel on 16 July.

although at nine o'clock we were only three or four leagues offshore, and the water had now an intense greenish colour.

During our recent short passage, particularly when making our landfall at Cape Suckling, we were much surprised by the variation, which had been found to be 26°40' in Port Mulgrave, when compared to Captain Cook's chart. In Puerto del Desengaño [Disenchantment Bay] and by meridian azimuths today and on the 6th we found it to be 32° NE. We did not adopt it and found our position to be very uncertain, but we saw it to be much less than that observed and used by the English captain for his charts.[1]

A few shearwaters[2] were encountered some distance from the coast, but they left us as soon as we altered course inshore again. In their place, or rather in place of any other species of birds, there only appeared a seal from time to time.

The land surveyed to the east of Cape Suckling consisted at the coast of an area covered with a pine forest as thick, unbroken and luxuriant as those we had seen around Port Mulgrave. It extended beyond the moderately high and snow covered hills, among which we could distinguish the one which (according to the English Captain) rose above the cape itself.[3] There was not the smallest opening to be seen on this stretch of coast and, from its eastern extremity which finished in an inconspicuous point, the coast appeared to trend gently once more rather to the north than to the south of west.

At half past ten in the evening, in soundings of thirty five and a half fathoms, ooze, we were only two leagues from Cape Suckling, which was now bearing N28°W by compass. We could clearly see the large rock lying in the middle[4] and all of Kaye's Island, the ends of which bore W26°N and S64°W. At the time both the moderate easterly breeze and fairly clear coast encouraged us to pass between Kaye's Island and Cape Suckling to survey Comptrollers Bay,[5] the English captain having attempted this in vain.[6] With this intention and also with the object of examining this passage

---

[1] Variation observed by Cook off Cape Suckling, as given in his journal, was 22°47'E (Cook and King, *Voyage to the Pacific Ocean*, III, p. 508) and on his 'Chart of the NW Coast of America and NE Coast of Asia explored in the Years 1778 & 1779' (David, *Charts and Coastal Views*, III, 3.95A) it was 22°45'.

[2] Possibly Sooty Shearwaters (*Puffinus griseus*) or Short-tailed Shearwater (*Puffinus tenuirostris*) which migrate northward in large numbers on completion of their breeding seasons. Lesser numbers of Pink-footed Shearwaters (*Puffinus carneipes*) might also have been encountered.

[3] According to Cook, 'The point of the Cape is low; but within it, is a tolerably high hill, which is disjoined from the mountains by low land; so that, at a distance, the Cape looks like an island.': Cook and King, *Voyage to the Pacific Ocean*, II, p. 349. A hill 1,500 feet high is shown behind the cape on current US charts.

[4] Malaspina is presumably referring to the 'elevated rocks between the Cape and the North East end of the island [Kayak Island]' seen by Cook (ibid.) and shown on Cook's 'Chart of Cooks River in the N. W. part of America': ibid., p. 353; possibly two above-water rocks, 1¾ miles ENE of Lemesurier Point, the NE extremity of Kayak Island.

[5] Named Comptroller Bay by Cook to complement his naming of the southern point of the bay after Maurice Suckling (see p. 141, n. 4 above). The spelling was modified to Controller Bay in Vancouver's published account of his voyage (W. Kaye Lamb, ed., *George Vancouver, A Voyage of Discovery to the North Pacific Ocean*, Hakluyt Society, 3 vols, 2nd ser. 163-6, London, 1984, p. 1322), which spelling has survived.

[6] The unnamed and shoal channel between Lemesurier Point and Okalee Spit, a 7-mile long sandy spit with dunes on it. Cook fortunately gave up the attempt when the wind shifted to north: Cook and King, *Voyage to the Pacific Ocean*, II, p. 349.

more carefully I decided to heave-to until two o'clock the next morning, so as not to submit blindly to the wind, which, although fair, threatened to freshen too much, keeping our position by means of soundings. Then, according to the conditions, enter the channel or pass to the south of Kaye's Island.

It was unnecessary to wait until then to see which course of action would suit us better. By midnight the wind was strong and gusty from ESE, the sea had risen, and it was overcast with drizzle and heavy cloud, hiding most of Kaye's Island, although it was not far off. Under these conditions it would have been unwise either to attempt entering a place which would be difficult to get out of, or to wait idly by for the wind to shift to the south and allow us to round Kaye's Island. Up to now, based on our soundings (as we could no longer take bearings), the tide had had little effect. We could therefore consider ourselves to be in almost the same spot where we had hove-to.

10 July
Accordingly, we first steered south and then slowly altered course into the third quadrant, away from the island, which runs approximately from SW to NE.

In 1779, the corvettes *Princesa* and *Favorita* from the Department of San Blas, sailing in these waters and coasting Kaye's Island, had discovered a shoal approximately WbyN from the islet off the point,[1] extending some two miles offshore. Although the wind was quite strong and the sky fairly dark, I thought it necessary to survey this danger, considering the future safety of shipping. In addition the existing heavy swell should make it visible from a greater distance. I also hoped to pass between Kaye's Island and Cape Suckling on our return, since conditions did not permit this at present. We continued on, therefore, with corresponding vigilance, and close enough, particularly on the bearing given, to ensure that we could not miss the said danger, and thus (as we did not sight it), we could only conclude in the end that these were the prominent rocks that Captain Cook had seen, though neither in the direction nor at the distance reported by our navigators.

Having cleared the southern point of Kaye's Island[2] at half past three, with the wind now much stronger and settled in from ENE, we shaped our course towards Prince William Sound, doing our best at the same time to survey a considerable stretch of the coast which runs from the above island to Cape Hinchinbrook (named on our charts as Cabo Español).[3] We continued cautiously, sounding twice without obtaining bottom. As we took advantage of every break in the clouds to observe for longitude,

---

[1] Presumably Pinnacle Rock, a remarkable pillar of rock, standing 2 cables SSW of Cape St Elias and not Roca Pamplona (see p. 141, n. 2 above). According to Cook, 'The South West point ... is very remarkable, being a naked rock, elevated considerably above the land within it. There is also an elevated rock lying off it, which, from some points of view, appears like a ruined castle.': Cook and King, *Voyage to the Pacific Ocean*, II, p. 350 and David, *Charts and Coastal Views* III, 3.120.

[2] Cape St Elias.

[3] The SW point of Hinchinbrook Island named Cape Hinchingbroke (Hinchingbrook on his 'Chart of Cooks River in the N. W. part of America') on 12 May 1778 by Cook (Cook and King, *Voyage to the Pacific Ocean*, II, f.p. 353) after Hinchingbrooke, the family seat of the Earl of Sandwich. It had been named Cabo Español by Fidalgo on 24 May 1790. Malaspina used both names, usually the latter, causing some confusion since, on his chart, he also named the southern point of Kayak Island Cabo Español: see p. 153, n. 1 below.

we were able to take several hour angles at half past five and half past ten to confirm our bearings and the bases we had run.

With the strong NE wind then blowing and with a fairly high sea, the view of the land had cleared considerably. Thus it was easy to make a detailed survey, but, considering the weather signs, it seemed that the wind, rather than backing to north, would soon veer to SE and south and become a full gale, forcing us to waste several days which we could use neither for hydrographic nor scientific work. As the murky weather would only allow the latter, I was inclined to anchor in Prince William Sound, with the intention of staying there while the contrary winds lasted, to deal with our work and attend meanwhile to botany, geology and the study of the natives. With this intention we continued on towards Cabo Español, making good a speed of eight to nine knots. We had closed the coast some four or five leagues east of Entrada de Menéndez[1] and, while running bases, we shaped our course so as to be only one or two miles offshore when coming up to Cape Español.

This stretch of coast, that Captain Cook, beset by bad weather, had surveyed in no great detail, had subsequently been sighted by our corvettes *Princesa* and *Favorita*, which, although coming no closer than six or seven leagues offshore (according to the journals of the commanding officer, Arteaga, and Piloto Mourelle) had enjoyed some long clear days and had plotted some prominent points with as much accuracy as possible. We could assume the accuracy to be much greater in the work done by Don Salvador Fidalgo the year before, as he had taken a launch from Puerto de la Magdalena[2] through the inner channel to Ensenada de Menéndez, observing the latitude of a prominent islet[3] with a very good sextant, sounding all around it and determining its size with some care. Given these circumstances our present work was aimed at determining longitudes, rather than the search for a passage which seemed, at best, highly unlikely to exist in these parts and which, of course, was not indicated in the details given by Ferrer Maldonado.

The high, broken ground, covered in ice which reflected the Sun, had already shown signs of other inlets to the east, like those we had seen in the vicinity of Port Mulgrave. However, with that experience we were somewhat sceptical in assuming them to be such, although we did not hasten to exclude the possibility, leaving it to our return to the east to dispel any hydrographic doubts in this regard.

By ten o'clock we could see Cabo Español and towards eleven the extremity of

---

[1] In the previous year, 1790, Fidalgo had explored present-day Orca Bay behind Hawkins Island and, when he performed the act of possession on 8 June, named what would seem to be today's Sheen Bay, Ensenada de Menéndez, after his second-in-command on the *San Carlos*, Salvador Menéndez Valdés: see Wagner, *Cartography*, p. 472. While the name appears on Malaspina's chart his location is clearly different from that of Fidalgo. From where he was positioned offshore, Malaspina merely gave the name to the opening that appeared NE between Hinchinbrook Island and the continent proper, in the general direction of where Fidalgo had been.

[2] Malaspina is referring to what is today Port Etches, a large bay on the western side of Hinchinbrook Island, named by Portlock in July 1787. Arteaga had named Hinchinbrook Island Isla Santa María Magdalena in July 1779, anchoring in the bay, which he named Puerto de Santiago, where he performed an act of possession. Fidalgo later anchored there in 1790: Wagner, *Cartography*, p. 194.

[3] The flat-topped and grass-covered westernmost of Porpoise Rocks, in the approaches to Port Etches.

Montagu Island[1] was also in sight, if indistinctly, although between us and this island there was an islet surrounded by reefs, not more than about three miles distant.[2] As we could also see above the cape some hillocks which Captain Cook did not mention, there might be some slight doubt as to our present position, particularly as the weather had closed in again with showers and strong gusts, requiring greater care in sailing. This itself would be very dangerous if the bay we were making for happened to be Ensenada de Menéndez. This being the situation, we lay-to for about a quarter of an hour on a southerly tack, a good mile off Cabo Español. We sounded at the time but obtained no bottom with eighty fathoms of line. When the clouds cleared a little, our ideas about our position were confirmed, enabling us to approach the cape and make for the anchorage[3] under topsails.

Because of the cloud cover it was impossible to observe the meridian altitude of the Sun at noon, as we so eagerly desired, for the latitude determined by Captain Cook was very different from that found by our navigators. We were then half a mile off the coast, which is extremely steep-to and runs NE and north from Cabo Español to the anchorage. By then the wind was blowing strongly with gusts down the gullies of the nearby ridges and, as we bore up, it dropped and varied in direction, according to the shape of the hills. Naturally, as will be imagined, we were not remiss in closing the coast and casting the lead to find either the depth of seventeen fathoms that Captain Cook had sounded off Cape Hinchinbrook,[4] or the depths found by the commanding officer Arteaga.

I would have anchored immediately to wait for a better moment to enter the harbour, but, although we were now two cables offshore, such a precaution would have been pointless, as we had to tack between some large rocks which our navigators called Los Negrillos[5] and the shore where we wished to anchor.

The very strong and variable gusts made these tacks not only uncomfortable and risky, but also fruitless, as the tide seemed at the time, and must have been, against us rather than with us. However, at such a short distance from the anchorage it would be disappointing to have to give up the attempt. I also thought it would be unwise to proceed further to the north or to look for shelter on Montagu Island if we were to make full use of the first favourable NW wind to make a detailed survey of the coast lying to the east.

I decided, therefore, to continue the attempt and straight away I sent Piloto Sánchez in the pinnace to examine the nearby coast to see if there was anywhere that we might anchor with some degree of safety. Soon afterwards, when on an easterly tack and only a cable and a half offshore, we had to go about, although the gusts remained very strong and variable, and we could not change the way the sails were

---

[1] The largest island fronting Prince William Sound; named by Cook on 18 May 1778 after John Montagu, the Earl of Sandwich. This is the Isla de Quirós of Ignacio Arteaga who named it in July 1779 after his second in command in the *Princesa*, Fernando Bernardo de Quirós y Miranda.

[2] Seal Rocks, which consist of two rocks, 9 metres and 11 metres high, 7 miles SW of Cape Hinchinbrook.

[3] Port Etches, Malaspina's Puerto de la Magdalena and Arteaga's Puerto de Santiago.

[4] Shown on Cook's 'Chart of Cooks River in the N. W. part of America' (Cook and King, *Voyage to the Pacific Ocean*, II, f.p. 353), but not mentioned in his journal.

[5] Porpoise Rocks; see p. 144, n. 5 above.

set, regardless of the fact that the wind at times had changed from favourable to adverse and back. The corvette remained in this position, still not falling off onto the other tack, when an excessively strong gust sprung the fore topsail yard at the slings,[1] forcing us to alter our plan. Having finally put about onto the starboard tack, with the wind continuing very gusty, our first aim was to try to keep on the offshore tack under foresail and main topsail, and to get the pinnace back and hoisted on board again. We then replaced the broken yard with a new one and at about three in the afternoon we were fully rigged again. We were, however, now some two cables off Cabo Español, with the breakers east of Isla Triste[2] bearing approximately south two miles distant.

By now the wind had slackened and the sky was much clearer, seeming to indicate that the wind would soon shift to north and NW, this being confirmed by the sight of all the mountains inland which were now quite free of cloud and haze. In these conditions we put about onto the starboard tack once more and ran along the northern end of Montagu Island, a short distance offshore. At six in the evening we were well inside the inlet, so that, lying only half a league from the shore, this morning's anchorage was already bearing east and ESE, giving us some hope of being able to reach it with the tide setting us east. The SE tack now seemed better and we quickly took it, meanwhile making use of the chance to take some accurate observations of latitude and variation and to extend our bearings towards the interior points as far as we were able. The wind and tide, however, soon raised fresh obstacles, the tide setting us back from the locality we were eager to reach, while the wind with further gusts and signs of foul weather obliging us to shorten sail. During the rest of the afternoon, therefore, our efforts to reach the anchorage were as vain as were our attempts to pass to the east of Isla Triste. Finally, at eleven o'clock that night, we had to decide to pass to the west of it, in order to get clear of the area.[3]

Three native canoes, covered with seal skins,[4] had already been seen when we

---

[1] That part of the yard where the slings are attached to support the yard.
[2] Seal Rocks: see p. 145, n. 2 above.
[3] Suria describes the problems and the attendant frustration in trying to get into Prince William Sound, 'we could not enter without danger with that wind and sea, which was very heavy'. He noted that Malaspina had to 'content himself with having reached the entrance of Principe Guillermo and thus exceeded the orders of the court which had commanded him to go up to 60° latitude. Here we were in 61° and some minutes, the season was advanced and he considered that we should prepare for our return to Acapulco ... All day we were working to get out and although we were afraid that we could not succeed in view of the strong wind, the heavy seas and the tide which was entering and carrying us on the rocks, the efforts of our excellent seamen who labored this day excellently well, together with the fact that our corvettes answered the helm, was sufficient to enable us to save ourselves by tacking in the channel and in keeping away from the coast.': Cutter, *Journal of Suria*, p. 52. Tova also mentions 'the intemperate weather, the heavy swell of the sea and very strong winds.': Porrúa, *Diary of Tova*, p. 401.
[4] Suria describes the three canoes in more detail. First the corvettes were approached by single canoe with two Indians, which was probably a two-man Chugach kayak. Then 'A little later about 6 in the afternoon two other large canoes could be seen and a great number of Indians who were armed with bows and lances held on the canoes by means of the thongs which passed through them. They made the greatest effort to approach us [*Descubierta*] but they also were unable to succeed, but they did get alongside of the *Atrevida*.': Cutter, *Journal of Suria*, pp. 52-3. Both Cardero and Suria sketched the kayaks and canoes encountered in the North Pacific. In drawings of the kayaks by Suria and also one by Bauzá it is possible to make out the lances and arrows secured by the thongs across the top of the craft: see Sotos, *Los pintores*, II, figs 567, 592 and 594. On his drawings of Bucareli Sound and Port Etches in the summer of 1779,

put about onto the port tack at six in the evening. They called out with their usual emphatic tone and gestures to the *Descubierta*, which was some distance off, and then reached the *Atrevida*, whose commanding officer signalled to me that their intentions appeared peaceful. All invitations and offerings to entice them on board were in vain, as that officer told me afterwards. They frequently uttered the word 'captain',[1] but seemed to have little or no knowledge of the language of Port Mulgrave.[2] All their gestures encouraged him to anchor in the lee of Montagu Island. Their canoes were more carefully made than those of Port Mulgrave. As it was difficult, or seemed imprudent, for either side to comply with the wishes of the other, they soon parted company, the natives making for Puerto de Santiago[3] while the *Atrevida* easily caught up with us.

It was about eleven o'clock at night when we decided to pass to the west of Isla Triste, the side on which we could see no reefs, while we would have been unable to clear those extending from the eastern side, which were at least half a mile long. At midnight we passed the island at a distance of two miles, obtaining no bottom with thirty fathoms of line. We then altered course to SE and hoisted more sail to make some distance from Montagu Island.

Spanish navigators had seen in these waters some islets (named Hijosa[4]) that neither Captain Cook nor Captain Dixon had included on their charts, for which the former could be excused, having passed to the west of Montagu Island,[5] but which cannot be overlooked in the latter, both because his route in his first year took him through these waters,[6] and because he rashly attributed to our former navigators

---

Primer Piloto José Camacho y Brenes made sketches of a Tlingit canoe and of both a one-man and a two-man Chugach kayak. These are the earliest extant Spanish depictions of native craft on the NW Coast: see Luisa Martín-Meras, 'The Evolution of Spanish Cartography on the Northwest Coast of America', in Inglis, *Spain and the North Pacific Coast*, pp. 18-28. For illustrations of such a craft encountered by Cook in Prince William Sound and drawn by John Webber see Rüdiger Joppien and Bernard Smith, *The Art of Captain Cook's Voyages*, 3 vols, New Haven and London, 1985-8, III, pp. 478 and 486.

[1] Although this word is rendered as *capitán* in the original MS it seems more likely that the natives used the English 'captain' due to their lengthy acquaintance with Meares in the winter of 1786-7 and with Portlock in the spring of 1787. In addition the relevant term in Spanish is *comandante* and not *capitán*.

[2] It is not surprising that these natives were unfamiliar with the language of Port Mulgrave since they belonged to the Chugach group of the Pacific Yuit who, with the Bering Yuit, continue to make up Alaska's most diverse family of natives – the Southern Eskimos or Inuit: see Langdon, *The Native People of Alaska*, pp. 40-53.

[3] Port Etches: see p. 144, n. 2 above.

[4] Middleton Island, 50 miles ESE of Cape Cleare, the SW extremity of Montague Island. The naming of this island is wrongly attributed to Vancouver in 1794 in Wagner, *Cartography*, p. 397. Vancouver did not sight this island in 1794, since the nearest he got to it was about 30 miles when he was off Kayak Island, nor did he mention Middleton Island in his journal. The island is not charted on Vancouver's large-scale chart from Prince William Sound to Mount St Elias (chart 11 in his published atlas), but is shown and named on his small-scale chart from Kodiak Island to San Diego (chart 14 in his published atlas). The island was probably named after Admiral Charles Middleton, one of the Lords Commissioners of the Admiralty at the time that Vancouver returned to England. Previously sighted by Martínez on 19 May 1788 and named Hijosa after Francisco Hijosa, the Commissary at the Naval Department of San Blas. For Hijosa see p. 223, n. 2 below.

[5] The nearest Cook got to Middleton Island was about 50 miles, when he was rounding Kayak Island.

[6] This is borne out by Dixon's chart showing his tracks in 1786 and 1787: [Beresford], *Voyage ... by Captain George Dixon*, f.p. iii.

the occasional error here and there in the hydrography of the endless number of coasts that they had surveyed.[1] Without this precedent, the course required in our present circumstances, with the wind now settled in the east and blowing hard with heavy cloud cover, might have led us into an error with disastrous consequences, as it would otherwise have been natural to continue close hauled in the second quadrant, not only to clear Montagu Island but also to reach the meridian at which our survey was to begin.

11 July
Indeed, shortly after sunrise the sky became extremely overcast, with the sea getting up and the wind freshening, so that we could not keep the topsails hoisted. We also had to attend to the repair of the foresail now bent on, whose bolt-rope[2] had been split since the previous afternoon. We therefore changed it for another foresail while making the repair, but bent it on again when this was done. Our course was approximately true south. With the heavy cloud cover the land was soon lost from sight and, as neither the sea, the wind nor the rain slackened, we continued on the same tack until noon, when we went about under the four principal sails, with one reef in the topsails, believing our latitude then to be 59°30'.

The wind soon dropped and even became very light, although without changing direction. The clouds cleared a little and, at two o'clock in the afternoon, we could make out a low island on our windward beam about three leagues distant, which we naturally assumed to be Hijosa, although its position in both latitude and longitude was very different and it appeared to be only a single island.

The calm did not last very long either. By seven in the evening the wind was once again fresh in the first quadrant and accompanied by heavy rain. This did not cease but the wind dropped after we had enjoyed breezes in the second quadrant for a time. At dawn, with the sky now largely clear of cloud and the heavy swell much reduced, we finally saw signs of improvement in the weather and the possibility of continuing with our work. Since the previous afternoon we had had the single aim of remaining south of both the island we had sighted and of Montagu Island, while the variable wind continued with occasional calms, accompanied by constant rain and cloud. As, however, a favourable change seemed imminent at dawn the next day [12th] we quickly took advantage of the light airs in the first quadrant under full sail, to make suitable use of the time.

By eight o'clock we managed to sight the low island again, now some four leagues distant. Our course of NWbyN took us towards it and at noon its northern and southern extremities bore N82°E and S86°E, barely two leagues distant. At the same time the southern point of Montagu Island bore S86½°W by compass and the *Atrevida* signalled a depth of sixty-seven fathoms, sand. By this time we had obtained a very satisfactory observation for variation of 26° NE by means of two sets of azimuths.

[1] Perhaps Dixon was referring to the fact that Mourelle did not encounter Queen Charlotte Islands and that the 'islands Los Majos, La Maso, and St. Maria la Gorta ... from a Spanish M.S. chart, were in vain looked for by us ... so that their intention has uniformly been to mislead rather than to be of service to future Navigators': [Beresford], *Voyage ... by Captain George Dixon*, pp. xiv-xv.
[2] The rope sewn all round the edge of a sail.

Although we failed to obtain an exact meridian altitude of the Sun, the results of the latitude calculations were of such a nature, and so consistent, that we were sure of it being 59°30', the longitude then being 6°58' west of Mulgrave.

The wind, although moderate, remained from NE all afternoon. We sailed close-hauled in the fourth quadrant, measuring bases to determine accurately the position of various points of both the low island and Montagu Island. According to signals from the *Atrevida* the depth was forty to fifty fathoms. Finally, at six o'clock, we found ourselves once more a mile and a half to the south of Isla Triste in depths of seventy-four fathoms, the NE point of Montagu Island then bearing N41°W and the inner extremity of Puerto de la Magdalena N36°W by compass. In this position we had to tack to the ESE. Even though the sky remained clear, the wind was gradually freshening, although without preventing us from making good easterly progress on our tacks, which we changed at midnight and then [13th] at four o'clock, when, steering ESE again, the points adjacent to Cabo Español bore N15°W by compass, only four leagues distant. Finally, at noon we had to shake out the two reefs that we had taken in the topsails at ten o'clock when the wind and sea had risen considerably, in order to clear the low island, which we sighted at S5°W to S10°W, at a distance of three leagues.

Our latitude and longitude completely confirmed the results of the previous day for the position of the island and, as they depended on the same calculations, for points on the eastern coast of Montagu Island, so it seemed that we need have no fears in settling their position with more than an average degree of accuracy. Thus, the SE point of Montagu Island was finally assigned a latitude of 59°47' and [longitude] 8°16' west of Mulgrave, our latitude differing from that of Captain Cook by the same figure of 11' further south that Captain Dixon had noted when making an approximate observation on its parallel.

14 and 15 July

Having cleared the low island, passing it at a good league's distance and continuing on our southerly tack, we were once again back in the same position as on the previous days. As the wind remained very strong and gusty with a heavy sea from NW all the next day and during the early hours of the 15th, our main intention was maintaining the correct trim of the sails, as we alternately reefed and unreefed the sails, rather than making any easting, which would have been extremely difficult. However, the clear skies now favoured our course somewhat more and we were able to continue our tacks to within two or three leagues of the low island

At last, on the morning of the 15th, (although not before some gusts, variable breezes and several hours of calm), light airs from SE got up, which, combined with the very good weather conditions and the bright appearance of the coast, seemed to promise that a favourable change was imminent. We were only two leagues off the low island, when we could clearly see breakers to the east. Montagu Island and the vicinity of Cabo Español were visible in the far distance, while the pleasantly smooth sea provided a spectacle that we had almost forgotten since leaving Port Mulgrave.

At about ten in the morning, to contribute variety to the splendour of the day, there appeared alongside us a covered canoe with two natives. They spoke, or rather shouted, to us, repeating the same words whose meaning we could not ascertain, while holding up on the end of a stick an otter skin which seemed to be one of the finest we had seen so far, and constantly indicating with the paddle that we should make for the island, on the western side of which we would find good shelter and an orderly trade in skins. It was impossible to entice them on board, although we not only gave the customary sign of peace with open arms, but also made sure to show them several pieces of iron and other trifles. They took their leave at eleven and set out very rapidly for the island.

With regard to the detailed survey of the eastern side [of the low island], the noon observations, consistent with those of the 12th and 13th, confirmed its size and astronomically determined position so clearly that we felt we had some right to give it a new name. We therefore called it after Galiano, the *teniente de navío* assigned to this mission, whose talent and love of his work give him a very distinguished place in our memories.[1] The latitude of its mid point was determined as 59°26' and its longitude as 6°37' west of Port Mulgrave. It is almost round, extending a little further to the NE and SW. The land all round the shore is fissured, the southern part being a little higher; only in the centre are there many trees. The reefs fringing the eastern side would discourage any mariner from attempting to land on that side. The western side, however, towards which the natives were leading us, is quite different. Seeing it to be entirely free of reefs and with a sandy bottom, that we found three leagues off, we believe that it offers good shelter in winds from the first and second quadrants, although we could not see any salient point to suggest that there might be a harbour or bay. Although the canoe I have mentioned came from the island, I cannot venture to affirm that it is permanently populated, but perhaps the otter-hunting brings the natives there at certain times of the year. During the four days in which the island was in sight we never saw any smoke. No doubt they would not have omitted such a signal, both in a the desire for trade that they later showed and because we had found this practice fairly common all along the coast.[2]

Until three in the afternoon the breeze remained light from SW and, either as a result of some current or of the slight short swell that continued from the east, we had to steer ENE to get clear of Isla Galiano. It was finally lost to view at seven in the

---

[1] Galiano was not on board at the time, having been sent to Mexico City: see p. 70 above. Malaspina's change of name was not accepted on his return to Spain, Isla de Hijosa being retained on chart no. 3 in the Atlas accompanying *Relación del viage hecho por las goletas Sutil y Mexicana*. Malaspina had earlier paid fulsome tribute to Galiano in his official letter of 28 April 1791 to Antonio Valdés: see p. 420 below.

[2] Suria commented on the visit of the natives. As a result of the clear weather 'a skin canoe like those at the Puerto de Mulgrave came out from the Isla Hijosa with two Indians in their respective holes and with their arrows and lances tied on the deck of the canoe by way of precaution. Notwithstanding the advantage in sailing of our ships they rowed with such spirit and swiftness that in a short time they were at our stern close to the rudder. We repeatedly entreated them to come on board but they excused themselves as being timid and gave the well-known signs of friendship by stretching out their arms and repeating this word *La li, La li!* which is equivalent to *koacan* or friend. At the same time they manifested to us their desires for us to come to anchor in a port which according to their signs lay on the west side of the island. Having lost hope of this they departed. The dress which the natives in Montague wear consists of sea-otter skins, a blouse of flexible and transparent gut, the folds of which are fastened around the hole in the canoe. Their hats are like Chinese hats, their hair is loose, covered with red ochre, their ears and nose are bored and hanging from these are some long narrow leather thongs like tape, while passing through the nose is a tooth or bone of some land animal.': Cutter, *Journal of Suria*, p. 55.

evening. At almost the same time a large canoe, with some twenty men on board, left us, having [earlier] approached us with the usual hymn of peace. The *Atrevida*, which was closer to it, luffed up and threw them a line so that they could come alongside, using every means to attract them. However, it was impossible to persuade them to take this step. Accordingly, as the breeze was freshening somewhat, we continued on our way and the canoe appeared to make for the island.[1]

We naturally set a course for the eastern side of Cabo Español, from which we began our survey at ten o'clock in the morning. The breeze remained moderate, the sea very smooth, and the weather, particularly after ten o'clock at night, very hazy.

16 July

Before three o'clock on the morning of the 16th, however, we could clearly make out the southern end of Kaye's Island, only four or five leagues to our east. Although the coast was rather hazy, as at the time the breeze was very light and variable, we very soon knew that our position with regard to hydrographic work was all that we could wish. We sounded seventy fathoms, ooze. Variation, as deduced from several azimuths the previous afternoon and this morning, seemed fairly constant at about 28°. Until half past nine we remained almost becalmed, but when the haze was finally dispersed by the first puffs of the sea breeze, we could not only make for the coast, but also extend our view and bearings as far as Cabo Español, and attempt the passage between Kaye's Island and the mainland.

On the morning of the 16th we believed we could see several large openings to the west of Punta Sarmiento[2] among the range of hills, not very high but entirely snow-covered, which runs from Ensenada de Menéndez to Cape Suckling or Cabo Chupador.[3] This belief was soon dispelled by the appearance of a stretch of low ground in front of the range, thickly forested and showing an unbroken shoreline without any salient points. However, the opposite occurred with another opening at the end of this coast, then bearing NNE, the existence of which seemed increasingly probable as we approached, because of a gap in the hills inland. At midday we were only three leagues off it, the extremities of Kaye's Island then bearing S75°E to N66°E by compass. Our soundings gave a depth of sixty-five fathoms, ooze, and our latitude by observation was 60°3′ and our longitude 5°20′ west of Mulgrave.

As our progress towards the coast was very slow with the light airs from SE and

---

[1] Tova mentions both the small canoe with two Indians and the big canoe 'with fourteen people in it who for some reason stopped rowing although they were very close and could have reached us in a short time despite the swell and the fact that we were travelling at 4 knots. We responded to their signs of friendship and urged them to come on board offering them all kinds of merchandise that we thought might arouse their curiosity or ambition; but to all of this they answered by showing us several very fine sea otter pelts which we would be able to buy in great quantity at the anchorage indicated on their island; this was clear proof that Europeans had anchored there or had engaged in trade with the natives of Prínce William Sound.': Porrúa, *Diary of Tova*, pp. 404-5.

[2] Cottonwood Point, 32 miles NNW of Cape St Elias. Malaspina probably named it in honour of Pedro Sarmiento de Gamboa, the 16th-century Spanish navigator whose *Voyage* he had consulted off the eastern entrance to Estrecho de Magallanes: see Vol. I of this edition, p. 112, n. 4. The 'large openings' are between the islets in the delta of the Copper River and Cottonwood Point.

[3] From now on Malaspina only uses the Spanish version of this name, which is the standard term in Spanish for sucker or teat of a bottle.

WSW, even during the early hours of the afternoon, it was not until after two o'clock that we abandoned our first thought of an opening towards Punta Sarmiento. Before it lay another sizeable stretch of coast, in parts flooded and in other fairly thickly forested. Although to the east, in the same low ground a small entrance projected, whose end we could not see, there was no doubt that this was the mouth of a river,[1] both on account of the breakers appearing from time to time nearby, and because there was no sign of any ravine in the hills behind it.

We could now bear away gradually to the east, the sea breeze having freshened somewhat, with our soundings continuing at sixty-five to sixty fathoms, ooze. A valley we had identified was given the name Valle de Ruesga[2] and that of Cabo Nodales[3] to the point which terminated it on its eastern side, the coast then turning towards Comptrollers Bay. Cabo Nodales is a low, sandy point, off which two conspicuous rocks stand out to the east. The coast then runs inwards, all its shore is sandy, but beautifully forested a short way inland. The hills, of moderate height, turn abruptly northward here, joining the cordillera behind Cabo Chupador before running almost due east to Mount St Elias.

At six in the evening, with the sea breeze still moderate, we were able to pass this cape and undertake the intended passage, since we could now clearly see Cabo Chupador and the northern end of Kaye's Island. Naturally we were proceeding cautiously with lead in hand, but soon afterwards were surprised to find only twelve fathoms, sand. However, believing that we must have closed the land, we immediately altered course to starboard. But the depth diminished rapidly and finally, at nine o'clock, we had only five fathoms. The speed at which it had shoaled, with a sandy bottom, led us to suspect that very soon we would be unable to continue. In this position, however, it was easy to examine all the inner parts of the bay and thus eliminate a preconception that had deceived us until now.

What we had thought to be Kaye's Island was only a peninsula joined to the mainland by a low spit, thickly forested and almost semicircular in shape.[4] Behind it was Cabo Chupador and the NE extremity of the peninsula and, if we were to judge by the internal formation of the bay, the same high steep islet that lay near us must also be joined to the peninsula by another short, low-lying strip of land, which at present would be difficult for us to investigate. On this account we called it Isla Dudosa.[5] We

---

[1] Possibly the mouth of Martin River, which enters the sea west of Cottonwood Point.

[2] The valley would appear to be upper reaches of the Copper River Delta, probably named after Valle de Ruesga in the Santander province in Northern Spain and birthplace of Tova Arredondo: see Bauzá's detailed survey between 10 and 18 July, 'Levantamiento en la costa NO desde los Negrillos y islas Triste hasta C° Español, en la península de Kaye por las corbetas': AMN, Sig. Borradores. Carp. XI. C-13 (42) (Higueras, *Catálogo crítico*, no. 1899).

[3] Now Point Martin, 22 miles north of Cape St Elias, named by Vancouver in 1794. Malaspina probably named it after the Nodales brothers whose *Derrotero* he had consulted off Tierra del Fuego: see Vol. I of this edition, p. 112, n. 7. Wagner suggests that this is the Punta Eguia noted by Arteaga in 1779: Wagner, *Cartography*, p. 449.

[4] Malaspina was too far away to determine that Kayak Island is separated from the mainland by an unnamed channel.

[5] Wingham Island, close west of the northern end of Kayak Island, and named on 13 June 1794 by Peter Puget, commanding officer of the Chatham, during Vancouver's voyage. Presumably Malaspina called it Isla Dudosa, which translates as Doubtful Island, because he was was unable to determine whether it was indeed an island or part of Kayak Island.

kept the name Kaye for the peninsula and called its southern point Cabo Español[1] and the bay where we were now Comptrollers Bay, the name given to it by Captain Cook, and called the bay formed to the east by Cabo Chupador and the steep projecting peninsula, Bahía de Burgos.[2]

There did not seem to be any inhabitants in these parts, although the nature of the terrain, the distance from the mountains and the shelter of the bay would certainly invite habitation. It would be difficult to determine whether or not there was a good harbour to the north of Isla Dudosa, given the lack of depth we had at no less than two miles [from it]. I would have liked to be able to find out by using the pinnaces, but the need to make use of the few clear days in continuing with our work persuaded me that it would be better to tack out of the bay as soon as possible and round Cabo Español to survey the coast to the east.

Our depth soon increased to seventeen fathoms, ooze, as we made for the high ground of the peninsula, but it diminished again as we approached Cabo Nodales, from which we were still a good two miles when the depth was only six or seven fathoms, sand.

17 July

With the tide against us, although the breeze continued light and the sea very smooth, we made little headway towards our destination until five in the morning, at which time the coast of the peninsula and the sky and horizon in general were thick with haze, and the depth was fifteen to seventeen fathoms, ooze. A few light airs from west then allowed us to make good progress to the south. At half past nine, the haze now gone, we saw the islet off Cabo Español,[3] and at half past eleven, when only two miles from it, we tacked to the west with a moderate breeze from SSW and clear skies.

As the afternoon wore on the gentle breeze gradually backed through south to SE and ESE, forcing us to continue close hauled on the port tack as we stood offshore. We did not change tack until three o'clock the next morning [18th]. Although our only object during this period was to clear Cabo Español, we had not yet done this by midday. Indeed we were still some six leagues off, and the cape was bearing N33°E, a course we could barely make. But as the breeze then veered to the SE, this tack became easier than we had expected, taking us to windward of the islet near the isolated rocks that we found in this survey to be the same ones, without any doubt, that Comandante Arteaga had thought to lie in another direction and at a greater distance from Cabo Español.

In this position, obtaining no bottom in sixty-five fathoms, we tacked to SbyE at six o'clock, continuing on the same tack until half past nine when, the breeze having settled in the south, we steered east for a while, before bearing off to the north to approach the headland at Cabo Chupador to continue our survey. Cabo Español,

---

[1] Cape Saint Elias, the southern point of Kayak Island. By using the name Español for this cape Malaspina creates some confusion as he had previously used the name Español for Cape Hinchinbrook: see p. 143, n. 3 above.

[2] No longer named as it is strictly not a bay.

[3] Pinnacle Rock: see p. 143, n. 1 above.

which will always be an important landmark for navigation on this coast, lies in latitude [blank] and longitude [blank]. If we consider the various observations made in sight of it, which agree exactly with the bearings, we may flatter ourselves that there is no possibility of any error which might affect, however remotely, the safety of navigation.

19 July
Our plans for the following day were thwarted by south and SE winds which had set in on the previous afternoon, as I have said. For the weather immediately closed in over the entire coast with rain and mist, so that surveying was no longer possible, nor could we tie in our bases as we wished without observations. At noon, in a depth of sixty-five fathoms, ooze, Cabo Chupador bore N10°W by compass, three or four leagues distant.

Although, for the verification of Ferrer Maldonado's passage, the necessity of assuming that the high lands to the west might also be excluded from our examination of the present stretch of coast between Cabo Chupador and Mount St Elias, I definitely could not disregard it in the plan adopted for our work, because this coast had been drawn by Captain Cook and our own navigators from a great distance. This being so, there was no doubt as to the best course of action in the present situation, which was to remain in these waters until the southerly winds dropped and we could benefit from favourable winds from NW, the brief duration of which made them more valuable to us at every step. During the 20th and until noon on the 21st, this was therefore the sole purpose of our manoeuvres, although we made some easting, so as to make as much use as possible of the first clearings in the clouds to the east and west. At noon on the 21st the meridian altitude of the Sun put us in latitude 59°36' and we believed ourselves to be some eight leagues east of Cabo Chupador.

As the weather continued overcast with rain, our imposed inactivity tended to oblige us to fall back somewhat to the west. During the afternoon we attempted to sail to the north, taking care to sound, while examining the western coast from close enough inshore to make up for the lack of visibility and give us some idea of at least its direction and nature as far as Cabo Chupador, given that, for the time being, it would not be possible to determine its position astronomically.

We did indeed sight it, two or three leagues off, at about half past five in the afternoon. Soon afterwards the *Atrevida*, which had been signalled to take charge of the soundings, indicated that they had sounded eighty-seven fathoms. The nearest shore to north and NW was forested, just like those we had seen to the east and west of Port Mulgrave. The extremely heavy cloud prevented us from seeing what lay beyond, but further west we could see other points which appeared to be steep-to, and which cannot have been far from Cabo Chupador. This imperfect idea of the coast (more accurate information being unobtainable at the time, even at only two leagues' distance) could not free us from returning to the west until eight o'clock and then heave-to on the port tack. Although the moderate wind from SE continued with heavy rain, the weather seemed to show signs of a fair change in the near future, which gave us even more encouragement to remain on a westerly course.

21 July

Appearances had not deceived us. On the morning of the 21st, after several hours of flat calm, light airs began to get up in the third quadrant, quickly clearing the sky and horizon and at last allowing us the view of the coast that we had been hoping to see. At noon, in latitude 59°49′, Cabo Español bore S59°W by compass and we could see the whole of the coast from Cabo Chupador, between S84°W to N21°E.

From the westernmost point of our surveys of the 10th (from which we were now about eight leagues) the coast appeared to continue with very few gaps, all low lying, forested on the shore and some way inland. It was backed by a cordillera of moderate height, snow covered down to the foot, which at one end joined the hills behind Comptrollers Bay to which we had taken bearings on the afternoon of the 17th, and at the other, after forming a large valley, ran up to a fairly high mountain which we named Monte de las Coronas for the shape of its summit.[1] There were no gaps of any size to be seen along this higher part. At our distance we had no way of telling if there might be a harbour or river mouth in the low ground in front of it, even if of little importance, according to the trend of the forest at either end.

This same forest, now in view again to the NW of our present position, continued without a break as far as Punta Verde,[2] not far from the foot of Mount St Elias, and along all this coast, which stretched at least ten leagues in an east/west direction, there was not even the slightest sign of an opening. At a distance of four leagues we generally found depths of [sixty-five][3] to seventy fathoms, ooze.

The few hours of twilight, the weather remaining extremely pleasant, had allowed us to continue measuring bases and taking bearings without interruption. The fruit of this constant labour were the surveys just mentioned, although the breeze remained very light throughout the previous afternoon and even at dawn on the 22nd. Thus at two o'clock, Mount St Elias bore N29°E and, at three o'clock, in a depth of fifty-five fathoms, pebbles, we were only some two leagues from the coast of Punta Verde, which is rocky, steep-to and extends from a high headland which fronts the majestic cordillera that includes Mount St Elias.

As may be imagined, we did not miss the opportunity of the present clarity of the sky to take all the observations within our reach.[4] Longitude by chronometers and by distances from the Moon to the Sun, variation and the continuation of the bases were consequently tasks which occupied us unceasingly in the early hours of the morning, during which we tried to make the best possible use of the breeze, sailing a mere two leagues offshore in depths of thirty-five to forty fathoms, ooze.

---

[1] Mount Nichawak behind Controller Bay at the foot of Bering Glacier.
[2] As Punta Verde is not shown on any of the surviving Malaspina charts it cannot be located with any certainty. It may be Cape Yakataga, situated about halfway between Cape Suckling and Icy Bay or possibly Claybluff Point, the western entrance point of Icy Bay.
[3] Indecipherable in the original MS, but sixty-five in Palau et al., *Diario de viaje de Malaspina*, p. 281.
[4] According to Suria, 'During these eight days the geographer [Bauzá] marked it [took bearings to Mount St Elias] to his full satisfaction from different points and I drew several views of it, one of them particularly exact which the geographer adopted for the collection.': Cutter, *Journal of Suria*, p. 58. This drawing has survived in the Bauzá Collection, Museo de América in Madrid; it shows the *Descubierta* and *Atrevida* in the foreground with the *ensenada* of Icy Bay behind, leading up to the majestic mass of Mount St Elias itself: see plate 17. It is wrongly attributed to Suria in Sotos, *Los pintores*, II, fig. 558.

At nine o'clock, contrary to our expectations and very much contrary to our hopes, the breeze dropped completely. From then on our progress was so slow and the breeze so light, that until dawn on the 26th it may be said that our position did not change. The few breaths of air that reached us at times were very weak and usually in the second or third quadrant. Our distance offshore was between two and four leagues, Mount St Elias bearing from NbyE to NbyW. This change was really the effect of the tides, which during the afternoon and evening appeared to set to the NE, and the rest of the time to WNW, at a speed of one or two knots.

The hilly country of moderate height close to the shore, fronting the cordillera, terminates at Punta Olavide,[1] or rather joins the foot of Mount St Elias, the summit of which (according to our trigonometric calculations) is seven and a half leagues inland and 2792 *toesas* above sea level.[2] From the cape the coast forms a comparatively shallow bay, given the name of Estremadura[3] on our charts, within which are to be seen only two small inlets or coves, one to the west, which appears to be permanently ice-bound, and one to the east near Punta del Indio,[4] sheltering a small native settlement. Between these two points the shore, although rocky, has some trees, which then give way to hummocky escarpments which run eastward by way of Punta Novales to Punta Barrientos and stand somewhat further from the cordillera, which runs, of course, towards the north of Puerto del Desengaño.

Our soundings during all this period ranged only from thirty to forty-seven fathoms, the bottom being soft ooze towards Punta Olavide and fine sand towards Punta del Indio. The crews having become tired from rowing with the sweeps, we had to take the decision to anchor with a large kedge on the night of the 24th and the morning of the 25th, to prevent the corvettes, trying to use the light airs, being set too far inshore. This manoeuvre, by a fortunate chance, gave rise to a visit on the 25th from one of the natives living near Punta del Indio.

Although we were at least seven miles offshore at the time, this robust young man ventured out to meet us in his covered canoe. However, when he was a mile from us he seemed to change his mind and was more inclined to go back than to approach us, but as Teniente de Navío Valdés was heading towards him in the pinnace, with the clearest signs of peace and friendship, he finally decided to let himself be overhauled and visit us [in company] with the pinnace. His lack of surprise and his eagerness to

---

[1] Vancouver's Point Riou, the eastern entrance point of Icy Bay. Named by Malaspina after Alférez de Navío Martín de Olavide of the *Atrevida*. In his journal Suria suggests that the crew were enthralled by the magnificence of the panorama of the cordillera in front of them and that this led to 'scientific reflections on the part of some of the persons on the ship', including Tadeo Haenke. The Mexican artist satisfied himself however that the 'admirable order of things ... cannot be the mere child of accidents which can often be seen in Nature but that of Divine Providence who, with hidden and sapient ends, impenetrable to men, has determined all things.': Cutter, *Journal of Suria*, pp. 56-7.

[2] For full details of the observations for the height of Mount St Elias see Espinosa, *Memorias* (1809), 2nd memoir, pp. 60-61 and Espinosa, *Memoria* (1805), pp. 5-6, in which he gives the height of the mountain as 2,793 *toesas* = the French *toise* of 6·3946 feet, which would make Malaspina's height 5,442 metres and Espinosa's 5,444 metres, both slightly below the actual 5,489 metres accepted today.

[3] Icy Bay, the name being adopted from the description in Vancouver's Journal. The bay is in fact much larger and deeper than Malaspina thought.

[4] Probably Tsimpshian Point, the extremity of a spit which extends 2½ miles NNW from Point Riou, which would provide shelter for an Indian settlement.

Plate 17. *Descubierta* and *Atrevida* at anchor off Mount St Elias, by Felipe Bauzá. Museo de América, Madrid

invite us to the nearby anchorage, as well as his spontaneous readiness to offer us food, as had so often been done to us in Port Mulgrave, left us in no doubt that we were not the first Europeans met by these natives, although when studying the previous voyages to these parts it seems more likely that their knowledge arose from contact with the inhabitants of Port Mulgrave than from any direct visit to their dwellings. The customs, facial features and language of this native seemed exactly the same as those we had seen in that harbour. He gave us some strawberries and exchanged his otter-skin cloak, although we did not give him the hatchet that he craved. At last, towards nine o'clock, with various trifles we had given him, he took his leave of us and returned ashore.[1]

During the almost complete inactivity of these days we had taken advantage of our unchanging position to confirm the longitudes, not only repeating the observations of lunar distances, but also examining the daily rate of the chronometers by comparing the longitudes to the bearings of Mount St Elias, and tying them in to the observed latitude. The lunar distances observed on both corvettes once again confirmed, much to our surprise, the results of the previous month, being approximately 1°15' east of the chronometers and, which was no less surprising, the change of rate in the latter being well proved by the discrepancy of only 2' between the present daily determination of the longitude of Mount St Elias and that which we had calculated in our geodetic operations in Port Mulgrave. These, which we had chosen because they depended on the theodolite, placed the high peak in latitude 60°7'40" and longitude 143°54'30" west of Paris (the [lunar] distance results having not been adopted). Captain Cook's determinations differ from ours by 19' to the north and 34' to the east.

26 July

Finally, at dawn on the 26th, when a moderate breeze set in from the first quadrant, we quickly set sail and were able to make some four or five leagues offshore, enabling us to consider ourselves beyond any need to anchor again. Towards noon, however, the breeze was very light from SSE and south and decreasing, while the horizon was obscured by cloud and some drizzle. At the time we were unable to obtain bottom with one hundred fathoms of line. We had obtained soundings of fifty-one to eighty-five fathoms, ooze, while only five leagues off the coast. Having again tied in Puntas Novales and Barrientos, which we had examined and fixed with the bearings taken in Port Mulgrave, or those taken on the afternoon of the 7th, left us in no doubt of either the nature or trend of the coast or its continuity to the east and west, as opposed to the assertions of Ferrer Maldonado.

---

[1] The expedition was again in Tlingit territory. According to Suria the visit of the intrepid Indian from Icy Bay was 'Without any fear and boldly he came on board showing much pleasure and confidence and signified to us by signs that he had come to visit us to tell us that all his countrymen were ready to entertain us, and that for that purpose we should raise the kedge anchor and follow him and he would conduct us to a large port which was behind the point where they had their town and where they would trade with us for sea-otter skins.': Cutter, *Journal of Suria*, p. 58. Tova adds 'His language was somewhat different from that of the inhabitants of Port Mulgrave of whom he spoke as being valiant fighters and, because of trade with them or with other Europeans who had preceded us, it is certain that he understood the use and workings of our arms.': Porrúa, *Diary of Tova*, p. 409.

Indeed, the more we examined these parts, the low ground running continuously along the shore and the higher parts running unbroken, without even a valley or a river of medium size, terminating in the noble and natural architecture of Mount St Elias at one end and Cape Fairweather at the other, the more we were surprised at either the source of Ferrer Maldonado's report or the ease with which M. de Buache gave it support so publicly expressed and so widely echoed. If our present survey, being subsequent to that of the distinguished English navigator, does not allow us the complacency of considering it as important for the progress of geography, let us hope at least it will put an end in the future to new speculations on the existence of a passage in these latitudes, and not risk so many lives and fortunes in such investigations.[1]

27 July

The weather had changed for the better again, suggesting the most suitable choice for our following tasks, since we could now consider ourselves to have achieved the principal object of coming to these latitudes. We made straight for Cape Fairweather, confirming with fresh bearings and observations the position and connection of the entire cordillera running from Mount St Elias to Cape Fairweather. Repeated observations gave the variation as 29° to 29½°NE. Although what we were enjoying really deserved to be called light airs rather than a breeze from NW, they gradually increased in strength, so that at noon on the 28th we were some three leagues west of Cape Fairweather.

28 July

From the trend of the coast, which we could see at the time almost continuous without any conspicuous feature jutting out to sea, it was difficult to be sure whether or not this is the same point that Captain Cook distinguished with this name. The one that terminates Bahía de Behring, however, is fairly hilly and steep-to, snow-covered down to the shore and lying approximately SW of the mountain of the same name. The summit of this is some five and a third leagues inshore, rising to [blank] *toesas*[2] above sea level, in latitude 59°0′43″ and longitude 2°4″[3] east of Port Mulgrave, our position agreeing well with that of the English captain.

Even though we had remained well offshore until now, we had been considerably affected by a current setting to the south, which seemed to cease when we again came close inshore to tie in the true position of the coast with new bases and observations. It was at least four o'clock when Mount St Elias was lost from sight, at which time we were sailing two or three leagues offshore with a fresh breeze from the fourth quadrant.[4]

---

[1] Suria, with little expertise or experience, criticized Malaspina's refusal to be drawn into further exploration to find Ferrer Maldonado's passage: see Cutter, *Journal of Suria*, p. 58. Two days later, Malaspina had ended his search for the strait. Writing to Valdés from San Blas on 12 October he stated that there was not 'the least hope' of such an opening: see p. 424 below.

[2] Mount Fairweather, whose height is given in Palau *et al.*, *Diario de viaje de Malaspina*, p. 285 as 5,368·3 *varas* (of 0·836 metres), which would make Malaspina's calculation of 4,488 metres, slightly below the actual 4,670 metres accepted today.

[3] 2°4″ in the original MS, which could represent either 2°00′04″ or 2°04′.

[4] Off Cape Fairweather Suria noted, 'All day many whales of all sizes accompanied us, giving us quite some diversion. Some of them were very large.': Cutter, *Journal of Suria*, p. 67. The expedition was

Beyond Cape Fairweather the coast is thickly forested but without the strip of flat ground that we had seen from Bahía de Behring onwards. On approaching the coast what seemed to be a number of gaps, joined by the low ground, disappeared. It is undoubtedly inhabited, to judge by the smoke we saw in the afternoon, and by another fire seen in the evening towards Cross Sound. We obtained soundings of seventy to eighty fathoms about two leagues off the cape,[1] after which point, at the same distance, we were out of soundings with ninety and one hundred fathoms of line. It was about ten o'clock at night when darkness obliged us to stop work. We made use of the remaining hours until dawn to approach Cross Sound, near which we encountered a piece of floating ice alongside. At three the following morning [29th], now very close to its southern extremity, we altered course and began to measure bases.[2]

The coast we were now examining was very different from that we had just left to the west and bore out Captain Cook's suspicion that it was formed of a large number of islets with several inlets and harbours very useful for navigation. Close to these islets are several small rocky islets which are also mostly tree-covered. Two or three miles off these the depth was fifty to sixty fathoms, rock.

The heavy haze, that had prevented us all morning from renewing our longitude observations, as we wished, and from studying the nature of the interior mountains, disappeared. Finally, as the Sun approached the meridian, Don Felipe Bauzá, with his usual keenness, was able to fix the number and position of this little archipelago, with little fear of error. At noon our latitude by observation was 57°29′ and longitude 3°28′. We then checked the position of Puertos de los Remedios[3] and Guadalupe,[4] off which we now lay.

The sight of these harbours could not fail to remind us, with gratification, of the courage shown by Comandante Bodega y Quadra, who had visited them with a schooner[5] in August 1775, and of the rights of priority that we had acquired over this coast and almost all of the Americas, since his voyage had preceded that of Captain Cook by some three years. If it were possible to relate this voyage properly in a few lines, I certainly could not fail to mention many creditable circumstances attached to

---

passing Lituya Bay, the Port des Français of La Pérouse who had anchored there in 1786 and visited Tlinglit Indians from Cross Sound who had a summer camp in the bay. See Robin Inglis, 'Lapérouse 1786: A French Naval Visit to Alaska', in Stephen Haycox, James K. Barnett and Caedmon Liburd, eds, *Enlightenment and Exploration in the North Pacific, 1741–1805*, University of Washington Press, Seattle, 1997, pp. 49–64.

[1] Probably Cape Bingham, the southern entrance point of Cross Sound.

[2] After passing Cross Sound the expedition was retracing the steps of its earlier passage along the Alexander Archipelago. Throughout this coastal run from the entrance of Prince William Sound, and extending south to Vancouver Island, Bauzá and his colleagues continued to chart the coast and to draw coastal views. Much of the work survives in the collection of the Museo Naval: see AMN, Sig. Borradores. Carp. XI, C-13 (33), (38-40); Sig. Vistas. Carp. VII (262-267), (268-285). (Higueras, *Catálogo crítico*, nos 1900–1903, 2755–2760, 2761-2788).

[3] Named by Bodega y Quadra, who anchored there on 18 August 1775; identified by Wagner as Sea Lion Bay (now Sealion Cove at the NW end of Kruzof Island, on the north side of the entrance to Sitka Sound): see Wagner, *Cartography*, p. 490.

[4] Named by Bodega y Quadra, who anchored there on 17 August 1775; identified by Wagner as Port Mary in Shelikof Bay (on the west side of Kruzof Island): see ibid., p. 460.

[5] The tiny *Sonora*: see also p. 16, n. 1 above.

it. But these will be related at greater length elsewhere and perhaps when illustrated by engravings will receive from the nation the proper tribute that it deserves.[1]

The weather cleared in the afternoon and, still helped by a fresh breeze from the NW and WNW, it was easy for us to continue with our survey by way of Cabo Engaño[2] and Ensenada del Susto[3] to the islands south of this bay. We were anxious to make a detailed examination of the entrance to Port Banks, visited by Captain Dixon.[4] We even lay-to for several hours during the next night, which was murky and rainy, but a fairly strong current setting to the east thwarted our plan. At six o'clock on the morning of the 30th, when we could see the coast quite clearly, we found that we had been carried past it. We therefore made for the SW point of Bahía del Principe,[5] which we reached at eight in the morning. We then went a little way into the bay, although in the end we chose to pass to the south of Captain Dixon's Hazy Islands,[6] from which we were a good mile at noon, in latitude 55°57′ and longitude 5°14′ [east] of Port Mulgrave. We could not obtain bottom at the time with ninety fathoms of line, but we had sounded ninety-five fathoms, small pebbles, the night before while in the early hours of the morning the *Atrevida* had signalled depths of seventy-six and eighty-two fathoms. Variation had dropped almost instantly to 26°NE.

Although the frequent gusts and the persistent cloud cover were clear indications that the westerly breeze would not last long, the good fortune that allowed us so far to describe the coast in great detail was too much of a temptation not to try to continue while we had the choice. Accordingly, we had no sooner cleared Hazy Islands than we came up on the breeze again to approach the beginning of Archipielago de Bucareli,[7] also surveyed by Comandante Bodega y Quadra in 1775 and then examined in detail in 1779 by Piloto Mourelle under the orders of Tenientes de Navío Arteaga and Bodega y Quadra.

At five in the afternoon we were already close to some of the islands, but because of the heavy cloud it was not easy for us to extend our bearings inland, and we could not link them to each other with the accuracy we desired. The breeze dropped and almost at the same time the sky clouded over even more with mist and drizzle.[8] Finally we had to stand offshore somewhat, particularly as the constant soundings of

---

[1] A full account of Bodega y Quadra's voyage has yet to be published. For brief accounts see Wagner, *Cartography*, pp. 175-9 and Cook, *Flood Tide of Empire*, pp. 72-83. See also Wallace M. Olson, *Through Spanish Eyes: Spanish Voyages to Alaska, 1774–1792*, Auke Bay, Alaska, 2002, pp. 45-53.

[2] Cape Edgecumbe: see also p. 85, n. 6 above.

[3] While not mentioned in Bodega y Quadra's narrative, it is laid down on his 1775 chart to the east of Cabo Engaño [Cape Edgecumbe]. It is the entrance to Sitka Sound through Necker Islands: see also p. 97, n. 7 above.

[4] See p. 97, n. 3 above.

[5] A large entrance shown on Bodega y Quadra's 1775 chart, which is the entrance to Chatham Strait.

[6] Malaspina's Islas Nubladas, a group of islands on Dixon's chart, 11 miles south of Cape Ommaney. The name was retained by Vancouver: see Wagner, *Cartography*, p. 391.

[7] Named by Bodega y Quadra in honour of Antonio María de Bucareli y Ursúa, the Viceroy of New Spain (1771-9); possibly Prince of Wales Island.

[8] On Cook's third voyage Charles Clerke had complained about 'the confounded foggy Weather ... was a devilish Impediment to our business': Beaglehole, *Cook's Journals: The Voyage of the Resolution and Discovery*, p. 345, n. 2. Suria also commented, 'All these days were foggy, obscure, and wet, and although we sailed along quite close to the coast we could not see more than a little of the beach on account of the fog and the low clouds which covered the surface of the mountains.': Cutter, *Journal of Suria*, p. 67.

fifty-five and sixty fathoms seemed to confirm our suspicion of a current or tidal stream setting towards the inner channels.

31 July
To the extreme variability of the light airs, which continued during the night and the following morning, was added a mist so thick that we had to fire guns to remain in company with the *Atrevida*. The soundings were from seventy to seventy-six fathoms, fine sand, and at noon it was still impossible to ascertain our position, either by observations or by bearings. This inactivity and unease, however, did not last long. At half past twelve the mist began to clear gradually and at last, at half past one, we were not only able to repeat our observations with confidence, but also to see the mainland, from approximately the points we had seen at noon the previous day to the first of the islands, these then stretching out close together in a line as far as the broad entrance and then to Isla de San Carlos.[1] This latter bore S50°E by compass, and Cape Bartolome[2] S87°E, three leagues distant. In the afternoon, although the breeze dropped entirely, we were quite satisfied with our position, as we could combine our astronomical tasks and some accurate views of the area of these anchorages with the useful and painstaking work of the Spanish navigators who had preceded us on this coast and whose knowledge and contribution (to judge by Captain Dixon's account and chart) could be considered completely unknown to European navigation.

Cape Bartolome is in latitude 55°17′ and longitude 6°5′ east of Mulgrave. It is a rocky point which drops abruptly from a fairly high and thickly forested hill. Lying a short distance to the east of the cape are three needle-shaped rocks or rather islets,[3] behind which can be seen through a fairly wide gap the far coast, which is also forested and which runs more to the west[4] to join the ends of this coast, which forms Dixon Entrance.[5]

Whether one considers this parallel on which so many good harbours are to be found, with its closeness to Queen Charlotte Sound[6] to the SE, or to the large numbers of natives who inhabit this area, it must undoubtedly be preferred to the other places seen so far for the establishment of the fur trade on a solid and permanent basis. Even so it seems highly doubtful that it could ever be sustained by the excessively risky, precarious and limited arrangements for trade of this type, particularly in the hands of a nation which, by necessity, may not be skilled in good

---

[1] Named by Bodega y Quadra, on 26 August 1775. Now Forrester Island, 30 miles WNW of Cape Muzon, the northern entrance point of Dixon Entrance; named by George Dixon in 1787 and adopted by Vancouver.
[2] See p. 96, n. 2 above.
[3] A number of small islands extend 7 cables south, not east, of the cape.
[4] A transcription error for south.
[5] Malaspina's Canal de Dixon, whose northern entrance point, Cape Muzon, lies about 46 miles SE of Cape Bartolome.
[6] Named by James Strange on 5 August 1786 (*James Strange's Journal and Narrative of the Commercial Expedition from Bombay to the Northwest Coast of America*, Fairfield, 1982, p. 95) and not by S. Wedgborough as given erroneously by Vancouver (Lamb, *George Vancouver's Voyage*, p. 647 and n. 1). Wedgborough was second in command and surveying officer of the *Experiment*, one of Strange's two ships. It seems unlikely that Malaspina would have been aware of this name at the time of his voyage and may have learned of it later from Galiano or Valdés, who in turn may have been told it by Vancouver.

FROM ACAPULCO TO PORT MULGRAVE AND NOOTKA SOUND

husbandry. But we will leave this political discussion to its proper place and return now to the narrative of the voyage.[1]

During the hours of calm the current had set us some way to the south, although at six in the evening we were still only about two leagues from the harbour mouth,[2] in a depth of seventy fathoms, fine dark sand, and variation, according to several azimuths, of 23°30′NE. At the time we felt a few light airs from the north, which soon afterwards veering to NE, seemed to encourage us only to stand further offshore, but not to stop work on the survey of the coast as far as Nootka,[3] so that future navigators might not censure us for neglecting a matter so directly relevant to the objects of this voyage. In truth, having assumed the necessity not only of visiting the new establishment at Nootka and one or two ports in our California, but also of not delaying beyond mid-October our arrival at the ports of San Blas and Acapulco, the survey of the inner coast of Queen Charlotte Sound could not be sufficiently detailed to describe the entire coast, particularly if, as seemed probable, this was formed of islands rather than a single mainland coast. Nevertheless our survey would at least ensure the safety of navigation and direct future investigations more wisely, if their aim was to perfect hydrographic knowledge, even if this might be of little utility in this part of the globe.

1 August

Having thus abandoned any thought of even a brief stay in Puerto de la Cruz[4] in Archipielago de Bucareli, we set a course so as to pass two or three leagues to the east of Isla de San Carlos [Forrester Island], then meaning to come up on the breeze towards the centre of the channel.[5] These intentions, however, were very soon entirely thwarted by the wind which, after midnight, set in fresh from ESE and SE raising the sea considerably and closing in the sky and horizon with fog and drizzle.[6] Our first tack to south and SSW took us out of sight of land from seven o'clock in the morning, at which time Isla de San Carlos was bearing EbyN, true, at about eight leagues. At noon, in latitude 54°32′, we calculated our longitude to be 4°44′[east] of Mulgrave and variation 24°23′NE.

This did not dissuade me altogether from the proposed survey which, although it seemed risky or too time-consuming to attempt along the inner channel, might at least be rewarding along the outer coast, on which the very different work of Captain Dixon could allow us to show a greater degree of accuracy, especially in sailing directions for the two most prominent points of the mainland coast. But in this regard I

---

[1] For a fuller reference to Malaspina's remarks on the fur trade see p. 119, n. 2 above.
[2] Here Malaspina has perpetrated a *non sequitur*, with no previous mention by him of a port or harbour in this vicinity. Perhaps he is referring to Bucareli Bay behind Cape Bartolome or Puerto de la Cruz in the same bay; see n. 4 below.
[3] Up to now Malaspina has used the spelling Nootka, no doubt derived from Cook and King, *Voyage to the Pacific Ocean*, but from here on he uses the Spanish spelling Nutka.
[4] According to Wagner a name no longer in use for a feature in Bucareli Bay: Wagner, *Cartography*, p. 445.
[5] Dixon Entrance.
[6] Tova suggests that it was the calm that accompanied the fog, followed by light airs as night fell, that caused Malapina to decide it was too late to enter Bucareli Bay as intended: Porrúa, *Diary of Tova*, p. 412.

was far from anticipating the gales that we were to encounter from now on. Soon after midday, with constant rain and heavy cloud accompanied by a very high sea, we had to take two reefs in the topsails as a precaution, and on the following day we still had to sail with two courses and reefed topsail.

3 August
Our tacks, however, had brought us to a point from which, at seven o'clock on the morning of the 3rd, we sighted the northernmost[1] of the Queen Charlotte Islands, five or six leagues distant, probably near Captain Dixon's Cloak Bay.[2] It was a coast of moderate elevation, with some inlets to the south, generally covered with fine forest. From our position at present it covered an arc bearing from N72°E to S87°E by compass.

Although the weather continued very gloomy and threatening, we closed the coast until nine o'clock in the morning, and then tacked back to SSW, having given up our hopes of making the required observations for latitude and longitude, while in sight of it. These were all the more necessary as recent observations had left us in no doubt of a considerable error in our dead reckoning, which would have influenced both determinations. If, this being the case, we could conjecture freely as to the longitude (having adopted Captain Dixon's latitude). We would be persuaded, by the combined dead reckoning from the 1st, and from the 4th, when we had made fairly reliable observations by chronometers, that the longitude of this point was 7°5′ east of Port Mulgrave. It was therefore somewhat further inland or to the east of that determined by Captain Dixon, according to the direction of Isla San Carlos, which he named Isla de For[r]ester.[3]

No sooner had we tacked than the breeze began to strengthen again, obliging us to shorten sail. From this moment until the afternoon of the 7th it may be said that we had nothing but a continuous gale from SE, which was, however, very much stronger on the night of the 5th, when the wind could more justly be called a fully developed hurricane. The extremely high seas, the continuous rain and the wind from ESE, certainly more tempestuous and gusty than any we had experienced since leaving Spain, demonstrated the excellent qualities of the corvettes, which did not suffer the least damage, while keeping a steady course under foresail and double-reefed main topsail.[4]

[1] Malaspina had sighted Langara Island, Dixon's North Island: see [Beresford], *Voyage ... by Captain George Dixon*, chart f.p. iii.

[2] In this instance Malaspina does not translate Cloak Bay into Spanish. This bay forms much of the western side of Langara Island at the northern end of Queen Charlotte Islands. Dixon named it on 4 July 1787 in recognition of the fact that he traded for good quality fur cloaks there: [Beresford], *Voyage ... by Captain George Dixon*, p. 202. On 18 July 1774, Alférez de Fragata Juan Pérez in the *Santiago* reached this point on the first Spanish voyage to the NW Coast, naming the northernmost point of Langara Island, Punta de Santa Margarita, today's St Margaret Point: see Herbert K. Beals, transl. and ed., *Juan Pérez on the Northwest Coast*, Oregon Historical Society, Portland, Oreg., 1989, p. 74.

[3] Malaspina's meaning is unclear. He may be referring to the geographical position on Dixon's chart of Forrester Island.

[4] Suria, not surprisingly for someone who was not used to going to sea, was overwhelmed by the experience: 'The wind kept getting stronger every instant with rain and a very heavy sea. The rolls were tremendous and the darkness terrifying.': Cutter, *Journal of Suria*, p. 71. See also Vol. 1 of this edition, p. lxi.

7 August

At noon on the 7th, the gale having abated, we were in latitude 53°20' and longitude 3°1', a long way offshore and south of the points we had identified, so that for the accomplishment of our hopes we would perhaps waste the first puffs of favourable wind if we steered NE, when further SE winds might find us in the same position as on the 1st. These considerations persuaded me that it would be better to make directly for Nootka, or at least for the northern extremity of its coast.[1] Therefore, when a moderate breeze set in from the SW and west at six in the evening, we altered course to ESE under full sail.

The weather continued moderate and even a little variable on the 8th and 9th, when we took advantage of very clear skies to observe up to 200 sets of lunar distances on each corvette. The results were to cause us further confusion, as they were so close to the longitude according to the chronometers that they differed by no less than a degree from the longitude deduced in June and July from observations made within sight of Mount Fairweather and Mount St Elias. We flattered ourselves, however, with the hope of making observations at Nootka that would settle with all certainty this new and very difficult question in the survey methods followed so far.

11 August

At ten o'clock on the morning of the 11th we sighted land, although dimly, and the latitude of 51°17' observed at noon convinced us that we were not far from the southern end of Queen Charlotte Sound, between Captain Dixon's Cape Cox and Cape Woody.[2] At half past three in the afternoon, near the latter cape, with a fresh breeze from SEbyS, we bore up for the coast and began to survey it in detail, as the course we had taken offshore had not allowed us to plot more than the higher points to the north of that cape.

This stretch of the coast is undoubtedly aligned more from NW to SE than indicated by the charts published so far. Cape Woody, which is more easily distinguished by its hummocky shape and thick forest than by the islet with a hole through it on its western side,[3] is in longitude 11°50' east of Port Mulgrave, so that the results according to our chronmeters in Nootka would have to be far closer to Captain Cook's longitudes than those we had found in Port Mulgrave and Prince William Sound. With the approach of darkness the breeze dropped considerably, and as the sky and horizon became clearer, during the following hours we always had the coast in sight.

---

[1] Cape Scott, the northernmost point on Vancouver Island. Prior to the Galiano and Vancouver reconnaissances of the next year, this cape was considered to be part of the continental mainland.

[2] From the position of Cape Cox on Dixon's general chart ([Beresford], *Voyage ... by Captain George Dixon*, chart f.p. iii), it would appear that Wagner is correct in identifying this point as Aristazabal Island, deep within Queen Charlotte Sound: Wagner, *Cartography*, p. 445. Woody Point, named by Cook on 29 March 1778, but now Cape Cook, is the northern point of Brooks Peninsula on the NW coast of Vancouver Island.

Suria notes that at this time Surgeon Flores ordered that both officers and men be given rations of lemonade to 'thank the sailors for the good work they had done and at the same time to keep them away from the scurvy which was insidiously threatening them': Cutter, *Journal of Suria*, p. 72.

[3] Solander Island, ¼ mile SW of Cape Cook. Its present description, however, merely states that it is 'a conical mass of rock nearly 91 m high', *British Columbia Pilot*, vol. I, Taunton, 1979, p. 230.

At the time we were some two leagues offshore in depths of fifty fathoms, pebbles, with the islet off Cape Woody bearing W20°N about six or seven leagues distant and the point that we assumed to be the entrance to Nootka bearing N88°E by compass. In this position we thought it more prudent to heave-to until first light the next day, on alternate tacks as required either by the soundings, which showed a depth of thirty-five fathoms, or the breeze, which dropped completely in the lee of the land.

12 August
Even before daybreak we made sail again, and although the breeze was extremely light, by eight o'clock in the morning we were off the entrance to Puerto de la Esperanza,[1] a league and a half from the islands inside it, and disillusioned as to what we had thought to be Punta de Nutka[2] the previous afternoon. This point, now bearing east by compass, was still four or five leagues distant, but several canoes had already approached us, and although they came apparently more for the purposes of fishing than trade, we saw, as on the night before, several large fires on the beach nearby.

The sea breeze did not set in until two in the afternoon. At first we had to stand offshore a little to avoid some eddies which were setting us onto the shoals off Maquinna Point.[3] Finally we bore away, in depths of seventeen and twenty fathoms, rock, having reached the edge of these shoals, which had been surveyed by Captain Cook.

Two or three canoes carrying natives had come alongside the corvettes by then, eager not only for the shells from Monterey[4] and some bread or other food, but also to show us that they were familiar with our flag, language and customs, and knew the names of Comandantes Martínez and Eliza. They gave us to understand that only one of our vessels was in the harbour and after a time they left us to return ashore.

At five o'clock in the afternoon we were only two leagues from the entrance to the harbour, the southern extremity[5] of which was bearing NE. I hauled the very light, variable breeze – what there was of it – to this bearing, and hoisted the ensigns, in the

---

[1] Malaspina may have been referring here in translation to Cook's reference on 29 March 1778, when rounding Estevan Point, to the large bight sweeping north to Woody Point [Cape Cook], which he 'called *Hope Bay*; hoping from the appearance of the land, to find in it a good harbour. The event proved, that we were not mistaken.': Cook and King, *Voyage to the Pacific Ocean*, II, p. 264. The harbour Cook referred to was his anchorage in Resolution Cove in Nootka Sound. The name Esperanza was later transferred to the inlet that links the open sea to Tahsis Inlet and Nootka Sound to create Nootka Island. It was explored by Cevallos and Espinosa during Malaspina's visit to Nootka, when it became clear that Malaspina's Puerto de la Esperanza was in fact either the entrance to Esperanza Inlet or Port Eliza on the northern side of the inlet close within its entrance.

[2] It is unclear to which point Malaspina is referring, but it was probably Bajo Point, the SW extremity of Nootka Island, particularly as he distinguishes it from Maquinna Point, the southern point of the island.

[3] Cook's Breakers Point. Named Punta de Macuina on contemporary Spanish charts after the principal chief of Nootka Sound, it guards Friendly Cove from the open ocean. Foul ground with rocks above and below water extends 1 mile SE of Maquinna Point.

[4] Abalone shells, often referred to as Monterey shells, as they were a prized trade item brought to the NW Coast by the Spanish supply ships and others from stopovers in California. Suria reports that the Indians clambered on board the *Descubierta* without the use of a ladder and immediately asked for shells using the words 'pachitle conchi' ('give us shells!'): Cutter, *Journal of Suria*, p. 72.

[5] Probably Yuquot Point.

hope that in the nearby settlement they would see them and know of our approach. Our feelings may be imagined on seeing the national flag,[1] shortly afterwards, flying from a small hill near the southern point, and on making out, through the trees, the three masts of an unrigged vessel. We knew of course about our settlement on this coast and how much money had been lavished and how much blood might have been spilt to sustain its legitimate possession. Nevertheless, such is the instinct of man towards society and his longing to find himself among his own people, free of all the shackles of envy, greed or a misunderstood sense of honour, that at this moment, what we should perhaps have considered a disastrous and unfortunate venture, seemed to us a great joy.

As the Sun sank below the horizon we found ourselves in flat calm, only half a league from the harbour entrance and barely a mile from the nearby shore. We sounded fifty-five fathoms, ooze, and dropped a kedge to wait for the sea breeze on the following day. Soon afterwards, to offer us assistance, the launch of the frigate *Concepción*[2] from San Blas reached us and remained alongside during the night.

13 August

The land breeze blew freshly in the early hours of the morning, but then dropped at sunrise. At last, towards seven o'clock, it was replaced by the first light airs of the sea breeze, with which we immediately set sail. We were closely followed by the *Atrevida*, and, having passed the western point of the harbour[3] at a ship's length, we successfully anchored inside it at half past nine. We quickly began the work of mooring with a line taken ashore from the stern to the base of the huts, an anchor NE to the harbour mouth and a holding kedge to the north. By midday the operation was complete and the topmasts and yards were struck.

---

[1] The Spanish flag flew over the battery of San Miguel on San Rafael Island, the largest of the San Miguel Islands, which form the southern side of Friendly Cove, in which the Spanish establishment had been created by Esteban José Martínez in 1789. Cardero's drawing of this scene is part of the artistic record that has survived from the visit to Nootka: see Sotos, *Los pintores*, II, fig. 603.

[2] One of the California supply ships that was being used at Nootka as a guard ship during the summer of 1791. It appears in Cardero's drawing noted above and figures prominently in Brambila's general view of the Spanish Establishment: see plate 18 and Sotos, *Los pintores*, II, fig. 602. Bauzá made a close-up sketch of it (later wrongly identified as a picture of *Atrevida*) during the visit: ibid., fig. 597.

[3] Malaspina was rounding San Rafael Island.

Plate 18. View of the Spanish Establishment in Friendly Cove, by Fernando Brambila. Museo de América, Madrid

CHAPTER 4

At Nootka Sound[1]

[13 August]
The commanding officer of the frigate *Concepción* at the time was Teniente de Navío Don Manuel Saavedra,[2] since Teniente de Navío Don Francisco Eliza[3] had taken charge of the snow *San Carlos*, with the aim of continuing the survey of the coast to the north and south of Nootka Sound with the schooner *Saturna*. The entire establishment[4] was under the command of that officer [Saavedra], including the batteries at

---

[1] In August 1774, Juan Pérez had anchored off Nooka Sound, off the NW coast of Vancouver Island, and traded with the local Nuu-Chah-Nulth Indians, but he did not enter: see Beals, *Juan Pérez*, pp. 144-9. On 29 March 1778, Cook became the first European to enter the sound, when he anchored in Resolution Cove, off Bligh Island, staying there for three weeks to rest, replenish his supplies and replace the foremast and mizzen mast of the *Resolution*. His expedition also visited and traded with the Mowachaht people at the village of Yuquot in Friendly Cove. From 1785 onwards fur traders began to arrive on the coast and at the same time there was a suspicion of Russian movement down the coast from Alaska. In consequence Spain established a fortified outpost at Yuquot in 1789. It was occupied on a continuous basis from April 1790 until March 1795 and during that time was the centre of Spanish activity on the coast north of California.

[2] Ramón (not Manuel) Saavedra was one of the six officers who had arrived in New Spain, in February 1789, with the new Viceroy, Conde de Revillagigedo and the new *Comandante* of the Naval Department of San Blas, Juan Francisco de la Bodega y Quadra. Their purpose was to strengthen Spain's naval abilities on the coast of California and farther north in view of Esteban Martínez's assertion, after his 1788 voyage to Alaska, that the Russians intended to occupy Nootka in 1789. Four members of the group - Jacinto Caamaño, Salvador Fidalgo, Francisco Eliza and Manuel Quimper - undertook important exploring expeditions in British Columbian and Alaskan waters. See Olson, *Through Spanish Eyes*.

[3] Francisco Eliza, for whom Saavedra was standing in as *Comandante*, had been given the difficult task of surveying the coast in detail from Mount St Elias to Alta California. Setting off in the summer of 1791, he encountered strong winds north of Nootka and so turned south, examining Clayoquot and Barkley Sounds before entering Juan de Fuca Strait. Here he was joined by the *Santa Saturnina* in which José María Narváez charted 'Canal de Nuestra Señora del Rosario', today's Strait of Georgia, to 49°50'N beyond the present-day city of Vancouver. Malaspina left Nootka two days before Eliza's return and it was not until he reached Acapulco that he learned of these latest Spanish discoveries: see pp. 237-9 below This resulted in his detaching Dionisio Alcalá Galiano and Cayetano Valdés from the main expedition and their exploration of Juan de Fuca Strait and subsequent circumnavigation of Vancouver Island in the summer of 1792: see John Kendrick, 'End of the Northern Mystery: the Spanish in Juan de Fuca and Beyond, 1790-1792', in Inglis, *Spain and the North Pacific Coast*, pp. 100-110.

[4] The establishment at Nootka set up by Martínez in May 1789 displaced the Indian village of Yuquot in Friendly Cove, visited by Cook in April 1778 and sketched by his artist John Webber (Joppien and Smith, *Art of Cook's Voyages*, III, p. 441). It was abandoned after the 'Crisis Summer' of 1789 but was quickly re-occupied in the spring of 1790 under the command of Eliza. Despite the construction of solid frame buildings and the agricultural activities of Alberni, it was never self-sufficient and was dependent on the

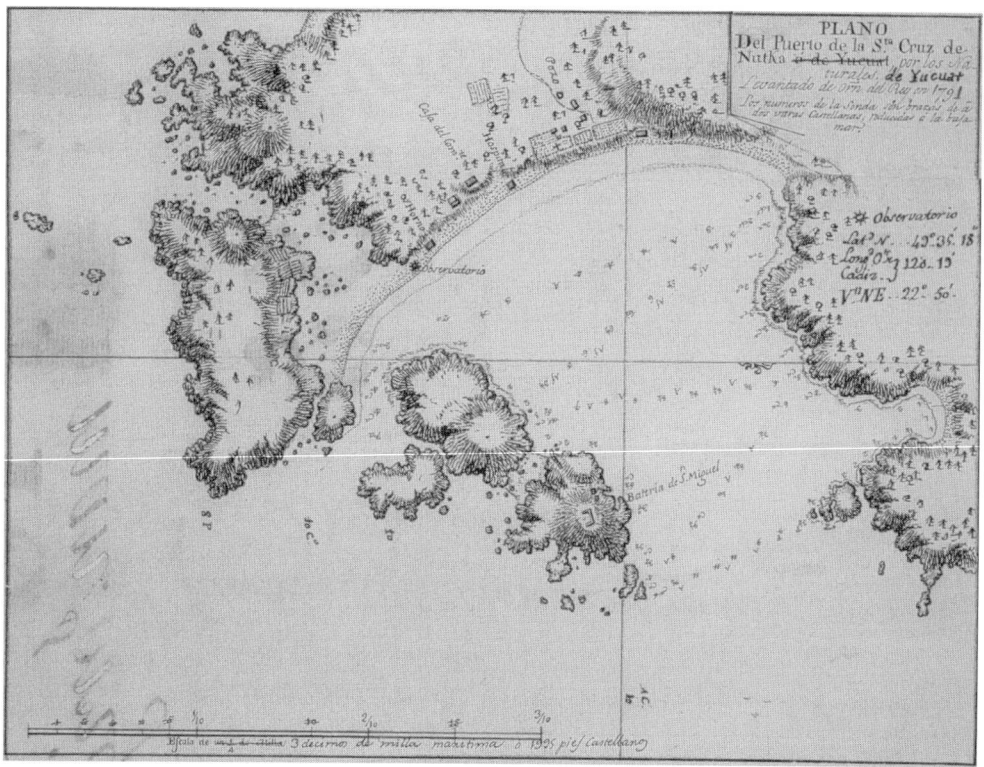

Plate 19. 'Plano del Puerto de la Sta Cruz de Nutka llamado por los naturales de Yucuat, levantado por orden del rey en 1791.' Museo Naval, Madrid

the entrance, since the independent company of Catalonian volunteers had been brought in an auxiliary capacity, their *capitán*, Don Pedro Alberní,[1] was also there, the *teniente* and *alférez* who had accompanied him having been withdrawn because of ill-health. All the sick, most of them suffering from scurvy and in a very bad way, had been taken back to San Blas in the frigate *Princesa*, under the orders of Teniente de Navío Don Jacinto Caamaño.[2] The establishment had received the necessary provisions from the snow *San Carlos* and the frigate *Aránzazu*. The return of the latter from

---

supply ships from San Blas and California. The inclement winter weather made it a miserable place for men used to a warmer and drier southern climate. See Christon Archer, 'The Transient Presence: a Reappraisal of Spanish Attitudes towards the Northwest Coast in the Eighteenth Century', *BC Studies*, #18, Summer 1973, pp. 3-32 and, for a survey of the Spanish occupation at Yuquot, Oakah L. Jones, 'The Spanish Occupation of Nootka Sound, 1790-1795', MA thesis, University of Oklahoma, 1960.

[1] For the story of the 'Primera Compañía franca de voluntarios de Cataluña' at Nootka see Joseph P. Sánchez, *Spanish Bluecoats: The Catalonian Volunteers in Northwestern New Spain, 1767–1810*, Albuquerque, 1990, pp. 71-88. A short biography of Alberni (1747-1802) by Christon Archer can be found in the *Dictionary of Canadian Biography*, V, Toronto, 1983, pp. 10-11. Suria referred to Alberni as 'the distinguished official who will occupy one of the most worthy places in the account of this voyage on account of his skill and management of these natives, and who was charged with sustaining the establishment and keeping it free from invasions': Cutter, *Journal of Suria*, p. 75.

[2] Jacinto Caamaño is best known for his explorations in southern Alaskan waters in 1792, where his investigations disproved the legend of the Strait of Admiral Fonte.

the port of Monterey, where she had been sent to collect fresh meat was to ensure for the following winter, with such an important commodity, the well being of the seamen and troops who were then in the presidio.

At the end of the harbour we could see various huts built of wooden planks, which were guarded and kept in good order by Alberni and the troops quartered ashore.[1] The bakery, which daily supplied fresh bread to all, the vegetable gardens, in which nature was already providing generously;[2] the protection of the stores and equipment against a highly destructive swarm of rats; the forges; the preservation of or additions to the dwellings with the necessary cutting of timber, were other duties in which the discipline and steadiness of the men and the good example and skill of Comandantes Eliza, Saavedra and Alberni, were consistently outstanding. These had a considerable influence on the preservation of health, and the harmony which reigned among them all.

We did not delay a moment in setting up the observatory at a suitable spot, not far from the huts, which I went to examine in the pinnace. We inspected the watering place, while Don Felipe Bauzá began taking bearings from the forecastle as the pleasant calm afternoon allowed a view of many distant objects, among which there stood out a peak inland,[3] a very conspicuous mark for the survey of the harbour.

The next day these operations continued, with the measurement of a base for the exact determination of the position of the harbour. Many more bearings were taken to several of the islands of the inner archipelago, which were all tied in with an equal number of azimuths, so that the great differences in variation, noted by Captain Cook, should not affect the accuracy of our work. Lastly we began replenishing our water supply with the two launches and the *bombos*, which, as they had to go a league, using the tides, without disturbing our good relationship with the natives,[4] were always sent in the charge of an officer, accompanied by two armed marines. Various causes (the origin of which is not part of this account) had brought about, on the part

---

[1] In addition to Cardero's drawing of the battery of San Miguel (see p. 167, n. 1 above), two sketches in the collection of the Museo de América give a sense of the small Spanish establishment in 1791. A new Comandante's house, used in 1792 by Bodega y Quadra, is shown under construction: Sotos, *Los pintores*, II, figs 599 and 600. The Expedition's plan of Friendly Cove, 'Cala de los Amigos', provides an excellent overview of the site, the placement of the various buildings, gardens and well, and the location of the observatory set up at the SW end of the beach on the first day: AMN, Sig.: II, D. (17), (Higueras, *Catálogo crítico*, no. 2069), plate 19.

[2] For a discussion of Alberni's agricultural efforts see Donald C. Cutter, 'Pedro Alberni y los primeros experimentos de agricultura científica en la costa Noroeste del Pacífico', *Revisita de historia naval*, V, 18, 1987, pp. 41–55; also comments in Cutter, *Malaspina and Galiano*, pp. 76–8.

[3] Pico de Tahsis (Tahsis Peak), now the 1,481-metre high Conuma Peak, a dramatic cone-shaped mountain, which dominates the view up Tlupana Inlet, inside Nootka Sound. It rises above the Sound when viewed from offshore. Its distinctive presence is depicted in Bauzá's coastal views: AMN, Sig. Vistas. Carp. VII (286 and 287) (Higueras, *Catálogo crítico*, nos 2779, 2780).

[4] Good relations with the natives encountered on the NW Coast were central to Spanish efforts to uphold sovereignty and to explore and undertake scientific activities: see Christon I. Archer, 'Seduction before Sovereignty: Spanish Efforts to Manipulate the Natives in their Claims to the Northwest Coast', in Robin Fisher and Hugh Johnston, eds, *From Maps to Metaphors: the Pacific World of George Vancouver*, Vancouver, 1993, pp. 127–59.

of the natives, a timid and cautious behaviour towards our establishment.¹ As a result we saw few fishermen coming to the corvettes. We wanted, however, to meet the various caciques, or *taguís*,² but none of these had appeared three days after our arrival, although various presents to those who came in canoes and many promises to those who visited us should have been a powerful incentive to attract them.³

14 August

At last, on the morning of the 14th, the secondary cacique, Tlupananú overcame this barrier, trusting in the constant friendship that had indeed reigned between him and ourselves, but he was shy and almost alarmed at the sight of such an assembly of forces.⁴ His portrait was drawn very accurately by Don Tomás de Suria.⁵ We gave him many presents and promised him even greater generosity if he visited us again in his large canoe, well manned, and ready to perform its manoeuvres, both martial and festive. [15th] With these incentives he was soon followed by various others, either subordinates or relatives of Macuina,⁶ the principal chief of the whole district. At

---

¹ Malaspina refers here to the murder on 13 July 1789 of Chief Callicum, a close ally of Maquinna, after a confrontation with Martínez. For four years Callicum had played an important role in the the fur trade at Nootka: see Cook, *Flood Tide of Empire*, pp. 179-81.

The botanist José Mariano Moziño, who accompanied Bodega y Quadra to Nootka in 1792, left a detailed account of the natives and the Spanish occupation in his *Noticias de Nutka*, in which he credited Alberni with re-opening the establishment's communication with Maquinna. To the tune of a popular folk song he taught his troops to sing a short verse in praise of Maquinna and of Spain's friendship with the Chief, a strategy that caught Maquinna's attention if not his trust: see Iris H. W. Engstrand, ed. and transl., *Noticias de Nutka: An Account of Nootka Sound in 1792 by José Mariano Moziño*, Seattle, 1991, p. 78, and Sánchez, *Spanish Bluecoats*, p. 95.

² *Taises*: see Engstrand, *Noticias de Nutka*, pp. 24-31.

³ It is not altogether surprising that the natives were apprehensive. With the arrival of the *Descubierta* and *Atrevida* the number of Spaniards at Friendly Cove and moving around the Sound with armed marines had more than quadrupled.

⁴ Tlupananutl, a relative of Maquinna and chief of a native group in Tlupana Inlet. Referred to as 'secondary' because of the primacy of Maquinna (see n. 6 below).

Although Suria's journal falters and then ends abruptly during the expedition's visit to Nootka, one remarkable passage recording Tlupananutl's speech on this occasion has survived; it is a long harangue about the genuineness of his friendship and the untrustworthiness of his rival Maquinna. 'Although you may marvel and believe me a barbarian I am not ignorant of the inviolable laws of friendship. They inspire me to tell you not to confide in nor feel safe from the dissimulated perfidy of Macuina. I tell you that he is crafty and overbearing and he looks on you with hatred and abhorrence. He shortly meditates dislodging you from this place which you have founded in our dominion, but he cannot do it while Tlupanamibo [Tlupananutl] lives, who, being experienced in this double-crossing game, will know how to oppose it as I have his malign projects up to the present. Although, as I am his subject, I could accompany him in his enterprises, I forbear to do it because my heart is filled with integrity and justice.': Cutter, *Journal of Suria*, pp. 74-5. The artist suggests that while the officials were impressed by this speech, he was less so 'as I remember the elegant way in which the Mexicans know how to make a harangue.': ibid., p. 75.

⁵ Suria's 'accurate portrait' is held in AMN, carp. I (47) (Higueras, *Catalogo critico*, no. 2937) and reproduced in Sotos, *Los pintores*, II, fig. 607. Tlupananutl also wears the Nootkan 'whaling hat' symbolic of his chiefly status; four examples of these are in the collection of the Museo de América: Sánchez, *Indios de América*, pp. 116-17, nos. 89-92.

⁶ Maquinna, principal chief in Nootka Sound and ranking chief of native groups living along the west coast of Vancouver Island; these included those subordinate to Chief Wickaninish centred on Clayoquot Sound and to Chief Tatoosh at the entrance to Juan de Fuca Strait. Contemporary accounts put

Plate 20. Maquinna, by Tomás de Suria. Museo Naval, Madrid

times they boasted of the extent of his dominions or the power of his authority, at others, however, with various pretexts or excuses, they gave us to understand that the said chief was afraid to visit us. This fear was particularly confirmed on the morning of the 15th when Don Cayetano Valdés and Don Felipe Bauzá went to Macuina's settlement as they travelled along the coast for geodetic purposes. They found the huts abandoned and, of the many people hiding in the forest nearby, hardly any could be persuaded to approach.[1]

18 August

Meanwhile both corvettes had finished taking on water and their crews had been given a good rest. They had received some soap and were allowed to prepare their meal ashore, with an increased ration of wine, so that they could eat as they wished and stroll in the woods nearby. I thought it time, therefore, to employ the launches for more important work, as a continuation of our stay in this harbour was necessary, both to assess fully its political and geographical situation[2] and because we had some time yet to wait for the favourable season to return to the ports of San Blas and Acapulco.[3] Furthermore, we did not yet know how far the many channels of this

---

Maquinna's age in the mid 30s and the most authenticated portrait of him, reproduced in 1802 as fig. 12 in the atlas accompanying *Relación del viage hecho por las goletas Sutil y Mexicana* and now in the Museo Naval, is by Suria: AMN, carp. I (27) (Higueras, *Catálogo crítico*, no. 2936) and reproduced in Sotos, *Los pintores*, II, fig. 606 (plate 20). Although other chiefs were his rivals, there was recognition of his primary rank and status – the first determined by primogeniture, the second by wealth and behaviour appropriate in a chiefly person such as generosity in the potlatch and skill in the whale hunt: see Inglis, Robin, 'Maquinna of Nootka: Portrait of an Indian Chief on the Edge of the Empire', in Alejandro R. Díez Torre, Tomás Mallo, Daniel Pacheco Fernández, eds, *De la ciencia ilustrada a la ciencia romántica: actas de las II Jornadas sobre España y las expediciones científicas en América y Filipinas*, Madrid, 1995, pp. 32-52. In a different account Malaspina reported that the chief's appearance 'was not in accord with his status', finding him short and thin with flabby muscles. He also found his character 'difficult to decipher ... his personality seems simultaneously fierce, suspicious and intrepid.': Novo y Colson, *Viaje político-científico*, p. 354.

[1] Bauzá and his colleagues had wasted no time in beginning their surveying activities; they soon left Friendly Cove to visit Cook's 1778 anchorage off Bligh Island and various other islands at the entrance to the Sound. They then set out to explore Tahsis Inlet at the head of which was Maquinna's winter village. Tova confirmed that they found that the Indians 'had abandoned the houses and it was with difficulty that they approached one or other of the many who had fled into the surrounding woods.': Porrúa, *Diary of Tova*, p. 415.
  Following the murder of Callicum, and particularly the installation of the Spanish establishment in Friendly Cove, Maquinna's approach to the Spaniards was pointedly guarded. He consistently refused to set up another 'outside' village near Yuquot fearing for the security of his band's women. See Novo y Colson, *Viaje político-científico*, p. 359.

[2] Malaspina is referring to his obligation to report on the situation at Nootka in light of the recently signed Convention (October, 1790) that formed the framework of a peaceful settlement of the Nootka Crisis of 1789: see Cook, *Flood Tide of Empire*, pp. 146-249. Malaspina wrote a lengthy commentary on Spain's political and commercial position on the NW Coast vis à vis the other European powers; 'Examen político de las costas Noroeste de la América': AMN, MS 330; see also Novo y Colson, *Viaje político-científico*, pp. 364-74.

[3] From April to September calms and light variable winds are experienced along the coast of lower California and as far south as the Gulf of Panamá.

archipelago extended inland, among which many conjectures led to the possible existence of one or another that might communicate with other harbours to the south, and perhaps with the inner channels of the Strait of [Juan] de Fuca. Finally, the most recent voyage of the American Capitán Kendrick[1] who had made his way by inner channels to Puerto de la Esperanza,[2] and the surveys, still incomplete, of these waters by Comandante Eliza, provided new objects for the work of the launches.

These were put under the orders of Tenientes de Navío Don José Espinosa and Don Ciriaco Cevallos.[3] They were fully armed and had rations for nine days. Although having with them the excellent Stancliffe[4] sextant belonging to Don José Espinosa made it unnecessary to take the astronomical quadrant, the Ramsden sextant, pocket chronometer number 351 and the theodolite were added, for the sake of accuracy in the work undertaken. They were also accompanied by a marine and the coxswain of the frigate *Concepción*'s launch as interpreters and by Piloto Inciarte, who was entrusted with noting the observations and bearings. Finally their instructions required that the surveying should always be undertaken to the right[5] and should continue, weather permitting, until reaching the open sea. These being the circumstances, both launches set sail that morning with a fair breeze and were soon lost from sight, making for Captain Cook's anchorage,[6] designated as their point of departure, as our triangulation included it among the places reliably linked to the observatory.

The absence, just mentioned, of the launches, although essential for the reasons given above, also allowed us to deal with other objects, equally important concerned partly with our own immediate needs and partly with those of the presidio or establishment. For our part, therefore, today we began cutting a large quantity of firewood, employing marines and seamen alternately, with a sergeant or corporal, and a petty officer, in charge. The carpenters of both corvettes worked not only on the replacement of any spars no longer serviceable, including the fore topsail yard of this

---

[1] John Kendrick (1740-94), the American fur trader from New England who frequented Nootka Sound 1788-91. A short biography of Kendrick by Richard Pierce can be found in *Dictionary of Canadian Biography*, IV, Toronto, 1979, pp. 410-12. He formally purchased land in 'Mawinna Cove' (Marvinas Bay) from Maquinna and was blamed for trading firearms to the Indians.

[2] See p. 166, n. 1 above.

[3] The orders given to this well armed and provisioned exploring party can be found in English translation (from 'Instrucciónes de Malaspina a Espinosa y Cevallos para su comisión de reconocer el brazo de mar existente al E. del golfo de Nutka': AMN, MS 427, ff. 91^v-92^v) in Cutter, *Malaspina and Galiano*, pp. 84-5. Suria records that Espinosa and Cevallos, having joined the expedition in Acapulco, were put in command so as to have 'a chance to participate in the glories which others had gained by such commissions which being dangerous and adventurous were worthy of such honoured office[r]s.': Cutter, *Journal of Suria*, p. 76. Suria records in his journal that he set out with the group but no extant drawings or any other mention of his presence confirm this and his own account tantalizingly ends at this point. He may have started the excursion and returned early to Friendly Cove as the evidence suggests that he was there at least two days before Espinosa and Cevallos returned on 25 August. The two officers made a full survey of the sound and its principal channels: see plate 23.

[4] The English instrument maker John Stancliffe (fl. 1770-1810).

[5] Presumably to survey the sound in an anti-clockwise direction.

[6] Resolution Cove on the SE side of Bligh Island, near its southern extremity. Malaspina would not have known the exact place where Cook set up his observatory unless it was indicated to him by one of the natives.

corvette, but also on making a new topmast,[1] while some seamen were employed in a complete check and repair of the sails in use. Finally, the surgeon, Don Francisco Flores took charge of the production of a moderate quantity of beer from spruce needles, which along with the French we shall call *sapineta*, to serve both as an aid to the preservation of health and to show those in the establishment how to make it, as an efficacious and agreeable remedy during the coming winter,[2] since it seemed probable that the frigate *Aránzazu* would not return, and they would have to support themselves on salt meat.

With regard to the establishment, undoubtedly an important task for us was to provide assistance with our forges, blacksmiths and armourer, since these essential crafts were lacking there. Their weapons and farming implements were in a very poor state, as were other implements required by the community. Alférez de Navío Saavedra and Capitán Alberni informed us of everything needed for the security of the establishment and ships until next year.[3] We reduced our own needs and handed over to them any of our spares that were not absolutely necessary for us. These included some lengths of cloth and baize, wax, several pea-jackets, instruments for the sick bay,

---

[1] After the long and arduous voyage from the Gulf of Alaska during which the fore topsail yard of *Descubierta* had sprung and was in need of replacement (see p. 146 above) the expedition was fortunate to have a safe anchorage and the support of the Nootka establishment to effect some necessary repairs. Malaspina reported on the timber to be found at both Mulgrave and Nootka with comments as to its value for ship construction: 'Maderas de construcción, de fábricas y muebles': AMN, MS 126; see also Vol. 1 of this edition, pp. lxvii-lxviii.

Concurrent with this attention to the ships and the astronomical observations and scientific experiments being undertaken at the Observatory, Haenke made a collection of plants whose classification was later credited to Luis Neé: 'Noticias de algunos de las plantas que se encuentran en las cercanías del Puerto de Santa Cruz de Nutka': AMN, MS 2296, f. 302 (Higueras, *Catálogo crítico*, no. 1495). In addition, in a report written in Latin, 'Physica constitutio insulae Nootkae' Haenke noted details of the flora and fauna, fishes, birds, soils and beaches: AMN, MS 1316, ff. 144-145 (Higueras, *Catálogo crítico*, no. 1496). Malaspina noted that Haenke also transcribed the music of native songs. The manuscript of one of these 'The Song of Joy' - 'Canto de la Alegría en Nutka' - has survived: AMN, MS 567, f. 390 (Higueras, *Catálogo crítico*, no. 1494). As at Mulgrave, artifacts were collected for the Real Gabinete, some of which can be found today in the collection of the Museo de América; they include fishing hooks, harpoons, gambling sticks, hats and masks.

There was also time for relaxation. Suria noted in his journal, 'Every afternoon for a respite from our labors we went to walk on the beaches. They are composed of small stones of various kinds of marble and jasper, the greater part black, like all the coast. They were in spherical and elliptical form, very pleasing and for curiosity's sake all of them were collected.': Cutter, *Journal of Suria*, p. 76. 'Suria stones' are still easily identifiable on the open ocean beach by visitors to Yuquot today.

[2] Spruce beer was called *Sapineta canadiense* from the French 'sapinette canadienne' made in Eastern Canada from the needle-like leaves of spruce and fir trees. Although Francisco Flores is mentioned, it was the surgeon of the *Atrevida*, Pedro María González, who provided the recipe, later published in his *Tratado de las enfermedades de la gente de mar en que se exponen sus causas y los medios de precaverlas*, Madrid, 1805. Jacinto Caamaño, visiting Nootka in 1792, suggested that this beer was used successfully as an anti-scorbutic during the winter of 1791-2, which was fortunate because the *Aránzazu* did not return until May 1792.

[3] For the full extent of Malaspina's concern for the welfare of the establishment see Cutter, *Malaspina and Galiano*, pp. 108-9. This help, he noted elsewhere, was 'in truth a small repayment to the troops and seamen of the detachment for the generosity displayed to our people in supplying greens from the gardens and assistance with their daily tasks.': Novo y Colson, *Viaje político-científico*, pp. 191-2.

Plate 21. Nootka Chief and his Wife, by José Cardero. Museo de América, Madrid

the pilotos and the boatswain, a large quantity of tablets of bouillon,[1] a similar amount of flour, the medicines that the surgeons considered useful for this climate and for the more common illnesses, four casks of San Lucar wine and a month's worth of supplies to last until the return of the snow *San Carlos*. These provisions for the well-being of the seamen and troops were surely in accordance with the intentions of His Majesty in supporting his deserving local subjects, while giving us the certain satisfaction that the stay in Nootka of the corvettes *Descubierta* and *Atrevida* would prevent, in the following winter, the illnesses suffered in the past.

Due to a error, which was difficult to find, the astronomical observations of our first days were useless for rating the chronometers, as they were based on a chronometer whose results agreed with neither the astronomical clock nor with the other chronometers. The deduction of longitude had therefore to be referred to our noon observation on the 17th, when we had begun to be sure of the rate of the astronomical clock, and the results were as follows:

	Chronometer 71	Chronometer 72	Pocket chronometer 105
Longitude E of Mulgrave	13° 9′ 59″	12° 55′ 54″	
Therefore from Paris	129° 36′ 36″	129° 50′ 41″	129° 33′ 45″

According to the daily comparisons at sea, and even according to the first period for the present comparison, we were in no doubt that chronometer 72 was gaining, and therefore we thought it better to rely on longitude by number 71, particularly as it was corroborated by 105 as closely as we could wish. As for chronometer 61, it had stopped some time ago due to the breakage of a single part of its workings, doubtless one of those that had arrived somewhat damaged in Cádiz, where the watchmaker Lozano had had to repair it.

This longitude differed by more than a degree not only from the results of the lunar distances observed in June and July, but also from those we calculated on the following two days, 401 sets having been observed ashore in the best conditions, giving a longitude of 128°26′ [west of Paris].[2] It was by pure chance and indeed unlucky, that during all this period there was no occultation of a visible star by the Moon. Nor could we make any other observations to determine longitude by a more accurate method, although our lunar distances, which were taken in large numbers and with very reliable sextants, seemed to have very little possibility of error. Meanwhile Señores Vernacci and Concha occupied themselves in determining the latitude by different stars to the north and south of the zenith,[3] the comparisons of the pendulum were undertaken by alternating groups of

---

[1] No doubt a form of portable soup, similar to that carried by Cook on his three voyages, made by preparing a soup from the offal of cattle, flavoured with salt and vegetables and then evaporated down into hard, glue-like cakes.

[2] A reference in this sentence to Captain Cook's longitude of Port Mulgrave, which he never visited, is incomprehensible and so has been omitted.

[3] For full details of these observations in which the position of the observatory at Nutka is calculated as 49°35′15″N and 120°18′52″ west of Cádiz, see Espinosa, *Memoria* (1805), pp. 6–7 and Espinosa, *Memorias* (1809), 2nd memoir, pp. 61–3 and 105–8. The latter memoir also gives details of obseravations for magnetic variation and inclination (p. 117) and a discussion the observations to determine the force of gravity (pp. 190–212).

officers, until there was no doubt of the exact relationship of its oscillations to the mean time of the observatory [i.e. the astronomical clock], and we took numerous observations for variation, because of differences we found in the results.

19 and 20 August

Our peaceful relationship with the natives was now more solidly established, although at the cost of various presents which were requested equally by the chiefs and their subjects, as well as a continual contribution of biscuit. The canoes no longer fled at the sight of our boats and we were daily surrounded by fishermen, with many fish of excellent quality, while some of the natives spent the night beside the observatory. There were few chiefs who had not visited us. We had received the same attention from chief Macuina, although there was considerable mistrust in his face, but he did not allow his three wives, who accompanied him, to come on board.[1] Nor did I overlook on this occasion that he had his own personal interest with the sale of a slave girl that he had brought with him.[2] The officers from the frigate *Concepción* usually bought them either for two muskets or for one or two sheets of copper. Dealings of this kind, too closely linked to questions of religion, morality and policy for discussion in a few lines, were at the time quite common in the establishment. As many as twenty-two children of both sexes had already been transported to San Blas or were soon to be taken there, entrusted for their future education and upbringing to one or another person of His Majesty's ships always chosen from among those who were of good conduct and married, with families in the Department.

The presents given to Macuina and to those who accompanied, or had preceded him, brought increasing numbers of natives to gather on the ships in the following days. Among them the chief Tlupananú always stood out. On the afternoon of the 20th he handed over letters and reports given to him the night before by Tenientes de

---

[1] Maquinna first appeared on 18 August when he visited the *Descubierta*. The next day he went on board both corvettes. No doubt it was at this time that Suria drew his portraits of the chief – three in all, each similar – now in the collection of the Museo Naval: see Sotos, *Los pintores*, II, figs 606, 608, 609. Another drawing of a Nootka chief and his wife by Cardero, in the collection of the Museo de América, seems likely to be Maquinna as the Indian portrayed is the right age for the Chief : see Sotos, *Los pintores*, II, fig. 617 and plate 21. The visits of Maquinna, despite his apparent fear and initial distrust of the visitors, prompted Tova to echo his captain's sentiment that one of the principal goals of the visit – to improve Spanish-Native relations – was meeting with some success: 'Our efforts to gain the confidence and friendship of the natives had not been unfruitful … .There was scarcely any chief who had not visited us several times, including the principal chief Macuyna.': Porrúa, *Diary of Tova*, p. 417.

[2] The practice of purchasing children or accepting those who sought Spanish protection had become common at Nootka, ostensibly to save them from cannibalism and to give them the benefits of civilization and the Christian religion. Malaspina accepted the trade but was uneasy about it: see Vol. 1 of this edition, p. lxv and Novo y Colson, *Viaje político-científico*, p. 361.

The influential opinions of Cook and the fur trader Meares that Maquinna and other Nootkan chiefs practised cannibalism was shared by the residents of the Spanish establishment and many of the other traders who came to Nootka Sound. Malaspina investigated the charge and concluded that there was no hard evidence to support it: see Novo y Colson, *Viaje político-científico*, pp. 355–6, Vol. 1 of this edition, pp. lxv-lxv and Jim McDowell, *Hamatsa: the Enigma of Cannibalism on the Pacific Northwest Coast*, Vancouver, 1997, for a broad discussion of this controversial yet compelling subject, in which reference is made to contemporary 18th- and 19th-century accounts, and analyses the various views of modern scholars.

Navío Espinosa and Cevallos, who were making for Tahsis Inlet,[1] having been unsuccessful in their attempts to survey the two branches or channels to the left.[2]

In return for this constant friendship towards the Spaniards and for the recently delivered letters, Tlupananú requested, as well as other presents, a large sail made of light canvas for his canoe. However, our desire to see the manoeuvres of that canoe was such that it restrained the impulses of gratitude on this occasion, so we gave him a few trifles, or even only one, deferring the gift of the sail until we should see the craft on which it was to be used.

23 August

Very early on the morning of the 23rd he finally came to visit us with the canoe we wished to see.[3] It was paddled by some thirty men, whose chants, manoeuvres and skill surprised us in their first turns around the corvettes. There followed several dances performed by the paddlers themselves on board the corvette, and then on the beach by the observatory, after which all his men came on board the *Descubierta* to sing and dance as we wished, while Don Tomás Suria drew from life all their actions.[4] Finally we sent them off, well content with our presents, among which were, of course, the promised sails.

25 August

Both launches returned by midday on the 25th, having reached the anchorage by an offshore route, as their surveying had led them by an inner channel to Puerto de la Esperanza, off which the corvettes had been at dawn on the 12th. As the result of this expedition, the clarity of the weather corresponding to the energy and intelligence of Tenientes de Navío Espinosa and Cevallos, these zealous officers had, in the brief period of eight days, enlarged our hydrographic and physical knowledge of these parts to such an extent that they may now be considered almost completely charted.[5]

The terrain of the archipelago is truly remarkable. As many as five channels or arms, usually no more than a third of a mile wide, run inland in different directions,

---

[1] Malaspina's Canales de Tasis.

[2] This statement is at variance with the facts. Espinosa and Cevallos were instructed to survey Nootka Sound in an anti-clockwise direction and therefore the two channels referred to would be Muchalat and Tlupana Inlets, which would have been to their right hand side as they rounded Bligh Island. These two inlets were successfully and competently surveyed. See the resulting chart made by the expedition, 'Canales interiores de Nutka levantados por Espinosa y Cevallos en el viaje de las Corbetas', AMN, Sig. Borradores. Carpeta. XI. C-13 (37) (Higueras, *Catálogo crítico*, no. 1908).

[3] An illustration of Tlupananutl's large canoe was introduced by Cardero into his drawing of Friendly Cove: Sotos, *Los pintores*, II, fig. 603. The same image, larger and in more detail, was inexplicably superimposed onto the same artist's 1792 sketch of the short-lived Spanish establishment at Nuñez Gaona [Neah Bay] in Juan de Fuca Strait, during the voyage of the *Sutil* and *Mexicana*: see Sotos, *Los pintores*, II, fig. 642.

[4] Two drawings of the 'Dance on the Beach at Nootka' one from the land, the other from the water are in the collection of the Museo Naval: see Sotos, *Los pintores*, II, figs 604 and 605. For the former see plate 22.

[5] Details of the Espinosa/Cevallos survey of Nootka Sound can be found in Espinosa's 'Diario de la comisión de reconocimiento de los canales interiores de Nutka en unión de D. Ciriaco Cevallos y noticias de los habitantes de estas costas, su lengua, sus costumbres y leyes': AMN, MS 95, ff. 149-76 (Higueras, *Catálogo crítico*, no. 1498). For a version of the resulting chart see plate 23.

Plate 22. Dance on the beach in Friendly Cove, Nootka, by Tomás de Suria. Museo Naval, Madrid

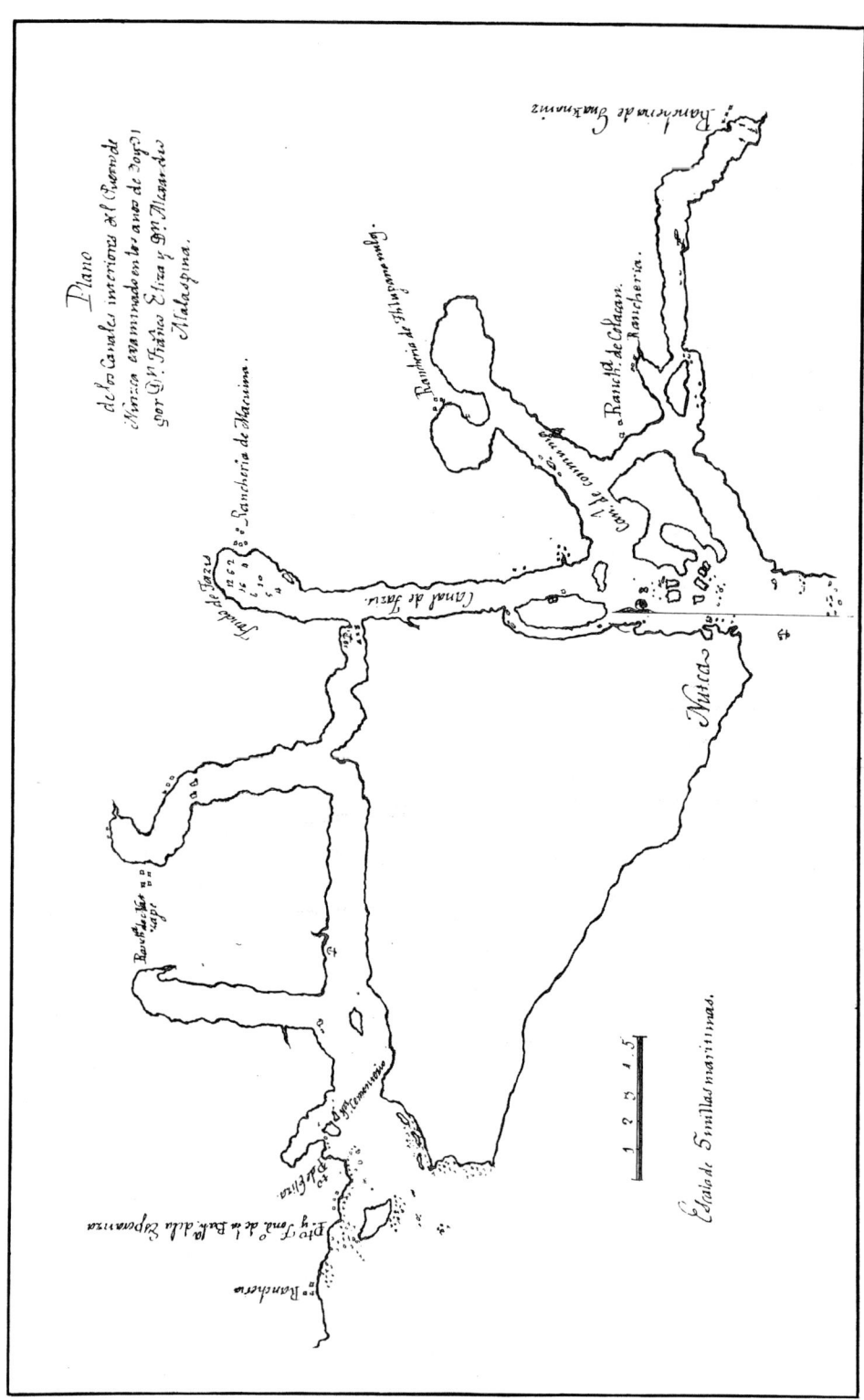

Plate 23. 'Plano de los Canales interiores del Puerto de Nutzca examinado en los años de 90 y 91 por Dⁿ Francisco Eliza y Dⁿ Alexandro Malaspina.' Courtesy of H. P. Kraus, Inc.

ending in small bays which are chosen by the natives for their settlements or habitations. The two channels to the east and ENE, the seaward ends of which had been investigated by Captain Cook, finish at Tlupananú's villages.[1] The channel leading to Puerto de la Esperanza [Port Eliza] divides into three branches to the north, the first, or easternmost, ends at Tahsis, residence of the supreme chief, Macuina, the second[2] leads toward the village of the subordinate chief, Natzapé,[3] and the third, although no smaller in size, appears to be deserted along both shores and around the bay at the end.[4] In all of the channels there is generally no bottom to be reached in sixty fathoms, even near the shore. This inconvenience can be overcome by running warps ashore to trees and rocks from any vessel wishing to enter them, proceeding either from Puerto de la Esperanza to Nootka or the other way.[5]

This harbour, the accurate plan of which is a real acquisition for hydrography, provides an excellent haven for vessels making for Nootka which find themselves driven to leeward by the easterlies. It combines good shelter with excellent holding, plenty of firewood nearby, and probably a watering place, there being various settlements of people in the area who were then occupied in fishing. The return of the launches leaves the trend of the coast between these two harbours equally well studied and confirms the true position of the shoal that we had seen on arrival, near which the above-mentioned officers had taken soundings, observed for latitude and took various bearings.[6] All this work was suitably tied in with daily observations for latitude, longitude and variation, taken from the same spot. They were then linked together with many other bearings, either taken on shore or confirmed by bases run with the log. Finally, for the plan of Puerto de la Esperanza, measuring a base with a surveying chain was not possible. Instead, not only was a base measured by log-line, but also by the speed of sound, with the time between the discharge and hearing the shot by chronometer, being measured twice (which agreed closely).[7]

Our launches, as their commanding officers reported, were at first received in the various settlements with signs of discontent and restlessness. In the village of Tlupananú (this chief being absent) they saw the women and children actually withdrawing while several men armed with sticks approached, deaf to any declarations of

---

[1] Muchalat and Tlupana Inlets.
[2] Zeballos Inlet. 'Canal de Efatizat' on the expedition's chart.
[3] Natzapé, a 'secondary chief' and brother-in-law to Maquinna became a favourite of Malaspina's officers. In a series of interviews just before the ships left Nootka, he provided details of the Indians' practices. (See p. 185, n. 3 below.) A preliminary sketch of him was made by Suria: see Sotos, *Los pintores*, II, fig. 610.
[4] Espinosa Inlet.
[5] Within the larger inlet the two officers identified and named Puerto Eliza (Port Eliza), another arm of Esperanza Inlet which they did not fully investigate. Here, on the NW entrance point to this port the Spaniards performed an act of possession.
[6] On their return to Friendly Cove from Esperanza Inlet via the open ocean, the two officers did not survey the large opening of Nuchatlitz Inlet. They did, however, fix the position of Inner Bajo Reef off Bajo Point. In 1778 Cook probably saw the larger Bajo Reef which is considerably farther out to sea. (Cook and King, *Voyage to the Pacific Ocean*, II, p. 265) The fact that a single reef only was placed on the charts of the respective navigators has led to some confusion; but it seems clear that they identified different parts of the shoal.
[7] The two measurements would have been made from each end of the base to cancel the effect of any wind.

peace and offers of presents. The number of armed men who appeared at Tahsis or Macuina's settlement was much greater, the natives, furthermore, took the precaution of firing several musket shots beforehand. Alarm had spread throughout the vicinity and the canoes stopped fishing at the moment of sighting them. Even after the two officers, in a show of confidence, jumped ashore alone, making the launches move a little way offshore, Macuina not only greeted them with a mixture of annoyance, coldness and fear, but also tried to demonstrate his power, showing them a gun rack holding fifteen muskets at his door, guarded by a native who stood beside it, leaning very ceremoniously on his weapon.[1]

This scene was enough, no doubt, to rouse the attention (and surprise) of our officers. Very soon, however, they had to attend to other spectacles worthy of greater admiration. The first of these was the sight of some panes of glass set up in Macuina's house[2] and then the pleasing face of his favourite wife. This was a young woman of twenty to twenty-five years, sister to Natzapé, who, for her affability, colouring and features, would stand out anywhere, even in places with well defined ideas about beauty. Meanwhile Macuina had become much more humane and pleasing, since he could not doubt the peaceful intentions of our officers. He took them to see his hoard of copper ingots and then accompanied them on a short walk, taking them passed the front of the huts, to visit Natzapé, his father-in-law.[3] Finally he decided to follow them right back to the launches, where he was presented with gifts, as was proper. From that moment our peaceful intentions were thoroughly understood and a solid and lasting friendship apparently established with much closer bonds between us.

Tlupananú did not share in this general mistrust. When he returned from fishing, although it was ten o'clock at night, he came alongside the launches with a confidence that demonstrated both the rectitude of his intentions and his conviction about our own. He paid them a visit early the next morning and only left when our officers set out for Tahsis. He must have feared that Macuina would be angered if he thought him to be either involved in or responsible for them going there. He took his leave with various excuses, although promising to deliver to me very soon the letter and credentials that they had entrusted to him.

Señores Espinosa and Cevallos carefully studied the number of inhabitants of the area, which formed, so to speak, the society subordinate to Macuina. They calculated that there were about four thousand, mostly reduced to living from fishing, which was not very abundant, particularly in winter, moving back and forth according to this necessity, towards the shore in summer and towards the inner channels in winter.[4]

---

[1] Tova noted that the sentry leaning on a musket 'looked as if he wished to imitate our sentries'; that the armoury and sentry were a sign of 'Maquinna's pride and superiority over the other chiefs' and that the chief 'was filled with vanity over the furnishing [of his house] with four window panes that the American Kendrik had installed for him and for which he had had to pay a good price.': Porrúa, *Diary of Tova*, p. 419.

[2] The interior of Maquinna's house was sketched by Antanasio Echeverría (Madrid, Archivo General y Biblioteca, Ministerio de Asuntos Exteriores) in September 1792 during the visit to Tahsis of Bodega y Quadra and Vancouver.

[3] This is presumably an error for brother-in-law.

[4] By the time of European contact the natives living in Nootka Sound, now the Mowachaht-Muchalaht of the Nuu-Chah-Nulth Nation, had developed a distinctive maritime culture based on a two-phase economic cycle. An 'outside' season began in February and March with whaling, the summer

To this information they added a study of the soil and vegetation, the geodetic location of several mountains inland and, finally, a visit to a cemetery on a deserted island,[1] all of which will allow us to give an accurate report of these lands, based on what we have learnt so far.[2]

26 and 27 August

With regard to this latter aim, the two days following the return of the launches, the 26th and 27th, were also extremely productive, as we were visited on board both corvettes by the two brothers, Natzapé and Nanikius, young men of remarkable talent, understanding and affability. They gave us information so clear and strange about their religion, origins, laws, customs and system of government, commerce and inland geography that we could hardly believe that we were understanding each other so quickly and that the door had been so easily opened to mysteries of the greatest importance. Among the many officers who, knowing the importance of these matters, naturally applied themselves with greater eagerness to extricating them from the obscurity which enveloped them, Teniente de Navío Don Antonio Tova will always deserve a special place in our report. His remarkable patience and affability, a fair knowledge of the language and, above all, a clear and orderly method of questioning, which guided us rapidly to the important scientific information that we shall set out clearly in the following chapters.[3]

---

bringing edible plants and berries, shore gathering and fishing for halibut, cod, herring and perch. Salmon spawning in the late summer signalled the move up the inlets for the 'inside' season and by September fishing in the numerous streams was in full swing. By mid November the salmon had been smoked and dried and the natives had settled into their winter villages: see Wayne Suttles, ed., 'Nootkans of Vancouver Island', *Handbook of North American Indians*, 7, 'Northwest Coast', Smithsonian Institution, Washington, D.C., 1990, pp. 391-411.

[1] Harbour Island which guards the entrance to Port Eliza (see p. 183, n. 5 above).

[2] Bustamante also carried out some ethnographic research. Attempting to confirm Cook's reports of cannibalism, the Spaniards discovered that this practice was a chiefly privilege. They learnt that the inhabitants believed in a creator-god but also worshipped the spirits of dead chiefs, that the common people spent the after-life in darkness, chiefs in the sky and chiefs' wives in a state of invisibility (in which they could sometimes be heard singing). Their enquiries about laws elicited that the death penalty applied in cases of repeated murder and adultery by males among the common people, whereas theft was punished by mutilation and exile. Succession to the throne was 'the same as among us' except that in default of an heir the people elected the founder of a new dynasty: Bustamante, *Diario general del viaje*, p. 271.

[3] Although the primary source for the history and culture of the natives of Nootka Sound at the end of the 18th century remains the *Noticias de Nutka* of José Mariano Moziño, the information gathered by the Malaspina expedition (like that of Cook thirteen years earlier) was substantial. There are, however, no 'following chapters' in this copy of Malaspina's journal. For results of the expedition's investigations it is necessary to refer to Tova's journal (Porrúa, *Diary of Tova*, pp. 420-22) and to Novo y Colson's edition of Malaspina journal and related documents: Novo y Colson, *Viaje político-científico*, pp. 353-62.

The written record describing the Nootka Indians is supplemented with six extant portraits which add to the artistic record already mentioned. There are portraits of four young girls by Suria and Cardero and similar pictures of an Indian with a herring rake by Bauzá and Suria: Sotos, *Los pintores*, II, figs 611-16.

One of the more interesting pieces of information learned from Natzapé and Nanikius was of a trade route across Vancouver Island which established contact with the 'Nuchimases' or Nimpkish Tribe of the Kwakiutl Nation: Porrúa, *Diary of Tova*, pp. 422-4 and Novo y Colson, *Viaje político-científico*, pp. 359-60. This was a 'grease trail' by which the Nimpkish supplied the Nootkans with eulachon oil and furs, and received European goods in return. In 1792, on the eastern side of Vancouver Island, George Vancouver found that this included arms: see Lamb, *George Vancouver's Voyage*, p. 627.

On the morning of the 27th we had another visit from Macuina, to whom we had sent various emissaries with invitations, hinting that we were anxious to ratify our friendship with him and to demonstrate, by means of gifts of great value, our desire for a solid and lasting peace between his people and that of our establishment. The conduct of the crews of the launches and the unvarying good treatment that the natives always received when on board the corvettes, could leave them in no doubt of the rectitude of our intentions, particularly as these were corroborated by our lack of insistence on buying furs and our prompt departure after taking on wood and water. So many motives and even more the hope of a fine present, had indeed had their effect on Macuina's sentiments, as his face now showed clearly the desired change of heart. He took several cups of tea on board the *Atrevida*, a custom now well-established among his relations and subordinate chiefs, his head adorned with a sort of strip of red cloth to which were sewn little stars of glass. He claimed that the fishing and his poor health had prevented him from visiting us more often. Finally he earnestly referred in the most vivid and noble terms to his present situation, which compelled him to live at some distance from the sea because we had settled on the site of his dwelling place. In consequence he did not have enough food, making him so weak and emaciated, although previously he had been strong and skilful enough to harpoon a whale by himself. Two canoe sails, four panes of window-glass, a sheet of copper, several *varas* of blue cloth and a few pieces of hardware, were the presents given him on board the *Descubierta*. On that occasion he confirmed the previous cession of the land for our present national establishment, assuring us that there would be lasting peace between us.[1] Finally on taking his leave, he showed by unmistakable signs that his gratitude and friendship were now as great as his anger and distrust had been at the beginning.

By this time all the instruments and stores had been taken on board and the crews of the launches had enjoyed a good rest and shore leave. The people were also in the best of health, and the officers Alberni and Saavedra, whose courtesies towards us had been from the first kind and constant, contributed to our well-being by giving us, for our supplies, most of the vegetables grown in the gardens, which until now we had all shared.

We therefore thought that it would be possible to set sail that very evening, with the first of the land breeze. To this end we arranged the ground tackle so as to lie on the seaward anchor alone.

In this regard, however, our hopes were ill-founded, depending too much as they did on the sailing qualities of the corvettes, since it was necessary to sail close hauled against a contrary current to clear the rocks near the point, from which we were only

---

[1] Maquinna's apparent acceptance of Spanish 'sovereignty' at Yuquot, no matter how suspect, was vital in the development of Spain's position vis à vis England in the aftermath of the Nootka Convention of 28 October 1790. Building on the efforts of Alberni, the successful Malaspina visit laid the groundwork for Bodega y Quadra's close alliance with Maquinna in the summer of 1792 and allowed the Spanish Commissioner, in his meetings with Vancouver, to pursue the strictest possible interpretation of British rights in Friendly Cove.

A year later Moziño could report as 'eternal' the Nootkan memory of Malaspina and Bustamante 'for the friendly and generous manner in which they behaved during the short time they remained among its inhabitants.': Engstrand, *Noticias de Nutka*, p. 80.

two ship's lengths when the anchor was up and down. The *Descubierta* set sail twice and twice she was set back towards the rocks, from which, however, they [the crew] were able to hold her off with the booms, as the bottom dropped off so steeply. The land breeze then freshened considerably and a warp that we had passed to the *Atrevida*, so that we could lie to her anchor, served only to make her drag her anchor in the same direction.

Towards midnight, therefore, having given up the idea of weighing anchor, we ran out some warps to keep us clear of the rocks and hold us in a better position, which we achieved without difficulty at about two in the morning, with both ships then settled in a reasonably safe position. We then sent the launch back to the frigate *Concepción* and allowed the men a good rest.

28 August
Having learnt from these difficulties, we cleared the harbour the following day by warping off when the land breeze was with us. Thus, after sunset, when we felt the first light airs from NE, we did not hesitate to get under way and set a course under full sail to clear the point and reefs[1] as quickly as possible.

---

[1] Yuquot Point and its off-lying reefs.

BOOK SEVEN

From Nootka Sound to Acapulco

CHAPTER 1

From Nootka Sound to Monterey

[28 August]
Although a fairly strong land breeze was blowing when we set sail from Nootka, we had no sooner completed the necessary work with the anchors and boats in the early hours of the night and made good a league on our course than the breeze began to drop. A fairly high sea from NW then threatened to set us onto the reefs off Estevan Point,[1] from which we were only two leagues distant at midnight, in a depth of thirty-two fathoms, sand. However, the outlook soon changed. With a light breeze from NNW and north favouring our SSW course from two in the morning, by sunrise we were well clear of the coast and able to begin running bases and our usual survey. Estevan Point then bore N52°E by compass five or six leagues distant, the land further east bore N87°E and the harbour entrance N15°E.

The coast, extending south from Nootka Sound as far as California, could now be seen in a very different light, with regard to the convenient management of our work, from that in which we had been obliged to view the more northerly coasts.[2] We were well aware that officers Martínez[3] and Quimper,[4] from the Department of San Blas, had sailed along the coast as far as the entrance to Juan de Fuca Strait during the previous year, that Teniente de Navío Eliza[5] was at present engaged in the same undertaking, that from there it was only a short distance to Puerto de los Mártires,[6] visited in 1775 by Comandante Bodega y Quadra; that in that same year Don Bruno

---

[1] The southern extremity of Hesquiat Peninsula about 13 miles south of the entrance to Nootka Sound. Named by Juan Pérez in August 1774 after Piloto Segundo Estéban José Martínez of the *Santiago*: see Beals, *Juan Pérez*, pp. 88–9. Cook's Breakers Point, a name which survived until 1849, when Pérez's name was restored on British Admiralty charts: John T. Walbran, *British Columbia Coast Names*, Vancouver, 1909, pp. 172–4.
[2] Malaspina was no longer looking for Ferrer Maldonado's supposed passage to the Atlantic.
[3] For Martínez see p. 54, n. 7 above.
[4] For Quimper see p. 54, n. 6 above.
[5] For Eliza see p. 169, n. 3 above. For an account of the Quimper and Eliza expeditions see Henry R. Wagner, *Spanish Explorations in the Strait of Juan de Fuca*, Santa Ana, Calif., 1933.
[6] Literally Port of the Martyrs, an unnamed indentation off the mouth of the River Quinault, south of Cape Elizabeth, situated 65 miles south of Cape Flattery, the southern entrance point of Juan de Fuca Strait. It was here that a boat's crew of the *Sonora*, commanded by Bodega y Quadra, was cut off and massacred in July 1775, while ashore seeking water and wood for the main topmast: Beals, *For Honor and Country*, pp. 74–8.

Hezeta[1] had continued these surveys as far as Trinidad Harbor[2] and that there it would then be possible to fix with confidence the starting point of the useful work done by Sebastián Vizcaíno in the year 1602.[3]

In view of this it would have been unwise to expose the corvettes to further risks, and to a further sacrifice of precious time, when the safety of navigation only required us to establish with greater certainty the direction of the coast, using the methods and the excellent instruments available to us. We therefore settled on a plan of keeping at a distance offshore that would put us in no danger either of grounding or of going off course. Thus we would be able to keep under way all night and during the day we would be able to repeat as many observations as possible, until we reached Cape Mendocino,[4] from which point our work would be carried out in more detail so as to provide all possible safety for navigation of the galleons from the Philippines and those of our San Blas vessels sent annually to relieve the presidios of California.

29 August
The morning, however, was extremely pleasant with a favourable sea breeze from nine o'clock. Being in the vicinity of Cayuclá[5] and Juan de Fuca Strait, it was too important to geography and trade for us to resist the lure of surveying, from close inshore, the stretch of coast that was now in sight. Therefore towards midday, in latitude 49°5′ and approximately on the meridian of Nootka Sound, we altered course to east and EbyN, so that by four in the afternoon we were only three leagues offshore.

The very clear weather on this course had enabled us, from two o'clock onwards, to see a vessel under full sail, close inshore, which after closing the coast, continued to the north close hauled. Having passed between a small island and the mainland,[6] she

---

[1] For Hezeta see, p. 58, n. 3 above.

[2] Trinidad Harbor, 110 miles south of Cape Blanco, named by Hezeta 11 June 1775 in honour of the feast of Santísima Trinidad: Beals, *For Honor & Country*, p. 63.

[3] On instructions from Gaspar de Zúñiga y Acevedo, Conde de Monterrey, Viceroy of New Spain, Sebastián Vizcaíno sailed from Acapulco on 5 May 1602 in the *San Diego*, accompanied by the *Santo Tomás* and *Tres Reyes*, to examine the coast to the north. After charting and naming San Diego Bay and refitting his ships in Monterey Harbor, named in honour of the Viceroy, he was forced to turn back when, on 19 January 1603 in 42°N, Vizcaíno sighted 'on the coast a cape of white earth close to some high sierras covered in snow. This was named [in honour of his personal saint] "Cabo Blanco de San Sebastián".': Henry R. Wagner, *Spanish Voyages to the Northwest Coast of America in the Sixteenth Century*, San Francisco, 1929, p. 253. This cape is possibly today's Point St George, 66 miles south of Cape Blanco. Malaspina was presumably hoping to identify where Vizcaíno was forced to turn back rather than his starting point. For a chart depicting Vizcaíno's discoveries see 'Carta de los reconocimientos hechos en 1602 por el Capitán Sebastián Vizcayno', chart no. 4 in the atlas accompanying *Relación del viage hecho por las goletas Sutil y Mexicana*. See also p. 195, n. 4 below.

[4] Cape Mendocino, probably named during the voyage of Juan Rodríguez Cabrillo in 1542–3 in honour of Viceroy Antonio de Mendoza, is the turning point for all vessels bound north or south along the coast. It also lies in the latitude of great climatic change. The winds do not blow so strongly south of the cape, where fog is also more prevalent, while north of the cape rainfall increases rapidly: *Pacific Coasts of Central America and United States Pilot*, Taunton, 1995, pp. 340–41.

[5] One of a number of alternative spellings of Clayoquot Sound on the west coast of Vancouver Island, south of Nootka Sound: Wagner, *Cartography*, pp. 353 and 440.

[6] The Spanish ships were off Clayoquot Sound, home of the Indian chief Wickaninnish and a favoured port of call for the fur traders after 1785. Its entrance is guarded by numerous small islands. The continent was of course not the mainland but Vancouver Island. It would be another year before the exploration of Vancouver and the joint exploration of Galiano and Valdés would establish its insularity.

finally anchored in the lee of some islets, or rather rocks, among which we could not make out a harbour or any gathering of natives, although we were only some five or six miles distant. From mid-afternoon, when still under sail, this vessel had hoisted an American ensign, which appeared consistent with her rigging, lines and gear. This gave us the information that, in addition to the *Columbia* and Captain Kendrick's *Lady Washington*, there was another vessel of that nationality in these waters destined for the fur trade.[1] We responded immediately with our ensign and, to avoid creating the suspicion of any aggressive intention if we came too close to the coast, we altered course so as to stand somewhat offshore rather than giving way to a navigator's natural impulse to approach, examine and speak to those who share the same lot amid solitude and dangers.

This stretch of the coast, to the SE of Estevan Point, consists of thickly forested islands, with various bays which, from their situation, look as though they might be good harbours. These islands are fringed by a number of small needle-shaped and barren rocks somewhat offshore. Behind the islands the mainland consists of low hills, free of snow, with many peaks making four parallel ranges running approximately north to south. For the most part they are thickly covered with trees, which also adorn the offshore islets. If we consider the gathering of foreign vessels in Cayuclá for the acquisition of furs, or the continual enmity between the peoples living south of Nootka and the inhabitants of this archipelago, we can only conclude that the population in these parts is not small and that in fact this may be the beginning of the larger numbers found south of Juan de Fuca Strait.

At the close of the afternoon we were in twenty-five to thirty fathoms, coarse dark sand, some three leagues offshore, with an observed variation of about 20°. Having sounded thirty-one fathoms, rock, at ten in the evening, we steered somewhat more southerly courses, as the currents appeared to be setting us towards the entrance to Juan de Fuca Strait. By midnight we obtained a sounding of sixty fathoms and at dawn the next day we were about five or six leagues offshore, in depths of fifty-eight fathoms, rock.

30 August

We were now in sight of the celebrated Juan de Fuca Strait, the mouth of which is some five or six leagues wide. It terminates on the one side in a point, fringed by hummocks or boulders which extend from a range of some height[2] and on the other, or southern side, there appears to be a fairly large, high island,[3] the extremities of which bore from 49° to 55° in the first quadrant.

The haze increased as the day advanced, obscuring the clear view of the coast, and

---

[1] Malaspina was mistaken, he had actually sighted the American fur-trading vessel *Columbia*, Captain Robert Gray, and not an additional American vessel. One of Gray's officers, John Box Hoskins reported on 29 August that 'at three in the afternoon saw two sail to the westward standing to the eastward': Frederic W. Howay, ed., *Voyages of the Columbia to the Northwest Coast 1787–1790 and 1790–1793*, Massachusetts Historical Society, Boston, 1941, p. 238. The American *Lady Washington*, Captain John Kendrick, was indeed also engaged in trading for furs on the coast in the summer of 1791.

[2] Possibly Bonilla Point, Punta de Bonilla on Quimper's survey, a copy of which Malaspina probably had on board the *Descubierta*: see Wagner, *Spanish Explorations*, f.p. 82.

[3] Tatoosh Island off Cape Flattery, the southern entrance point of Juan de Fuca Strait.

since the outlook was not promising we kept our distance offshore, abandoning, not without hesitation and regret, this entrance so important for hydrography and the opening (as had been imagined in days past) of a new communication between the Pacific and Atlantic Oceans in this latitude.[1]

Light and variable airs soon set in from all points, interspersed with many calms and an almost constant mist, which was so thick, particularly at night, that we were often obliged to sound the bell on both ships in order to keep company. The breezes tended to settle in the first and second quadrant. We were continually out of sight of land, although at times the haze seemed to indicate that it was near and, guided by the lead, we tried to keep in depths of not less than sixty fathoms, maintaining our course under all possible sail.

3 September

When the moderate breeze shifted to the north at noon on the 3rd, promising better conditions for the following days, our latitude was 45°3' and our longitude 1°40' east of Nootka, variation 17°30'NE, our distance offshore being fifteen to twenty leagues. In this position we resumed our survey of the coast, making our way towards it during the following afternoon and night, although taking some care with our course because of the haze which enveloped us again. At about midnight both corvettes obtained sounding of forty-seven fathoms, fine sand. We were surrounded by considerable numbers of bonito and albacore, of which we had caught a great many since the night we had left Juan de Fuca Strait. At times there was a strong smell of shellfish, and at others we were accompanied by *aguas malas*[2] or molluscs of the same species that Don Tadeo Haenke had studied in the Gulf on our northern passage.[3]

4 September

At dawn on the 4th the sky was quite clear and accordingly, having sighted the coast six or seven leagues off, we were able to begin measuring bases and repeat our observations. The latitude of 43°50' that we observed at noon left us in no doubt that the stretch of coast was the same as that sighted by Captain Cook between Cape Perpetua and Cape Flattery, ending at Cape Foulweather, the description of which, as was that of the rest of the coast, could not have been more clear and accurate.[4] The English captain was not mistaken in believing, unlike others, that what appeared to be banks of ice were actually ravines. In fact, the entire coast is intersected by gullies, or rather

---

[1] A reference to the apocryphal voyage of Juan de Fuca in 1592, which was not entirely discounted until the surveys of Vancouver and Galiano and Valdés in 1792: see John Kendrick, trans. and ed., *The Voyage of the Sutil and Mexicana 1792: The Last Spanish Exploration of the Northwest Coast of America*, Spokane, 1991.

[2] Literally bad waters, possibly plankton which is sometimes killed more or less suddenly by changes in sea temperature, producing dirty-brown or grey-brown discolouration and 'stinking water': *The Mariner's Handbook*, Taunton, 1979, p. 88.

[3] See p. 91, notes 3 and 4 and p. 92, n. 1 above. Malaspina was off an open stretch of coastline at the time.

[4] Cook spent most of the month of March 1778 examining this part of the coast, naming Cape Foulweather after the very bad weather he encountered soon after he sighted it, Cape Perpetua on account of its being sighted on the day of St Perpetua, an African martyr, and Cape Flattery because it 'flattered us with the hopes of finding an harbour': Cook and King, *Voyage to the Pacific Ocean*, II, p. 263.

large patches of white sand, along the shore. It is of medium height further inland, rather uneven, thickly forested, with various small ranges of hills which join and finish at some higher mountains to the north. Although we were only four leagues offshore we no longer obtained soundings with eighty fathoms of line. Variation seemed to have decreased to 16°. There were a great many whales and seals swimming about us, the former particularly being much larger and more numerous than those we had seen at higher latitudes.[1]

To the view of the coast and a fair breeze from the north and NNW was added in the afternoon the opportunity to observe, much to our satisfaction, a series of distances from the Sun to the Moon. The results, both in this corvette and in the *Atrevida*, were entirely consistent with each other and with the chronometers, thus differing considerably with the longitude observed in Nootka. This result was confirmed on board the *Descubierta* by other observations made the previous afternoon, which were repeated on the 6th. The discrepancy of more than one degree between the longitudes, either by the lunar distances alone, observed during the waxing and waning quarter,[2] or by the chronometers, was to cause us ever more surprise each day, as the results which should have dispelled our doubts only increased them.

The settled breeze from north and NNW, and the surveying we had carried out this day allowed us to sail through the following night with greater accuracy and confidence, even though we had no soundings at all. We passed through several shoals of fish and tide-rips, without losing for one moment the company of the bonito and whales. Finally, at dawn on the 5th, we found ourselves two or three miles from a large group of small islands which fringed a cape running well out to sea. We thought it must be Comandante Hezeta's Cabo Diligencia.[3] The *Atrevida* sounded fifty fathoms, rock, and, following the course required by the trend of the coast, we began the survey that was to lead us to Cape Blanco[4] and Río de Martín de Aguilar.[5]

The coast that we were now examining was high and tree-covered, forming as

---

[1] For a general account of Spanish exploration and charting of the coast of Oregon see Donald C. Cutter, 'Spain and the Oregon Coast', in Thomas Vaughan, ed., *The Western Shore: Essays Honoring the American Revolution*, Portland, Oreg., 1976, pp. 28-46.

[2] Presumably some days before or after the full Moon when the distance between the Sun and the Moon was less than 120°, the maximum angular distance that can be measured with a sextant.

[3] Today's Cape Blanco: see Beals, *For Honor & Country*, p. 147, n. 62. See also n. 4 below. Cape Blanco, which is fringed by various above-water rocks and islets, projects 1½ miles from the general line of the coast.

[4] According to Wagner Cabo Blanco was 'a favorite name in the imaginary geography of the north-west coast'. The name appears to have appeared first on Ortelius's 'Maris Pacifici' of 1589, where it was placed in 33°N. In other maps its position varied from 30° to 58°N: Wagner, *Cartography*, pp. 432-3. In his instructions Vizcaíno was given permission 'to pass beyond Cabo Mendocino as far as Cabo Blanco': Wagner, *Spanish Voyages*, p. 178. See also p. 192, n. 3 above.

[5] Martín de Aguilar commanded the *Tres Reyes*, during Vizcaíno's expedition, but the ships got separated in a storm, during which Aguilar died. Estéban López then took command of the *Tres Reyes* and on the way south reported that he had discovered a large river, which was named Río de Martín Aguilar in honour of the dead captain. This discovery gave rise to the idea of a great river north of Cape Mendocino. Hezeta searched in vain for it in 1775: see Beals, *For Honor and Country*, pp. 89-91. The identity of this river is uncertain: see Cook, *Flood Tide of Empire*, pp. 13-14 and Lamb, *George Vancouver's Voyage*, p. 494, n. 2.

many as three ranges running north-south and rising gradually in height. Several prominent capes allowed the appropriate hydrographic observations to be made, but the shore appeared difficult of access, being fringed with large rocks, among which we saw, before midday, some which were more than three leagues offshore with channels between them that seemed fairly clear. By this time we were in no doubt that a cape lying to our east, fringed by needle-shaped rocks and not far south of the mouth of a large river, was the Cape Blanco of Martín Aguilar.[1] We therefore saw that Comandante Bodega y Quadra's suspicions that such a river did exist in the short stretch of coast near the parallel of 42°, which he had not been able to examine, were well founded.

At noon our latitude was 41°59' and our longitude 2°11' east of Nootka; variation 15°45'. At the time no bottom with obtained with eighty fathoms of line, although we were no more than two miles from the small islands and boulders already mentioned.

We hoped that afternoon to get a view of Trinidad Harbor which Comandante Hezeta visited. Considering just the breeze, which was fresh and fair, it seemed that we would achieve this modest desire. However, a dense haze soon disillusioned us and throughout the afternoon we could see nothing of the land beyond the shore or most of the coast, having to sail from one conspicuous point to the next simply to confirm the trend of the coast.

6 September

By dawn the following day we could trim our sails and adjust our course to bring us into sight of Cape Mendocino. The strong breeze continued to blow, causing some minor damage to the running rigging of the studding sails. The weather was hazy and the current setting to the east so that the view of the coast at daybreak, and the longitude observations made later, convinced us that we had accumulated a considerable error during the previous night.

Cape Mendocino must be considered the true final point of the surveys made by Sebastian Vizcaíno, for although the *fragata* in company with him[2] reached Cape Blanco and the mouth of Río de Martín de Aguilar this voyage was made with too much risk and haste to be able to describe the intermediate coast with the same scrupulous care and accuracy as the *Almirante*[3] had displayed as far as Cape Mendocino. However, owing either to the natural loss of the original documents or the negligence of the navigators who followed him, we could see with much regret that on the various manuscript charts of the Californian coast, the directions, distances and configuration of the coast were at this point very different from these in the original description. For our part, having to validate these for the sake both of safe navigation

---

[1] Malaspina's subsequent noon latitude of 41°59' indicates that he was in fact off Cape Sebastian in 42°19'N, a name given by the US Coast survey at the suggestion of George Davidson, probably because its latitude corresponds closely to that of Cabo San Sebastián on some of the Spanish maps, especially those of Hezeta of 1775: Wagner, *Cartography*, p. 416. Rogue River enters the sea 6 miles north of Cape Sebastian.

[2] The *Tres Reyes*: see p. 195, n. 5 above.

[3] This appears to be a lapse by Malaspina. In fact for this expedition Vizcaíno had been appointed as general and in overall command of the voyage. His *almirante* or second in command of the fleet was Toribio Gómez de Corbán. In his 'Disertación' (Appendix 2, p. 474) Malaspina correctly describes Vizcaíno as General.

and the good reputation of that enlightened navigator, we have begun by restoring the name Cape Mendocino to the northern extremity the reddish headland known in recent times as Punta Gorda, and we have designated the other extremity with the name Cape Vizcaíno,[1] as, despite this *almirante*'s skill, his modesty had prevented him from naming any point on this coast after himself.

Before seven o'clock in the morning not only was the islet to seaward of the cape clearly in sight, but also a shoal not far off it, two or three miles from us.[2] At the same time the *Atrevida* sounded forty-eight fathoms. As we continued surveying the headland, the breeze slackened almost at that moment and the fairly heavy westerly swell seemed to be setting us onto the coast. Our manoeuvres until noon were largely directed towards standing offshore, from which we were at this time some seven miles, obtaining no bottom with 120 fathoms of line. Our latitude was 40°20', our longitude 2°2' east of Nootka and variation 15°30'NE.

By noon various bearings taken to the shore had convinced us that the current was setting us to the south.[3] This current was further confirmed in the early hours of the afternoon when, on a southerly heading, we tried in vain to make use of some light airs. Even so we were some four leagues offshore. Finally some light airs from NW and NNW gave us steerage way from four in the afternoon, allowing us to consider ourselves a safe distance offshore by sunset.

At nightfall the light airs in the fourth quadrant dropped again, and were then succeeded by a moderate breeze in the second quadrant. The sky and horizon were immediately obscured by haze, making it a little difficult to keep company with the *Atrevida*. We hauled the breeze on alternate tacks, as suited our course, without standing too close inshore. When this breeze also finally dropped during the night of the 7th, we could make good our course once more with light airs from NW, with the intention of identifying Point Reyes[4] and the vicinity of San Francisco Harbor.

8 and 9 September

In spite of strong and settled NW winds, the haze did not clear. On the morning of the 9th it concealed Point Reyes from us entirely, although we believed ourselves to be very close to it, given the large numbers of whales, seals, otters, geese etc and the depth of sixty-five fathoms, ooze, that we obtained at 10 o'clock. We hove-to at times, and at others we altered course to make use of any breaks in the cloud. At last, after eleven o'clock, we were fortunate enough to be able to use some clearings to observe the necessary altitudes for hour angles and at the same time, despite the haze, we managed to take a latitude observation when we sighted all of the coast running north from Point Reyes past Río Grande de San Sebastián or Bodega Harbor.[5]

The breeze was now fresher and, with the coast in sight a short distance off, this enabled us to be abeam of Point Reyes before two o'clock that afternoon. At that

---

[1] The name Punta Gorda has, however, survived, together with Cape Mendocino and Cape Vizcaino; Cape Gorda being 11 miles south and Cape Vizcaino 52 miles SSE, respectively, of Cape Mendocino.
[2] Blunts Reef lies 2¾ miles west of Cape Mendocino.
[3] Off Cape Mendocino the current sets to the south at about ¼ knot.
[4] Point Reyes, a bold, dark rocky headland, 26 miles WNW of the Golden Gate.
[5] Bodega Bay, 20 miles north of Point Reyes.

time it was bearing N55°E, four to five miles distant when, according to the *Atrevida*'s signals we remained in depths of forty-four to forty-five fathoms, ooze. We were then sailing among molluscs in numbers beyond description.

Our course, taking us between the *farallones*[1] off San Francisco and the mainland, led us naturally to spend the remaining hours of the afternoon making a good survey of these *farallones* and the harbour entrance,[2] including the stretch of coast extending to the west as far as Point Reyes and to the SE to Punta de Almejas.[3] The bases neatly linked various points together, while the mist, although thick in parts, allowed us a good view of the coast. Even though we could not make any longitude observations during the afternoon, we could none the less flatter ourselves that our work had been done with more than a common degree of accuracy.

Until now our usual method of sailing had preserved us from all those incidents to which a vessel is naturally subject when compelled never to sail far from the coast, and a coast which had not yet thoroughly surveyed. To extreme vigilance under easy sail and steering with care at night, we also took constant soundings and paid attention to the information and surveys of the navigators who had preceded us, considering and comparing them whenever possible. We had not yet been able to compare Vizcaíno's sailing directions in such detail, as Cape Mendocino was the only place so far included in his descriptions. We found a considerable error in his latitudes, but that was hardly surprising, given the instruments used for this purpose in the last century. We would therefore have to continue taking the same precautions, probably with the same success, had we not suffered a mishap that was difficult to guard against.

In Nootka the commanding officer of the frigate *Concepción*, without any prompting on my part, had offered me one of his petty officers who, having sailed these coasts for the lengthy period of twenty-one years, could be considered a local pilot and could therefore serve me in that capacity during the passage along the coast of California. In these circumstances it would have been careless either to doubt his ability or not to take him on board. So far his responses and reasoning (as his practical knowledge began at Point Reyes) had given me no cause for anything but satisfaction with the measures he took. The man had twice anchored in San Francisco Harbor and he listed the names of the surrounding points one by one, describing very confidently the courses taken by the San Blas ships from Point Reyes to Punta de Almejas, and from there to Point Año Nuevo, the northern extremity of Monterey Bay.

It was already six o'clock in the evening when we set a course for Punta de Almejas, according to his information. Being prevented by extremely heavy mist from examining the trend of the following stretch of the coast, we had for the first time to follow his instructions on the choice of courses to steer so as to be within sight of Point Año Nuevo at dawn. With a fresh breeze and in depths of twenty-five fathoms, sand, we steered SE, so as to increase the depth to forty fathoms, while sailing two or

---

[1] The Farallon Islands, two groups of small rocky Islands, between 18 miles south and 14½ miles SSW of Point Reyes.
[2] The Golden Gate.
[3] Point San Pedro, a dark rocky promontory, 13 miles south of the Golden Gate.

three leagues from the coast, which is low and consists entirely of sand and consequently so is easily obscured or misidentified in the mist.

Fortunately Piloto Maqueda, when comparing the latest bearings on one of the many charts that we had to hand, found such a discrepancy in the bearings and distances that he thought it best to inform me and even to insist that the soundings that I had ordered for eight o'clock should be brought forward to seven o'clock. We found, indeed, no more than eighteen fathoms, sand, which, according to the information we had, placed us only one league offshore, convincing us that we had misidentified Punta de Almejas and that our course was taking us onshore. We altered course immediately to SbyW and fired pistol shots to advise the *Atrevida* of our course and of the need to follow us. The fresh breeze, the decidedly heavy mist, the time difference in altering our respective courses and the difficulty of determining a true bearing by sound alone, now caused the corvettes to become separated. Thus, despite firing our guns, with the *Atrevida* sailing closer to the wind, by nine o'clock that night we had lost company.

Our heading took us gradually into a depth of forty fathoms and by ten at night we were once again able to alter course parallel to the coast in the hope of sighting Point Año Nuevo at dawn. At half past one, the mist having cleared somewhat, we also sighted the *Atrevida* and joined company with her. Soon afterwards, having got clear of depths of sixteen to seventeen fathoms in which we found ourselves again, we finally sighted a low point of land at five in the morning, during a break in the clouds, which we thought to be Point Año Nuevo. We immediately closed it to a distance of one and a half miles, when the *Atrevida* signalled to us that they had sounded thirty-five fathoms, upon which we altered course to continue our survey of the coast, for we had so much information at our disposal that instead of easing our path to Monterey Harbor it actually made it harder to find.

10 September

Not even its latitude had been positively determined since there was a difference of 10′ between the charts and log books in San Blas, the harbour plan of the port communicated by Piloto Tovar to Mr Dalrymple, who had sent it to me already engraved,[1] and the chart drawn up by Piloto Mendizábal on his passages from Asia to

---

[1] On 14 January 1789 Alexander Dalrymple published a sheet of plans 'taken from a Spanish MSS communicated by John Henry Cox Esqr.', one of which was titled 'Plan of Monterey on California by Don Josef Tobar y Tamariz, 7th December 1786'. This sheet, together with several other charts of the NW Coast of America published by Dalrymple, was probably obtained in London for the expedition before its departure from Cádiz through the good offices of Teniente de Navío José Mendoza y Ríos, the noted mathematician and astronomer, who lived in London for many years. José Tovar y Tamáriz was brought from Callao by Bodega y Quadra in 1778. In 1789 he served under Martínez in the *Princessa* and was present at the confrontations with the British fur traders in Nootka, being in charge of the party which arrested the *Iphigenia*. Later that year he took the *Argonaut* to San Blas with a prize crew. In 1794, in command of the *Aránzazu*, he made two round trips to the NW Coast with supplies and in 1796 he was sent north in command of the *Sutil* with instructions to reconnoitre the coast as far as Bucareli Bay. Unfavourable weather forced him to call at Nootka, where he befriended Thomas Muir, a passenger on board the American trader *Otter*. On his return to San Blas, Tovar was arrested and court-martialled, when he was sentenced to exclusion from further positions in command: Cook, *Flood Tide of Empire*, pp. 93, 153, 177 and 428.

New Spain.¹ As for the sailing directions and the original depiction of the coast by Vizcaíno himself, it seemed absurd to consult them at this time when we had so many recent reports at hand, which, even if relating to a different date could never be bettered by the judgments of an ancient navigator, deprived of all the means which contribute so greatly to the reliability of hydrographic work today. As may be imagined, with such a profusion of possibilities we did not hesitate to heed the opinion of our pilot, who, although he might have been mistaken in the area of San Francisco Harbor, having not frequented it in the last six or seven years, would never mistake the entrance to Monterey which he had entered almost every year, and particularly in the past year, 1790, under the orders of Teniente de Navío Don Salvador Fidalgo.

The weather prospects had now improved, much of the mist had cleared enabling the Sun to light up a considerable stretch of the nearby coast, so that nothing could remain concealed of the features which distinguished one spot from another, from which we could therefore make a choice unhindered by Delphic ambiguity.

It was clear that the port and the site of the presidio were beside some hills which then lay ahead, that we were now abeam of Pajaro River, off which Don Salvador Fidalgo had mistakenly anchored the year before and, finally, that if we fired a blank from a cannon this would certainly be answered from the presidio and we would then know its whereabouts. The cannon was fired, the national ensigns were hoisted and our attention was indeed proportionate to our hopes for the occasion. Meanwhile the mist cleared more and more and the light, fair breeze soon gave us a sight of new objects. We therefore passed the hills, the river disappeared from view and a long stretch of the coast was revealed, showing not the slightest sign of a bay. We were then only two miles offshore in depths of eighteen to twenty fathoms, shell, and the land in sight was steep-to at the coast with low hills inland, the lack of trees and the sparseness of the vegetation giving an arid and desolate appearance.

However, we came to consider this new mistake as more of a stroke of luck than a misfortune as we were able to survey the coast in great detail, the longitude observations allowing us to determine its direction exactly relative to the nearby Monterey Harbor. We also acquired clear evidence for distrusting the local pilot and, above all, being now certain of being north of Monterey, we could not doubt that we would soon sight it, favoured as we were by the beautiful clarity of the day and by the light fair breeze from WNW and NW. Towards nine o'clock in the evening this dropped and even left us for a brief time without steerage way, but by ten o'clock we were making two to three knots again, with which we continued under way, a short distance offshore, without seeing the slightest sign of the anchorage.

Finally, at half past eleven, we no longer doubted that we were in the large bay which lies between Point Año Nuevo and Point Pinos.² We had already made considerable easting and although we were a long way from the shore opposite, which we saw to be backed by hills of medium height, we took bearings to several hills to the south, not doubting that they were the ones near Point Pinos and the presidio of

---

¹ For Mendizábal and his chart see p. 38, n. 3 above.
² The northern and southern entrance points of Monterey Bay, with the *presidio* close north of Point Pinos.

Monterey. This belief was supported by the latitude of 36°49′ observed at noon, in soundings of [blank] fathoms, ooze, and thus it seemed that, steering towards the last land sighted and taking the precaution of firing a few blank cannon shots, we would soon be able to continue in perfect safety.

However, we were fated to fall into a further series of almost inevitable errors in our conception of this locality. After midday the breeze freshened considerably and at the same time the sky and horizon became covered in a thick mist, which according to reports was almost constant. We thought it best, therefore, to hasten our arrival at our destination before the mist grew thicker and before the current could upset our dead reckoning. We were aware that as soon as we encountered the seaweed off the Pinos coast,[1] we could make for the anchorage, and that the presidio was always very prompt in responding to cannon shots. Indeed, when we fired the first blanks at half past one, we heard them answered from the SE, although at a considerable distance. we were therefore able to continue at a speed of six to seven knots on the same southerly course that we had held since noon, with the same purpose of approaching Point Pinos.

As we proceeded, however, we felt more and more conscious of not knowing the true distance from the anchorage to Point Pinos nor the latitude of either. Since the breeze continued strong and the mist extremely heavy, we thought it better to depend on cannon fire and a good lookout than on dead reckoning and bearings. Consequently we shortened sail, the cannons were fired frequently, and finally, at about a quarter past two, we altered course to east, as the answering shots from the presidio, although distant, were perceived to be from that direction. There was no time to keep to this last course for long, for almost at the same moment we sighted at about two miles a short stretch of coast, with a few breakers, bearing from SE to south, which the local pilot, although not asked, immediately identified as Point Pinos and insisted that we should close it so that it could serve as a marker in case the coast were hidden again.

Everything seemed to confirm this suspicion, above all my belief that the coast running out to the west was Point Pinos itself. We altered course to south, therefore, having sounded forty fathoms, shell, and quickly approached to within a mile of the said point, the coast now very close abeam, bearing ENE. This position allowed for new possibilities, even though the mist continued heavy, among which I finally thought it most plausible that we had passed Point Pinos and were now in Carmel Bay, where I knew other ships had anchored in the same circumstances as we were in at present. In this belief, with soundings of twenty-five to thirty fathoms, sand and shell, I ordered an anchor to be dropped with the intention of returning to the anchorage off Monterey as soon as either circumstances or more tranquil conditions revealed the true position of the corvettes. As the *Atrevida* followed our manoeuvres exactly, the corvettes were now anchored a mile and a third off the shore, which we could see to

---

[1] According to Captain Beechey, '... some immense beds of sea weed (*Fucus pyriformis*) lie off the coast [near Point Pinos], and are so impenetrable that they are said to have saved several vessels which were driven into them by the swell during calm and foggy weather', F. W. Beechey, *Narrative of a Voyage to the Pacific and Beering's Strait ... in the Years 1825, 26, 27, 28*, London, 1831, p. 408.

be entirely lined with reefs, with the most westerly point now bearing south and the breakers running from north to NE.¹ A high sea was running from NW to SW, the breeze still fairly strong and our hopes of the mist clearing more and more remote.

The examination of our noon bearing,² our subsequent course, and the confused ideas that came to mind, soon supported my first belief that we had passed Point Pinos, and that this was the same point now bearing NE two miles distant. I recognized furthermore that our present anchorage could not be more exposed, since both the bottom, which we found to be extremely uneven and suspect, and the types of fish that we caught, which were typical of a rocky bottom. So at about half past three in the afternoon, although the breeze was falling and the sea very high and contrary, I signalled to the *Atrevida* that we would set sail, deciding that the risk of losing an anchor and cable was better than being driven completely to leeward of the harbour. This manoeuvre was extremely hazardous because of the difficulty, with a heavy swell from the SW, of being driven to port, the anchor being set out to that side, to which was then added the anchor pulling off the bottom before it was up and down. With so many difficulties that could not be overcome under sail alone, no sooner had the anchor began to drag than we saw that we were being driven to starboard onto a lee shore. It was then necessary to pay out cable again and signal to the *Atrevida* my intention of remaining here until conditions improved.

The commanding officer of that corvette, when informed of this decision, which he also deemed necessary and even commendable, used the last of the daylight to send Teniente de Fragata Don Francisco Viana in the pinnace to tell me that the cable of their main anchor had parted on anchoring. He was now lying to the second anchor, the loss of which would have considerable consequences if he were forced to cut the cable. For this reason he required further instructions, although he did not doubt the need to cut the cable, while making use of a spring,³ thinking it highly probable that he was on, or very near, a bottom encumbered with stones. I replied that in these circumstances he should manoeuvre quite independently of the *Descubierta* and that he should understand that it was my intention to make fresh efforts to reach the nearby harbour the following morning, even though it was to windward and might finally result in the sacrifice of the anchor.

Meanwhile darkness had fallen and the mist had thickened so much that despite the Moon it was difficult for us to see each other. We spent the night with the vigilance appropriate to our unpleasant situation and although the swell continued very high from SW and west, the breeze was light and so we were able to maintain our position until dawn.

---

¹ Malaspina was mistaken in thinking he was anchored in Carmel Bay. His subsequent distance of 2 miles from Point Pinos places his anchorage between that point and Cypress Point, the NW entrance point of Carmel Bay.

² Malaspina may have meant his noon observation for latitude: see p. 201 above.

³ It would appear that in the difficult situation in which the *Atrevida* found herself, Bustamante intended to use a spring to turn the corvette in the desired direction. To achieve this a hawser would be led out from the stern by boat to a kedge anchor laid in an appropriate position. The spring would then be hauled in and when the ship's head was pointing in the desired direction the sails would be hoisted, the cable cut and the spring slipped, when the boat would recover the kedge anchor: see John Harland, *Seamanship in the Age of Sail*, London, 1984, p. 276.

12 September

At that time the breeze shifted to the NNW and north, but without producing even a moderate clearing of the mist. This made me suspect that this would be a land breeze of brief duration and that a failure to take advantage of it might have disastrous consequences. I thought it necessary, therefore, to prepare to get under way, with the use of a spring, hailing the *Atrevida* to inform her that we would cut our cable. When both corvettes had done this at almost the same moment, we were under full sail before seven o'clock steering west and WbyN.

We continued on this tack until one o'clock in the afternoon with a fresh breeze at first, although not strong enough for us to make way against the high sea running directly towards us. The breeze then became much stronger, hardly allowing us to keep the topsails hoisted. The mist that still enveloped us made us somewhat uncertain of the latitude, deduced on board both ships to be 36°33′. Finally we altered course to the first quadrant with the breeze still fairly strong from NW and continued close hauled until three in the afternoon.

By this time we were in no doubt of being once more to windward of the harbour, whatever its latitude might be, so we bore off to the east. When, at a quarter past four in the afternoon, we calculated by dead reckoning that we were close to the meridian of Point Pinos, we fired cannon again, to which the presidio promptly replied. This told us that we were considerably to the north of it and, furthermore, by the sight of a stretch of low land at five o'clock, undoubtedly well to the west.[1] We therefore quickly altered course to south, but were soon thwarted in this attempt by the breeze dropping and becoming unusually weak, with a shift from NW to WSW and SW. By then the fog was extremely thick, the depth thirty-five to forty fathoms, and the sea fairly high from offshore.

Two or three tacks under full sail, guided either by the cannon shots or by the sound of the breakers on the beach, brought us much closer to the anchorage in the remaining hours of the afternoon. Finally, the breeze having dropped entirely soon after nightfall, we anchored with the large kedge in twenty fathoms, sand, and shortly afterwards the *Atrevida* did the same. By then the sight of the flashes compared with the range of the sound had shown us that we were less than a mile and a half from the anchorage, which was bearing SSW.

Our first step, therefore, was to send a pinnace to examine it, so as to find in advance the best spot for anchoring. When the pinnace returned at midnight, we began the task of warping into position, as the swell and the complete calm left us no alternative to ensure the safety of the corvettes.

It was necessary to increase the use of cannon fire and pistol shots during the night so as not to leave the pinnaces without a marker in the dense fog that enveloped them, but at last, the crews having worked very hard, by first light we were in the anchorage and soon moored with two anchors to east and west some three or four cables from the shore.

---

[1] 'E' in the original MS, but this is clearly a transcription error for 'O' for '*oeste* = west, since 'well to the east' would place the *Descubierta* well inland.

Plate 24. Presidio of Monterey, by José Cardero. Museo Naval, Madrid

CHAPTER 2

At Monterey

13 September
Our opinion so far of this harbour differed utterly from the favourable impression that it had made when viewed from a distance. We thought that navigators from the Philippines were justified in their desire to stop calling at this roadstead despite the shortages which would inevitably inconvenience them until Acapulco after such a long passage. A difficult entrance due to a lack of landmarks, a sky constantly overcast and foggy, the very dangerous proximity of Point Pinos and finally the position of the anchorage itself, the northern extremity of which gave little shelter from the prevailing winds, being some ten leagues from Point Año Nuevo, were other obstacles to forming even a passable opinion of these parts.

Our conjectures proved to be unfounded. However, with a quick change in all these circumstances we had to recognize that one could hardly hope for a better port of call for ships coming from the north coast of America at the end of summer to approach the milder climes of the tropics.

In compiling the administrative and natural history of California,[1] we will deal at due length with everything that relates to the discovery and subsequent subjection of the coast and its inhabitants to the Spanish crown. For the present we will limit ourselves to reporting that the presidio of Monterey, residence of the governor of the province, consists of an enclosed and fortified rectangle affording accommodation to a company of sixty-three horsemen with its *teniente* and *alférez*, with enough room, although in rather cramped conditions, for each man to live with his wife and children. Near the shore is a small storeroom, no doubt provided for the use of the ships from the Department of San Blas which annually arrive at the roadstead. Not more than two leagues to the SE lies the Misión de San Carlos, on the Carmel River,[2] which, under the guidance of the Franciscan fathers, has gathered together a considerable number of Indians recently drawn to religion and a communal life.[3]

Consequently, our stay at the port combined various objectives of no little

---

[1] See 'Estado de las misiones de la Nueva California', AMN, MS 330, dated 31 December 1785, ff. 4-5, and 'Establecimientos de la California Septentrional. Presidios, misiones, pueblos y número de sus habitantes', AMN, MS 330, f. 1.

[2] Carmel River, which discharges into Carmel Bay.

[3] The Misión del Carmelo was founded in 1770 by Father Junípero Serra, with the name San Carlos de Monterrey. In August 1771 it was moved close to the banks of a nearby river that the Carmelite priests who had accompanied the expedition of Vizcaíno had named the Carmelo.

importance for the nation's wealth as well as meeting the need both to give the crews a good rest before braving the climates of San Blas and Acapulco and to allow time for the unhealthy rainy season on the coast of New Spain to abate somewhat. And, of course, if we were able at the same time to give an accurate report of these shores, so that in the future there would not be the slightest danger in approaching them, and to examine the ways in which this province, until now a heavy burden on the Royal Treasury, could contribute to general prosperity, we could flatter ourselves that this part of our work would not be considered fruitless.

Once the corvettes were properly anchored and moored, the beauty of the day (which presented Nature's most smiling face once the fog had cleared) and some refreshments sent to us by Don José Argüello,[1] the *teniente* in command of the company and at present the acting governor of the presidio, soon combined to cast a favourable light upon our tasks. The latter gave us an excellent impression of the taste and abundance of the foodstuffs, and the former gave us hope that our investigations in the various branches of science that we tried to cover had nothing to fear from any comparison with those which had been made here some years before by the French frigates *La Boussole* and *L'Astrolabe* under the command of Comte de la Pérouse.

As soon as the mist had lifted, Don Juan Vernacci, with the necessary instruments ready on the beach, was able to take equal altitudes of the Sun and deduce its longitude by the chronometers and to establish the first period for obtaining their rates. The results of this observation were as follows:

	Chronometer 72	Chronometer 71
Longitude east of Nootka	4°43′32″	4°46′38″

Accordingly, continuing the series of our longitudes, preferring that of chronometer 72 as its present rate was very close to that which had been determined in Nootka, the longitude of the observatory, which had been moved for greater convenience to a good room in the courtyard, was 124°23′14″ west of Paris.[2] Having achieved this objective, which we considered most desirable, and with the confirmation soon afterwards of all the information and appearances regarding this harbour, which although seemingly lacking in shelter was nonetheless quite safe because of the mildness of the climate, we could attend to other objectives. To this end the measures that seemed to us most suitable were undertaken that very day. Both crews were given a larger amount of fresh meat each day, without diminishing either their daily rations or their bonus of wine. The proximity of the mission and the ease of using the troops' horses

---

[1] Don José Dario Argüello, who received Vancouver so courteously in 1792: Lamb, *George Vancouver's Voyage*, pp. 740-41. He came to California in 1781, subsequently serving consecutively at San Gabriel and Santa Barbara and as *comandante* of San Francisco until March 1791. From 1791 to 1796 he served as *comandante* at Monterey. He later served again at San Francisco and Santa Barbara, was acting governor of California 1814-15 and governor of Baja California 1815-22. He died at Guadalajara in 1828: Donald C. Cutter, *California in 1792: A Spanish Naval Visit*, Norman and London, 1990, p. 84 and Richard A. Pierce, *Russian America: A Biographical Dictionary*, Kingston, Ontario and Fairbanks, Alaska, 1990, p. 9.

[2] For full details of these observations in which the longitude of Monterey is calculated as 115°34′53″ west of Cádiz, see Espinosa, *Memoria* (1805), p. 7 and Espinosa, *Memorias* (1809), 2nd memoir, pp. 63-4 and 108-9. The latter memoir also gives details of observations for magnetic variation and inclination (p. 117) and a discussion on the observations to determine the force of gravity (pp. 190-212).

Plate 25. Misión del Carmelo at Monterey, by José Cardero. Museo Naval, Madrid

gave everyone the chance to enjoy more than once the recreation and healthful exercise of riding, combining this, of course, with that mettle, love of freedom, and liberality with money which are always to be found amongst sailors. Finally, a daily corrida with bullocks in the courtyard of the presidio allowed each as he wished to show off his inclinations towards prudence or agility, or a certain love of danger, all nevertheless enjoying vigorous exercise without the distraction of the vices so common in large cities. To be truthful, on the first evenings there were a few episodes of drunkenness which might have disturbed this general state of well-being, but these were easily stopped by the *comandante* of the presidio forbidding the sale of alcoholic drinks while we, at the same time, punished with some severity those who were rash enough to drink to excess.

In addition to these circumstances, which in themselves were very agreeable, the weather, almost from the day of anchoring, was constantly clear and calm, which helped a great deal in our other objectives. Thus Señor Haenke's botanical collection was very soon considerably enriched, zoology did not fall far behind and the astronomical observations were continued with all necessary eagerness and accuracy.

It was also natural, whether in a spirit of honourable rivalry or because of that social instinct that unites the interests of those who find themselves in the same situation, that we were not indifferent even to the most insignifant reports of the mishaps of the French expedition under the command of Comte de la Pérouse.[1] Several [members of the presidio] had known him and all were unanimous in admiring the attributes that distinguished the members of that expedition. M. Dagelet's[2] observatory remained in the storeroom by the beach. M. Lamanon[3] and Padre Mongez[4] stayed for some days at the mission, from where they used to start their scientific examinations and botanical expeditions. M. de Vancy[5] left a small engraving with a most skilful representation of the reception of M. La Pérouse and M. Langle[6] at the same mission, with many of their officers. Finally, we found, as a fitting record of that expedition and the humanity of its leaders, a number of seeds and fruit trees already propagated at the mission and at those nearby, as well as a small machine for grinding wheat which Vicomte Langle had given to the mission fathers. As for the results of their scientific investigations, the reticence they had shown was no less than what we had found in Concepción, Chile, and accordingly it was impossible for us to make a careful comparison which would have allowed the perfection we desired, particularly in the hydrography of the coast. There were different ideas about the locality and the causes of the sad loss of the two launches of that expedition. The officers kept completely silent about it and only one or two of the lower ranks dared to speak to our people about this unhappy event. Any interpretations of these rumours therefore proved highly ambiguous and confused.[7]

---

[1] For an account of La Pérouse's visit to Monterey see Dunmore, *Journal of La Pérouse*, pp. 167-200. This account makes no reference to mishaps at Monterey; Malaspina must have been referring to the disaster that befell La Pérouse's expedition in Lituya Bay: see n. 7 below.

[2] Joseph Lepaute Dagelet, member of the Académie Royale des Sciences and astronomer to the expedition.

[3] Jean-Honoré-Robert de Paul de Lamanon, physicist, mineralogist and meteorologist.

[4] Abbé Jean-André Mongez, chaplain on board *La Boussole*.

[5] Gaspard Duche de Vancy, portrait and landscape artist.

[6] Capitaine de Vaisseau Paul-Antoine-Marie Fleuriot de Langle, commanding officer of *L'Astrolabe*.

[7] Malaspina is referring to the capsizing of two of La Pérouse's launches in Lituya Bay, Alaska, in July 1786, with the loss of six officers and fifteen seamen.

Among those who could satisfy our natural curiosity in this regard, with more judgment and knowledge, we first turned to the *Presidente* of the Missions, Father Matías de Lasuén,[1] of the Order of St Francis, a man of truly apostolic learning, demeanour and conduct and of singular courtesy and education. This friar had with good reason earned the esteem and friendship of both the French commanding officers and most of the men. He succeeded in giving them an idea of the religious organization of our missions, which surprised them all the more given the present unfounded malice against this system on the part of many modern writers, a malice which sometimes includes accusations of superstition and at other times considers only the personal vices of this or that individual or the errors inevitably born of distance and territorial vastness.

We were indebted therefore to Father Lasuén who, when he knew of our arrival in Monterey, quickly moved from the new missions being established between this presidio and that of San Francisco to the nearest one. As soon as he arrived he was very active in helping us with our natural history collections and very meticulous and detailed in his information and thoughts on the success of these missions. His hospitality was so affectionate, natural and according to traditions of his order, whatever hour either officers or men of other ranks might visit him at the mission, that nothing but perpetual gratitude and appreciation can describe our feelings for him.

Against all expectations it was really fortunate for Señor Haenke, in a climate so favourable to vegetation, that a recent fruiting almost as complete as that of spring had occurred. The leafy shores of Río Carmelo had mingled plants near the sea in such a variety (their seeds no doubt carried down by the winter rains) that they seemed to come from a territory over one hundred leagues wide rather than from the small area that our excursions could cover.

Meanwhile Señores Bauzá and Suria had made it their business to acquire all information likely to widen our knowledge. Thus, on the one hand, bearings had been linked with distant points whenever clarity made it possible and, on the other, we now had a good representation of the features and customs of new converts recently brought to the mission. For my part, I took every opportunity to acquire knowledge concerning their language and ancient customs and any ideas that might throw some light on our understanding of the obscure past and of the migration and civilization of mankind. Everything seemed to confirm that these peoples can be considered as among the most unintelligent and limited to inhabit the globe, with no similarity to those we had visited to the north of Nootka. Certainly they were not ready for any rapid advance of civilization, as the poor quality of the soil, the narrowness of the peninsula (which prevents them from getting any distance away from their enemies) and the almost constant state of warfare which seemed to prevail, unhindered by rivers, mountains or differences in their lives, must all lead to the reciprocal animosities which, on a national scale, contribute so much to the self destruction of mankind.

16 September
At midday on the 16th we had the pleasure of seeing the appearance near the harbour

---

[1] Fermín Francisco de Lasuén, who had been Father President of a growing chain of Franciscan missions since 1785.

Plate 26. Indian of Monterey, by Tomás de Suria?
Museo Naval, Madrid

of a Spanish schooner, which by two o'clock had already anchored near the corvettes. It was the schooner *Santa Saturnina* from the Department of San Blas which, in company with the snow *San Carlos*, and under the orders of Teniente de Navío Francisco Eliza, had left Nootka to continue surveying the coast to the north and the south. The winds had obliged both ships to begin their work from Juan de Fuca Strait, where they had then spent the whole summer, because of the great length of the inner channels, the ends of which they had not been able to find, although sailing to the north they had reached a latitude of about 49°40' along a branch some six or seven leagues wide. After finally emerging [from the strait] to return to Nootka, the ships had become separated. The schooner, after struggling in vain for many days to reach the necessary latitude, had been forced for want of water to bear away and make for Monterey Harbor. The lack of log books and the poor skills of Pilotín Carrasco,[1] who was in command, prevented us from acquiring all the information we needed to include these parts, so interesting to geography, to our own work in this area, although one could imagine that the lack of reliable observations and bearings, as the *pilotín* himself stated, was bound to contribute greatly to inaccuracy, even after Teniente de Navío Eliza submitted the systematic summary of these surveys.

Although most of the benefits to our hydrographic knowledge expected from the arrival of this schooner had not materialized, we still thought it afforded a good opportunity for the attempt under consideration to recover with the launches the anchors lost to the south of Point Pinos. In truth I thought this undertaking was not only difficult to achieve but also somewhat hazardous because of the risk of being driven to leeward of the harbour, which might force vessels of lesser tonnage and

---

[1] Juan Carrasco, who had also taken part in Quimper's expedition to Juan de Fuca Strait in 1790. Initially José María Narváez had been in command of the schooner, but he was transferred to the *San Carlos*, probably because Eliza needed him to draw the surveys and because of doubts that the schooner would be able to return to Nootka: Wagner, *Spanish Explorations*, p. 34.

endurance to run to other presidios, but as these obstacles did not seem insurmountable to the commanding officer of the *Atrevida* nor to the other officers who would take charge of the attempt, I thought it would be wrong not to try, at least, to recover items of such value.

The schooner was to anchor some distance from the area to be dragged to serve as a depot for any provisions and equipment required and to receive the anchors and cables if they were recovered, and finally to escort the launches if any mishap should oblige them to run to the south, unable to rejoin the corvettes. She was accordingly supplied with water, stores and the necessary ground tackle and given orders to be ready, from the following day, to assist with our attempt.

On the night of the 18th the launches set sail. The operation was directed by Teniente de Navío Don Cayetano Valdés on board the *Descubierta*'s launch with Don José Robredo in charge of the *Atrevida*'s launch; and Don Francisco Viana was to take charge of the schooner to direct her operations and movements so that the launches were never without the help and shelter that were so necessary to them. They were to be away for only two days, with strict instructions that the launches were not to be exposed to the least danger of shipwreck, and that the crews of both boats were to be made up of those men who had shown the greatest degree of intelligence, calmness and endurance at work.

It was certainly remarkable that while the sky and horizon in port were extremely clear, particularly after nine o'clock in the morning, our launches, only a short distance away, should have been in such a dense and constant fog that at times they could not see each other, although they were joined by the drag-line. A problem of this kind alone could have led to the failure of the attempt, if it had not been for the remarkable energy and expertise shown by those in charge of carrying it out. They worked day and night whenever a momentary clearing allowed them to look for the bearings of the anchorage. The cannon shots of the anchored schooner helped them find their position in the fog, while the sound of the breakers and the lead line also gave them a guide to the distances. The dragging went on continuously, when possible, at times without interruption for eight or ten hours. However, the quantity of rocks on the bottom was an insurmountable obstacle to success. This problem also made them lose a great deal of time as they had to change the direction of the drag, which was becoming chaffed. In the end all hope of finding even one of the anchors was abandoned and they returned to port at the pre-arranged time.

21 September

By then our main objectives had been accomplished at the observatory, namely a satisfactory rating of the chronometers, gravity experiments with the pendulum, observations for latitude and the determination of longitude by all the methods within our reach at the time. These were in fact not very favourable, because of the constant mist at night. Furthermore they were limited to the lunar distances and the occultation of 231 of Mayer[1] by the Moon, observed by Señores Concha and Vernacci with little confidence because of the amount of cloud.

---

[1] No. 231 in the star catalogue of Tobias Mayer (1723-62), the Göttingen astronomer.

We had also acquired from the mission stores several *quintals* of dried vegetables, of which we had very few at the time. The presidio troops, by means of unceasing labour, had provided us with a good supply of salt, with which to make new salted provisions in Acapulco, if convenient in the circumstances, while the schooner *Saturnina* had been given every help in the form of victuals and equipment to ensure her arrival at Acapulco.

Having thus achieved the various objectives that we had proposed for this port of call, it seemed that the time had come for departure, so as to make our way gradually to Acapulco. We fixed the date for the morning of the 25th, occupying ourselves in the few remaining days by extending the soundings in the bay along different headings, by supplying ourselves with some live animals [to provide fresh meat] for the crew, in gathering more samples for the Real Gabinete, and in showing both at the presidio and in the mission nearby the extent of our gratitude and appreciation for the friendship and generosity with which they had welcomed us and contributed to our well-being.

25 September

The corvettes were indeed up and down on one anchor by nine o'clock on the morning of the chosen day. Shortly afterwards, with the first breath of the sea breeze we set sail, close hauled in the first quadrant under full sail, and during the following night after several tacks, we were close enough together to continue on a southerly course.

CHAPTER 3

From Monterey to Acapulco and visit by *Descubierta* to Isla Guadalupe and San Blas

25 September
On getting under way we set a course in the first quadrant in order to use the tide which was [expected] to remain favourable until two in the afternoon. However, we found the sea breeze so light and the swell so high against us, that we made very little progress until noon, when were obliged to tack into the third quadrant when two miles offshore to clear Point Pinos, which was then bearing S30°W six to seven miles distant.

However, soon afterwards, when the sea breeze freshened once again we were able to tack closer to our route, in spite of a moderately heavy swell, and by three in the afternoon we were approaching the rocks to seaward of Point Pinos.[1] Having tacked to the north again at four o'clock, when the point was bearing south, we were well offshore and able to continue on the same course all afternoon. By sunset this had taken us some four leagues to the north of Point Pinos and two leagues from the coast, which we could only see vaguely because the mist had closed in again and the breeze had dropped entirely.

Until midnight the breeze alternated between breaths of land breeze and light airs from NW, with the occasional calm which left us without steerage way. We had maintained an approximately westerly course, so as to clear the land. By the time we had achieved this we obtained no bottom with ninety fathoms of line, when previously we had been in depths of fifty-eight to sixty-three fathoms, ooze. The swell remained moderately heavy from the NW, indicating that the breeze would soon get up from that quarter.

26 September
By daybreak it had indeed set in from that direction and at sunrise, being out of sight of land with a fairly clear horizon, we could set a course to continue with the tasks we intended to carry out.

The latitude of 36°19' that we observed at noon confirmed that the high land now in view, its base deep in haze, was that which follows Punta del Carmelo,[2] this being

---

[1] Above-water rocks extend 2½ cables NW of Point Pinos.
[2] Now Pinnacle Point, the southern entrance point of Carmel Bay. To the south of the bay the coast is backed by high land, which attains an elevation of almost 1,350 metres 6 miles inland.

as far as our survey from the port had reached. The fresh breeze from the NW helped us greatly in surveying the high land, which we soon approached on an easterly course and immediately began to measure bases and make observations to different points along this stretch of the coast, the ends of which we could now see clearly, three leagues distant. These tasks continued until darkness fell when, in latitude about 34°55′and on the meridian of Monterey, we altered course somewhat further offshore to make good progress on our route during the night, while being able to get some rest in safety.

The coast of California from Monterey had been well surveyed and accurately described by Almirante Sebastián Vizcaíno,[1] whose accuracy we had already been able to judge in Monterey and which we found even more worthy of admiration and praise at every step. Furthermore it was visited annually by ships from the Department of San Blas, either for stopping over or to provision the presidios. As for the galleon from the Philippines this coast was the object of all their desires and their most welcome and sought for sight, so that on our part we could now only add to what had been done previously by giving more exact astronomical positions for the points of landfall or ports of call, without sacrificing the time that we had to consider valuable during the longer dark nights.

From nightfall, in fact, the mist usually left the trend of the coast somewhat too indistinct for us to be able to choose the most suitable courses, but this disadvantage was made up for by the strong and constantly favourable breeze from the NW, with which we could stand on or offshore as we wished.

Thus once our work was done for the 26th our intention was to approach Point Pedernales[2] so as to be able to observe the meridian altitude of the Sun within sight of it, and in this manner fix the landmarks for the entrance to Santa Barbara Channel[3] and the presidio. Accordingly we sailed some twenty leagues during the night, lay-to until first light and then altered course to east, as we knew we had stood too far offshore during the night.

27 September

By ten o'clock we managed to sight Point Pedernales and at noon we were only three leagues WNW of it in latitude 34°34′ and longitude 1°8′ east of Monterey, with variation 11°NE. This point is low and fissured, running down from a bare hill of moderate height which finishes to the north shortly before reaching the head of a small, shallow bay surrounded by low, flat ground along the shore. From it the coast runs almost due east, by way of Point Conception,[4] where Santa Barbara Channel begins, formed by the mainland and several islands[5] which are heavily populated by hard-

---

[1] For Vizcaíno see p. 192, n. 3 above.

[2] From Malaspina's description of this point it would appear that he was referring to Point Arguello, a narrow rocky point which extends 4 cables west from the general run of the coast 138 miles SSE of Pinos Point, rather than Point Pedernales, a dark and prominent point 1½ miles further north.

[3] The channel that leads between the mainland and Santa Barbara Islands, the northern group of the Channel Islands.

[4] A point 12 miles SE of Point Arguello.

[5] San Miguel, Santa Rosa, Santa Cruz and Anacapa Islands, forming the Santa Barbara Islands, the northern group of the Channel Islands.

working native Indians, by whom our missionaries have been kindly welcomed, finding religion, industriousness and agriculture to be well established among them.

Having adopted our original plan of not wasting the nights in going over unnecessary details of the coast, I now put aside any desire to sail up the inner part of the above mentioned channel, a passage which, if it were to be of any use, would have obliged me to anchor a couple of times, which I considered somewhat unwise with our present shortage of anchors. Thus, as soon as we had completed a thorough survey of the above-mentioned points, we crossed to Isla de San Bernardo[1] under full sail and employed the rest of the afternoon in surveying it, while managing to fix the position of Farallón de Bajas[2] and a considerable part of the adjacent Isla de San Vicente.[3]

The breeze was strong and favourable during the following night. We made good some twenty leagues to the south and then altered course to east at three o'clock in the morning, with the intention of continuing under shortened sail until dawn, then to pass between the islands of Santa Barbara[4] and Santa Catalina,[5] and finally to steer for the entrance to the port of San Diego.

28 September

As soon as day had dawned we saw, three leagues ahead, an island of moderate height and circumference, which we could hardly believe to be Santa Barbara as we could not see Santa Catalina which, according to the coasting pilot, was separated from other island by a channel only five leagues wide. Vizcaíno's sailing directions dispelled our doubts in this regard, showing that what we could see was San Nicolas Island which lies some five leagues west of Santa Barbara and is omitted on all recent charts.[6]

By now accustomed to settled and favourable conditions, we had no doubt of being able, in the long hours of daylight, to reach the above-mentioned channel, from which we could not be more than eight or ten leagues, but on this occasion the closeness of the full Moon thwarted our plans.[7] The breeze soon dropped almost entirely and then veered to east and ESE. Some flashes of lightning and the heavy cloud cover and haze limited our work that day to the mere survey of the island [San Nicholas Island] and determination of its position, while seeming to threaten an unfavourable change in the weather for the following night. At noon our position had been latitude 33°2′ and longitude 2°27′ from Monterey and therefore very close to the island.

In these circumstances it seemed preferable to abandon our first idea of approaching the port of San Diego and instead make use of the night breezes, as far as possible,

---

[1] San Miguel Island.
[2] Probably Richardson Rock, a 16-metre high isolated pinnacle 5½ miles NW of Point Bennett, the western extremity of San Miguel Island.
[3] Santa Rosa Island.
[4] Santa Barbara Island, one of the southern group of the Channel Islands, is 1½ miles long and one mile wide, rising to an elevation of 193 metres.
[5] Santa Catalina Island, another of the southern group of the Channel Islands, lies 21 miles east of Santa Barbara Island. It is 23 miles offshore and separated from the modern city of Los Angeles by San Pedro Channel.
[6] San Nicholas Island, the outermost of the southern group, is eight miles long and 3 miles wide and rises to an elevation of 276 metres. It lies 27 miles WSW of Santa Barbara Island.
[7] It is not clear why the closeness of the full Moon should have thwarted Malaspina's plans. Although tidal streams further north are strong, they are not significant in the vicinity of the Channel Islands.

to steer directly for Isla Guadalupe, the exact position of which I considered very important as it was the usual landfall for ships coming from Asia bound for the west coast of New Spain.

The breezes were very favourable for this purpose, with all threat of gales dispelled after midnight when a settled, moderate NW breeze soon cleared away the mist which had veiled the sky and horizon. We continued under full sail for the next two days, our speed increased by the strong current setting to the SE.[1] To avoid all risk of sighting the land to the east too soon, we took the precaution of sailing twenty leagues to the west of the distance [from the island] indicated by most of the charts of the coast of California.[2] By four o'clock on the afternoon of the 30th we had already reached approximately the parallel of the island, eight or ten leagues to the west, without the slightest sign of land with a fairly clear horizon. We hauled the breeze to the east, therefore, and at sunset the *Atrevida* signalled us that she had sighted the island, her commanding officer hailing me shortly afterwards to say that although he was not sure because of the haze, he thought it lay some thirteen leagues E5°S.

Mindful of the current, we were cautious during the night and hove-to well to the north of the island and some five leagues to the west, so as to be able to survey it at dawn and establish its position with certainty, choosing to pass to the north or south as the circumstances required. [1 October] However, by five in the morning the current had set us so far off course that its northern end bore NE, four or five leagues distant.

It was not possible, nor would it have been useful, for us to coast the northern side of the island; it was the southern part, in fact, which must be considered as the more important, because ships coming from the west at the time have to identify it with certainty. Furthermore the dense haze prevented the astronomical and geodetic work that we had been contemplating, as none of the higher points or those on the shore could be seen clearly for taking bearings. Intending to wait for more favourable conditions after sunrise, we hauled the breeze under very little sail so as to gradually approach the northern end, from which we were only two miles at eight o'clock. As the haze had not yet cleared we lay-to for a time for this purpose.

At last at nine o'clock the breeze, which continued strong NW, finally looked as if it wanted to favour us. The mist dispersed, the island came beautifully into view, and the Sun, now completely unveiled, allowed us the observations of latitude, longitude and azimuths that we so desired. At noon, all of the western side having been well surveyed, we steered SE, taking bearings to the *farallones*[3] at the southern end, a short distance off in the first quadrant. Soon afterwards, having rounded the southern extremity of the island, we were able to continue on our way under full sail.

Isla Guadalupe can been seen from the deck at some thirteen or fourteen leagues, being particularly high on its northern side. Its coast is steep-to and offers no shelter at all, nor is there the slightest sign of vegetation to be seen on its western side. Thus, in such a mild climate rain must be extremely rare. The *Atrevida* sounded twice when

---

[1] The California Current sets to the SSE at about ten miles a day throughout the year.
[2] Malaspina was adopting the well established principle of steering well to the west or east of an isolated island, whose longitude was in doubt, and then running down its latitude.
[3] Isla de Adentro and Isla de Afuera, two prominent islets off the south coast of Isla Guadalupe.

a mile and a half offshore without obtaining bottom. The two southern islets or crags to the south appear also to be very steep, so that it may safely be stated that all approaches to the island are free of dangers. According to our observations its longitude is 3°23' east of Monterey. The latitude of its southern extremity is 28°48'30" and variation, according to various azimuths, was [blank] NE.

Having surveyed this island accurately, our next intention was to close the coast again and follow it with great attention as far as Cabo San Lucas, as by age-long custom shipping from Asia to these coasts usually kept closer inshore after passing Guadalupe. The breeze continued to blow strongly and the weather prospects seemed good. We had trimmed the sails a little, steering EbyN, so that by dawn we would have sighted the islands near Isla Cerros,[1] were it not for the fact that the distance given from Guadalupe on the San Blas and Manila charts was much greater, as Piloto Mendizábal[2] had deduced from his own dead reckoning.

2 October

As we neared the shore the wind slackened somewhat from its strength of the previous night. We knew from the sailing directions of Sebastián Vizcaíno that the coast formed a large bay[3] which ended south of Isla Cerros at Morro Hermoso,[4] but we were left in some doubt of the existence of two islands called the Islas San Benito included in some recent charts, but not in those sailing directions.

The confirmation of the existence of these islands was therefore the main objective of this day's work, so we remained on a higher latitude than that of Isla Cerros until, having sighted the islets,[5] we bore away to south at ten o'clock to examine them from a short distance. At noon our latitude was 28°22' and our longitude 6°12' [east] of Monterey. At that time one of Islas San Benito bore SE and some high mountains on Isla Cerros could be seen vaguely in the distance bearing SEbyS. We altered course immediately to approach this latter island, and at half past three in the afternoon we were some two or three leagues abeam of its Cabo San Agustín.[6] We could now confirm once more the accuracy of Sebastián Vizcaíno in the description of this coast, and we certainly felt more envy than surprise at seeing described with such precision at so early a period in navigation and hydrography the approaches to a harbour of such importance to the nation in its conquests.

The favourable breeze that we made use of under full sail had placed us by sunset abeam of Isla Natividad[7] and in sight of the vicinity of Puerto de San Bartolomé.[8]

---

[1] Isla Cedros, a large island of volcanic origin off the west coast of Baja California, 435 miles NW of Cabo San Lucas.
[2] For Mendizábal and his chart see p. 38, n. 3 above.
[3] Bahía Sebastián Vizcaíno.
[4] The SW entrance point of Bahía Sebastián Vizcaíno is Punta Eugenia, with the 210-metre Monte Eugenia, 7 miles SE, the most conspicuous of a number of sharp bare hills in the approaches to Punta Eugenia; present day Morro Hermoso is situated 27 miles SE of the same point.
[5] Islas San Benito lie about 15 miles west of Isla Cedros.
[6] The SW extremity of Isla Cedros.
[7] A barren and hilly island 4 miles west of Punta Eugenia.
[8] Bahía Tortugas, 15 miles SE of Punta Eugenia; it is one of the best harbours on the west coast of Baja California.

Here we shortened sail and even hove-to for a few hours during the night, as it was our intention to follow the trend of the coast by way of Los Abreojos, which is surrounded by dangers and where it is important to know the exact longitude.[1]

3 October

The mists which enveloped the coast made this investigation, which we began on the following day, somewhat difficult and incomplete. By midday we could still hardly see Punta Abreojos itself clearly. We never sighted the outer islets and reefs, although we could be satisfied with their description from the directions of Vizcaíno, whose *almiranta*[2] had anchored in their lee.

In the afternoon the coast was soon lost from view for, as well as being shrouded in mist, in these parallels it forms a large bay,[3] the shores of which are generally low, sandy and shelving. On the other hand, it was difficult to infer from the various charts that we had to hand the real direction of the coast, because the closer they came to coincide as to the true position of Cabo San Lucas, the more they varied from each other and the more they deviated from the truth.

4 October

The night was calm and our vigilance matched our uncertainty about the position of the coast, particularly as the Morro de San Lázaro,[4] which we wanted to survey, ran out to the west for a considerable distance, like an island. We hove-to at midnight therefore, so as not to pass it, and at dawn the next day we saw it a long way off to the east, which was approximately our course at the time.

By this time both the wind and the sea, which would have made communication by means of the pinnaces somewhat risky during the previous days, had fallen considerably. Consequently, I took advantage of the moment to call the *Atrevida*'s pinnace over so as to send instructions to her commanding officer that in view of her shortage of anchors and the earliness of the season she did not need to go to San Blas with the *Descubierta*. There the latter would take on board the necessary official letters and stores for the continuation of the voyage, while the *Atrevida*, making directly for Cabo Corrientes, could complete her April survey as far as Puerto de Acapulco, where she could anchor in perfect safety. I left it up to Don José Bustamante to decide upon the moment of this separation, from when he could consider himself independent of the *Descubierta*, but he hailed me to say that only when he had reached Cabo San Lucas would he head straight for Cabo Corrientes, and therefore he would sail in company with us as far as that point, where, without affecting his intentions, he would perhaps be able to make a reliable comparison of the longitudes according to number 105.

So, after the pinnace was hoisted, we set full sail again, with a rather stronger breeze,

---

[1] Dangerous rocks extend up to 5½ miles WSW and from 1 to 1½ miles south and SE of Punta Abreojos, 106 miles SE of Punta Eugenia.

[2] The ship that flew the flag of the *almirante* or second in command of a fleet: see p. 196, n. 3 above.

[3] From Cabo Abreojos to Cabo San Lázaro, 135 miles SE, the coast recedes for about 40 miles to form a large unnamed bay.

[4] Monte San Lázaro, which rise above Cabo San Lázaro, is a bold headland which appears as an island when first sighted.

and continued on our course to determine the position of the Morro de San Lázaro with all possible accuracy at noon, by which time it was bearing E11°S by compass, while the following stretch of coast was visible as far as Bahía Santa Marina,[1] our latitude being 24°55′ and our longitude 9°8′ from Monterey.

The afternoon was exceptionally pleasant. We closed the coast and continued along it, surveying the mouths of [Bahía] Santa Marina[2] and several other important points towards [Punta] Magdalena,[3] which we tried to fix with all possible accuracy. As the night was equally clear and agreeable we progressively altered course to the east to follow the trend of the coast.[5th] At dawn Punta Santa Margarita[4] was bearing N31°W about six leagues distant. The rest of the coast to the ESE was so low, pale and veiled in haze that we could not see clearly where it ended. We therefore decided to keep two leagues offshore, so as not to interrupt our bases nor to leave ourselves without points of known position to confirm our observations, which we repeated frequently.

By the afternoon we were off Bahía de Todos los Santos,[5] and could see clearly both the mission of that name and also the river near the stretch of coast that runs from there towards Cabo Falso de San Lucas,[6] which at sunset was bearing S51°E about six leagues distant.

We kept under way for part of the following night until two o'clock in the morning when we thought we must be close to Cabo San Lucas. We then hove-to and at first light found ourselves only two leagues offshore, with the *farallones* off the cape[7] bearing N72°E about three leagues distant.

6 October

Here the commanding officer of the *Atrevida* hailed me to say that as soon as we had both taken observations on the meridian of Cabo San Lucas he would send his pinnace over to us[8] and he would then set a course for Cabo Corrientes, according to the instructions that he had been given. Having achieved the first aim, with the cape bearing true north two to three miles distant, we hove-to for a short time. At about half past eight, after the *Atrevida*'s pinnace had returned and been hoisted inboard,

---

[1] Bahía Santa María, situated a short distance north of Bahía Magdalena, a large enclosed harbour protected on its southern side by Isla Santa Margarita, an island 20 miles in length. Bahía Magdalena is the largest and best sheltered harbour on the west coast of Baja California.

[2] From a distance the centre of Isla Santa Margarita, which is low, is sometimes mistaken for another entrance to Bahía Magdalana.

[3] A point 2 miles north of Punta Entrada, the northern entrance point to Bahía Magdalena.

[4] Probably Cabo Tosco, the southern extremity of Isla Santa Margarita.

[5] The coastline in the vicinity of the present town of Todos Santos has no indentation that could be described as a bay nor is one charted on either 'Carta esférica de los reconocimientos hechos en la costa NO de América en 1791 y 92 por las goletas Sutil y Mexicana y otros buques de S.M.' or 'Carta de los reconocimientos hechos en 1602 por el Capitán Sebastián Vizcayno', charts nos 1 and 4 in the atlas accompanying *Relación del viage hecho por las goletas Sutil y Mexicana*.

[6] Cabo Falso, a steep rocky bluff forming the SW extremity of Baja California, 4½ miles west of Cabo San Lucas, a rocky peninsula 1 mile in length, usually regarded as the southern extremity of Baja California and so depicted on most modern maps.

[7] Two rocks stand at the extremity of Cabo San Lucas, the highest 89 metres in height, while the cape itself is fringed with detached rocks, the highest 37 metres in height.

[8] Presumably to pass over copies of the *Atrevida*'s observations before she headed for Acapulco and the *Descubierta* continued to San Blas.

the two corvettes continued on their separate ways, the *Atrevida* steering SE while we followed the coast of Cabo San Lucas to fix, if possible, the mission of San José, where Don Vicente Doz and Abbé Chappe had made their observations.[1]

Many sets of distances from the Sun to the Moon observed on board both corvettes during the previous days had indicated a longitude much closer to that of the chronometers than shown by the observations at Monterey. Even after consulting the charts in general to find the distance from the mission to Cabo San Lucas we finally concluded that the results of our series of longitudes could hardly be called an error when compared with those of the mission. Among these latter we were inclined, as was M. Cassini, to prefer those resulting from the transit of Venus across the Sun's disk, observed by Abbé Chappe with all the precision that one might want from an astronomer. This was 112°2′30″ west of Paris, with a difference of only 2′ to the west of that deduced by Don Vicente Doz from the emersions of the first satellite of Jupiter. It did indeed seem strange that in the latitude determined by the French astronomer and by ourselves there should also be a difference of 2′, and finally for this datum we also preferred the results of Abbé Chappe, as we found in the printed account of his voyage[2] all the factors that he had used to calculate it.[3]

It had been important to settle this point beforehand since our bases were extremely unreliable all day because of contrary currents and it became necessary to subject all our work to these observations to achieve the accuracy we desired.

As has been mentioned we had already observed longitudes on the meridian of Cabo San Lucas. We repeated these observations the following morning to the south of Cabo Pulmo,[4] and, having taken a latitude observation at noon, by one o'clock we could see the mission bearing N35°15′W distant nine and two-third miles, at which time we observed hour angles for comparison.

These precautions had already convinced us that the mission was only fourteen miles N38° E true from Cabo San Lucas and therefore that the error deduced from this comparison in our series of longitudes would be considerable. Fortunately, although the *Atrevida* was not with us, we could include number 105 in this comparison as we had, as usual, at noon on the 5th compared its difference in rate with that of chronometer 72 by means of pistol shots.

Consequently, having calculated hour angles for five in the afternoon, it was then easy to work out the longitude assigned to the mission according to the two chronometers and the pocket chronometer and to see how far these were from the truth. The results, which have been set out in full in the astronomic log-book, were as follows:

	Chronometer 72	Chronometer 71	Pocket chronometer 105
Difference to the west from the true longitude:	35′57″	28′55″	33′44″

[1] For Vicente Doz and Abbé Chappe and their observations see p. 38, n. 2.
[2] Jean Baptiste Chappe d'Auteroche, *Voyage en Californie pour l'observation de Vénus sur le disque du soleil*, Paris, 1772.
[3] For full details of these observations in which the longitude of Cabo San Lucas is calculated as 103°34′05″ west of Cádiz, see Espinosa, *Memoria* (1805), pp. 8-9 and Espinosa, *Memorias* (1809), 2nd memoir, pp. 64-6.
[4] Situated 43 miles NE of Cabo San Lucas.

The mean of which, 32'55",[1] seemed to be the absolute error of all our longitudes on the Northwest Coast of America, if we considered not only the observations of distances from the Sun to the Moon since the end of May, which showed an equal or greater difference, but also the longitude assigned to Nootka by Captain Cook, which was justly considered highly reliable by that illustrious navigator.

In our present latitude and, to a greater extent, due to the weather now prevailing on the coast of New Spain, we had every reason to fear that the men would catch colds, which would then become intermittent fevers, usually spread by the rapid change from cold to hot. Fortunately neither the rains nor the calms had reached us yet, but as the thermometer could be seen at 85° and 90° in the open air, the consequences of such excessive heat could only be disastrous. From an early stage we had taken care, adding to our daily precautions the serving *gazpacho* for dinner and a refreshing drink of *chicha*, or fermented corn liquor, at three in the afternoon, the repeated ventilation of the hammocks, not an onerous task but one frequently carried out, and finally the continuation of a daily ration of wine. Don Francisco Flores also had to use alternate blood-letting with refreshments, and it gave us much pleasure to see that these mild preventative measures sufficed to keep both crews, in their appearance, good humour and readiness to work, in as healthy a state as we could desire, apart from a few chronically ill men on both corvettes.

By midday the *Atrevida* had been lost from sight on her southerly course.[2] During the afternoon, as has been mentioned, we were able to continue surveying as far as Cabo Pulmo, the [south-]eastern end of the headland of the peninsula. By sunset it was bearing N17°E five leagues distant, with the mission also in sight, bearing N45°W at about eleven miles.

The breeze then dropped and the coast became shrouded in haze, which continued nearly all night. Dawn would have found us in almost the same position had we not been set considerably to the south by the current, which no doubt came from Golfo de California.[3] [7th] From the early morning we had light breezes from west and WNW, with which we set a course under full sail and at noon, still in sight of land, our latitude was [blank] and our longitude [blank] east of the mission of San José.

9 October

Although accompanied by very pleasant conditions and a clear horizon, the falling winds slowed our progress so that we did not sight Islas [Tres] Marías[4] until the afternoon of the 9th. The current had obliged us to take some care with our latitude by

---

[1] The mean is actually 32°52'.

[2] For the *Atrevida* the period of the separation was uneventful. Bustamante experienced stormy conditions and confirmed the aptness of the name Cabo Corrientes [cape of currents], while successfully accomplishing the survey entrusted to him: Bustamante, *Diario general del viaje*, pp. 288–92.

[3] In the centre of the gulf the current normally sets SE, but it is weak and greatly influenced by the tide.

[4] Islas Tres Marias consist of a group of three high islands of volcanic origin and a fourth smaller island, which extend NW over a distance of 40 miles. Isla María Cleofas, the southern island, lies 60 miles NNW of Cabo Corrientes.

observing various meridian altitudes of stars during the night. The sea was extremely smooth and every day we saw seals and different species of birds. The heat, however, became increasingly hard to bear, particularly at night.

The Marías were sighted at two in the afternoon, and immediately we altered course to approach the westernmost island,[1] the extremities of which bore S39½E to S49°E, seven leagues distant. At four o'clock we were able to run some bases, when we then observed some hour angles and azimuths. By sunset we had surveyed in detail Islote Juanico[2] and the anchorage of the first island, with several points of the second island in view,[3] which we therefore also included in our bearings.

During the following night our choice of course naturally led us to coast the islands at a moderate distance, choosing to pass between them and Isla Isabela[4] and Piedra Blanca,[5] so as to finish the hydrographic description of that side, given that the *Atrevida* on her route from Acapulco had coasted the southern side of the islands.

The night was rather murky and rainy and, to judge by the thunder and lightning, very stormy over San Blas. We had a fair breeze, however, and by dawn the next day we were already two leagues south of Isla Isabela and, at the same time, we could see the whole of the coast of the Marías that we had plotted the previous afternoon.

Hour angles were observed and, until ten o'clock, we made use of the variable breezes to counter a strong south-going current. Then, with the first breaths of the sea breeze, we altered course for the roadstead of San Blas. At noon, in latitude of 21°30', Piedra Blanca bore N68°E three or four leagues distant and Isla Isabela, almost out of sight, N32°W by compass. Finally, after passing one mile north of Piedra Blanca, having observed some hour angles on its meridian, with a fresh sea breeze from EbyN, we dropped anchor in six fathoms, sand, at about four in the afternoon, with the outer Piedra Blanca[6] bearing N81°15'W,[7] the point of the harbour N17°E, and Punta Matanchel[8] S72°E, all by compass.

Soon afterwards a launch came out from the dockyard with a kedge and hawser. We lowered our boats and by six we had set out a second anchor and were moored lying almost east/west to two very reliable cables.

I had a number of ideas in mind for our stay in San Blas. It was not only necessary to provide the corvettes with some anchors and cables, timber, paint, tallow and other stores, but also to escort, if it was ready, the schooner which was to complete the work on the coast of Teguantepeque.[9] In addition I wished to discuss with Comandante Bodega y Quadra,[10] all the surveys made so far to the NW, so as to obtain a thorough description of the coast and to compile some good sailing directions. On the other

[1] Isla María Madre, the NW of the three high islands.
[2] Isla San Juanito, the smallest and NW island of the group.
[3] Isla María Magdalena.
[4] A small high island 35 miles WNW of San Blas and about 17 miles offshore.
[5] Piedra Blanca del Mar, 14 miles WNW of San Blas.
[6] Blanca de Tierra, about 6 cables SW of San Blas.
[7] N81°15'E in the MS journal which is clearly an error for N81°15'W.
[8] Possibly Punta Camarón, the northern entrance point of Ensenada Matenchén, 2½ miles SE of San Blas.
[9] Tehuantepec.
[10] For Bodega y Quadra see p. 16, n. 1 above.

hand, our present indifferent anchorage as much as this most insalubrious climate compelled me to stay here for as short a time as possible.[1] We were naturally urged to greater haste by the news which we had just received that the rains were extraordinarily late this year and could not yet be considered as finished.

As I was informed by Comandante Francisco Hijosa,[2] the commissary, who very soon came on board in the barge, Capitán de Navío Don Juan Francisco de la Bodega y Quadra had had to leave for Mexico City a few days earlier at the summons of the Viceroy and that the Department was consequently under the care and command of Teniente de Navío Salvador Fidalgo,[3] who at the time was in Tepic.[4] There would be no delay, however, in providing the necessities we had requested, of which I now gave a list in person to the commissary, asking him to send a copy to Fidalgo by special messenger so that his arrival in this port would not be postponed. We made arrangements for the best way to transport all the supplies requested, starting the next morning. Don Secundino Salamanca, whom I put in charge, worked with such energy that by the afternoon of the 12th our launch and that of the dockyard had already brought us all the required provisions, in spite of their considerable quantity.

However, we could not arrange to accompany the schooner,[5] although it was ready, as the Viceroy had given instructions for it to be sent to another destination under the command of Don Francisco Mourelle,[6] and we were assigned another one of equal tonnage which was at present on the stocks in the shipyard and due to be launched in November.[7]

The time spent being delayed in this anchorage was a most convenient occasion to inform His Excellency the Ministro de Marina of the essential occurrences of the past cruise. I therefore speedily sent a special messenger to Mexico City with these official reports,[8] to which was added, for greater detail, a comprehensive Mercator chart of

---

[1] San Blas was developed as a naval station in 1767 to support the campaign to control the province of Sonora, and to supply settlements in Alta California which were planned to counter the threat of a Russian advance down the coast towards New Spain: see Cook, *Flood Tide*, pp. 50-51. As a port and naval department it had many deficiencies, not least its unhealthy climate, but despite a number of plans to relocate it, it survived until 1803. The place made an unfavourable impression on Viana: see Francisco Xavier Viana, *Diario de viaje*, ed. H. Martínez Montero, 2 vols, Montevideo, 1958, II, pp. 16-25.

[2] Francisco Hijosa y Rodríguez came to New Spain in 1766 and was appointed by Viceroy Marqués de Croix to be treasurer and war Commissary for the Sonora campaign to pacify the native tribes on the northern frontier. When that campaign ended he had three tours of duty at San Blas where, as Commissary, he served with such figures as Bodega y Quadra and throughout the period of the NW Coast exploration: 'Relación de los Servicios y Merítos de Don Francisco Hijosa y Rodríguez', Archivo General de Indias, Guadalajara 520.

[3] For Fidalgo see p. 54, n. 4 above.

[4] A village 40 miles east of San Blas, in the interior highlands, where the air was clean and fresh and where officers of the Department were permitted to maintain temporary quarters to escape the insalubrious conditions in San Blas.

[5] The recently constructed *Mexicana*.

[6] For Mourelle see p. 51, n. 4. His orders were to explore Juan de Fuca Strait, but Malaspina, on his arrival in Acapulco, persuaded the Viceroy to mount a more ambitious expedition under the command of Dionisio Alcalá Galiano in the *Mexicana* accompanied by Cayetano Valdés in the *Sutil*.

[7] The *Sutil*.

[8] See p. 422 below for the text of Malaspina's report of 12 October 1791.

the coasts surveyed between Montagu Island and Monte San Jacinto or Mount Edgecumbe, so as to dispel any doubts regarding the existence of the passage to the Atlantic suggested by Ferrer Maldonado and supported by M. de Buache. At the same time I tried to make arrangements with Señores Galiano and Pineda, who would probably be in Mexico City, to meet and then compare the results of our respective labours.[1] I also asked the Viceroy for assistance in the form of either money or provisions which would take longer to arrive at Acapulco. An important part of the latter was a large quantity of flour which was to be taken to Manila to be made into bread, as in those islands [the Philippines] this important item was generally poor and often scarce. As for the former, chronometer 61 certainly deserved our special attention, and I sent it carefully packed to Don Dionisio Galiano, so that he could oversee its repair in Mexico City if, as seemed probable, this was simple enough to be within the powers of the craftsmen of that city.

It seemed injudicious [at first] to set up an observatory ashore just to rate the chronometers considering our haste to leave this anchorage and the insalubrious conditions in the town. We therefore began rating the chronometers on board by means of absolute altitudes, and later, in the early afternoon of the 10th, we could refer the longitude of the mission of San José to our observatory in this port, so as to study the second hydrographic question, no less important than the first: that is, the degree to which the observations of Abbé Chappe agreed with our own series of longitudes determined on shore. It would have been unwise to take the rate of the chronometers determined in Monterey to calculate the difference between San José and San Blas, when the present comparisons suggested that the heat had had a considerable effect on these instruments. The second rating, then, was the one adopted, and the difference between the meridians of the two towns was 4°24′18″. That is, the longitude of the observatory of San Blas, according to the observations made at the mission of San José, was 107°38′12″ west of Paris.

This result gave us much pleasure, as it not only agreed with several emersions of the first satellite of Jupiter observed by Don Juan de la Concha, but was also very close to the observations made in Acapulco[2] which, when referred to San Blas with number 10, had given a longitude for that observatory of 107°40′30″ west of Paris. In fact when leaving Acapulco we had preferred a longitude 6½′ greater than this, because certain satellite observations had indicated as much. It was now clear that these observations had not been very reliable, while the error of the chronometers in the past cruise would be less than this. This detailed account of our longitudes should not be considered inappropriate, as on a voyage dedicated essentially to hydrography it is a subject on which the safety of mariners depends. It would therefore be most reprehensible not to take meticulous care.[3]

---

[1] Galiano was in Mexico City to determine the geographical coordinates of the capital, long a subject of controversy. Antonio Pineda was conducting a land survey: see Iris H. W. Engstrand 'Antonio Pineda and his Environmental Impact Survey of 1791', *Colonial Latin American Historical Review*, 9, 2000, pp. 487-508.

[2] Malaspina is referring to observations taken later in the month when he returned to Acapulco.

[3] For full details of these observations in which the longitude of San Blas is calculated as 99°01′30″ west of Cádiz, see Espinosa, *Memoria* (1805), p. 9 and Espinosa, *Memorias*, 2nd memoir, pp. 66-7. The latter memoir also gives details of observations for magnetic variation and inclination (pp. 116-17) and a discussion on the observations to determine the force of gravity (pp. 190-212).

11 October

On the afternoon of the 11th Teniente de Navío Don Salvador Fidalgo at last arrived from Tepic. The almost impassable roads had exposed him to countless risks, which he could only overcome by sacrificing much needed rest. I owed his immediate arrival on board to his devotion to the service. It was an essential part of the planned method of work that this officer should report minutely all the accounts, observations and plans relating to his previous year's expedition towards the coasts of Prince William Sound, Cook River and Kodiak Island, since I had omitted some surveys which might have been needed for a decision regarding the passage of Ferrer Maldonado, if Fidalgo had not verified them the previous year.[1]

Time seemed too short while this officer was on board to give us a detailed account of his observations. Finally he handed over to us his journal so that we could read it at leisure and summarize it. We also made the fortunate acquisition of some plans belonging to Pilotos Tovar[2] and Pantoja,[3] which appeared very complete for both Golfo de California and stretches of the exterior coast, on the basis of many accurate surveys. There was no pilot of even moderate competence in the province at the time who would have been able to accompany us to Acapulco as I had requested.

13 October

By the afternoon of the 13th, therefore, we considered ourselves entirely ready to set sail, having received all the provisions and some twenty casks of water. We postponed the moment of unmooring, however, as at sunset the weather had begun to look very squally, but later these fears were dispelled to some extent and we weighed the eastern anchor and hoisted the launch inboard, so at three in the morning we were able to set sail, with a fresh SE breeze. We were no more than a league and a half from the anchorage, steering WSW and SW, when the sky, until then covered with dense mist, opened with a squall with heavy rain and some flashes of lightning not far off, the breeze having dropped almost completely meanwhile. We considered ourselves lucky to have encountered this squall while under sail, and were pleased to think that it would soon clear after sunrise.

14 October

This in fact is what happened. At the same time light airs got up from south, which we made use of immediately. By noon the southern extremity of the easternmost of Islas [Tres] Marías[4] bore S82°30′W and Cabo Tintoque[5] S26°E, the coast being some three or four leagues distant. A moderate sea breeze from the WNW and west soon

---

[1] For Fidalgo's 1790 expedition to Alaska see Cook, *Flood Tide of Empire*, pp. 277-8 and Olson, *Through Spanish Eyes*, pp. 300-41.

[2] For Tovar see p. 199, n. 1 above.

[3] Juan Pantoja y Arriaga, a graduate from Seville's Seminario de San Telmo, was brought from Callao by Bodega y Quadra in 1778. He took part in Arteaga's 1779 expedition to Alaska and Eliza's 1791 expedition to Juan de Fuca Strait. Pantoja later commanded vessels sailing to the NW Coast. He was still attached to the Department of San Blas in 1803; Cook, *Flood Tide of Empire*, pp. 93, 429.

[4] Isla María Cleofas.

[5] Punta de Pontoque on 'Carta esférica desde el Golfo Dulce en la Costa Rica hasta S^n Blas en Nueva Galica ... construida con las observaciones executadas en las corvetas *Descubierta* y *Atrevida*', Madrid, 1822. Now Punta de Mita, 25 miles NNE of Cabo Corrientes.

set in, which we hauled to on the starboard tack. But it did not last long and by sunset it had backed to the SW and WSW and was so light that we hardly had steerage way, leaving the current to set us to SSE, so that we had to try to keep our heading in the fourth quadrant to counteract it, if possible, and not to fall off towards Ensenada del Cabo Corrientes.[1] The clarity of the day had allowed us to confirm various important points on this coast by observations for latitude and longitude. The night was very calm. [15th] At dawn the next day we were three leagues SE of the islet[2] off Cabo Tintoque, with Cabo Corrientes bearing S10°E, but because of the lack of wind we could not continue on our heading until half past eight, when a moderate sea breeze got up from the WNW and NW, with which we proceeded under full sail and continued with all the survey work within our reach.

At ten o'clock we sighted the shoal or group of rocks that the *Atrevida* had already surveyed[3] and to which for that reason we gave her name. We chose to pass to seaward of them, because between them and the coast we could see a great many floating trees,[4] which had already obliged us to alter course frequently, and because in this way we could survey a greater extent of sea to the east. We would also be able to find out if there were another shoal farther out, as a merchant captain had suggested when we were together at anchor in Acapulco. Having dispelled these doubts and observed for latitude and longitude in sight of Islote Atrevida, soon after midday we bore up to the SE and SSE for the rest of the afternoon to make use of the fresh sea breeze and to approach Cabo Corrientes. At sunset it bore N30°E some four or five leagues distant and as our course was now easterly, following the coast steering approximately SEbyS, it was now only two leagues distant on our beam.

All night and the following morning the breeze continued strong and favourable. We did not lose sight of the coast until after midnight. [16th] As the morning was very hazy, it was difficult to make out any conspicuous marks except Volcán de Colima[5] until noon, when we saw the *farallón* or outer islet[6] off Puerto de Navidad,[7] which bore approximately N7°E four or five leagues distant.

The following day's run was equally successful. The afternoon was spent in surveying the coast of Suchiché,[8] although it was rather hazy. During the night we stood somewhat further offshore to have the benefit of the stronger sea breeze. [17th] Having closed the coast again in the morning, by midday we were near Los Motines,[9] which at the time were shrouded in haze. After making such good time, it was easy

[1] Bahía de Banderas, a deep bay between Cabo Corrientes and Punta de Mita, site of present day Puerto Vallarta.
[2] Roca Corbeteña, a steep-to whitish coloured rock, 22 miles NNW of Cabo Corrientes.
[3] Islas Tres Marietas, a group of islets, rocks and shoals, 10 miles SW of Punta de Mita.
[4] The bay is 'where foreign ships sometimes take in the Brazil-wood, with which the coast abounds': Alexander G. Findlay, *A Directory for the Navigation of the Pacific Ocean*, 2 vols, London, 1851, I, p. 276.
[5] Volcán de Colima, the westernmost of the Mexican volcanoes, 132 miles ESE of Cabo Corrientes.
[6] Roco Cono, a high reddish coloured conical rock, off Punta Graham, the western entrance point of Bahía Navidad.
[7] Bahía Navidad, a well protected harbour, 90 miles SE of Cabo Corrientes.
[8] The coast of Suchiché has not been identified.
[9] Possibly Islas Blancas, a group of above-water rocks, 112 miles WNW of Acapulco or Isla Grande, 2 miles farther NW.

for us to be abeam of Puerto de Zihuantanejo[1] by the evening, and to examine its vicinity and take several views to show all the features which might guide the mariner in these waters, although it is most unlikely that this harbour will ever be of any use for national navigation, as it is to leeward of, and such a short distance from, the Puerto de Acapulco.

In this position it was justifiable to assume that we would reach this latter port on the following day, particularly as our daily experience gave us almost certain grounds to count on a considerable advantage in keeping on course thanks to the SE current. However, the breeze dropped almost entirely during the night, and we were threatened by several squalls from the land, which combined extreme heat with a great deal of thunder and lightning in all four quadrants. Our progress therefore was quite slow and at dawn we found ourselves, more as a result of the current than the wind, at the beginning of Playas de Coyuca[2] and only four miles from Punta de Petatlan.[3]

18 October

The sea breeze did not get up until noon, when Punta de Tequepa[4] bore N44½°W three leagues distant, with an observed latitude of 17°1′N. We set a course at once under full sail, but made little progress in shortening the distance, both because the breeze was light and because it was necessary to take precautions against the dangerous effects of the currents, which, with any negligence on our part, might set us to leeward of the port. To this end, as we were now only about ten leagues from the port, we shortened sail at nightfall and closed the beach to a distance of two miles, so that the view of it during the coming night, and the soundings we took of sixty to sixty-five fathoms, mud, would serve as a continuous guide to make up for any odd effects of the currents.

The land breeze set in freshly at nine in the evening. We hove-to at times and otherwise continued close hauled on alternating tacks. At last at dawn, being one league off the beach and some six leagues from the port, we set a course under full sail to approach Isla del Grifo,[5] which bore E7°S.

Contrary to our hopes the sea breeze did not set in until after midday, when we were only a league from Isla del Grifo. We made for it immediately to enter the port and, having finally overcome a very strong current which set us very close to Punta de la Bruja,[6] by four in the afternoon we had passed Punta Grifo.[7] The sight of the corvette *Atrevida*, which had been at anchor since the afternoon of the 16th, added greatly to our pleasure. By tacking repeatedly, despite the very light breeze, we managed to reach the anchorage by prayers, and at nine o'clock in the evening we were moored at last, the yards and topmasts struck and the sails unbent.

[1] Bahía de Zihuatanejo, a small but excellent harbour, 108 miles WNW of Acapulco.
[2] A sandy beach, which extends 14 miles WNW from Bahía de Acapulco.
[3] Morro de Petatlan, a prominent point, situated 100 miles WNW of Acapulco.
[4] Possibly Morro de Papanoa, a bold, rocky headland, on the south side of Bahía de Tequepa, 73 miles WNW of Acapulco.
[5] Isla Roqueta, a prominent island off the western side of the entrance to Bahía de Acapulco.
[6] The NW entrance point of Bahía de Puerto del Marqués, a small sheltered inlet near the eastern entrance to Bahía de Acapulco.
[7] The western entrance point of Bahía de Acapulco.

CHAPTER 4

Return to Acapulco and preparations for crossing the Pacific

[19 October]
For a great many reasons our stay in Acapulco was most agreeable. Not only because all the nearby mountains, which had been parched by the Sun last April, were now clothed in beautiful green and showed no sign of aridity and burning, but also because our arrival in this port also marked the end of a considerable part of our work, the reunion of absent companions, and the imminent departure from this coast. Nor did we appreciate it any less for the ease of unloading the ships at this place, the convenience of the observatory, the safety of the anchorage and the difficulty of desertion, all of which seemed to offer an unusual degree of rest and tranquillity. The purposes we intended for this stay, which would necessarily be at least two months long, were equally important. To the above-mentioned return of absent officers and the receipt of the money and flour we had asked for from San Blas must be added arranging the material from the past cruise, fitting out the schooner to be sent to the coast of Teguantepeque [Tehuantepec] and Guatemala, preparing a large quantity of salt pork, making the necessary repairs to the boats and casks, and, lastly, performing reliable repetitions of the pendulum experiments,[1] the results of which, during the previous stay in April, did not satisfy us at all when referred to the observations made in Port Mulgrave, Nootka and Monterey.

We could certainly view the state of our ships and both crews with considerable pleasure, particularly when we compared the robust, cheerful and amiable appearance of the latter with the jaundiced complexion and natural indolence, dejection and melancholy of the inhabitants of the port. As for the ships, the fact that we needed no one apart from our crews for the repairs, and that these did not amount to much, also added to our satisfaction I have described.

20 October
Accordingly we were quick to make the most of such an agreeable situation. From the following day the supply of victuals was suspended, substituting a payment of money for rations; Señor Haenke began his botanical excursions; both corvettes were moved to convenient berths to attend to the inspection of their stores, cooperage repairs, taking on water and landing ammunition. Finally, an observatory was set up in

---

[1] Experiments for gravity: see also pp. 66-7 and Vol. 1 of this edition, pp. 327-9.

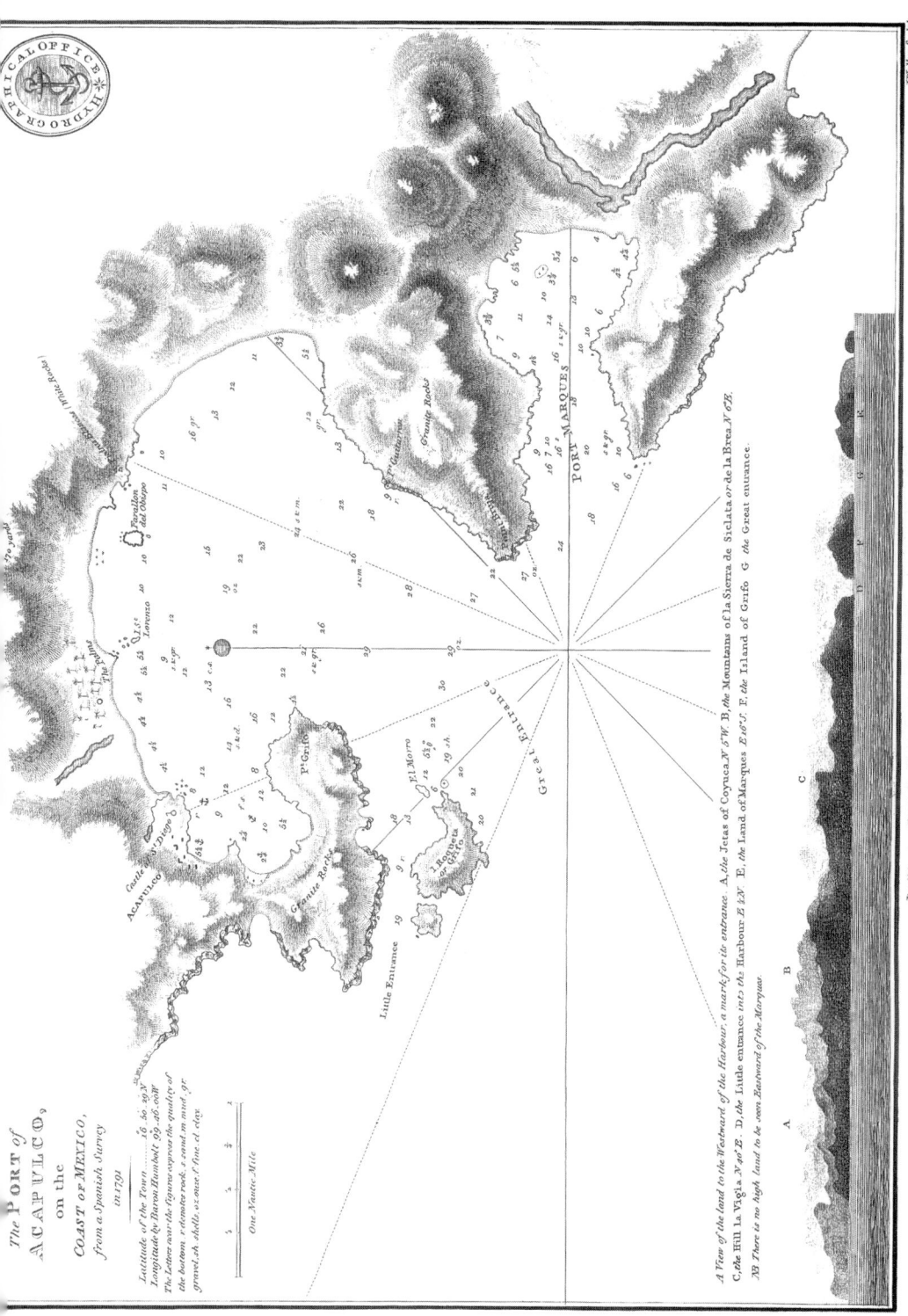

Plate 27. 'The Port of Acapulco, on the coast of Mexico, from a Spanish Survey in 1791.' British Admiralty chart based on Malaspina's survey. Private collection

a house close to the quay, as it seemed no longer wise to use the house of the warden of the castle, who would soon arrive at his post, His Majesty having appointed Teniente Coronel Pedro de Tueros,[1] who was obliged to live continuously in the fort or nearby.

The first equal altitudes were naturally used to calculate longitude with the chronometers. We saw with much satisfaction that not only did chronometers 71 and 72 give the same meridian difference of 5°21′ between San Blas and Acapulco as that determined by number 10 on the *Atrevida*'s previous passage, but also that the same chronometers agreed, with remarkable precision, with pocket chronometer 105, in determining the difference of longitude as 9°45′18″ between Cabo San Lucas and our observatory in Acapulco.

On the other hand the surveys of the corvette *Atrevida* during her last separation from us were also quite important for the accuracy of our own work, which now, linking the determinations of both voyages of that corvette and those of the last voyage of the *Descubierta*, made the calculation of latitude and longitude for each point along the coast almost independent of our bases, and immune to the many errors that the strength and constancy of the SE current I had to contend with, as can be expected.[2]

The currents experienced by the *Atrevida* had been even greater.[3] They not only had to repeat the longitude observations continually, but also had to guard against latitude errors by taking various meridian altitudes of stars both in the early and final hours of the night.[4] After our separation on the morning of the 6th off Cabo San Lucas, they had made good speed towards Cabo Corrientes, without stopping for a new and fruitless examination of Islas Marías. It had therefore been easy for them to approach that cape on the morning of the 11th after a heavy squall, and fortunately to anchor in this port by the night of the 16th, shortly before a violent storm broke from the NE and SE, obliging them to drop the sheet anchor.

The presence of the *Atrevida*, with all the advantages I had foreseen, seemed all the more fortunate when Don José Bustamante told me of his chance meeting four or five leagues from the port, on the afternoon of the 16th, with the port barge and two large canoes, coupled together and towing a spare topmast from the spares left by the corvettes. They were being rowed by a large crew in search of a merchant vessel from the Guayaquil trade that had been dismasted a few days before in this area, and left like a buoy without rudder or spare spars for repairs. Bustamante, seeing no ship from the masthead, ordered them to return immediately. No sooner had they reached the entrance to the port than the aforesaid squall showed the danger to which they had thoughtlessly been exposed.

---

[1] Many references to Teniente Coronel Pedro Tueros can be found in Luis Navarro García, *Don José Gálvez y la Comandancia General de las Provincias Internas del norte de Nueva España*, Seville, 1964

[2] For full details of the astronomical observations at Acapulco and the geographical positions of various places on the NW coast of America in which longitude is given west of Cádiz, see Espinosa, *Memoria* (1805), pp. 9-20 and Espinosa, *Memorias* (1809), 2nd memoir, pp. 67-74 and 104. The latter memoir also gives details of tidal observations (p. 124), observations for magnetic variation and inclination (p. 116) and a discussion on the observations to determine the force of gravity (pp. 190-212).

[3] The two corvettes had experienced unusually strong currents. Normally between Cabo San Lucas the currents are very irregular both in direction and strength.

[4] I.e. at evening and morning twilight, the best time to take star sights as the horizon is still clearly visible.

This unsuitable form of assistance had been ordered by the Superintendent of the Real Casa de Moneda [the Royal Mint] in Lima, Don José de la Riva Aguero, who happened to be a passenger on board the dismasted vessel. He had been able to reach the shore near the port in the ship's pinnace and set in motion the measures described. Never has it been more obvious that on such an occasion it is better to abstain completely from meddling in an art than to have vague rudiments of it mistaken for real skill: Don José de la Riva, his ventures bolstered with distances, courses, latitude observations and bearings that no mariner could make sense of, had not realized how great were the risks for inexperienced and unseamanlike men, who had to set off to travel a considerable distance out to sea in canoes, and how useless a single topmast would be for a vessel which had neither rudder, sails, nor rigging.

Our fears for the safety of the crew were largely dispelled the next day by the news that they had finally abandoned ship and, with the launch, reached the shores of Río Papagallo, about eighteen leagues east of the port, thus saving their lives and some twenty thousand pesos of silver coins which made up the most valuable part of the cargo. The captain took the precaution of setting out an anchor with 130 fathoms of the best cable, with the result that the ship, dismasted and at the mercy of the sea, was also safe and moored near beaches not far from the spot when the launch had come ashore.

Meanwhile the fact that the rains had been very late this year and that heavy downpours had come with SE winds during the last days of the month, had led us to discover the illusory nature of our pleasant hopes with regard to the good health that we then enjoyed up to then. The mildness of the weather returning on the morning of the 28th together with the complete clearing of the rain allowed constant sunshine to cause an indescribable evaporation of miasmas, which, with the mountains so close and the vegetation so luxuriant, could not be dissipated by the beneficent sea breezes, and in both crews and all around fevers began to break out, typical of that season in these dreadful climates.[1]

Very soon the epidemic was intensified by the excesses inevitable among sailors, that is, the use of liquor and the preference for their own home-made remedies to the helpful hand of the surgeon. In consequence as the number of the sick in the hospital grew, so it correspondingly increased the work for those who remained healthy. The artificers of both ships were fully occupied at the time in rebuilding the *Atrevida*'s launch, which had been made in San Blas, and the main defects of which had been noticed on several occasions. The *Descubierta*'s *bombo*, which was riddled with worm and damaged after two years of constant service, also needed to be entirely restored. The forges, the cooperage and the armoury could hardly meet the demand for their respective workers. With these demands, the unloading of the ships and various scientific tasks, the boats were never at rest apart from the daily period granted their crews from mid-afternoon to eight in the evening for recreation and free time.

30 October
For this reason, it would have been impossible at that time to help with the recovery

---

[1] Probably a mild intermittent or tertian malaria, which responds to quinine.

and fitting out of the dismasted ship, the *Sacramento*, which, as already mentioned, was anchored near the mouth of Río Papagallo, if the appearance on the afternoon of the 30th of the frigate *Santa Gertrudis* of the royal navy, fully armed for war, had not provided greater manpower to reinforce our efforts to repair her. Capitán de Fragata Alonso de Torres y Guerra, the commanding officer of the *Santa Gertrudis*,[1] told us that he had taken fifty-six days from the port of Callao, where the frigates *Liebre* and *Santa Bárbara* of the royal navy were lying. This length of time resulted, however, from having to make landfall to leeward of the port, because twenty-two days out they were in sight of the Playas de Naguala,[2] and the recent SE gales had inconvenienced him considerably, causing one of his topmasts to spring and setting him onto the coast of Zihuantanejo.[3] He had been fortunate enough to keep his crew healthy during all this time and give free rein to his humanitarian instincts by helping an English whaler off Paita whose crew was severely afflicted by scurvy and threatened with destruction.

3 November

Thanks to this assistance, and with the return of Capitán de Fragata Cayetano Valdés in the *Descubierta*'s launch after a careful inspection of the abandoned vessel, which he found to be in a fit state for sailing once supplied with crew, provisions, spars and rudder, it became possible to start working hard on fitting her out. So on the afternoon of 3 November a small convoy of two launches and two pinnaces under the command of Teniente de Navío Juan Gutiérrez de la Concha sailed from the port with the artificers, provisions and tools necessary for repairing the rigging and rudder. The officers and crew of that ship had been brought together beforehand and their complement made up with volunteers from the frigate *Santa Gertrudis*. An excellent topman had stood in for the sick boatswain, Alférez de Fragata Francisco Benítez had been sent over to command the other launch, and orders given for communication with the port to be as reliable and swift as possible, so that everything should be directed to the achievement of our purpose with all economy and dispatch.

It was very odd at the time that the currents offshore, which had run against us so persistently last February and March, were now setting to the west, sometimes at no less than two knots, seeming to encourage us to put our efforts towards navigating the vessel to Acapulco rather than making for Realejo. With this in mind I left to Concha the choice of the best course of action, although I instructed him not to weigh anchor until the ship was completely ready to sail, so as not to risk her at any greater distance from the port until the pinnaces and launches were able to assist her.

Concha soon found that the only course of action was for the ship to sail to Realejo, or perhaps to Guayaquil, particularly as contrary currents would prevent the passage to Acapulco. Her captain agreed. The alternative was also encouraged by commercial considerations, but it would require on our part the major sacrifice of the launch, without which the crew could not be regarded as safe if anything happened nor could they obtain from the coasts of Guatemala and *Tierra firme*[4] the

---

[1] See Cutter, *California in 1792*, pp. 91–2.
[2] The beaches to the east of Acapulco.
[3] Now Bahía de Zihuantanejo, 108 miles WNW of Acapulco.
[4] I.e. the north coast of South America, including Panamá.

assistance and communications that would contribute to a rapid and successful passage and above all to ensure that the ship would not be untimely abandoned. The replacement of the launch would not in fact be impossible in Acapulco but it would be necessary to start cutting the timber required and setting to work the few healthy men we still had left and perhaps delaying our departure.

In the end, the protection that the royal navy owes to merchant vessels had to prevail over these considerations and at midday on the 10th, the launch having been handed over, the jury masts constructed, the steering oar fixed, water and provisions replaced, the anchor weighed, although the depth was twenty-six fathoms, and the ship's speed and steering tested with satisfactory results, Don Juan de la Concha returned to this port, having carried out his mission with all the energy and intelligence that could be desired.

The merchants commissioned in Mexico City by the owner of the vessel immediately paid the value of the effects supplied by the Royal Treasury, and the wages due to the artificers and seamen. They also agreed to meet the cost, whatever that might be, of the new launch, on which work would be started immediately, and showed us in repeated letters how grateful they felt on this occasion for the royal navy's exertions on their behalf. They gave us the pleasure of carrying out His Majesty's general orders regarding assistance to the commerce of his subjects and also of putting into effect the measures taken by His Excellency the Viceroy of Mexico, who, moved by a remarkable energy and humanity, considered first the safety of individuals, and then that of ships, if they appeared near the coast.

Perhaps such a lengthy and, I may even say, excessively detailed account will seem out of place or contrived to extol what are no more than moral duties. That is not the case. I have been specific only to demonstrate how much can sometimes be achieved by efforts concentrated on a single just purpose, and how much mariners can take satisfaction in seeing benefits flow to society from armed forces which might otherwise be designed only for destruction.

10 November

Not wanting at that time were circumstances, for good or ill, which had thoroughly changed the prospects of the expedition requiring new measures totally at variance with what at first sight we would have proposed. If in great monarchies,[1] fear of the consequences were reason enough to refrain from one's original orders, despite the dictates of conscience, the mature examination of facts and the approval of proper advisers, our conduct at that time would indeed have been reprehensible. But let it be noted how blameworthy we should be if, owing to such inhibitions, we were to forfeit any of the benefit which the crown might properly expect from our efforts after the expenditure of so many resources. And it will be seen that, if indeed the outcome of these efforts, for good or ill, depended absolutely on a thousand circumstances, which were hard to anticipate, it would in any event have been truly culpable and reprehensible to stand by and watch the waste of valuable achievements, for

---

[1] Probably a reference to France, Great Britain and Spain, the only nations that could afford to mount a naval expedition devoted to scientific objectives at a time that war could break out at any moment.

which I was responsible, merely through fear of laying an inexperienced hand to the wheel.

Moreover, I was under even further obligation by reason of the King's kindness in having approved, so far, my feeble efforts for the honour of his flag and the prosperity of his subjects, by his liberality in granting new favours to those who had not had a share in those of 1789[1] and finally by his generosity in promising, so as to bring our work to a fast and successful conclusion, to commission other ships for the surveys that we would be unable to undertake ourselves during the first months of 1794.

This, then, was the pleasant news brought to us by the first mail from Europe that we received soon after our arrival in Acapulco. The commanding officer of the *Atrevida* and Tenientes de Navío Dionisio Galiano, Antonio Tova and Cayetano Valdés had been promoted to the next rank and Don Antonio Pineda had been awarded a good pension over and above his military entitlements. Don Felipe Bauzá had been commissioned Alférez de Navío, and the paymasters, the *pilotos* and *pilotines*, the sergeants and master gunners were also promoted, the two surgeons and the senior boatswains were given a bonus, the families of the excellent artificers from Galicia[2] on board both ships were given an extra month's pay. Finally, all were told how much His Majesty's thoughts were with us, and how great would be his future expectations of the further services to the nation to be made by the corvettes *Atrevida* and *Descubierta*.

At the same time His Majesty authorized me to fix an amount for a gratuity, and to distribute it, to all the other men of every rank who had thrown in their lot with the corvettes since Spain, having served reliably, willingly and honourably. However, I thought it best to delay this reward until reaching Manila, because there were many good men who should not be subject to any unfair comparison, having joined the service in Buenos Aires or Lima. In addition if either four months' pay or all the arrears had to be paid to the crew here, the small increase of this gratuity would hardly be perceptible and would not achieve the proposed intention of prompting stronger feelings of love and gratitude towards the sovereign.

Meanwhile, the news from Mexico City grew better at every moment. The letters from there, which reached us at the same time, were no less satisfactory. His Excellency the Conde de Revillagigedo had already arranged for the remittance of the funds requested and the supply of bread and flour. Don Antonio Pineda and Don Luis Neé, with tireless activity, had enriched their natural history collections, covering some 400 leagues of varied terrain, extending from Acapulco to Mexico City by Chilpancingo, Tixtla, Río Azul, Real de Taxco and Cuernavaca, and from Mexico City to Guanajuato by San Juan Teotihuacán, Zempoala, Pachuca, Real de Monte, Santa Rosa, Ixmiquilpán, Querétaro, the hot springs of Atotonilco el Grande and San Bartolo, Queréjuaro, Acámbaro, the hot springs of Ucarco, Salvatierra and Salamanca. On receiving word from me they prepared to return to Mexico City and Acapulco; they left thirteen boxes of specimens in the capital for the Real Gabinete in Madrid, having also enriched the important account of their voyages with many physical experiments, and with various perspective views taken by a Mexican painter whom

---

[1] The year that *Descubierta* and *Arevida* were commissioned.
[2] Probably recruited from the naval dockyard at El Ferrol.

Plate 28. The Waterfall at Querétaro (120 miles NW of Mexico City), by José Gutiérrez. Museo Naval, Madrid

they had taken with them.[1] They had also made a useful comparison of the operation of the mines in this kingdom with the most carefully developed ideas of Europe and with the methods adopted in Peru, all aims of the greatest importance for the true enlightenment of the nation regarding such an essential part of its wealth.[2]

Don Dionisio Galiano had been equally active and successful during his stay in Mexico City, occupying himself efficiently by putting all the material from the past voyage in order, continuing his series of astronomical observations, collecting new hydrographic information and giving the final touches to his calculation of latitude at sea by two altitudes of the Sun. Finally Don Arcadio Pineda, with equal energy and insight, had collected a large number of important and useful documents for the proper understanding of the present state of prosperity in the kingdom, that would stimulate our desire to be of use to the nation in every way within our reach. Don Manuel Novales was now in his original state of good health, owing to the intelligence and care of Dr O'Sullivan of Mexico City, and although the painter Guio, racked by fever, no longer had thoughts of anything but his return to Spain. Don Juan

---

[1] Because José Guio was suffering from some sort of fever Pineda hired the artist Francisco Lindo in Mexico City to accompany him to Guanajuato, during which he painted over seventy botanical subjects. However, Malaspina appears to be referring to José Gutiérrez, who accompanied the expedition at his own expense and who sketched all the important places visited: Engstrand, *Spanish Scientists*, p. 98. Several of Gutiérrez's sketches are held in the Museo Naval.

[2] For a summary of Pineda's expeditions see Engstrand, *Spanish Scientists*, pp. 76-102. See also Virginia González Claverán, 'Antonio Pineda: Naturalist and Pre-Archaeologist' in Inglis, *Spain and the North Pacific Coast*, pp. 60-68.

Ravenet and Don Fernando Brambila, appointed by His Majesty, with the same pay and prerogatives, to replace Don José del Pozo, both skilful Italian masters of painting, had arrived conveniently in Mexico City to join the expedition.

The friendly reunion of so many and such useful men, with whom it would not be difficult to face new fatigues and dangers in the future, did much to make our longer stay in Acapulco most pleasant, particularly as both the astronomical and geodetic work had been finished during the previous stay, while the lack of haste in making the preparations allowed us a real rest. The commanding officer of the *Atrevida*, Don Tadeo Haenke, Don Fernando Quintano and Don Francisco Viana took advantage of this last circumstance to make a scientific excursion to Mexico City, and the others arranged for a moderate amount of work putting in order and reviewing the latest hydrographic material or the pendulum experiments, while waiting for the chance to make any observations which might correspond to those taken in Mexico City by Don Dionisio Galiano.

However, the inevitable mixture of good and evil in human affairs inevitably balanced out, perhaps excessively, the advantages of our situation that I have just described.

15 November

The prevalent fevers, which seemed of little account at first, now set in with intermittent inflammations, complicated at times with putrefaction, and at times accompanied by delirium, bilious colic and bloody dysentery, the conclusion of which, at the tertiary stage, seemed to be the best point at which to take advantage of the beneficial use of the excellent quinine that the Don José Villalengua, ex-Presidente [de la Audiencia de] Quito and present Regente de Guatemala, had so generously given us the year before.[1]

Very soon some ninety men from the frigate *Santa Gertrudis* and at least fifty from the corvettes were attacked by this disease. A good half of the officers from the former, and from our complement Don Ciriaco Cevallos, Don José Robredo, Don Felipe Bauzá and the surgeon of the *Atrevida* added to our cares and troubles. Although on one hand it had seemed better to care for the infected on board, for the healthier air, better order and even for the better help for the sick, on the other hand, the lack of space, the almost continual noise and the close proximity of those still healthy appeared to argue against such a measure. The workshops could not be abandoned, even though this cost us many sacrifices. The construction of the new launch proceeded slowly, while the *Atrevida*'s was still not yet finished. The cutting of firewood could no longer continue, and there were hardly enough men on board to carry out the indispensable tasks of fetching water, stowage, work on the rigging and mending the sails. Meanwhile the seamen, never ready to learn from experience and never satisfied, added new problems to those of the harmful influences of noxious air, by trying to cover their fear and anxiety in a thick veil of profligacy and wastefulness.

---

[1] See p. 33, n. 5 above and Vol. I of this edition, p. 261, where his first name is given erroneously as Juan. A more serious form of malaria, which can prove fatal, but which responds to quinine. 'Putrefaction' was a term used when symptoms included foul breath, vomiting and diarrhoea and its use in this context implies a falciparum infection.

But as they continued to appear for work at the right time it seemed particularly unjust and even unwise on our part to subject them to a discipline as useless as it would be irksome. Nor did we have any soldiers, since those who had been transferred to us last April as auxiliaries had been returned to the castle[1] and a corporal from the *Atrevida* and three marines, chronic and incurable invalids from the *Descubierta*, had been given passports to return to Spain. The few remaining, as well as suffering greatly from diseases, had to share with the seamen the hard work on the ships and boats.

Fortunately the method followed by our surgeons from the start, and imitated in the hospital and on board the frigate *Santa Gertrudis*, had dispelled all fears of a fatal end to the illnesses mentioned, however much this seemed inevitable from the painful symptoms that accompanied them. But as the remedies depended principally on frequent repetition of bleedings, many purges and emetics and a strict diet, the convalescents found themselves so weak that either the slightest excess of food caused new and dreadful attacks of colic, or the atmospheric conditions caused new relapses into tertian fever. To this most unpleasant distraction, which constantly threatened us with more suffering for those already sick as well as the imminent possibility of disease for those who were still well, was added a new circumstance, soon to deprive us of a considerable and much-needed number of officers and friends.

Orders very recently sent by His Majesty to His Excellency the Viceroy of Mexico required that while the recent differences over territorial rights between our monarchy and that of Britain should be resolved in Nootka, a detailed survey should be made of what is known as Juan de Fuca Strait, which, according to recent passages by Captains Barkley, Meares and Quimper, seemed to lead to a further arm of the sea, which the imprudent believed reached nearly to, or as far as, a connection to the Atlantic Ocean.[2] His Excellency was kind enough to notify us of these orders, and to inform us that the schooner *Mexicana* of the Department of San Blas, under the orders of Teniente de Fragata Francisco Mourelle would soon sail to undertake that survey, while Capitán de Navío Juan de la Bodega y Quadra, with the frigates *Gertrudis* and *Princesa* and a schooner, would make for Nootka, there to find or wait for the English ships sent to conclude a convention.[3] The schooner *Sutil* was still assigned to the conclusion of the unfinished survey of the coast from Aquatulco[4] to Teguantepeque, Soconusco[5] and the mouths of the Lempa,[6] thus combining the various duties of the Department so that they could be carried out with the same thoroughness. Don Francisco Mourelle certainly combined his considerable maritime experience and the standard knowledge of pilotage, with a resolution and enthusiasm which would have been equal to the greatest ventures, but his health was not up to them. Nor did he have that useful knowledge of nautical astronomy without which his expedition would cause new hydrographic disputes rather than resolving

---

[1] See p. 71 above.
[2] See p. 53, notes 2 and 6 and p. 54, n. 6 above.
[3] See p. 53, n. 2 above.
[4] Puerto de Huatulco, 58 miles WSW of Salina Cruz.
[5] The vicinity of Paredones de Soconusco, a group of hills 85 miles ESE of Salina Cruz.
[6] Río Lempa, which enters the sea 50 miles west of Punta de Amapala.

the old ones. In addition to which the lack of astronomic and geodetic instruments, and therefore of all reliable means of determining latitude and longitude, remained an obstacle to the undertaking, the outcome of which could not fail to be affected by the fact of Mourelle being alone, without even a [second] schooner under his orders.

These reflections could no longer conceal the irremediable risk to His Majesty's exchequer and national honour, if our expedition, with its excellent officers and instruments, could not contribute to the suggestions of His Excellency the Viceroy. All the officers were of the same mind and every day one or another would demonstrate his energy and probity of character by adding new tasks to those already in hand, undertaking to carry them out promptly and thoroughly, whatever the hardships, discomforts and risks they had to face. Our nation would be cheated of one of the brightest adornments of the present expedition if I failed to make public the daring projects that gave rise to an honourable and commendable rivalry though never divorced from a remarkable friendship and esteem among all the officers. The completion of the survey of the inner waters of Juan de Fuca Strait, the final touches to the parts not yet fully surveyed of the coasts of Teguantepeque and Guatemala, the survey of Golfos de Nicoya and Amapala, the reliable determination of the position of the Galapagos, the subsequent passages to Chiloé, the coast of Patagonia and Estrecho de Magallanes and the final survey of Golfo de San Jorge were all included in these proposals. They could certainly be easily achieved by a team of officers who, after two and a half years of uninterrupted labours, nevertheless were now quite ready to tackle anything they might encounter with these two schooners, only forty-four feet in the keel and just capable of accommodating two officers and a small number of seamen.

However, it would have been unwise to agree to all of these operations, exposing to grave risks people of whom the nation could expect, in good time, further laurels, and further delaying the final publication of our voyage beyond the year 1794. Accordingly I proposed to His Excellency the Viceroy that Capitanes de Fragata Dionisio Galiano and Cayetano Valdés, with Tenientes de Fragata Juan Vernacci and Secundino Salamanca, should sail from Acapulco in the schooners, after transferring to that port from San Blas. They should make directly for Nootka Sound, from where, having taken on water, provisions and men, they should enter Juan de Fuca Strait by the middle or end of April, surveying it, if necessary, until September or October, and then sail for San Francisco Harbour in California to complete the survey undertaken by the corvettes, returning to the coast of New Spain after the rainy season. Galiano and Valdés, in one of the schooners, would then be able to survey the coast from Acapulco to Barra de Iztapa,[1] and then make their way back to Spain by way of Guatemala and Vera Cruz to begin the revision and putting in order the astronomical log-book and other material from the voyage. Vernacci and Salamanca would be able to take the other schooner to run along the parts of the coast of New Spain, Golfos de Nicoya and Amapala, not yet well surveyed, then leave her near the narrow Istmo de Nicaragua and possibly examine its height and extent in order to decide the question of a connection between the two oceans. Finally [Vernacci and Salamanca] would be able to draw up a very accurate hydrographic chart of Golfo de Nicaragua and the

---

[1] Situated at the mouth of Río Michatoya, 56 miles WNW of Punta Remedios.

navigation of Río San Juan as far as its discharge into the Atlantic Ocean, an object of great importance for national prosperity and which could very well be completed by the time of our arrival in Spain, so as to conclude our entire work.

His Excellency approved the proposed plan immediately and gave the necessary orders for the complete fitting out and return of the schooners *Mexicana* and *Sutil*. Meanwhile we devoted all our efforts to the supply of everything they needed. They were to use the astronomical quadrant, the Ellicott astronomical clock, the large achromatic telescope and the pocket chronometer, which were at present in Don Dionisio's charge. To these were added chronometer 61, already repaired in Mexico City, a second achromatic telescope, a barometer, some thermometers, a reflecting circle with a stand, a theodolite, an azimuth compass and a mariner's compass. They were also supplied, drawn on various charts, not only with our surveys of the last voyage, but also those of Captains Meares and Dixon, and of Teniente de Navío Eliza in Juan de Fuca Strait. Finally, some nine volunteer seamen from the frigate *Santa Gertrudis* having been received on board the *Descubierta*, ten of the best seamen from the latter transferred as volunteers to the schooners, choosing to lend their service in all the dangerous situations that would inevitably arise in the planned voyage.

On my part, while I could only envy these officers their new and honourable opportunity to multiply the benefits of the expedition, for the well-being of society and the glory of the nation, I could not omit to describe it thus to His Majesty, then joining all the others who were to accompany me in wishing this useful part of the expedition all the good fortune which might immortalize their names.

The complements of the corvettes were therefore now made up as follows:

Descubierta	*Atrevida*
Don Alejandro Malaspina	Don José Bustamante
Don José Espinosa	Don Antonio Tova
Don Manuel Novales	Don Juan de la Concha
Don Francisco Viana	Don José Robredo
Don Martín Olavide	Don Ciriaco Cevallos
Don Fabio Ali-Ponzoni	Don Arcadio Pineda
Don José de Mesa	Don Jacobo Murphy
Don Rafael de Arias	Don José Ezquerra
Don Francisco Flores	Don Pedro González
Don Felipe Bauzá	Don José Añino
Don Juan Maqueda	Don José María Sánchez
Don Gerónimo Delgado	Don Juan Inciarte
Don Joaquín Hurtado	Don Luis Neé
Don Antonio Pineda	Don Fernando Brambila
Don Tadeo Haenke	
Don Juan Ravenet	

In our present state of weakness and unease, Teniente de Navío Fernando Quintano finally gave in to our appeals and the advice of Dr O'Sullivan for a thorough cure of his chronic and severe stomach disorder, since it would not be difficult for him to rejoin the expedition in Manila by the Manila galleon the *San Andrés*, which had just arrived in port under the command of Teniente de Fragata Don Joaquín Berenguer de Marquina.

The arrival of this ship was very convenient, to help with our protracted fitting out. It owed the remarkable speed of its crossing to the well-planned new route which made use of the *colla* or SW Monsoon directly from San Bernardino Strait[1] to the Marianas Islands, then running down the parallels of 14° and 15°, until the favourable westerlies gave way to the easterly trade winds with which, when more than 10° east of the said islands, they continued close hauled to the north to reach the westerlies again, from where they could make rapidly for the coast of California. It was also fortunate that they had sighted Farallones de Vázquez, a group of islets well off the Californian coast in latitude of about 26°, the position of which was therefore no longer uncertain, as several series of lunar distances had been observed shortly before sighting them.[2]

With this help we redoubled our efforts in cutting timber in Puerto Marqués, sawing it and preparing it for the construction of the launch. Thus we were able, although its interior was not yet finished, to count on having it ready to be taken alongside and hoisted inboard by the middle of December at least. For this purpose we used the carpenters of two merchant vessels from Guayaquil, at present anchored in the port with a cargo of cocoa, despite the fact that the presence of the galleon made it necessary to take many precautions to avoid smuggling. The recently arrived governor[3] was nonetheless good enough to allow us to continue with the same method of work that we had used so far, in the certainty that we would not take unfair advantage of such a concession.

8 December

These and many other kindnesses that we had received from Teniente Coronel Pedro Tueros from the moment of his arrival, combined with the remarkable work that he had done in the inner provinces of Nueva España, made it a very heavy blow to us when the epidemic, to which he soon fell victim, brought his life to an unexpected end within a fortnight. The epidemic continued its ravages with the same intensity as at the beginning of November, and neither a calm and methodical life nor preventative bleedings, nor clearing out the undergrowth that the rains had caused to grow and multiply in the vicinity of the town, according to a well established custom, were enough to stop it. There was nothing else to be done, therefore, but to hasten our departure, particularly as we had managed to obtain, from the Observatory of Mexico City a good corresponding observation of the first satellite of Jupiter. We had repeated with great care the pendulum observations, embarked most of the instruments and begun a new rating of the chronometers. Thus, counting on the galleon to transport to Manila the stores that we could not yet obtain, there was nothing essential to detain us once the launch was ready to be taken on board.

---

[1] Between the islands of Luzon and Samar.

[2] Almost certainly Rocas Alijos (24°57′N, 115°45′W), a group of four high and remarkable rocks, which lie about 150 miles off the coast of Baja California.

[3] Teniente Coronel Pedro Tueros: see below and p. 230, n. 1 above.

Bread was, in fact, very scarce on board because, in addition to having to supply the merchant frigate *Sacramento*, the *Atrevida* had had to discard some fifty *quintales* and the *Descubierta* twenty. Since the hundred *quintales* and the flour requested from Mexico City had not yet arrived, there was hardly more than a bare two months of this essential part of our provisions in each corvette. Our hopes of being able to collect a good store of salt pork had also been dashed, the dried beef which we could have substituted for it was still very scarce, and eighty *quintales* of chickpeas that we were expecting for our stock of dried vegetables were late in arriving.

It was by chance that we became aware of a misfortune in the preparation of salt pork, for which we had preferred to choose the method described by Captain Cook[1] rather than that normally used by Comte de la Pérouse with the addition of vinegar. Although we put heavy weights on the layers of pork, and the salt was very effective, it did not penetrate far enough, so that part of the pork was spoilt at the beginning of the process. We would probably have lost all of it if we had not immediately taken the precaution of cutting the pieces into smaller sizes and infusing them with boiling water before covering them with the salt and putting the weights on top. This mishap, although trivial, is recorded to remind those who are preparing their provisions for long passages how hazardous it is to follow any method blindly, even one that has been thoroughly tested, and how necessary it is to pay constant attention to the various eventualities which cannot be foreseen.

The method of preparing dried beef on all our Pacific coasts and in Río de la Plata is well known. The animal is killed and divided into several slabs; the meat is then left in brine for twenty-four hours and then exposed to the Sun until it is completely dry. The resulting meat tastes very good and not too salty, so that it does not lose any of its nutritional value. But for this precise reason its useful life is short, because the meat has not been stripped of those parts which are useful as food at first, but are then very likely to rot.

Having stored four or five months' worth of meat and salt pork, it was not difficult to persuade the commanding officer of the frigate *Santa Gertrudis* to part with as many as 150 *quintales* of bread that he had just received from Mexico City which he would easily be able to replace in San Blas if I notified His Excellency the Viceroy. Also from the commanding officer of the galleon we received sixty *quintales* of mungo beans and rice from Manila, both of excellent quality, of which he had no need at the time. It was left to the latter to use the hundred *quintales* of bread and carry the 800 [*quintales*] of flour and seventy [*quintales*] of chickpeas to Manila, which I most earnestly urged him to preserve, since this depended to a great extent the success of the last, and very arduous, part of our voyage.

It was not as easy to solve with either of these commanding officers our need for a number of marines and seamen. It would have been unwise in the weakened state and reduced numbers of both our crews not to make up our complement, considering that our coming excursions through the Philippine channels demanded the

---

[1] James Cook, *A Voyage towards the South Pole and around the World*, 2 vols, London, 1777, I, pp. 247-8.

greatest attention to the safety of the launches, which would be continuously exposed to the piracy of the Joloanos Indians.[1] I was only asking for five marines from the frigate *Santa Gertrudis*, on which they could very well be considered redundant or perhaps even detrimental, given the present peaceful conditions and the many good seamen remaining to her, while the crowded conditions on board that ship hardly left room for four months of water and provisions.

I had reduced to fifteen voluntary seamen my request to the commanding officer of the galleon, which beside, having been made ready for war, had brought seventy or eighty stowaways and, having only to make the direct and very peaceable return passage to Manila in the most suitable season, was obliged to carry four or five hundred soldiers sentenced to serve there. It would therefore be to her own advantage not only to part with these fifteen, but also with as many again for the frigate *Santa Gertrudis*, whose commanding officer insisted that he was unwilling to break up any part of his present complement.

These considerations had no influence on either commanding officer, both being timid and inclined to a servile interpretation of the laws and ordinances and, above all, being very much given to excuse their own advantages by citing a supposed lack of authority and documents.

In the end it was necessary to produce these in the form of some official replies [on my part], as I thought it unsuitable to resort to military authority in a matter which should not require it. However, while such pleas and conduct did finally convince them, the obstacles, difficulties and schemes that they laid in our path were so troublesome, reviving our memories of what had happened in Lima with the frigate *Liebre*,[2] that we would henceforth have considered the encounter with other ships of the royal navy as something to be dreaded, had not the efficient help and kindness of Capitán de Navío Don José Orozco in Río de la Plata reminded us in good time and gratitude of the convenient benefits to naval service that may arise with a commanding officer who is also a friend and companion.

At the time the corvettes were indeed in a deplorable state, as regards the complement of seamen. Apart from the fact that the majority of them were either gravely ill or unfit for service, the *Atrevida* had just lost in hospital a second carpenter of the greatest skill.[3] Three excellent seamen from the *Descubierta* probably would not escape the same fate, one of them being ravaged by venereal disease, another suffering from a hemiplegia[4] so far incurable, and the third from a putrid fever due in great part to his excesses during a previous convalescence.

Not even the pursuit of deserters was proceeding with the success that we had had earlier. Indeed on our return to this port, not only had we been handed over the only deserter from the *Atrevida* on the previous voyage, but also we had now seen, led by two militiamen, two deserting seamen from the frigate *Santa Gertrudis*, although they

---

[1] See page 270, n. 6 below.
[2] On the eve of the expedition's departure from Callao six seamen missing from the *Atrevida* were precisely those that had just transferred voluntarily from the *Liebre*: see Vol. 1 of this edition, pp. 229 and 235.
[3] Identified by Bustamante as Juan Barral: Bustamante, *Diaro general del viaje*, p. 300.
[4] Paralysis of one side.

were carrying some 300 pesos, with which they had not been able to break the loyalty of these honest subjects. The *Atrevida* was now missing at least four seamen, most of them Filipinos. It was discovered that one of those from the *Descubierta* recently recruited in Monterey had gone to Guayaquil in the merchant ship of that trade.[1] Finally, it was necessary to take the greatest care to avoid the desertion of others, whose minds were more influenced by the incitements of a disorderly life among the most horrible objects of nature, than by the almost daily warning offered by their companions and by our pleas, punishments and reprimands.

14 December

At noon on the 14th the shipment of money arrived from Mexico City, of which part was taken on board and part was shared out in four payments to the officers, marines and seamen, settling in full, until the end of the year, all payments and bonuses due to those who were leaving the corvettes, either because of illness or to serve in the schooners *Mexicana* and *Sutil*. The muleteers who brought the money assured us that the flour would not arrive until the 24th. As this meant not only waiting for a period, albeit short, of four days, with the increasing epidemic and the proximity of the Christmas holiday, it was finally decided, for fear of further excesses and desertions, that we should set sail on the morning of the 20th, without waiting for the schooners, the flour, or anything else.

19 December

The frigate *Santa Gertrudis* sailed on the 19th for Puerto de San Blas, having received all the provisions assigned to her. On the same day we hoisted the launches and embarked the sick, these being no fewer than thirty or thirty-five on each corvette. We also took this opportunity to send to Capitán de Navío Don Juan de la Bodega y Quadra not only our charts from Nootka to Acapulco, duly completed, but also two sextants and the ephemeris for the next year, all things that he needed greatly, but we were not able to part with a chronometer he had also requested.

On the same date I sent to His Excellency the Ministro de Marina a report of all that we had been able to prepare for the present consignment to His Majesty of the results of the expedition so far, which, although not organized as we might have wished, had the double advantage of being forwarded free of any risk and likely to arrive more quickly at Court.[2] It was, of course, entrusted to the efficient protection of His Excellency the Viceroy. At the same time I begged him to be kind enough to arrange for the return of the painter, Guio, to Spain and to consider as highly praiseworthy the conduct of the draughtsman Don Tomás Suria, who had accompanied us on the last cruise and had now returned to Mexico City. The following items, then, were those now be forwarded:

With the first packet boat

In a tin cylinder: Three Mercator charts, covering the coasts from Acapulco to the entrance to Bucareli Bay. The chart sent from San Blas should

---

[1] The two ships of the Guayaquil trade in the harbour (see p. 240 above).
[2] Malaspina to Valdés, 20 December 1791: AMN, MS 583, ff. 97–8.

include the short stretch of coast from Bucareli Bay to Cabo Engaño [Cape Edgecumbe].

Nine plans of the harbours of Mulgrave, Desengaño [Disenchantment Bay], Nootka, Cayucuat,[1] Monterey and San Blas.

A sketchbook of views of the coasts surveyed on the last cruise.

Two perspective drawings by Señores Ravenet and Brambila: the first of Puerto del Desengaño[see plate 13], the second of Acapulco [see plate 4].

In a packet or bound book:
Sailing directions from Coquimbo to Lima.
Memoir for the charts from Lima to Realejo.
The journal of our stay in Acapulco last April.
The log book of the passages from Acapulco to the Northwest Coast of America until our return to that port.
The astronomical journal of the same voyage, including the gravity experiments with the pendulum, arranged and compared by Don José Espinosa.
The meteorological journal of the same voyage.
The summary of the magnetic variations observed on both corvettes.
The physical description of the coasts surveyed to the north of Cape Blanco in latitude of 43°.
Political study of these.
A discussion of the most convenient harbour for a depot for naval forces in the Pacific.
The copy of a letter to the Mexican trade inviting them to make a trial of trading in otter-skins.[2]
The continuation of Don Tadeo Haenke's botanical treatise.

In a small box, number 1, marked D.A.[3]
The drawings by Don Tomás Suria and José Cardero of the most important things seen during the last cruise. Those done in pencil have been glazed, so as not to be smudged. Some have not yet been completed, and fair copies are being made of these.
The botanical and insect illustrations by José Guio.
The perspective views by the two painters who accompanied

[1] Probably a copy of Piloto Gonzalo López de Haro's survey 'Plano del Puerto de Cayuela' carried out during Eliza's 1790 expedition to Juan de Fuca Strait. Cayuela and Cayucuat were two of a number of alternative spellings of Clayoquot Sound on the west coast of Vancouver Island south of Nootka Sound: Wagner, *Cartography*, pp. 353 and 440.

[2] After his visit to the NW Coast Malaspina wrote a detailed report on the possibilities of active participation in the fur trade as a way of upholding Spanish sovereignty in the North Pacific: 'Carta al comercio de México convidándole a un ensayo sobre el comercio de las pieles de nutria', AMN, MS 335, ff. 53-5. See also James Gibson, 'Nootka and Nutria: Spain and the Maritime Fur Trade of the Northwest Coast', in Mercedes Palau Baquero and Antonio Orozco Acuaviva, eds, *Malaspina '92*, Cádiz, 1994, particularly pp. 150-53.

[3] The *Descubierta* and *Atrevida*.

Don Antonio Pineda on his excursions through the kingdom of Mexico.[1]

In another packet boat
For the accurate collection and arrangement of the whole:

General mark D.A.

13 boxes: Nos 1 to 13	Containing herbariums, minerals, crystals, spars, insects, and a few birds from the collections of Señores Pineda and Neé.
No 14	Continuation of Don Tadeo Haenke's herbarium.
No 15	Collection of utensils of all kinds from Port Mulgrave. The large canoe from Tinaja[2] will be sent from Manila.
No 16	A similar collection from Nootka and otter skins from various latitudes.
No 17	A similar collection from Monterey and several mounted birds.
No 18	Small bundle of bows and arrows from the harbours visited.
No 19	Papers and books belonging to Don Antonio Pineda.
No 20	Notebooks and books from officers of various branches of the navy.

Boxes 14 to 20 were entrusted to royal officials; the tin cylinder and the packet of papers were sent by the packet boat and the small box of drawings, with Don Antonio Pineda's thirteen boxes, were left for complete preparation in charge of the judge of the Real Audiencia de Mexico, Don Ciriaco González Carvajal.

One cannot go further here without a brief but most grateful reference to the important services that the expedition received from this worthy Minister. His house was rather like a lyceum and his magnificent natural history collections were at all times available to Don Antonio Pineda. Furthermore he also allowed full use of his library to Don Arcadio Pineda. His excellent political intelligence and careful enquiries among his friends, that is, among the majority of the cultivated people of Mexico City whose knowledge might make our account useful to the nation [was put at our disposal]. He made daily visits to our sick officers. Such fond memories would in themselves suffice to secure our most lasting gratitude in Mexico City. But there is also in equal measure and weight the kind, constant and efficient assistance of His Excellency the Viceroy, and the remarkable action of the Super Intendente de la Real Casa de Moneda [Royal Mint],[3] who devised the stratagem of snatching almost from the hands of the makers various objects that we had commissioned and paying for them from his own funds so as to have the pleasure, as he said, of presenting them to the expedition.

A colony which, as well as contributing by its great affluence to the nation's prosperity, gives such proof of its love of the sciences and its loyalty to the sovereign, and

---

[1] Francisco Lindo and José Gutiérrez: see p. 235, n. 1 above.
[2] Not identified.
[3] Dr José Francisco Fernández Cordova: see p. 63, n. 2 above.

is ruled by leaders so devoted to the common good, cannot fail to call to itself the attention of the moral philosopher, and arouse his ardent wishes for the growth and strengthening of its social links not only with the mother country, but also with the other provinces which, scattered across the globe, form the immense Spanish monarchy.

20 December

At dawn on the 20th the work of unmooring had already begun. We waited for the first breath of the sea breeze in order to make our immediate departure from the port, having hoisted the launches, completed rating the chronometers on the 18th and taken on board all the correspondence for the Marianas and Philippines received by that date from Mexico City. There were more than a few seamen missing at the time. Don Francisco Viana had to go and drag out of wretched dens of vice six or eight of them, cunningly hidden, although his energetic labours did not allow him to detain two seamen deserters who had kept very quiet until then but had now given in to disorderly conduct. Finally, at ten o'clock in the morning, with the sea breeze having set in, the anchor weighed and the spring taken in, we set sail, with the deserters and the remainder of the crew, as follows:

Present complement

	Descubierta	*Atrevida*
Commissioned officers, other officers,[1] naturalists and artists	16	14
Petty officers	16	16
Seamen of all ranks	47	44
Marines	13	14
Marine gunners	3	3
Servants	7	5
Total	102	96

Losses since the previous departure from Acapulco:

	Descubierta	*Atrevida*	Total
Deserters	2	3	5
Died on board or in hospitals		2	2
Left in hospitals	3	1	4
Transferred to the schooners	9	0	9
Discharged for usual mishaps	4	2	6
Total	18	8	26

---

[1] Paymasters, chaplains, surgeons, *pilotos* and *pilotines*.

BOOK EIGHT

From Acapulco to Manila

CHAPTER 1

Acapulco to Guam

20 December 1791
We were still inside the port, recovering our ground tackle, under shortened sail, when Don Cayetano Valdés approached in the port barge to inform me that the mule trains carrying our flour were just arriving. I felt, however, that it was neither useful nor necessary to stop to take on board the flour as it could be carried by the galleon more quickly and with less inconvenience. We could very well make up any shortage with rice from the Marianas or the Philippines or with wheat from China, if an extended duration of our cruise so required.

This time we were much luckier in our departure from this port than we had been the previous April with the sea breeze more favourable both in strength and direction, so that by midday we were off the outer point of Puerto del Marqués,[1] without a single tack, and past any risk of grounding. The sea breeze continued fresh until nightfall, by which time we were a good six leagues from the port, with Punta del Grifo[2] bearing N15°E by compass and variation by observation 7°0′NE.

The usual distractions on the day of departure, the somewhat high sea from SE, and the general satisfaction of breathing clean air, so visible not only in the sick but also on the previously unrecognized faces of the healthy, had persuaded us to leave until the next day our eudiometer experiments with various samples of air, taken shortly before sailing, in the Plaza Mayor in front of the hospital and in the spacious and well ventilated ward where three of our sick men had laid. [21st] We performed the experiments, with great attention to detail, the following day with the Fontana eudiometer.[3] The degree of salubrity obtained was 0·81 for the first two samples, 0·79 in the hospital ward and 0·82 for the air that we were now breathing ten leagues off the coast, in calm conditions with haze on the horizon.

We hardly moved all day, as both the breeze and current were very slight, and a high swell from SE caused us to roll heavily, counteracting any headway, let us say, we might otherwise have made to the south. However, by the early morning of the 22nd, more because of the haze than the distance, we were out of sight of land, and shortly afterwards we began to feel light airs from the first and second quadrants, enabling us

---

[1] Punta del Diamante.
[2] The western entrance point of Puerto de Acapulco.
[3] For Fontana see p. 69, n. 1.

to steer WbyS, with the pleasant prospect of soon encountering the trade winds[1] on which we depended for the complete recovery of our sick men.

There were no fewer than twenty-five of these on each of the corvettes at the time of departure and several more had now joined this number. Although we had no cause for alarm regarding the majority, some of whom were convalescent and others not seriously ill, there were many who were suffering considerably from a bilious colic which threatened to have a lasting effect on the bowels even when the air had cured them of the illness itself. All our efforts, therefore, were concentrated upon the essential object of cleanliness in order to support the skill of Don Francisco Flores, who had carried out his work with much success until now. Two more servants were assigned to the sick bay, and those among the sick who did not have all the comfort they needed in the waist were accommodated in the deck-house, which was kept very clean, cool and quiet. The English cots[2] were properly arranged, the livestock was housed in the gangways, the decks were thoroughly cleared as often as possible, Málaga or Sanlúcar wine was distributed to the convalescents, and everything possible was done to make them more comfortable.

23 December
Only a few birds, mostly boobies,[3] were to be seen around us, while the number of turtles that we had encountered since our departure had begun to decline. Shortly before noon on the 23rd we had the pleasure of sighting a large vessel about four leagues to the west, whose position and NW course left us in no doubt that it was the frigate *Santa Gertrudis*.[4]

24 December
We hoped to be able to make use the very light NE breeze to approach this vessel, which was sailing almost close hauled, but we were separated during the following night most probably by a wind shift and an unexpected northerly current, which had caused an error of no less than 28' in our dead reckoning of latitude in the last twenty-four hours. Rain was in sight to the west and finally, by noon on the 24th in latitude 15°50', we had made one degree to the west. The trade wind seemed imminent, given the constancy of wind from the first and second quadrants, although it had so far been weak and interspersed with calms.

[1] The North-east Trade Wind which is encountered from about 25°N during the winter months.

[2] A ship's bed made of canvas stretched on wooden frame and slung like a hammock from the deck beams. Used by officers before the introduction of cabins, but also more suitable for the sick than conventional hammocks.

[3] Brown Boobies (*Sula leucogaster*), Red-footed Boobies (*Sula sula*) and Masked Boobies (*Sula dactylatra*) occur off the coast of Mexico: Gerald Tuck, *A Guide to Seabirds on the Ocean Routes*, London, 1980, p. 118. Nicknamed 'booby' (Spanish '*bobo*') because they are trustful of humans and 'suffer themselves to be catch'd by the Hand' (Hans Sloane, *Voyage to Jamaica*, I, London, 1707, p. 31). Since they never stray far from land, they were a welcome sign to sailors. See Robert C. Murphy, *Oceanic Birds of South America*, 2 vols, New York, 1936, II, pp. 827-70.

[4] Commanded by Capitán de Navío Alonso de Torres, the frigate *Santa Gertrudis* had been sent from Spain for the express purpose of reinforcing Spanish naval strength during the crucial negotiations to settle the terms of the Nootka Convention. Bodega y Quadra sailed in her for Nootka on 29 February 1792. It seems likely therefore that the *Santa Gertrudis* was bound for San Blas to pick him up before proceeding to Nootka.

These signs did not deceive us, and once the effects of the new Moon had passed with only some cloud cover on the horizon, giving way to a variable, but fresher, wind from SSE to east, we had the pleasure of encountering the trade wind at noon on the 26th in latitude 15° 22′ and longitude 4° west of Acapulco. At noon we compared our chronometers with those of the *Atrevida* for the second time that day. We had decided to repeat these comparisons frequently, not so much for the sake of having exact results each day, as for the purpose of a continuing examination of the degree of accuracy of these instruments and checking as well their respective differences daily for our hydrographic calculations.

On the following morning the sight of two large trees, serving as a natural resting place for birds, caused us no surprise, as we were now off the coast near San Blas, where we knew from previous experience that many tributaries of large rivers, now swollen with the winter rains, discharge into the sea. We began to see a few tropicbirds[1] and, although the trade wind on the following days did not have the strength or consistency that we had hoped, we had reason to think that it would last. Our progress had been far from negligible, when compared with the usual times made by the galleons.

Many considerations induced me not to stray from the well-tried route. Our stores of food and water were not sufficient to allow for any delays in reaching the Marianas, nor were the crews in a condition to bear any extra work in watch-keeping, unexpected manoeuvres, etc. Furthermore, the rainy season, which we assumed would start in the Philippines at the beginning of June, would not leave us time for any useful work in those waters if we wasted time searching for one or another of the uninhabited islands which are known to abound below the parallel of 10°.[2] As for a brief call at Hawaii, which I had previously proposed, it seemed now most untimely for the above reasons and the fact that Teniente de Fragata Quimper of the Department of San Blas had recently spent a month there acquiring the knowledge we needed concerning the politics and natural history of that island.[3]

Accordingly I now gave the commanding officer of the *Atrevida* instructions about a rendezvous, in case we should unexpectedly become separated. He was to steer directly for the Marianas, where he was to wait for me for fifteen days in the port of San Ignacio de Agaña.[4] When that time had elapsed, so as not to waste the good season, he was to sail directly to Cape Bojeador[5] and from there follow the east coast of Luzon[6] and, after passing through San Bernardino Strait, finally make for Manila.[7]

---

[1] Red-billed Tropicbirds (*Phaethon aethereus*): Tuck, *Guide to Seabirds*, p. 118.

[2] A wise decision. At the time and for most of the 19th-century charts of the central Pacific featured numerous islands, whose existence has now been disproved or whose longitudes were badly in error: see Henry Stommel, *Lost Islands: The Story of Islands that have Vanished from Nautical Charts*, Vancouver, 1984.

[3] See Cook, *Flood Tide of Empire*, pp. 298-9.

[4] Agaña is the capital and administrative centre of Guam, the largest and southernmost of the Mariana Islands in the NW Pacific. Agaña is on the west coast, north of Apra Harbor, which is the only good anchorage on that coast. For a description in 1887 see Luis Ibáñez y García, *History of the Marianas, Caroline and Palau Islands*, trans. Marjorie G. Driver, Guam, 1992; for fortifications see Driver, op. cit., and Omaira Brunal-Perry, *Architectural Sketches of the Spanish Era Forts of Guam*, Guam, 1994. (Both these references come from Richard J. Shell.) See also P. Carano and P. C. Sánchez, *A Complete History of Guam*, Rutland-Tokyo, 1964.

[5] The NW extremity of Luzon.

[6] The largest of the 7,000 Philippine Islands, about 2,000 of which are inhabited.

[7] Manila, capital of the Philippines, founded by Miguel de Legazpi in 1571, is on the River Pasig in

31 December

When the *Atrevida*'s pinnace came alongside to take the instruction we learnt that there had been a considerable improvement among all the sick men on board her, who had lately included Señores Neé and Brambila and the chaplain among their number.[1] Our own progress in this regard was much slower, as we had no fewer than thirty-five sick on board, among whom there were at least six who were seriously affected by the illness or by excessive weakness.[2]

As in fact we had been mistaken earlier on in taking as the trade wind the light breezes from the second quadrant rather than from the first, our progress along our route in the last few days had not fulfilled our expectations nor, I should say our needs.

1 January 1792

By New Year's Day 1792 we had only reached latitude 13°24' and longitude 12°28' west of Acapulco, with variation approximately 7°30'.

The following days' runs were also poor, with a very heavy sea from north and NW, the winds light and variable. The seven degrees of longitude achieved by noon on the 6th had cost us considerable wear to the rigging, sails and hull and even to the few men who remained in good health. In these conditions it was impossible to air or clean the waist properly, as was our custom. It was also impossible to avoid tiring the crew frequently either by mending the torn sails or by repairing the damaged cordage. On the 3rd and 4th there were gales from SW to NW, accompanied by continual rain, so that it was difficult to dry drenched clothing or to avoid more work and damage. On the afternoon of the 2nd, the weather being still very boisterous, we took in two reefs in the main topsail, hoping that we might get some rest during the night under that and the foresail, but it was not enough to prevent the topsail from splitting when loosened. The *Atrevida* suffered the same misfortune when striking the fore topsail, so that new sails had to be fitted on board both ships.

6 January

At noon on the 6th, in latitude 12°41' and [longitude] 20°38' west of Acapulco, we

---

SW Luzon and has the best natural harbour in eastern Asia. For an 18th-century description, and some French reflections on the city and its society, see Dunmore, *Journal of La Pérouse*, pp. 236-49.

[1] The following day, however, Bustamante recorded a further deterioration in the condition of the sick, due to the high seas and the movement of the corvette in variable winds: Bustamante, *Diario general del viaje*, p. 304.

[2] Malaspina, like every good commander, was concerned for the welfare of his crew, stressing the need for regular hot meals, physical exercise, fermented drinks and frequent bathing: Cook, *Flood Tide of Empire*, p. 119. These voyages took a toll on seamen. La Pérouse wrote from Botany Bay that he had lost his teeth and hair, warning, 'You will take me for a centenarian when I return.' Scurvy was a serious problem, though James Lind (1716-94), 'the father of nautical hygiene', having confirmed his predecessors' intuitions, showed that fruit was essential in a sailor's diet: S. O. Waife, *Notable Medical Books*, Indianapolis, 1976, p. 119. Lind's work was known to Pedro María González, whose *Tratado de las enfermedades* is a primary source for contemporary Spanish maritime medico-sociological studies. Although he refers to the *Atrevida*, González is not to be confused with a namesake who served as a surgeon on the Malaspina expedition. For a summary account see C. C. Lloyd, 'The Conquest of Scurvy', *British Journal of the History of Science*, 1, 1963, pp. 357-63, and Randolph Cock, 'Precursors of Cook: The Voyages of the *Dolphin*, 1764-68', *The Mariner's Mirror*, 85, 1999, pp. 30-52, especially pp. 41-4.

once again believed that we were close to the zone of trade winds, although they remained somewhat variable and rainy, while the heavy swell from north caused the usual rolling. We made use of a few intervals of calm to clean the interior of the ship. We were now under full sail and at last, at four o'clock in the afternoon, after a heavy squall from WNW the wind veered to the north, when we encountered a steady trade wind. At midnight, under full sail and with a clear sky and horizon, we were making eight to nine knots. This favourable change was heralded, shortly beforehand, by the sight of great numbers of flying fish,[1] which continued to accompany us afterwards. The sick men gave credit to these fish for the purer and brisker air, and the following morning they all showed a considerable improvement and alleviation of their symptoms.

10 January
The weather answered all our hopes until the 10th. The trade wind remained steady from ENE and both corvettes were making seven knots. There were a few showers of no great strength which promised fresher and more lasting winds, if we were to judge by our recent voyage in the frigate *Astrea* in these waters.[2] It gave us no small satisfaction on board the *Descubierta* on this day to have unequivocal proof that even though the *Atrevida* was usually sailing in company with us, without studding-sails, the advantage she sacrificed was very little, as these sails had no effect on our respective speeds.

The experiments with the eudiometer at that time demonstrated that our hopes of finding better air as we got further offshore were not unfounded. The salubrity in the open air was now measured at 0·89, having been only 0·81 at our departure from Acapulco. We were now in latitude 12°42′ and longitude 32°30′ [west] of Acapulco; variation 5°NE.

However, we still felt uneasy about the outcome and success of the crossing, which very much depended on preserving the health of our crew and efficiently planning our forthcoming tasks in the Marianas and Philippines. The trade wind, far from remaining constant from ENE, veered to the second quadrant, bringing heavy and humid air, with frequent calms and with such a heavy swell from the NW and north that the increased rolling impeded our work below decks and reduced our speed considerably. By midday on the 20th, in latitude 13° and longitude 55° [west of Acapulco] according to number 72, we could only just consider ourselves to have reached the meridian of Hawaii, yet our dead reckoning error was no less than 7°E, which, with the long log line[3] that we were using, was not the maximum that might

---

[1] Linnaeus's *Exocaetus evolans*.

[2] From 1786 to 1788 Malaspina commanded the *Astrea* on a commercial voyage to Manila on behalf of the Real Compañía de Filipinas (see Vol. 1 of this edition, p. xxxvii), as a result of which he gained a reputation as one of the most competent of Spanish navigators. Here he refers to observations made by him at that time, some of which were incorporated into the *Carta nueva de navegar a las Marianas* (Madrid, 1794) by the Cartographer Royal, Tomás López (1731-1802). The Real Compañía de Filipinas, founded by Carlos III (1785), had the right to trade directly with Spain and to deal with China and the Indian states; see M. L. Díaz-Trechuelo, *La Real Compañía de Filipinas*, Seville, 1965 and Holden Furber, *Rival Empires of Trade in the Orient, 1600–1800*, Minneapolis and Oxford, 1976, pp. 182 and 226; see also E. H. Blair and J. A. Robertson, *The Philippine Islands, 1493–1898*, 55 vols, Cleveland, Ohio, 1903-9, LIV, pp. 235-6.

[3] See Vol. 1 of this edition, p. 5, n. 1 and p. 33, n. 1.

be made on the crossing. This strongly supported our suspicions that Sandwich Islands of Captain Cook were those named as Monje, Ulua etc on Spanish charts. They were discovered by Juan de Gaitán in 1555 and located some 10° east of the new position determined by the English.[1]

Variation remained at about 5° or 6°NE, and the distances from the Sun to the Moon, only established satisfactorily on the morning of the 18th, made us suspect a small westerly error in number 72, confirmed by frequent comparisons with number 71 and with number 105 of the *Atrevida*.

The weather, Don Francisco Flores's skill and, above all, the strict diet which was imposed on the most seriously ill, who were kept, as already noted, in the clean and well-ventilated deckhouse, had at last triumphed over the persistent epidemic, contracted in Acapulco. Until now we had believed that three or four men of the lower ranks to be so weak that their lives were in grave danger. Another thirty, at least, who could not be considered fit for duty, needed special rations while the least disturbance, either of diet or tranquillity or exposure to the Sun or rain, would inevitably cause fresh relapses which might be fatal. This number included the two carpenters' mates, which would have greatly delayed the completion of our launch if the caulkers had not exerted themselves to replace them, with a good degree of success. With great satisfaction we could now consider it ready for use. Such a measure was necessary for many reasons, and the more so because of the long delays we were experiencing on this crossing. The truth is that it seemed as if our luck was improving to a certain extent now that we had passed the meridian of the Sandwich Islands. The outlook seemed better now that the trade wind had returned to the first quadrant, the sea comparatively smooth and the weather pleasant, all of which, with the sight of increased numbers of flying fish, bonito[2] and many birds of species common to the tropics, made our situation more agreeable. However, in the end the only material advantage in our favour was a state of orderly calm for the classification of information collected during the past cruises. Any hope of shortening the crossing was already lost, as the trade wind was mostly very light, while a swell from the NW, which made itself felt again during the last days of the month, dispelled any doubts that the wind would have been more favourable in higher latitudes.[3]

27 January

On the evening of the 27th we were able to repeat satisfactorily our observations of lunar distances, forty-eight sets of these giving a longitude of 20' less than that indicated by number 72. On the same day the eudiometers showed a new degree of salubrity in the open air and also in the other places where we usually took samples.

---

[1] Juan de Gaetán was a member of the Spanish exploratory expedition in the Pacific under Rui Lopez de Villalobos (1542). On the controversial question of a possible Spanish discovery of the Hawaiian Islands, see vol. 1, p. lviii; E. W. Dahlgren, *Were the Hawaiian Islands Visited by the Spaniards before their Discovery by Captain Cook in 1778?*, Stockholm, 1916, and O. H. K. Spate, *The Spanish Lake*, Canberra, 1979, pp. 108-9 and p. 316, n. 72.

[2] A fish (*Thynnus pelamys*) of the same family (Scombridae) as mackerel and tuna.

[3] This is a reference to Malaspina's decision to keep to the well-tried route.

The open air gave a result of 0·94, the sick bay 0·90 at ten o'clock in the evening and the main deck 0·87 at the same time.

31 January

Such was our situation at the end of January. Our latitude was the usual 12°45' and our longitude 81°37 [west] of Acapulco; variation was about 11° and our distance from the Marianas not less than 600 leagues.

It was difficult to verify the changes in the rates of the chronometers from those determined in Acapulco, as the equations deduced from the comparisons were contradicted by the results of the [lunar] distances, which were now corroborated by four more sets of observations with Pollux, in very good conditions.[1]

As the full Moon approached, the welcome signs of settled favourable weather increased, which we made the best of under full sail, with a state of cheerful tranquillity which is difficult to describe. On the nights of the 3rd and the 4th we repeated the observations of lunar distances with eastern and western stars.[2] The results indicated a somewhat greater difference to the east compared with number 72 than that previously shown by the distances observed from the Sun to the Moon. Variation had already reached its maximum of 11½° to 12½°NE and now began to diminish again in longitude 90° and 91° [west] of Acapulco, where our observations had resulted in 10 ½° to 11° with an acceptable degree of precision and reliability.

We continued to follow religiously, so to speak, the track of the Manila galleon and that of the frigate *Astrea*. We might be accused of some neglect or excessive caution in not having tried to identify or position accurately any of the many islands and dangers which the Spanish charts of these waters show to the north and south of the prescribed route, but I had constantly to decide against such an idea in view of the great uncertainty of the true latitude of such dangers, the length of the nights and the compelling need to keep as much time as possible allotted for the coming work, which would be difficult to combine with other than reckless attempts at discovery.[3]

5 February

At noon on the 5th, in latitude 13° and longitude 97° [west of Acapulco], we had to alter course for the islands of Saipan and Tinian,[4] which I only wished to include in our current work in order to determine their longitude as their latitude had been accurately fixed by Commodore Wallis in 1767.[5] It was necessary to disregard the more southerly islands or rocks, whose exact position seemed of no great importance

---

[1] Malaspina is clearly referring to lunar distances to Pollux, one of ten stars listed in the *Nautical Almanac*. With the approach of the full Moon distances between the Sun and the Moon would be too great to observe.

[2] I.e. to stars to the east or west of the Moon as tabulated in the *Nautical Almanac*.

[3] Malaspina has sometimes been criticized for lack of daring but his explanation here shows that this was not so much timidity as policy. See also p. 251, n. 2 above.

[4] Two of the Mariana Islands.

[5] Captain Samuel Wallis (1728-95), was the first European navigator to visit Tahiti during his cirumnavigation of the globe in 1766-8. As a result of his visit the Royal Society chose this island for the site of their expedition, under Lieutenant James Cook, to observe the Transit of Venus there in 1769. According to Wallis, Tinian was in latitude 14°58'N: John Hawkesworth, ed., *An Account of the Voyages undertaken by the Order of His Present Majesty for Making Discoveries in the Southern Hemisphere*, 3 vols, London, 1773, I, p. 521.

for navigation and would be fairly well established when that of Saipan was known. The remaining months of the favourable season urged us to hasten towards the Philippine and China Seas, where our hydrographic tasks were numerous and important.

11 February

At noon on the 11th, in latitude 14°54′, we estimated that we were 113°15′ west of Acapulco. We therefore took for this meridian the longitude determined by our observations as 102°26′15″ west of Paris and, according to Captain Wallis' calculation that the southern tip of Tinian lay 114°6′ from Acapulco,[1] we were only 51′ of longitude distant from it. Indications of its proximity were also given simultaneously by the many tropicbirds and gulls[2] which flew around us from the morning onwards, variation, which we now calculated at 5°25′, a constant cloud cover to the west and, above all, the advantageous position of the island of Saipan which, being both higher and further west than Tinian, would bring us closer to the happy sight of land. To hasten the successful outcome of such promising signs, we altered course to the fourth quadrant to take us more directly to the latter island, and at two o'clock we could indeed see it clearly about fifteen leagues distant.

We continued to steer towards it and, as the wind was fairly strong, by four o'clock we could take bearings of the two extremities of the island, bearing between 58° and 75° in the fourth quadrant,[3] while the islands of Tinian and Aguiguan[4] could be seen from the mastheads in the third quadrant. We now altered course towards them so as to determine their distance from Saipan by triangulation and to approach these other islands more closely.

At five o'clock they could be distinguished easily, the extremities of Tinian now bearing from S71°W to N84°W by compass. We therefore began the determination of our distance from this island and at the same time, having signalled to the *Atrevida* to do the same, we observed hour angles so as to relate these longitudes to that of the observatory on Guam.[5] Don Felipe Bauzá took views of both islands with his usual accuracy. Before nightfall we were only five leagues off Tinian, where the channels between that island and the other two islands were clearly visible, Aguiguan now bearing S66°W. This latter island is of moderate height and size. To reach the anchorage at Tinian it is usual to pass through the channel formed by these two islands, passing a short distance from the second one.

We concluded these tasks at nightfall when we altered course to the south, under shortened sail, to cross the parallel of the island of Rota,[6] intending then to alter course again to the west to pass between this island and Guam and make for the anchorage. The wind was fresh and there was cloud on the horizon, so we kept a very

---

[1] According to Wallis, Tinian was in longitude 214°10′W by Dr Maskelyne's method (i.e. by lunar distances): ibid. Taking into account Paris Observatory being 2°20′00″east of Greenwich (*Tables Requisite*, 2nd edn, London, 1781, p. 161), Wallis's figure actually places Tinian 114°03′45″ west of Acapulco.
[2] Probably White-tailed Tropicbirds (*Phaethon lepturus*), Red-tailed Tropicbirds (*Phaethon rubricauda*) and possibly various species of terns and noddies: Tuck, *Seabirds on Ocean Routes*, p. 94.
[3] Presumably between N58°W and N75°W.
[4] Aguijan, separated from Tinian by a channel 5 miles wide.
[5] The largest and southernmost of the Mariana Islands.
[6] A small island about halfway between Guam and Tinian.

careful lookout, which this locality required. At four o'clock in the morning we were able to set courses in the third quadrant and, shortly afterwards, to the west. [12th] At first light the island of Rota was in sight five leagues distant, bearing N37°W. We observed hour angles on its meridian and, assisted by the favourable trade wind, interspersed with a few passing showers and a fairly rough sea, we continued steering W5°S towards a position from which we were soon able to take bearings of the northern extremity of Guam.

The Spanish charts showed an islet or rock between Guam and Rota, which we searched for very carefully, both for our own safety and that of later navigators. However, we found no sign of it and had to conclude that it had been confused for an islet that we could see not far off the SW extremity of Rota. There was certainly no danger overlooked by us between these islands.

At ten o'clock in the morning we were on the meridian of the NE extremity of Guam, which is high and somewhat rocky, with sheer cliffs down to the water's edge. New hour angles were observed, our ensigns were hoisted, as we ranged the coast about a league offshore, altering course gradually to the south as we rounded the north of the island to sail down its western[1] coast. From one end to the other this is an attractive coast, whether one considers the lush vegetation, the gently rounded contours of its hills or the always calm sea into which many streams discharge their crystalline waters. At about half past eleven we could easily make out the buildings of the capital, Agaña, and at midday, no bottom being obtained with one hundred fathoms of line one league offshore, the NW point bore N43°W, the capital S6°W and Orote Point[2] S41°W by the compass.

A chart of the San Luis anchorage[3] published by Mr Dalrymple[4] based on Spanish manuscripts,[5] and information, although confused, from M. de Crozet,[6] would eventually induce me to discard this anchorage in favour of the one at Umatac,[7] which I knew from my previous voyage to be fairly comfortable and safe, particularly in the present season.[8] Nevertheless the desire to examine carefully the only place which offered shelter from the SW, its greater proximity to the capital and particularly its

---

[1] E = *este* or eastern in the original MS, which is clearly a transcription error for O = *oeste* or western, the side of Guam which is sheltered from the North-east Trade Wind.

[2] The southern entrance point of Apra Harbor.

[3] Apra Harbor.

[4] Alexander Dalrymple (1737-1808), the first hydrographer to serve both the East India Company and the Admiralty, spent years in India and South East Asia, including the Philippines. On 23 November 1762 he proposed a 'Plan of an Expedition for the Conquest of the Southern Philippines': BL, Add MSS, 19,298.

[5] 'Puerto de Apra on the Island Guahan vulgo Guam by Antonio Rodrigues 1733 from a Spanish MS', London, 20 May 1781.

[6] Julien-Marie Crozet (1728-82), who sailed in the *Mascarin* under Marion du Fresne to New Zealand in 1772. After the latter was killed by Maori warriors at the Bay of Islands, Crozet assumed command. Homeward bound, he met Cook at the Cape in 1775 and shared his charts with him. Despite Malaspina's remarks, Crozet was enthusiastic about Guam, which he called a 'terrestrial paradise': Julien Marie Crozet, *Crozet's Voyage to Tasmania, New Zealand, the Landrone Islands, and the Philippines in the Years 1771–1772*, transl. H. L. Roth, London, 1891, pp. 88-100.

[7] Umatac, a town and bay on the SW coast of Guam Island, 9 miles south of Orote Point.

[8] See 'Plan of Umatac Bay on the Island Guahan or Guam, laid down geometrically by the Officers of the Frigate *Astrea* belonging to the Royal Company of the Philipinas ... by the Observations of the Chevalier Malespina [*sic*]' published by A. Dalrymple, London, 31 May 1796.

central position, which would enable our hydrographic and natural history excursions easily to cover all parts of the island, could have determined our choice, but the complete lack of any buildings nearby for the observatory and for the accommodation of the convalescents was a serious inconvenience, of which we had just now become aware.

At one o'clock in the afternoon we were only a league and a half from Orote Point, forming the southern entrance to the port. At that moment we saw a proa[1] under sail coming from Agaña which appeared to be making for us. We therefore hove-to, to wait for it, in the hope that it would be able to guide us more safely through the many shoals in the port and save us this extra work. The proa did not reach us until half past two, as it approached with great caution, still fearing that we might be enemies, and because of the frequent tacking and sail-trimming made necessary by its construction made it difficult to sail without the risk of being pooped[2] in the fairly rough sea raised by the wind at the time. I did not think it prudent to hand over to this frail craft the sealed documents and letters for Manila given to me in Acapulco. There was no one on board who had any practical knowledge of the port of San Luis. Consequently this visit was of no use to ourselves and only served to allay the fears of the inhabitants at our arrival and prevent them taking measures for their defence which had been prudently established by Don José Aslegui, the present Governor of these islands.[3] With hopes of obtaining useful information about the anchorage thwarted and in no doubt as to the direction of the reefs near Orote Point,[4] we hoisted more sail to approach it until we were close to the breakers. From there we continued under topsails only, so as to be able to examine the bottom more easily.

At about half past three, even before our soundings warned us, we saw that we were passing over the extension to SSW of the reef, which closes off the good holding ground about a cable from the entrance to the harbour. We could see some enormous rocks four fathoms below the surface, but we bore up to avoid them and obtained depths of thirty and thirty-five fathoms, gravel. We hailed the *Atrevida* to warn her of this considerable danger and she made almost the same manoeuvre. We then luffed to get to windward and, as we were now close to Orote Point, we came about to the other tack under topsails. Finally, at half past four, we dropped anchor in twenty-seven fathoms, gravel, about half a mile to the NE of the abandoned Orote battery. The *Atrevida* was delayed by a kink in her cable and fell back to the stopper,[5] with her anchor

---

[1] The flying proa of the Marianas, a double-ended vessel with a single outrigger and a large triangular sail. When going about the former stern becomes the bow and she is trimmed on the other tack. Two of the crew who are placed in the bows and the stern steer the vessel alternately with a steering oar depending on the particular tack. For a full description see Williams, *Anson's Voyage round the World*, pp. 305-8 and sketch f.p. 340.

[2] The danger of a sea breaking over the stern of the proa in a following sea, causing it to capsize.

[3] José Arlegue y León, Governor of Guam (1786-94), undertook an index to royal orders relating to the Marianas, which was continued by others down to 1843. There is a copy (161 leaves) in the Library of Congress, according to Blair and Robertson, *The Philippine Islands*, LIII, pp. 363-4.

[4] At the time of Malaspina's visit shoals and reefs extended across the entrance to Apra Harbor except for a channel about 5 cables wide between Orote Point and Catalan Reefs, the usual entrance. The shoals and reefs have now been dredged away, making the harbour into a major US naval base.

[5] A piece of rope having a large knot at one end and secured to a ring bolt at the other end. It is attached to the cable by a lanyard, enabling the cable to be restrained when at anchor.

caught on rock not far from the reef and lying too close to Orote Point. By then I had fully realized that this locality did not suit our needs in any way. There was not a single building nearby, the very rocky shore would make landing dangerous if not impossible, the watering place was far away, and to find sufficient shelter would require warping for nearly a league while still exposing our anchors and cables to the numerous rocks which lay everywhere about.

For this reason the boats were lowered immediately and I informed the commanding officer of the *Atrevida* of my plan to move to the roadstead of Umatac the following day. Don Francisco Viana was sent to examine in greater detail the shore and soundings of the surrounding area, while both corvettes paid out long warps to the NE, we to help our anchor hold until the next morning, the *Atrevida* to fall back to a better position and to lessen the risk to her anchor in the dangerously poor holding ground.

Don Francisco Viana confirmed all the disadvantages of this place that we had observed. The muddy channel which led between the shoals and the shore to the basin,[1] was so narrow that even when warping through it, sternfasts would be necessary at times. We had every reason, therefore, to decide upon making the proposed move at first light on the following morning.

During the earlier part of the night the land breeze or a north wind blew quite strongly. Later two officers from the island came on board and I gave them the sealed documents and letters we had brought. Finally, at dawn, the wind having dropped considerably, we weighed anchor and both corvettes hove to windward on the warps. [13th] By nine o'clock the *Descubierta* was under way, under the foresail, fore topsail and topgallants passing within a cable of Orote Point, where the whitish colour of the water warned us of the considerable length of the reef. The danger was the greater because we had not yet finished getting the kedge anchor on board. The *Atrevida* was at some risk of losing her own kedge, but at last, like ourselves, she managed to bring it on board. Under full sail and towing the launches both ships then made for the anchorage at Umatac, keeping a short distance offshore. After some troublesome tacking in light and variable winds the *Atrevida* dropped anchor on the parallel of the battery, two thirds of a mile distant. Soon afterwards we did the same a cable's length to the north, the only mishap being that our shoreward anchor was lying on rock.

---

[1] 'The anchorage usually occupied by ships ... is a basin surrounded by coral patches of 2 or 3 feet beneath the surface. The channels leading to it are frequently narrow, the last before entering the basin not more than 120 yards wide.': Findlay, *Directory*, II, p. 1112.

CHAPTER 2

At Guam

[13 February]
The previous evening, when forwarding the correspondence to the Governor, we had informed him of our main reasons for visiting this roadstead. Soon after anchoring I received from him a very courteous message advising me that he would arrive in person at the roadstead in a few hours time, when it would be easier for him to attend as required, with instructions and advice that might contribute to the success of our mission. Indeed, by nine o'clock he had arrived at the small town,[1] accompanied by some priests from the nearby missions,[2] but by then we had returned on board after a pleasant and productive walk through surrounding area.

14 February
This active intercession by the Governor was bound to be of great benefit to us. Early the next morning fourteen men from the *Descubierta* and six from the *Atrevida*, some gravely ill and others convalescent, were very comfortably lodged in the guards' quarters of the Governor's own house. Señores Cevallos and Bauzá, who also needed some peace and rest to restore their health, found good lodgings in a house near the mission, in which we were also able to set up both the pendulum and astronomical clock and safely store the other instruments. The astronomical quadrant, sheltered by the portable observatory, was positioned a short distance away, so that everything was now arranged for our tasks in this area to begin immediately with the usual steadiness and bustle.

Those responsible for natural history studies were not idle either: Señor Haenke set out that same day for Agaña and the southern extremity of the island,[3] Don Luis Neé made for the Vigia Mountains,[4] not far from this bay, while Don Antonio Pineda

---

[1] Umatac.
[2] Initially, the Marianas had been a Jesuit mission, but in 1767 the Society was temporarily expelled from the Spanish possessions and replaced by priests of other communities, in this case by the Augustinian Recollects.
[3] Colleagues later published some of Haenke's papers relating to the Marianas: see *Reliquiae Haenkeanae seu descriptiones et icones plantarum, quas ... in insulis Phillipinis* [sic] *et Marianis collegit Thaddeus Haenke*, Prague, 1827.
[4] Possibly Mount Bolanos, 379 metres high, backing Umatac Bay.

Plate 29. The anchorage of Umatac in the island of Guam, by Fernando Brambila. Museo Naval, Madrid

occupied himself particularly with the lithology and zoology of these parts, which appeared to be most relevant and curious.[1]

The epidemic contracted in Acapulco, the backlash of which accounted for most of the sick men that we were trying to restore to health, was now considerably aggravated by the disorders inevitable among sailors, little inclined to accept any regimen, privation or diet. It had now established itself so firmly that it would have been in vain to attempt to cure on board those who had suffered repeated bouts of tertian fever. One of the *Descubierta*'s seaman was so weak that at times we doubted that he would last more than twenty-four hours. Another seaman from the same ship and one from the *Atrevida* had relapsed with dangerous attacks of dysentery, the *Atrevida* having already lost a seaman to this disease during the crossing. A variety of illnesses conspired to worsen the epidemic. Thus in addition to the above, on the *Descubierta* a marine was suffering from a severe colic and a seaman was gravely affected by scurvy, already of the second degree. We could only hope that the fresh air, the rest ashore, healthy food and, in particular, daily exercise, would soon help them towards a complete recovery. To this end both ourselves and the Governor took every measure for the well-being and care of these unfortunates.

The principal occupation of both launches during this day was obtaining water. A stream with an abundant supply of water was situated only a short distance from the corvettes. By working hard the crews were able to make two trips, so that by nightfall we had replaced nearly half of our supply of water and we proposed to make this our main task for the following day.

15 February
Although the day dawned fairly cloudy, the officers of both corvettes went to the observatory, which was now properly set up, with the intention of observing many sets of distances from the Sun to the Moon to calculate its longitude. Our attempts were fruitless, however, owing to the continuing cloud cover, although the astronomers were able to obtain the time of noon by observing equal altitudes of the Sun, so that it was easy to calculate the longitude by the chronometers. On this occasion it would have been unwise to assume the rates of the chronometers as being the same as that determined in Acapulco, since daily comparisons had shown their rates to be very different. The ones to be determined now seemed all the more preferable considering that the differences observed at sea remained constant in the comparisons.

16 February
Meanwhile, the new Moon was approaching; the wind was now stormy from north

---

[1] Spanish interest in natural history had lapsed, so that only six books on the subject were published during the entire reign of Carlos II (1661-1700): See J. M. López Piñero, 'Los comienzos de las ciencias modernas en España', in *Actas del segundo congreso de historia de la medicina*, Madrid, 1965, I, p. 287). The Enlightenment brought a change, and Malaspina, asking Joseph Banks (1789) for advice for his planned expedition, stated his purpose to be the 'study [of] Natural History and of the Human Race and the world it inhabits': BL Add. MSS., 8097, ff. 216-220 and Warren R. Dawson, ed., *The Banks Letters*, London, 1958, pp. 569 and 654. For a general study see Juan Carlos Arias Divito, *Las expediciones científicas durante el siglo XVIII: Expedición botánica de Nueva España*, Madrid, 1968.

and NNE with rain, strong gusts and a high sea. Since the *Descubierta*'s anchor was still lying on rock it seemed prudent not to defer beyond the next day the task of weighing the anchor to examine the cable and to anchor again this time on sand, particularly as the pinnaces sent to take soundings found that there was good holding only a third of a cable away towards the *Atrevida*. Early on the morning of the 16th, therefore, having passed a warp to the *Atrevida*, the launch was sent to lay another anchor and then weight the first from the rocks by the buoy-rope. We found that one strand of the cable had already parted, although only a short distance from the clinch.[1] We also moved the western kedge [to a better position] and now considered ourselves secure for the remaining days that we might have to spend in the anchorage.

Our dismay may be imagined, therefore, when the lead informed us that despite all our labours, the anchor was once again lying on rock. The only result that had been achieved was that now both our anchors were in depths of ten or twelve fathoms greater than before. It was necessary to set to work again early the next morning, when it was made more difficult by the strong wind and a high sea from the north, continuous rain, and the need to anchor on a steeply sloping bottom while trying to avoid disturbing the *Atrevida*, which appeared to be satisfactorily moored.

17 February

At three o'clock in the afternoon everything seemed to have been achieved with the eastern anchor laid out on a warp and in nineteen fathoms, sand, with the large kedge moved to the NW, so that we were now only a cable to starboard of the *Atrevida*, with the small fort bearing NEbyE, half a mile distant. Having been broken at the crown, the anchor recovered from the rocky bottom was not used and was replaced by a bronze one from San Blas. The men were given leave and the following day we only occupied ourselves finishing watering ship, for which purpose the launch was sent out very early to fill the remaining casks.

18 February

However, a number of tiresome tasks still awaited us. A moderate gale had been blowing in gusts from the NE since dawn, and by eight o'clock we began to drag the anchor and then the kedge. We were already in forty-two fathoms and too close to the shore to the south, so that it seemed unwise to drop a second anchor. It was therefore necessary to get under way, paying out the hawser [marked] by a good buoy so as to ensure that we would later be able to recover the cable, of which we now had no less than 120 fathoms out. Fortunately the launch had come alongside a little earlier, which we unloaded at once. The few officers who were occupied ashore at the observatory or in the study of natural history arrived soon afterwards in the Governor's barge, so we could set to with a will to haul in the cable over the starboard bow under eased fore topsail, jibs and mizzen.

---

[1] A method of fastening the cable to the ring of the anchor by a half hitch with the end stopped back to its own part and secured by seizings.

The wind, far from dropping, increased in the afternoon with heavy squalls and rain, making our work much harder. To this were added the difficulties of hauling in the cable over the starboard bow, the necessity of hoisting all the boats and the misfortune of having a useless fore topsail bent on, which was rapidly being torn to shreds, while the corvette was becoming impossible to steer in these conditions. To overcome these obstacles as far as possible our first action, once the boats were hoisted, was to change tack, falling off to leeward somewhat in order to keep a league away from the breakers off Cocos Island[1] and then lying-to on the same tack so as to be able to work more calmly and easily.

It was already seven o'clock in the evening when we brought the anchor inboard at last. It was necessary to bend on another fore topsail immediately, but finally, at eight o'clock, we were able to set a course in the fourth quadrant under the four principal sails, giving the crew some respite, even though this might be interrupted by the heavy sea and frequent squalls and showers from the NE.

The moment I realized that we were at risk of having to abandon the anchorage, I took the opportunity to use the *Atrevida*'s pinnace, which was with us at the time, to send the necessary orders to Don José Bustamante, informing him of the next steps to be taken. I instructed him to cut short the excursions of Señores Neé, Pineda and Haenke, to send a *piloto* by land, if it were not possible by sea, to make a detailed survey of Puerto de San Luis, fixing the soundings and delineating the shoals, to embark the sick, the instruments and other tools belonging to both corvettes and to make for the anchorage of Palapag[2] on Samar Island, to which I would sail if I considered it too difficult or tiring to return to our present anchorage.

I did not, however, wish to be separated at this time from the *Atrevida*, which would be put to great inconvenience by having on board sick men, instruments and equipment belonging to the *Descubierta*. Accordingly, I tacked to the SE at about four o'clock in the morning so that at least they would see us from the higher ground around the anchorage. The sea was still high and the wind strong, but it was now from ENE [19th] and there were intervals of fine clear weather which allowed us a view of the whole island after sunrise, although we were not less than seven leagues from its southern extremity, now bearing ESE.

By now we now had a better understanding of the shifts of the trade wind at different hours of the day and night. We could therefore plan our tacks more effectively, remaining on the starboard tack all that day and part of the night, and putting about to the second quadrant at eleven o'clock.

20 February

Thus by dawn we managed to be nine leagues from Orote Point, which bore SE. As the sea was becoming calmer and wind, by now a fresh breeze, was backing a little towards north, our progress towards the port was so rapid and direct that by ten o'clock we were hardly two leagues from the point. By eleven we could see the anchorage and the *Atrevida* and, by noon, having made a tack towards the breakers

---

[1] A small island, 2 miles off the SW coast of Guam.
[2] Palapag on the NE coast of Samar, one of the central islands of the Philippines.

off Cocos Island, we were able to haul the wind on the starboard tack under full sail only three or four miles from the little fort at Umatac, which bore N63°E, observed latitude 13°15′30″.

My first idea was to stand off and on until the *Atrevida* could set sail, and then use the launches to bring our men and belongings over to the *Descubierta*, thereby causing as little inconvenience as possible to the *Atrevida* and avoiding the necessity of anchoring immediately. However, in that case we would not be able to finish taking on water and cutting firewood, of which we were in great need at the time. On the other hand, all the observatory and hydrographic work would fall on the crew of the *Atrevida*, who would have less time to attend to their own need to rest and restore their health.

With these considerations and as the trade wind was particularly favourable, I decided to anchor. At four o'clock we passed ahead of the *Atrevida* and anchored nearby in fourteen fathoms, sand, in approximately the same place where we had begun to drag our anchor on the morning of the 18th. The *Atrevida*'s launch, which had managed to pick up our kedge by dragging for it, brought the anchor back to us and immediately laid it out to the NW. We lowered the boats, then allowed the marines and sailors complete rest for the remainder of the afternoon and the following night.

During the past few days Don José Bustamante, the Governor, Don José Aslegui and others had been very active in the discharge of their various duties. Most of the sick showed a considerable improvement, and Señores Pineda and Haenke, having been as busy as usual in the vicinity of Agaña, had just returned to Umatac. Don Felipe Bauzá had embarked on his geodetic operations, Piloto Inciarte had been to Puerto de San Luis, and the abundant stores of fresh food that the Governor had ordered for us had just arrived from Agaña. At the observatory Señores Concha and Cevallos had checked the rate of number 105 and observed the immersion of the second satellite [of Jupiter] on the night of the 18th, and had set up the pendulum and astronomical clock for the gravity experiments, regretting that an untimely cloud had prevented them from observing the immersion of the first satellite on the following night.[1]

With everything now in good order, but with much less of the favourable season now left for the continuation of our tasks, it seemed wiser to leave the roadstead as soon as possible. With this intention we endeavoured to complete watering the next morning (the 21st), then observed a series of equal altitudes for the first period for rating the chronometers, and began the comparisons of the astronomical clock with mean times. The Governor brought on board the fresh food and other provisions collected for us, refusing to accept any payment as they came from crown property. At the same time Piloto Sánchez was sent to the shore opposite with a theodolite to take accurate bearings to tie in the outer extremities of the surveys we had made under sail. A huntsman soldier acquired as many species of birds as he could shoot for Don Antonio Pineda, while Don Juan Ravenet took an accurate likeness of two natives of the islands, one of each sex, and of a native of the Carolines who was on the island at

---

[1] Espinosa, *Memorias* (1809), 2nd memoir, gives details of tidal observations (p. 125), observations for magnetic variation and inclination (p. 118) and a discussion on the observations to determine the force of gravity (pp. 190-212), while the 3rd memoir gives details of the observations for geographical positions (pp. 1-4).

the time.[1] Finally, Señor Brambila began a perspective view of these pleasant surroundings,[2] although he had hardly yet recovered from an illness.

22 February
With the equal altitudes taken on the 22nd, the chronometers on both corvettes were considered to have been accurately rated. On that afternoon, accordingly, we brought on board all the instruments and the sick men, of whom only three from the *Descubierta* and one from the *Atrevida* had to stay behind, to join us later in Manila by the galleon. By nightfall both corvettes had a good supply of firewood, but the marines and seamen worked equally hard the next day when another wood-collecting party was sent ashore. By the afternoon of the 23rd the kedge had been weighed and we could consider ourselves completely ready to set sail.

The comparisons of the chronometers with mean time had indicated, as we suspected, a gain of approximately 5″ in numbers 71 and 105, and a loss of 1″ in number 72. Given the observations we had made at sea, it was this latter rate at which the chronometers had run rather than that determined in Acapulco. It therefore seemed more suitable to adopt it for the calculation of longitude by the chronometers and for the total equation for these variations. It made no difference if we rated number 105 according to the calculations made in Acapulco, as the equations would correct its irregularities and, once this was done, it would then be easy to apply the corresponding correction to 351, which had been compared daily with 105 during the crossing. These were our results for noon on the 15th:

	No 71	No 72	No 105	No 351
Difference of longitude west of Acapulco	7h 40m 54s 39	7h 42m 13s 50	7h 43m 50s 00	7h 40m 31s 17
Comparison equation	+ 54 21	− 24 50	− 2 01 00	+ 1 17 43
Corrected longitude	7h 41m 49s 00	7h 41m 49s 00	7h 41m 49s 00	7h 41 49 00

The averages according to the series of satellite longitudes taken in Acapulco were as follows:

Longitude west of Cádiz	209° 17′ 30″
Observation of 2nd satellite on the night of the 18th (according to tables)	209° 21′ 55″
Distances from the Moon to Aldebaran and Regulus, observed on the nights of the 3rd and 4th, taken with chronometer 72	209°[3] 26′ 30″
My calculation on the Frigate *Astrea*, by 44 series of distances	209° 3′ 30″
Commodore Wallis' calculation on Tinian, carried forward [to our observatory] by our chronometers	209° 9′ 45″
Unreliable longitude by the first satellite, as it could be seen clearly at 2h7′, and when the cloud passed at 2h9′50″, the immersion had already taken place	209° 18′ 00″
Latitude of the observatory by observations to stars to the south and north	13° 17′ 42″

[1] AMN, carp. I (31), (32) and (35) and Museo de América, No Inv. 2.289 and 2.290; reproduced in Sotos, *Los pintores*, II, figs 668–72. For the native of the Carolines see plate 30.
[2] AMN, MS 1724 (17) and Museo de América, No Inv. 2.287 and 2.288; reproduced in Sotos, *Los pintores*, II, figs 662–4. For the anchorage of Umatac by Brambila see plate 29.
[3] 208° in the original MS, which is clearly an error.

Plate 30. Man of the Caroline Islands, by Juan Ravenet. Museo Naval, Madrid

Variation	(By theodolite ashore . . . . 3° 15' NE
	(By the Gilbert and Martínez compasses on board . . . . 2° 45' NE

The longitude as determined by the chronometers was adopted. With regard to the slight doubts which might arise concerning its accuracy, it seemed preferable to leave the decision to the chronometers themselves, so as to relate it to the many known points of longitude which we would pass on our passage to Manila, whose longitude, already accurately determined by Monsieurs Le Gentil[1] and Dagelet,[2] could be confirmed by our observations.

Night had already fallen and the boats had been hoisted when the roll was called on the *Descubierta*. It was found that the huntsman soldier assigned to Don Antonio Pineda to help with his natural history collections was missing. Some of the men had seen him that day and, although there had been signs of a connection of some sort with the head man of a small village nearby, we all believed that his absence owed more to exhaustion or the effects of wine than to any desire to desert in a country so lacking in attractions. However, I sent the sergeant ashore to look for him, with instructions to inform the Governor if he could not be found, so that he could have the villages searched for the missing man, particularly the one where it was suspected he might be.

The investigation was fruitless, as he could not be found in Umatac or any of the nearby villages. Thus at dawn on the 24th, with the Governor's assurance that he would have the man sent on by the galleon *San Andrés*, having to abandon any hope of finding him, we lost no more time in getting under way. It is difficult to explain a sailor's humours, and it is strange that this soldier, one of the strongest and best liked among those on board at present, who had volunteered to leave his permanent regiment in Lima for service on the corvettes, now preferred this island to that delightful country and all the other places we had seen since then, an island, whose advantages, particularly for a European soldier, were most uncertain.

At daybreak, therefore, after the boats had been hoisted and the anchor weighed, we hove-to briefly to bring the corvettes to windward, and then, with a moderate ENE wind, under full sail, we set our course W 5°N by compass.

---

[1] Guillaume-Joseph Le Gentil de la Galaisière (1725-92), French astronomer and scientist, who spent eighteen months in Manila (1766-7) and left an account of conditions there in his *Voyage dans les mers de l'Inde*, Paris, 1779-81, II, pp. 1-366.

[2] Joseph Lepaute Dagelet, French mathematician and astronomer, studied astronomy under Lalande. After sailing with Kerguelen (1773-4), he joined La Pérouse's expedition, perishing with the rest of the *Boussole*'s crew in 1788 on Vanikoro.

CHAPTER 3

From Guam to Port Palapag in the Philippines

The nearer we came to the Philippines, weighing the great importance to our nation of its exact hydrographic description against the short time allowed for this kind of work by the favourable North-east Monsoon,[1] the greater was my preoccupation regarding good planning to ensure that the expedition produced the best results without risking failure by being excessively adventurous in an effort to avoid accusations of negligence. For a good number of reasons the period ahead had to include a voyage to Canton.[2] The survey of the opposite [i.e. eastern] coast of Luzon seemed extremely important and so was the passage round Cape Espíritu Santo[3] and through San Bernardino Strait, with the many ports it encompasses to east and west on the Camarines coast at the southern end of the island of Luzon. Finally the excursions of the three naturalists through the whole island would assume great significance, if they landed at the same time, one at the northern extremity at Apary,[4] in Cayagan Province, another at the southern extremity in Sorsogon,[5] and the third at Lampon,[6] not far to the east of Laguna de Bay[7] and the vicinity of Manila, their three routes then converging on this capital, while during the rainy season[8] both corvettes would be making their way towards Cavite.[9]

The separation of the corvettes was, however, unavoidable if so many different tasks were to be undertaken. This being the case, it seemed best that one corvette should

[1] In the Philippines the North-east Trade Wind gives way to the North-east Monsoon, which blows from October to April, while the South-west Monsoon blows from May to September. In the archipelago the term 'monsoon' refers to both the season and the dominant wind. Malaspina, however, continues to refer to the *brisa* for the North-east Trade Wind instead of *monzón* for the North-east Monsoon and *vendavales* for the South-west Monsoon.

[2] Now Guangzhou.
[3] The NE extremity of the island of Samar.
[4] Aparri, on the northernmost coast of Luzon.
[5] A sheltered harbour on the western side of the SE extremity of Luzon.
[6] Port Lampon on the east coast of Luzon, almost due east of Manila.
[7] A large lake SE of Manila.
[8] Rainfall is abundant over the whole of the Philippines, though relatively dry spells occur over the northern part of the archipelago in spring during the North-east Monsoon.
[9] The small but important naval establishment and harbour, 9 miles SSW of Manila. It is protected on its seaward side by a spit running NNE/SSW. As a result of the occupation of Manila and Cavite by the British in 1762, efforts were made to improve their defences by sending artificers and special personnel from San Blas and shipwrights from Havana: Hugo O'Donnell, *España en el descubrimiento, conquista y defensa del Mar del Sur*, Madrid, 1992, pp. 259-60. Cavite el Viejo, a village on the south of Cavite bay, contained the port brothel, much frequented by sailors on leave. This would concern the health-conscious Malaspina.

make straight for Port Lampon, continuing along the eastern coast to Capes Engaño and Bojeador,[1] then to Canton, finally returning to Manila by the Iloco coast.[2] Meanwhile the other, having sighted Catanduanes Island[3] and Cape Espíritu Santo, would first produce a plan of the port of Palapag, then after entering San Bernardino Strait would make for Sosorgon. Once there, having set up camp, so to speak, parties would be sent out by land and sea to chart the nearby harbours, including those on the islands of Ticao and Burias,[4] after which the corvette would gradually make its way back by the coasts of Mindoro and Luzon, to reach Manila before the middle of May, the earliest date for the onset of the South-west Monsoon.[5]

There were two arguments against this separation of the corvettes. First the poor state of health of both crews whom we had not been able to free from the epidemic fevers caught in Acapulco, even during our stay in the Marianas; the slightest indigestion still caused very severe attacks of bilious colic. A second consideration, not to be overlooked, was the continued presence of the Joloanos pirates in the archipelago,[6] so that a solitary launch sent out to obtain soundings or take bearings some distance away would be continually at risk. Finally, it would create a better impression of our armed forces if the two corvettes were to appear simultaneously in the port of Macau[7] and this was the combined view of all the officers of the expedition.

These latter reflections prevailed upon the commanding officer of the *Atrevida* and myself and as a result it was resolved that the corvettes should sail in company, first to

[1] Taken by Malaspina to be the NE and NW capes, respectively, of the north coast of Luzon.
[2] The NW coast of Luzon.
[3] An island off the eastern side of the SE extremity of Luzon, north of the eastern entrance to San Bernardino Strait.
[4] Two small islands off the western side of the SE extremity of Luzon.
[5] From May to September.
[6] Muslim pirates who terrorized the Filipino coasts from the island of Jolo (also formerly known as Sooloo or Sulu) in the Sulu Archipelago between SW Mindanao and NE Borneo. In the late 18th century 'pirates swarmed all over the Archipelago ... and in the Sulu Group, where the "Illanos" were considered the most dangerous of all.', Howard T. Fry, *Alexander Dalrymple and the Expansion of British Trade*, London, 1970, p. 15. See also Blair and Robertson, *The Philippine Islands*, LV, p. 733, and José Montero y Vidal, *Historia de la piratería muslim-mahometana en Mindanao, Jolo y Borneo*, 2 vols, Madrid, 1880. On the problem in the South China Sea at this time, see Louis Dermigny, *La Chine et l'occident: le commerce à Canton au XVIIIe siècle, 1719–1833*, 4 vols, Paris, 1964, III, pp. 1323-39, 1490-91; and Dian H. Murray, *Pirates of the South China Coast, 1790–1810*, Stanford, 1987; for a succinct survey with bibliography, see C. R. Boxer's 'Piracy in the South China Sea, 1550-1950' in *History Today*, December, 1980, pp. 40-44.
[7] Macau, formerly known as Macao, was founded in 1557 by the Portuguese on the south China coast, was the oldest permanent European settlement in East Asia, and the easternmost outpost of the Portuguese 'State of India': it was also an important commercial centre. It has since been increased by the addition of the islands of Taipa and Coloane, now linked to the old city by a bridge and a causeway respectively. For bibliography, see J. M. Braga, *The Western Pioneers and their Discovery of Macao*, Macau, 1949; G. W. Keaton, 'International Status of Macao before 1887', in *Chinese Social and Political Science Review*, XI, Peking, 1927, pp. 404-13. For a highly readable account, see Austin Coates, *A Macao Narrative*, London, 1978; also C. R. Boxer, *Fidalgos in the Far East, 1550–1770*, London, 1969; Anders Ljungstedt, *A Historic Sketch of the Portuguese in China*, Boston, 1836; Hong Kong, 1992; M. Martins do Vale, *Os Portugueses em Macau, 1750–1780*, Macau, 1997, is a scholarly account. La Pérouse gives an interesting contemporary account of the town, Dunmore, *Journal of La Pérouse*, I, pp. 218-26; Manuel Teixeira, *Macau no séc. XVIII*, Macau, 1984, is a year-by-year (1700-1799) chronicle of rather parochial events in the city; for the year 1792 - see his pp. 689-91.

Palapag and then to Sorsogon, where they were to continue their hydrographic tasks. After anchoring next at the mouth of the Mariveles[1] to hand over sealed orders from Acapulco they would then sail directly to Macau, returning to Manila in the middle of May, after ranging the coasts of the provinces of Cayagan and Ilocos,[2] in order to undertake the lengthy preparations for the following cruises. Meanwhile local conditions might indicate other possible advantages in broadening the scope of the expedition of which, at the moment, we could not be aware.

In these circumstances, our most direct course was to sail to Cape Espíritu Santo, omitting the investigation of some shoals on the way, which probably would have achieved nothing more than the sacrifice of a few nights' sleep. We kept to the same parallels as those I had followed in 1787 in the Frigate *Astrea*, but although we were now doing it at a better time of year the [North-east] Trade Wind was very light, tending to the second quadrant at times, with some squalls.

28 and 29 February

On the 28th and 29th we were very pleased to be able to observe several distances from the Sun to the Moon which, according to chronometer 76, gave the longitude of the observatory at Umatac as 209°17' west of Cádiz, as previously supposed; those taken on board the *Atrevida* and referred in the same way to chronometer 105 gave the observatory's longitude as [blank].

1 March

The strange calms which had accompanied us until now could not last long. From noon the next day a heavy sea began to roll in from NE, soon followed in the evening by a fresh breeze from the same quarter, with strong gusts and showers, so that we had to run under topsails and foresails. The wind then dropped a little, leaving the sky and horizon with an appearance that promised a good [North-east] Trade Wind. We made the most of it under full sail, and by noon on the 3rd we were at latitude [blank] and longitude [blank] west of Umatac.

On our departure from Umatac variation had again been 5° to 5½°NE. It then had gradually diminished to 1°30', as indicated by some azimuth observations made on this day, although the rolling made this difficult. Some experiments with air samples taken on board were carried out with the Fontana eudiometer, the results being both exact and satisfactory, as shown in the table drawn up for these experiments.

The latitude that I had calculated for Cape Espíritu Santo on my previous voyage, although based upon calculations made by Admiral Anson and those of several *pilotos* from Manila, seemed suspect when I studied either my own course on that night or the sailing directions of Cabrera Bueno.[3] There was also a possible error of longitude,

---

[1] Mariveles Bay, a small bay fronted by the island of Corregidor, at the NW entrance to Manila Bay. Corregidor had a watchtower that gave warning by fire signals of the approach of any vessel.

[2] Provinces in the NE and NW part, respectively, of Luzon.

[3] José González Cabrera Bueno, a Spanish navigator who travelled widely in the Pacific and East Asia in the 18th century, was the author of the *Navegación especulativa y práctica*, Manila, 1734 (facsimile edition ed. by W. M. Mathes, Madrid, 1970). González Cabrera included in his treatise practical sea routes for Pacific voyages, e.g. Acapulco to Manila.

which I was able to determine with sufficient certainty when comparing our observations with those made in Manila by M. Le Gentil.[1] At sunset I was able to calculate, with these figures, the approximate true distance to that cape, and to sail that night, at times under a press of canvas and at times under shortened sail, steering WSW, so that at sunrise, we sighted the coast at a distance of five leagues.

4 March
From Cape Espíritu Santo, which is rocky and of moderate height, this coast runs SE for five or six leagues, decreasing in height gradually so that the furthest visible point is very low. Both the mountains and the lower parts are beautifully clothed in green. There are a few isolated rocks close in to the shore, but only two leagues off the cape we still could not obtain bottom with 120 fathoms of line.

We made use of a favourable moderate breeze from ENE under full sail, which took us to the meridian of the SE extremity and in sight of the cape itself and eventually to the entrance to Port Palapag, where I intended to stay for a few days. We observed hour angles at several of the more prominent points, while the *Atrevida* continued sounding, although without obtaining bottom. We continued to measure bases as we steadily approached Batag Island,[2] whose rocky points surrounded by reefs could be clearly seen at nine o'clock in the morning.

A vessel coming from the east may enter Port Palapag by passing either side of the island. The southern entrance leads more directly to the river, but in the channel there are several banks with very little depth. The northern entrance between the islands of Batag and Cagahiaga,[3] although it has reefs on either side and often very little wind, leads into a wider channel clear of dangerous sandbanks. This latter channel was the one we now chose for entering harbour, particularly as the wind was almost ENE so that it could be accomplished in one short, safe tack. We rounded the north side of Batag Island, two cables from the reef off the island at the same distance, and then stood to the south close hauled in depths of fourteen and fifteen fathoms, ooze, to make way against the tide, which was setting us toward Cagahiaga. At about midday, when we were well into the harbour, we dropped the bower anchor in nine fathoms, ooze, about two-thirds of a mile from the coast of Batag and in sight of the mouth of the Palapag River. We then lowered the launch and laid out the large kedge to the SW.

[1] For M. Le Gentil see p. 268, n. 1 above.
[2] Fronting Port Palapag.
[3] Cahayagan Island at the entrance to Port Palapag.

CHAPTER 4

At Port Palapag

[4 March]
The more we considered the excellent qualities of this harbour, with its good shelter, the abundance of water and firewood, the villages nearby, and its position in the outer part of the river mouth, the greater was our desire to ensure by means of a thorough survey that this fine harbour could be safely used by the nation's shipping. It was equally important to examine its natural products and wealth, while not losing sight of the need to make the fullest use of the valuable time available and to provide for our own safety during the various excursions which naturally had to be made, keeping in mind the ferocity of the pirates in these parts.

As far as we could see, the area around the harbour was entirely deserted. To make the best use of the afternoon in gathering the necessary information on which to base a well-conceived plan for our future activities, I took the *Descubierta*'s launch, fully armed, to Palapag, the nearest town,[1] where the missionary or parish priest would be able to tell me all I needed to know. As an immersion of the first satellite of Jupiter was to take place that night, Teniente de Navío Concha accompanied me, so that we could observe it together and take the opportunity of being ashore after dark to determine the latitude of the town by the meridian passages of different stars.

Although the tide was against us it was not difficult to row to the mouth of the Palapag river before nightfall, but that did not add to our local knowledge since we had seen little more than a roofless and apparently deserted house. As the nearby fish pens were seen to be abandoned and we did not meet a single canoe, we began to suspect that the local inhabitants, unaccustomed to the sight of large ships and constantly harassed by pirates, had mistaken us for these. Finally, when night was already drawing on we saw a native at the foot of the turret or house that we had sighted before. Although he was extremely suspicious, in the end he gave in to our persuasion and proofs that we were indeed Spaniards and even more to our offers of generous presents if he would get into the launch. He spoke very little Spanish, but we had some sailors from these islands on board who were most useful to us, as

---

[1] *Pueblo* in the original MS, which can be translated as small town or village. However, Malaspina and his officers refer to almost every settlement that they visited as *pueblos* irrespective of apparent size. *Pueblo* has therefore been translated throughout the Philippines section of this work as town, except when it is clear from the context that village is more appropriate.

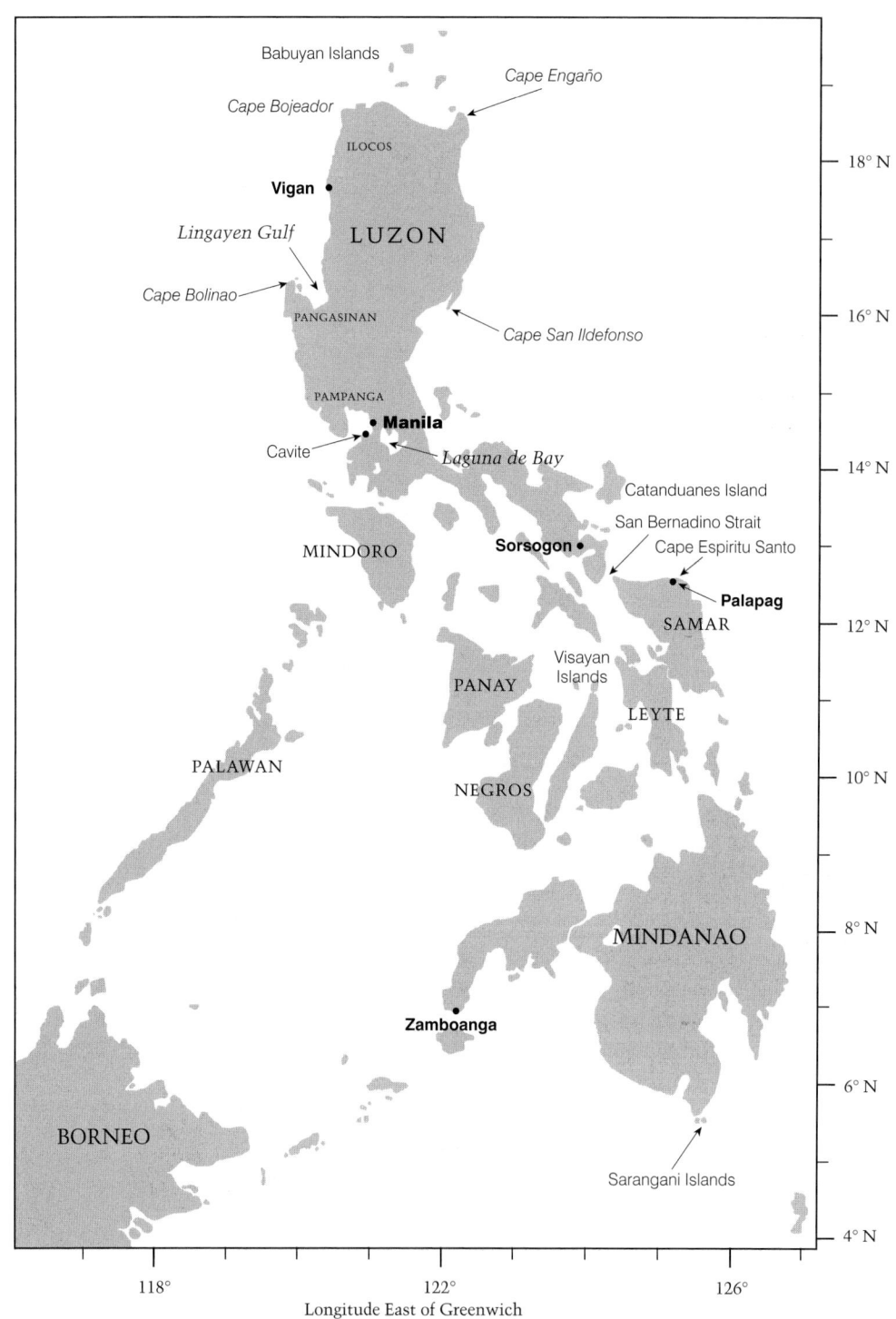

Fig. 4. The Philippine Islands, March to December 1792

although they only spoke the dialect Tagalog,[1] they were nonetheless able to make themselves understood with the new arrival. He informed us that all the people in the vicinity had indeed thought us to be pirates, confused as they were by our ensign[2] rather than by the structure of our ships. He himself had warned the village people, for whom he had been keeping watch with some others in the house that we had seen. Now that he was sure that we were *Castellanos*,[3] he was willing to lead us in the launch to the town of Palapag, which was only an hour away.

The situation was now much changed, and we could flatter ourselves that our plans might be achieved, particularly as the outlook for the night was calm and clear. We left the steering of the launch to our new pilot, and at first he fulfilled our expectations. We had not gone more than half a league upstream, however, when we found ourselves aground on a muddy bottom, when the helmsman assured us that there was no better depth of water to be found on this kind of bar and that as the tide was ebbing rapidly we would be stranded until after the Moon had set at about three in the morning. We were unable to free ourselves from the mud with our oars and thus, with all our plans upset, it now seemed unlikely that we would be able to make any observations or to speak to the missionary father. Some canoes or *banquillas*[4] passed along near the shore on either side of the river, but although our helmsman, whose voice they knew, called them over with assurances that we were Spanish, they answered that we were Moros,[5] and on no account would they approach us to judge the truth of our claims.

At last the constant shouts and assertions of our guide, and particularly our offers of money, tipped the balance in our favour. Two small canoes approached the launch, and in them Don Juan Concha, myself and Piloto Hurtado, with the achromatic telescopes and pocket chronometer number 351, were able to continue towards Palapag, leaving the launch in the care of Don Felipe Bauzá, who was to be notified from Palapag of the best time and place in which to start his hydrographic work.

After making our way thus along a good stretch of the river, we then continued on foot for half a league on a track which ran between pleasant, leafy fields, before finally reaching the town of Palapag that we sought. Here we asked to be presented to the missionary father, who was a Franciscan friar. We then considered our troubles to be

---

[1] One of the principal native languages in the Philippines; for a cultural-linguistic map of the Islands see Nena Vreeland *et al.*, eds, *Area Handbook for the Philippines*, Washington, D.C., 1976, pp. 77, 450-51, 453. On the fate of the Spanish language in the islands see K. Whinnom, 'Spanish in the Philippines', in *Journal of Oriental Studies*, I, 1954, pp. 129-94.

[2] In 1785 Carlos III chose the present Spanish colours (red-yellow-red) for the naval ensign from twelve models submitted to him by Antonio Valdés and promulgated by Royal Decree dated 28 May. The purpose was to have an ensign easy to identify and distinguish at a good distance. The naval ensign became the present Spanish national flag in 1843 after considerable resistance, particularly by the Army.

[3] Even in more recent times Filipinos use the term *Castellanos* (i.e. Castilians) to describe people from Spain.

[4] A dugout Filipino canoe, fitted with outriggers, propelled by oars, paddles or a quadrangular sail.

[5] Inhabitants of Mindanao, known to the Spaniards as Moros, because of their Muslim faith who, together the inhabitants of Jolo, carried out piratical raids against the rest of the Philippines. Bustamante noted that they came from Jolo and Mindanao, confirmed later by Malaspina (see pp. 288-9 below) and that the latter regretted his inability to be of service against them, except by giving the missionaries some powder and weapons: Bustamante, *Diario general del viaje*, p. 314.

at an end, but another awkward situation, of equal difficulty, now arose. The friar was ill, and his very illness was causing him to lapse into a state of apathy and mental incoherence which was all the more unfortunate for us since there was no one else with the essential knowledge of the language. In vain did we question him about the nature of the surrounding country, the refreshments and other supplies which we might obtain, or a suitable place for us to make our astronomical observations. His ailments, the destruction caused last November by a terrible hurricane, and the almost daily depredations of the pirates were the only subjects of his replies.¹ After a long hour of fruitless conversation we were obliged to take our leave, if we were not to miss the chance of observing the immersion, even if it were only from the public square. Our pleasure and surprise can be imagined, therefore, on hearing the friar give the unexpected order to have us taken to the nearby monastery, where the damage caused by the hurricane had already been partially repaired, to be served an abundant meal and offered all possible assistance by the town people.

As far as we could ascertain in the darkness, our trigonometric operations would be quite impossible in the thick forest which lay between the harbour and the town. I informed Don Felipe Bauzá of this immediately, so that he would not try to join us. At the same time I asked him for the theodolite and told him to get the launch afloat when the tide allowed, as we would join him there as soon as we could.

As for our observation, by now the only remaining objective in our mind, we were still dogged by a series of doubts and misfortunes. Clouds began to cover the sky, which increased as the time for the observation approached, and it seemed certain that we would miss our opportunity. However, luck was with us in the end, as there were two brief breaks in the clouds in quick succession which limited the immersion phase to a period of a few seconds, and accordingly we could calculate the longitude as approximately 228°54' west of Cádiz. We immediately returned to the launch, which was now afloat, and by sunrise we were on board once more, very pleased that our perambulations during the night had not been entirely fruitless.

By then the natives had put aside all their fears and, attracted both by our willingness to buy whatever they offered and the high prices we paid in silver coin, they flocked to us in their canoes to sell everything they could find. In this way we obtained an extraordinary abundance of provisions, among which the cockerels were the most sought after, as they were useful both as food and as an amusement for the crew during their hours of leisure, since these fierce creatures entertained them with cock-fights,² [a pastime] still enjoyed in Europe.

Señores Pineda and Haenke were quick to take advantage of the amenities of the

---

[1] Loneliness would afflict men previously accustomed to community life. Anxiety, depression, the daily struggle for chastity amidst exotic Asian temptations, and the fear of death, alone, without Confession and the Last Rites, would all cause stress: see Blair and Robertson, *The Philippine Islands*, I, p. 78, note, XXVIII, pp. 244, 294-5; XLIV, p. 85

[2] Cock-fighting involved gambling and, despite protests by the clergy, it remained popular among Filipinos; heavily taxed, it was a considerable source of state revenue: see Artemio R. Guillermo and May Kyi Win, *Historical Dictionary of the Philippines*, London, 1987, p. 60. Malaspina later records (see p. 289 below) that cock-fights were especially frequent in Sorsogon, for which he was grateful, since they entertained the crew and distracted them from worse pastimes.

Plate 31. View of the port of Palapag in the island of Samar, by Fernando Brambila. Museo de América, Madrid

surrounding countryside and the good will of the natives, previously mentioned, for their natural history excursions, as did Don Felipe Bauzá for his hydrographic operations, which were extended to include Laguan[1] and the outer part of the harbour, as far as the area of Baliquatro[2] in San Bernardino Strait. The armed launches were sent out, the two *pilotos* alternately taking charge, to continue carefully sounding the inner part of the harbour and the channels leading to it. A small island with a good view of the horizon, not far from the anchorage, gave the astronomers an excellent place for any observations to be made.

These included particularly the occultation by the Moon of number 414 in Mayer's star catalogue,[3] observed to our complete satisfaction on the night of the 5th, and also a further immersion of the first satellite of Jupiter which took place on the following night, observed by Señores Espinosa, Concha and Cevallos, although somewhat interrupted by the frequent passage of clouds. The method of absolute altitudes was preferred for rating the chronometers, as we had a good clear horizon in the morning, enabling us to allow the crew a good rest at night, it being unnecessary to keep watch ashore at the observatory.

The results of these important observations were as follows:

Longitude of the anchorage by the four chronometers, and by the assumed meridian of Umatac, west of Cádiz.	228° 53′ 5″
By satellite on the night of the 4th.	228° 53′ 48″
By satellite on the night of the 6th	228° 53′ 13″
Latitude	N 12° 37′ 5″
Variation	NE 0° 20′ 0″

7 March
The beauty of the weather, which we were enjoying continuously was too much of a gift of nature to be wasted, so we were diligent in making the best use of it. It seemed better therefore that Don Felipe Bauzá, who had finished measuring a base and taking most of the bearings within the inner harbour, should proceed to the outer coast of Laguan using local craft, to gather information about soundings, tides and suitable anchorages.[4] This left the launches, with the help of the pinnaces, free to be used for sounding inside the harbour and by the morning of the 9th they had finished taking soundings in the area near the corvettes' anchorage.

Among the more important objects which the natives daily brought on board to sell we particularly valued the shells which were found, equal in beauty, abundance and variety, throughout these parts. Many of the officers were quick to join the natives in this useful search, and the hours of low tide, whatever the height of the Sun, gave the strongest incentive not to remain peacefully on board if daily occupations

---

[1] Probably Laoang Island close westward of the entrance to Port Palapag.
[2] Baliquatro Point, 45 miles west of the entrance to Port Palapag, is the NW extremity of Samar, with Baliquatro Islands close north.
[3] The Göttingen astronomer Johann Tobias Mayer (1723-62), whose star catalogue was much used by Malaspina and his astronomers.
[4] Espinosa, *Memorias* (1809), 2nd memoir, gives details of tidal observations (p. 125), while the 3rd memoir gives details of the observations for geographical positions (pp. 40-42).

allowed. It is certain that within three days not a stone remained unturned on the nearby shores, nor was there a single species of the shells of these waters that we did not find. The assemblage of specimens gathered for the Real Gabinete and the study of this pleasant field of natural history were thus considerably enriched.[1]

8 March

By now the news of our arrival and of the benefits of trade with us, so to speak, had spread among the villages near Palapag. For this reason, and at my request, another three or four Franciscan friars decided to visit us on board, and our conversation with them was most useful in giving us an accurate idea of the island of Samar, its products and inhabitants. This information brought a further increase of the already inexhaustible supplies of good provisions which daily arrived on board. As the crews of some of the canoes were armed it was easy for us to ask for a demonstration of their war dances,[2] which they performed several times on board and which Señor Ravenet faithfully represented.[3]

In these conversations with the missionary fathers I was interested above all in acquiring exact information about the incursions of the Joloanos and Mindanao pirates on these coasts. Their ravages are a real scourge in the Visayas,[4] and are certainly the only reason which prevents these islands from adding to the strength of the monarchy. Excessive delay in finding a drastic remedy to eradicate such ravages could well mean the total ruin of really wealthy islands, and of natives who constantly claim protection from their attackers. We would have liked to be able to make a useful start to this national effort, but we were obliged to concentrate our efforts on the peaceful tasks we had undertaken. We could make no other contribution than the offer, in the King's name, of some iron and gunpowder to these unfortunate missionaries, who had to deal almost daily with the conduct of a dangerous and bloody defence rather than the peaceful spreading of the gospel.[5]

Don Felipe Bauzá soon joined us and began examining the small channel between the islands of Laguan and Cagahiaga, which was the only remaining task of those we had undertaken in this harbour. While taking soundings on the more prominent reefs at the entrance to the harbour, the launches had anchored and taken important bearings to link up all our surveying work.

---

[1] Shells were collected as scientific 'curiosities'. Malaspina considered that this was a useful form of research, his finds being intended for the royal natural-history collection (the Real Gabinete), just as some of Cook's went to Lord Bristol (J. C. Beaglehole, ed., *The Journals of Captain James Cook on His Voyages of Discovery*. II. *The Voyage of the* Resolution *and* Adventure, *1772–1775*, Hakluyt Society, extra ser. 35, Cambridge, 1961 (repr. 1969), p. 961). For a contemporary account of conchology see Peter J. P. Whitehead, 'Emmanuel Mendes da Costa (1717-91), and the Natural History of Shells (1778)', *Bulletin of the British Museum (Natural History)*, VI (1977), pp. 1-24. On conchology in general, see Hugh Stix, *The Shell*, London, 1978.

[2] On native dances in general, see Blair and Robertson, *The Philippine Islands*, LIV, p. 381.

[3] AMN, carp 1 (40); reproduced in Sotos, *Los pintores*, II, fig. 685.

[4] The group of islands between Luzon and Mindanao, comprising Samar, Leyte, Cebu, Negros, Bohol, Masbate and Panay.

[5] An aspect of the old controversy over peaceful or forceful methods of conversion.

I had still intended to try leaving the next day by the same channel, but its narrowness showed it to be an unwise choice if the wind was favourable for the channel by which we had entered the harbour.

9 March
The naturalists had sent word that they could not rejoin us until the evening of the 9th, after having roamed at their pleasure through the vicinity of Palapag. They counted this excursion as one of the happiest they had made until now. The abundance of plants and animals that they had collected more than compensated for the heat and exhaustion that they had suffered. There was now nothing to delay our departure, and the continuation of our work.

10 March
The next day dawned calm, as usual. We brought the cable up and down. Then at half past ten, with the first puffs of the [North-east] Trade Wind, we made for the entrance to the harbour under full sail, and by midday we were about a mile from it.

During our stay in the anchorage we had been careful to study the flow of the tides and had been surprised to find that the tide ebbed towards San Bernardino Strait, so that the best time to leave harbour at this time [of year] and pass between Capul and the Calantas shoal[1] was in the morning.

The tidal stream in Port Palapag was not as strong as that usually experienced in the Strait. It ran at a fair rate, however, particularly when one of the many channels leading into the harbour ran counter to the free flow of the stream. As for the times of its ebb and flood, as related to the phases of the Moon, according to the tables set out by Señor de Armenteros[2] in Manila rather than the general laws established by the scientists, it was not easy on this day to obtain new values which would have corroborated either of these, because the former assigned the same period of exactly six hours for the month of May as the latter, and this was the period of its least rate and height.

---

[1] Capul Island and Calantas Rock at the western end of the San Bernardino Strait, 11 miles SW and 12 miles WSW, respectively of Baliquatro Point.

[2] José Armenteros, Secretary of the Manila branch of the Real Compañía de Filipinas (Royal Philippine [Trading] Company), which had overseas factories in Canton (from 1793) and Calcutta, but the Company had failed long before its official demise in 1834: see Díaz-Trechuelo, *La Real Compañía de Filipinas*.

CHAPTER 5

From Port Palapag to Manila and at Sorsogon

10 March
The bearings taken from the village of Laguan clearly showed that the distance from Palapag to San Bernardino Strait was not more than fifteen or sixteen leagues, as confirmed by my previous voyage in the frigate *Astrea*, although the charts of this coast generally showed it as being much greater. Everything urged us, therefore, to make the most of the very pleasant afternoon to continue our survey, approaching the entrance to the strait during the night and thus, with a favourable wind and tide, reaching the entrance to the port of Sorsogon the next morning. Nature appeared in her most pleasing aspect around us. The Moon seemed almost to compete with the Sun for brilliance, and the fresh [NE] Trade Wind still blowing from a cloudless sky gave the passage that security which we would not have enjoyed in calm weather, given the strong currents in the strait.

By nightfall Tabones Island[1] already bore S82°E, four leagues distant, where we sounded, obtaining a depth of fifty fathoms, sand. In this position the tide was barely perceptible. We were now only about seven leagues from Biri Point,[2] bearing N83°W, which therefore seemed a good place to wait until early the next morning. In a fresh east to ESE breeze, at times close hauled, but otherwise lying-to, we managed to avoid the effects of the currents and tides. At three o'clock in the morning, heading towards Samar again, we obtained soundings of forty fathoms, sand and gravel. The welcome daylight brought into view the many points, to which we wished to take bearings, and allowed us to crowd on sail and set our course. By sunrise we were already only a league and a half from San Bernardino Isle,[3] which now bore S67°W, while Biri Point bore 27° in the same quadrant.

11 March
After passing within a mile of this islet and fixing the longitude of the salient part of the strait by taking several hour angles, we altered course directly for Galeras Point on

[1] Cabaun Island, off the north coast of Samar, about 14 miles east of Baliquatro Point.
[2] Biri Head, the NW extremity of Biri Island, the northernmost and largest of the Baliquatro Islands.
[3] Two islets close together in the north entrance to San Bernardino Strait, 5 miles NNW of Biri Head.

Plate 32. 'Carta general del archipiélago de Filipinas' (northern sheet, detail), showing the corvettes' track from San Bernardino Strait to Manila. UKHO, E939. Reproduced by permission of the Controller of Her Majesty's Stationery Office and the UK Hydrographic Office. *See overleaf.*

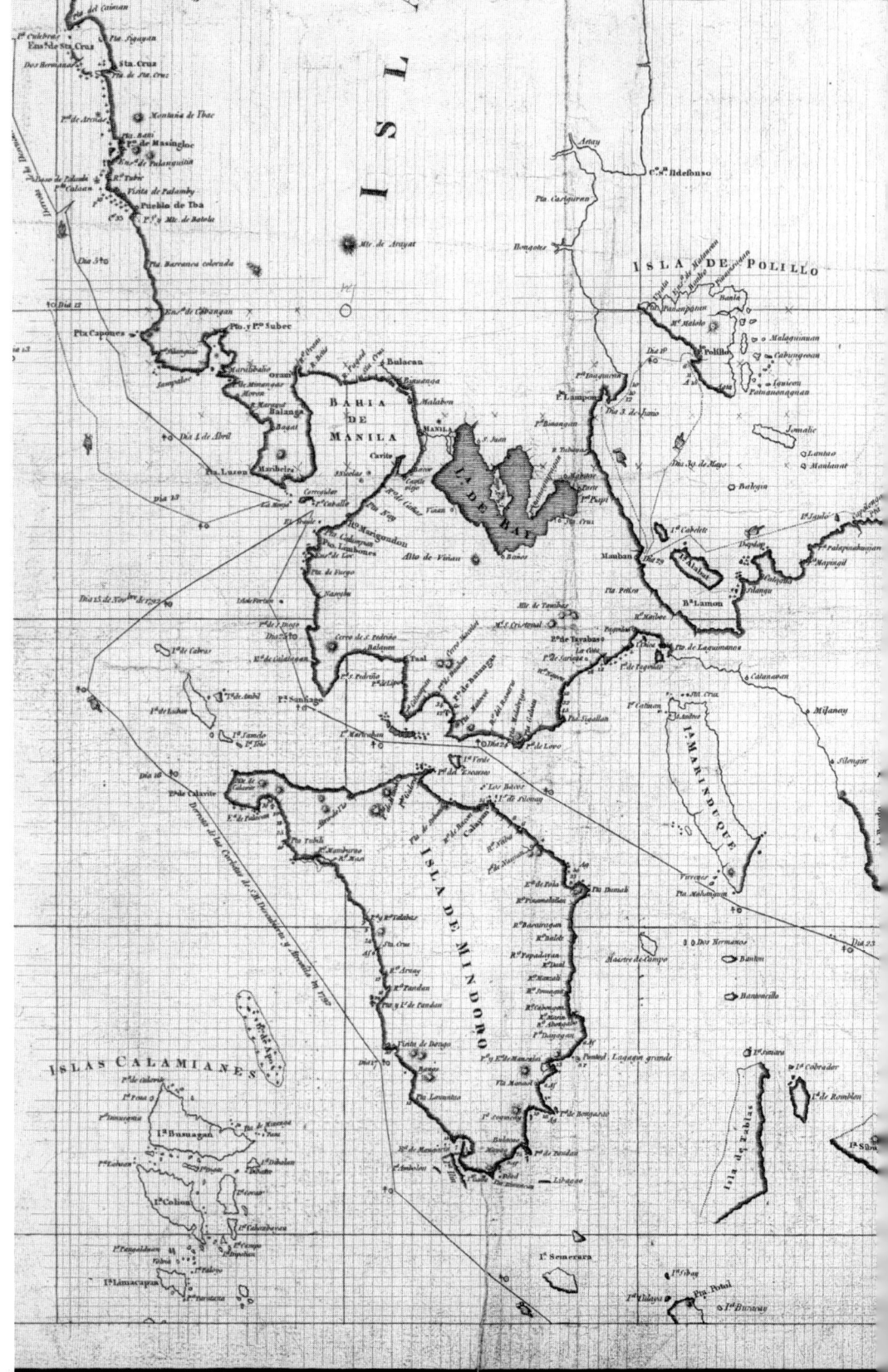

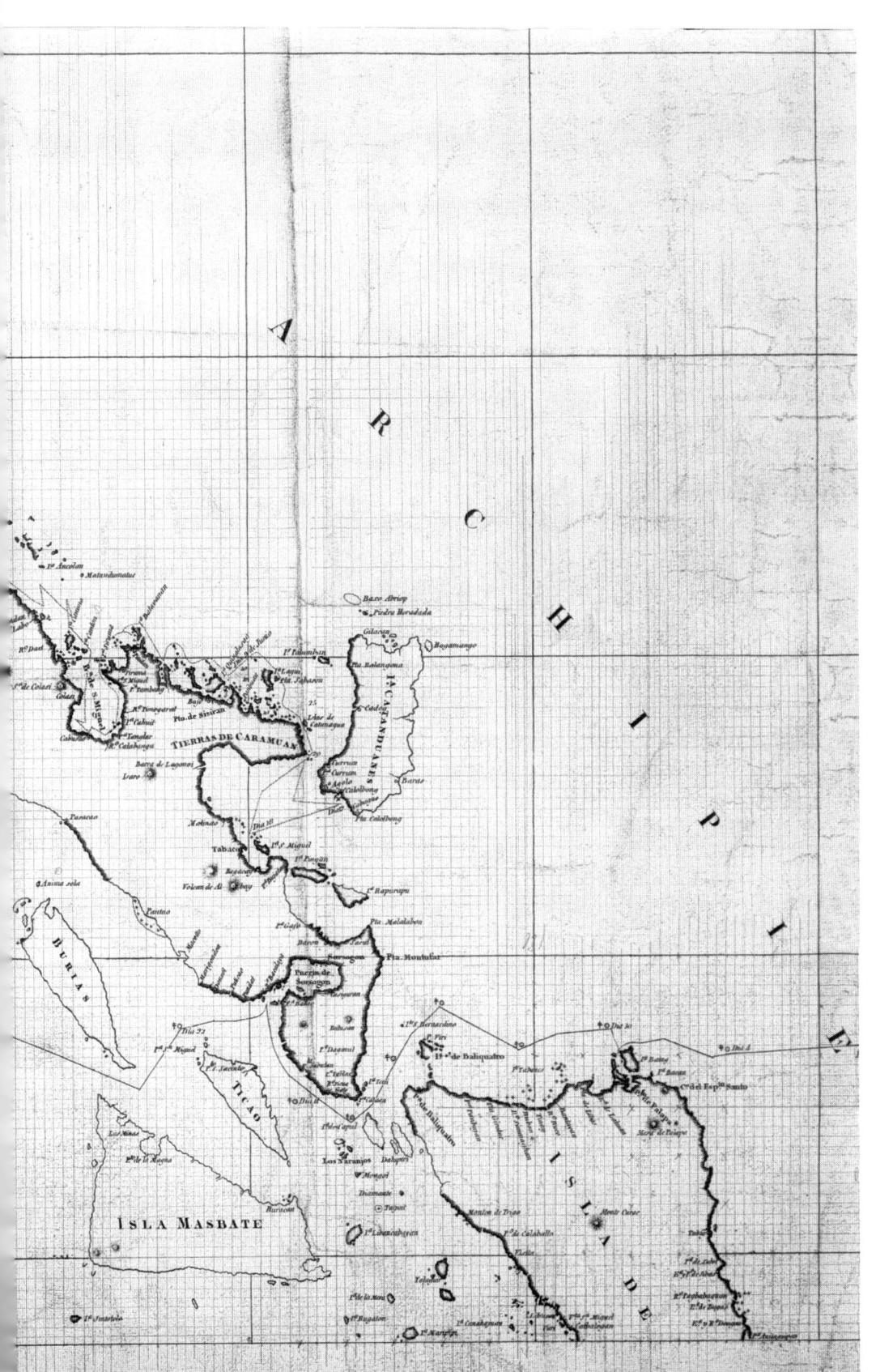

THE MALASPINA EXPEDITION 1789-1794

Capul Island.[1] It is well known that the flood tide, which was now in our favour, sets very strongly towards this island and may drive vessels ashore through carelessness or a lack of wind, by forcing them to pass to the south [of the island] or finding themselves caught in an eddy among the Naranjos.[2] This consideration led us to stand in closer to the coast of Luzon, where we could see the village of Calantas not far off. Meanwhile we continued to take bearings and transits of all the more important points surrounding us in this archipelago. Thus the many islets of Baliquatro, the point of the same name, Biri Point, the two extremities of Capul Island, Muertos or Dalupiri Island,[3] the volcanoes of Albay[4] and Balusan[5] and the coast of the island of Luzon were all linked together, little by little, independent of any bases which in these waters would be useless, if not dangerous [to run].

At eight o'clock in the morning we were no more than two leagues from Calantas Shoal,[6] whose position we could now determine safely. For a while we were delayed by light airs from NW and north, and were even forced to make some tacks which did little to assist our progress, but the wind soon veered to ENE and east and at ten o'clock we were already in the channel between Capul Island and the Calantas Point[7] and Shoal. By noon we had passed the Naranjos and were sailing between Ticao Island and the coast of Luzon, standing close in to the latter so as not to fall too far to leeward of Bagatao Island, which forms the entrance to the port of Sorsogon. A clear horizon to the south allowed us to take a good meridian altitude of the Sun, and this, with the longitude observations that we had made in the morning and repeated shortly afterwards, gave our survey a firmer basis, the more so in that it was later tied in with those we observed in Sorsogon with great astronomical detail. The volcanoes of Albay and Bulusan were the principal links in this important chain.

It is not easy for anyone who has not travelled in these parts to get a true idea of its pleasures when, in the good season, the peaceful skies and the gentle easterly breezes seem almost to vie for ascendancy, leaving the admiring sailor hardly time to take in all the joy of his voyage. The scenes that meet the eye are so many and varied: a uniformly luxuriant vegetation, the terrain either gently rounded or steeply rising to volcanoes and other higher mountains, the many channels formed by the sea in its fruitless search for equilibrium among the islands and the watchtowers of each of the towns of Calantas, Capul and Ticao. In addition the philosophic recollection of the vicissitudes suffered by the inhabitants and the great possibility of the expansion of humanity which could take place in these parts, without shedding any blood on the

---

[1] On the southern side of the southern entrance to San Bernardino Strait, 11 miles SW of Baliquatro Point.

[2] Three small islands about 7 miles SW of Capul Island.

[3] An island between Capul Island and NW coast of Samar.

[4] Mayon Volcano, an active volcano 26 miles NW of the town of Sorsogon, is a perfect cone 2,421 metres in height and is the most prominent in Albay Gulf.

[5] Bulusan Volcano, an active volcano 12 miles south of Sorsogon, is 1,559 metres in height, and is an excellent mark when not obscured by clouds. There are 22 volcanoes in the Philippines, 13 of which are active; they are mostly on the Pacific Rim of the Islands: Blair and Robertson, *The Philippine Islands*, LV, p. 955.

[6] Malaspina may be referring to a shoal which extends ¾ mile SSE of the 2-metre high Calantas Rock, situated about 4 miles north of Capul Island, rather than the rock itself.

[7] Possibly Colasi Point, situated 1½ north of Calantas Rock, at the southern extremity of Luzon.

Plate 33. View of Sorsogon in the island of Luzon, by Fernando Brambila. Museo Naval, Madrid

land which should only feed it, all make almost vexing and disturbing the favourable wind which removes the sailor from such agreeable and thought-provoking scenes as suddenly as the dropping of a theatre curtain.

Meanwhile we were approaching the port of Sorsogon, close hauled in the falling ENE breeze and standing two miles off the coast of Luzon in depths of fifteen to eighteen fathoms, fine sand, according to soundings taken either on this corvette or the *Atrevida*. By four o'clock in the afternoon we were only two leagues from the northern extremity of Bagatao Island, which forms the entrance to the port, but as the wind was now very light and the tide strongly against us, our progress was slower than we desired. We made some way by tacking, however, during the few hours of daylight left to us. At nightfall both corvettes were coasting along Bagatao Island at a distance of one or two cables, and soon afterwards, having cleared the mouth of the harbour, we could consider ourselves ready to anchor at any time. However, a strong NE wind had set in and since we were not familiar with the coast opposite, where we had noticed some reefs during the afternoon, and realizing that the strength of the tide would be greater if we anchored in the middle of the entrance, we decided to bear away towards the shelter of the island to find a good anchorage for the night. We anchored shortly afterwards in fourteen fathoms, fine sand, some three cables from the northern end of the island. The *Atrevida* soon did the same, and there we spent the night, keeping the usual careful watch, all the more necessary here owing to the frequent raids by the Mindanao pirates.

12 March
When the Sun rose the wind was still falling, obliging us to wait for the tide, which was not favourable either. So we lowered the launch and I instructed the commanding officer of the *Atrevida* to use her launch to obtain soundings in the furthest points of the harbour, while Don Felipe Bauzá, in the *Descubierta*'s launch, took bearings to the extremity of Bagatao [island] and to some watchtowers of a moderate height we could see inland overlooking various parts of the harbour. A canoe came alongside, and the native dissuaded us from arming the launches as strongly as we had first intended, informing us that there were no pirates in those parts at the time and that the watchtowers were manned by people who paid taxes to Spain. The *cura doctrinero*[1] of Sorsogon was that day vising one of them and Comandante Gómez had just left the area with the small privateering squadron commissioned in Cavite.[2] I took the opportunity offered by this favourable news to advise the Alcalde[3] of Albay[4] and the *cura doctrinero* beforehand of our plan of operations, so that they could assist us with

---
[1] The missionary priest with the specific task of teaching the Christian doctrine to the natives. According to Viana his monastery was called San Diego, which suggests he was a Franciscan: Viana, *Diario*, II, p. 121.
[2] During the 17th century privateering vessels performed a major defensive role in the Philippines, which the Spanish navy's inadequate forces could not manage on their own. From 1674 onwards, the Governors licenced privateers subject to certain conditions. In the 18th century the number of pirates declined, but not those of smugglers, as a result the authorities continued to issue privateering licences to counter their activities.
[3] The magistrate or mayor of a Spanish town.
[4] The provincial capital.

guides and local knowledge. I thought it unwise to risk sending the sealed orders received in Acapulco to the capital from such a distance, but I took care to inform the government and colony as quickly as possible of the most important news from Europe regarding our recent disagreements with England, and of the safe arrival of the galleon.[1]

After eight o'clock in the morning we felt the first breaths of the [NE] Trade Wind, when both ships set sail at once and began tacking towards the interior of the harbour with the tide. The frequent tacks and the somewhat gusty wind inclined us towards caution in the amount of sail, but shortly after midday we had made a good league into the harbour and were close to the southern shore, at a spot which gave promise of a sheltered and comfortable anchorage, particularly for our extensive hydrographic work in this beautiful harbour. We anchored in seven fathoms, mud, near a small promontory halfway between the two watchtowers of the town of Casiguran.[2] From our anchorage Bulusan Volcano bore S70°E, the Albay Volcano N23°W, the watchtower nearer Casiguran N44°E and the nearest point ESE, two to three cables distant. The *Atrevida* anchored half a cable from us.

The port of Sorsogon is, without doubt, one of the most beautiful that nature has created. It is capable of holding numberless squadrons, in depths not exceeding fifteen or sixteen fathoms, ooze, its shores being fairly steep-to with a few towns not far away which can supply all necessities. There is an abundance of good fish and it offers truly commodious and agreeable shelter, particularly during the season of the *vendavales*.[3] During the period of the [NE] Trade Winds,[4] if no more than water, firewood and a little fresh food are needed, it is perhaps more comfortable to anchor outside the harbour a little to the south of Bagatao, by a small but conspicuous waterfall. The very size and beauty of the harbour were, however, something of a hindrance to our work, which at first we had hoped would be quickly accomplished. The hydrographic tasks were not the only work which was to occupy us: the lush vegetation, the two volcanoes in sight, the proximity of these terrains to the more distant areas watered by the muddy Pasig [River] in the vicinity of Manila, were too strong an incentive for the naturalists to curb their impatience to be free, and for me to restrain my eagerness not to lose a single moment for their important tasks.

The launches were back by sunset, the *Atrevida*'s launch bringing on board the parish priest of Sorsogon, who was to return to his place of residence the next day in his own boat, having completed his visit to these parts. This good friar soon offered to take with him Señores Pineda and Haenke, who planned to extend their excursions to take in Albay, the provincial capital, and the nearby volcano, whose nearly continuous eruptions were visible from nightfall onwards. [13th] Indeed they departed at the intended hour, and although their route was to include a long stretch on foot

---

[1] News of the safe arrival of the galleon from Acapulco, the lifeline of the Philippine colony, was always greeted with relief and Te Deums. The Anglo-Spanish differences here referred to arose out of their respective relations with Revolutionary France.

[2] A town on the south side of Sorsogon Bay.

[3] The South-west Monsoon from May to September.

[4] The North-east Monsoon from October to April.

through swampy terrain to the opposite coast and then a coastal passage with considerable risk of attack by pirates, they were nonetheless very pleased to be leaving without delay to reach the desired area on the following day.

For our part we had not been idle to produce an accurate chart of the harbour, with a combination of many methods, as quickly as possible. To this end the two armed launches, with Señores Viana, Murphy and Bauzá, with Piloto Sánchez, had set out early on the morning of the 14th for Sorsogon and Casiguran to chart all the interior part of the harbour which, we surmised, extended no more than five leagues beyond the corvettes' anchorage. Don Francisco Viana, who was in charge of the launches, had orders then to make his way to the opposite coast to fix the extremities of the island as far as possible in the short time available.[1] Pocket chronometer number 351 and a sextant were to be used to confirm these results. Meanwhile Don Jacobo Murphy and Piloto Sánchez were to be responsible for taking soundings with both launches, using long tacks to make this tiring operation somewhat shorter.

At the beginning the weather prospects seemed to promise a continuing calm, although the present season was generally the wettest in these parts. The first day could not have dawned more brightly, and we felt sure of being able to observe an immersion of the first satellite of Jupiter on the following night. We missed it, however, because clouds covered the sky shortly before the beginning of the immersion. A place very close to the anchorage had been chosen for the observatory on a small cleared patch of land, a little higher than the surrounding area. The chronometers were to be rated by means of absolute altitudes taken on board both corvettes. Consequently the determination of latitude by the astronomical quadrant was almost the only calculation which had to be made by celestial observations. In truth, any undertaking ashore was particularly trying, especially at night, as the usual custom of the pirates was to hide themselves upriver and attack indiscriminately to landward or seaward, compelling us to double our vigilance to the detriment of the rest which we had hoped to give the crew. On the evening of the 12th we had already determined the longitude of the anchorage with the first of the absolute altitudes by taking the mean of the four chronometers, and correcting the equations as follows:

	No. 72	No. 71	No. 105	No. 351
Longitude west of Palapag......	4′ 42″ 33‴	4′ 38″ 58‴	5′ 00″ 30‴	4′ 32″ 50‴
Comparison equations.........	0 00 00	+ 6 00	− 18 00	+ 9 40
Corrected longitudes..........	4 42 33	4 44 58	4 42 30	4 42 30
Average in degrees .... 1° 10′ 46″ 56‴[2]				

Two other missionary friars who visited us on board and were accommodated in the corvette, gave us more information about the area surrounding the bay. They were assigned as curates to the districts of Casiguran and Bulusan, and were daily witnesses to the havoc wrought by the frequent raids of the Joloanos and Mindanao pirates, although the construction of the watchtowers mentioned above had held them off

---

[1] I.e. he was to make his way, with Bauzá, back through San Bernadino Strait, round the SE extremity of Luzon and as far as Albay Gulf.

[2] Espinosa, *Memorias* (1809), 3rd memoir gives details of the observations for geographical positions (pp. 42-3).

for some time. Various families who had fled to the mountains had returned to live in this area under their protection.

14 March

The astronomers had no better luck on the night of the 14th than on previous nights. They could only take the meridian altitudes of a few stars between the clouds, giving the resulting latitude as 12°52′10″. Their preparations for the observation of the immersions of the first and second satellites of Jupiter were in vain.

By now the natives of the region had discovered the benefits of trading with us, whether in food or clothing. A sailor's cravings are inexhaustible and to this powerful incentive were added the very low prices over here compared with the coasts of Peru and New Spain that we had recently visited. It is true that this province is not the most outstanding for woven goods, particularly compared with those of Samar, but there was an abundance of domestic fowls, and the cockerels, which are the object of the natives' constant attention, occupy a large part of the market. It had to be considered an advantage, therefore, that the useful diversion of the cock-fights continued throughout our stay in this port, distracting the men from other vices and providing a quantity of healthy food for the cooking-pot. We also had some deer[1] and a copious supply of delicious fish and, as the officers took great pleasure in the collection of natural history specimens, they did not neglect this very interesting branch of trade in their work and their transactions with the natives.

We had now added to the more urgent undertaking of completing the plan of this port, begun on the 13th, the secondary tasks of sounding in the vicinity of the anchorage, taking bearings and examining suitable places to obtain water. The diversion of the pinnaces to this task achieved no useful object, as there was no convenient watering place close by, so from the following day we occupied ourselves in cutting firewood, of which there was a great abundance easily obtainable on the nearby shores. It was the custom of the marines and seamen to take this work in turns. Generally they cut wood until ten o'clock in the morning, after which they had their meal in peace and rested under a tree, waiting for the afternoon to bring the results of their labours on board, little by little. An officer or a sergeant was always present to keep order, with a few men who could take charge of the loaded firearms and use them if necessary.

18 March

Both launches returned on the 18th, their allotted tasks completed. Don Francisco Viana and Don Felipe Bauzá had reached the opposite coast, where they had measured a base near the town of Bacon[2] and made some observations which

---

[1] In earlier times deer were common in the Philippines, and deer-skins were exported to Japan. For an earlier appreciation of the rich fishing in the Islands see J. S. Cummins, ed., *Sucesos de las Islas Filipinas by Antonio de Morga*, Hakluyt Society, 2nd ser. 140, Cambridge, 1971, p. 257. Fish were abundant and varied and figured prominently in the Filipinos' diet, providing their proteins: J. L. Phelan, *Hispanization of the Philippines*, Madison, 1959, pp. 110, 112. Vreeland, *Area Handbook for the Philippines*, p. 23 counts 750 species of edible fish in the Islands. On fishing in the Philippines in general, see Vreeland op. cit., p. 445, and Blair and Robertson, *The Philippine Islands*, LIV, p. 400.

[2] In Albay Gulf, 5 miles NE of Sorsogon.

brought the survey of one side into exact agreement with the other. For lack of a suitable boat they had not extended their work to include Albay, but the inner part of the harbour had now been carefully examined, including the soundings for which Don Jacobo Murphy was responsible. We were greatly assisted by the measures taken by the *alcalde mayor*[1] of the province, which enabled us to work with greater speed and convenience. Although he was too busy to leave the capital at present, he had ordered some of his people to take every care of us, so that we were provided with all the necessary provisions and everything we needed for our excursions. In his letters he recommended that we take to Manila a good quantity of *abacá*[2] cordage which, being stored in poor conditions in warehouses as part of the taxes paid to the royal exchequer by the natives, was exposed to many risks and would attract a considerable cost in freight if carried by private vessels. We immediately offered to take 300 *quintales* on board each corvette, which was brought to us by boat from Sorsogon.

20 March
The measurement of a base, to tie in the more distant points and relate trigonometrically the astronomical calculations to the geodetic ones, was the only task left for the completion of our work in this harbour. The clouds which usually covered the volcano of Albay had prevented us from measuring its height with the theodolite, although we had waited daily for a chance to make the attempt. We now had the pleasure of seeing both objectives attained and we could therefore prepare for our departure with added eagerness now that Señores Pineda and Haenke had returned, with a vast number of acquisitions and much useful information.[3]

21 March
These industrious naturalists had, in the short space of eight days, travelled through a considerable part of the province and, at some risk, had made a close study of the volcano of Albay and the molten rock which forms the greater part of the material thrown up during its eruptions. After this, botany and zoology had been the principal object of their investigations, and although the rain, the rough tracks and the short time available were obstacles to the success of the excursion, their survey could nonetheless be considered complete, particularly as Don Luis Neé had explored the area surrounding the harbour with his usual zeal.

Despite these achievements, it was clear to all of these gentlemen that an island so remarkably favoured by nature's generous hand, and probably destined to be one of the principal supports of the Monarchy, deserved a much more detailed study than could be provided by the corvettes during their short stay in one harbour or another.

---

[1] A trained magistrate who was responsible for civil jurisdiction in a town. In certain provinces he also had administrative and financial responsibilities.

[2] A Tagalog word for a species of banana fibre (*Musa textilis*) used for making manila ropes, which float in water and which, not being subject to rot, do not require to be tarred. 'This useful plant' (Neé, 17 March, 1792) was used for making ropes, marine cordage, and rigging.

[3] What is useful (*lo útil*) and what is practical (*lo práctico*) are two key words in this period when a Spanish minister (Campomanes) could declare that the invention of the sewing needle was more useful to humanity than Aristotle's *Logic*. On this attitude see Jean Sarrailh, 'La Notion de l'utile dans la culture espagnole à la fin du XVIIIe siècle', *Bulletin hispanique*, 50, 1948, pp. 495–510.

It was the best season of the year, and the overland route from Albay to Manila was easy and pleasant owing to the assistance which could be expected from the towns along the way. Furthermore it crossed the rich province of Camarines and the intermediate mountains and the time available was not limited, as the road led to Manila, where the corvettes were to be laid up during the rainy season for several months. Don Luis Neé took up this enterprise with enthusiasm and set out from Sorsogon that very day, provided beforehand with all the assistance, documents and instructions that might contribute to the success of the journey.

22 March

The following day there was nothing to delay our departure. In the early morning calm both corvettes weighed the kedges laid out to the south and, with the boats hoisted and the wind from the NE with a few brief squalls, we set sail at nine o'clock. It was our intention to sail directly towards the entrance to the port of San Jacinto[1] on the island of Ticao, to examine it in detail, and then to continue to Manila without anchoring again, since the description of the interior of this small port of limited uses was within the powers of the many vessels, particularly the galleons, that frequented it on their way to the Visayan Islands or San Bernardino Strait.

The wind, however, was not as favourable as we had hoped. Instead of being from NE we only had variable light airs, which by two o'clock in the afternoon these were tending increasingly to the NW and west, so that we were still some three leagues from the fortified house of San Jacinto. We were making little way by tacking, while the tide was visibly setting us to the north. The clarity of the day was of considerable help to us, nevertheless, as we could clearly see the outline of this house and refer its bearings to other points around us, so that we could consider our principal object to have been achieved. At three o'clock, when the light airs were backing to the third quadrant, we were making good a course under full sail for the passage or channel between the islands of Burias and Masbate. We obtained no bottom with one hundred fathoms of line.

At four o'clock in the afternoon we had the satisfaction, at last, of finding a moderate ENE wind. Although it was of variable strength, because of the high mountains on Luzon, it enabled us to make good progress, so that by five the small islands near Diablo Point[2] on the island of Ticao bore west two leagues distant. At nightfall, now with a fresh easterly wind, we were only two leagues from the west point of Burias. We had taken numerous bearings of this island and of Masbate. The transit of this latter island with Diablo Point would guard against any risk of an error in determining the position of either by relating them both to the surveying work undertaken since Sorsogon.

It was not until eight o'clock at night that we entered the channel. It is not less than three and a half leagues wide, all of it clear and, to judge by this passage and my previous one in the *Astrea*, the tides appear to be neither strong nor dangerous. During this passage we stood close in to Burias, whose beaches, even at night, looked peaceful and thickly forested. At ten o'clock, under only the main topsails and foresail,

---

[1] An anchorage on the east coast of the island, used by Manila and Acapulco galleons.
[2] Now Nunan Point, the northern extremity of Ticao, off which lie the islands of Bagababoy and San Miguel and an unnamed islet.

we were through the channel and could set a course for the island of Marinduque.[1] We did not want to waste the fresh and favourable breeze, as we were still in the early hours of the night, but the NW end of Burias, the adjacent parts of Luzon, and Cape Bondoc or Head,[2] deserved a detailed survey, particularly as their exact position could be determined by reference to some other islands opposite.

Given these considerations it seemed wiser to heave-to at midnight four leagues from the entrance to the strait,[3] where we eagerly waited to begin our survey once more early the next morning.

23 March
There could have been no finer sight than the rising Sun as it appeared to us this day. Not far the island of Burias, gently elevated, the coast of Luzon beyond it as far as Bondoc Head, a magnificent range of mountains behind that coast, the island of Masbate, and the islands of Cobrador, Romblon and Sibuyan,[4] higher and further off, could only delight the eye with their beauty and variety, while we strove to plot their positions accurately.

We had crowded on sail since first light to see if we could reach Mindoro that day, but the wind did not answer our hopes. During the whole of the morning we could barely make two knots and at noon, when the north point of Sibuyan bore S4°W, we were still five leagues from the south point of Marinduque, which bore N63°W.

The calm continued during the afternoon and our progress was very slow. At sunset we were on the meridian of Elefante Island,[5] while the islands of Hermosa and Rey[6] lay further west bearing S75°W and N70°W, respectively, the latter three to three and a half leagues distant. The wind, however, increased somewhat after dark so that we were soon able to pass Tres Reyes Islands and approach the coast of Mindoro at a distance of two to three miles from Dumali Point.[7] We shortened sail there and, after making another two or three leagues, we hove-to and waited for the morning.

24 March
The next day began very pleasantly; the south point of Marinduque bore S71°W, Dumali Point S19°W, the outermost of the Baco Rocks[8] N83°W, and Verde Island[9] WNW about five leagues distant. Everything was clothed in beautiful green, and the light breeze was favourable. We did not obtain bottom with one hundred fathoms of line.

[1] A mountainous and volcanic island to the east of Mindoro.
[2] Bondoc Head, a prominent point 405 metres high, with Bondoc Point, a 15-metre high limestone bluff 1½ mile SSE, at the southern extremity of Bondoc Peninsula on the south coast of Luzon midway between the islands of Burias and Marinduque.
[3] The channel between Mindoro and Marinduque.
[4] Three islands on the south side of the Sibuyan Sea.
[5] Four cables south of the southern extremity of Marinduque.
[6] Dos Hermanas Islands, on the south side of the fairway, and one of the Tres Reyes Islands, on the north side of the fairway, 10 miles SSW and 11 miles WNW, respectively, of the southern extremity of Marinduque.
[7] The eastern extremity of Mindoro, 27 miles west of the southern extremity of Marinduque.
[8] On the south side of the eastern entrance to Verde Island Passage between the north side of Mindoro and Luzon.
[9] In the centre of the fairway at the eastern entrance to Verde Island Passage.

A new encounter contributed to give this day a special interest. It was the sight of three *pancos*[1] at sunrise, less than a mile off our bows to the north. The local pilot we had brought with us from Sorsogon to help us identify the correct names of all the points and islands, assured us that they were Joloanos pirates. We immediately hauled the wind on the starboard tack under full sail, preparing to use the cannon and side arms. The *Atrevida* followed, and to evade us the suspect craft altered course under oars, which they used very skilfully, passing about two cannon-shot lengths from our bows. We put about as soon as they were eight or nine points to windward of us, signalling to the *Atrevida* to maintain her first tack. Although we were not within range, both corvettes fired several cannon shots with the intention of frightening them and perhaps confusing them as to the best move to make. We soon realized, however, that we would not achieve our aim. With considerable skill the three craft had scattered as soon as they took flight, but continued to manoeuvre as one, going about at the same moment as the corvettes while keeping to the same tack, but only two or three points off the wind. They realized at once that they would be better off under oars again, and lowered their masts. Finally, after an hour of tacking, the two larger and faster craft had made a mile and a half to windward, and the third one, although much less nimble, had also gained considerably on us. In these circumstances only a breeze fresh enough to overcome their advantage under oars could have given us any hope of reaching even the last and less nimble boat, but as there was no sign of such a breeze there was nothing to be achieved but the waste of precious time. Accordingly we abandoned the chase and bore round to resume our course, making for the coast of Luzon in order to pass between it and Verde Island.[2]

In the slight to gentle breeze we could not reach this strait until past midday, but we could not regard this as a misfortune when we found that we had an excellent horizon to the south to observe the meridian altitude of the Sun, so that the confirmed latitude of that position also gave us a more exact result for the longitude observations that we had made during the morning.

The wind steadily increased in strength and at the same time the tide set us imperceptibly towards the other side of Verde Island, where we passed close to a naval schooner at anchor, which set sail again shortly afterwards. While coasting along Maricaban Island[3] we carefully examined the shoals running out from the shore, which make its western coast somewhat dangerous. We also took hour angles on the meridian of each point whose exact position we thought it important to determine and at four o'clock in the afternoon we were approaching Cape Santiago[4] on Luzon Island.

The wind was then blowing freshly from the ENE and NE, obliging us to proceed under foresail and topsails. It then veered aft once more and slackened as the evening

---

[1] Armed coastal vessels using both sails and oars, and carrying a crew of fifty. Widely used both for coastal trade and piracy, they originated among the Muslims of Borneo.
[2] Now known as North Pass.
[3] An island in Verde Island Passage, 10 miles NW of Verde Island.
[4] The SW extremity of Luzon at the western entrance to Verde Island Passage.

drew on, but by nightfall we were only a league from Fortune Island,[1] while Corregidor[2] was bearing N5°E and the highest point of Mariveles[3] N6°W. The night began with a gentle breeze so that we were unable to follow our original intention of continuing under shortened sail. We made the most of a few small gusts from the south under full sail, which led us to believe towards midnight that we might enter the bay before daylight, as Corregidor Island was already in sight and we were close to the coast of Limbones,[4] in depths of sixty-five to sixty fathoms, sand. After half an hour of calm, when we lost all steerage and were at risk of running foul of the *Atrevida*, the wind at last got up freshly from ENE. We then tacked close hauled under the three topsails with eased sheets, so as not to be carried back by the contrary tide.

25 March
The dawn promised a beautiful day. While tacking into the bay we could see different coastal vessels, among which we could distinguish by the King's flag the two privateer schooners. A merchant frigate had anchored in Mariveles [Bay],[5] and some *pontines*[6] were sailing out of port. The sky was clear over the land, El Fraile Island[7] bore N65°E, Caballo Island[8] N43°E, La Monja Island[9] N5°E and the mid-point of Fortune Island S5°W.

From there we began tacking under full sail to enter [Manila Bay], taking care at first not to approach Corregidor or the coast of Marigondon[10] too closely as the tide was against us. By noon we had made considerable progress and at two in the afternoon we passed Caballo Island, then passing half a mile to the east of Corregidor.

As is usual in Manila Bay, the wind freshened and shifted to the ESE and SE as the afternoon wore on, so we could remain on the starboard tack. At sunset Manila bore N71°E four leagues distant, when the depth was ten fathoms, ooze. Soon afterwards we obtained soundings of eight and a half fathoms one league offshore, when we put about and made for the coast near Cavite[11] under topsails and foresail. For the rest of that very beautiful night we alternated between heaving-to and sailing close hauled under topsails to keep in depths of eleven, twelve and thirteen fathoms, ooze. Thus dawn found us only a league from the entrance to Manila Harbour, now bearing approximately NE.

26 March
Until eight o'clock we had calm or light variable airs, which hardly gave us steerage

---

[1] A small wooded island, 119 metres high, 19 miles WNW of Cape Santiago.
[2] A island in the entrance to Manila Bay with navigable channels on either side.
[3] Mariveles Mountains, rising to 1,420 metres, near the southern end of Bataan Peninsula, which forms the western side of Manila Bay.
[4] An island and cove near the southern entrance point of Manila Bay.
[5] A harbour at the southern end of Bataan Peninsula.
[6] A two-masted coaster used for inter-island trade.
[7] A rocky islet, 12 metres high, in the southern approaches to Manila Bay.
[8] A bluff rocky island, 116 metres high, 1 mile south of the eastern extremity of Corregidor Island.
[9] A rocky islet, 37 metres high, 2¼ miles WSW of the western extremity of Corregidor Island.
[10] The SE side of Manila Bay near its southern entrance, east of Limbones.
[11] See p. 269, n. 9.

way, even when we resorted to being towed by the pinnace under oars. At last, however, a few timely gusts from SE allowed us to anchor at half past nine a mile off the beach in six fathoms, ooze, with the large kedge laid out to the west. The cathedral bore N55°E, the western knuckle at the entrance [to Manila Harbour][1] N32°E and Caballo Island S53°W. The view of various Chinese junks and a few large trading vessels made the anchorage all the more pleasant.

---

[1] *Martillo O. de la barra* in the original. However, 'Carta esférica de bahía de Manila trabajada ... á bordo de las corvetas Descubierta y Atrevida ... en 1792 y publicada en ... Madrid año 1807' has the legend 'Barra de Manila' against two jetties extending some distance from the mouth of the Pasig River, from which it seems clear that Malaspina's bearing was to a *martillo* or knuckle (the outer edge of a sharp bend in a jetty or pier-head) at the western end of these jetties. The Manila Harbour entrance formed by the jetties was known as Barra de Manila.

BOOK NINE

AT MANILA
AND THE SEPARATION OF THE CORVETTES

CHAPTER 1

Events in Manila Bay

[26 March]
At the time [of our visit][1] the important command of the Philippines was held by Brigadier de Real Armada Don Felix Berenguer de Marquina,[2] while in the capital Capitán de Navío Don Francisco Muñoz de San Clemente held the positions of *Teniente de Rey*,[3] Inspector of Troops, and *Comandante* of the Cavite Dockyard. Everything, therefore, led us to anticipate that this stay would be one of the most agreeable we were to have, among officers who were not only of the same corps, but were also men of qualities well proven in the different posts in which they had served, either as scientists or as members of the armed forces. A nine-gun salute to the city was fired immediately, and answered according to regulations. At the same time Teniente de Navío Don José Espinosa went ashore to pay his respects to these senior officers to appraise them of the assistance which would be most necessary for the prompt continuation of our work and to arrange for the delivery of the mail from Acapulco to the post office.

We found out afterwards that the Governor was absent in the nearby province of Bulacan in an attempt to restore his health, and that the command of the city was entrusted to the *Teniente de Rey*. Consequently our first courtesies were directed to him, as well as those of our requests that seemed most urgent.

I was soon visited by the Secretary of the Real Compañía de Filipinas, Don José Armenteros,[4] whose knowledge of the political conditions and natural history of these islands has been frequently praised both here and in the [American] continent. It was with much pleasure that I received from his hands an official letter in which His Excellency Señor Bailio Don Antonio Valdés advised him that, for as long as the

---

[1] This was Malaspina's fourth visit to Manila. In 1777-9 he had served as an *Alférez de Navío* in the frigate *Astrea*, commanded by Antonio Mesía, who was taking the new Governor of the Philippines, Don José Vasco y Vargas, to Manila. In 1783-4 as *Capitán de Fragata* he was second in command in the frigate *Asunción*, Capitán de Fragata Juan Ruiz de Apodaca, which was sent to Manila to take the news of the 1783 Treaty of Paris. This voyage, via the Cape of Good Hope, caused much interest because it only took five months to reach Cavite, one month shorter than usual. In 1786-8 Malaspina completed a successful commercial voyage to the Philippines in command of the *Astrea* on charter to the Real Compañía de Filipinas from the Spanish Navy; for the later voyage see Vol. 1 of this edition, p. xxxvii.

[2] Félix Berenguer de Marquina (1788-93), an active reformer, was later Viceroy of Mexico; for his biography, see Blair and Robertson, *The Philippine Islands*, XVII, pp. 299-300.

[3] The officer in charge of supervising a port or naval base in the absence of the appointed Governor.

[4] See p. 280, n. 2 above.

corvettes remained in the archipelago, he should combine his our work with ours and thereby broaden the scope and benefits accrued to the expedition. It was, indeed, a truly valuable addition to our expedition since the zeal and vigour of this most loyal subject allowed him to make light of any inconvenience and labours likely to come his way as he helped us in hastening the pace of our transactions. In fact his visit on that very first day was most rewarding as we were given there and then precise and detailed information regarding the kind of winds and currents that we could expect in the present season, which would allow us to determine more accurately the tasks to be attempted in the short time remaining of the favourable season.

This information gave me to understand, contrary to my first assumptions, that the return from the port of Macau in May would not only be excessively slow, but that it would also be impossible to follow the coast from Cape Bojeador to the entrance to Manila [Bay]. Yet the survey of this coast was essential for the sake of coastal shipping and the route of the galleon, and because of the necessity for shipping on its way to Canton [Guangzhou] towards the end of the South-west Monsoon to make calls at ports on this coast. These were not reasons, however, for omitting the voyage to Macau, where we were to carry out important gravity experiments with the pendulum for the proposed agreement on uniform measurements.[1] We also planned to make a better profit there from the sale of the furs acquired by the crew on the NW coast of America. It was also important that a close study of national interests there should take place at a time when all the factors[2] of different nations were present and not otherwise occupied with the preparation of shipments for Europe in Canton.

These considerations naturally led to the conclusion that a further separation of the corvettes was unavoidable if we were to achieve our two original objectives – a visit to Macau and the survey of the northern coasts of Luzon – without finding ourselves at sea at the start of the rains, which would be most detrimental to the crew and might cause irretrievable delays in the refitting prior to the coming cruises. Sending a single corvette to Macau now seemed more appropriate to [naval] discipline, a matter which could not to be overlooked on an expedition of this nature. There would also fewer chances of trouble on the part of the marines and sailors, so often the cause of heated arguments with the officers or the rapacious Chinese police officials in the [Boca] Tigris.[3] A single crew could be assembled more easily with a selection of steady, robust and smart seamen, since there were now few left of our original complements. There were now no fewer than thirteen sick between the two corvettes, all of whom had to be kept in hospital suffering from severe intestinal obstruction and in great need of aperients and continuous exercise, particularly as this disorder was, by its very nature, complicated by intermittent fevers. Finally, as the operations entrusted to the corvette [the *Atrevida*] which was to examine certain

---

[1] For international co-operation between scientists in the 18th and early 19th centuries see Gavin de Beer, *The Sciences were never at War*, London, 1960.

[2] A Factor was the executive head of a 'Factory', i.e. a trading establishment at a foreign port or mart.

[3] A narrow passage, which was guarded by forts on either side, at the entrance to Zhujiang, the river leading to Guangzhou.

designated coasts of Luzon were not of great complexity, it would be possible to transfer some of its crew and to assign them to tasks just as important in this vicinity.

27 March

Against this background it was decided early on the following morning that Don José Bustamante would undertake the voyage to Macau in the *Atrevida*, returning as quickly as possible without deviating from the direct route for any reason. The *Descubierta* would survey the outer coasts of Luzon, as far as was prudent or feasible in the circumstances. Alférez de Fragata Don Fabio Ali Ponzoni and Alférez de Navío Don Felipe Bauzá were instructed to make a detailed chart of this bay and then proceed to the islands of Cabra, Lubang and Ambil[1] and the coasts of Mindoro and Tayabas [Bay].[2] Don Antonio Pineda, with his tireless devotion to natural history, agreed to start at once upon his important excursions in the vicinity of the capital, while Don Tadeo Haenke would remain on board the *Descubierta* as far as the coasts of Ilocos[3] or Cagayan,[4] from where he would begin his botanical survey while making his way south along the Igorrotes and Pampanga Mountains.[5]

For the sake of greater accuracy in the gravity experiments with the pendulum, the astronomical quadrant was added to chronometer 72 and the astronomical clock, which had already been transferred to the *Atrevida*. Pocket chronometer 351 and a theodolite were entrusted to Señores Ali Ponzoni and Bauzá, while Don Antonio Pineda was given every assistance and freedom of action necessary to carry out his mission with all decorum and efficiency.

The Governor, who was kind enough to return to the capital that very day, was quick to render us all the assistance in his power for the execution of this plan. He gave us a letter for the Governor-General of Macau[6] inviting his support for the *Atrevida*'s mission and provided us with two well-equipped schooners for our survey of Lubang, Ambil and Mindoro. At the same time he gave wide ranging instructions that we should be helped promptly in the provinces, measures which were to be of considerable benefit to the expedition. The directors of the Real Compañía de Filipinas likewise directed their factor in Macau to assist us in our work, and the Provincial Fathers of the religious houses of Santo Domingo and San Agustín, whose parishes

---

[1] The three principal islands of the Lubang Islands off the NW extremity of Mindoro.
[2] A large bay on the south coast of Luzon, NW of the island of Marinduque.
[3] The province at the NW end of Luzon, north of Lingayen Gulf.
[4] The province at the NE end of Luzon, east of Cagayan River, one of the major rivers of Luzon, flowing from south to north and entering the sea west of Aparri on the north coast of the island.
[5] Possibly the two mountain ranges in the north of the island separated by the great valley of the Cagayan River. The eastern range is Sierra Madre and the western range Cordillera Central. Madre Ygorrotes (Igorots), a Tagalog word meaning 'mountain men'; they are an unassimilated group in central and northern Luzon; for these and other pagan groups in the modern Philippines see Vreeland, *Area Handbook for the Philippines*, pp. 90, 446, 450 and Blair and Robertson, *The Philippine Islands*, LIV, pp. 443-4. Pampanga is in central Luzon, N of Manila. The Pampangans were considered especially loyal to Spain: 'They are as good and faithful here as are the Burgundians in Flanders', wrote Governor Corcuera to Philip IV in 1636: Blair and Robertson, op. cit., XXVI, p. 197.
[6] The Governor of Macau was Vasco Luís Carneiro de Sousa e Faro (1790-93); followed by Jose Manuel Pinto.

and missions would lie on the route to be taken by our naturalists, urged their subordinates to show us the hospitality and good conduct required by [Christian] charity and by devotion to the service of His Majesty.

Such unanimous support for the expedition could only expedite the departure of the corvettes for their new destinations, particularly as we had not lost a moment in replenishing our water supplies, which was now necessary, stocking two months' worth of provisions, and in taking on a considerable number of native volunteer sailors, so that our complement was now almost complete in numbers, if not in vigour and discipline. Two marines and a marine gunner from the *Descubierta* made up the numbers of these important members of *Atrevida*'s crew. Don Alexo Blanchat of the Merchant Marine of these islands joined her as a pilot for the Chinese coasts, and two native pilots who were familiar with the names, soundings, rivers and bays of the northern coasts of the island of Luzon joined the *Descubierta* in the same rank.

Meanwhile we had continued with our usual astronomical work. The method of absolute altitudes used on both corvettes since our arrival at this anchorage had allowed us to continue the series of longitudes referred from the meridian of Palapag to longitude west of Cádiz, which we had retained in our calculations. Disregarding the daily equations because of the short time span, the results from both ships were as follows:

	Chronometer 71	Chronometer 72	Pocket chronometer 105	Pocket chronometer 351
Longitude west of Palapag in time)	16' 5" 34'''	16' 16" 01'''	16' 35" 12'''	16' 19" 6'''

This being the case, it seemed better to use only the results of the two chronometers whose rate in present comparisons was closer to that determined in Sorsogon. Allowing for the difference of meridian between the anchorage and the cathedral, the results refer to the position of the latter.

By our series of longitudes west of Cádiz..232° 53' 29"
By M. le Gentil's observations ....232° 50' 30"
By the calculations of Comte de Roseli,[1]
    Comandante of the French Frigate [blank]...232° 52' 45"
Immersion of the 1st satellite of Jupiter on the night of the 27th..............232° 50' 15"
Immersion occurring on the night of the 29th ....232° 56' 15"

Teniente de Rey Don Francisco Muñoz de San Clemente had offered his house to the astronomers for these latter observations, combining kind and generous hospitality with an almost innate love of the sciences, particularly astronomy. Not only did he wish to share with our officers in all the work necessary for the greatest possible accuracy of the observation, but also, on the 29th, he observed the immersion phase through a bronze telescope, the results of which are shown above. Now, as on many

---

[1] François-Etienne de Rosily (1748-1832) commanded the *Venus* (1784-8). see Olivier Chapuis, *A la mer comme au ciel*, Paris, 1999, pp. 789-90; Dermigny, *La Chine*, III, p. 1087.

other occasions, we regretted that we did not have the results of M. Dagelet's calculations on the ill-fated expedition of the Comte de La Pérouse,¹ although we had no doubt that they would have been similar to our own.

30 March
Another fortunate coincidence was to engage our attention during this part of our stay in the capital. Two months previously the French doctor, Dr Robert, had arrived from the Île de France [Mauritius]. He treated various nervous complaints with Señor Mesmer's animal magnetism, which in recent years has been the cause of so much argument and even invective among scholars.² As is well known, the object of animal magnetism is the cure of illnesses of nervous origin by the use of remedies which are purely external, but more efficacious than the usual ones.

The doctor applying the magnetic treatment establishes a connection or contact with the patient by touch and then, by means of gentle compression of the head with the thumbs on the forehead and of other compressions on the hypochondrium³ with the fingers on the solar plexus, he transmits an oscillation to the nerves, which he intensifies and maintains through his finger-tips with hand movements in different directions. When the patient is prepared to receive the magnetism the treatment is effective. The compression of the head and the solar plexus cause a gentle warmth in the brain and after a time, which varies according to the individual, the patient lapses into a kind of sleep. This state, whose result is somnambulism, is well known and respected in Europe as a symptom of a disease, but has been very little studied by physicians until now.

The somnambulism is accompanied by the most extraordinary effects. The coherent dialogue between the doctor and patient during this state, the consistent and satisfactory answers given to the doctor's questions about the origin and nature of the illness, the signs of relief, and the foreknowledge of the effect, are other incidental characteristics which accompany this treatment, and which can be neither doubted nor understood by an unprejudiced witness of the cures almost daily effected by this method.

According to the reports of M. Robert and others among the more enlightened members of the colony, magnetism has had even more remarkable results here, either

---

[1] Joseph Lepaute Dagelet, La Pérouse's astronomer, whose longitude of Cavite by lunar distances was 118°50′40″ east of Paris and 118°46′08″ by chronometer: Dunmore, *Journal of La Pérouse*, p. 248.

[2] The Austrian physician, Franz Anton Mesmer (1733–1815), asserted (1772) the existence of 'animal magnetism' as a cure for some nervous diseases. His theory (an aspect of Enlightenment para-science) was first rejected (1785) by the French medical establishment, and then validated 50 years later when it returned as mesmerism, which continued to be fashionable into the last pre-Darwinian decades (1830s and 1840s): see Alison Winter, *Mesmerism: Powers of Mind in Victorian Britain*, Chicago, 1998. 'Dr Robert from Île de France' (Mauritius) cannot be identified. There was also a 'French Island' between Canton and Macau, but that cannot be meant here. The writer's interest in electro-physiology is shown by his detailed description of the procedures, his close questioning of the doctors involved, and his return to the subject later (pp. 325–6). All this suggests a willingness to experiment, shows a dislike of medical and religious conservatism, and is further evidence of a new temper in Old Spain, although the Inquisition had prohibited experiments with electricity, circa 1760 (Le Gentil in Blair and Robertson, *The Philippine Islands*, LI, p. 99). On early magnetism and electricity see R. W. Home, *Electricity and Experimental Physics in 18th-century Europe*, Aldershot, 1992; see also Jean-Paul Marat, *Mémoire sur l'électricité médicale*, Paris, 1784.

[3] Those parts of the human abdomen which lie immediately under the ribs.

because of the influence of the atmosphere and soil or because of an extraordinary nervous sensitivity in the other sex, among whom these treatments are very frequently performed, to good effect.

Meanwhile, there was a great variety of opinion as to the method adopted. Other doctors, as is their habit, rejected or even disparaged it, and the common people attributed almost infinite virtues to it. Nor was there any lack of those who appealed to the sanctity of religion, declaring it to be nothing more than trickery and incapable of providing the desired cure.

The arrival of the corvettes at this juncture seemed destined to do away with such doubts. Accustomed to hear of this method in Europe and not deluding ourselves by any confusion of cause and effect, we observed in silence and with a respect born of experience, the great works of nature, whose causes we cannot fathom, having also among us several people who had performed careful and, I should say, scientific experiments.

Our surgeons and most of the officers were, of course, present at these experiments from the beginning in various places. Teniente de Navío Juan de la Concha, who had suffered from severe nervous attacks for a long time, consented to try this method, just as an experiment. Considering that most of our sick suffered from intestinal obstructions, which are directly connected to the nervous functions this new method was proposed as the treatment, and two of them volunteered to try it. Don Juan de la Concha, either because he was not a suitable subject for magnetism, or because of the noise made by the onlookers, or some other cause, experienced the lethargy or preliminary sleepiness but was not able to fall fast asleep, although everything showed him to be very close to the desired state. The other two men, who were a quartermaster and a topman from the *Descubierta*, were transferred to another hospital in the charge of M. Robert himself, and I asked Don Antonio Pineda to attend these treatments as often as his occupations would allow him, as our own impending departure would not give us time to do so.

1 April
The *Atrevida* was able to set sail for her destination with a favourable breeze early on the morning of 1 April, while the *Descubierta* had to wait until the afternoon of the 3rd for favourable conditions.

BOOK TEN

THE ISLAND OF LUZON AND ATREVIDA'S VISIT TO MACAU[1]

[1] For Tova y Arredondo's account of his surveying activities south of Manila and Laguna de Bay, which Malaspina does not include or even mention in his journal, see Appendix 3.

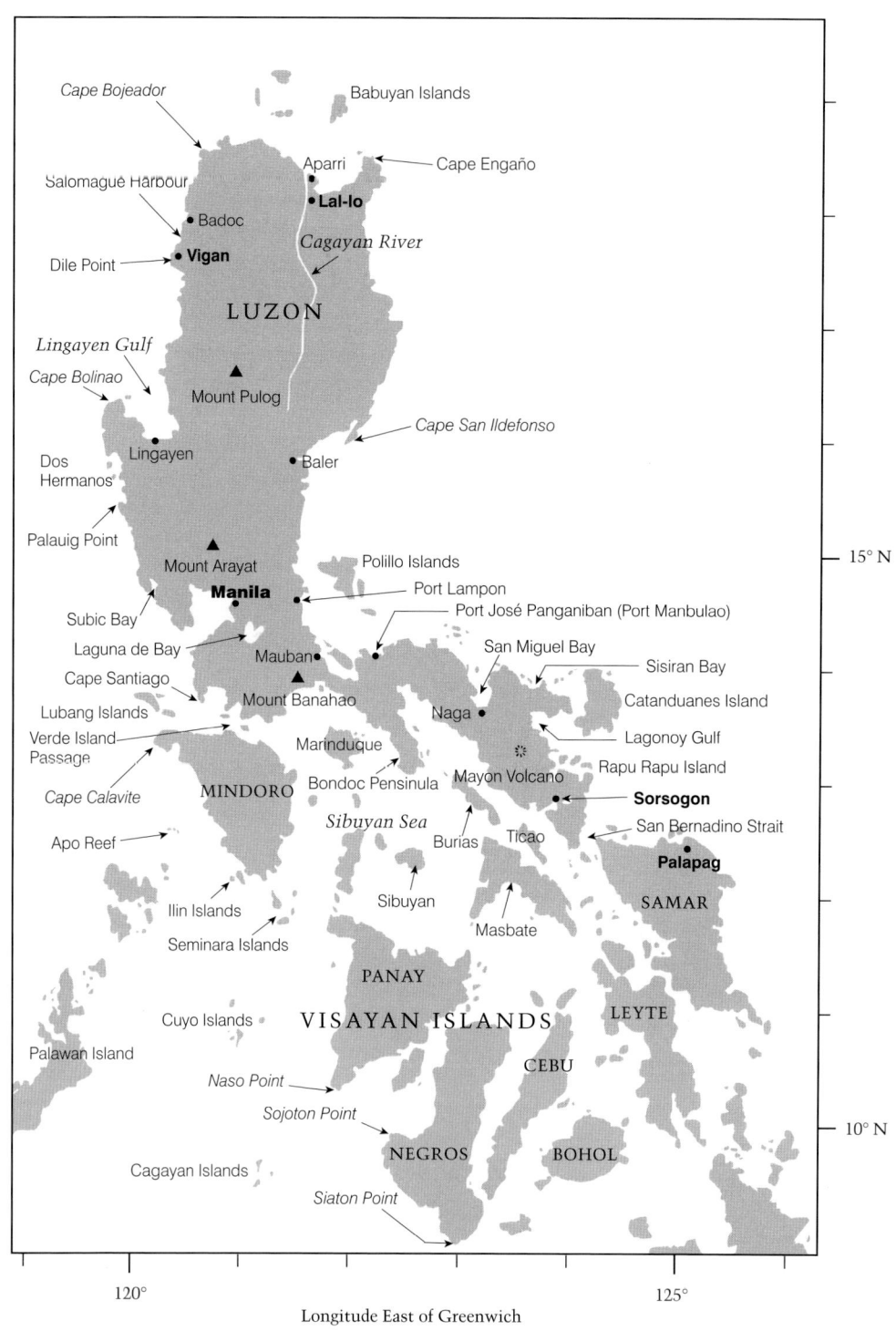

Fig. 5. Luzon and the Visayan Islands, March to November 1792

CHAPTER 1

Survey of the Coast of Ilocos[1] by *Descubierta* and her return to Manila Bay

3 April
The NE wind which was to carry us towards the entrance to Manila Bay[2] did not set in until half past one in the afternoon, when it was so variable in strength and direction that we did not reach the vicinity of the entrance to the bay until night was falling. Having passed very close to Corregidor Island, we then altered course to south, giving La Monja Island a good berth. At eight o'clock, when it was bearing N58°E, one and a half leagues distant, and Caballo Island was bearing E8°N, we altered course to WNW under easy sail.[3]

It was a very pleasant night, with a light and sometimes a fresh breeze. A brilliant Moon promised further good fortune for our tasks the following morning. We heard repeated cannon fire or shots from the inner part of the bay, but as we had not seen the least sign of pirates before dark, we attributed these to some festival in the nearby towns, particularly as a considerable consumption of gunpowder is generally an essential part of these celebrations.

4 April
The position of the coast from the anchorage in Mariveles Bay to Capones Point,[4] that encloses the beautiful port of Subec,[5] varied greatly on different charts. We therefore had to consider fixing the position of this particular point as an essential part of our survey to ensure that navigators could neither fail to identify it when making for this port nor find themselves in the sort of doubt that up to now has exposed them to many dangers during the frequent sightings of land when making for Manila. Bearings taken during surveys of the interior as far as Corregidor Island and in the harbour of Limbones[6] could be extended as far as the vicinity of Subec [Bay], but they could never provide details of the more distant localities with the accuracy that we required.

[1] Province in the NW part of Luzon, north of Lingayen Gulf.
[2] Here and elsewhere Malaspina uses 'Boca de Mariveles' to refer to the entrance to Manila Bay.
[3] Having passed close north of Corregidor and then west of La Monja island.
[4] A bare reddish headland, 12 miles NW of the western entrance point to Subic Bay.
[5] An excellent natural harbour on the north side of Subic Bay.
[6] Now Limbones Cove.

These considerations had already persuaded us not to make too much distance during the night. Indeed we had earlier altered course much more to the north[1] to keep offshore. At ten o'clock and again at four in the morning we obtained no bottom with one hundred fathoms of line. We lay-to on alternate tacks during the last hours of the night and dawn found us in a position as advantageous as we could desire. We were no more than three or four leagues from the port of Subec, the head of Mariveles Bay S71°E, and the outermost islet off Capones Point[2] bore true north, some four to five leagues distant.

We began at once on our usual tasks of delineating the coastline, measuring bases with the log line and taking observations for longitude. The wind was light, and we did not make as much progress as we had expected, but by noon the centre of Capones [Capon Grande] Island bore E14°S three leagues distant, when our observations placed us at latitude 14°58′ and longitude 1°7′ west of Manila Cathedral.

The coast as far as Capones Point is steep-to and of moderate height, with a few small islands close inshore, particularly towards the port of Subec. The few lights or bonfires, or none at all, indicate that it is thinly populated, although it constitutes most of the province of Zambales, next to that of Pangasinan, which includes Cape Bolinao[3] and the port of Lingayen, the latter [coast] being the usual landfall for shipping from Chinese ports bound for Manila Bay.

We had already been warned in Manila that once having doubled Capones Point we would probably encounter a mixture of calms and gentle land and sea breezes. This was borne out that afternoon by a moderate breeze which slowly shifted from south through west to NW, which we used in the late afternoon, when we were three leagues offshore with Capones Point bearing S28°E, tacking to the third quadrant under full sail. A Chinese junk that we had sighted near Manila before midday had now disappeared from view, as the same winds which were contrary to our course were favourable to her.

The last of the sea-breeze died at nightfall. After several hours of calm a light land breeze set in, which we made use of to close the coast and by dawn we were four to five leagues offshore. The height of the coast diminishes markedly in this vicinity. Its irregularity and ruggedness indicate the presence of shoals, making it a dangerous one for shipping. Capones Point and its island were still clearly in sight, now bearing SE, while our northerly course was bringing us considerably closer to Playa Honda.[4]

5 April
Despite the haze still present at seven o'clock in the morning we sighted a Spanish merchant vessel which passed us about one league to starboard bound for Manila. Before midday it was lost from sight.

The land breeze dropped and was followed by a brief period of calm, but shortly

---

[1] Malaspina had altered course from WNW to NW.
[2] Capon Grande Island
[3] The northern part of the peninsula that forms the western side of Lingayen Gulf.
[4] Literally 'Low Beach', an extensive plain in Zambales province, on the western side of Luzon, north of Bataan Peninsula see Blair and Robertson, *The Philippine Islands*, XLVII, p. 291; LIII, p. 129; LV, p. 747.

before noon a fresh sea breeze set in from the west, allowing us to continue measuring bases. The noon observations gave latitude 15°9′23″ and longitude 1°10′ [west of Manila Cathedral], confirming that we had made very little progress since the previous morning. The only useful achievement of the rest of the day was the confirmation of the position of Bagalahuá shoal[1] near Bagaluban.[2] The moderate NW breeze was against us, obliging us to tack until the wind veered to the north, NNE and NE. [6th] Early the next morning the latter finally compelled us to put about on the starboard tack and set a course in the fourth quadrant, close hauled.

We were then some seven or eight leagues from the coast, which the haze prevented us from seeing clearly. Towards midday the NE breeze was followed by a calm in which we were unable to approach the coast, so that it was not until the afternoon that we caught sight of Dos Hermanas,[3] islets which lie not far offshore to the north of Calagan Point.[4] Even this small progress was due to the effect of the almost constant northward set of the current. We soon became aware that the east/west ebb and flood of the tide at right angles to the coast undoubtedly also affected our progress.[5]

7 April

The following day was little better, at least at the beginning. The land breeze had been so light during the previous night that we had hardly made enough offing to clear Dos Hermanas with safety. The calm now prevented us from continuing our work and we could only fix our hopes on a squall that we could see approaching us from the south. The squall brought a light but favourable wind when it reached us, enabling us to make progress to the north once more. With our noon observations we were able to fix the position of Dos Hermanas as accurately as possible, our own position at the time being latitude 15°51′ and longitude 1°26′ west [of Manila Cathedral], with the highest point of one of the Hermanas[6] bearing S72°E, four to five leagues, distant, although we could not see it very clearly. The squall was soon over and the wind veered through SSW and SW to west, so that conditions in the afternoon were somewhat better than they had been on previous days. We surveyed a good stretch of the coast as far as the vicinity of Cape Bolinao by taking bearings and observations. Cabatugan Point[7] then bore N54½°E, about seven leagues distant.

---

[1] Baxo de Palaubi on 'Carta general del archipiélago de Filipinas levantada en 1792 y 93 por los comandantes y oficiales de las corbetas de S.M. Descubierta y Atrevida ... publicada en 1808', 2 sheets (northern sheet), which Malaspina closed to identify. Now called Palauig Reef, on which the sea usually breaks heavily, 1 mile west of Paluaig Point. No wonder Horsburgh doubted the existence of such a shoal since 'A Spanish M.S. Chart in my possession ... places a shoal in lat, 15°28′N., about 2 leagues off shore, named Baxos Bagalagua, but its existence seems very doubtful.', James Horsburgh, *India Directory*, 3rd edn, II, London, 1827, p. 375.

[2] Palauig Point.

[3] Hermana Major and Hermana Menor Islands, in the approaches to Santa Cruz Harbour.

[4] Not named on 'Carta general del archipiélago de Filipinas (northern sheet)', but probably Santa Cruz Point, 18 miles north of Palauig Point.

[5] In March the current sets north at rates rarely exceeding one knot, but offshore the effect of the tide is negligible.

[6] Hermana Mayor Island.

[7] Not named on 'Carta general del archipiélago de Filipinas (northern sheet)', but possibly San Fernando Point, 30 miles NE of Cape Bolinao.

As the night was very clear we kept the coast in sight until we were about three leagues off. By then the wind had shifted to the north, obliging us to alter course from ENE to the fourth quadrant. We kept on this tack only until midnight, when the wind dropped entirely. As we were then not far offshore, we brought the bows round to the west.

8 April
The day dawned with a flat calm. The horizon and sky were very hazy, but the land could be seen very clearly as far as Cape Bolinao, at a distance of four or five leagues. Our bearings showed us that the current had carried us a considerable way to the north during the night, so that Balingasay Point,[1] which forms the end of that coast, now bore ESE.

In this position, which I had failed to reach in less than six days sailing, I had now to turn my thoughts to new considerations, based upon our more accurate knowledge of the winds now prevailing on this coast. All the evidence led me to believe that the currents and the extraordinarily variable winds would greatly prolong the cruise, subjecting it to the risk of innumerable errors in charting the principal points of the coast. Port Sual,[2] and many other roadsteads which provided essential shelter from the northerlies, could not be accurately described unless the corvette anchored in Salomague[3] for the launch to make lengthy excursions. It was very doubtful whether we could undertake any surveying of the northern part of the island, where the currents were very strong in this season.[4] In addition the state of the corvette, infested with cockroaches and manned only by those few officers whose health had stood up to the present inclement weather, would not allow for the prolongation of the present cruise. All these considerations, and the essential fact that, if the corvette were laid up, we would more easily be able to undertake various excursions to other parts of the island, thus making the best use of the season, finally persuaded me to return to port and work from there with different parties so as to complete our tasks as accurately as possible.

It was not until eleven o'clock in the morning that a gentle breeze set in from the west, when we at once altered course to south, steering a little to the east to close the coast. At noon we were in latitude 16°24′ and longitude 1°22′ and, having measured some bases, we were able to fix the position of Balinasay Point with a degree of certainty. The wind was favourable for the whole of this afternoon, enabling us to confirm or rather correct any doubtful determinations made while making our way north. We were now able to sail much closer to the coast and measure bases more regularly, although at night we had to take the precaution of standing off to the west, as the tide would have set us too close onshore.

By nightfall we had already lost sight of the frigate *Concepción* of the Real Compañía de Filipinas, which had sailed from Manila a day later than us and was now

---

[1] A low wooded point formng the northern extremity of Cape Bolinao.
[2] A village and harbour in the SW corner Lingayen Gulf.
[3] A harbour 44 miles SSW of Cape Bojeador, which affords shelter from all but west and SW winds.
[4] See p. 309, n. 5 above.

9 April

The night was very peaceful, with the wind falling, making our progress so slow that the following morning Tambobo Point[1] still bore S31½°E, six to seven leagues, distant. We altered course to SSW and then SbyW to give the Hermanas a berth of two or three leagues. We could not confirm their position that night as there was still haze, and the current was setting us offshore.

10 April

On the morning of the 10th we waited anxiously for dawn expecting it would reveal Capones Point and thus help us to make for the entrance to the port,[2] as a fresh breeze had now set in from NNW, backing to north and NE. But since neither [Capones Point and Island] were in sight, we knew for certain that we were further offshore than we had thought and so came about to SEbyS. At noon our position was latitude 15°10' and longitude 1°16', less than six leagues offshore, with Mount Iba[3] bearing N82°E.

We soon sighted Capones Point and Island and continued to close them. At nightfall when we were only two leagues off them, we altered course for the port.[4] The wind remained strong and favourable for some time, but at two o'clock in the morning it blew strongly from east and ESE, obliging us to alter course to the southward, close hauled, standing well off the entrance to Manila Bay.

11 April

Indeed at sunrise we were less than five leagues off Corregidor Island, the extremities of which were now bearing N72°E and N76°E. Other conspicuous points near the entrance could be clearly seen and our position allowed us to extend our bearings to the islands of Cabra, Lubang and Mindoro, linking in the surrounding area very nicely. At eight in the morning we tacked to the first quadrant and before noon we tacked again to SSE under full sail, but we had made little progress as the wind remained no more than a gentle breeze and contrary.

Thus towards three in the afternoon, while on the same tack, we had crossed to the Limbones Coast[5] when the wind began backing into the first quadrant, allowing us to alter course to the west.[6] Finally a squall from SSE enabled us to make for Corregidor under full sail. The light airs that followed prevented us from steering a direct course for some time, but by nightfall we were only a mile off La Monja, which

---

[1] Situated 23 miles south of Cape Bolinao.
[2] Presumably the entrance to Manila Bay.
[3] A 1,905-metre peak 63 miles SSE of Cape Bolinao.
[4] See n. 2 above.
[5] I.e. the southern side of the entrance to Manila Bay: see p. 294, n. 4 above.
[6] E in the MS journal, which is clearly an error for O = west, which would take Malaspina back towards Corregidor Island.

now bore N21°E. In this position, having sounded thirty-seven fathoms, sand, we dropped the port anchor with half a cable of line.

12 April
At first light the next morning we set sail to enter [Manila Bay] through Boca Grande.[1] The tide was against us, but with a smooth sea and a moderate breeze we made good progress and by half past six we were on the meridian of La Monja, where we took an observation for longitude which confirmed the excellent rate of number 71 and the accuracy of our previous calculations. The wind shifted to the north which allowed us to steer a more direct course, so that by noon the western extremity of Caballo Island bore N37°W, one league distant. The Marigondon or southern coast[2] was scarcely two miles distant, the depth twenty-two fathoms, sand.

It would have been most unwise to continue our easterly course from this position, given Nichelson's warnings[3] and the recent experiences of His Most Christian Majesty's Frigate *Calipso*.[4] We therefore put about, with the wind still moderate from the north, and sent the pinnace in charge of Piloto Don Juan Maqueda, to take soundings in the immediate area, where the local pilot assured us, using known bearings, he would soon find the reported shoal.[5]

At two o'clock the pinnace was still searching in vain for the shoal. We lay-to and fired a gun to recall it, as we were too close to the southern coast and would now have to beat offshore under full sail in the continuing NE breeze. The pinnace returned and was hoisted inboard. Shortly afterwards a fresh SE breeze set in and we continued, sailing free, until we were able to confirm the position of the shoal. We then made for Cavite, close hauled, and by sunset we were some five leagues from our destination. The sky looked squally in the early hours of the night, and we proceeded under courses and topsails until sounding fourteen fathoms, ooze, where we anchored, at about eleven o'clock at night. Manila was then bearing NE5°N and Sangley Point[6] SSE5°S.

13 April
The hope, or rather, the certainty, that we would have a land breeze the following morning, had prevailed upon me to anchor overnight, so as to be able to make Cavite on a single tack. My intention was to lay up [the *Descubierta*] there immediately and employ the officers and crew on other more important tasks. There was no land

---

[1] South Channel between Caballo Island and El Fraile Island.
[2] To the east of Limbones.
[3] 'In this passage [from Corregidor to Manila] you must be very careful of a dangerous shoal that lies in the Fairway, called St Nicholas's Shoal, which has but 11 feet on the shoallest part of it, & is steep to.': William Nichelson, *Sundry Remarks and Observations made on a Voyage to the East Indies*, 2nd edn, London, 1773, p. 84.
[4] The *Calipso* was one of a French fleet of hydrographic research vessels sent to China and the East Indies in 1785 under Captain Thibaut-René de Kergariou-Locmaria: see Dermigny, *La Chine*, III, pp. 1087, 1106.
[5] San Nicholas Shoals, which extend 4½ miles offshore from the SE side of Manila Bay: see p. 316 below.
[6] The NE extremity of the peninsula protecting Cavite Harbour.

Plate 34. View of Cavite and the city of Manila, by Fernando Brambila. Museo Naval, Madrid

breeze at all, however, and as the wind was either falling or variable from east through to south until late in the afternoon, we spent the whole day in this unpleasant situation aggravated by an ever greater number of circumstances.

Nevertheless, the day was not entirely wasted. Don Francisco Viana, Segundo Piloto Don Gerónimo Delgado and Don Tadeo Haenke left for Manila in the pinnace early in the morning, intending to set out on their trip to [province of] Pampanga.[1] The first two were to work along the coast from Lingayen or the interior of [Cape] Bolinao to Cape Bojeador and Cape Engaño, and the third was to carry out his botanical investigations for as long as possible before the rains began. Don Francisco Viana was to take with him the chronometer previously used by Don Felipe Bauzá, who, with Alférez de Fragata Ali Ponzoni, now restricted his work to the bay alone. A seaman from the province of Ilocos was assigned to each of these two parties to serve as interpreter, guide and servant, while the Governor and the provincial fathers in charge of the monasteries there were asked to provide them with the necessary letters of introduction.

Don Francisco Viana returned in the pinnace in the afternoon and told me that he had made all necessary preparations for his trip and that a boat sent out promptly would soon reach Don Felipe Bauzá so that the chronometer could be sent back. He also informed me that the Governor was now restoring his health at a farm not far from Cavite.

We remained at anchor there for most of the night, but as it would have been reprehensible to waste any wind, we set sail at three in the morning and set a course to NE, close hauled. The wind was fresh from SE, but at first light it backed a little towards the east, allowing us to make for Cavite close hauled on the port tack, passing two miles from the bar to Manila [Harbour], near which several junks, and a few merchant vessels or smaller Spanish vessels were still anchored. Finally, towed by the pinnace and with the help of frequent light airs from east and SW, we dropped anchor in Cavite at ten o'clock in the morning, in three fathoms, ooze.

---

[1] A province NW of Manila Bay.

CHAPTER 2

Laying up *Descubierta* in Cavite and the survey of Manila Bay

14 April
The Bonoy cables[1] that had been ordered in Cavite to be used for mooring cables were brought on board that same afternoon and so contributed to speeding up our mooring and unrigging, which tasks were almost completed by the following day. Furthermore we had sent to Manila the greater part our equipment, books and instruments so that all the officers, whose first and essential duty now was to recover their health, could follow them without delay.

Don Felipe Bauzá had already returned from the vicinity of Bulacan,[2] having previously sent the schooner he commanded to inform her consort under the orders of Alférez de Fragata Ali Ponzoni, who was at the time examining the depths near San Nicholas Shoals, that she should rendezvous in Mariveles Bay before proceeding to the islands of Mindoro, Luban and Cabra. Don Francisco Viana received the chronometer and then set out for his destination. He was preceded by Don Tadeo Haenke, who was making his way little by little through the pleasant province of Bulacan, while Viana proceeded directly to the further parts of [the province of] Pampanga by sea.

Don Felipe Bauzá was to be joined as an assistant by Don Vicente Llanos, *Segundo Piloto* of the royal navy, a loyal subject with a good training and so dedicated to the royal service that he disregarded the risk to his uncertain health in his eagerness to work with us. Neither Bauzá nor Ali Ponzoni were in the best of health, but there was nobody to replace them as Don Manuel Novales and Don Martín de Olavide were already under the doctor's care, while Don José Espinosa, as well as having taken charge of the astronomical work, was often much affected by his unremitting devotion to its study and by the dreadful climate.

19 April
The condition of the officers, the lack of additional chronometers and the short time left to us, led me to decide that it would be unwise to send both schooners out of the bay. Bauzá, therefore, resumed his survey, sailing from Cavite along the Marigondon coast as far as Limbones and Mariveles Bay[3] in the schooner *Santa Ana*, a better sailer, while I prepared to obtain soundings inside Manila Bay itself.

[1] Possibly a type of hemp from the island of Cebu.
[2] A town 15 miles NNW of Manila in the province of the same name.
[3] This would entail Bauzá crossing from the south side of the entrance to Manila bay to the north side of the bay.

To this end I took charge of the other schooner, the *San Juaquín*, a vessel with many poor qualities, adding a barge from the dockyard and the *Descubierta*'s launch, both manned by our own seamen, so that the soundings could be taken in three lines covering at least a mile, at intervals to be determined by timing, by dead reckoning and by bearings, and could thus be more accurately charted.

I made first for San Nicholas Shoals where, with the help of a fisherman, I was able to take bearings from the spot where the frigate *Calipso* of His Most Christian Majesty had run aground in 1787. I then continued taking soundings towards the coast of Marigondon. After examining the waters around El Fraile, at a launch's length from the island, I then took the schooner past the western end of Corregidor Island to Mariveles Bay. Despite all the efforts of Piloto Hurtado, the launch was unable to close the coast from Caballo Island onwards because of the strong NE wind and the contrary tide.

20 April

We used the few remaining hours of the afternoon to chart and sound the bay, although the work turned out to be superfluous, as the parish priest told me in the late afternoon that Don Felipe Bauzá had left this bay only on the previous afternoon, to continue working towards Corregidor Island.

With these operations both parties slowly made their way further into the bay until the 26th. During this period Don Felipe Bauzá examined the coast from Mariveles Point[1] to the extremities of [the province of] Bulacan while I followed a different course to take soundings in the middle of [Manila] Bay. On the last day Pilot Hurtado was sent with the launch and the barge to examine once more San Nicholas Shoals in order to fix its position and establish its limits as precisely as possible.

The schooners were then laid up and the launch sent back to Cavite. Don Felipe Bauzá took the barge, with a fresh crew, to complete his chart of the coast and rivers of Bulacan, whose position had not yet been accurately fixed. This task was successfully concluded, and by 2 May we had fully discharged this important part of our duties.

The method adopted this time for the detailed survey of the bay was undoubtedly the simplest, but also the safest. From the first base measured on the jetty at the entrance to Manila [Harbour][2] triangles were gradually extended towards El Polvorista,[3] Parañaque[4] and Cavite. The various mountains in sight, and the higher points around the entrance to the bay, were fixed with further bases, so that it would be easy by taking bearings to them to determine from anywhere the true position of the schooner. From such positions we could then fix precisely the shores of the bay, which are mostly low and easily confused because of the mangrove swamps. The port of Cavite and the nearby port of Cañacao[5] had been the object of specific operations, as had the bays of

---

[1] Presumably Cochinos Point, the SW entrance point of Mariveles Bay.

[2] 'Barra de Manila' in the original; for an explanation of this term see p. 295, n. 1 above.

[3] A settlement 2½ miles south of Manila at the time of Malaspina's visit, possibly the site of a gunpowder factory.

[4] A coastal village, 5 miles south of Manila, now part of metropolitan Manila.

[5] A bay formed by the two arms at the extremity of the peninsula forming the northern side of Cavite Harbour.

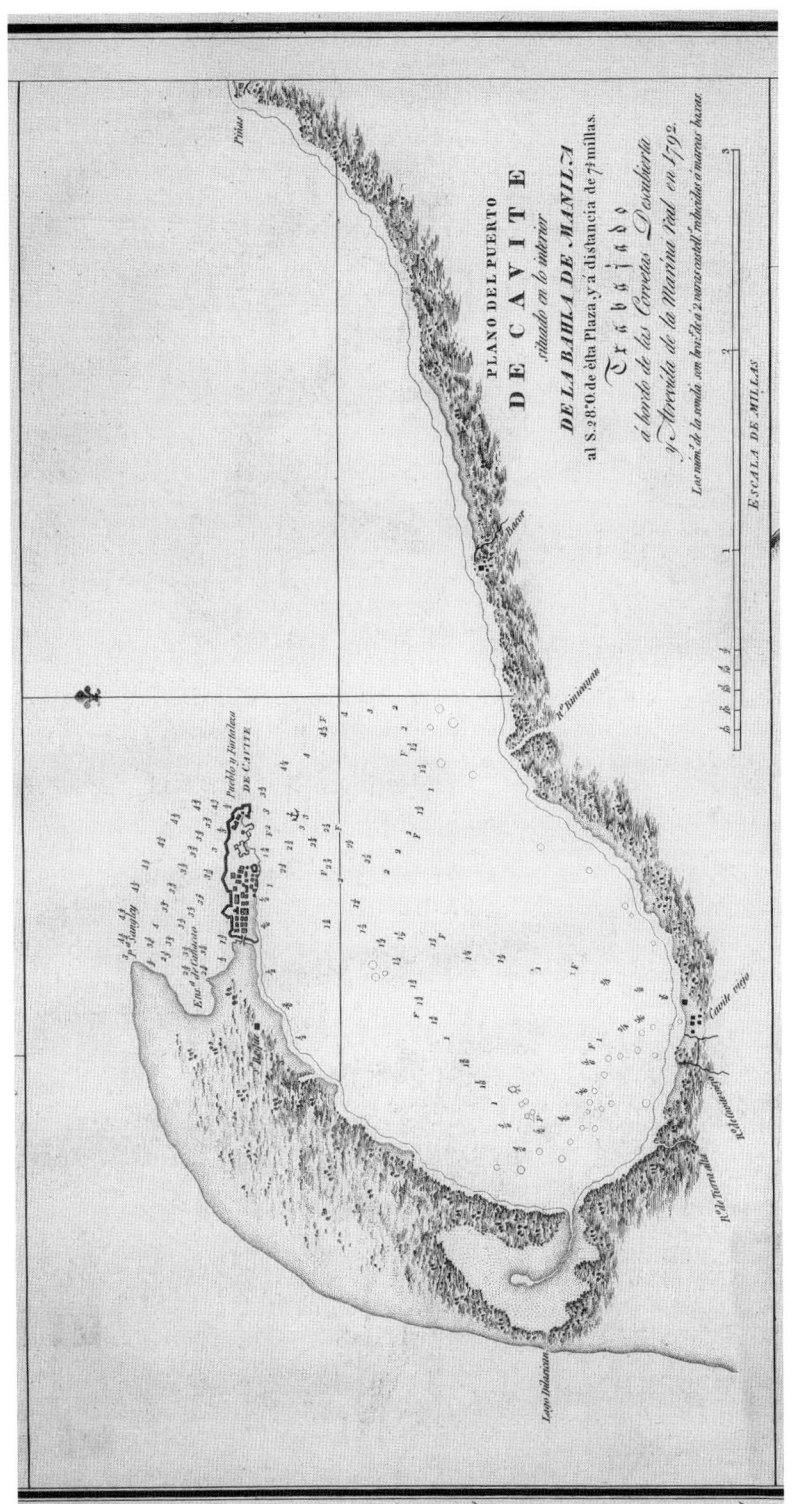

Plate 35. 'Plano del puerto de Cavite.' UKHO, E932. Reproduced by permission of the Controller of Her Majesty's Stationery Office and the UK Hydrographic Office.

Limbones and Mariveles. The principal rivers of Orani, Pampanga and Bulacan[1] were also fixed geometrically along their courses. A more detailed examination of the lower reaches of the river[2] from the entrance to the bridge, and the vicinity of the Plaza[3] from seaward to beyond the range of a cannon shot would have to wait for a more suitable opportunity.

A new and particular benefit of these tasks was undoubtedly the fact that the geometric positions of the mountains in sight allowed us to tie in our survey outside the city with the astronomical determination of Manila's position. Mount Arayat[4] could be seen from Lingayen,[5] where Don Francisco Viana began his work. The peak on Talim Island[6] served admirably to tie in the whole of Laguna de Bay. Mount Luyban[7] both confirmed the position of this latter and linked the triangulation of the other side of the island, through Mauban, Lampon, and Polillo[8] to the north, and through Atemonan and Mamburao[9] to the east. It was now easy to make out Mount Albay before it was lost to sight,[10] and this mountain, with its highest points and elevation accurately determined, allowed us to place many inland towns in the province of Tayabas. From there we turned to the extinct volcano of Taal[11] to link the triangles to the south[12] also, as far as Burias Island and including the two large bays of Taal[13] and Tayabas.

Considering the above, it will be understood how much detail was involved in determining astronomically the position of Manila. Don José Espinosa, accompanied at times by Teniente de Rey Don Francisco Muñoz, took charge of this important mission. Although the best instruments had been recently handed over to the *Atrevida*, we had, however, more than sufficient means to achieve this end with the Ramsden[14] astronomical quadrant, chronometer 71, and a good achromatic telescope which had often been tested against the bronze one. Don José Espinosa also made frequent use of

---

[1] These three rivers flow into the NW and north part of Manila Bay.
[2] Pasig River which flows from Laguna de Bay to the sea through Manila Harbour.
[3] The main square of Manila in front of the Cathedral.
[4] A 1,030-metre high peak 38 miles NNW of Manila.
[5] A town on the southern shores of Lingayen Gulf.
[6] A large island in Laguna de Bay, with Mount Susundalaga, its highest peak, positioned centrally in the lake
[7] Not named on 'Carta general del archipiélago de Filipinas (northern sheet)', but the 2,001-metre high Mount Banahao, 15 miles SE of Laguna de Bay.
[8] A town on the east coast of Luzon, 50 miles SE of Manila.
[9] Atimonan and Port José Panganiban, formerly Port Mambulao, both situated on the south side of Lamon Bay.
[10] Mayon Volcano, which was sighted by Malaspina from the approaches to Sorsogon (see p. 284, n. 4 above).
[11] Malaspina is apparently referring to a 957-metre height on the SE shore of Lake Taal: see p. 498 below. Present day Mount Taal is the active volcano on Volcano Island in the centre of Lake Taal, 35 miles south of Manila.
[12] O = west in the MS journal, which is clearly a transcription error for S, since Burias Island and Taal and Tayabas Bays are situated well to the south of Manila.
[13] A large bay on the south coast of Luzon, west of Cape Santiago.
[14] Jesse Ramsden (1735-1800) was acknowledged as one of the most skilled instrument-makers in 18th-century England: see Charles C. Gillispie, *Dictionary of Scientific Biography*, XI, New York, pp. 284-5; and Allan Chapman, 'The Achievement of Jesse Ramsden', in R. G. W. Anderson et al., eds, *Making Instruments Count*, Aldershot, 1993, pp. 418-30.

his own excellent sextant with an artificial horizon to determine apparent time and to rate the chronometer. As this was precisely the time when Jupiter was nearly in opposition, resulting in the greatest number of visible immersions of its first satellite, the almost constant clarity of the atmosphere gave us the opportunity to take an important series of observations which contributed greatly to the accomplishment of our object. With a number of meridian altitudes of stars taken to the south and north we were able to determine with equal accuracy the latitude of the observatory, which, for greater convenience, had now been set up in the house we occupied some two cables SE of the cathedral tower.[1]

The fact that all the senior officers had to live some distance from the corvette and the need to prepare thoroughly for the complete refitting of both vessels, while attending in Cavite to the problems which had emerged in the course of three successive cruises, required me to take numerous precautions. I will describe these in some detail, as a necessary justification not only of the measures eventually taken, but also as an indication of actions required in the future, to ensure that the concentration of ships of the royal navy in this part of His Majesty's dominions should enhance the discipline and true efficiency of the service.

The corvette remained in the fairway from the start, anchored in barely three fathoms of water, with two moorings laid out to the [blank] with two Bonoy cables, or black rope, recently made in the dockyard to fit our hawse holes, which we were now using instead of our hemp cables,[2] which we wanted to preserve. A sheet anchor was then laid out using a hemp cable and all the other mooring lines were then stowed. The ordnance was also stowed in the hold, after we had washed the ballast and gathered it into two piles in the bows and the stern. To get rid of the cockroaches the cabins were dismantled and everything possible was removed from the ship to make it easier to track down these noxious insects.

The ship was left in the charge of a warrant officer, commanding a small party of seamen. They were provided with arms and the necessary ammunition, with orders that from sunset to the following morning a detachment of marines was to remain on board with a sergeant, the gunner, and a corporal to take command by turns. The division of the marines, the seamen and the other petty officers seemed to be unavoidable, as it was necessary to find quarters for all the ship's company. The seamen's quarters being near the shore, the boatswain's gear was deposited there, enabling work to start at once overhauling the rigging. Another building some distance away was assigned to the marines. The provisions were stored separately, in a building where the steward's mates were to prepare the supplies. In all these arrangements we had, of course, to provide enough room for the requirements of both ships. The sails, the cooperage, the spare spars and three of the boats that had been repaired or remade in Acapulco were stored in the dockyard, protected from Sun and rain. All the Filipino sailors taken on at the entrance to Manila [Harbour] were discharged by

---

[1] Espinosa, *Memoria* (1809) 2nd memoir, gives details of tidal observations at Cavite (p. 126), observations for magnetic variation and inclination at Manila (p. 119) and a discussion on the observations at Manila to determine the force of gravity (pp. 190-212), while the 3rd memoir gives details of the observations for geographical positions at Manila (pp. 43-6).

[2] Presumably tarred.

Plate 36. Manila Cathedral, by Fernando Brambila. Museo Naval, Madrid

Plate 37. The *Descubierta* careened in the port of Cavite, detail from View of the port of Cavite and Manila Bay by Fernando Brambila. Whereabouts unknown

Plate 38. Dwellings in the outskirts of Manila, by Fernando Brambila. Museo de América, Madrid

the end of the month. Finally the senior artificer rates were given leave to find lodgings where they wished, on condition that they conducted themselves as befitting their positions, and that they were not otherwise required for service duties.

Several important disciplinary measures were taken. The marines were ordered to perform firearms drill twice a week and to have a clothing inspection once a week. Any seamen who missed roll call without leave for three days was to be considered a deserter. All the men were to receive their monthly pay from, and including, May, which would give them a total of four months' earnings. The hospital would remain in Manila, although administered at our expense and according to our own methods. Anyone who transgressed these very moderate regulations or caused any public disorder, would be condemned to the Cavite galley, a harsh punishment for the offender and less of a burden to those charged with guarding them.

The daily allowance continued to be paid in kind during the month of May. As an encouragement the *segundo pilotos* were assigned a house in Manila with double rations, so that their proximity to us [the officers] would encourage them to apply themselves daily to their studies and hydrographic work, and thus be of greater service to the King and to their commission.

The construction of a large new pinnace for each corvette was an essential task, as those we now had were entirely useless as being too small, having been built to fit into the launch, which had a fixed deck. With the substitution of a removable deck the pinnaces could be made considerably longer, so that henceforward they could be sent out on longer excursions with much greater safety and benefit.

The timber from Laguan,[1] the only kind used in the royal dockyard at Cavite, was entirely unsuitable for us, being inflexible and not long-lasting, and it was therefore necessary to use María and Baticulin timber[2] instead. As we had to arrange to procure it, and charge to the expedition accounts all other costs relating to the corvettes, the choice of a construction site was of no great importance, but we decided to use the Manila River[3] because the selection and laying off of workers would be easier. In addition the storage of the timber, which had to come from Laguna [de Bay], would not be delayed during the season of the *vendavales*,[4] as might occur if the timber had to be taken [by sea] to Cavite.

7 May

Having thus dealt with most of the tasks relative to the refitting and mindful of the need for the expedition to achieve as much as possible, it was arranged that Don Juan Ravenet would use the last of the good season to visit the settlements of the *Negrillos*,[5] the former inhabitants of these islands, who were not yet subjects of our monarchy. He would thereby be able to describe them with greater accuracy and the comparison of this information with that gathered on our subsequent cruises would perhaps give us a firmer basis for the history of mankind and its migrations. The *Negrillos* live in a good half of the country around Manila Bay; that is, all the mountainous area from the Mariveles [Mountains] to the Upper Pampanga,[6] including the provinces of Bataan and Pampanga. The former, and Orani[7] in particular, was not far away and easily reached by sea, and also had the advantage of a factor of the Real Compañía [de Filipinas], who was in charge of the production and purchase of indigo.

Don Juan Ravenet went to Orani by sea, having a short and comfortable trip. He carried with him wide-ranging orders from the directors [Real Compañía], but the kindness and hospitality of the factor, Don Antonio Aguirre, made them unnecessary. This loyal subject had already established a peaceful relationship with the nearby families of the *Negrillos*. In consequence, no sooner had Ravenet reached the foothills of Mt Jollo[8] than some eight or ten natives arrived to visit him. This little group

---

[1] Probably Laoang Island, close westward of the entrance to Port Palapag.
[2] Two types of timber used for shipping and in carving: Blair and Robertson, *The Philippine Islands*, XVIII, p. 172 and XLIII, pp. 299-300.
[3] Pasig River.
[4] The South-west Monsoon, which blows from May to September.
[5] The Aetas, or Negritos, thought to be the aboriginal inhabitants of the Philippines: see Guillermo, *Historical Dictionary of the Philippines*, p. 15, and Blair and Robertson, *The Philippine Islands*, LV, pp. 631-2. There is an interesting analysis of their resistance to the Spanish in Phelan, *Hispanization of the Philippines*, pp. 142-4.
[6] Not identified, but possibly the upper reaches of Pampanga River, which discharges into the NW part of Manila Bay, just east of the mouth of Orani River.
[7] On the NW shore of Manila Bay at the mouth of Orani River.
[8] Not identified on either 'Carta de bahía de Manila' or 'Carta general del archipiélago de Filipinas (northern sheet)', but presumably at the northern end of Bataan Peninsula.

Plate 39. *Negrillos* from the mountainous area around Manila Bay, by Juan Ravenet. Museo de América, Madrid

included people of both sexes and a range of ages, all of whom were very obedient to their chief.[1]

Although they were armed[2] they showed not the slightest distrust or ill will, and indeed, having been given a few trinkets, they were happy to exchange their weapons and adornments and then to demonstrate their dances and songs. The dances were slow, with little variation because of their lack of agility. Their songs were equally slow and melancholy evoking (according to the interpretation of Don Antonio de Aguirre) their present lamentable situation and their hopes that a leader would come one day to give new strength to their weakened power. Don Juan Ravenet sketched their movements as accurately as possible and also had the satisfaction of taking the likenesses of two or three of the more distinguished among them.[3] The merest hint that Their Majesties would see the portraits was enough to persuade them to sit for him, and it was clear that they would not object to a meeting on the following day simply to confirm his impressions.

[1] According to the title of one of Ravenet's drawings his name was Andahuat: AMN, carp. 1 (11); the title of another of Ravenet's drawings gives the name of Andahaut's young daughter as Mindato: AMN, carp. 1 (14). Plate 39 shows Andahuat and family (left) with a group of Negrillos dancing (right)
[2] With bows and arrows.
[3] Eleven drawings by Ravenet of the *Negrillos* have survived: see Sotos, *Los pintores*, II, figs 728–38.

When this second visit had been made, Ravenet showed his sincere gratitude to Aguirre in every way he could. He then returned to Manila to describe to us all that he had seen in the six or seven days of his excursion.

In the hospital the skill of the surgeon, Don Francisco Flores, had by then almost entirely cured the effects of the last cruises on the patients from both corvettes. The blockages had yielded to a course of baths and the diarrhoea had been successfully treated with mercury, which was also most effective against the dreadful symptoms of venereal disease that had appeared in a few of the men.[1] The magnetic treatment had been no less effective when administered, as mentioned above, by M. Robert to two of the sick men from the *Descubierta*, who were suffering from severe blockages. In the absence of Don Antonio Pineda who, with his usual tireless energy, had started on new and difficult excursions before the return of the *Descubierta* to [Manila] Bay it was now necessary, in order to give our disinterested support to the search for the truth and continue our careful investigations of the effects of magnetism, to authorize the two cured patients to make a declaration on the course of the treatment, with the surgeon's intervention.

This declaration was all the more satisfactory in that, particularly in the case of Quartermaster Palmero,[2] it was made by an unprejudiced person, endowed with a good natural intellect, whose previous condition, after three dangerous relapses, and present restoration to health, could not be doubted by anyone on board. Three days after the removal of the two patients to the Hospital of San Juan de Dios,[3] they were both taken out into the garden every day, where there was a magnetized tree with a length of Manila rope[4] tied to it, which was passed two or three times around the patient's waist to channel more of the magnetic force to him. After this the treatment was administered directly by M. Robert to the two men, one after the other. On the first day Palmero experienced a gradual weakening of his sight until he could see nothing but tiny motes or blue and white stars before his eyes, even when open, or nothing at all, when the mesmerist moved his hands in front of his eyes. Soon after these strange symptoms began, he felt his eyes closing suddenly and he fell against the wall as if stunned, with great pain in the spleen and gasping for breath. He could hear all that was said around him but was unable to answer. Meanwhile M. Robert relieved the effects of this violent convulsion by blowing on the patient's heart and holding his hand to the patient's stomach, until he was completely calm and could speak once more. During this time he could feel all that was being done to him, but he could neither speak nor open his eyes. When it was over he attempted to rise, but found his legs to be so weak and numb, with such acute pain in his right knee (from which,

---

[1] Mercury, by drinking, inhaling, or inunction, enjoyed a long popularity as a cure for venereal diseases – hence the saying, 'Venus for a night, Mercury for life': see J. S. Cummins, 'Pox and Paranoia in Renaissance Europe', *History Today*, August, 1988, pp. 28–35. For the venereal disease hospital of Los Baños, see Blair and Robertson, *The Philippine Islands*, XLVII, p. 227 and LIV, pp. 295–6.

[2] Antonio Palermo of the *Descubierta*: Antón Solé, 'Los padrones de cumplimiento pascual', p. 197.

[3] The Hospitallers of St John of God, a 16th-century Spanish nursing order, worked both at home and in the colonies: see the *New Catholic Encyclopedia*, New York, 1967, VII, p. 158 and Blair and Robertson, *The Philippine Islands*, LIV, p. 437.

[4] Rope made from the *abacá* fibre: see p. 290, n. 2.

however, he had suffered somewhat previously), that without the help of those present he would doubtless have fallen to the ground. M. Robert immediately began his magnetic treatment on the knee, and soon the pain left him and he was able to walk without difficulty.

The following day he received the same treatment, and suddenly experienced the same sensation as on the day before, but he came to himself again calmly, and had no pain at all in his knees.

After these two days he continued the treatment for another fourteen days, tying himself to the tree every afternoon at three, and then being subject to the same magnetic treatment by M. Robert from five to six. The convulsions ceased, and little by little the shortness of breath and the hardness of the spleen disappeared. From the second day onwards he was also given five grains of tartar emetic, dissolved in half a bottle of emollient mixture, from which he took two spoonfuls morning and afternoon, mixed with a glass of mallow-water. This medicinal drink caused him considerable pain in the stomach, until he vomited up a variety of noxious material.

The effects on the topman were no different, apart from the first convulsions and a greater resistance to bilious evacuation, although both of them were able to leave hospital, fully cured, after eighteen days, needing only to take the precaution of river-bathing in the future.

This was the only trial that we could perform at present, until the return of the *Atrevida* would provide subjects for new tests to clarify the results of these experiments and to determine the true effects of magnetism. However, M. Robert was duly thanked and paid a suitable consideration in His Majesty's name.

12 May
Meanwhile the departure of two ships of the Department of San Blas for the port of Acapulco was approaching, as was the arrival of the *Atrevida*. The two ships were the frigate [blank],[1] fitted out in Cavite under the orders of Teniente de Fragata Don Manuel Quimper, who, during the past year, had brought the sloop *Princesa Real* to Macau to return her to the English,[2] and the schooner *Valdés*, which some months earlier under the command of Alférez de Navío Don Cosme Bertodano had brought to these islands the first news of an imminent rupture with England.[3] I thought it right to take this opportunity to inform His Excellency Señor Bailio Valdés of the state of the expedition and to send the Viceroy of Mexico[4] some of our hydrographic

---

[1] The *San José y las Animas*: see p. 358 below. She was probably a merchant vessel rather than a frigate of the Spanish navy, which Quimper would have been too junior to command.
[2] Malaspina is mistaken. Quimper took the *Princesa Real*, formerly the *Princess Royal*, to Manila, from where she was taken to Macau by Vicente de Llano y Valdéz to be returned to representatives of her rightful owners, under the terms of the Nootka Sound Convention: Thurman, *Naval Department of San Blas*, pp. 321–5. The *Princess Royal* had been seized in Nootka Sound in 1789 by Estéban José Martínez, the Spanish commandant. For a full account of this affair and its consequences see Cook, *Flood Tide of Empire*.
[3] Although relations between Spain and Britain were deteriorating, war between the countries was not declared until October 1796.
[4] The Viceroy of Mexico was the Conde de Revillagigedo (1789–94).

work with descriptions of California and inland provinces. There they could be carefully examined by experts before reaching the Court, thus lessening the risk of error in the news and conjectures that we had necessarily received from others.

19 May
It was most fortunate that various unexpected incidents delayed the departure of these ships for several days, as it was therefore possible to inform the Ministro de Marina of the arrival of the *Atrevida* in this port. To the satisfaction of all she anchored in Cavite on the morning of the 19th, having carried out the voyage to Macau, and the various important associated assignments, with the greatest success.

CHAPTER 3

Bustamante's Account of *Atrevida*'s Visit to Macau[1] and her return to Manila

30 March
Today we finished taking on water and provisions and when the astronomical instruments to be used in Macau had been brought on board, there was nothing to delay our departure except the delivery from the Cavite dockyard of an anchor, bought from the Real Compañía de Filipinas, with another for the *Descubierta*. They arrived in the afternoon, but without the stocks. Ours weighed nineteen *quintales* and immediately we attached the stock of the fourth anchor to it, so as to have two reliable small bower anchors ready for use.

31 March
At nightfall, having received our orders from Don Alejandro Malaspina, we were completely ready to get under way early in the morning with the first puffs of the land breeze, or the trade wind.[2] The *comandante* entrusted me with a letter from him to the Governor of Macau[3] and I also carried another for him from the *Capitán General* of these islands, both informing the Governor of the object of the *Atrevida*'s voyage to the establishment under his command and requesting that he offer me all the assistance we might need to fulfil the aims of the voyage. Chief among these were the gravity experiments with the pendulum.[4] Since these were considered to be of too great an interest for the whole of Europe to be omitted, our obligation was to carry out His Majesty's intentions and to ask to perform them in the presence of the Governor and other experts, so as to give the seal of respectable authenticity to the accuracy we sought in such experiments.

1 April
At dawn, with the anchor up and down, the SW kedge was weighed. We got under

---

[1] Known to the Chinese as Aomen.
[2] The North-east Monsoon which blows from October to April: see p. 269, n. 1 above .
[3] The Governor of Macau was Vasco Luís Carneiro de Sousa e Faro (1790-93).
[4] Espinosa, *Memorias* (1809), 2nd memoir, gives details of observations for magnetic variation and inclination at Macau (p. 118) and a discussion on the observations there to determine the force of gravity (pp. 190-212).

way at eight at 8 o'clock with a fresh ESE wind, steering WSW 5°W for Boca Chica[1] between Mariveles and Corregidor Island, under fore topsail and mizzen while the anchors were secured and the boats brought inboard. These tasks concluded, we made more sail with a strong and settled trade wind. We then altered course to WbyS to close Mariveles Point[2] and to give a good berth to San Nicholas Shoals, whose position on the plan we were using was not very accurate, according to the pilot. At ten o'clock, when we were ESE of a conspicuous hill on the Mariveles coast, we altered course to SW to make for the northern extremity of Corregidor Island or the narrow channel,[3] steering WSW to pass to the north of La Monja.

At noon the northernmost point of Corregidor bore E2°N, its SW extremity S72°E and La Monja in transit with Fuego Point[4] S16°E. We were then one mile distant from the islets on the western side of Mariveles Bay.[5] From here we altered course to run along the coast as far as Luzon Point,[6] and when on the meridian of that point and three miles distant from it we altered course to NW 5°W and made for Silanguin Point.[7]

The fresh trade wind remained with us until sunset, when it backed to north. The most salient point of Capones Island[8] now bore N14°W and Silanguin Point N20°E, one and a half leagues distant. The calm and fine weather continued all night, but at half past two the NNE wind, now less moderate, veered to the SSE, still weak. With this we altered course to NNW to keep three leagues offshore and [2nd] at dawn we were this distance from Capones Island, bearing EbyS. From nine o'clock the wind began to drop and veer to the third quadrant, becoming the sea breeze which often blows at this time. At noon we were able to make out Dos Hermanas bearing N13°E, our latitude by observation being 15°24′48″ and our longitude by number 105, 1°9′30″ west of Manila; variation by western amplitude was 1°50′NW.

In the afternoon the westerly wind dropped, having been fresher when the Sun was close to the meridian. To pass the westernmost of the Hermanas we altered course to NNW, but could not maintain this course and so tacked to the third quadrant. The northernmost point of the southern Hermana[9] bore NEbyE, one and a half leagues distant and the NW point of the northern one[10] bore north. We sighted, sailing near the coast, some of the small vessels which trade with the province of Ilocos.

---

[1] Present-day North Channel.
[2] Not named on 'Carta de bahía de Manila', but presumably Cochinos Point, the SW entrance point of Mariveles Bay.
[3] I.e. North Channel, Bustamante's Boca Chica.
[4] A high rocky point in the southern approaches to Manila Bay, 15 miles south of La Monja.
[5] Los Cochinos, five above-water rocks which extend 4 cables south of Cochinos Point, the western entrance point of Mariveles Bay, and Palomonti Rocks, which extend 4 cables SE of the same point.
[6] The SW extremity of Bataan Peninsula.
[7] Silanguin Island, which is joined to the mainland by a reef, is situated in the western approaches to Subic Bay, 25 miles NW of Luzon Point.
[8] Capones Islands, a group of three small islands 10 miles NNW of Silanguin Island, the largest of which, Capon Grande, is very prominent.
[9] Hermana Menor Island.
[10] Hermana Mayor Island.

Until half past ten we could barely maintain steerage way, when a light SE wind got up, which we took advantage of by crowding on sail and steering NNW, to run along the coast, [3rd] but at dawn it backed to ENE, becoming very light from all point of the compass until about midday, when it settled in the west. Consequently we had made little progress during the night. Cape Bolinao now bore N4°E and the NW part of the northern Hermana N87°E. Until noon we had not been able to increase the bearing of Cape Bolinao to more than N11°E, at which time Culebra Island[1] bore S39°E, our latitude by observation was 15°52'07" N and our longitude 1°10'3" west of Manila.

The sea breeze, which usually begins in the third quadrant and finishes in the fourth, allowed us until half past one to keep barely a league offshore, attempting to remain close inshore in order to make the best use of the northerly current which becomes perceptible from Cape Bolinao. With this aim we continued tacking, as the wind was still blowing from the direction in which we had to make good. At sunset Cape Bolinao bore NbyE, two to three leagues distant. We then put about, the breeze being fresh, to stand in very close to shore. We then sighted a merchant vessel, whose course and appearance suggested that it was a Manila trading vessel steering south from the province of Ilocos.

During the night we made some progress by tacking immediately at every slight shift in the breeze, as it remained fresh, [4th] so that in the morning Cape Bolinao bore E5°S, but until midday we gained no more than 3° on this bearing. We had continued on our offshore tack until we were five or six leagues offshore so as to be at a better angle to tack inshore when the sea breeze began, but in fact we waited in vain all day for the opportunity to do this, as a gentle northerly breeze dogged us during the whole day's run.

5 April
Our observations also confirmed that the current had favoured us, as we had hoped;, our latitude by observation being 16°22'45" and variation 1°10'NW. At that time Salomague Point,[2] which we were eager to reach, bore ENE, as the northward set becomes stronger from there. As before, we continued our exertions under full sail, calculating the best tacks to make. Despite this and our hopes of finding the current, by noon we were no further north than latitude 16°45' and longitude by observation 41'01" west [of Manila].[3]

In the afternoon the wind increased in strength from NNW. We remained on the shoreward tack until we were so close that we had to go about. At nine o'clock, however, we tacked again to keep inshore and search for the north-going currents, [6th] tacking once again at midnight, with the wind still from the ESE and almost calm. The lack of steerage way led us to suspect that there was a strong current, [6th] a suspicion later contradicted by the bearings taken in the morning and the noon observation of 17°12'30", which, far from showing a discrepancy to the north, gave it as 9' to the south; our longitude by observation was 0°37'22"[west of Manila]. Mount

---

[1] Situated 5 miles north of Hermana Mayor Island.
[2] Situated 43 miles SSW of Cape Bojeador.
[3] But still some 60 miles south of Salomague Point.

Vigan[1] was then bearing N35°E and Santa Catalina Point[2] N43°E; we were then about five leagues offshore.[3]

Keeping on the shoreward tack, we sighted Santa anchorage[4] at four in the afternoon, in which there were three small craft which carry on the rice trade with the capital. At sunset the town was bearing NE5°E and Gorda de Santa María Point[5] S72°E. The fresh breeze from the fourth quadrant now dropped; the air and the land were covered with haze, making the latter seem much further off than it really was, as we realized later during the night when we could judge the distance by eye with the accuracy allowed by some fires we saw on the beach. When a moderate SE breeze set in, which lasted until after midnight, we tacked offshore, steering NbyW in order to avoid Salomague Shoal,[6] which extends more than a league offshore. Passing it at the same distance, we kept a somewhat lesser distance from the coast, which we were now closing near the conspicuous Vigan Inlet,[7] where we could hear the surf on the beach. When we could take its bearing by the light of the full Moon it bore EbyS, noting that it was fairly open, being formed by two sloping headlands of good height.

7 April

In the morning it [Vigan Inlet] was bearing S26°E, Salomague Island,[8] which is low, S 42°E and Sinay Island,[9] also low, bore N62°E. These bearings immediately showed noticeable discrepancies to the north, which confirmed that, however slow our speed, we would sight Cape Bojeador during the day. Our latitude at noon by observation was 18°9′15″, which supported our theory regarding the current, as it placed us 17′ further north than by dead reckoning.

At nine o'clock the southerly breeze set in, at the same time as a swell from the north, which slowed our progress, although the current compensated for this delay. The wind veered to SW at noon, when we had expected to sight Cape Bojeador, as we were in latitude 18°5′15″ and longitude 37′ 57″ [west of Manila] according to the mean of numbers 72 and 105, but the haze, which seems frequent in these parts, made this impossible. We continued steering north, determined to sight the cape, with the

---

[1] Situated about 15 miles east of Point Dile according to 'Carta general del archipiélago de Filipinas (northern sheet)'.
[2] Situated about 6 miles NE of Point Dile according to 'Carta general del archipiélago de Filipinas (northern sheet)', possibly the western extremity of Pinget Island.
[3] There is a major discrepancy here if Bustamante's latitude and longitude are reasonably correct, since they place him less than five miles offshore in a position where it would be impossible for him to sight Point Santa Catalina. However, it seems probable that his longitude is in error and that he misidentified Mount Vigan and that his Santa Catalina Point is actually Dile Point. This would indeed place him farther offshore.
[4] Presumably an anchorage off the coastal village of Santa, 8 miles SE of Dile Point.
[5] Not named on 'Carta general del archipiélago de Filipinas (northern sheet)', possibly San Esteban Point, 15 miles SSE of Dile Point.
[6] South-West Shoal, the outer of several shoals fronting Salommague Harbour.
[7] Charted 9 miles NE of Dile Point on 'Carta general del archipiélago de Filipinas (northern sheet)', possibly present day San Ildefonso Harbour, 4 miles north of Dile Point.
[8] Probably present day Pinget Island, 7 miles north of Dile Point, but 14 miles NNE of the point on 'Carta general del archipiélago de Filipinas (northern sheet)'.
[9] Now Badoc Island.

aim of either correcting its position or of comparing any position we gave it with that determined by the *Descubierta*, which was to survey it.

Towards four in the afternoon we sighted the extremity, or low projecting point, of Cape Bojeador, which was bearing N43°E, distant five leagues. The wind then dropped completely and it remained calm all afternoon, so that we had no way of measuring a base by which to fix its position. However, we used our estimation of the distance to determine its position, which I still consider to be very close, or at least much more accurate than the latitude shown on Mr Dalrymple's charts.[1]

Latitude observed on board at noon	18° 5' 15"
By dead reckoning to the north until six in the evening, adding only two miles for the current to the distance made, as there was hardly any difference in the bearing from four to six, when a final bearing was taken	10' 00"
Latitude of the ship at six in the evening	18° 15' 15"
Difference in latitude to the north according to the bearing of the Cape and the estimated distance of fourteen miles	+ 9' 40"
Latitude of the Cape	18° 24' 55"
Observed longitude west of Manila at noon according to the chronometers (almost the average of the two)	00° 37' 57"
Difference in longitude to the Cape, according to bearings	13' 00"
Resulting longitude of Cape Bojeador west [of Manila]	24' 57"[2]

The accuracy of this longitude may be affirmed, although hour angles were not observed when the bearings were taken. It was felt of no use to do so, since we had continued on our northerly course without alteration since the morning's observations and also because the current runs in the same direction. The latitude may also be accepted with sufficient confidence, since the only errors involved were in estimating the distance to the cape and the need to allow for the negligible effect of the current, as it was only a short time before noon. Thus I believe that the latitude given to this point cannot be exceeded by more than 2' and should be much preferred to Dalrymple's, which is 17' further north. We will establish the greater or lesser degree of accuracy of these calculations when we rejoin the *Descubierta*, which has been sent to chart the island of Luzon from Manila to Cape Bojeador and Cape Engaño, and I flatter myself that there will be little difference between their results and ours.[3]

We believed that the sight of Cape Bojeador would mark the end of the contrary winds that we had experienced since Manila. In the present season here they generally blow from the first quadrant, and the crossing to Macau usually does not take more than four to five days for slower vessels than this corvette. This information, based upon the pilot's repeated experience, and the fact that the settled trade wind had blown freshly from NE all night, left us in no doubt that we would soon reach our destination. [8th] We steered NNW5°N until noon, when we altered course to

[1] 'A Chart of the China Sea ... ', published 19 April 1771, which places Cape Bojeador in 18°40'N.
[2] On modern charts Cape Bojeador is placed in 18°30'N, 120°34'E or 24½' west of Manila.
[3] Bustamante was not to know that Malaspina was forced to abandon his survey before reaching Cape Bojeador, while Viana, who was later sent to carry it out, does not give a position for the cape: see p. 363 below.

NWbyN, as the wind had dropped almost completely. We assumed that the calm was due to the effects of the Sun's rays, but we later found this belief to be mistaken. Our observed latitude indicated a difference of 33' to the north, and the longitude according to the chronometers, or the mean of the two, which differ by 2', was 1°02'40" west of Manila.

A few hours of calm were succeeded in the afternoon by light airs from the fourth quadrant. The atmosphere was extremely hazy, which gave the stars an extraordinary degree of apparent refraction, a phenomenon which seldom occurs with the trade wind and almost always with calm conditions. We tacked to keep as close as possible to a northerly course,[9th] and the night passed in calm or with very light, variable airs from the NNE to NNW. We trusted that the trade wind would re-establish itself on the following morning, so as to free us from the necessity of continual and irksome trimming the sails. In the night we had also heard the loud noise of currents running in different directions, and this continued during the day, with eddies and the heavy impact of water against the hull, without us being able to determine which way they were carrying us. While the currents were toying with us in this manner, the weather gave no signs of improvement, being exactly the same as on the previous afternoon. Our observed latitude of 19°53'30" agreed with our dead reckoning, but the observed longitude of 1°50' by number 105 and 1°48' by number 72 showed a difference of 30' to the west.

According to the position given by these observations the NE extremity of Plata Shoal[1] bore N60°W of us distant 130 miles, relying on its position as established in 1779 by His Britannic Majesty's British corvettes *Resolution* and *Descubierta [Discovery]*, then commanded by Captains Gore and King, following the death of Messrs Cook and Clerke. In the last volume of their voyages, King's description of this shoal may be seen, as they surveyed it from its NE extremity, which they placed in latitude 20°45' although unable to determine its western limits, and longitude 116°44".[2] Mr Dalrymple conjectures that this danger covers an area six leagues square[3] which, as nature has placed it on the direct route from the Philippines to Canton [Guangzhou], is marked on our charts with the accuracy so important to shipping, thanks to the zeal shown by those illustrious navigators during their voyage.

At nightfall the wind, although no more than a gentle breeze, began to settle in the NNE, and we hauled the wind on the starboard tack, as it was my intention to pass to the north of Plata Shoal. It freshened somewhat during the night, [10th] so that by noon our observed latitude was 20°45'N, that is, on the parallel of the southern part of the shoal, and our longitude 3°08' by number 105, which gave the same difference of 30' to the west.

Assuming we were to continue on the same course, our position was somewhat critical should the wind drop when we had the shoal abeam at the same time as the

---

[1] Dongsha Jiao, formerly known as Pratas Reef, 180 miles SE of Hong Kong.
[2] Bustamante misquotes King whose entry reads 'The North East extremity we place in latitude 20° 58', and longitude 117°; and the South West in latitude 20° 45', and longitude 116° 44'.': Cook and King, *Voyage to the Pacific Ocean*, III, p. 414.
[3] Bustamante appears to have misinterpreted Dalrymple's 'A Chart of the China Sea' on which the reef is depicted as being circular with a radius of about five leagues.

swell abated and the strong westerly currents continued. But this was not so much to be feared since the monsoon wind was sure to follow the calms. Furthermore, it was my intention to fix the position of Piedra Blanca,[1] as it is the point where ships bound for Canton in this season stand inshore or determine their position and, if we passed south of it, we would find it impossible with the prevailing winds, to carry out my intentions.

The current maintained the same speed and set, as shown by the breaking of the waves on the surface. At the same time the wind was moderately fresh and increasing gradually, although it did not shift to ENE, and at times was lighter. After midday, however, we altered course to NWbyN to reduce the leeway and increase the corvette's speed, while keeping a very careful look-out from the mastheads, since it would not have been surprising to sight the shoal by half past four, allowing for the current proportional to the distance run, when we should be off its easternmost[2] point, [allowing us] to pass between five and five and a half leagues off its northern point.

The clouds which soon gathered over the shoal made it impossible to see more than two leagues. The wind was freshening and the weather did not look promising, and by half past five we were obliged to reduce sail to the four principal sails. At nightfall it was blowing a moderate gale from NE, with a fairly high sea. We continued under the four principal sails, with the main topsails eased a little and the main sheet eased as much as necessary to give us better steerage. Not only did the gale remain strong until after dark, but the heavy gusts obliged us to sail with great attention to the rigging, which was not an unnecessary precaution, given the constant squalls and the threatening appearance of the weather. However, in order to be able to survey the coast in the morning and sight Great Lema,[3] it was necessary to carry a press of canvas in the afternoon. Piedra Blanca bore N51°W fifty-one leagues distant at midday, and thus, depending on our being able to make good NW, true, we stood eight leagues to the east of it to ensure that we could identify it even if the current continued setting us as strongly to the west.

At eight o'clock at night the foot-rope of the foresail parted during a squall, and consequently the sail immediately split from top to bottom. We proceeded to bend on a new one which was set and drawing at half past nine, after which we continued under the four principal sails, with the topsails half reefed, since in these conditions it was only just possible to keep them set.

11 April

Early in the morning we sighted various vessels, or Chinese fishing lorchas.[4] Although these usually go out as far out as Plata shoal, we were surprised to see them so far offshore in weather which seemed heavier than they could take. As a result we judged ourselves to be nearer the coast than our dead reckoning had indicated, considering

---

[1] Zhenyantou, a rock islet with a white summit (hence its name), which when seen from south appears as two rocks, making it a useful landmark; known variously in the past as Pedra Branca, Pedro Blanco and Tai-Sing-Chau. It is situated 49 miles east of Hong Kong Island.

[2] N in the original MS which is surely a transcription error for E.

[3] Dangan Dao, the largest and NE island of Dangan Liedao, a group of five islands, 11 miles south of Hong Kong Island.

[4] A vessel developed by the Portuguese in Macau with a European hull and a junk rig.

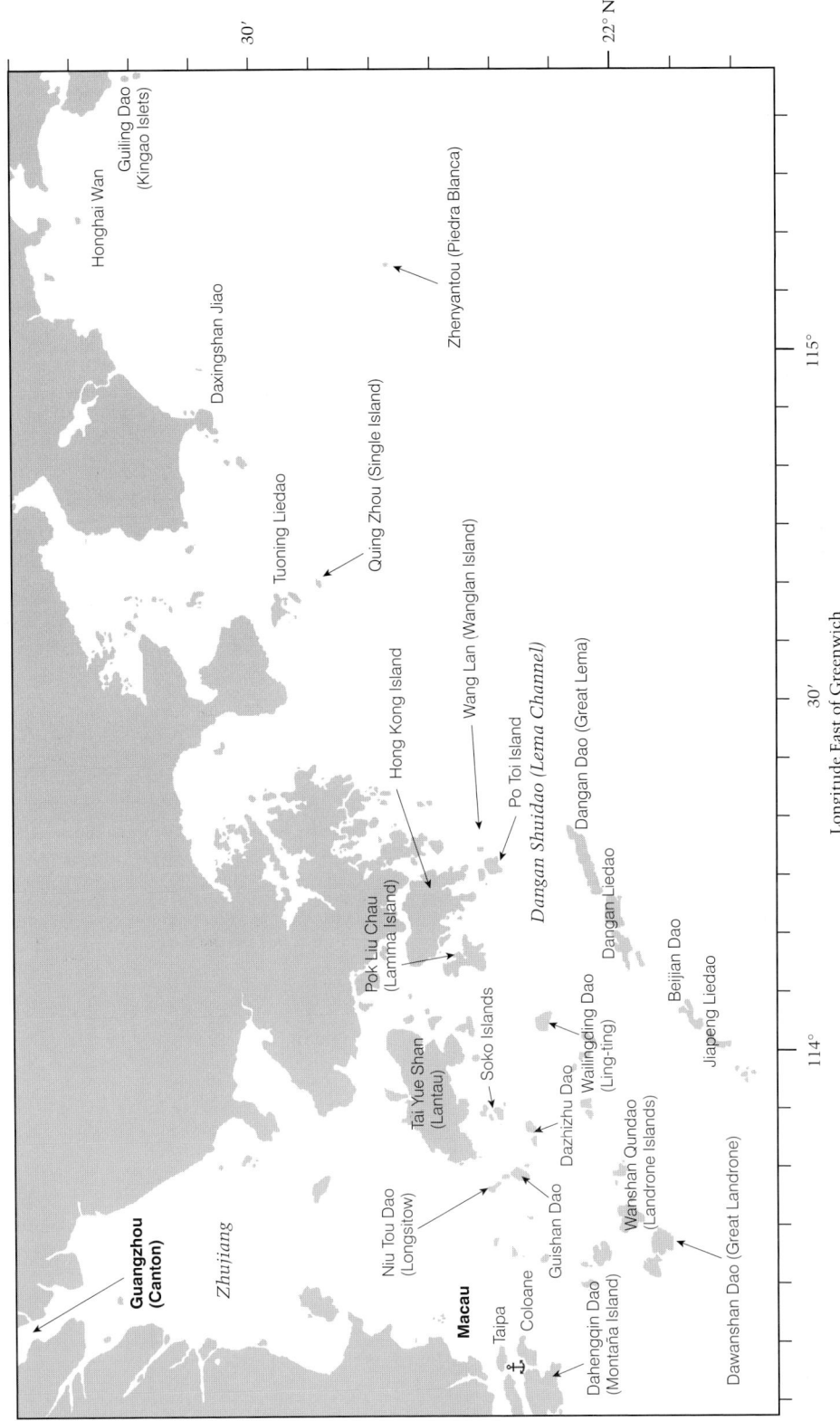

Fig. 6. The approaches to Macau, April 1792

the usual errors that this method always involves, particularly in waters where there are currents and very variable and gusty winds.

Our thoughts were not unfounded, as was soon confirmed by the changing colour of the water and the sight of land off the bows at eight o'clock. By waiting for a break in the clouds I was able to take a single altitude, calculating the hour angle with our dead reckoning latitude of 22°00′, which gave us a longitude of 5°01′ west of Manila or approximately 2° east of Macau. We were therefore sure of being able to determine the position of Piedra Blanca if the Sun was visible, which seemed unlikely, as the sky was overcast. Our subsequent courses of WNW and NW 5°W were directed towards this object and, as the wind remained strong until noon, we continued under full sail, so that our latitude observation would be as close as possible to that point.

The sight of Kingao Islets[1] bearing N 5°E, distant about four leagues, confirmed to the pilot that our longitude observed to the east of Piedra Blanca was correct. Hour angles were then taken, that is, almost on its meridian, to determine its longitude by the mean of the two chronometers, which were within a minute of 5°19′30″ west of Manila. Although the wind slackened near noon, the Sun was clearly visible, allowing us to observe a reliable latitude of 22°30′30″. Shortly afterwards we sighted Piedra Blanca to the SSW, looking, from a distance of three to four leagues, like a vessel under sail. We immediately made for it, and at a quarter past one we were on its meridian a little more than a league away from it. In this position the observed longitude, by the two chronometers, and consequently that of Piedra Blanca was 5°47′ west of Manila. According to the dead reckoning carefully kept up from noon until the hour angles were taken at 1.39 in the afternoon, we established the latitude of Piedra Blanca as 22°20′N. From then onwards we steered WSW 5°W, measuring bases to various points or islands close inshore.

At half past five, when we were one and a half leagues south of Single Island,[2] we sighted Great Lema to WSW. We continued steering the same course in order to pass through the channel that separates it from Pootoy Island.[3] After sunset, the southernmost extremity of the former [island] bore SWbyW and that of Single Island north, two and a half leagues distant. We continued steering WSW 5°W, under shortened sails and topsails, even though the wind was fresh. After nightfall we took frequent soundings, keeping in the channel in depths of eighteen or nineteen fathoms, mud. The night was dark and the Moon rose too late to light our way in the various channels through which we had to make our way to Macau. At half past ten [Grand] Lema was close to our port side, with other islands to starboard. We therefore altered course little by little towards the former[4] so as to stay in the centre of the channel.

It had been my intention to anchor in the shelter of some of these islands during the night, as the darkness before moonrise would certainly make the passage

---

[1] Guiling Dao, 3 miles SE of the eastern entrance point of Honghai Wan.
[2] Quing Zhou, the southern island of Tuoning Liedao, a group of islands 25 miles NE of Hong Kong Island.
[3] Po Toi Island, the largest of the Po Toi Group, 6 miles NNW of Dangan Dao from which it is separated by Dangan Shuidao (Lema Channel).
[4] Surely Bustamante means the latter.

hazardous. As a precaution two anchors were cleared away ready to be dropped at the moment that a calm or current should make it necessary. However, I decided to proceed with the topsails reefed and braced against each other, so as to be in sight of Macau at dawn and avoid the irksome necessity of anchoring and then weighing anchor soon afterwards. At half past eleven the Moon gave us enough light to make out the channels through which we had to pass and to take a few transits to draw up a separate plan of the entrance. When the NE point of Lema bore S28°E and Waglan Island[1] bore north, we steered WNW and then NWbyW. [12th] At half past twelve we altered course to west to pass to the north of Ling[-ting],[2] which was on the same bearing to us as the highest point of Lamma [Island][3] at WNW 5°W,[4] with the westernmost point of Lema bearing south. At a quarter past one we were on the meridian of the western [extremity] of Lamma, when the most salient part of Ling-ting bore WSW 5°S. We then altered course to WbyN to stand a little way off Ling-ting and also to approach the southern end of Chamchow.[5] At two o'clock we were to the west of it, seeking the passage between Chichow[6] and the islets to the north, called Chow.[7] To approach Chow Island[8] we luffed up at three o'clock, not far off it, steering W 5°S and then WSW 5°W, sounding eleven fathoms, soft mud, when Ling-ting bore SEbyE. At half past four, off the westernmost of the Chow Islands, we bore up to the NW to pass to the east of Latsanze[9] and hoisted all sail. At dawn we were between the islands of Lantau[10] and Longsitow,[11] with the same light breeze from ENE that had accompanied us during the night.

It is not easy to describe the delightful scene we saw as the light strengthened. From our position in the middle of a chain of islands, even though they were arid or barren, they could not fail to please us by their number, symmetry and varied sizes. Added to this was the multitude of fishing lorchas surrounding them, which at a certain distance appeared, in their various groupings as a very large fleet. The fishing in these waters being as plentiful as it is necessary to sustain the natives, as a principal source of food, it is not surprising that it is a matter of the greatest importance for them. We altered course to pass two miles to the north of Longsitow and when we were off that island we could already see the entrance to the port of Typa[12] bearing WbyS. As the currents were setting southward at the time, it was necessary to steer to

---

[1] Wang Lan.
[2] Wailingding Dao.
[3] Pok Liu Chau.
[4] Bustmanante means that Pok Liu Chau (Lamma Island) and Wailingding Dao are on reciprocal bearings.
[5] Not identified.
[6] Dazhizhu Dao, the eastern island of Zhizhu Liedao.
[7] Soko Islands; the passage Bustamante was making for was Dahao Shuidao (Lantau Channel), leading between the Soko Islands and Dazhizhu Dao and then SW of Tai Yue Shan.
[8] Probably Tai A Chau, the SW island of Soko Islands.
[9] Guishan Dao.
[10] Tai Yue Shau.
[11] Niu Tou Dao, 2½ miles SW of the south point of Tai Yue Shau.
[12] At the time of Bustamante's visit the Typa was an important anchorage for Macau, between the islands of Taipa, 1½ miles south of Macau and the island of Coloane, 1 mile farther SSW. By 1834, however, the Typa had shoaled to such an extent that it was no longer usable as an anchorage. As a result of reclamation the two islands are effectively one island. They are joined to Macau by a bridge.

the NW. At seven o'clock, with the city of Macau in sight, we headed for the port, firing a gun and hoisting our ensign. The wind freshened a little from ESE to SE, so that by nine o'clock we were between Cabaret Point[1] and the northern islet[2] at the entrance to Typa. From here we passed to the west of its southern extremity in depths of three to four fathoms, reaching the northern entrance at ten and continuing until we could see Macau through it, when we anchored in four fathoms, mud. The boats were lowered immediately and a second anchor was laid out to the north, so that we were lying north/south. The fortress, which is the most conspicuous building of the city, bore N2°W and the north point of the entrance E5°N.

STAY IN TYPA

As soon as we had dropped anchor the Portuguese harbour pilot, who combines with these duties those of harbour master, arrived on board with a customs official. The former came at the orders of the Governor of Macau to ask the usual questions regarding the class of the ship, her route and destination, etc. He also wished to ask other questions to which, considering them inappropriate for warships, I replied that the officer whom I would send immediately to convey our compliments to the Governor would give him all the information he desired. The second official told me that he came as directed by the Customs Office to establish whether or not this was a warship and, even if it were, to proceed to inspect the cargo and assign guards to remain on board, as is customary with merchant ships.

When the ship had been secured our officer went ashore with the letters for the Governor, from which he was to learn the reasons that had brought His Most Catholic Majesty's corvette *Atrevida* to this port. At the same time he was also to inform him that I was ready to salute the city if I were assured of this being answered, gun for gun. I advised him that I would immediately call upon the Commissioners of the Real Compañía de Filipinas, so that they, as the only agents of Spain in these dominions, could make arrangements to expedite, during the few days that I intended to remain in the port, the various objects described, which were necessary for the continuation of the voyage. Meanwhile, with the Governor's agreement, it was essential that we were provided with a suitable building in which to set up our observatory.

Shortly afterwards I received a letter from the Commissioners themselves, Don Manuel de Agote[3] and Don Julian de Fuentes, offering to do everything within their

---

[1] Bustamante appears to be referring to Ponta de Ka-hó, the eastern extremity of the island of Coloane, whereas the name Cabarreta Point formerly referred to the eastern extremity of the island of Taipa.

[2] Island of Taipa.

[3] Manuel de Agote, First Factor of the Real Compañía de Filipinas in Macau, dedicated his 1792 map of Macau to Malaspina. The British Library's copy (Add. MSS. 17641B) gives statistics for 1792 (population 11,871, including 7,500 Chinese living in their own quarter) and shows forts, colleges, hospitals, churches, convents and two Chinese temples. For the manuscript of a log-book by Agote ('Diario de Navegación ... desde Guayaquil ... a Macao ... con el navío Hercules ... (1783-87)' with charts, tables, coastal profiles, cargoes carried, and with notes on Chinese philosophy etc., see the London auctioneer Sotheby's Catalogue 93607 (*Natural History, Atlases, and Travel*), 7 December 1993, 147. Agote travelled to Manila with Malaspina in 1786-7 in the *Astrea*: John Kendrick, *Alejandro Malaspina – Portrait of a Visionary*, Montreal and Kingston, 1991, p. 27.

power to help us during our stay here. I answered them immediately, thanking them for the kind intentions they had expressed. In the afternoon both of them came on board to invite me to dine with all the officers at the Company's office. I then gave them the particulars of our urgent necessities: the repair of chronometer number 10 by a skilled craftsman familiar with this type of instrument. In addition the acquisition of another chronometer and paint of all types were matters of the greatest necessity for us, requiring immediate action, my intention being to leave this port by the 24th of this month.

The Governor, and Captain General, Don Vasco Luis Carneyro de Sousa y Faro, Knight of the Order of Christ and Rear Admiral of the Indian Ocean, received with unmistakable signs of courtesy and civility the officer who went to convey our compliments, bidding him assure me that I could count upon all the assistance within his own power and that of his staff for everything I might need.

Our stay in this port, which is frequented by all the nations of Europe, required that our military discipline be that appropriate for a warship. The King's ensign had not yet been seen in these waters, a circumstance which doubled our efforts to ensure that the crew adhered to the conduct and moderation that this principle required. To this end my orders were extremely strict, the crew and marines being warned that the slightest grounds for complaint arising from their behaviour ashore would not be tolerated, and I was subsequently pleased to find that these measures had had the desired effect.

The following morning we saluted the city with nine guns, as prescribed by our own regulations, and the salute was immediately returned with the same number. I then went ashore with the officers to call on the Governor, and the Bishop,[1] as a sign of the respect due to his sacred office. The Governor told me with the greatest politeness how much pleasure it would give him to be able to contribute to the progress of an expedition of this nature, and that for this purpose he had asked Don Manuel de Agote to suggest to him every measure which might help to achieve this end. With regard to an appropriate house for the observatory, Señor Antonio José de Acosta very willingly offered us to use his own, as its situation nearby and suitability for the purpose made it preferable to others. The owner's requests and the Governor's wishes that I should accept made me decide to establish our observatory in it. Accordingly, all the instruments were taken there the next day. Chronometer 72 and the pendulum were set in motion straight away, but the experiments were suspended for a few days to allow them to settle. The altitudes taken on the 14th by the officers Don Juan de la Concha and Don Ciriaco de Cevallos gave the following differences of meridian with Manila:

	Number 72	Number 105
Difference on mean time at noon on the 14th ...	1' 26"·86	+ 3h 26' 31"·24
From the [chronometer] log at Manila........	27' 47"·86	+ 3 55' 41"·00
Difference between the meridians..........	29' 14"·72	0 29' 09"·76
Longitude west of Manila................	7° 18' 45"	7° 17' 25"
Longitude of Manila [east of Greenwich]	120° 53' 30"[2]	

This difference of meridians found over a period of a few days, and within the figures

[1] The bishop was Marcelino José da Silva (1789-1802): R. Ritzler and P. Sefrin, *Hierarchia catholica medii et recentioris aevi*, VI (1730-1799), Padua, 1958, p. 270.

[2] Bustamante was making his calculations using the British *Nautical Almanac* and has given his longitude for Manila, and thus of Macau, east of Greenwich to enable a comparison to be made with the

for the two chronometers, gives a certain degree of confidence in establishing a longitude for Macau preferable to that of Captain King, as he did not make any observations at all in this city, and his longitude was determined by means of distances observed with a single chronometer before and after leaving this port. Mr Bayly agrees with us, but his longitude is also calculated by distances, taking the average of several series which differ considerably among themselves.[1]

When we went ashore we frequently made our way to the house of Señores Agote and Fuentes, where we were immediately visited by the Governor, the Syndic,[2] the leading supercargoes, and the subordinate members of the French, Swedish and Danish companies, with some from the English company, and various private individuals of the city. The Governor, and these companies, invited us to dine on alternate days, deserving on each occasion a gratitude and appreciation which words can hardly convey. These civilities being so general, it could only surprise everyone that Mr Harrison,[3] the Chief Supercargo of the English company, should refuse to take part in them, in the name of a nation which, due to its affluence, occupies the first place here among the other European countries. This discourtesy, however, would have been much less remarkable if I had not been assured that he had been expressly ordered by the Commander-in-Chief of the Indian establishments to offer every assistance requested or needed by His Catholic Majesty's corvettes *Descubierta* and *Atrevida*. Such strange behaviour could not fail to be condemned as much as it was regretted by his compatriots, and they urged him to comply, if not with good manners, at least with the orders he had been given. Giving way at last to their petitions, after some days he left a note at the Company offices.

I considered that I should not fail to inform myself about this Mr Harrison and if such orders were authentic and in what sense they had been conceived, so as to report on them with due accuracy. Although His Excellency the Ministro de Marina had sent to Don Alejandro Malaspina in Lima a copy of a general order issued by His Britannic Majesty to all the governors of his overseas possessions and the commanding officers of warships, requiring them to offer our expedition all the assistance in their power, I thought that perhaps it had not reached as far as these dominions, where the English nation has neither possessions nor military commanders to represent royal authority. With this purpose I went to his house the day before our departure, when he thought it proper to show me at once the original order from Lord Cornwallis, Commander-in-Chief in India,[4] in which he referred to the order he had

---

observations by James King during Cook's third voyage (see below). To obtain longitudes west of Cádiz Bustamante would need to add 6°11′, making the longitude of Manila 127°02′15″ west of Cádiz and that of Macau as 113°35′25″. For his final calculation of the longitude of Macau see p. 359 below.

[1] King's longitude for the anchorage in the Typa was 113°48′34″ east of Greenwich: Cook and King, *Voyage to the Pacific Ocean*, III, p. 442. On the other hand Bayly's longitude, based on sixteen sets of lunar distances, was 113°37′15″ and thus in close agreement with Bustamante's value: William Bayly, *The Original Astronomical Observations made in the course of a Voyage to the Northern Pacific Ocean ... in His Majesty's Ships the Resolution and Discovery*, London, 1782, p. 77.

[2] A term used for a type of official, differing in different countries and times.

[3] John Harrison, an English Factor: see H. B. Morse, *Chronicles of the East India Company Trading to China, 1635-1834*, 5 vols, Oxford, 1926, IV, p. 404.

[4] Charles Cornwallis, first Marquis and second Earl Cornwallis (1738-1805), Governor General 1786-93.

received from Lord Grenville, Minister for Foreign Affairs,[1] dated in the year '89. It would have been as unpardonable not to inquire into this very generous measure of Lord Cornwallis as it would have been unjust to take no notice of its origin. Our nation itself would blame our ingratitude if we concealed from its knowledge so worthy a reason for remembering our sincere feelings of gratitude to the British Government, for its zeal in defending the success of this enterprise.

While the principal representative of the English nation was behaving in this manner, his second in command, and other subordinates of the same company, extended to us the same courteous attentions as did the others. Among all of these Mr Daniel Beale, the present Prussian Consul,[2] distinguished himself; with an equal kindness he allowed us, with particular generosity, the use of various books and public documents that interested us. He also quickly sent to Canton for chronometer number 11[3] belonging to the late Mr Cox,[4] whose partner he had been in a company trading in furs from the Northwest Coast of America, where he had used it during his voyages. This was the only instrument of this type which we could find, and although there was little time left for an examination of its movement, I decided to buy it, considering our experience with the quality of other machines from the same maker.

When we arrived here Don Manuel Agote informed me of the strict prohibition imposed by the [Chinese] Emperor,[5] to the extent of capital punishment, on the sale of any type of furs throughout his dominions, a new measure which obliged him to keep in store 3,333 [furs] which had been sent to him by the government of Manila for sale, being crown property brought from the coast of California by the officers

---

[1] William Wyndham Grenville, Baron Grenville (1759-1834), Minister for Foreign Affairs, 1791-1801.

[2] Daniel Beale came to Canton in 1785 as purser of the East India Company's ship *General Coote*. Apart from being Prussian Consul at Canton and Macau he was also a merchant at Canton and co-adventurer with Meares in the later's expedition of 1788; see also Dermigny, *La Chine*, III, pp. 1156, 1241-2, 1267. For Beale and other consuls at this time see Austin Coates, *Prelude to Hong Kong*, London, 1966 (rpt. as *Macao and the British 1637-1842: Prelude to Hong Kong*, Hong Kong, 1988), pp. 72-3.

[3] According to George Mortimer in *Observations and Remarks made during a Voyage ... in the brig Mercury commanded by John Cox, Esq*, London, 1791, p. 73, Cox owned a watch made by Mr Hughes of Holborn. This watch, however, was made by Thomas Earnshaw, but sold by William Hughes, who then sold it to Cox as explained by Earnshaw in his *Longitude. An Appeal to the Public*, London, 1808, p. 264. Number 11, however, is an unlikely number for an Earnshaw watch and it therefore seems likely that this watch was a series III box chronometer by John Arnold as subsequently referred to by Malaspina: Jonathan Betts, Curator of Horology, National Maritime Museum *in lit.*, 7 January 1998. This is confirmed by Bustamante referring to the quality of the chronometers on board by the maker of number 11. Neither the *Descubierta* nor the *Atrevida* carried chronometers by Earnshaw.

[4] John Henry Cox became established in Canton about 1781. In 1785, together with three supercargoes of the East India Company he financed Captain James Hanna's voyage to the NW Coast of America in the brig *Harmon*, the first of the fur trading voyages. After financing several other voyages he became a partner of Daniel Beale. In 1787 or 1788 he was expelled from Canton and returned to Europe. Here he acquired the British snow *Mercury*, which sailed for the NW Coast of American under Swedish colours and was renamed *Gustavus III*. In January 1790 the *Gustavus III* reached Canton, where Cox died shortly afterwards: see Pierce, *Russian America: a Biographical Dictionary*, pp. 101-3 and Mortimer, *Observations and Remarks*.

[5] From 1757 the Chinese confined all overseas trade to Canton, and imposed severe restrictions on the European (and after 1784, American) factors. In 1793 the British sent the Macartney mission to Peking, vainly requesting new trade agreements and wider contacts with the Chinese.

Don Manuel Quimper and Don Cosme Bertodano of the royal navy.[1] It seems that the cause of this prohibition arose from the assumption that all the furs from America were considered to be from Russian dominions, there being some friction between these two empires.[2] The Chinese were so apprehensive of the punishment threatened by the edict that none of them dared to participate in negotiations of this nature. Mr Beale, tired of trying various means of selling a cargo brought by the brigantine *Argonaut*, found himself obliged to send them to the islands of Japan, preferring this measure, unlikely to be successful, as was indeed the case, to running the risk of them spoiling if they were kept on board.[3]

Various other vessels from the Northwest Coast of America have experienced the same difficulties. The Chinese were aware that we had brought some furs from those parts, but they did not dare to reprimand us as they had done to privately owned ships, going so far as to suggest that they leave the port. No doubt the respect or fear they feel towards any warship may have been the cause of their silence and, so as not to presume upon this information, I felt it more fitting to refrain from taking any but the most lawful measures so that our factors would not request the owners [of the furs] to sell them in any way possible. On the contrary, I informed them of these matters, in case they were contemplating other methods which might bring unfortunate consequences, which would involve exposing themselves to the frequent outrages which the Mandarins were always ready to commit for the sake of the base self-interest which dominates them. The most suitable step, therefore, would be to return the furs to Manila, where they could be sold, if not as profitably, at least both easily and safely.

All the otter, sable and ermine furs which had been gathered on this ship since leaving Manila, belonging to the crews of both corvettes, would come to about 300, more or less, all of which had been assembled in the hands of a few since Acapulco, where the news brought by the galleon of the drop in prices in Canton had caused some to part with their furs at little profit and others to take advantage of this opportunity for lucrative speculation.[4] Both Don Alejandro Malaspina and I were aware of this type of contract and it did not seem fair to prohibit them when the furs had been acquired with our permission, following orders from His Majesty. As the *Atrevida* had

---

[1] See pp. 326 above.

[2] Here Bustamante adds his own footnote 'In Manila we later found out that on the 28th of May the Emperor had permitted the introduction of furs, and the extraction of rhubarb, which had also been prohibited.' According to Lo-shu Fu, *A Documentary Chronicle of Sino-Western Relations (1644–1820)*, Tucson, 1966, this date should read 12th of May. The late 18th century witnessed the Rhubarb Mania. At a time when purging was one of the most common medical interventions, rhubarb was valued as a wonder drug. On its commercial importance, see Ljungstedt, *A Historic Sketch*, p. 258 and Lo-shu Fu, op. cit., pp. 303–5, 323. The Chinese claimed (1821) that they sold it as 'a favour to Europeans who need it to keep alive', since without it they would die of constipation: *The Chinese Repository*, VII, Oct. 1838, p. 311; Morse, *Chronicles of the East India Company*, IV, p. 48). See also the study by Clifford Foust, *Rhubarb: The Wonder Drug*, Princeton, 1992.

[3] In 1650, Japan deliberately isolated herself from all contact with the outer world (except for annual visits permitted to the Dutch) and it could be fatal to land there. Occasionally, however, ships were wrecked there, particularly whalers.

[4] The thick pelt of the sea otter (*Enhydra lutris*) was highly valued but the intensity of the fur trade almost wiped out the otter; see Dermigny, *La Chine*, III, p. 1493. For Malaspina's plans for Spanish participation in this rich trade see Cook, *Flood Tide*, pp. 315–16.

to go to Macau alone, interested parties on the *Descubierta* asked the commanding officer if they could transfer to her, which request was granted without objection.

The present value of furs has been considerably reduced since the last voyage of Captain Cook. According to King there were sailors at that time who sold their stock of furs at eight hundred pesos, and the value of the good ones was not less than 120 a piece.[1] Today they hardly reach half that price, because the excessive number of people trading has lowered the profits which they offered at the beginning. The truth is that it is now difficult to defray the cost of expeditions of this type, and many predict that they will soon have to be abandoned.

Nature appears to have granted exclusively to Spain the trade in this branch of commerce. Our establishments in San Francisco and Monterey, as well as being an abundant source of furs, allow us to acquire them at each place with ease as far as Cook River [Cook Inlet] at lower cost and with greater safety and speed. Their transport to China benefits from the same advantages, for when the Manila galleon reaches the coasts of New Spain in November or December, the vessels assigned for this purpose are back in Acapulco. The freight and costs as far as Manila must be very moderate, as this ship returns without cargo and has a considerable carrying capacity.

Let us now compare the possibilities of profit in this trade with that of the foreigners who dedicate themselves to it. Their expeditions must either travel directly from Europe by Cabo de Hornos or go by Asia, making expensive stops in Macau and the Sandwich Islands or wintering in one of the harbours in the high northern latitudes of America, at the risk of a thousand dangers and sinkings, as Captain Meares experienced in the year of 86 and described so vividly. The goods they carry for exchange lose their value in the natives' eyes, as experience has taught them that the traders want only furs, and as these are in their hands they can dictate the conditions, secure in the knowledge that the traders will have to accept them. This is not the case for us. The coast of California not only produces them for us, eliminating the need of receiving them [from others], but also provides another product, the shells,[2] which are peculiar to that territory and of great value among them if they are offered economically.[3] In addition to these, the copper from New Spain and the ordinary cloth used for clothing which is made there, are very much sought after by the Indians, as we found on the corvettes.

Although foreigners are not fully conscious of these excellent opportunities, being still unaware of their favourable effects for Spain, they have admitted to me without hesitation that our competition in this type of commerce will always defeat their ventures, however well planned and directed they may be. Furs are considered an article of the highest necessity and luxury among the Chinese. All ranks of people use them for warmth and many for adornment. Therefore, although their abundance may

---

[1] 'One of our seamen sold his stock, alone, for eight hundred dollars; and a few prime skins, which were clean, and had been well preserved, were sold for one hundred and twenty each': Cook and King, *Voyage to the Pacific Ocean*, III, p. 437.

[2] Shells of the edible mollusc Abalone (*Haliotis cracherodii*) found off the coast of California, whose ear-shaped shell lined with mother-of-pearl, usually known as Monterey Shells, was much prized as an item of trade: see James R. Gibson, *Otter Skins, Boston Ships, and China Goods*, Montreal and London, 1992, pp. 8, 228–9.

[3] It is not clear whether Bustamante means at a reasonable price or in small amounts so as to maintain a reasonable price-level.

have lowered their value, they will always be a highly esteemed article of consumption. Thus, every circumstance invites our country to participate in a trade in which not only can no other nation cause us harm, but neither can it be equalled in the profit that it promises.[1]

Our arrival here could not but alarm the Chinese, as usually happens when a warship comes in to this port. The Mandarin of Casa blanca (a town near Macau)[2] presented himself to hear from Don Manuel Agote the reasons which brought us to these waters and, reassured by the fact that we would soon depart, asked no further questions. They are more anxious at present regarding the many pirates who harassed these parts last month. The continual robberies and outrages committed against any Chinese vessel they encountered, not excepting the fishing craft, obliged the government to ask the Portuguese to arm vessels capable of pursuing and exterminating them. This measure explains, in fact, the backwardness of the navy in this empire, which is, to say the least, in the same deplorable state as in the sixteenth century when, in similar difficulties, they called on the Portuguese to expel the famous pirate Tchang-Silao[3] from Macau and its environs, by means of which service that European nation succeeded in establishing itself in these dominions.

The Portuguese government, after examining the request in the Senate, agreed to it, with the same idea of obtaining some privilege from the Chinese. It immediately bought two brigantines, one Portuguese owned, but not particularly suitable, and another from Mr Beale, copper-sheathed and built in London expressly for the fur trade; an excellent ship, and moreover more appropriate for the purpose.

While these ships were being prepared, Señor Botello[4] went to Canton, commissioned by the government to obtain, in recompense for this service, the right to build houses in Macau without paying any taxes to the Mandarins and to allow Portuguese vessels to anchor and sail freely between Canton and Macau, needing only the permission of the Senate. However, either these concessions seemed excessive or the pirates had indeed disappeared, since Botello returned at the end of last month without having achieved anything more than being able to inform the Governor and Senate of the gratitude of the Emperor for arming the ships. In addition, although the cause no longer existed, he would not forget the particular merit of the Portuguese nation so as to recompense it appropriately. The ships, of course, now have no purpose, and up to now they have cost no less than 22,000 *pesos*. The Portuguese attribute this inconsistency of the Chinese to the perfidy of the Mandarin of Giang-Chang[5] who, seeking to impress his worth upon the Emperor by obtaining this assistance, had promised the Portuguese even greater exemptions than those which Botello sought.

---

[1] The Spanish trade in sea otter skins never flourished: see Gibson, *Otter Skins*, pp. 18–21.
[2] Casa Branca: see n. 5 below.
[3] Chang Si-lao, a pirate allegedly driven out of Macau by the Portuguese, in return for which the Chinese allowed them to settle there; but on this, and for the origin of Macau, see C. R. Boxer, *South China in the Sixteenth Century*, Hakluyt Society, 2nd ser. 106, London, 1953, p. xxxv.
[4] A judge in Macau of whom nothing more is known.
[5] Possibly Zhuhai, a town about 5 miles north of Macau; the mandarin of the place (known as the 'Mandarin of Casa Branca') was the official overseer of the city and responsible for the conduct of affairs there. These mandarins acted as intermediaries between the Macau traders and Peking [Beijing].

THE ISLAND OF LUZON AND ATREVIDA'S VISIT TO MACAU

The city of Macau is on a peninsula of the island of Un-zao.[1] It runs back from the sea shore on uneven terrain, elevated in parts. The streets are irregular and narrow, with few public buildings. The Europeans' houses have little architectural merit, although inside they are arranged and decorated according to the custom and elegance of Europe. The city has five fortresses, some of which rise high above it, called Nuestra Señora del Monte Carmelo, Nuestra Señora de la Guia, Nuestra Señora del Buen Parto, San Francisco and Fortín de San Pedro, all of which, I have been informed, are in very poor condition. There is a cathedral, as well as three parish churches, two colleges (San José and San Pablo, which used to belong to the Jesuits[2]), three monasteries (Augustinian, Franciscan and Dominican), the convent of Santa Clara, a church and the Casa de Misericordia,[3] two hospitals, and three hermitages, of which San Lazaro is outside the city. Don Fernando Brambila, with his usual skill, took two views of the city from the best places from which to depict it most accurately.[4] The praise which his work earned from the Governor emboldened me to offer him a copy, which I sent to him from Manila.

The political administration of the city lies with the Senate Chamber, composed of three *Veedores*,[5] two examining magistrates, a court clerk, who serves as standard bearer, another clerk of the Board [of Conscience[6]] and a treasurer who also both serve in the customs office. The Senate is presided over by the Governor and *Capitán General* and the present judge or Syndic, Señor Lazaro de Silva Ferreyra, Knight of the Order of Christ, *Desembargador de los Agravos*[7] of the Lisbon Court of Appeal. The sessions of this tribunal are held in the building known as the Senate House, which was built for that purpose in the year 1786 and is the finest building in this city.

The police come under the administration of the judge and the two examining magistrates, while the city attorney is responsible for dealing with matters relating to the Chinese. The posts of the *Veedores*, judges, attorney and treasurer are annual and appointed in the capital of Goa, by a selection held every three years. These posts are always conferred upon highly regarded citizens, who must be married and either Portuguese, or born in Macau.

Military authority rests with the Governor. The junior officers consist of a *comandante*, a *sargento mayor*[8] with four *tenientes*, who command 150 sepoys and gunners, the same number of militia with a *maestro de campo*,[9] a *sargento mayor*, two militia *capitanes*

---

[1] Aomen Dao.
[2] When the Society of Jesus was temporarily suppressed by the papacy (1773-1814) Jesuit properties were transferred to other orders.
[3] 'House of Mercy', a charitable brotherhood, for whose history see Boxer, *Fidalgos*, pp. 217-21.
[4] Both views have survived; for one see plate 40, for the other and another version of plate 40 see Sotos, *Los pintores*, II, figs 748-9. In addition Brambila drew a Chinese pagoda: ibid., fig. 750.
[5] Senior administrators attached to the senate chamber; elected by leading citizens, they controlled the town's finances.
[6] The Mesa de Conciencia, or Board of Conscience, who advised the crown on religious policy at home and abroad.
[7] A crown lawyer.
[8] Although the literal translation of this rank is sergeant-major, by context he is senior to the *tenientes* and is probably equivalent to a major in the British army.
[9] Since by context he is senior to a *sargento mayor* he is probably equivalent to a lieutenant colonel in the British army.

Plate 40. View of Macau, by Fernando Brambila. Museo Naval, Madrid

and another known as *mor de campo*.¹ The five fortress *comandantes* have the rank of *capitán*, with the exception of the *comandante* of the principal fortress, Our Lady of Mount Carmel, who has the rank of *sargento mayor*.

Despite the small cost of running this establishment, owing both to the small staff and to the low wages that they earn, the income of the treasury is barely sufficient to defray these expenses. The return from this is unreliable being dependant on the number of vessels which arrive and the value of their cargoes. In the two years of 1789 and 1791 the income of the various funds administered by the Senate reached the sum of 30,000 *taeles*.²

The duty received on goods from foreign ports does not exceed six per cent of customs income, on a conservative assumption, and four per cent on those from domestic ports. Silver and gold pay two per cent, dropping to one per cent, as a special concession, for Spanish ships coming from Manila. Of the six per cent for wholesale goods whose value does not reach ten *taeles* a *pico*,³ one and a half per cent is taken for the Convent of Santa Clara and the Casa de la Misericordia. For the benefit of the proceeds of the funds administered by the Senate, it gives from its maritime claims fund up to 4,000 *taeles* guaranteed by properties, to provide short-term loans at a premium of five per cent per annum.

To encourage shipping, His Most Faithful Majesty, allows national shipping a reduction of twenty-two per cent on the royal duty payable in this port and those of Bengal, the Coromandel coast and Malabar, when the goods they are carrying are consigned to foreign ports, according to the valuation given by the Casa de India, but despite this allowance the number of ships used in this trade is not large. Last year the number reached twenty-two, fourteen of them from 350 to 800 tons burden, and the rest smaller. Only one of the vessels came from Lisbon, while the others came from Asian ports. The European companies receive thirty to forty ships each year in Bampú,⁴ none being of less than 800 tons, and twenty per cent of those are English.

To continue with the account of our journey to the west. By the 21st we had replenished our water supplies and drawn up a plan of the port⁵ with several lines of soundings, and I would have attempted to do the same at Macau had we not suspected a certain reluctance on the part of the Governor, of whose unfailing kindness and courtesy I did not wish to take the slightest unfair advantage. I kept in mind the opposition to the same type of hydrographic work on the Portuguese coasts, when Señor Don Vicente Tofiño⁶ was commissioned to produce charts of our peninsula. The experiments with the pendulum had been carried out to our complete satisfaction and we now had only to wait for the arrival of the paints from Canton, as we

---

¹ Aide-de-camp to a senior officer or a colonel in charge of military discipline.
² Here Bustamante adds his own footnote 'Equivalent to 40,000 *pesos*, at an exchange rate of 75 *cuntrines* to the *peso*, which is the standard rate used by the Senate.'
³ Here Bustamante adds another footnote 'Each *pico* has 137½ units'.
⁴ Huangpu, formerly Whampoa, the anchorage for all foreign vessels a few miles downstream from Guangzhou (Canton).
⁵ I.e. the Typa.
⁶ For Tofiño see Vol. 1 of this edition, p. xxxviii, n. 3.

had given up hope of repairing number 10 without entrusting it to unskilled hands. We had not been as successful in our celestial observations as we had wished, for the weather was either cloudy or rainy, preventing us from taking observations of the two satellites [of Jupiter] which would otherwise have been visible. However, we can affirm that the longitude of Macau is now established, in the absence of absolute observations, with all possible accuracy, by the agreement of the two chronometers.

We cannot leave this port without making public the obliging and amiable conduct of the Governor. This officer unites the excellent personal qualities which distinguish his character with the learning, rectitude and firmness which are necessary to command successfully in all circumstances such a complex establishment. The moderation and wisdom with which he is also endowed have enabled him to ensure peace and tranquillity for this sensitive government, enabling the foreign companies to extol with praise, in no way excessive, his singular merits. All of this has earned him the appreciation of foreigners, the respect of the inhabitants and the particular esteem of all who know him. Thus, I could not fail to acknowledge in some fashion the gratitude we keenly felt for all the kind attentions he had paid us. To this end I asked the Governor if he would like to visit the corvette one day, as his fondness for all things naval encouraged me to invite him (despite the inconvenience of our distance from Macau) to do us the kindness of dining on board on the 22nd. He accepted the invitation with much pleasure, declaring that he could not conceal from me his desire to see a vessel built expressly for a voyage around the world. In order to do him the greatest possible honour, of which other principal persons were also deserving, I invited for the same day the Syndic, the leading supercargoes of the companies which had already dined with us, the second in charge of the English company, Señor Antonio José de Acosta, Mr Beale, and the factors of our company.

The corvette, painted and cleaned, was prepared to receive them with all possible comfort. At the table, following the foreign custom of these countries, a toast was drunk to the Governor's health and then to the prosperity of commerce, with a five gun salute for each toast. On leaving the ship the Governor was saluted with cheers and a gun salute, according to the honours due to a *Capitán General*, his rank in his jurisdiction. The city immediately answered these salutes, gun for gun. Some officers and I accompanied him ashore, the Governor showing he was as satisfied as he was grateful for what was no more on our part than a small mark of our own obligation to him and a duty regarding his noble character.

Nor could I omit to mention, without committing a most reprehensible fault, the energy and care with which Don Manuel de Agote has assisted us in all we have needed in this country. We cannot deny that without his help I would not have been able to carry out my mission so quickly, nor obtain information as accurate as that he has given me. His learning and knowledge of commercial matters are too well known for me to pause to praise them. Likewise, he unites a disposition to hard work, activity and application with qualities which will make him always worthy of the highest posts in the company, and for which he enjoys here the public esteem that he deserves, in the opinion of all who know him.

RETURN TO MANILA

24 April
The instruments having been brought on board yesterday and the painting materials having arrived from Canton the previous day, there was now nothing left to be done in this port to fulfil the orders given to us. It was, therefore, my intention to leave today, using the ebb tide in the early morning, but the ESE wind was too strong for this manoeuvre, either by sailing or warping out. So as not to lose any time, we began weighing the southern anchor, with the rising tide, to get it up and down. We then laid out a long warp on which to come about when the flood tide began to lose strength around midday. However, this did not have the desired result because, with both anchor buoys not watching,[1] it became necessary to [attempt to] weigh the northern anchor by its crown,[2] which would cause further delay even if we could manage it, the anchor having presumably been buried deeply in the soft ground. In fact the buoy-rope parted and the diver could not find the anchor to pass a line around the shank and so we were obliged to use the corvette to weigh it. Despite these setbacks, at midday we began to warp round, and at half past two we laid out another warp, but the tide was soon ebbing so strongly that shortly afterwards it carried us to seaward over the kedge, so that to get it hove up and down it was necessary to set the jibs and mizzen topsail, with which we succeeded in weighing it. All of these unexpected incidents delayed us somewhat in proceeding to sea, but at five o'clock a fresh SE breeze set in to compensate for the delay. We then set a course to ENE under full sail to clear both islands before the turn of the tide, which was now helping us very little. At sunset we were on the meridian of the northern point of the entrance, distant two miles. We continued to steer ENE until half past seven, when we tacked to SSW in the hope of clearing Montaña Island,[3] if the wind continued with sufficient strength, to allow us to make headway against the current. As we were running along the coast of Typa Island we sighted Montaña Island, which we attempted to pass, but the wind slackened and then dropped, obliging us to anchor at eleven o'clock in five fathoms, mud. Although there was a steady moderate breeze all night, it was from SE and not strong enough to give us headway against the current, which here sets to the east. [25th] At dawn the western point of Montaña Island bore N60°W and Peack Point[4] NE.

In the morning the breeze freshened from the south and when the current eased we set sail on a SE tack, with the wind from SSW, which took us through a crowd of fishing boats. Meanwhile the current did not gain strength and we tacked twice, as until then we had not been able to clear the Great Ladrone.[5] At nine we sighted a merchant vessel to the SSE, whose size and the fact that she had not yet arrived from Manila, led us to believe at first that it was the *Concepción*. So as to confirm this and to

---

[1] I.e. a buoy which has been dragged below the surface by the tide.
[2] I.e. to weigh the anchor by means of a line attached (by a diver) to the crown of the anchor.
[3] Dahengqin Dao, formerly Montanha Island, a large island SW of the island of Coloane, together forming the southern side of the Typa.
[4] Not identified.
[5] Dawanshan Dao, the largest of the Wanshan Qundao (Landrone Islands).

be able to pass the news to the Real Compañía, we hoisted our ensign when closer to her, to which she responded with the English ensign. This vessel, as Mr Harrison had informed me, was expected at any moment, coming from the northern part of New Holland, New Guinea and the island of Borneo where she had been sent by the East India Company to investigate their commercial possibilities.[1] We regretted that we had missed by so little the chance to meet in Macau and learn of the results of this mission concerning the geography of places either little known or poorly surveyed.

Our latitude at noon was 21°45′00″, at which time the westernmost of the Ladrones lay to our north. A fresh breeze accompanied us, allowing us to clear the Asses Islands[2] and islets[3] steering SEbyS, and by sunset they were lost to sight. At nightfall frequent flashes of lightning lit the entire horizon. However, since the breeze remained fresh from SW and there was no sign of worsening weather, we continued under full sail. Such were the conditions until two o'clock, when the wind freshened markedly; the lightning had not stopped and the sea was now high. By dawn a moderate gale had sprung up, the weather looked threatening and it began to rain very heavily. Shortly afterwards the wind shifted suddenly to NNW, now blowing strongly, but dropping at intervals, only to return with greater strength in squalls, accompanied by loud and repeated thunderclaps and lightning flashes which made us proceed with great care. We steered SEbyS under foresail and topsails, easing them as the circumstances required. Although the wind varied between the second and third quadrants, conditions remained similar until three in the afternoon, when the weather cleared and the wind shifted to the south, freshening at nightfall. We made more sail, tacking to WSW, as in these parts the current sets strongly to the east in this season. The night was mild, although the heavy cloud cover did not lift, and it was still overcast in the morning.

27 April

As we later confirmed, this unsettled weather, whose effects still threatened us, was a sign that in these waters the North-east Monsoon was coming to an end. Furthermore M. D'Après [de Mannevillette][4] and Captain King affirm that the South-west Monsoon begins, or may be expected, in April. It was necessary, therefore, to change

---

[1] In April 1791 the East India Company's snow *Panther*, Captain John McCluer, had visited Macau for supplies. McCluer had been sent to the Palau Islands by the company to inform the King of the death in London of his son Prince Lee Boo. McCluer reached the Palau Islands on 21 January 1791, before proceeding to Macau for supplies. On returning to the islands to deliver them he then sailed for New Guinea, where he discovered an extensive inlet at the SW end of the island, which was subsequently named McCluer Inlet (Teluk Berau). During December 1791 and January 1792 he ran a line of soundings off the north coast of Australia, before proceeding to Bencoolen (Bengkulu), on the west coast of Sumatra, to report his discoveries to the East India Company. It seems that news of McCluer's proceedings had reached Macau and that Harrison was expecting his imminent return. McCluer, however, returned to the Palau Islands via the island of Sulu (Cagayan Sulu) and did not return to Macau until 1794: Andrew C. F. David, 'John McCluer', *Oxford Dictionary of National Biography* (forthcoming).

[2] Jiapeng Liedao, with the Ass's Ears, two remarkable peaks rising to 300 metres near the SW extremity of Beijian Dao, the largest and NE island of the group.

[3] Dajitou Dao, a white rock 34 metres high and Eyanshi Dao, a rocky islet 40 metres high, ¾ mile east of the eastern extremity of Beijian Dao and 1 mile north of the island, respectively.

[4] Jean-Baptiste-Nicolas-Denis d'Après de Mannevillette, French sea-captain and hydrographer; author of the *Neptune oriental* (Paris, 1745).

our plan of taking a direct route to the island of Luzon, in case the *vendavales* began early. At eight o'clock, with a fresh north to NE breeze, we altered course to south. At ten o'clock it began to rain, and the sky took on the same ominous appearance as it had yesterday. After midday it became completely overcast, with frightful thunderclaps and flashes of lightning which made the violent rain that accompanied them more obvious. The wind remained gusty, between east and south, and we tacked as close to a southerly course as possible. During the night it continued overcast, with variable wind, thunder and lightning, but without squalls,[28th] and at dawn we made more sail steering SSW and SW5°S, with a fresh SSE breeze. At eleven o'clock, with several claps of thunder and flashes of lightning, we had a hard shower from NW which we took with lowered topsails, steering SSE. The wind soon dropped and backed to a moderate south to WSW, with drizzle which continued through the afternoon with few interruptions.

After nightfall the weather showed signs of improvement, as the horizon was clear and the thunder and lightning had left us, except in the distance in the second quadrant, showing that the conditions would improve as we proceeded further to the south.

29 April

With winds from SSE and south we steered in the third quadrant all night under full sail, but at half past six we tacked to ESE so as not to stand so far to the west and to keep to more easterly meridians until the wind had settled. The appearance of the Sun, of which we had been deprived for the last three days, allowed us to make observations for both latitude and longitude, the former being 19°07′00″N at noon and the latter 2′18″ east of Macau, by number 72, which corresponded to our dead reckoning longitude.

With light airs from the second quadrant and a fairly clear sky we tacked to the SW. After sunset a light breeze settled in from ENE, with which we steered SE, close-hauled. Towards midnight the sky looked threatening in the fourth quadrant, dashing the hopes raised by the favourable conditions of the afternoon.[30th] However, the appearances were much worse than the effects, as we had only light rain and little wind from that quadrant until three o'clock, which was followed by a light breeze from ENE.

In the morning it seemed that the calm weather was to compensate for the unsettled weather of the previous days, although the wind remained variable and not very favourable, obliging us to tack frequently, in about latitude 18°43′50″N and longitude 00′48″ west of Macau by number 72.

Although we had thought, in the morning, that the conditions were no longer against us, as they had been until now, in the afternoon the weather took on almost the same aspect again, with showers in sight on the horizon. At four o'clock one of these came upon us from SSW, but it soon passed. Although it was a dark night, with thunder and lightning, these were a good distance off, and the weather now did not look as bad as it had on the previous nights. [1 May] From eleven to twelve o'clock the wind freshened from WNW, and then dropped, with a brief downpour which was followed by a moderate breeze from north and NNE. With this we steered SEbyE, keeping this course during the morning with light airs from WSW, under full sail. By making the best use of the wind shifts with as much canvas as possible, we were able to reach latitude 18°13′16″ and longitude 37′51″ east of Macau by number 72; variation by western amplitude was 1°30′NE.

We were now left in no doubt that good weather had set in, the more so in that the wind had shifted from WSW through north to NNE. It remained light during the afternoon and for some hours of the night, [2nd] freshening a little from the NE towards eleven o'clock, while the sky remained clear and calm.

In the morning the weather looked most promising, except that the wind was rather light to steer directly to Mariveles,[1] as I had intended, and it would probably drop still more at midday, when we would be further south, because the North-east Monsoon ends by veering to SE and SSE. Our observed latitude at noon was 17°28′10″, 9′ further south and longitude 17′00″ further west than our dead reckoning position, and 1°29′03″[east of Macau] by number 72. These discrepancies are very odd, because at the advanced stage of the season they would usually be in the other direction. However, during the night we noted the slowing of the current, which was not as noisy as it had been on the passage from Cape Bojeador to the coast of China.

During the whole day's run the weather has been pleasant, the sea smooth and the breeze, sometimes fresh and at other times light, between NE and east. We have continued under full sail, close hauled on the port tack. The night, with the Moon almost full, has been very clear and calm, [3rd] and in these agreeable conditions when the Sun rose above the horizon, the strength of its rays was perceptible at this height, increasing with its proximity to the zenith.

The observed latitude at noon was 16°40′N, almost the same as by dead reckoning, but with the large difference to the east of 30′, according to the longitude of 2°36′29″ east of Macau by number 72, which confirmed our opinion of the previous day on the set of the currents in these waters at this time of year. We had suspected an error in the calculation of the hour angles but, after checking them carefully, we found none.

With the wind settled between EbyN and EbyS for the whole of the day's run, we remained on the port tack, as this heading was the best we could manage towards our intended track. Although it was not very favourable, we trusted that the marked differences of position to the east would compensate for the contrary winds, if they continued, or at least that the constant fair weather would reduce their effect and would allow the crew to rest from the discomforts experienced soon after our departure.

4 May

As we expected, the noon observations gave a latitude of 15°47′46″, with a difference of 13′ to the south, and longitude 2°59′34″ by number 72, showed a difference of 18′ to the east.

Since after midday the wind began to veer to ESE and even SE, it seemed preferable in these conditions to tack into the first quadrant. However, since I was given to

---

[1] I.e. to make for North Channel between Mariveles and Corregidor Island, Bustamante's Boca Chica.

understand by the pilot that the wind would continue from SE, and probably from further to the south, it would be better to remain on the port tack for the day's run, to pass south of Scarborough Reef,[1] tacking again to the east from latitude 14°40′ to approach land wherever possible with winds from the second quadrant. This plan seemed possible in the present conditions, as the wind showed signs of shifting to the south, dropping at night, contrary to our experience of previous nights. But our hopes were thwarted and our conjectures shown to be false, as in the morning the wind settled in the east once more. Nor was this to be the last of the trials in store for us, as when we eagerly made our observations, to console ourselves over the differences to the east, we found that they were in the opposite direction.

Latitude by observation was 15°3′34″, approximately the same as by the dead reckoning, and longitude, by number 72, was 2°33′36″, that is 19′ west of our position by dead reckoning. This information could not fail to surprise me and I suspected an error in the calculations, but when the hour angles were repeated at half past one in the afternoon, not only did they confirm the difference to the west, but during the interval of four hours between the two sets of observations, the currents had carried us four miles in the same direction. Variation by western amplitude was 1°23′NW.

We continued on our tack to SSE with the easterly breeze, so as to pass to the south of Scarborough Reef and either reach 14°25′, the parallel of Mariveles, or stand further to the south, if the wind made the second quadrant preferable for our course, allowing us to make more easting than would have been possible in the first quadrant. However, the wind was firmly settled, as it had been yesterday, leaving us no option in choosing our tack. [6th] We therefore went about to NbyE at eight in the morning, and shortly afterwards we tacked again to SEbyE as the wind had dropped.

According to our observed latitude of 14°29′N we were 31′ south of the southern edge of Scarborough Reef, but a considerable distance from its meridian, assuming that the pilot is correct in assuring us that it lies thirty-five to forty leagues from Luzon. In this case it will be necessary to remove from Mr Dalrymple's chart[2] the reef of the same name which he places at the greater distance of fifty-seven leagues from that island, and establish as the true and only Scarborough Reef another reef which he places in the same latitude, but closer to land than does the same report.[3] I would have been pleased if the winds had allowed us to run along its parallel, as we would have been able to have surveyed this reef, without too much delay, on which Spanish and foreign ships have been lost, for if the *Descubierta* had had the same conditions as we had off Luzon, as is probable, it would have been impossible for them to confirm

[1] A dangerous reef, on which the *Scarborough* struck on 12 September 1784, which lies with its eastern extremity in 15°07′N; 117°51′E, 120 miles west of the western coast of Luzon.
[2] 'A Chart of the China Sea' in which Dalrymple places a reef named Scarboro, with its southern extremity in 15°N and 180 miles west of Luzon and with two other possible positions in the same latitude 75 and 130 miles farther west and an unnamed reef in the same latitude about 50 miles west of Luzon.
[3] The track of the Spanish frigate *Santa Lucía* which fixed the position of Scarborough Reef on 1 May 1800, in approximately its present position, is shown on 'Carta general del archipiélago de Filipinas (northern sheet)'.

its position as her commanding officer had intended. [7th] Our longitude was 2°31′00″ by number 72, 18′ to the west of our dead reckoning position, and variation by western amplitude was 1°37′NW and by eastern amplitude 1°45′.

10 May

There has been no change in the wind or the appearance of the weather since the 7th; the differences to the west, although not as great, have continued at 12′ for the 7th and 8th, and yesterday, when there were only 7′ of difference, there was a difference of 18′ to the north. These appear to result from the fact that the South-west Monsoon is still some time off, which will inevitably cause us considerable delay in reaching Manila.

This well-founded conjecture, in addition to the paucity of our provisions, particularly bread, of which we have only sixteen days' supply, has obliged us to reduce the daily ration of this food by a quarter and add three ounces to the ration of dried vegetables, in which we are better supplied. We can no longer hope to reach port before the *vendavales* set in and we are setting a course in accordance with this assumption. The differences to the north and the need to reach the parallel of 13°54′, on which lies Cabra Island,[1] which must be surveyed, have persuaded us to take the southern tack when the wind has backed to ESE.

The noon observations gave a latitude of 13°52′23″, which was 9′ north of the dead reckoning latitude, while the longitude of 3°09′05″ was only 7′ west. This allowed us to flatter ourselves with the hope that the current would no longer be against us and, as the southerly winds had eased somewhat, we could anticipate an earlier arrival at Manila.

The longitude according to chronometer 105 was 42′ further west than we had calculated with number 72, which we considered more reliable, and number 11 gave a result 30′ further in the same direction. We therefore hoped to take lunar distances during the final quarter of the Moon, to establish a reasonable probability of error and to determine the course to be steered towards our landfall. The conditions tonight were not good for taking these distances, as the cloud cover hid the stars, nor could they be calculated by the refraction and parallax tables, preventing us from following our usual custom of taking several sets of observations in quick succession. However, during a brief break in the clouds one set was taken, which gave a longitude of 13′ further west than by number 72, when calculated by M. Borda's method,[2] which thus, to a certain degree, confirmed our preference for the results achieved with this instrument over those of the other two, even though more observations were still necessary to corroborate the calculations made with the first one.

11 May

However, the following morning the longitude given by the mean of fourteen sets of distances, 29′ west of number 72 and 49′ in the same direction the next day, led us to assume that it had an error to the east, and that our approximate longitude was

---

[1] The NW of the three principal islands of the Lubang Islands off the NW extremity of Mindoro.
[2] For Borda see Vol. I of this edition, p. 7, n. 1 and p. 240, n. 6.

halfway between those given by the two chronometers and the distances of 2°44'55" east of Macau or 4°22' west of Manila, adjusting the difference of meridian according to the absolute observations made by M. Gentil[1] in that capital, and by Captain King in Macau.

The light airs from SE and south were hardly enough to fill the small sails, but the sea was so calm that this was the only way to make any easting. The weather could not have been more pleasant or agreeable by day and by night,[12th] so the conditions were the best possible for the distances that I took this morning, and accordingly I may declare that there is undoubtedly an easterly error in the distances taken with number 72. Nevertheless, we continue to calculate our daily longitude, which today was 4°01'45" at noon, and our latitude 14°33'30", both agreeing with our dead reckoning position. Variation by western amplitude was 2°45'NW.

While the light airs continued from south to SE, as they did yesterday, we set a course on the port tack, until they backed to ESE, when we changed to the starboard tack for the four hours that they blew from that direction. It was important that we made the most of these shifts, even if brief, to make some distance to the south, which we would probably lose making leeway to the north, as the wind appeared to be settled in the second quadrant.

13 May
At midnight we put about to steer ENE5°N, and from then until noon the following day we steered between this course and east, according to the direction of the light airs on the quarter. By noon, therefore, we had got no further than latitude 14°44' and longitude 4°44'30", both agreeing with our dead reckoning position and almost confirming that we were no longer at the mercy of adverse currents.

In the early hours of the afternoon the wind shifted to SEbyE, when we went about to SbyW. It was to be assumed that on successive days the wind would veer further south as the new monsoon approached. Consequently we used this light breeze to make some distance to the south, as today's observations placed us at least 16' north of the latitude of the Mariveles entrance, according to M. D'Après' chart. 105 [14th] In fact, by remaining on the same tack until four o'clock in the morning, when the breeze set in from the south, we were able to reach the latitude of 14°28'23" by noon the next day. The longitude by number 72 was 4°48'20" and variation by western amplitude 1°33'NW in pleasant weather.

Before noon we repeated the observations of lunar distances to confirm, for the third time, whether the differences to the west according to number 72 remained constant. The mean of sixteen sets of distances was 1°15' to the west of the result given by the chronometer. Therefore we could no longer doubt that we were further from our destination. If we add to this the weakness and scarcity of the wind, the few signs of improvement before the end of this lunar cycle, the continuing discrepancies of position to the west and the excessive heat, reaching 86·8° by the wardroom thermometer, it is certain that this passage, although brief, is becoming one of the most uncomfortable and laborious that we have had.

[1] For Gentil see p. 268, n. 1.

15 May

However, the weather was so constantly fine that its mildness compensated, in part, for the tedious delays caused by the adverse winds and currents. The observed longitude of 5°13'58" still indicated 10' of difference to the west and on reaching latitude 14°32'23", there was a difference of 6' to the north. The continuing light airs from between SSW and SE, with a few intervals when they were slightly fresher, inevitably caused errors in our dead reckoning which we perhaps attributed to the currents. On this day's run, at least, it would not have been easy to calculate the distance made good, to even a moderate degree of accuracy, with the log-line. [16th] The truth is, that either for this reason or because of the effects of the currents, our observed longitude at noon of 5°23' was 8' west of our dead reckoning position, while our latitude of 13°31'27" was in agreement with it.

The light airs from the second quadrant did not set in until nightfall, when the breeze freshened from ESE, backing to ENE, and then, at midnight, to NNE. [17th] We altered course accordingly, steering east, close hauled, when possible. By this means we were able to reach the longitude of 5°46', although our position by dead reckoning was 15' further to the east. Latitude by observation was 14°16'42", as it was by dead reckoning. We could no longer doubt that these differences to the west were caused by the currents for, as well as these discrepancies, the effects of the currents were apparent on the surface at times, as we noted this morning. When we took observations for longitude at half-past five this afternoon, however, we noted that up to that time the currents had not had any effect.

At the time of these last hour angles the longitude was 6°00' east of Macau by number 72 and 5°14' by number 105. If the former were correct our proximity to land obliged us to keep a good look-out during the night, although at sunset there was no land in sight with visibility eight leagues. Our confidence in the distances, which have seldom differed by as much as they do now, and the longitude as given by number 72, which we had considered the more reliable, led us firmly to believe that the results given by number 105, being closer to the distances run, were in fact more dependable.

The night was clear, with lightning to the NE and SE and the wind light from north and NbyE. [18th] At dawn there was no land in sight, bearing out my conjectures, as we had sailed thirty-four miles steering EbyN and ENE and, in good visibility, we still could not see the coast when, according to number 72, it should have been in sight. Shortly afterwards the wind dropped and veered to NE, leaving only a few light airs around noon, when our observed latitude was 14°13'45", 8' south of our dead reckoning position. The longitude by number 72 of 6°35' showed the same difference to the west.

At three o'clock a fresh breeze set in from NW, enabling us to steer east under full sail, but soon the sky began to darken, with thunder and lightning from the SE and east. At a quarter to six we thought we could see either Lubang or Cabra Island, bearing S36°E, five or six leagues, distant. The darkness increased in that quarter, so that we were unable to sight it again, as we had hoped to do. By sunset the weather was looking worse, with closer and more frequent thunder and lightning. As a result we had no choice at nightfall but to continue under topsails alone while waiting to see where the wind would settle, as it was now threatening us from different points of the compass between NE and south. At half past seven the light airs backed to SE and immediately fell calm, and then veered to NW and freshened a little. We continued to steer to the east until half past eight, when it shifted suddenly, forcing us to tack to NNE under lowered topsails. The wind was not long in returning to the NNE, when it began to rain very heavily, with brief pauses. The night could not have looked worse, making it clear that we could not increase sail with the aim of being off the entrance to Manila Bay at dawn. It was certainly hazardous to steer to the east on such a dark night in conditions which appeared to portend the beginning of a *colla* (as the South-west Monsoon gales are called), but our lack of bread and the poor state of the stores gave us no room to consider other measures which the safety of the ship would demand in different circumstances.

The showers, and what little wind there was, ceased entirely after midnight, [19th] and at half past one light airs got up from SW when, with conditions having improved somewhat, we hoisted all sail. This did not last long as at daybreak the weather looked as threatening as it had the previous evening at sunset. This reduced the visibility and thus prevented us from sighting land. The wind, accompanied with heavy downpours, was variable from the second and third quadrant, and strong at times. At seven o'clock it backed to south and although it was still squally from various directions, principally from east, we crowded on sail, while we could see showers in the distance as the wind was settling between south and SSW, with brief downpours.

In our assumed position at about noon, by dead reckoning from our observed position yesterday, we were surprised that we could still not see land, particularly Lubang Islands or Fortune island,[1] which according to our latitude could not be far off, unless there were strong currents setting us either offshore or to the north. This could not be verified, as the Sun was invisible and it was unlikely that the sky would clear, as was indeed the case.

While we were in this state of uncertainty as to our true position, at about midday the Lubang Islands, and then the Fortune Island, came into view. To make up for the lack of observations of both latitude and longitude, we measured a base to determine our distance from the former and, consequently, the bearing and distance to the entrance to Manila Bay. We assumed that the position of these islands in relation to Manila was accurate enough for us to be able to steer directly for the entrance, in case the weather closed in again, as seemed likely. The base gave a distance of twenty-two miles from the SE extremity of Lubang, which bore SSE.

At noon we had reached a position where the main entrance [to Manila Bay] bore EbyN, where we were delayed. The SW wind had dropped considerably, and on the horizon a few showers concealed the land. At one o'clock Corregidor Island bore ENE, and accordingly, at two o'clock, we altered course to ENE5°N, making for Boca Chica of Mariveles[2] and Corregidor, which was now in transit with La Monja.[3] A few brief downpours then began to fall, hiding the entrance marks, but we continued towards the entrance with wind of very variable strength from the third to the fourth quadrant.

---

[1] Not identified.
[2] A small wooded island, 119 metres high, 19 miles WNW of Cape Santiago.
[3] I.e. present day North Channel between Mariveles Bay and Corregidor Island.

Before nightfall we were between Mariveles Bay and La Monja.[1] From there we steered NEbyE, noting a considerable error in the position of these parts of the entrance on M. D'Après' chart,[2] for if we had followed it we would have had to steer two points further east from this position, a very surprising error for a navigator of such repute who has sailed in these waters. From the moment when the eastern point of Corregidor bore south, we kept on the same course to clear San Nicholas Shoals. When we had run this distance we altered course to ESE, sounding fifteen fathoms, and continuing under topsails and foresail. [20th] After midnight we came up on the wind with the intention of making for the Cavite anchorage, if the wind continued and the lights showed us the position of the town. We were soon deprived of both these aids, and anchored in ten fathoms, soft clay. The calm continued until dawn, when we set sail with light airs from SSE, but we made little ground to windward. However, during a squall the wind settled in WSW, and we made our way towards the *Descubierta* (which we saw to be completely unrigged), and anchored near her in five fathoms. The frigate *San José y las Animas* was ready to set sail for the entrance, being bound for San Blas in company with the schooner *Mexicana*,[3] under the command of the naval officers Don Manuel Quimper and Don Cosme Bertodano.

Don Alejandro Malaspina then arrived on board, informing me that he had been obliged to return to this port on the 12th of last month, after recognizing that it was impossible to survey the coast from here to Cape Bojeador with reasonable accuracy, either going or returning. He added that he had sent Don Francisco Viana, with coastal pilots, in a small vessel to carry out this mission by land or by sea. At the same time Don Fabio Ali Ponzini and Don Felipe Bauzá had been employed before the return of the *Descubierta*, in compiling a chart of this great bay, with soundings, while the Pilotos Maqueda and Llanos[4] had linked together the results of previous partial surveys of the opposite coast [of Luzon]. In the afternoon the chronometers were taken to Manila; the different longitudes calculated by them are shown by comparison with number 71, which has maintained a uniform rate for a considerable period.

Difference of longitude between Macau and Manila, according to chronometers 72 and 105, compared on the 21st with number 71 from the *Descubierta*.

Number 71 fast on mean time	−	2h 45′	59″⅓
Number 72 slow on number 71	+	2	59	21
Difference or number 72 slow on mean time	+	0	13	21⅔
From [chronometer] log at Macau		0	20	29
Difference between the meridians in time			33	50⅔
Longitude east from Macau		8°	27	40
Longitude of Manila[5]		120	53	30

[1] La Montaña in the original MS, which is clearly a transcription error for La Monja, which is confirmed by Bustamente, *Diario general del viaje*, p. 350.

[2] It must have given satisfaction to detect 'a considerable error' in D'Après de Mannevillette's reckoning, especially if Bustamante was aware of French views of Spanish geographical inefficiency: 'they do not even know the shoals surrounding the island of Luçon': Dunmore, *Journal of La Pérouse*, p. 522.

[3] According to Malaspina the name of this schooner was the *Valdés*: see p.326. A vessel with this name was transferred from San Blas to Manila in 1791: Thurman, *Naval Department of San Blas*, p. 203, n. 1.

[4] Segundo Piloto Vicente Llanos, who had assisted Bauzá in his survey of Manila Bay: see p.315.

[5] The longitudes of Manila and Macau have been computed from Greenwich and not Cádiz: see p. 339, n. 2.

Difference or longitude of Macau		112 25 50	

Number 105

Number 71 fast on mean time	−	2h 45′ 59″½	
Number 105 slow on number 71	+	6 03 24½	
Difference or number 105 slow on mean time	+	3 17 25	
From [chronometer] log at Macau	+	2 46 44	
Difference between the meridians in time		0 30 41	
Longitude east from Macau		7° 40 15	
Longitude of Manila		120 53 30	
Difference, or longitude of Macau		113 13 15	

Number 11

Number 71 fast on mean time	−	2h 45′ 59″⅓	
Number 11 slow on number 71	+	3 25 59⅓	
Difference or number 11 slow on mean time[1]	+	40 00	
From [chronometer] log at Macau	+	08 13	
difference between the meridians in time		0 31 47	
Longitude east from Macau		7° 56 45	
Longitude of Manila		120 53 30	
Difference, or longitude of Macau		112 56 45	

21 May

The identical meridian difference between Manila and Macau of 7°18′, given unanimously on the passage to that port by chronometers 72 and 105 differs, as may be seen, from that of the return trip, by 1°10′ for the former and 22′ for the latter. The longitude ascribed to Macau by Captain King[2] differs by 11′ to the east from that of our outward passage, but as it was taken from distances previously observed and then calculated with a single chronometer after reaching port, the difference is not surprising, nor is the fact that ours is the longitude chosen for charts, as, having been taken in a period of only twelve days at sea by two chronometers of uniform rate, ours is still preferable to that taken from King's distances. Furthermore, our distances observed on the 11th, 13th and 14th of this month also agree closely with this assumption; the same meridian difference found on the outward trip is also found to within a minute of the time differences given for the year '88, but we do not know who made the observations, nor to which absolute observation in Macau it refers.[3]

---

[1] 'tpo verdº' = *tiempo veradero* (apparent time) in the original MS which is surely a transcription error for 'tiempo medio' (mean time) to agree with the computations for chronometers 72 and 105 and the corresponding entry in Bustamante, *Diario general del viaje*, p. 351.

[2] 113°47′: Cook and King, *Voyage to the Pacific Ocean*, III, p. 442.

[3] Macau is approximately 113°33′ east of Greenwich and Manila 120°57′, making the meridian distance between them 7°24′ which compares favourably with 7°18′ obtained by Bustamante on his passage to Macau.

CHAPTER 4

Viana's Account of his survey of the Coasts of Pangasinan, Ilocos and Cagayan

18 April
Having received the final orders from the Comandante, a wide-ranging passport from the Governor, and the kind letters of introduction from the Very Reverend Provincial Fathers of San Agustín and Santo Domingo, whose friars administer the provinces that I was to pass through, I departed from Manila River at seven o'clock in the morning of 18 April, accompanied by Segundo Piloto Don Gerónimo Delgado and Seaman Gerónimo Arcangel. I carried with me pocket chronometer number 351 by Arnold, which had been rated in Manila, theodolite number 3, a sextant made by Nairne, a marine compass and a log-line. Our route was to take us directly to Arayat,[1] crossing the bay to the mouth of the Betis River.[2]

Accordingly, we followed the coast along the NE part of the bay in a *panga*,[3] and, after a run of eight leagues, we reached the bar at the entrance [to the river]. Once we had crossed the bar we continued between the leafy banks of the Betis River, with groups of huts here and there, used for cutting firewood and nipa palms.[4] The lower reaches of the river trend north to NNW for about the first five miles, then continue in the direction of the first and fourth quadrants as far as the town of Guagua, which is well placed on the river bank at a distance of about four leagues from the bar.

After making all the necessary arrangements in this town for the safe transport of the instruments, we set out the following day on our journey by land, passing through the province of Pampanga to Lingayen,[5] the principal town of the province of Pangasinan. The road is extremely agreeable, both because of the delightful luxuriance of the vegetation throughout and also because of the hospitality, as obliging as it is unobtrusive, and the most active assistance to be found at every step.

---

[1] Present day Arayat is situated close SE of Mount Arayat (p. 318, n. 4). Viana's route was not direct, taking him through the low-lying land to the east of Zambeles and Cabusilan Mountains.
[2] Betis River flows into the NW part of Manila Bay 4 miles east of Orani River.
[3] A local craft propelled by sails and oars.
[4] Used for thatching houses, but nipa palm was also used in producing Pampanga wine; in addition it had various medicinal uses.
[5] Situated at the southern end of Lingayen Gulf.

The *alcalde mayor* of the province of Pampanga, Don Pablo Biron, who lives in the principal town, Bacolor,[1] moved by a sincere desire to serve His Majesty to the best of his ability, sent instructions round the entire district for us to be given all the help we might need. The Reverend Fathers of Santo Domingo and San Agustín carried out this order with benevolent zeal as well as lodging us most kindly in their monasteries and showing, by their active measures, the extent of their influence over the natives, undoubtedly won by gentleness, love and kindness, all these being virtues that I have observed to be most characteristic of the members of both orders. The nature of the native priests is not comparable since, sharing the customs of the Indians, they are as the mass of the people. It is clear, at first glance, that they have little influence, not only in being unable to uphold the dignity of their office, but also because of their inactivity which prevents them from putting any idea into effect, however limited it may be. I became increasingly fixed in this opinion when I noticed the difference between the towns administered by the Spanish missionaries and those under the native Filipino parish priests. The former, one can often see, are orderly, their towns are well situated and kept clean, the people are hard working, public schools are well attended and natives well dressed, while in the latter one sees widespread idleness, indolence, neglect and laxity, evils which cannot be corrected until the parishes are returned to more industrious hands, whose efficacy is already thoroughly proven and whose principles are well known in these islands.[2]

Don Alejandro Malaspina's instructions included the acquisition of political information as well as the exercise of our professional skills, although preference was always to be given to the latter. In view of this and the fact that the season was fairly advanced, to carry out the former instruction would require me to spend longer in the towns and thus misuse our very limited time. It therefore seemed to me more prudent to suggest that the *alcaldes mayores* give prompt and carefully considered answers to various questions which I left in writing with the *alcalde mayor* of Pampanga for that purpose, intending to check them against those of the *alcaldes mayores* of the other provinces, whom I likewise implored to have their answers ready for my return at the end of May.

20 April

We would undoubtedly have reached the town of Lingayen on the 20th if I had not found, from Arayat to Paniqui,[3] a state of apathy among the native leaders and clergy, in whom I observed, despite having informed them of my destination and shown them my passport, a boundless indolence and a most reprehensible neglect of their duties. In these circumstances we were very eager to reach the towns administered by the Dominican Fathers, as there we would be able to see most of our wishes fulfilled.

---

[1] Bacolor, 35 miles NW of Manila, was the seat of the Spanish government during the British invasion of the Philippines (1762–4).

[2] No native Filipino would accept this rosy picture, which is typically Eurocentric, as is the contempt for the native clergy. This widespread attitude, one of the colonizers' greatest mistakes, continued into modern times and is denounced by the Filipino Jesuit Father Hilario Lim in his *Memorial to Pius XII* (Manila, 1957); see also J. S. Cummins, ed., *Christianity and Missions 1450–1800*, Aldershot, 1997, p. xxiii.

[3] A town 31 miles SE of Lingayen.

We did indeed reach Paniqui on the afternoon of the 20th, and on the afternoon of the 22nd we arrived in Lingayen.[1]

It is not easy to give a description likely to do justice to the propitious situation of these places, and particularly to the great fertility of the soil; it is fair to say, however, that not a single space can be seen whose luxuriance does not proclaim earth's bounty and the generous hand of nature. The perfect situation of the towns, close to each other, made the scene more picturesque, with the excellent paved roads that lead to them, the blending of colour in the fields, surrounded by high mountains, and the arrangement of the towns, which, with their external adornments, remind us of the felicity of rustic life. In general the houses are built of nipa palms and cane, some are of boards, most of the monasteries are of stone, and the streets are perfectly straight, running between cane fences, and planted with bonga,[2] manga,[3] camachil[4] and other trees which make the air aromatic, soft, and pleasant to breathe.

According to the information we had acquired since our departure from Manila, we had thought that it would be easy to survey the greater part of the coast linking various places together by a series of triangles. However, on our arrival at Lingayen these hopes were thwarted when we were told by Don Manuel Martínez and the Fathers of local conditions and the slow pace of any work performed in that district. These considerations persuaded us that we should carry out the survey by sea, which would undoubtedly take much less time, without compromising the accuracy of the work. Furthermore, Don Alejandro Malaspina had left all these considerations to my judgement and had told me that in the port of Salomague or at Solot[5] I would receive word from Don Juan Ker, the *capitán* and owner of the schooner *Santa Isabel*, which he would place at my disposal. The weather would also favour our intentions, and accordingly I asked Don Manuel Martínez, the present *alcalde mayor*, to provide me with a vessel capable of making the passage to Cape Engaño[6] and return. He immediately applied himself to this task with great energy, but his efforts were in vain as it was impossible to find a suitable craft. It seemed preferable, however, even at the cost of greater expenditure, to go to Vigan[7] by sea and undertake the operation from there, either with Ker's vessel or with a *pontín*, so we did not hesitate for a moment when deciding upon our departure. I asked him to supply me with a *parao*[8] and, with all preparations completed, we set sail on the morning of the 24th with a light southerly breeze and followed the delightful banks of the Agno River,[9] crossing its bar at half past ten in the morning.

---

[1] These two paragraphs throw interesting light on both Malaspina and Viana, showing the former's interests and his practical methods and the latter's contempt for the natives, especially the native clergy.

[2] The fruit of the areca palm: see Blair and Robertson, *The Philippine Islands*, LV, pp. 736-8.

[3] For the manga tree (*mangifera indica*), see Blair and Robertson, *The Philippine Islands*, LV, p. 742.

[4] The Camachil (*Pithecolobium dulce*) is one of the commonest trees in the Philippines; besides producing fruit it has various medicinal usages and its bark is used for dyeing.

[5] A sheltered anchorage off the mouth of a cove, 1¼ miles SSE of Solot Point, 9 miles north of Salomague Harbour.

[6] The NE point of Luzon.

[7] Close east of Dile point.

[8] A Malay word for a small vessel.

[9] The southern shore of Lingayen Gulf is formed by the delta of the Agno River. Presumably Viana made his departure from one of the mouths of the river near the town of Lingayen.

Although I was not fully satisfied with pocket chronometer number 351, as its movement might have been affected by the overland journey to Lingayen, it did not seem necessary, nevertheless, to stop to verify and correct its rate. We therefore contented ourselves with taking hour angles on the meridian of the church of San Isidro,[1] where I intended to rate it by absolute altitudes on our return. We were further encouraged in this decision by our confidence in the position of Cape Bojeador, which would probably be confirmed by the *Atrevida* on the voyage to Canton, and that of Balingasay Point,[2] the northernmost[3] point of the Zambales coast,[4] which we had fixed from the *Descubierta* at the beginning of April.

The breeze continued steady from south and SE until twelve o'clock, when it backed to north but remained light. At noon we were in latitude 16°5′15″ and longitude 0°51′49″ west of Manila. The mouth of the Agno River, in transit with the church of San Isidro, then bore S5°W, Santo Tomás[5] N63°E, and the northernmost point of land N20°E.

25 April
As the fresh northerly breeze would enable us to reach the vicinity of Cape Bolinao by dawn, and definitely did not allow any other course which might have been preferable, we decided to continue towards that point with the dual object of using it on our return to confirm the results of our subsequent work, and to make best use of the sea breeze in the morning. We were able to carry out this plan, even though there was a calm early on the morning of the 25th and a few squalls from the SW, because these were brief, and were dissipated as the Sun rose and the land breeze set in. Although the wind was moderate, we were able to make observations for longitude one and a half miles from Cape Bolinao, and at noon, on the parallel of the point, we were in latitude 16°25′4″ and longitude 1°6′00″.

Having concluded our observations and with the breeze now settled in the west, we altered course to EbyN and ENE, heading for Arigayo Point[6] with the intention of anchoring in its lee and collecting firewood and water nearby. As the wind allowed us to make five or six knots, we were able to anchor in the early hours of the afternoon and, early the following morning, we were ready to set sail with the land breeze. When we had cleared the points we tried to measure bases for the purpose of surveying the coast, as we had done the previous day, but all our attempts were in vain. Bearings could not be taken in less than a quarter of an hour, nor could they be observed within less than three or four degrees. We therefore abandoned the attempt, and only

---

[1] A village adjacent to Mount San Isidro, an 800-metre peak 4 miles SSW of the western mouth of the Agno River.
[2] A low wooded point forming the northern extremity of Cape Bolinao.
[3] 'la mas occidental' = the most western, which seems to be a slip for 'la mas septentrional' = the most northern, a slip Viana repeated on the way south: see p. 370, n. 6 below.
[4] The Zambales coast appears to extend to the northern extremity of the peninsula forming the western side of Lingayen Gulf rather than the northern border of Zambales Province.
[5] A town on the eastern shores of Lingayen Gulf, 18 miles NE of Lingayen.
[6] Darigayos Point, 40 miles NE of Bolinao Point. On his way south Viana referred to Darigayos Point as Namapacan Point: see p. 370, n. 1 below.

took observations for longitude on the meridians of prominent features and of latitude on the parallels of others, with the double objective of using them as a comparison for our work on our return and to allow us to make good the most convenient course at night.

At noon Santa Cruz River[1] bore S85°E, the entrance to Candon Bay[2] N38°E, Santa María Point[3] N20°E, and Mount Sobobalo[4] N16°E, at which time our position was latitude 17°2'48" and longitude 0°35'20"[west of Manila].

27 April
With the land breeze and the sea breeze constantly in our favour, we were able to reach Cambayan River,[5] as we desired, at eight in the morning of the 27th. Horses were immediately provided, and at nine o'clock I greeted Don José Sánchez, the present *alcalde mayor* of the province of Ilocos, who resides in the town of Vigan. He gave me the satisfactory news that Capitán Ker was at anchor in the port of Solot. Accordingly, I begged him to send an urgent message to the *capitán*, assuring him that however unfavourable the weather I would reach the port between eight and nine in the evening. With this intention I returned as quickly as possible to Cambayan, and between eleven and twelve o'clock we had crossed the bar. At first the northerly wind, although light, was favourable to our course, but it soon veered to the NE and dropped. However, we were able to reach the port under oars at ten thirty that night, anchoring near the schooner *Santa Isabel*, whose *capitán* had left early for Vigan on private business.

In order to produce a plan of the harbour we measured a base line of 986 English feet[6] on its NE beach at dawn on the 28th, having previously placed flags at the extremities of the reefs and in the middle of the shoals. Before we began to take bearings we saw Capitán Ker, who immediately made a sincere offer of help with any of our work. I therefore asked him if he would use his launch to take soundings in the harbour, if I determined for him the points to which he was to take the bearings, at the time of obtaining soundings, which had to be at intervals of five minutes.

At noon our observed latitude was 17°41'20" and in the afternoon we took hour angles which gave a longitude of 0°32'57"[west of Manila]. Having completed our observations and taken bearings to Solot Point, we returned on board at three o'clock and shortly afterwards Capitán Ker also arrived, having completed his task. With our work now finished, we proposed to get under way, the wind being then from NE, but the attempt was soon frustrated by a contrary wind from west and WNW.

We weighed anchor at first light and set sail with a light easterly breeze. Once clear of the shoals we set a course for Salomague Harbour. At sunrise the wind fell to a flat calm, but with the aid of a tow from the launch we reached the harbour at half past

---

[1] Situated 30 miles south of Dile Point.
[2] Candon Anchorage, situated south of Candon Point and 22 miles south of Dile Point.
[3] Situated 14 miles SSE of Dile Point.
[4] Tetas de Santa, prominent twin peaks 650 metres in height, 7 miles SE of Dile Point.
[5] One of several rivers, possibly the Abra River, which enter the sea through a delta between Dile point and Santa, 8 miles SE.
[6] Viana was presumably using an English Gunter's chain, developed in 1620 by Edmund Gunter, professor of astronomy at Gresham College, London.

ten. The launch was immediately sent to place flags on the shoals and at the extremities of the reefs. At noon our observed latitude was 17°44′42″ and the hour angles gave a longitude of 0°33′12″[west of Manila].

At one o'clock we took the launch to the SE beach of the harbour, where we measured a base of 675 English feet with the intention of making a plan of the harbour. We then took bearings of the second point of Solot, finishing just at sunset. Capitán Ker, who was in charge of taking soundings of the entire anchorage, also completed his work at the same moment. When he returned to the point we went on board together.

30 April

That night we came to an agreement with Capitán Ker that on the morning of the 30th he would take Segundo Piloto Delgado and myself to Salomague Point, from where we planned to take additional bearings to fix the NE extremity of the island of that name. Meanwhile he would make his way to the anchorage off that island, where we intended to measure another base in order to fix the position of the outer shoal, over which a *parao* was to station itself with a flag flying from its mainmast. I asked him to send us the launch as soon as we hoisted a flag, which we did at eight o'clock, and soon after that we went over to the island, where we measured a base of 928 English feet on its eastern beach. After taking the bearings we made an observation for longitude of 0°34′31″[west of Manila] and at noon our latitude was 17°45′15″.

At two o'clock in the afternoon, a fresh breeze having set in from west and WNW, we set sail, clearing Salomague Island, and then setting a course parallel to the coast at a distance of two to three leagues. During the night the wind dropped completely until the early morning of 1 May, when a fresh breeze set in from ENE. We began our survey, measuring bases and taking hour angles on the meridians of prominent features. At noon, when on the parallel of Port Currimoa,[1] we sighted the higher ground of Cape Bojeador. Our position was then latitude 18°1′59″ and longitude 0°38′37″[west of Manila], while Vigan Inlet bore S21°E, the western point of Currimao S89°E, Mount Llarra[2] N59°E and the higher ground of Cape Bojeador N38°E.

The information that we had received about the schooner *Santa Isabel* before our departure from Manila led us to expect that we would probably complete our work on board her, but on leaving the harbours of Solot and Salomague we found that this was not to be the case, when we noticed that the pumps were too frequently in use. Surprised by this, we made inquiries of the *capitán*, who told us that the schooner would soon need to be careened for a complete repair, as all the seams were sprung. With this news we realized that we could only make use of her with the wind astern and, as the season was now so advanced, that we could not lose an instant in carrying out our mission, I assured him that the voyage would be over upon our arrival at Aparri.[3]

---

[1] A cove, which provides indifferent shelter during the North-east Monsoon, 29 miles south of Cape Bojeador.
[2] Situated 10 miles SSE of Cape Bojeador on 'Carta general del archipiélago de Filipinas (northern sheet)', but not identifiable on modern charts and maps.
[3] Situated on the north coast of the island, 60 miles east of Cape Bojeador.

From midday the wind began veering to the fourth quadrant, and at half past three we were obliged to tack to seaward, on which we measured bases, repeating the bearings taken previously. We finished at five o'clock, when we tacked back towards the land with a northerly breeze, intending to approach the cape so as to allow for a course overnight which would place us in a favourable position at dawn, but our efforts were all in vain. Our intentions were thwarted by the weakness and variability of the wind, forcing us to abandon the measurement of bases and observe only latitudes and longitudes at suitable positions.

Although the unsettled weather was an inconvenience for us, our anxiety was allayed by our knowledge of the exact positions of Cape Bojeador, Bangui Point,[1] the most NE point of Luzon Island,[2] and some of the Babuyan Islands.

5 May
At dawn on the 5th Linao Point[3] was visible, although indistinctly, and soon we could see the church of Aparri. We would undoubtedly have reached the anchorage if the wind had not dropped completely. Very early in the morning a *panga* came alongside and took us to the north beach of the islet, which lies in the mouth of the Cagayan or Tajo River, where we measured a base of 1,272 English feet, remaining there to fix all the points in sight.

At two o'clock in the afternoon we were able to reach the schooner *Santa Isabel*, which was anchored near the Santo Domingo monastery, where we intended to land with the intention of paying our respects to the fathers and of finding out if a reply had arrived from the present *alcalde mayor* of the province of Cagayan, Don Manuel Garray, to whom I had written beforehand to ask his help in finding us a vessel with which to finish our survey and return to Lingayen. Soon after our arrival we were informed that the *alcalde mayor* was already in the town and, on finding him in the monastery, he assured me that he had come down from Lal-lo,[4] the principal town of the province, with the sole object of helping me in any way possible.

6 May
Although there were *pontines* on the river, they were all laid up at present, and none could be made ready for us until the 8th or 9th. For this reason, and so as not to waste the 7th and 8th, we came to an agreement with Capitan Ker to leave for Cape Engaño on the night of the 6th, which we managed with the help of a tow from the two *pangas* and the small launch. Once clear of the island in the river-mouth, and with a fresh breeze that had set in from the south, we steered directly for the island of Cape Engaño[5] and at dawn it was in sight, about four leagues distant. As there was no wind at all at the time, except for light airs from various directions, we approached it

---

[1] Situated 21 miles NE of Cape Bojeador on 'Carta general del archipiélago de Filipinas (northern sheet)', which corresponds to Mayraira Point on modern charts and maps.
[2] Escarpada Point, the NE extremity of a grey, rocky promontory, which forms the NE extremity of Luzon.
[3] The western entrance point of Cagayan River, one of the major rivers of Luzon, flowing from south to north and entering the sea west of Aparri, its eastern entrance point.
[4] Situated on the Cagayan River, 9 miles south of Aparri.
[5] Cape Engaño is the northern point of Palaui Island, off the NE extremity of Luzon.

being towed by the launch. At noon the SW extremity of the island bore N65°E, five miles distant, and our observed latitude was 18°32′11″.

These conditions remained unchanged until four o'clock in the afternoon, when, with a moderate breeze from SE, we made for Machon Point,[1] and at ten o'clock that night we dropped anchor in six fathoms, clay, half a mile from the mainland shore, and the same distance from San Vicente Island.[2]

The *Segundo Piloto* and I set out in the small launch at dawn on the 8th with the intention of identifying Cape Engaño and drawing up a plan of Port San Vicente.[3] Having passed Machon Point and sighted the cape, we soon saw Malaque Point,[4] the westernmost point of land that we managed to survey. We then made our way to the NE beach of the island, where we measured a base of 880 English feet, after which we went over to a small island near the cape[5] and took new bearings. We then made for Machon Point and measured a base of 1,024 feet on the nearby beach, with the aim of beginning our survey of the port, taking our soundings with the small launch.

Having concluded our survey at four in the afternoon, we set sail for Aparri with the wind settled in the SE, and began measuring bases when we were on the meridian of the SW point[6] of [Palaui] island. By sunset we had already linked Fuyay Point[7] into our survey, as we had wished, so as to be able to make six or eight leagues during the night and be in sight of it, and close to Aparri, at dawn. We began measuring bases as soon as the Sun had risen, taking Fuyay Point for our first bearing.

9 May
At noon on the 9th we were in latitude 18°24′26″ and longitude 0°47′50″ east of Manila; the church of Aparri bore S69°W, the westernmost point of Camiguin Island[8] N17°E, and Linao Point N89°W.

The weather conditions were entirely favourable for the course we were steering and at three o'clock in the afternoon we were able to anchor near the monastery. The [missionary] father came on board soon afterwards, and informed us that the *alcalde mayor* had held to his undertaking and that the *pontín* was completely ready. The wind at the time was against us for our departure and it would not have been possible to leave until the tide changed and the land breeze set in. For this reason it seemed a suitable occasion for me to show, in some way, my gratitude to Don Manuel Garray and to acquire some information regarding the country, either immediately or by having him send a reply to me in Manila. Accordingly I decided to go to the town of Lal-lo in the schooner *Santa Isabel*, which was to winter there. At five o'clock we set

---

[1] Not identified, but possibly New Orleans Point, the southern extremity of San Vicente Island.
[2] A small island off the southern side of Palaui Island.
[3] Port San Vicente lies between the north coast of Luzon and the south coast of Palaui island. It is the only harbour in northern Luzon available as a refuge during the typhoon season.
[4] Not identified.
[5] Dos Hermanos, two islets close NE of Cape Engaño, of which the southern island is 46 metres high.
[6] Puerto Point.
[7] Situated 16 miles ESE of Aparri on 'Carta general del archipiélago de Filipinas (northern sheet)', near present day Buguay.
[8] The SE island of the Babuyan Islands, 21 miles NW of Cape Engaño.

out and, helped at times by the breeze and at other times under tow, we arrived and anchored near the quay.

At midnight, the tide now being with us, I returned to Aparri in a *panga*, reaching the *pontín* at four o'clock in the morning. The land breeze had by then set in. We immediately hove in the cable until it was up and down, setting sail shortly afterwards. Once out of the river mouth and clear of Linao Point we altered course to NW and, on the morning of the 10th, we began measuring bases and taking hour angles on the meridian of the point.

At noon, in latitude 18°32'13" and longitude 0°28'56"[east of Manila], we took the following bearings: Pata Point[1] N68°W, Bangan Point[2] N77°W, Masi Point[3] S67°W, and Aboluc River[4] S15°E. The wind then began shifting towards the fourth quadrant. By two o'clock it was fresh from NNW and with it we tried to clear Pata Point, which lay to windward of us. However, while on the shoreward tack during the early hours of the night, we found ourselves in six fathoms, fine sand. The wind was then almost calm and the tide was setting us strongly towards the Aboluc River. Despite using the oars we had no steerage way. For this reason, so as to wait for the ebb tide, we then anchored and, using the log line, we measured the strength of the tide, which was setting at one and a half knots to the SE.

We remained there until midnight when, having the tide now with us and the wind settled from WSW, we got under way and set a course in the fourth quadrant towards Pata Point. At dawn on the 11th we were in sight of the point and could also see the Babuyan Islands which, with Bangui Point, we linked to today's survey, although the weather was not very favourable.

At noon we were in latitude 18°46'40" and longitude 0°2'20" west of Manila; Datupire Island bore N26°E, the eastern point of Cuga N65°E, *idem* of Calaya N31°E,[5] Pata Point S40°E and the highest point of Bangui S58°W.

As darkness fell the weather became squally and threatening. The wind, which in the afternoon had been a moderate westerly breeze, settled in the south during the night, allowing us to identify Cape Bojeador at dawn on the 12th and very clearly the low ground of Bangui Point which we took as our first bearing, having steered towards it during the night.

At noon Bangui Point bore N81°E, the harbour of that name[6] S89°E, and Cape Bojeador south. According to these bearings our latitude was 18°39'13" and our longitude 0°24'42" [west of Manila]. Although the Sun was very close to the zenith, we had full confidence in our latitude observation.

The breeze remained with us until the early hours of the night, when it veered to SW and dropped, obliging us to take to the oars to keep offshore. These conditions continued until midnight, when the land breeze set in and we were able to steer

[1] Situated 32 miles WNW of Aparri.
[2] Situated 25 miles WNW of Aparri.
[3] Not identified.
[4] Abulug River, which enters the sea 12 miles WNW of Aparri.
[5] Dalupiri, Fuga and Calayan, respectively, three of the Babuyan Islands.
[6] Situated 17 miles NW of Cape Bojeador on 'Carta general del archipiélago de Filipinas (northern sheet)', but not identified on modern charts and maps. It can hardly be present day Bangui Bay, which lies between 6 and 15 miles NE of Cape Bojeador.

towards Mount Llarra, which was in sight at dawn on the 13th, as was the entire coast as far as Salomague. When the Sun had risen we began measuring bases with the land breeze, which was replaced at nine o'clock by one from NNW.

At noon we were in latitude 18°5'10" and longitude 0°35'12", when Mount Llarra bore N40°E, Culili Point[1] N73°E, and the NW point of Port Currimao S70°E.

It was now necessary for us go into either the port of Salomague or that of Solot to replenish our water and firewood. As conditions were entirely favourable, having linked Badoc and Salomague Islands during our day's survey, we altered course for the latter port. At six o'clock we anchored close to the shore so as to be able take on wood and water as quickly as possible.

These tasks were concluded by dawn on the 14th, when we got under way with a light easterly breeze, which veered to the SSW as the sun rose, obliging us to haul the wind on the port tack until twelve o'clock. It then settled in the west, when we changed tack and began measuring bases while keeping parallel to the coast.

At noon the port of Solot bore N82°E, Mount Bulagao[2] S67°E, and Vigan Inlet S39°E when, according to these bearings, our position was latitude 17°41'20" and longitude 0°41'46".

Towards sunset the wind increased and the weather outlook altered, leading us to expect an imminent and adverse change. Nevertheless we continued our work and, having linked our surveys of Santa María, San Vicente[3] and Santiago[4] Points, we finished measuring bases by the end of the afternoon.

At nightfall the weather looked ominous. There was a stiff breeze from the first and fourth quadrants and the appearances were most unpromising, but we continued under way, keeping parallel to the coast and three leagues offshore. From ten o'clock, having made twenty miles, we made alternate tacks, close hauled, with the intention of being in sight of Santiago Point by dawn.

The weather appeared threatening to midnight, with a stiff breeze from the fourth quadrant. The fact that the Moon was on the penultimate day of its cycle, seemed to herald the beginning of the new monsoon, but this did not occur. As daylight approached, conditions changed and the wind slackened somewhat, so that by dawn it was very calm, by which time the wind had veered to SE. When the Sun rose the sky cleared over the land, enabling us to begin our work without the least inconvenience.

15 May

At noon on the 15th our latitude by observation was 17°6'20" and our longitude 0°43'36", in which position Mount Abot[5] bore N33°E, the bay and town of Candon N85°E and Tagudin Point[6] S25°E.

---

[1] Situated 25 miles south of Cape Bojeador.
[2] A prominent landmark on account of its comparative isolation, 11 miles NE of Dile Point.
[3] There is no San Vicente Point on modern charts. Viana is probably referring to Dile Point since the town of San Vicente lies 2 miles NE of this point.
[4] Situated close south of Esteban Point, 15 miles SSE of Dile Point, on 'Carta general del archipiélago de Filipinas (northern sheet)', but only Santiago Cove and town are shown on modern charts and maps.
[5] Not identified.
[6] Faycudin in the original MS, which is clearly a transcription error since it is Tagudin on 'Carta general del archipiélago de Filipinas (northern sheet)' and modern charts and maps.

As darkness fell conditions seemed that same as on the previous afternoon, the breeze remaining fresh from SW until four o'clock in the morning, when the sky became completely dark, the wind rose, and we were struck by a violent squall, with loud thunderclaps and continual flashes of lightning. At dawn the sky and horizon were overcast, and we could hardly make out the land, but at sunrise the high ground on Namapacan Point[1] was visible, and at eleven, with the wind settled in the WSW, we could begin on our work.

16 May
On the 16th our position at noon was latitude 16°38′55″ and longitude 0°54′26″; Namapacan Point bore N52°E, San Fernando Point[2] S35°E, and Santo Tomás Point[3] S25°E.

At four o'clock in the afternoon, having confirmed the position of San Fernando Point, in the northernmost[4] part of Lingayen Gulf, we then altered course for Cape Bolinao. At five o'clock we sighted the islet of that name[5] and soon afterwards the cape, whose bearing at half past six was S70°E, two to three leagues distant.

We tacked all night, hoping to be close to the point by dawn. The night, although it did not look very promising, gave us no cause for alarm. At daybreak we were well placed and, with a fresh NE breeze we steered for Balingasay Point, the northernmost[6] point of the Zambales Coast. At half past seven we began measuring bases and taking observations for longitude on the meridian of the point.

17 May
At noon on the 17th we were in latitude 16°26′30″ and longitude 1°14′00″, Balingasay Point bearing S17°E, the church and town of Bolinao S69°E, and the islet of that name N83°E.

The wind, which had been variable and dropping since ten o'clock, settled in the north in the late afternoon. As we were a reasonable distance from Bolinao Harbour,[7] we made for it and were able to reach the anchorage by nightfall. Shortly afterwards I went to the town of the same name, which lies a quarter of a league from the anchorage, with the intention of chartering three *paraos*, which at dawn were to be positioned at the end of the reefs which form the entrance channel.

Immediately after day break we went ashore and measured bases on the southern and western beaches, the first being 997 English feet in length and the second 738. Having completed the plan of the harbour and taken a few soundings in it, we set sail between ten and eleven o'clock on the 18th with the wind settled in the north. At

---

[1] Darigayos Point.
[2] The NE entrance point of Lingayen Gulf.
[3] Presumably off the town of Santo Tomás on the eastern shores of Lingayen Gulf.
[4] 'la más meridional' = the most southern in the original MS, clearly a slip for 'la más septentrional' = the most northern since San Fernando Point is the NE entrance point of Lingayen Gulf.
[5] Now Santiago Island.
[6] 'la más Occid¹' = the most western in the original MS, which seems to be a slip for 'la más septentrional' = the most northern, a slip Viana made earlier on the way north: see p. 363, n. 3 above.
[7] An unimportant harbour situated between Santiago Island (see n. 5 above) and the NE side of Cape Bolinao.

noon our latitude was 16°26′20″ and longitude 1°9′20″; Cape Bolinao bore east, the town of that name south, and Balingasay Point S22°W. In this position we began measuring bases and at half past one we were able to take hour angles on the meridian of Bolinao Island. After this observation had been completed we were well placed to make for the port of Sual,[1] which we regarded as the final point of our survey, while a fresh NE wind led us to hope that we would arrive there by the end of the afternoon. These hopes, however, were dashed by the fearsome aspect which the weather took on at half past five, when the horizon in the second and third quadrants became so overcast that, although we were close to shore, we could not see the land. By then we had already fixed the position of Calamitian Island[2] and considered our survey at an end, so that our only object was to attempt to reach the anchorage while the wind was still in the NW. However, it soon swung to SE when it began to rain heavily, followed by thunder and lightning. Shortly afterwards the wind veered to SW, with equally threatening appearances. We immediately tacked out to sea and, when half way along the channel leading to the gulf,[3] hove to on the port tack, in a moderate gale from that quarter which then shifted to the west with several strong gusts. The wind then veered to the fourth quadrant, when a dreadful scene met our eyes. The fact that the Moon was in the last day of its cycle and the variability of the weather during the preceding days, led us to suspect that the new monsoon was beginning with a typhoon. In this unpleasant situation we were prepared as much for ill fortune as for good. However, the wind began to slacken at midnight and, at one o'clock, after a heavy downpour and violent thunderclaps, accompanied by lightning which left us dazzled for a considerable time, the night became tranquil. The wind, although feeble, was now settled in the east and with this and the help of the oars, we were able to reach Calamitian Island at nine in the morning, from where, tacking with the wind in the SW, we were able to make the long-desired port of Sual.[4]

At 10 o'clock we landed and, although a thin drizzle was falling, we nevertheless measured a base of 530 English feet on the SW beach of the port after which we made our way to Mangas Point.[5] Here we took bearings to the Monastery of Santo Domingo in the town of San Isidro, where we intended to rate the pocket chronometer.

Constant rain, generally with winds from the third quadrant, prevented us from measuring bases near the river to fix some of the points which we had not yet been able to link with other surveys; the rain also obscured the Sun. These conditions continued from the 19th until the 22nd when the sky cleared, although the wind

---

[1] A village and harbour in the SW corner of Lingayen Gulf. 'Jual' in the original MS which is probably a transcription error since it is 'Sual' both on 'Carta general del archipiélago de Filipinas (northern sheet)' and at an earlier mention of this port: see p. 310, n. 2 above.

[2] Cabalitian Island, 105 metres in height and wooded, in the SW corner of Lingayen Gulf, 4 miles NNE of Port Sual.

[3] Viana's meaning is not entirely clear. It seems that he had been attempting to reach Port Sual, which would have been dead to windward when the wind veered to SW, forcing him to make for the open waters of the gulf.

[4] 'Tual' in the original MS, yet another transcription error for Sual: see n. 1 above.

[5] The southern entrance point to Port Sual.

remained in the same quarter. We were then able to take hour angles and make a reliable observation of latitude. Shortly after noon the rain began again, so for the time being we abandoned our idea of going out to measure a base. On the 23rd the day dawned clear and, after taking hour angles, we went over to the SE beach of the Ayno River, where we measured a base of 1,497 feet. Having completed this and taking bearings from both ends, we measured another base of 1,264 feet on the NW beach, enabling us to tie other points into our survey. We returned to the monastery at three o'clock in the afternoon very tired after all our labours, as was only natural. In addition we were both now suffering from a high fever. This caused us to fall into a sleep, or state of lethargy, so deep that neither hunger nor the tender and careful attentions of the missionary father could wake us until one o'clock the following morning. My feelings may be imagined when I saw that the time to wind the pocket chronometer had passed and it had stopped.

This might have rendered useless all our previous work, if we had not correlated its results with more exact calculations, and if we had not always preferred these to the rate assigned to the chronometer here, and the longitude determined on our return to that observed on departure from the capital, which would probably be inaccurate because of the effects on its movement of both of the difficult and uncomfortable overland voyages. For this reason and the fact that there was now nothing we could do to rate the chronometer, we decided to return to Manila. We set out on the morning of the 24th, without omitting to note the bearing of Mount Arayat, now obscured, by means of the alignment that the Dominican fathers had established from their monastery to the Tribunal de los Mestizos using two crossed poles on the courthouse. Its bearing should have been S34°E which, having been corrected on our return, in the presence of the fathers, could not be far from the truth.

At four o'clock in the afternoon, with the instruments secured, we set out once again, choosing to travel overland through the provinces of Pampanga and Bulacan, finally reaching Manila on the afternoon of the 30th, with the legitimate satisfaction of having fully carried out our instructions, even though at the cost of considerable damage to our health.

CHAPTER 5

The Survey of the Eastern Coast of Luzon from Cape San Ildefonso to Rapu Rapu Island

The survey of the eastern coast of the island we were now visiting was an essential objective of our present tasks, particularly because until now it had been very little frequented by modern shipping although it was subject, like all other parts of the island, to a great number of commercial or military projects. This survey implied, unavoidably, in the eyes of the government the kind of scepticism necessarily linked to a lack of preliminary information. The most suitable season for work of this nature was, without doubt, the period from the middle of May until the end of July, during which the NE gales give way either to favourable calm seas or to SW breezes, already established on the coast opposite, which blow offshore with only moderate strength on this side, leaving the sea on the lee of the island smooth and easy for rowing. This tranquility of the sea, however, has its disadvantages, as it also encourages the dangerous presence of a considerable number of pirate vessels, which annually infest these waters and imperil not only shipping in general but also any vessel standing anywhere along this coast.

These reflections, and the information received in Manila regarding the position of the towns, the nature of pirate vessels and the methods of defence to be found or suitable for this coast, finally decided me in favour of a plan of operations which, for this survey, would combine the greatest possible accuracy in the shortest period of time with the safety of those who were to take part in it, for whose selection there was not the slightest doubt, as there was nobody left who was fit for work of this kind except Primer Piloto Don Juan Maqueda, and myself. The other few remaining officers of the *Descubierta* were either engaged in more important tasks, as already mentioned, or were recovering from their previous labours. The *Atrevida* had not yet rejoined us, and it would not have been be fair to set to work again immediately a group of officers still suffering from the effects of the heat, rain and hardships of the recent passages to Macau and back.

Consequently it fell to Don Juan Maqueda to examine the coast running east and south from Mauban to San Bernardino Strait, while I chose to survey the northern coast, through Lampon and Polillo [Strait] until in sight of Cape San Ildefonso. This would not keep me away from the corvettes for as long, and would allow me on my return, to chart the entire Laguna de Bay, so as to link it with the bearings taken along the banks of the Pasig River as far as its mouth and at Tagui[1] in the lagoon itself. We would both, therefore, have to travel to Mauban partially by water and partially by way of the tongue of land which includes the beautiful Mount Lucban or Majaijay[2] and then continue with the *balancianes* found there, which may well be compared with the feluccas of the coasts of Naples and Sicily.[3]

One difficulty of no small consequence complicated these operations, which was the complete lack of chronometers, with which we could have linked the work carried out by both of us with latitudes observed in the lagoon and referred to Manila. The astronomical clock in the observatory had been replaced by chronometer 71 and [in any case] it would not have been easy to carry a chronometer carefully along the routes we were to use; pocket chronometer 351 was in the hands of Don Francisco Viana.[4] The rest of the chronometers had been passed to the *Atrevida*, so we would have to be satisfied with differences of latitude. These, of course, would be calculated and linked together by an uninterrupted series of trigonometrical operations.

Maqueda was to be accompanied by Segundo Piloto Don Vicente Llanos, who had already shown an uncommon degree of zeal and application in his previous work with Don Felipe Bauzá, and by a marine in charge of the various weapons and munitions necessary to arm the *balancian*, with two trustworthy members of our crew to lead the other natives in any conflict. I was to be followed by Piloto Hurtado and other selected sailors, whose numbers I might have to increase, as the barge would have to take to the lagoon [via the Pasig River] all the instruments and tools necessary for the subsequent passages at sea along the opposite coast.

We had naturally taken the precaution of obtaining wide-ranging orders from His Excellency the Governor for the towns along our route across the island and along the coast that we were to survey. The Franciscan Father Provincial had also sent out circulars regarding both parties, to remind the parish priests of the provinces of Laguna, Tayabas and Camarines how important it was for the service of His Majesty to assist us to the full extent of their powers in all of our undertakings.

With all arrangements now made and with Maqueda provided with a theodolite, a sextant and an azimuth compass, I had no reason to delay his departure, particularly as his instructions specifically stated that he was not to impose himself on either the good will or customs of the natives. In addition, without omitting the survey of Catanduanes Island, he was to pay great attention to his own safety and that of all those who accompanied him. Finally he was to return to Manila not later than the end of July.

---

[1] A village close to where the Pasig River flows out of Laguna de Bay.

[2] Named after the nearby villages of Lucban and Maja-ya. Now Mount Banahao, a truncated cone 2,165 metres in height, 17 miles WSW of Mauban. Malaspina and Maqueda would have passed through the 10-mile wide strip of land between the mountain and Laguna de Bay.

[3] In comparing the local *balancian* with the Italian felucca (a small lateen rigged sailing boat), Malaspina was evidently recalling Italian experiences.

[4] Pocket chronometers, being smaller and more robust than box chronometers, were much more suitable for being transported long distances by land.

16 May

Accordingly he left before dawn on the 16th with the two *pangas* that were to transport him across the lagoon to Pagsanjan,[1] the principal town of the province. Hindered by NE winds, he was obliged to stop at the towns of Binangonan[2] and Jalajala.[3] However, there was some advantage to these delays, since he took bearings to various points around the lagoon from a hill close to the former town, and near the latter he measured a base, taking bearings from both ends to the peak of Talim [Island][4] which, since it was also visible from Manila, now served to join the survey of that area with the triangulation already undertaken in the [Manila] bay.

18 May

It was past 10 o'clock on the morning of the 18th when, having navigated a long stretch of the beautiful Lumban River, Don Juan Maqueda reached the town of Pagsanjan. Here, with the help of its *alcalde mayor*, he arranged for the continuation of his journey as far as Mauban, which was inevitably slow and laborious due to the rocky and difficult tracks and the necessity of transporting the arms and equipment by *carabaos*.[5]

20 May

Maqueda himself informed me of this when the *pangas* returned. The satisfactory report that he gave me made the planning for my own journey the more agreeable, in that the arrival of the *Atrevida*, which took place on the morning of the 20th, as I have mentioned, allowed me to see the complements of both vessels in perfect order and to provide myself with chronometer number 11 by Arnold, the acquisition of which in Macau, by Don José Bustamante, was due to the efficient assistance of Mr Beale, an English merchant who had undertaken various expeditions to the Northwest Coast of America in search of [sea] otter skins. This chronometer appeared to run very well, according to the comparisons made in the *Atrevida*'s last crossing and now, a comparison over two days with the observatory chronometer, indicated that it was losing at an average daily rate of 21 seconds.

25 May

With nothing remaining to delay our departure for the lagoon we left early in the morning of the 25th with a *panga* and a barge from the dockyard, manned by a crew from the *Descubierta*. I had the double satisfaction of finding that the weather now seemed settled again and very suitable for our astronomical work, while Don José Armenteros[6] had decided to accompany me. The latter had the two objects of continuing his examination of the physical geography of the island and of carefully observing the tides, in the study of which, and in the most novel and interesting comparisons, he had been occupied for several years with a remarkable and truly scientific perseverance.

---

[1] Situated on the Lumban River at the SE end of the lagoon.
[2] A town on a promontory extending from the north side of the lagoon.
[3] A town on a promontory extending from the NE side of the lagoon.
[4] The island in the middle of the lagoon.
[5] Water buffalo.
[6] See p. 280, n. 2 above.

A brief and highly enjoyable passage between the leafy banks of the Pasig River brought us to Tagui before midday, and by five o'clock in the afternoon we had reached the town of Binangonan, where we stayed until three o'clock the next morning. We then had no difficulty in reaching Jalajala Point by ten o'clock, where we measured a base and took an observation for longitude. A fresh squall from the WSW then carried us directly to the Pagsanjan bar,[1] and thus, before sunset, we had reached this provincial capital and had made the necessary arrangements for an overland crossing the following morning.

I was concerned to meet Piloto Llanos here who, despite a serious illness, had wished to accompany Don Juan Maqueda to Mauban, but finally had to give up in this town in order to speedily restore his health. He gave me a detailed account of their journey as far as Mauban, of the most recent news about the incursions of the Joloanos and of the subsequent measures taken by Maqueda until their separation, which events Don Juan Maqueda also explained to me in a letter.

Indeed, the measures taken by this most able subject [of His Majesty] could not have been more shrewd. He had not wasted a moment and, despite rain, the nature of the road and the need for care with the instruments he had managed to observe very useful bearings to various points on the lagoon from the tower of Majaijay, a large and pleasant town at the foot of the high mountain of that name. He had also asked the alcalde of Tayabas for the help he needed, and had even given notice everywhere of my own impending journey, so that I would not suffer the delays and inconveniences which he had naturally encountered. Finally, on reaching Mauban at midday on the 22nd and finding that either two *balancianes* from the town, which could be made ready in a few hours or a galley belonging to the *alcalde mayor* of Camarines, who had to return to Naga,[2] were available for the continuation of his voyage, he had chosen the latter, after consulting the parish priest, and on the afternoon of the 24th, having discharged Piloto Llanos, he set out for Naga with a favourable breeze.

Maqueda advised me that he would begin his work at the north point of Alabat [Island].[3] I had asked him to indicate this point to me beforehand, so that I could confirm the results of my observations of longitude with greater certainty. However, the information given by Llanos made this precision less necessary, as he told me that it was possible to see for a great distance from the other side of Mount Lucban itself, whose well shaped peak would serve as a very useful apex[4] for the triangulations on both sides.

27 May

The journey to Mauban of the second party, of which I was in charge, was considerably more complex than Maqueda's, because of the greater numbers of people, provisions, tools and instruments that I took with me. The Ramsden astronomical

---

[1] I.e. the mouth of the Lumban River.
[2] Situated about 90 miles ESE of Mauban, at the head of San Miguel Bay, about 8 miles NW of present day Naga City.
[3] Situated 11 miles east of Mauban.
[4] I.e. the connecting point between two systems of triangulation.

quadrant, a theodolite, a sextant, an azimuth compass, and the indispensable instruments for the following passage by sea, were all objects needing to be transported with the utmost care. We would also have to provide ourselves with all the necessary stores for about a fortnight, as the friars had warned us that the greater part of the coast we were making for was uninhabited and that the people of Polillo would be able to supply us with little or nothing. Six seamen did not seem excessive, in the end, considering that they had to undertake not only to work and defend two vessels, but also bear the responsibility for our safety when we were in uninhabited parts, at some distance from the vessel for the purpose of taking bearings, or at night when we would need to sleep after our labours.

In these circumstances it seemed to me more suitable, rather than using *carabaos*, to have our goods carried on the men's shoulders which, according to the alcalde and headmen, would be much safer and faster. In addition it would not be at all onerous for the natives, the distances between towns being very short, the loads could be divided and even the number of men for each load doubled, so that they would be able to rest as necessary.[1] The public duties payable in each province prevent any disputes in voluntary contracts of this nature. Furthermore, the *governadorcillo*[2] named two or three *cabezas de barangay*[3] to see that the goods were punctually delivered by the natives, that they were paid what they had earned and that the money was distributed correctly by the person who had contracted them for work of this kind.

It was at least eight o'clock when the party was able to leave. We reached the town of Majaijay by midday, shortly before a violent storm broke on us from the west, which would otherwise have spoilt all our bread. At four in the afternoon, when it had passed, we immediately set out again on our route for Lucban, where we arrived at nightfall.

These two towns are indeed worthy of the traveller's attention for the excellence of their position, their large population, and the good administration, public order and affluence which distinguish them. The first is enriched by immense plantations of coconut palms, from which a liquor is made of which thirty to forty *quintales* is sent annually to Manila. A double harvest of rice and resources with which to conduct a profitable trade with both the Mambulao mines and Paracale[4] in the province of Camarines on one hand and with the towns on the lagoon and the capital on the other, supply Lucban with everything necessary for its comfortable existence. In both towns one may see that most of the houses are built of wood, the streets are straight and well-paved and have pure water running in pipes on either side. The church, monastery and the town hall are well built and respectable. Finally, the inhabitants show the health, cleanliness and good spirits which are the invariable signs of affluence. Their advantageous position undoubtedly favours this well-being, for from Majaijay, which lies at a moderate elevation, the country rises rapidly to Lucban,

---

[1] An example of humane treatment of the native carriers. Similarly on 29 May Malaspina intervened to protect an over-zealous Maqueda from harming his health: see pp. 379-80 below.
[2] A kind of native justice of the peace or similar petty official, with minor executive powers.
[3] Chiefs of kinship groups consisting of between 30 and 100 families.
[4] Situated 62 miles east of Mauban. Like Mambulao (see p. 379, n. 4 below), it was formerly famous for its gold fields, but Spanish fiscal policies and the abundance of American silver prevented Philippine

where the Fahrenheit thermometer showed the temperature at sunrise to be 76°, when it would certainly not have been less than 87° or 88° in Manila at that hour. From Lucban the road to Tayabas[1] is very short and straight and the friars tell us that this town is even finer than the previous ones, lying close to the sea on the west coast,[2] near Galvan Point[3] and Marinduque Island, which we had previously surveyed with the corvettes. The road leading to Mauban descends directly ENE and, running through gullies with which the annual rains compensate for the complete lack of paths, meets the Mauban River at the foot of the mountain. The ravines through which this river flows, if followed for some distance, lead to the coast on which the town stands.

A few years ago the wealth of this town was considerable, largely arising from coastal shipping and the bartering of *balate*[4] in Polillo, Binangonan,[5] Baler[6] and Casiguran,[7] and from the women's constant labours in making mats, which are easily sold in Manila. A widespread fire and the repeated attacks by the pirates, have obliged them [the inhabitants of Mauban] to divide their efforts between repairs and defence, but everything indicates that the inhabitants will very soon recover their prosperity.

28 May
For this final part of the journey, Don José Armenteros and I had chosen to use the *jamaca* slung from men's shoulders rather than horses. The two ends of a length of strong linen, about the size of a man, are secured to a thick cane, long enough to provide enough space at either end for it to be carried on the shoulders of four natives, each carrying a stout stick in the other hand to keep his balance. All of them are extremely agile and accustomed to travelling in this way, changing places frequently with their companions. They carry the traveller in perfect safety, lying on the piece of linen, sheltered from the heat by a small roof of palm leaves, fastened to the cane itself and open on both sides.

The road was quite long, and, having taken a brief rest in a timber building which the friars have had built for shelter from storms and sudden floods, we were unable to reach Mauban until after midday. However, as we went straight to the monastery and were offered there the same welcoming hospitality that we had found in the previous towns, it was easy for us to occupy the remaining hours until nightfall in various important matters, which had to be examined.

It was indeed most unfortunate that the chronometer, which had withstood all the

---

gold from acquiring importance: Pierre Vilar, *A History of Gold and Money, 1450–1920*, London, 1976, p. 95.

[1] Situated a few miles north of Tayabas Bay on the south coast of Luzon.
[2] Actually on the south coast of Luzon.
[3] Now Bantigui Point, a wooded headland 109 metres in height, forming the western entrance point of Tayabas Bay.
[4] *Bêche-de-mer*, also known as trepang, sea-cucumber etc. An echinoderm of the genus *Holothuria* which is caught by night when, attracted by the light of a torch, it is then speared, dried and smoked. It is regarded as a luxury food by the Chinese, who usually make it into soup.
[5] A coastal village 6 miles south of Port Lampon, not to be confused with the village of the same name on the shores of Laguna de Bay.
[6] On the east coast of Luzon, 95 miles north of Mauban.
[7] A village on the north coast of Jomalig, one of the Polillo Islands.

swaying motion on horseback and in the *jamaca* without the least problem, should now stop on being placed on a table in the monastery, thus thwarting my original intention of making a direct calculation of the longitude of this spot. On realizing what had happened we shook it to set it going again, but in vain. Finally we achieved this by giving a slight push to the balance mechanism. We could satisfy ourselves with the conclusion that, having determined the same discrepancy on our return, this mishap would have no effect on the accuracy of our work.

With the arrival of the instruments, which followed close behind us, my first intention was to take a bearing to Mount Lucban and measure a base to link this spot with Alabat Island, the adjacent bay[1] and, above all, the furthest points of the coast which we could see as far as Dapdap Point, some seven or eight leagues [east] of the anchorage.[2] After sunset, a most peaceful and beautiful sight, I took the opportunity to measure some meridian altitudes of stars with the astronomical quadrant. I was still engaged in this useful task when I was interrupted, much to my pleasure, by the appearance of the botanist, Don Luis Neé, from whom I had received no word since he had disembarked in Sorsogon in March.

This skilful subject [of his Majesty], persevering as always in his work and strength, had made valuable collections for botany and other branches of natural history, exploring tirelessly along the coast and through the nearby mountains of the provinces of Albay and Camarines. Then, having embarked at Naga where there was a small flotilla of *vintas*,[3] which was ready to range the entire coast to drive off any pirates, he had made a quick crossing to the mouth of the river, where the *vintas* were now anchored. Piloto Maqueda, whom he had seen on board the galley when it was anchored at Mambulao,[4] had told him of my impending arrival, adding that two or three of the *vintas* might be employed under my orders, to sail along the north coast.

This was an opportunity not to be lost. [29th] On the following morning it was arranged that three of the seven launches would take me to Polillo and Lampon and, as the day was very calm and beautiful I observed equal altitudes of the Sun to determine our longitude, and took some meridian altitudes of other stars in the early hours of the night to calculate our latitude. As there was nothing else to do but to take bearings again from a nearby hill and study the surroundings as far as possible, at dawn on the 30th I was already under sail and making for Polillo Island.

I had of course taken care to inform the *alcalde mayor* of Camarines of these arrangements. At the same time I advised Don Juan Maqueda that, in the absence of Piloto Llanos, he should not attempt to carry out his arduous enough tasks as meticulously as might otherwise have been expected. He should therefore omit the circumnavigation of Catanduanes Island and, above all, he should make certain not to

---

[1] Probably the unnamed expanse of water between Alabat Island and the mainland.
[2] On the northernmost point of Camarines Norte Province, 30 miles east of Mauban and to the east of Alabat Island.
[3] A craft the size of a launch, small fleets of which, known as *vintas del corso*, were used to drive off the pirates. Malaspina refers to them as launches in the next paragraph.
[4] Now Port José Panganiban, a well sheltered harbour from the South-west Monsoon, on the north coast of Camarines Norte Province, 55 miles east of Mauban.

delay his return to Manila beyond the beginning of July, thus cutting short by about a month the time I had allowed him in my first instructions. These measures, which I considered very necessary, were suggested by my fear that his excessive zeal could lead him to sacrifice his health and even his life.

Having set sail for Polillo, the highest point of which was already in sight by seven o'clock in the morning, we took as many bearings and transits that we could, and repeated our observations for longitude. At midday we could clearly see the extremities of the island and the area surrounding the port of Lampon. The fresh breeze from ESE and SE continued to favour us. It was no later than three in the afternoon when we approached the southern end of the island and began coasting along the western side, half a mile off and in depths of ten to twenty fathoms, sometimes sand but generally rock.

Polillo Island is gently ridged, rising gradually towards the centre and displaying everywhere a remarkable luxuriance of vegetation that it retains throughout the year. Running northward from Mauban the coast of Luzon is much higher than this. Mount Binangonan[1] stands out among the others. It is easy to make out the majestic heights of Lucban in one direction and, in the other, the Ilongotes Mountains, which mark the end of Cape San Ildefonso at Casiguran Sound.[2]

At half past four, after having sailed a short distance, we very soon expected to reach the town on the island, which was already in sight, at the end of a small bay opening to the NNW that is formed here by the coast. However, our course was blocked by a reef running out to the west from the outer point of the harbour, with a lengthy spur to the north. As the tide was now halfway into the ebb, we could not find the entrance channel although we made several attempts to do so. It was necessary, therefore, to sail considerably further NE before we could find a suitable entrance. When we had finally succeeded to do so we made for the town in depths of seventeen to fifteen fathoms, clay, reaching it shortly before prayers.[3]

A first and very natural fear that Joloanos pirate craft were approaching had only just been dispelled among the few families that make up the town. They were aware that there were nine *pancos* belonging to privateers among the small islands lying immediately to the east;[4] they did not know of the *vintas* and had never even been visited by the coastal *balancianes*, which might have been mistaken for the launches. The friar reassured them, however, particularly when he saw our ensign, and his assumption was not unfounded.

The presbytery was immediately put at our disposal. After agreeing that early the following morning all the boys would go to the beaches at low water to collect as many as possible of the shells that we knew to be abundant in these parts, with rare

---

[1] A 1,096-metre high mountain, 5 miles SW of Port Lampon.
[2] Cape San Ildefonso is situated at the southern extremity of San Ildefonso Peninsula, which extends SSW for 18 miles. Casiguran Sound, which is 6 miles wide at its entrance, lies between San Ildefonso Peninsula and the mainland.
[3] The evening Angelus at 6 p.m. There was a chaplain with Malaspina but religious devotions on board ships were not a particularly Spanish custom.
[4] A reference to the chain of islands extending east from Polillo Island, including Patnanongan and Jomalig Islands.

species to be found, we were finally able to take the rest that we needed and prepare for the tasks of the next day.

31 May

These would not differ from our usual methods in other ports, which was to measure a base, then to verify with the theodolite, from a suitable position, the points fixed from this base or those that needed a longer one [to be measured]. Longitude would be obtained by observing equal altitudes of the Sun, [latitude] by observing the meridian altitude of the Sun with the astronomical quadrant and the variation with the theodolite and finally sounding the port and studying its possible utility.

The very fine weather enabled us to carry out all of this as planned. We were also able to include in our bearings the high ground of Baler and Casiguran and even Cape San Ildefonso, as the natives pointed out landmarks nearby to indicate their direction. Finally, we had the unexpected pleasure of finding that the most experienced headmen of the town had agreed to occupy themselves in drawing up, with all possible detail, a sort of comprehensive map of the eastern coast of the island and all the other islets and reefs, which form there a small archipelago as unpleasant and dangerous for shipping as it is useful for the very lucrative collection of *balate*.

In these circumstances I would have been wrong to sacrifice as many as fifteen or twenty days to a survey which would have had no useful result for shipping. Nor would it have taken any less time to make a detailed study of the vicinity of Baler and Casiguran, as far as Cape San Ildefonso, whose steep shores did not provide any shelter for launches. Consequently I thought it better to cross directly to Lampon, during which it would be easy for me to fix with some accuracy all the more distant points and even the northern extremities of Polillo Island, by means of bases and longitude observations.

1 June

We set out on the crossing at three o'clock the following morning, at high water, so as to be able to steer directly across the reefs. We were led by a canoe, which guided us through the various channels formed by the rocks. When it left us, about half a league from the point, we continued under oars, with the three launches close together and keeping a careful watch, to avoid any assaults by the pirates.

The somewhat heavy head sea slowed our progress, however, and at sunrise we were hardly a league and a half from the anchorage of Polillo. Although we had the satisfaction of having Mount Lucban and Cape San Ildefonso in sight at the same time, the bases which were to link them were unsatisfactory, both because of the irregularity of the currents and our slow and indirect course. Fortunately we could substitute the closer and well positioned points on the island and on the coast opposite for the bases for determining positions to which bearings of distant points were taken, these also being confirmed by observed longitudes. Thus we were not excessively disturbed by the unavoidable error. At eleven o'clock we finally approached Dinahican Point,[1] which lies between the river[2] leading to [Mount] Binangonan and

---

[1] A low, densely wooded point, 7 miles ENE of Port Lampon.
[2] Agos River, which flows into the sea 6½ miles NW of Dinahican Point.

the coast where it trends to the WNW towards Lampon, choosing to make for the latter, and shortly after midday we anchored there, not far from a wooden tower recently erected to guard the port and watch over the cultivated fields of Binangonan.

This then was the famous port of Lampon, which during the last century had been for some years the depot for the galleons and for the wealth of Manila, which it was now hoped to reestablish so as to enjoy freer and safer communication across the vast ocean to New Spain. My principal object was to survey this port and all my work was consequently directed to this end.

My first action, therefore, was to seek information from the friar at Binangonan so as to know the exact position of this area. A dense forest of mangroves made it inaccessible except for a small channel running approximately northward from Bantay or Vigia[1] which, at high water, allows canoes to come very close to Binangonan besides the cultivated fields. One of the natives undertook to carry the letter I wrote. We occupied the rest of the afternoon in taking a few bearings and soundings. One of the two friars from the town reached us before midnight, enabling us to work more energetically and accurately the next day.

2 and 3 June
We investigated the watering place and the sites of the old powder factory and the town hall. The security and capacity of the port was also examined. Despite the frequent showers we were able to repeat the equal altitudes and the meridian altitude of the Sun. The former observations gave us a period of two days to rate the chronometer, which was now $23''{\cdot}8$ slow, a loss somewhat greater than that previously noted in Manila.

It was not long before the other friar and the parish priest of Binangonan came to visit us in this dismal wilderness.[2] He, on hearing soon afterwards of my idea of crossing the lagoon by a shorter route than the one from Mauban, advised me to take, instead of the well known road through Piapi[3] and San Antonio,[4] the one from Tinuan Point, some three leagues from this port,[5] from which the natives of Binangonan could guide us to Siniloan on the lagoon[6] in a single day. We therefore decided upon this plan and, by the early afternoon of the 3rd, we had made observations of equal altitudes and everything was ready for us to set out as soon as the people requested arrived from the town.

By five o'clock, however, nobody had arrived from the town and we did not have the slightest news about them coming. This being so, with a light favourable breeze blowing from the NNE and north, I thought it better to set sail for Mauban with the three launches, abandoning this desolate place, which will always serve as a melancholy warning for those considering such projects, founded only upon old and distant accounts.

At eight in the evening we were off Point Tinuan, and at ten we were not far from the Piapi River. It was constantly necessary to resort to the oars, but after midnight we

[1] Not identified.
[2] Elsewhere, however, the lonelier places of Nature are welcomed as a means of avoiding temptation: see p. 276 n. 1 above. Once again the priests show an eagerness to meet the travellers, which suggests their own loneliness in 'these solitudes'.
[3] Piapi River enters the sea 13 miles NNW of Mauban.
[4] Not identified.
[5] No longer shown on modern charts and maps.
[6] Situated 2 miles north of the NE arm of Laguna de Bay.

were struck by violent squalls, which finally dropped at dawn, allowing us to anchor in the Mauban River and discharge the launches immediately.

4 June

Don Luis Neé was still in this town, having scoured the surrounding parts, but was preparing to cross the high sierras of Cavinti[1] the next day for a fortnight's work in the vicinity of the lagoon, until the rainy season began in earnest. After bidding him farewell, I was able, with the efficient assistance of the parish priest, to set out before nine in the morning with my people and baggage for Lucban, from where I made my way back to Pagsanjan on the lagoon on the following afternoon, with no occurrences worthy of mention on the way.

5 June

The news of the arrival of the [Acapulco] galleon at Cavite spread very quickly in this provincial capital and I was in great hopes that it would bring new orders from His Majesty for our future missions, as well as important news of the two schooners which were to sail to [Juan de] Fuca Strait next summer under the orders of Señores Galiano and Valdés. With these considerations in mind and given the fact that Don José Armenteros would probably be needed at his posting, I thought it better that he should bring forward his voyage with the barge and return directly to Manila. I would soon follow him, particularly as a good *guilalo* – a large, well manned canoe –[2] would be more useful for our coming work in the lagoon. Furthermore, Don Vicente Llanos, who was now recovered and had visited me in Pagsanjan, was now in Santa Cruz,[3] He was to carry out elsewhere some important geodetic operations, for which purpose I had given him the compass and a lead-line.

6 June

I spent all the next day in the town of Paete,[4] where a base was measured to confirm the position of all the points in that area. Altitudes of the Sun were observed to determine the latitude and longitude of the monastery, and I repeated the bearings taken at the mouth of the Lumban River. Llanos was to measure another base at Santa Cruz for the same purpose of confirming the delineation of the coast to the left, towards Bay[5] and Calamba.[6] I was therefore able to set sail for Binan[7] after midnight, and, [7th] having arrived by nine o'clock in the morning, I repeated the same astronomical and geodetic operations there. When these were finally concluded I sailed for Tagui,

---

[1] The mountainous area SE of Laguna de Bay.
[2] A smaller craft than a *pontin* with a matting sail and outriggers, used for traffic between Manila and Cavite.
[3] On the SE shores of Laguna de Bay, a short distance north of Pagsanjan.
[4] On the eastern shore of Laguna de Bay, 6 miles north of Pagsanjan.
[5] On the southern shore of Laguna de Bay, about 10 WSW of Pagsanjan.
[6] In the SW corner of Laguna de Bay, 17 miles west of Pagsanjan.
[7] On the western shore of Laguna de Bay, 22 miles WNW of Pagsanjan.

where again I took bearings to link our work with another base measured in Angono[1] by Don Vicente Llanos. Well before sunset I was in that town, with time to take some hour angles with the astronomical quadrant and observe some meridian altitudes of stars to the north and south of the zenith to determine our latitude.

8 June

The following morning a very few hours on the river found me once more in Manila, where I disembarked at nine o'clock. Here I had the satisfaction of hearing that Don José Armenteros had arrived as easily, and well before me, and that Don Vicente Llanos would arrive in two days' time.

Don Juan Maqueda, who had received in Naga my last instructions from Mauban, had by now made great progress in his work. The voyage from Mauban to Mambulao had taken him only one day and as the *alcalde mayor*'s galley had to pause in the latter town for reasons of trade, he was able to measure two bases and observe for latitude on shore. He also managed to repeat those same bearings on another point, more prominent and further from the town, to which he had to be accompanied by twelve well-armed men, as there were several pirates' *pancos* in the vicinity.

During his voyage to Naga Maqueda had not been able to survey the entire coast from close inshore, although he was able to survey the intermediate coast from a short distance off and to pass through the channels between the islands of Quinamanocon, Cavimog and Canton.[2] These coasts and the inshore waters are so strewn with reefs and, in addition, so infested with pirates, that they are dreaded for the former reason by larger vessels, which cannot be rowed, and for the latter reason smaller craft are obliged to sail with the greatest care, while still at considerable risk.

On reaching Naga by dawn on the 30th, Maqueda had to give up the galley which had brought him and fit out other vessels with which to continue his voyage. The *alcalde mayor* Don Manuel Lecaroz was most active and even generous in the measures taken to fit out another small galley of his own and two launches belonging to the province, chosen from among those that had helped me. Meanwhile His Excellency the Bishop[3] and the factor of the Real Compañía, had offered him every assistance in their powers, as well as much important information. Don Juan Maqueda was thus able, not only to arrange his departure for 5 June, but also, on the preceding days, to complete a highly detailed plan of the bay. He was also able to make a brief and very useful excursion to Pasacao[4] on the opposite coast, where he repeated from a high islet his bearings to the extremities of Burias Island, to Bondoc Head[5] and various other places that, to a great extent, we had already surveyed and charted on our voyage from Sorsogon to Manila. Crossing from one coast to the other is undoubtedly much easier and more convenient here than at any other part of the island, although the sandbanks and shoals which extend from inside Dapdap Point towards

[1] Not identified.
[2] The small islands of Quinapagyan, Caringo and Canton off the NW entrance point of San Miguel Bay.
[3] Domingo Collantes, OP. (1788–1809).
[4] Situated 21 miles north of the northern extremity of Burias Island.
[5] A 405-metre bluff at the southern extremity of Bondoc Peninsula.

the other coast make a very short route which is generally preferred by the pirates for crossing the island, and sometimes even with their own boats.[1]

The present *alcalde mayor* has built a well sited town and a hard road for this communication with Pasacao that it takes scarcely three hours to get from Naga to the new town by water,[2] and travellers and goods take as many hours again along easy and well-made paths for the journey from this town to Pasacao, where vessels going directly to Manila come close inshore.

Having left the vicinity of Naga on the 5th, with a small flotilla consisting of the galley and the two launches, Maqueda set out to continue his survey towards the southern end of the bay, before sailing for the port of Sisiran.[3] There are so many islands of varying heights and sizes to be found on this passage that it always is dangerous to stand inshore, however much of a detailed hydrographic survey of these waters might be made with all possible clarity and accuracy. Light airs were already blowing from SW, the tides were at springs and Albay [Mayon] Volcano was in sight to link the coming surveys neatly with the bearings taken on board the corvettes from the port of Sorsogon. As well as this mountain, the notorious Mount Isarog[4] stands out in the Naga area, with the impenetrable luxuriance of vegetation and isolated position which have caused it to become the haunt of a considerable number of Christian vagabonds and *Negrillos* who give themselves over to a wild and barbarous life, frequently resorting to robbery and treachery, with the prospect of an existence ill-founded on idleness and vice.[5]

Until the 8th all three vessels had to be rowed constantly to reach the port of Sisiran, anchoring at times and hindered by contrary winds and rain and by the need to guard against the proximity of the Joloanos *pangos*, a danger which urged them to exercise great vigilance. They made their way through channels between various islands, particularly Butauanan Channel,[6] finally managed to anchor in the port in order to survey it in detail and take on water and firewood.

9 June
The port of Sisiran gives better than average shelter and should be considered equally as good as the other ports of the eastern coast from which, in any season, to begin an eastward passage bound for the western coasts of America. It has taken on a greater importance in recent years, having been chosen in 1780 by the Governor, Don José Basco [y Vargas], as the departure point for a vessel [the *Princesa*] which was to take sealed documents to New Spain in November of that year. Don Francisco Mourelle, her commanding officer, was gradually set to the southward by the winds and

---
[1] The distance from the head of San Miguel Bay to Pasacao is 15 miles, whereas from the head of shoal encumbered Basiad Bay (to the east of Dapdap Point) to the head of Ragay Gulf is 12 miles and from the head of Calauag Bay (to the west of Dapdap Point) to the head of Ragay Gulf is about 7 miles. If the pirates intended to carry their boats overland they would obviously prefer the shorter route.
[2] Via the navigable Bicol River, which flows into the head of San Miguel Bay.
[3] Sisiran Bay, which provides good sheltered anchorage SE of Quinalasag Island, about 30 miles ESE of the NE entrance to San Miguel Bay.
[4] An extinct volcano about 17 miles east of the mouth of the Bicol River.
[5] Renegade Spaniards who 'turned native' aroused horror because they were thereby rejecting their civil status, and worse, abandoning their religious faith and with it all hope of salvation.
[6] Quinalasag Passage, south of Quinalasag Island.

currents as far as the latitude of 28° S, where, fortunately coming upon the Friendly Isles [Tonga], he was able to make good to some extent a sudden shortage of water and wood, and then to return, after five months, to the Marianas and to take the usual route from there to San Blas.[1]

Don Juan Maqueda's survey work in the port of Sisiran was somewhat difficult, as the few inhabitants had previously mistaken his vessels for enemy craft. Then the presence of five Joloanos *pangos* had forced him to obtain water and take bearings under their very eyes. For that reason he was obliged to berth his three vessels together at night, so as to ensure that the enemy would be met by brisk fire [if they were approached] from any direction. The soundings, bases and observations for latitude occupied him throughout the day. On one of his excursions to an islet not far off Maqueda saw, with horror, the melancholy remains of these savage attacks, finding the bones of two recently murdered bodies, the flesh no doubt devoured[2] after some nine *pangos* had been driven off by the town of Pambuan[3] and had come to rest on this islet with only two captives as their paltry spoils.

11 June

Having completed these surveys, he set out again to pass between Catanduanes Island and the large number of islands to his right,[4] lying close to the shore of Luzon. He was hampered during this passage, even more than by the variable and squally winds, by the constant north-going current, which at times made it impossible to continue under oars. It was, however, by a most fortunate accident that they sighted eight pirate *pangos* the following morning. They gave chase immediately, although the *pangos* were two miles to windward among the Canatuan Islands,[5] forcing them to flee from the beach near which they were gathered, inadvertently leaving ashore two Christian prisoners, who were thus freed from slavery. These were both natives, one from Mauban and the other from Mambulao, who had been captured a little less than a month before in the fields near their respective towns. Their only clothing, or rather adornment, was a necklace made from *bejuco*[6] and a halter with which their head, feet and hands were tied at night. They told us that there were some fifty captives, and many women, on board the eight *pangos*. About ten of each sex had been captured only two nights before, during a raid on Porong Looc[7] in Catanduanes Island.

12 June

The strong and contrary currents, the lack of water on board both launches and the

---

[1] For Mourelle see p. 51, n. 4 above: for his voyage see Landín Carrasco, 'Mourelle de la Rúa in the South Sea', pp. 141–4 and for his discoveries in the South Pacific see Andrew Sharp, *The Discovery of the Pacific Islands*, Oxford, 1960, pp. 147–51.
[2] Allegations of cannibalism were not infrequent, though the evidence is disputed.
[3] Not identified.
[4] I.e. to the west; Maqueda was passing through Maqueda Channel, clearly named in his honour.
[5] Catanaguan Islands, two small islands on the western side of Maqueda Channel.
[6] Rattan, which was used for making wickerwork baskets and furniture. It was highly appreciated in the Philippines for its many other uses.
[7] Not identified.

continuous weary labour at the oars, obliged Maqueda to abandon the idea of anchoring at Rapu Rapu Island, which was now in sight and to which Señores Viana and Bauzá had taken their final bearings last March. He decided accordingly to anchor off Catanduanes Island, near the town of Calolbon on its southern extremity, where he replenished his stock of water and wood. Here he noted the poor condition of one of the two launches which, by all evidence, would certainly not withstand even a moderate gale in the future.

With the prevailing squally winds from ENE to SE, he considered it safest to cross to the border port of Tabaco,[1] which is situated in the province of Albay. By this means he was soon able to take new and important bearings which, when linked with a good observation of latitude and a number of soundings around San Miguel Island, not only enabled him to make good use of the day, but also allowed him to secure the vessels in the inner part of the port, within a shallow inlet sheltered from winds from every direction.

This was a very suitable place from which to carry out further trigonometrical work with all possible safety and speed. Two bases and some more bearings determined, in great detail, the true outline of the port and its considerable utility for shipping. Various excursions ashore to the nearby towns then established, with equal accuracy, the exact extent of the gulfs of Albay and Lagonoy. The former, incompletely surveyed by Señores Viana and Bauzá in March and once a port of call for certain galleons, is almost inaccessible to shipping because of the many rocks scattered on the bottom.

18 June
With these most useful undertakings the small flotilla was not able to set sail until the morning of the 18th. The moderate breeze from the second quadrant was fairly favourable for their intended course. By nightfall they had already taken bearings to the eastern extremities of Caramoan [Peninsula][2] and anchored in nineteen fathoms, sand, so as to be in an advantageous position for the survey of Taebun Channel[3] the following morning.

Their soundings soon indicated that this channel was entirely useless.[4] They continued on their course, passing between various islands lying off the port of Sisiran, which they reached at nightfall after sounding the channels in detail and confirming the bearings previously taken. [21st] The launches were able to replenish their supplies of water and wood without difficulty. The three vessels were then able to continue the survey they had begun, during which they examined a very deep bay[5] to the north of Bagata or Quinasalang Island and the islands of Tambong and Bantilan.[6] Having taken some useful bearings with the theodolite from the salient points on the coast, while continuing to sound with great care, they finally anchored at Naga on the afternoon of the 25th. During this passage Maqueda's work had been highly

[1] Situated in the SW part of Lagonoy Gulf, sheltered by San Miguel Island.
[2] The peninsula forming the western side of Maqueda Channel.
[3] The channel separating Catanaguan Islands from Caramoan Peninsula.
[4] Maqueda was mistaken; its fairway is deep and is now frequently used by local vessels.
[5] Binagasbasan Bay, between Lamit Islands and Quinalasag Island.
[6] Lamit Islands, two densely wooded islands which, with Quinalasag Island, are three of a number of offlying islands between the entrance to San Miguel Bay and Maqueda Channel.

accurate, as he zigzagged his way along the coast, so to speak, as its outline required, generally transferring to one of the launches to obtain soundings inshore while the galley took soundings further out.

It was necessary to remain in the bay[1] until early on the morning of the 29th to have enough time to obtain another launch in better condition for the entirely useless one that they had been using, to their peril. Maqueda, wishing to survey a very dangerous shoal[2] and the entrance to the bay, chose to separate the launches from the galley, taking only the latter to carry out the proposed survey, leaving the launches to sail, more safely, inshore. This choice was all the more necessary in that the new South-west Monsoon winds, which had been moderate for some five days, had now increased considerably, accompanied by gusts, squalls and overcast skies, as demonstrated by the galley's unfortunate experience, which might also have befallen the launches if they had followed her.

Indeed, after surveying the shoal, the galley made for the shore again, but as the wind had unexpectedly veered to the west she had to beat back close hauled, which was enough to increase greatly the amount of water she had been making every day and to subject the rigging to such strain that the crew were hard put to repair the constant breakages.

30 June
At last on the 30th, on obtaining a depth of twenty-four fathoms near the coast, opposite Caliño Island,[3] it was easy to continue without being set offshore again, enabling them to survey the coast accurately before reaching Mambulao Roads, where they were able to check all the bearings taken previously.

2 July
The *vendavales* kept Maqueda in Mambulao the following day. The wind finally eased during the night, allowing him to leave early on the morning of the 2nd. However, as the contrary wind and current prevented him from making the passage through Silangan [Pass] or narrow channel between Alabat Island and the coast,[4] he had to pass north of that island to reach Mauban at midday on the 4th.

4 July
Having completed his tasks with the greatest accuracy and success, Don Juan Maqueda was now only concerned with keeping, as far as possible, to the time limits prescribed. Thus, after a fast journey to Pagsanjan, and an equally rapid crossing of the lagoon in a *guilalo*, he was able to join us once more in Manila on the morning of the 7th, having carried out his orders most thoroughly, and having shown by his skill, judgement and conduct that he would always deserve any honours and distinctions that might be graciously bestowed upon him in the future by His Majesty.

[1] I.e. San Miguel Bay.
[2] Bicol Rock, which dries 0·6 metres, which constricts the navigable entrance channel to 4 miles.
[3] Possibly Canimo Island or Caringo Island off the NW entrance point of San Miguel Bay.
[4] The only reason that Maqueda would have attempted this passage would have been to survey Alabat Island, but his track on 'Carta general del archipiélago de Filipinas (northern sheet)' suggests that he made directly for Mauban.

CHAPTER 6

Neé's[1] account of his journey from Sorsogon through the provinces of Albay, Camarines, Tayabas and Manila

The mere visual examination – at best hasty and superficial – of the successive coastlines we had sailed along during our voyage, was in itself inadequate to fulfill the extensive aims of the expedition, whose main interest was to foster the progress of all sciences. Among them, that of natural sciences was preeminent.

This being so, we could not fail to eagerly seize the occasion which now arose and which could hardly have been more opportune. The corvettes had just entered San Bernardo Strait, where we were to spend some time in surveying the adjoining area before continuing to Manila, where they would have to spend the season of SW gales, during which sailing in the archipelago is impracticable, at least for hydrographic purposes.

As Señores Pineda and Haenke were to remain on board to accompany the expedition with their respective duties, it was decided that I should disembark in Sorsogon, so that I could make my way to Manila overland and thereby add to our botanical collections. The instructions I received did not limit my investigations to this object alone. I was also to include the cultivation and plantations of cocoa, mulberries, indigo, pepper, sugar and cotton, the survey of the various types of terrain that I would encounter and, as far as possible, the advancement of the branches of zoology and conchology. Don Antonio Pineda, who was responsible for natural history, had added these to his own when I saw him for the last time in the town of Sorsogon on my return from Albay Volcano.

Vitae summa brevis spem nos vetat inchoare longam[2]

17 March
On 17 March I left the corvettes and made for Sorsogon, where I arrived safely at

---

[1] For more on Luis Neé see Vol. 1 of this edition, pp. xlv-vi. For some details of his finds and successes see Antonio José Cavanilles, *Descripción de las plantas*, Madrid, 1802, pp. 239-80 and Félix Muñoz Garmendia, ed., *La expedición Malaspina, 1789-94. Tomo III: Diarios y trabajos botánicos de Luis Neé*, Madrid, 1992.

[2] 'Life's brief span forbids our entertaining far-reaching hopes': Horace, *Odes*, I: 4, 15.

dawn on the 18th. Sorsogon is a town in decline: its resident population is not more than 200. Although small, the many streams which rise in the nearby mountains make much of the area swampy and subject to flooding. The soil, however, is generally good and suitable for the cultivation of all types of grain, although at present only rice is planted. The forests are full of excellent timber for construction and buildings. The cultivation of *abacá*[1] is the only form of local industry and commerce practiced by the inhabitants in the provinces of Camarines and Albay. This useful plant grows everywhere in the area bounded by the Isarog and Albay Mountains,[2] but flourishes best in Ligao,[3] particularly near the volcano, where it thrives in heavy soil, dampness and shade. It is very similar to the common banana, but its fruit is useless. Like that plant, it reproduces by shoots which sprout at its foot, multiplying prodigiously without cultivation. It bears fruit at two years, having reached its full size, but for the best yield it must be cut off at the root at eighteen months, when the trunk has the girth of a man's thigh. It does not exceed four fathoms in height, and it is composed of layers of bark which are easily separated, exposing the tender, white spongy heart, seven to eight inches in circumference; these are joined by longitudinal bands two or three inches wide which produce a very fine thread, known as *lupin*, from which the *nipis* cloth is made, while the outer layers of bark provide the *bandala* fibre, used for cordage, and the inner layers provide the *tupon*[4] fibre, from which the cloth known as *guinara*[5] is made. The exploitation of the second species consists in pulling out the flesh and pulp that cover the fibres, separating them from the slimy secretion that surrounds them, and drying them in the Sun. The process, however, for the *lupin* and *tupon* fibres is much longer and more laborious: they must be crushed to make them flexible, they are then separated and joined by almost invisible knots to give them the required length. Once the cloth has been woven, it is soaked in lime for twenty-four hours and for the same length of time in rice water, which softens and whitens it, although this whiteness disappears with use and the cloth becomes a yellowish colour, with a reddish tinge. In the *alcaldías*[6] of Camarines and Albay 6,000 *quintales* of cordage are made up annually for the King, at a cost of 13,000 *pesos* in Cavite. At the same time as many as 120 pieces of *guinara* cloth are made, the price varying between two to five *pesos*, according to the quality.

Having made a sizeable collection of plants here, I next went to Bacon, whose terrain is almost the same. Its forests, which I crossed, contain rare and precious botanical specimens and are inhabited by innumerable monkeys.

The rains had made the road from Bacon to Albay impassable, and I was obliged to make the journey by sea. We made the crossing successfully on the night of the 28th,[7]

---

[1] See p. 290, n. 2 above.
[2] Mount Isarog (see p. 385, n. 4 above) and Mayon Volcano (see p. 284, n. 4 above) are situated 55 miles and 26 miles NW of Sorsogon respectively.
[3] Situated 11 miles west of Mayon Volcano and 33 miles NW of Sorsogon.
[4] The meanings of these four terms have not been found.
[5] A cloth made from Manila hemp.
[6] A borough or municipality under the jurisdiction of an *alcalde*.
[7] Presumably landing at the head of Albay Gulf near present day Libog, 5½ miles east of Mayon Volcano.

guarding against attacks by the Moros[1] who constantly infest these coasts. At dawn we were seen by the *vantallas*, or look-outs, who sounded the alarm, and within a few minutes the beach was covered with armed men, who did not withdraw until we were recognized. The inhabitants grow rice, pepper and a little cocoa but, as in Sorsogon, the general occupation is the exploitation of the *abacá*, from which they make cloth of some value by mixing the fibre with silk or cotton.

My first step was to examine Albay Volcano, in the hills of the same name, where it rises in pyramidal shape to a considerable height, although not proportional to its base, whose circumference is more than sixteen leagues. A luxuriant vegetation grows from its base to halfway up, the rest being completely bare as far as the peak, with a thick layer of coarse black sand and a few gypsum rocks. At various points there are large fissures and gullies formed by the lava and a column of smoke may be seen rising constantly from the summit, often with flames at night. I judged the crater to be fifty *toesas*[2] in diameter, and I noted that it was more open to the north and south than to other directions. The smoke alone is whitish in colour, similar to that of a lime oven, but brown when accompanied by ash and darker when accompanied by flames. The volcano frequently belches forth large masses of lava which rain down upon the surrounding fields, razing to the ground whatever they strike and withering the trees, which are covered with sand and ashes. These eruptions always give off such a brilliant light that one may read a paper by it on the darkest night. When a great deal of matter is thrown up it overflows the crater and rises up above it for a time until it pours over the edge, forming rivers of fire of varying sizes which can be seen from Nueva Cáceres.[3] Yet despite these risks the lower slopes are thickly populated, as the many rivers running down from the volcano irrigate and fertilize the fields around, while the minerals in the water and the deposits they leave, make the atmosphere particularly salubrious. The long and laborious treatment of *abacá* and the almost continual raids of the Moros, divert the natives from other more productive crops which, if managed with energy and skill, would make this beautiful terrain yield all the benefits of which it is capable.

I left this town for Guinobatan,[4] having successfully completed my botanical excursions. Surrounded on all sides by scrub and high mountains, Guinobatan appeared fairly substantial to me in size. The landscape is pleasing, and very well irrigated by fine streams. I was assured that the plantations of pepper and mulberries were in a flourishing condition several years ago. At present there are only a few plants of each of these two species, which probably will go the way of the rest.

I went on to Ligao, a settlement of medium size where rice is successfully cultivated, and from there to Oas,[5] which has extremely fertile soils and whose inhabitants are said to work hard at farming and making *guinara* cloth. I visited the famous Bologo mountain nearby,[6] but I found nothing to indicate that it was not the volcano

---

[1] I.e. Joloanos or Mindanaon pirates: see p. 275, n. 5 above.
[2] The French *toise* of 6·3946 feet, which would make the diameter of the crater just under 100 metres.
[3] An alternative name for Naga, which is no longer used: see p. 393, n. 7 below.
[4] Situated 7 miles SW of Mayon Volcano.
[5] Situated 4 miles NW of Ligao.
[6] A 1,328-metre high mountain 6 miles NW of Mayon Volcano and the same distance ENE of Oas.

it was assumed to be. The dense forest that surrounds its slopes is so thick that much of it is impenetrable, but the variety of precious plants growing in its shade, are enough to reward the keenest botanist for the fatigues of his labours.

23 April

The road from Oas, through Polangui to Iraga,[1] which I followed on the 23rd of April, is rough and very different from the previous ones. The bare mountains covered with half burnt rocks and dry, blackened earth incapable of fertilizing a seed, broken everywhere by steep escarpments and fearsome precipices, are a desolate reminder for the weary traveller of the beautiful and luxuriant forests through which he has just passed, images of natural fertility as it sprang from the Creator's hand.

Having been told in Iraga of the proximity of mountain *Negritos*,[2] I arranged to be accompanied by seven armed men and two interpreters, with the intention of seeking them out and observing at close quarters this peaceable and unfortunate race. I passed through several groves planted with pawpaws, coconuts, and guavas, but without water. A short distance further on we came across one of them, of middle age, armed with a spear, a bow and arrows, some poisoned, and wearing only a loincloth. He was accompanied by his young wife, who was not entirely without the attractions of her sex. My gifts and cordial greetings allayed the fears they had shown upon seeing us and won their trust. After a few moments they led me to one of their settlements, a short distance off, where the women and children were in the care of a single armed man. I gave presents to all of them and asked them various questions, to which they responded in a prompt and spirited manner. It seems that they have no notion of a creator, nor of any other type of divinity, and consequently they have no form of worship or of religious awareness. They suffer from few illnesses, but I noticed that some of the women were covered with the scaly rash that is so common in the Marianas. They are monogamous and avoid marriages between close relations. Their weddings consist only of the union of the two parties, with no ceremony or previous requirement other than the consent of the bride's parents. They give birth with little pain and never with fatal consequences, simply washing themselves immediately afterwards in the nearest river without suffering any ill effects. They are excessively fond of *tuba*,[3] the juice extracted from the trunks of palm trees and left to ferment until it becomes as strong as liquor, and also of the tobacco that they grow in the mountains and smoke ceaselessly, despite the persecution suffered by the agents of this industry since the establishment of the state monopoly.[4] The guavas, coconuts, pawpaws and bananas that they gather in the valleys form their usual diet, to which they often add a boar or deer which they catch with their dogs or shoot with arrows.

---

[1] Situated 2½ miles north and 11 miles NNW, respectively, of Oas.

[2] For the *Negritos* see p. 323, n. 5 above. Neé's determination to make contact with them is noticeable.

[3] A brandy-like liquor obtained by distillation from various palm trees: see Blair and Robertson, *The Philippine Islands*, XLIII, p. 273.

[4] Tobacco was widely grown and prospered and, until the tax was abolished in 1882, it enabled the Islands to make a contribution to the Spanish treasury; in part it helped to offset the loss of Mexican silver: Blair and Robertson, *The Philippine Islands*, LV, p. 790.

They bury their dead in the remotest parts of the mountains, placing beside the body food, weapons and other chattels for the use of the deceased.

A large number of these unfortunates were previously employed on nearby farms, greatly to the benefit of the owners, but the difficulty of providing them with the quantity of tobacco that they need, since the establishment of the state monopoly, has deprived them of this resource. This also had the advantage of moderating their habits through social intercourse, gradually weaning them from their barbarous state and giving them a taste for agriculture which could make their lives less wretched and precarious.[1]

With my curiosity partially satisfied, I made for Nabua, one league west of Iraga; the fields along the way, mostly under cultivation, are sown with rice, and are well tended and of an agreeable symmetry. The prized hats made of *nito* fern[2] are produced in this hard-working and industrious town. Here one may see everywhere, laboriously woven on a loom held at the waist, a cloth called *cambra*,[3] reputed to be hard-wearing and of good quality, made in different types some of which are very fine and in tolerably good taste. The land is very fertile but not widely cleared. There are no mulberries or other useful plants to be seen, except for a few stands of cacao trees[4] which show little hope of improvement.

The continual assaults by the Igorots[5] on travellers on the road from Nabua[6] to Nueva Cáceres made me take the necessary precautions to avoid them. For this reason I set out on the morning of 27 April accompanied by ten lancers, four bowmen and a leader, arriving safely in Naga at six o'clock in the evening. The terrain is rugged, mountainous and formed by nature for ambushes. There is little cultivation, owing to the lack of water, and only a few common plants are to be seen. Near the provincial capital, however, there are some good fields where large herds of cattle and horses graze.

Naga or Nueva Cáceres,[7] capital of the province of Camarines, can hardly be called a town, being no more than a disorderly group of small houses made of nipa palm, among which stand out the cathedral, the episcopal residence, the town hall and the seminary, which are partially built of stone, although their only value lies in the contrast with the paltriness of the other buildings. The surrounding country is moderately cultivated. In the town many types of cloth are woven, mainly from *abacá*, either alone or mixed with silk or cotton. A large quantity of cordage is made up and transported by water to a point half way along the route to Pasacao,[8] then taken in carts or by *carabaos* to this town, from where it is taken by sea to Cavite.

The river leading to Pasacao is uncommonly beautiful: its exquisite water, always

---

[1] These paragraphs differentiate Neé's interests from those of many of the other seamen, who were mainly concerned with practical marine matters.
[2] The stem of the climbing fern Nito (*Lygodium scandens*).
[3] A cotton cloth.
[4] Cocoa and chocolate are made from the seeds of this tree.
[5] For Igorots see p. 301, n. 5 above.
[6] Naga in the original MS, which is clearly an error as Neé was travelling from Nabua.
[7] Nueva Cáceres, almost adjoining Naga on Murillo Velarde's 1734 map, was originally the capital of Camarines Province. At the time of Neé's visit the two towns appeared to have merged.
[8] Via the navigable Bicol River, which flows into the head of San Miguel Bay.

pure and crystalline, runs peacefully through level country, keeping it perennially green and fertile, while the strong and vigorous growth of vegetation all around proclaims the eternal springtime of this privileged spot. The ground is carpeted with small plants, covered with flowers of countless shapes and the brightest colours, which scent the air with delightful perfumes. They are sheltered from the winds and storms, whose violence would no doubt be fatal to their tender structure, by a natural vault of medium sized trees of various species, their branches thickly interlaced and heavy with fruit. Above this second level of growth the robust *narra* trees rise majestically, lifting their enormous canopy and spreading wide their long knotted limbs, ignoring the hurricanes and the passage of centuries. The deer, boar and *carabaos,* which live in great numbers beneath their protective shade, thrive on the succulent pasture offered by these smiling meadows, safe from the assaults of man the destroyer. Flocks of tiny, beautiful birds perch on the smaller branches where, hidden among the leaves, they greet the dawn with song and wait joyfully for that life-giving star whose first rays soon appear above the peaks of the high mountains which, at a distance, surround this enchanting place.[1]

The quay where the cordage is embarked is protected by a small fort which contains a warehouse for its storage; the port is small and only accessible to vessels of shallow draught.

The road to Nueva Cáceres, along which I returned on the same day from Pasacao,[2] is equally vulnerable to attacks from the fierce Igorots. It was necessary to travel with the same precautions, which allowed little opportunity for botanical work. I therefore decided to avoid useless expense and on the 18th [May] I embarked with the small flotilla sent to cruise in pursuit of pirates. We sailed downriver all day, past fertile meadows full of livestock or through impenetrable mountains crowned with immense trees as old as themselves. At times we could admire large rice fields in excellent condition and there were many cane fields in just as flourishing a state.

The strong northerly breeze that set in at dawn obliged us to anchor. This allowed me to explore this area which I had been eager to see and had left with regret the previous day. I found the *Casuarina equisetifolia,*[3] and other valuable plants. The palm of the type known as *busil*[4] is common in the forests, and of great use to the natives: with the fibres separated from the pith they make up ropes for small craft. They also use the pith, in particular, from shoots which are cut in horizontal slices, dried and ground, stirred in water for a long time and left to soak. When the sediment has settled the water is poured off, leaving a very white, floury paste which, when dried or mixed with rice, is one of the most nourishing, healthy and frequently eaten foods of these parts.

---

[1] This rather sententious prose passage is quite as good as much Spanish poetry of this period.

[2] Mambulao in the original MS, which is clearly an error. Mambulao [Port José Panganiban] is too far away for Neé to have travelled to in a day from Pasacao.

[3] A willow-like plant common in Ilocos Province and in the SW Pacific as far as Fiji. In some places it was used for making blowpipes and spears.

[4] One of the nine species of palm found in the Philippines: Blair and Robertson, *The Philippine Islands*, LV, p. 743.

20 May

On 20 May[1] we continued our voyage and arrived at Capalonga,[2] a small town which only supports itself by transporting *bonga*[3] to the market at Mambulao. The frequent surprise attacks they suffer from the Moros lying in ambush among the islets all along the coast have forced them to give up the profitable fishing for *balate*,[4] which is more abundant here than anywhere else and which previously provided the principal occupation of the inhabitants.

Paracal,[5] which I then visited on my way to Mambulao, is a town of medium size situated at the end of a large bay. The mountains behind it are yet to be cleared and abound in gold mines, previously worked for profit but now abandoned. The fishing for *balate* is considerable and occupies the whole neighbourhood from June to September. It comes in three different grades, whose prices vary accordingly: the black is the most highly prized and is sold at two and a half *pesos* the *chinanta*,[6] a weight of thirteen pounds two grams. The *manungtung*, of the same colour, holds the second place and is worth two *pesos*, and the white costs from one to one and a half *pesos* for the same quantity. The first type is caught in eleven fathoms, the second in five and the third in one and two fathoms.

22 May

On the 22nd I reached Mambulao, a famous mining camp on a bay with a small narrow beach at the bottom of an escarpment falling from higher ground. The population is sizeable, mostly living in tents. The mines are a quarter of a league from the beach and are generally very productive, although the fineness of the gold is not of the highest quality. The metal is crushed and the gold is then extracted by the washing method. To melt the gold, instead of a crucible, they use a certain species of shell, which fulfils the purpose perfectly, and for the separation of the heterogeneous materials the bark of a tree called the *gogo*[7] is mixed in as a fixative, without which ingredient, they assure me, it cannot be done. Despite the wealth of these mines, most of the time they are not being worked. The Spaniards do not undertake work of this kind, which they have left entirely to the Indians and the *Sangleyes*[8] of mixed blood. The capital cost and the continual lawsuits brought by each group against the other are two insurmountable obstacles to the advancement of this industry. The nearby mountains have an abundance of excellent timber, likely [in the future] to facilitate the working of the mines, while the nature of the natives makes them suitable for all types of work.[9]

---

[1] *2 de Mayo* in the original MS, which is clearly an error. By the sequence of dates it must be either 20 or 21 May.
[2] Situated 45 miles east of Mauban and 9 miles WNW of Mambulao [Port José Panganiban].
[3] The fruit of the areca palm: Blair and Robertson, *The Philippine Islands*, LV, p. 743.
[4] *Bêche-de-mer*: see p. 378, n. 4 above.
[5] Situated 5½ miles east of Mambulao [Port José Panganiban].
[6] Not identified, but for other Filipino weights and measures see Blair and Robertson, *The Philippine Islands*, LV, p. 957.
[7] A tree (*Entada pursaeta*) which provided a soapy foam which was used for washing.
[8] Chinese living in the Philippines, or persons of Chinese-Filipino blood. The term is discussed in Boxer, *South China*, p. 260.
[9] On mining in the Islands, see Díaz-Trechuelo, *Philippine Studies*, 13 (1965), pp. 763-97 and Ronald E. Dolan, ed., *The Philippines. A Country Study*, Washington: Army Dept., 1993, p. 155.

25 May

On the 25th I continued towards Mauban, still travelling by sea. The following day I reached Apag,[1] a small town of twenty-six taxpayers, situated at the end of a bay under the protection of a small fort, among pleasant fields almost entirely covered with coconut. There are a few fields of rice and *camote*,[2] European figs trees are grown, bearing fruit two and three times a year. There is a small amount of fishing for *balate*, and the mountain *Negritos* bring down a little honey and a larger quantity of wax, which they exchange for tobacco and *camote*. The sea abounds in fish and shellfish, while mangroves grow all along the entire seashore.

27 May

On the 27th, having concluded these examinations, I had embarked once again for Mauban, but the beautiful forests that came into sight soon after gave me hopes of a plentiful collection, so I decided to walk through them for two leagues. I had hardly come to the first hills when I met two young mountain *Negritos*, armed with spears and arrows, who approached me, repeating the word '*señor*' among other words of their language. I gave half a *real* to each and they departed, content, assuring me through the interpreter that they were going to defend Castillo de Santa Cruz[3] against the Moros. Half a league further on I found some of their huts, but no people. Near them there was a half-built canoe, which I judged to be constructed with a greater skill and delicacy than their limited knowledge would have led me to expect. Meanwhile, three *Negritos*, similarly armed, came out of the scrub a musket shot away from us, followed by seven dogs of medium size. I asked them where they had come from, and they replied that they had been hunting the boar and deer which are only too common in these mountains. On my arrival at the fort I was told by the keeper that the *Negritos* invariably stood to arms at the first sign of attack by the Moros. Having passed Alimoxan[4] on the 28th, on the night of the 29th I finally managed to reach Mauban River, the end of the journey by sea. These two settlements are of a considerable size, surrounded by stockades with a few bastions, with tiled roofs on the houses and straight streets, the principal ones being paved. They stand on the shore among ranges of high mountains, densely forested with trees and thick scrub, but nevertheless have good pastures where the horses they breed, although small, are highly thought of, strong, and of excellent gait.

If its development had not been held back by frequent fires, Mauban would have become quite a wealthy town from the production of mats and even more from the profits of coastal navigation, in which a fair number of *balancianes* are used for trading along the entire coast as far as Cape San Ildefonso. However, it is now growing at a considerable rate and the greater amount of traffic between the opposite [i.e. eastern] coast and the Manila area must doubtless contribute to this expansion.

Immediately after my arrival I began to examine the famous mountains which

---

[1] Probably Apat Bay in the NE corner of Calauag Bay, between Alabat Island and the mainland of Luzon to the east.
[2] The sweet potato (*Batata edulis*): see Blair and Robertson, *The Philippine Islands*, LV, p. 738.
[3] Not identified.
[4] Not identified.

circle the town from west to NE. The astonishing height of the trees, their girth, their unfading verdure and luxuriance, are enough to amaze the most seasoned observer, each of which may be considered as a new and fertile territory. A thick layer formed by moisture and other materials of various kinds covers their gigantic trunks, sustaining and nourishing an infinite number of parasitic plants, whose light green foliage contrasts admirably with the dark trunks, displaying to the marvelling traveller a labyrinth of leaves and branches which adds to their size and majesty. The collection of plants that I made in these forests met all my expectations. Those that I made in the neighbouring valleys, where there are quarries providing excellent stone now used for building, was of equal quality.

On the beaches of Mauban there are several curious types of rock: silex quartz[1] is found, astrite strata,[2] and black ash which is thought to come from the sea, but which I consider to be volcanic.

Having explored the area surrounding the town to my satisfaction, I extended the range of my excursions to the more distant mountains of this municipality.[3] The exceptional density of their vegetation frequently subjects the passionate botanist to the torments of Tantalus.[4] The Sun's rays, stronger here than at any other part of this coast, never penetrate the natural barrier of undergrowth, and the fertile soil, with the moisture that the rays would otherwise evaporate, constantly renews its growth.

My desire to continue to enlarge my collection spurred me on to undertake the crossing of these mountains at this point, despite the roughness of the terrain, most of which is marshy and unhealthy. I set out on my journey, having arranged to be accompanied by five men to carry the plant collection, baggage and food. Soon we were obliged to take off our shoes and wade for two long leagues through swamps, submerged to mid-thigh, which took us six hours. The rest of the route was less arduous, and the additions to the collection consoled me entirely.

These mountains are infested with snakes of extraordinary size and there are indescribable numbers of leeches, which fasten themselves particularly to the legs and cause considerable discomfort. I had to endure no fewer than two dozen of these on each leg during this trip, until they dropped off by themselves. I am firmly persuaded, however, that the abundant loss of blood prevented me from a fever or other inflammatory illness, which the fierce Sun that I have been exposed to during most of my journey would otherwise have inevitably caused.

6 June

On 6 June I reached Cavinti, a small town on a hill between two streams. There is excellent grazing in the vicinity, and the natives grow a little rice and *camote*. There is, however, no industry or activity to be seen, a circumstance all the stranger for the fact

---

[1] Flint.

[2] Possibly a slip for astroides, a type of madrepore or aetite (eaglestone). For minerals in the Philippines see Manuel Buzeta, OSA, *Diccionario geográfico, estadístico, histórico de las islas Filipinas*, 2 vols, Madrid, 1850, II, p. 377.

[3] It is surprising that Neé makes no mention of his meetings with Malaspina at Mauban on 28 May and 4 June (see pp. 379 and 383 above).

[4] An interesting personal note, which together with the following paragraph shows the intensity of the writer's vocation.

that various embroideries worked for a specific use led me to believe that they have an aptitude for such an occupation.

On my way to Pagsanjan I passed through rice fields of considerable size, spread out on either side of the track as far as the eye could see. Near the town there is a very steep hill, on which there are to be found some unusual rocks from an extinct volcano.

Pagsanjan owes its establishment to a few *Sangleyes* families on the opposite bank of the [Lumban] river, with some Japanese[1] and natives, who were ordered in 1673 to settle on the present site of the town. It is of medium size, with fields sown with rice, their only crop, apart from the production of a substantial amount of indigo of excellent quality.

The road to Santa Cruz, a league away, is fairly even and [the land is] well cultivated, with large rice fields and some of indigo. From time to time there are small, luxuriant forests which vary the scene agreeably. The town stands on a beautiful and fertile plain, inundated by the lagoon when it floods. It consists of isolated houses of some height, fenced with stockades. The land belonging to their owners is used for orchards and is generally planted with *bonga* palms, indigo and cocoa, all of the finest quality. The frequent floods, destroying everything, limit the natural industry of the inhabitants, who would extend the plantations considerably if it were not for this risk.

The women make a type of colourful cloth of silk and palm fibre that they call *naghavit*. The *tiangue*,[2] or market, which runs from Wednesday to Thursday, attracts a large crowd of people from both Manila and the rest of the lagoon area. The articles that sell best are *guinara* cloth, cambray, raw silk and cotton in different colours, ribbons, *bejuco* hats (woven from liana vines), handkerchiefs and various kinds of embroidery. There is an abundance of food, much of which goes to providing for the capital. At last, on 20 June, with the rainy season setting in, I had to conclude my botanical work at the lagoon and sail for Manila, where I arrived safely at three o'clock in the afternoon of the next day, in the agreeable expectation of having carried out my instructions most thoroughly.

---

[1] For the Japanese in the Philippines see Blair and Robertson, *The Philippine Islands*, LV, p. 490.
[2] Mexican name for a small market.

CHAPTER 7

Haenke's[1] account of his journey from Manila to Bangui, near Cape Bojeador

14 April

On 14 April I disembarked in Manila Bay even before the *Descubierta*, to which I had been assigned, had anchored. That same day I made the necessary preparations in the capital and on the following day I set out in a *panga* for Bulacan, Malolos[2] and Arayat, to continue my journey more quickly, as far as possible, by way of the estuaries or the small river tributaries.[3] On this part of the journey we made a collection of the species of trees and bushes which are common in the tidal zone of the estuaries along the coast of this island.[4] We were now well into the dry season and therefore the approach of the rainy season only allowed me time to attend to the plant kingdom, of which the extraordinary abundance of species produced by nature in the various terrains studied would provide a lifetime's work for the most diligent and practised of botanists.

I stopped in Arayat for a few days to visit the solitary mountain[5] which can be seen at a great distance from both north and south, making a considerable collection in its vicinity. This beginning led me to hope that my subsequent acquisitions would be equally successful. By chance I met the Reverend Father Provincial of Santo Domingo,[6] returning from a long visit who, upon learning of the object of our expedition, was kind enough to recommend us to his subordinates by means of a circular which he wrote with the greatest zeal.

I continued to botanize[7] my way across this sandy plain, which is covered with

---

[1] For more on Bohemian-born Tadeo Haenke see Vol. 1 of this edition, pp. xlii–xlv and Ibáñez, *Trabajos de Tadeo Haenke*.

[2] Situated 5 miles NW of Bulacan.

[3] The north and NE shores of Manila Bay are formed by the delta of Pampanga River.

[4] I.e. the north coast of Manila Bay.

[5] Mount Arayat.

[6] At this time (1790-94) the Dominican Friar Provincial, or Superior, of the Philippines was Antonio Robles.

[7] Here Haenke uses an 18th-century neologism, *herborizando*. Hitherto, botany had been a mere adjunct of medicine, but in the 18th century it was coming into its own, especially after the publication of the major works of Carl Linnaeus (1707-78). The first attempt at a compendium of Philippine botany was the *Flora de Filipinas, según el sistema sexual linneo*, 2 vols. (1837), enlarged into 4 vols (1877) by the self-taught Augustinian friar Manuel Blanco.

dense forests of many species of trees and majestic palms, and extends in a north/south direction as far as the large bay[1] where the province of Pangasinan ends between Cape Bolinao and the coast of Ilocos.

The unsafe route from Arayat to the town of Tarlac[2] is constantly infested with *Igorots* and *Negritos* from [the province of] Zambales, causing me to hurry through this part of the [province of] Pampanga and to take various precautions. It is well known that travellers are at great risk of their lives in these parts, if we are to credit the pitiful tales of local people and the considerable number of recent misadventures.

At a first glance it is clear that these towns are administered by native priests, as there is nothing seen to equal the good order, regularity and discipline which characterise those in the charge of the friars, which have rightly won them the veneration of the inhabitants and universal respect.[3]

I made several excursions from the town of San Jacinto[4] to the nearby mountains, going as far as safety would allow me, and avoiding as much as possible any proximity to the *Igorots*, a fierce, wild people who inhabit the range of high mountains which run northward from Pangasinan,[5] close to the sea, leaving to the east an extensive area of flat, fertile land which is bounded on that side by the equally high and mountainous territory of Cagayan.[6] This delightful plain,[7] which nature seems to protect with so many obstacles, abounds with gold mines and other riches that they own, and which they defend well. However, they often bring their goods down to neighbouring villages for exchange, although always taking the greatest precautions.

I cannot speak highly enough of the generous hospitality extended to me by Father Fray Manuel del Barrio,[8] whose vast erudition and love of science make him a true philosopher in this remote region. His goodness extended even to accompanying me on my tiring excursions, which proved richly rewarding.

23 April

On 23 April I left San Jacinto to continue towards the northern extremity of the island, always following the western coast which forms virtually the whole of the province of Ilocos, which is bordered by the mountain range[9] a short distance from the sea. To the north this range extends as far as the coast. In the south it is inhabited by the *Igorots* and in the north by the *Tinguianes*,[10] a people still pagan but less savage than the former and closer to a civilised state.

The very extensive cultivation of various kinds of cotton, the pleasing and durable

---

[1] Lingayen Gulf.
[2] Situated 22 miles NW of Arayat.
[3] Another eulogy of the Spanish friars, at the expense of the Filipino native clergy.
[4] Situated 46 miles north of Tarlac, near the SE corner of Lingayen Gulf.
[5] The Cordillera Central.
[6] The Sierra Madre.
[7] The great valley of the Cagayan River.
[8] Fray Manuel Barrios y Ravago (d. 1802) noted as a distinguished poet by Pablo Fernández, *Dominicos donde nace el sol*, Barcelona, 1958, p. 343.
[9] Another reference to Cordillera Central.
[10] The Tingguians (Itneg), a people living as farmers, in the Abra valley in NW Luzon. They are related to the Igorot group. See Guillermo, *Historical Dictionary*, p. 14 and Vreeland, *Area Handbook*, p. 91.

cloth for which they are used, the plentiful harvest of the finest rice, as well as their diligence and skill, are the best tribute to the good character of the inhabitants of Ilocos and the fertility of their territory. My collection grew noticeably every day with the addition of new and precious species of plants and fruit trees, in which this province abounds more than any other.

I reached its capital, Vigan, on the 27th, and visited the lower [part of the] range, which is free of infidels between the towns of Narvacan and Santa,[1] whence I departed with a much larger collection than I had expected.

Both the Bishop of Vigan[2] and the *alcalde mayor*, Don José Sánchez, took a most enthusiastic interest in the success of my subsequent travels, giving me letters of introduction for the governors and ministers of the towns through which I was to pass, offering me all the help that was in their power.

30 April

On the 30th I left Vigan, making for the extremity of the island, and on 2 May, despite the burning heat from which I suffered excessively, I reached Bangui,[3] a town behind Cape Bojeador. I spent more than three weeks in this place, which was certainly the most suitable for my purpose. The NE rains, which affect this area as well as those from the SW, had finished a few days earlier. The vegetation was flourishing and the variety of terrain in this happy spot daily supplied me, in an abundance I had not found elsewhere, with new acquisitions which rapidly enriched my collection.

Only the fear of delaying my return and rendering it impossible if the rains set in hard, as well as the serious warnings of knowledgeable people, were capable of limiting my excursions and desires, making me think carefully about my return to the south of the island. However, before setting off I was still able to make a brief excursion to the Cabicungan River,[4] returning on foot with indescribable exertions across the high, rugged and almost impassable mountain of Tabug.[5] I collected everything I considered important, as far as time would allow me. On 20 May the change in the monsoon took place in Bangui with heavy downpours and squalls, but both ceased after a few days. I must declare my deep gratitude to the activity of Father Fray Miguel Sam, an Augustinian friar,[6] who provided me with all the help and equipment I needed for my excursions and my return journey.[7]

Thus, laden with a large collection of well-dried plants of about 2,000 species, I left Bangui on the 25th, passing through Pasuquin, Bacarra and Badoc,[8] and reached Vigan on 31 May. I spent a few days ensuring that the collections were protected from

---

[1] Situated 10 and 6 miles, respectively, SSE of Vigan.
[2] The diocese of Nueva Segovia in Cagayan. The bishop referred to was José de San Agustín, OSA (bishop in 1784-96).
[3] On the north coast of Luzon, 11 miles east of Cape Bojeador.
[4] A small river, which enters the sea 30 miles ENE of Cape Bojeador.
[5] Not identified, but probably part of the Caraballo Mountains.
[6] Nothing is known of the Augustinian friar Sam who was too late for inclusion in the biographies in the *Osario venerable* by A. M. de Castro, Manila, 1780: see Blair and Robertson, *The Philippine Islands*, LIII, p. 347.
[7] Another instance of the travellers' desire to acknowledge help received.
[8] Situated 10, 14 and 33 miles, respectively, south of Cape Bojeador.

the effects of humidity and other risks on the journey, and then set out for the capital, collecting on the way any plants which had come into flower with the change of season.

13 June
On 13 June I arrived at the southern extremity of Ilocos, which is administered by the Reverend Augustinian Fathers, to whom I owe my public thanks, as I do equally to the Dominican Fathers for their help on my passage through the province of Pangasinan.

I spent several days in the town of San Jacinto as I was in a poor state of health. A rare opportunity allowed me to make some observations on the little known fruition of the palms, which are plentiful here and greatly embellish the fields.

To the south of Mangavol[1] a long, broad strip of land which floods every year was passable at the time, although some parts of it were already flooded.

On 23 June I reached Arayat, still collecting, and after several successful excursions I proceeded downstream in a *casco*[2] and arrived in Manila on the 28th.

---

[1] Not identified.
[2] A flat-bottomed Filipino boat.

CHAPTER 8

An account of Pineda's journey to various provinces east and north of Manila and his death in Badoc[1]

Don Antonio Pineda, having decided to undertake his scientific excursions in the northern part of the island, wished to combine the most useful objectives with the largest possible area of country in the short time left before the onset of the rainy season. To this end he consulted the best informed and most experienced people on the spot. Don Juan de Cuellar, a keen naturalist commissioned by the Real Compañía in these islands, wanted to accompany him on the first part of the journey and together they drew up a plan. After a detailed study of the pleasant shores of Laguna de Bay and an examination of the cinnamon plantations in Calauan[2] and the thermal baths at Maquilin,[3] Don Antonio Pineda planned to cross the lagoon and Upper Pampanga [Province] from south to north, continuing afterwards along the entire length of the Cagayan River, but first to the missions in Ituy[4] and Paniqui[5] before continuing to Lallo[6] and Aparri at the northern end of the island. He would then turn westward to return to Manila through the provinces of Ilocos and Pangasinan, diverging from the projected route to a greater or lesser degree whenever there was good reason to do so.

It was true that this plan was hindered by the excessive heat, which keeps the thermometer at 24° to 25° on the Réaumur[7] scale and makes the climate intolerable, enervating and weakening to the memory, due to the continual dissipation of animal spirits that drags the traveller down into a sort of lethargy, broken only by annoying skin rashes and bites of insects, impeding any sustained period of reflective work. Nevertheless Don Antonio Pineda, untroubled by similar inconveniences in other

---

[1] This account, written by Neé from Pineda's notes and journals, is one of the most interesting sections both from a human point of view, and from the pathos of his end. It also makes interesting observations on up-country life and conditions. There are revealing details of Pineda's earlier work in Mexico in González Claverán, *Malaspina en Nueva España*. For details of Pineda's appointment to the expedition see Vol. 1 of this edition, p. xlii.
[2] Situated 3 miles south of the southern shore of Laguna de Bay.
[3] Now Los Baños (The Baths) near the southern shore of Laguna de Bay, 3 miles WNW of Calauan.
[4] In the present day province of Nueva Vizcaya on one of the tributaries of the Cagayan River; for the vicissitudes of this mission, see Fernández, *Dominicos*, pp. 204-5.
[5] Situated 31 miles SE of Lingayen.
[6] Situated on the Cagayan River, 12 miles south of Aparri.
[7] René Antoine Ferchault de Réaumur (1683-1757), French physicist who devised a thermometer that used spirit instead of mercury, in which the freezing point of water was 0° and the boiling point 80°.

unhealthy countries, faced them all with vigour. His talented creativity stands out among his useful observations, as well as his polished descriptions, of which we shall summarise those parts that will illustrate the course of his travels.

11 April

Accompanied by a young painter of middling ability[1] to sketch the most interesting subjects, he left the capital on 11 April. The densely forested shores of Laguna de Bay, whose fertile terrain is frequently broken by streams and groves of trees, offered delightful scenes to his eye. The towns, hidden among palms and banana plantations, with ingeniously paved roads, surrounded by rice fields, preserved traces of the more luxuriant vegetation, while the many houses and tiny stalls, scattered irregularly about, constitute a ribbon-like settlement, while the square and oblong plots which hold back the water and divide the land for the cultivation of rice, give the aspect of a garden artfully disordered.[2] To this may be added the structure of the houses, well adapted to the climate and the natives' manner of life, with a continuous activity linked to harvesting the rice. In this swampy country the *carabao* is of marvellous use to man, where any other animal working knee-deep in mud would become bogged down, exhausted and overworked. The phlegmatic *carabao* is in its element, enjoying the moisture and stimulated by its coolness. Whether it is due to disease, itching or the particular nature of its skin, it loves being sprayed with cool water and delights in being rubbed, and even in its muddy colour it seems to have been bred to inhabit the swamps.

Eleven leagues from Manila and five from the lagoon lies the *hacienda* of Calauan, belonging to Don Francisco Salgado and provided with good workshops. On the eastern side it is bounded by more than two leagues of mountains. The Calavang, San Nicolás and Lamot Rivers, and seventeen springs, irrigate more than 5,000 cinnamon trees, now yielding a crop, with another 500,000 trees of various species, in excellent condition and soon to bear fruit. On all sides one may see fields in good use, promising their owner an increased return for his considerable and patriotic expenses.

The thermal springs at Maquilin, a specific for tumours, the stone and all types of obstruction,[3] had been analysed according to Bergmann's[4] method by the learned M. Mongez,[5] on the ill-fated expedition of Comte de la La Pérouse, and a new examination was now made, the results of which, compared with those of that skilful chemist, confirmed his opinion and understanding of the waters, to which he added a description of the local terrain, omitted by that voyager.

---

[1] Presumably Ravenet, since he painted the scene of Pineda's death: see plate 41.

[2] Another late-18th-century touch. In Europe there was now a growing reaction against the formal, classical gardens of the past, and 'artificial disorder' was becoming fashionable. In time it became an aspect of the Romantic Movement.

[3] There are a number of hot springs and waterfalls in the area, some of which were credited with mystical powers.

[4] The Swedish scientist Torbern Olof Bergmann (1735-84), author of the *De analysi aquarum* (1778). Once again, the citation reveals the breadth and modernity of the research carried out in preparation for the Malaspina expedition.

[5] Abbé Jean-André Mongez, editor of the *Journal de physique* and a man of wide scientific interests.

22 April

Leaving Cuellar behind, he [Pineda] crossed the lagoon, spending the night on Talim Island, and on the following day he reached Binangonan, a town situated on a point extending from the north coast, near which, some three-quarters of a league to the NE, there is a rugged pinnacle and a spring whose waters have earned it the name of Frescas de Foselo.[1] The pinnacle is formed of *argilacea amarillosa*,[2] with a subsidence at its foot where the water gathers, filtering through drop by drop. In the open air the temperature reaches 25° to 27° by the thermometer, but remains at 18° or 19° in this delightful spot and, having tested the water with reagents, at the request of its conscientious guardian, Father Perdigón of the Franciscan order, who accompanied him in his examination, he determined that it may be considered as among the purest waters to be found.

A mile and a half SSW of Morong,[3] which is on the mainland but is nevertheless reached by water from the lagoon, there is a factory for making bullets whose owner has signed a contract for supplying Manila and, by means of a subcontract with a *Sangley*, provides the bullets at very good prices. The factory is extremely simple and the operations, of which there are only five, even more so, employing no more than that number of workmen, who have only to refine, mill, smelt, cast and finish the formed bullets on an anvil, the structure of the bellows and furnace, as he [Pineda] described them, being equally simple.[4]

On the following days our naturalist made an excursion to the Santa Inés Mountains, twelve leagues NE of Morong, to study the mines which supply the factory. He passed through the wretched town of Bosoboso and, leaving the greater part of his equipment there, he ascended to the higher parts along rough and almost impassable tracks, where horses could not be used without great risk and even on foot it was very hard going. Although consisting only of blanket, a pillow, a barometer, a hydrometer, boxes, some unhulled rice and a mere pittance to eat, his baggage hindered him considerably in such difficult terrain. Nor were his agonies to end. After climbing to the top by hauling himself up on tufts of grass, he spent the night in the open with no other shelter than a blanket and, above all, with nothing to eat but cold food, which he could not stomach. The damage to his health resulting from these hardships was to be beyond recovery.

Two lofty ranges running from south to north and from SW to NE until they unite or come close at Mount Pola,[5] towards the centre of the island, form the boundaries of the luxuriant plain on which Manila stands. From the base of Caraballo,[6] through

---

[1] *Foselo* from the medieval Latin *fossellum* – a holy water stoup, used here to emphasize the purity of the water of Laguna de Bay; the largest fresh-water lake in the Philippines, which provided fish in large quantities. The island is Talim, which abounded in game.

[2] Yellow clay.

[3] Situated about 5 miles NE of Binangonan.

[4] *bala* = bullet or shot in the original MS, but the operation seems much more like the production of cannon-balls.

[5] Mount Pulog, 2928 metres high and the highest mountain in Luzon, 36 miles east of the NE entrance point of Lingayen Gulf.

[6] The Sierra Madre and the Cordillera Central merge in north central Luzon to form the Carabelllo Mountains.

the provinces of Tondo,[1] Bulcan and both Pampangas, the fine open country is broken by delightful rivers in whose calm waters the trees along their banks are reflected. Many parts of this level country are low and are flooded to such a depth in the rainy seasons that they become navigable, so that the interrupted trade by land can be continued by water. A great number of settlements occupy this vast expanse of land, in which our traveller sated his curiosity with useful observations while the natives carried on their work of growing rice, corn, indigo and tobacco. This in spite of the fact that the monopoly of the latter lures many armed assailants, who harry them [the natives] and lay waste the country. Some of the settlements have been fortified with double rows of staked embankments against these raids. The Gapan[2] Factory offered a view of the entire scene and from it bearings were taken to the lofty Mount Arayat, which bore S56°W.

The dangerous Caraballo Gorge or mountain pass is the only means of reaching the Dominican missions of Irinayas or Ituy. On 10 May Don Antonio Pineda set out to visit the missions, which obliged him to abandon for the time being his studies of nature for those of the arts of war, no less demanding and much more destructive. The proximity of the Igorots,[3] who inhabited these mountainous areas and, until now, had been deaf to the attractions of a less barbarous and savage life, obliged travellers to take various military precautions. Fortunately, however, these treacherous assailants are incapable of attacking an armed man if he remains alert. They also show such a horror of firearms that a single musket shot fired on entering the narrow passes will give the alarm to the whole mountain, thus preventing an attack. But any travellers who undress, drop their guard or fall asleep, are almost sure to have their throats cut by dawn, thus any precautions taken will have been in vain. Lamps, guards and sentinels to give the alarm were all used in their little camp for a night in the wilderness. The escort was composed of a European servant, a dragoon and the painter, all carrying firearms, that rendered their force more respectable. The rest consisted of twenty recently converted Indians, carrying spears, arrows, bolas and a wooden shield to protect their naked bodies, in whom little trust could placed, despite their promises of loyalty. The progress of this little party was very slow, their speed being limited to that of its escort. The extremely steep slopes and the dark and tortuous tracks, intersected by the streams and waterfalls which pour down from every part of the mountain, made the going extremely uncomfortable, but this was balanced by the beauty of the lush spring growth and the multitude of rare birds and trees which doubly delighted the senses. In this strange region, where danger vies with pleasure, the barometer settled at 24 inches, 6 and 4/12 lines[4] at the highest point, but the thermometer showed no more than 18° on the Réaumur scale. The true summit of Caraballo is, however, not this but another mountain to the left of it, which appears to rise more than 500 *varas* above the col in the shape of a sugar-loaf.

---

[1] A former name for the province of Manila named after a 18th-century town on the eastern shore of Manila Bay close north of the the capital.

[2] Situated 42 miles north of Manila.

[3] For the heroic efforts of the local Dominicans to make fruitful contact with the Igorots at this time, see Fernández, *Dominicos*, p. 200 ff.

[4] A twelfth of an inch, a term no longer in general use.

Having overcome these obstacles, which the friars themselves repeatedly described as insuperable, the continuation of Don Antonio Pineda's work became relatively less arduous and more convivial, but the constant vapours arising from the earth, here rich in minerals and full of moisture, made it much more unhealthy. New and highly interesting objects of attention were to be seen along the pleasant banks of the New Tajo River,[1] on the fertile terrain where the Dominican friars have, for half a century, established numerous settlements known as missions. In these recently founded societies, under a semi-patriarchal rule, man is displayed in various aspects of his civilization. The savage's simple customs, his frugality, his resentments, his reciprocal needs, his docility and his inconstancy may be openly examined. These lamentable but constant proofs of man's weaknesses, when he does not subordinate his passions to enlightened reason, were frequently contemplated by our philosophical observer, whose admiration was earned, above all, by the prudent missionaries who civilize these wild natives by the kindness of their treatment. These beneficent men, condemned by the synod to live perpetually[2] among infidels, removed from all society in unhealthy or dangerous parts and always exposed to the guile and inconstancy of the barbarians, patiently endure their repeated deceptions and, impervious to hunger, thirst and exhaustion, climb the most rugged mountains on foot, either swinging, or pulling themselves, across rivers on liana vines, ever mindful of the horrible martyrdom which many others have suffered.[3]

In these parts the terrain consists of a continuous series of valleys, becoming successively narrower as the two ranges, between which they run, approach each other. Cotton cloth and cocoa provide their inhabitants with a comfortable subsistence, in which they begin to be productive at the age of twelve. This provides the Pangasinanes (the hard-working Catalans[4] of these islands) with a lucrative trade in the barter of clothing. Not a single object escaped the attentive and philosophical speculation of Don Antonio Pineda, but his health began to be unequal to his desires. From the outset it had been affected and the sudden change of climate in this new terrain to the cold weather of Caraballo caused a swelling of his left eye socket, while a troublesome flux confined him for several days.

The mutual enmity which exists among the various peoples of Luzon prevents peaceful travel, except through the maritime provinces, as the interior roads are always harassed by armed horsemen brandishing large spears and provided with cuirasses or curved rectangular shields, arrows, bows, cane pikes and hand pikes made from the heavy *buri* palm.[5] To avoid ambushes in the passes and mountains, the help of the

---

[1] A former name for the Cagayan River.
[2] In the beginning, the Dominican rule forbade their missionaries from ever returning to Spain, but this was relaxed in 1654. Note again the eulogy of the Spanish Dominican missionaries, their trials, courage and patience.
[3] Praise for the missionaries was politically advisable; but, in any case, the travellers would have seen the best side of the friars, who would welcome the newcomers warmly, seeking news from home, gossip from Manila, and relief from loneliness. Pineda's reference to the foundation of mission stations along the banks of the New Tajo River is revealing. Such stations as developed into villages or towns were named by their friar-founders, though some were later re-named by the secular authorities.
[4] The Catalans were popularly perceived as the most hard-working and reliable people in the Spanish peninsula.
[5] The sago palm. For its many uses see Buzeta, *Diccionario geográfico*, I, pp. 419-20, and Blair and Robertson, *The Philippine Islands*, LV, pp. 737-8.

alcalde or *teniente* of the district must be requested to provide an escort and the necessary arms. In the thickly forested parts it is necessary to dismount, sending the guides ahead and having the files of soldiers follow exactly in their footprints, which are then wiped away to conceal the traces of their passage. The pastures are sometimes sown with sharp points against the enemy. They cannot be crossed without a careful reconnaissance and nobody sets foot there except in the footprint of another. At night a small camp is set up, with pikes stuck into the ground to serve as a barricade for the cordon of sentries.[1]

The slopes of Abungul and Mamparang, lying ENE of Bagabag[2] in the extensive cordillera which runs from SW to NE,[3] form a high pass at the end of the broad valleys of Ituy,[4] where our traveller once again put his military training into practice. This elevated locality, although somewhat lower than Caraballo, offers equally pleasing views within a horizon, ten to twelve leagues distant, containing woods, plains, rough terrain, rivers and distant mountainous areas, which add charm and variety to the scene.

In the foothills of Mamparang a party of more than forty people from the towns of Bayonbong[5] and Bagabag were resting. They were on their way to get supplies of salt, coconut oil, lati[6] and cotton in the lowlands. The party consisted of armed men and women, each with two horses, who were entrenched with their leather-covered hampers in front of their encampment, from which we see how the laboriously this trade progresses, and how scant are the resources of these inland provinces.

From Mamparang the country begins to descend towards Cagayan [River] and the hills flatten out and become progressively lower. A chain of ridges, which can be seen intermittently, occupies the whole area from Carig[7] to Saniu. These villages and those of Camarag and Cauayan,[8] which lie on these ridges, lack vegetation and good grazing land. From a cocoa plantation of 3,000 plants scarcely 300 take root, but these bear fruit of the finest quality. The bends of the river irrigate the rice fields, and upon these their living depends. In describing this part of the country that he passed through, Don Antonio Pineda laments the deplorable situation of some of the villages or settlements, whose people, just for the convenience of communication, have been forcibly moved from their original sites, depriving them of the advantages of irrigation.

Our tireless traveller had not yet seen the end of the difficulties which had dogged him so persistently until now. His collections were almost destroyed in Carig by a sudden fire which reduced the monastery to ashes. This mishap, although his own activity and intelligence would have been to no avail in preventing it, nevertheless enabled the avoidance of many others in the future, by means of a set of regulations

[1] This paragraph illustrates the dangers and consequent strain of travelling up country.
[2] At the southern end of present day Magat Reservoir and 108 miles SSW of Aparri.
[3] The Sierra Madre.
[4] A pass leading to the great valley of the Cagayan River.
[5] Situated 10 miles SW of Bagabag.
[6] Neé explains in a footnote 'Lati is the fried flesh of the coconut after the oil has been extracted.'
[7] It has not been possible to identify this and several other villages along the banks of the Cagayan river, which Pineda appears to have followed, since some of them were very small.
[8] On the west bank of the Cagayan River, 38 miles NE of Bagabag and 85 miles south of Aparri.

which he gave to the missionary father for such cases and which the latter offered to pass on immediately to the other settlements.

30 May

From Ganni, the first town in the Cagayan jurisdiction, where he arrived on 30 May, navigation commences on the broad river, whose width along its middle reaches is not less than 700 to 750 *varas* and whose leafy banks offer much for admiration. The villages of Ilagan,[1] Tamavien, Guagua and various others which either lie on its banks or may be reached by shallow inlets, have nearly all a quay or landing ramp, where a few floating *camarines*[2] and one or two *pangas* may often be seen. These strange keel-less craft are trough-shaped with a flat bottom, two solid knees at bow and stern, reinforced upper works, and a canopy neatly woven of bamboo and palm. All the villages that form this province previously carried on a good trade in tobacco, whose reputation as the best on the island attracted the Pangasines and Ilocos, who were eager to buy it. The introduction of a monopoly has brought little benefit to the revenue, with a staff of ten employees, and has completely destroyed the original trade. The collection of wax, which requires a temperate climate, neither too dry nor too rainy, has also diminished, and cocoa does not progress.

The villages of Fupiparao, Iguig,[3] Amulung,[4] Nassiping[5] and Gattaran[6] all gave our traveller the opportunity to study the large Calinga tribe.[7] He was greatly assisted by the vicar of the first of these villages, Father Lobato, whose advanced age, venerable air and unkempt appearance gave him a monkish aspect, to which were added the reverence due to his remarkable apostolic work in these provinces, and the various books he has already had published.[8] Don Antonio found in him a man of real merit, worthy of his particular affection, and whose experience and continuous observations supplied him with a great quantity of interesting information with which to augment and compare his own work.

Lal-lo,[9] the principal town of the province and the residence of the *alcalde mayor*, is classified as a town for these two circumstances alone, without any other reason to deserve the title. A few Spaniards live there and use their boats for trading, but the paucity of this commerce, resulting from the sorry state of the province, does not provide them with a good living. Their fellow inhabitants have little taste for agriculture and dedicate themselves to the trade in salt and other minor merchandise that

---

[1] Situated 75 miles south of Aparri.
[2] Possibly a type of enclosed craft.
[3] On the Cagayan River 38 miles south of Aparri.
[4] On the Cagayan River 33 miles south of Aparri.
[5] On the Cagayan River 23 miles south of Aparri.
[6] On the Cagayan River 17 miles south of Aparri.
[7] For these native people of Luzon, see Buzeta, *Diccionario geográfico*, I, p. 464.
[8] Fray Antonio Lobato (d. 1794), a Dominican friar, philologist, poet, architect (he built his own church) and town planner (Tuguegarao, in Cagayan); for details of his eleven scholarly works (unpublished through Dominican indifference) see Robert Streit, ed., *Bibliotheca missionum*, Aachen, 1916-, VI (1931), pp. 366-7. Fernández, *Dominicos*, pp. 343, 345, amplifies Pineda's praise of this unusual friar.
[9] On the Cagayan River, 9 miles south of Aparri.

they transport by river. They work quite hard at their weaving, however, and hardly a woman is to be seen without her loom, but these are so inefficient that their work is doubled and their labours greatly prolonged. They will make, on commission, handkerchiefs which compare with the fine ones made on the coast, but they are sold at a low price because of the lack of promotion and a ready market.

The town stands in a grove of banana trees, with a high cordillera[1] barring the way to the east, some ten or twelve leagues distant, and to the south the plain stretches to the horizon. Don Antonio Pineda gave on every occasion unmistakable proof of his diligent attention to all useful tasks, noting bearings, and taking distances from every tower and high point to all conspicuous objects in view. These bearings will be doubly useful when there is time to correlate them with those taken by Don Francisco Viana in these same parts, thus linking points in the interior of the island with the geodetic work on the coast.[2]

Our observer notes that the impure waters of the Cagayan cause obstructions of the liver in the inhabitants, among whom young men and women of all ages may be seen suffering from this disease. Swollen bellies and constipation are common and, in all his peregrinations, he did not find half a dozen people with a sanguine complexion, an observation all the more valid when its truth became sadly apparent among those of their own party. The painter was unwell from the time he drank its waters and grew steadily worse and Pineda himself, already plagued by fever for several days, could continue his work only with considerable discomfort.

The towns of Aparri and Bangui[3] provided no more than a few insignificant observations.[4] In the latter town it rains for most of the year, and does so ceaselessly for six months. The climate is so humid that the hygrometer showed 6° more than in the previous towns. Its idle inhabitants, having no boats or anything indicative of a knowledge of watercraft, fish with hand lines and live in great poverty.

17 June

The departure from this town may be considered by our country as marking the moment it lost one of its brightest lights and, by the expedition, the greatest misfortune that could have befallen it. Don Antonio Pineda's notes, drafted in some confusion, bearings incorrectly given or duplicated in contradiction, began to show the first signs of the writer's fatal condition. His memory weakened, he confused species with each other and, his body lying exhausted on a litter or portable bed (carried by Indians), he was left powerless but for his will. This too was sapped by the constant work he tried in vain to continue. With his organs debilitated and his mind confused, he acted at times inconsequently, revealing all the signs of a man nearing the end. Racked by a high fever, which drove him towards his death, he mistakenly attempted to reduce it with lemonade and other refreshments which, as well as being extremely

---

[1] The Sierra Madre.
[2] For Viana's visit to Lal-lo see pp. 367-8 above.
[3] Situated 12 miles east of Cape Bojeador and 55 miles WNW of Lal-lo.
[4] A clear indication of Pineda's failing health.

acid, may perhaps have been very harmful to him. In vain did all those who saw him exhort him to rest and obtain more suitable medicines but, swayed by the fleeting pleasure these gave him, he demanded to continue his work and return to Manila.

He was carried onwards in a state of lethargy, with frequent lapses in his judgement, which even the Indians noticed, struggling all the time with the fate which had already overcome him, but never ceasing to describe the country and plan his itinerary. [20th] At last he reached Badoc, a town in the province of Ilocos administered by the Augustinian fathers. At times again he fell into a stupor, but he was constantly anxious about the continuation of his journey for which he had made the most active preparations. In his few untroubled moments he was still eager to discuss the ill-fated object of his work with the friar, but he was not easily persuaded by the Father's suggestions about the kind of food he should have or the necessity of rest. Nor did he attend to the dictates of his own medical knowledge with regard to the effectiveness of blood letting. Either he did not realize how close was his end or, having long been in the grip of patriotic zeal and an untiring love of science, he regarded its proximity with philosophic transcendence and tranquillity.

In this manner the day passed. That night he suffered an apoplectic attack from which, perhaps owing to the lack of skill of the native doctor, he recovered only enough to indicate to the Father that his soul was as steadfast in religion as it had been in his duties to society. Thus, on the night of the 23rd, the illustrious course of his life was brought to an end at the age of thirty-eight.

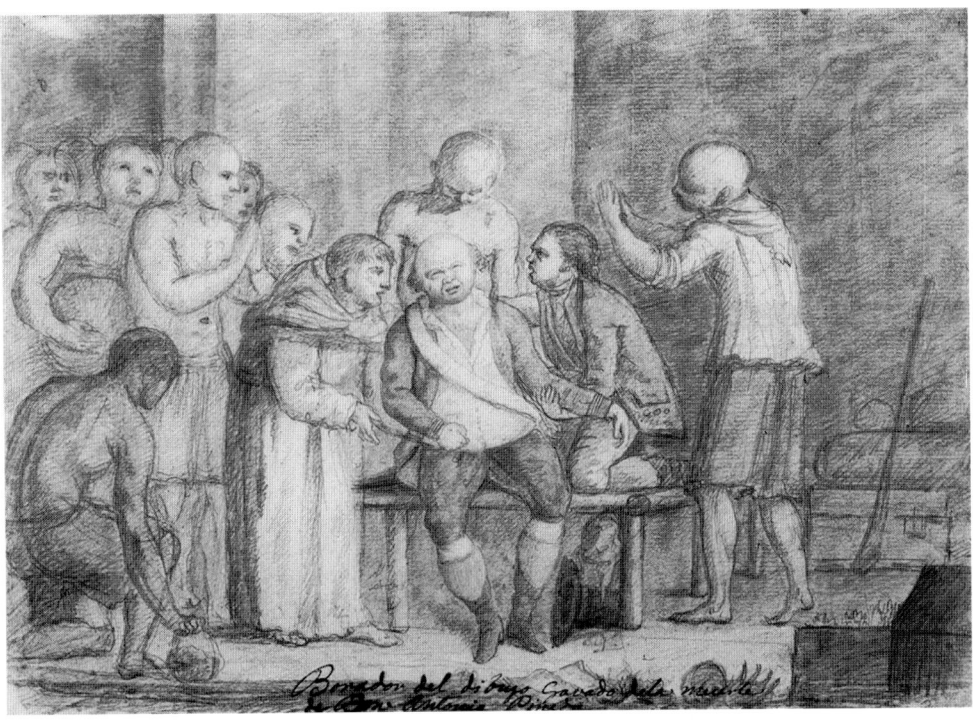

Plate 41. The death of Antonio Pineda, by Juan Ravenet. Museo Naval, Madrid

It is not easy to encompass in a few lines either the praise of such a distinguished subject, or the even more remarkable events of his life.

After an education befitting his birth, Don Antonio Pineda had entered the army as a cadet in the Regimiento de Reales Guardias of the Spanish Infantry. His sociable nature, his love of study and clear understanding of his duty to his country, soon urged upon him the need to broaden his education as much as possible. He chose the art of war and this became obvious in the attacks on Gibraltar during the war of 1779.[1] Indeed, his military science was acknowledged anonymously. A plan of his was implemented, detailing military operations aimed opening a new parallel[2] on the night of 1 August. His service was again distinguished and his life exposed to extraordinary danger on the floating battery *La Pastora* on board which, and in succeeding encounters between the two [opposing] squadrons not far from Cape Espartel,[3] when serving under Jefe de Esquadra Don Buenaventura Moreno. When peace was finally declared he rejected the thought of boring idleness or making the destruction of his fellow-men the only object of his efforts. Instead he turned his mind to physics and natural history, in which sciences he had already acquired a good grounding. His diligence and talent soon took him to higher levels in both sciences. In consequence his patriotic zeal and honour moved him to take the opportunity of joining the expedition of the corvettes *Descubierta* and *Atrevida* to the Pacific Ocean. The subsequent course of his useful work for mankind in general and for his fellow citizens in particular is revealed in the narrative of the voyage and the inscription engraved on the monument erected in his memory near Manila. It will be further demonstrated by the publication of all his observations, whose variety, quantity and utility were rightly reiterated with the thanks of the sovereign and the applause of the whole country. A rich inheritance for his family's property and, above all, the constant pleas of his travelling companions had reminded him of the honourable rewards awaiting him on his return to his native land.

After such a sudden and irreparable loss to the expedition, his companions could not fail to dwell thereafter upon his memory. At one blow had they lost the purest example of a man of great humanity, a philosopher of exceptional learning and diligence, a constantly convivial friend and an ever pleasant and good natured companion. To these personal and irreparable losses must be added the loss to the nation as a whole. His ideas, as ambitious as they were viable, about the land and inhabitants of almost the entire continent of the Americas subject to the monarchy, the comparative exploitation of its minerals, the analysis of its languages, the administration, situation

---

[1] Pineda had started life as a soldier fighting the British at the third siege of Gibraltar (1779), when the Spaniards made their most serious attempt to recover Gibraltar. For a laudatory comment on Pineda's work, and on his papers 'left in cypher at his death', see *Remarks on the Philippine Islands, and the Capital Manila (1819–1822), by an Englishman*, Calcutta, 1828; the Library of Congress copy is reprinted in Blair and Robertson, *The Philippine Islands*, LI, pp. 73-181. See also Marjorie G. Driver, ed., *The Guam Diary of Naturalist Antonio de Pineda*, Guam, 1990. He had hoped to return to Europe by land or via the Cape of Good Hope: Bruce Cruikshank, *Filipiniana in Madrid*, Honolulu, 1984, p. 261.

[2] In a siege a trench parallel to the general face of the works attacked, serving as a way of communication between the different parts of the siege-works.

[3] A prominent cape on the coast of Morocco and the SW entrance point of the Strait of Gibraltar.

and customs of our colonies, although partially described in his notebooks, have largely perished with him. Unhappy is the lot of man who, deriving his happiness only from the happiness of others, suffers countless troubles by this very desire and is doomed to failure by his own weakness.

This news did not reach Manila until the afternoon of 13 July. On the 16th tribute was paid to his memory with the most solemn funeral and obsequies in the Church of Saint Augustine. Immediately afterwards Don Juan Ravenet and Don Fernando Brambila set to work, the former in representing accurately the extraordinary achievements of this worthy subject to the nation that has lost him, and the latter in the design and construction in Malate Park, owned by the Real Compañia, of a monument to record for posterity our loss and our tears, which Don Tadeo Haenke engraved with the following elegant Latin inscription:[1]

Antonio Pineda,
Tribuno Militum
Virtute in Patriam Bello. Armisque Insigni
Naturæ demum indefesso scrutatori.
Trienni arduo itinere, Orbis Extrema adiit.
Telluris, Viscera. Pelagi. Abyssos. andiumque Cacumina Lustrans.
Vitæ simul, et Laborum Gravium.
Diem supremum obiit in Luconia Philippicarum
VI Calendas Iulii MDCCXCII.[2]
Præmaturam Optimi Mortem
Luget Patria Luget Fauna Lugent Amici
Qui Hocce Posuere Monumentum.[3]

Don Agustin de Emparan, the *regente* [presiding magistrate] of the Real Audiencia, on seeing the drawing of this sad event, moved by a true patriotism and the natural goodwill that he had constantly shown us here and in Mexico, had the kindness to write and send me the following inscription:

Studiis. Belli.
Asperrimo. Exercitus. Chiliarco.
Antonio Pineda
Qui et Columnas. oppugnavit. Herculeas.

---

[1] The entire cost of the monument was met by all the officers: Malaspina to Valdés, 20 October 1792, AMN, MS 583, ff. 107-108.

[2] Haenke is in error; VI Calends July is 26 June and not 23 June, the date of Pineda's death: for details of Roman dating see E. G. Richards, *Mapping Time: The Calendar and its History*, Oxford, 1998, p. 213.

[3] Antonio Pineda, a military commander who was outstanding in his love of his country in war. Distinguished in arms, he was, in addition, a tireless researcher into the ways of Nature. In a laborious journey of three years, he reached the limits of the globe, where he investigated the bowels of the earth, the depths of the ocean, and the peaks of the Andes. The last day of his life and heavy labours came upon him in Luzon in the Philippines on VI Calends July MDCCXCII. His homeland mourns, Nature mourns, as do his friends, who set up this monument, lamenting the premature death of this, the best of men.

Et de rerum Indole.
Plura conscripsit Eleganter.
Naturæ solers Arcana retexens
Ignotos idcirco
Trans Pontum utrumque penetrans
Extremos in Indos
Et qui tandem. Badocho Luconiarum.
Fatis concessit.
VI Kalendas Julias[1]
Diva Bellatrix
Docta Minerva
Lugens.[2]

---

[1] An error; VI Calends July is 26 June and not 23 June, the date of Pineda's death: see p.413, n. 2 above.

[2] Antonio Pineda. A student of war, a bold and experienced leader of men, he not only attacked the Pillars of Hercules, but also skilfully unravelled the secrets of Nature. He wrote copiously and elegantly on the nature of things, for which purpose he passed among unknown peoples, crossing both Oceans as far as the utmost Indies, until at length he yielded to Fate at Badoc in Luzon on VI Calends July, mourned by Minerva, who is the goddess of both war and learning.

APPENDIXES

APPENDIX 1

The Malaspina–Valdés Correspondence

Throughout the voyage Malaspina and Antonio Valdés y Bázan, Ministro de Marina,[1] were in regular correspondence with each other. Malaspina sent reports of his proceedings to Valdés from his various ports of call, while the minister responded with comments and, on occasion, further instructions. The four letters printed here explain the diversion of Malaspina's ships north to Alaska in the summer of 1791 to search for the strait described by Lorenzo Ferrer Maldonado, and the consequent alterations to the planned schedule of the voyage.

1. Valdés to Malaspina. Madrid, 22 December 1790.[2]

I informed the King of the contents of your last two letters of 27 April and 3 June last, the former written in the port of Coquimbo and the latter in Lima, regarding the proceedings of the corvettes *Descubierta* and *Atrevida* under your command since your departure from Santiago de Chile to return to Valparaíso. His Majesty was pleased with the skill with which you have so far led this expedition, and although before your departure from Cádiz he left it to your judgment whether, according to circumstances, you should carry out the expedition to the north of Kamchatka in search of the passage to the Atlantic recorded by Ferrer Maldonado, the royal wish now is that you should verify this, making use for this purpose the information contained in the attached copy of a report published in France on this venture.[3] I advise you of this by order of His Majesty for your information and for action.

May God &c. Madrid, 22 December 1790.

[Copies sent to Acapulco and San Blas]

2. Valdés to Malaspina. Madrid, 23 March 1791.[4]

The King has considered in detail what you wrote from Callao on 15 September regarding the plans which it was proposed to follow from there on your voyage, changing the basis of the expedition in the light of new insights and considerations, and His Majesty has agreed entirely with what you proposed.[5] Consequently, after

---

[1] For a short biographical sketch of Valdés see Vol. I of this edition, p. 311 and n. 1.
[2] AMN, MS 278, f. 87.
[3] A reference to the memoir on the Ferrer Maldonado account presented by the French geographer, Jean-Nicolas Buache de la Neuville, to the Académie Royale des Sciences of Paris on 13 November 1790. It is printed on pp. 453–60 below.
[4] AMN, MS 278, ff. 109–111.
[5] For the letter in question see Vol. I of this edition, pp. 319–23.

the corvettes return from the north next October or November to San Blas or Acapulco, where you will receive these letters, you may omit the visits to the Islas de Sandwich [Hawaiian Islands], the Pescadores[1] and the Carolinas, as well as the detailed survey of the Marianas. Instead, you should substitute for this route the one which you consider more suitable, that is to say, a short stay at Owihee [Hawaii], one of the said Islas de Sandwich, together with whatever is needed to determine the true astronomical position of Guajan [Guam] and Tinian in the Marianas. You should then use the months from January to May 1792 working on the Mercator-projection chart of the Philippines, and spend the following months in Manila in order to refit the ships and put in order your previous work. Likewise, the survey of Estrecho de Malaca [Malacca Strait] may be omitted, considering how often it is frequented by our vessels of the Manila trade and by foreign ships. Instead, the corvettes should proceed from Canton [Guangzhou] to survey the opposite [i.e. eastern] coast of Luzón and otherwise do all that you propose until you call at Islas de los Amigos [Friendly Islands] and de la Sociedad [Society Islands]. You should then set course from there in October 1793, as the season permits, direct to Chiloé, and meet in Montevideo in March or April 1794 in order to return to Spain that summer.

It is thus agreed that you should not carry out the circumnavigation by way of Cabo de Buena Esperanza [Cape of Good Hope]. However, since the detailed survey of that area, which as a result of this change you will not be undertaking, is still required, His Majesty has decided that the best way would be to carry this out from Spain with another ship which will be sent for this purpose.

For the important survey of the Golfo de San Jorge it will be arranged, as you have suggested,[2] that at the beginning of 1794 two launches or *sumacas* will leave Río de la Plata for this purpose in charge of Pilotos Tafor, Peña and Catalá, with good instruments. On this assumption you will draw up, and send to me, the orders which the said *pilotos* must follow for successfully accomplishing this task, which I shall forward in good time to Buenos Aires, where I am notifying the Viceroy of these plans so that at the appointed time the above personnel are in position and everything is ready.

Finally, I must inform you that the King agrees that the accounts should be settled at Montevideo, and the crews paid in full, in readiness for their return to Spain.

May God &c. Madrid, 23 March 1791.

3. Malaspina to Valdés. Acapulco, 28 April 1791.[3]

Excellency.

You will already have been informed, through the various dispatches of Capitán de Fragata José Bustamante y Guerra in command of the corvette *Atrevida*, of the very energetic and successful measures taken by that officer to give full effect to the

---

[1] A group of islands or large atolls discovered in 1537 by Hernando de Grijalva; their exact location is uncertain. They are placed in 10°40′N, 165°E in 'A General Chart Exhibiting the Discoveries made by Captn James Cook in this and his two preceeding Voyages …'. As Plate 1 in the atlas accompanying Cook and King, *Voyage to the Pacific Ocean*, this chart would have been held on board the *Descubierta*. The islands have been variously identified as being in the Marshall Islands (Findlay, *Directory*, II, p. 1068) and in the Gilbert Islands (Sharp, *Discovery of the Pacific Islands*, p. 26).

[2] See Vol. I of this edition, p. 322.

[3] AMN, MS 583, ff. 86–87v.

instructions which I had given him when he parted company with the *Descubierta* on the Nicaraguan coast, and afterwards to His Majesty's orders, transmitted by Your Excellency, which he received in this port, or which reached him subsequently at San Blas. As regards the *Descubierta*, Your Excellency will also have seen by the duplicate letter written from Realejo, and the dispatch which reported our arrival at this port,[1] that unseasonable weather and contrary currents had largely frustrated my work, requiring me not only to abandon almost two months of the next part of the programme but also to give up the work of correcting, as I had promised, the hydrographic description of various stretches of coast between Guatemala and this port, and to omit the marine survey of Golfos de Amapala [Fonseca] and Nicoya.

By a strange chance both copies of His Majesty's orders regarding our sailing programme for this year had been forwarded to San Blas with the result that Bustamante alone received them a few days after his arrival in that department, and I did not get them until he sent them on to me by special courier. They reached me in Mexico [City] where I had gone to inform His Excellency the Viceroy of our forthcoming operations and to fix the precise geographical position of that capital by astronomical observations. All our activities since the closing months of last year have been directed to the same end, namely to be in a position to give the fullest effect to all of His Majesty's orders. At the same time the dispositions already made by His Excellency the Viceroy greatly contributed to that purpose, as did the most active practical work of Capitán de Navío Don Juan de la Bodega y Quadra.[2] Bustamante, having received his launch and some supplies, and having carried out a refit that had become necessary, was able to sail immediately and joined us in this port on the morning of the 20th. This corvette continued its preparations and repairs with all speed, checking the launch and its fittings, and putting everything in order. Thus I have the satisfaction of informing Your Excellency that both ships will set sail on 1 or 2 May.

Thus it will be the most recent orders of His Majesty regarding the exploration of the passage of Maldonado that we shall now put into effect. The season, it is true, is somewhat advanced; nevertheless, we are now intent on this one objective. Since I have already informed Your Excellency in my dispatches from Lima[3] that it was in our minds to combine, in a single cruise, not only the clarification of the truth about this passage but also the limits of the permanent ice north of the continents both of Asia and America, we shall therefore neither lack time for the task nor shall we fail to carry it out in precisely the same months as the navigator Ferrer Maldonado claims to have made his entry [into the strait] from the Pacific on his return passage.

The report presented by M. de Buache to the Academy of Sciences of Paris which Your Excellency was kind enough to send us at the same time, should nevertheless avail us of all the options open to any person entrusted with this project. We can assure Your Excellency that as regards the Pacific entry to the strait we have been wholly in agreement since Lima with the ideas of M. de Buache, only excluding from our discussions the area around Shoal Ness and Cabo Newenham (on Cook's chart).

---

[1] The two letters are in AMN, MS 583, ff. 83–83v.
[2] Commandant of the Department of San Blas.
[3] See Vol. I of this edition, pp. 319–23.

We have concentrated on the area around the opening east of Oonalaska [Unalaska] near Cook's River, since only in that vicinity is it possible to make sense of two related points: the distance west from the mouth of the river to the coast which Ferrer believed to belong to Asia, and his claim to have kept the coast in sight on his return for the voyage back to Europe. The encounter with the Hanseatic or Asian ships whose sailors spoke Latin, the abundance of succulent fruits where now only snow is found, the ease with which he reached 71° in winter when whalers at that time indicated the same limits of ice at the North Pole as can be seen now, and finally the improbability that victuals were available for an extra year in a vessel engaged in cod fishing on Bancos de Terranova [the Newfoundland Banks] – these are all difficulties in the way of accepting the reality of this passage. I wonder how Señores Buache and Mendoza[1] have dealt with them.

But, be that as it may, Your Excellency will see from our activities this year that we wish to carry out His Majesty's orders as faithfully as possible and to prove worthy of the confidence with which the nation has honoured us. The plan, nevertheless, should not allow us to overlook the still incomplete state of the principal task entrusted to us, that of charting the Pacific Ocean. Nor, on an expedition in which His Majesty had invested large sums, with a generosity matching his sponsorship of the sciences, should we lose sight of the need to provide the maximum benefit for the advancement of geography, navigation and the natural sciences consistent with the minimum delay in completing the voyage. Consequently, Don José Bustamante and I agreed that a division of responsibilities was now necessary which would overcome these difficulties without any increase in cost. Meanwhile none of the many able officers serving at the moment in both corvettes who would be made redundant for the next stage of the campaign, limited as it would be to launches operating under the guns of the vessels, ought to stand idle and frustrated in the use of their abilities. We had also to consider the exceptional qualities that Teniente de Navío Don Dionisio Galiano had brought to the expedition, which have caused him to be entrusted with tasks more as a leader than as a subordinate. We owe to him many important innovations in astronomical navigation, which he will soon be in a position to put in order, and will be to the great honour of the nation. Finally, there is also the necessity of bringing some order to our collected materials, and of making it possible for this or that officer gradually to become involved in the essentials of our task by adding the finishing touches so as to ensure publication as soon as possible after our return.

In these circumstances it was arranged that Don Dionisio Galiano, with Don Arcadio Pineda and Don Martín de Olavide under his orders, would use the greater

---

[1] José de Mendoza y Ríos, the naval officer who while in Paris in 1789 gave Buache de la Neuville a copy of the Ferrer Maldonado account made by Juan Bautista Muñoz, apparently unaware of a royal command that no foreigners should be told about the account. Martín Fernández de Navarette noted that 'From the Muñoz copy teniente de navío D. José Espinosa made a further copy to have for his own use during his voyage round the world under the command of D. Alejandro Malaspina; and another one was made by capitán de fragata D. José de Mendoza, and this copy was then used in Paris by M. Buache for the composition of his *Memoir*.' Spanish text in D. Miguel Salvá and D. Pedro Sainz de Baranda, eds, *Colección de documentos inéditos para la historia de España*, XV, Madrid, 1849, p. 93.

part of this year either arranging and refining the many elements of our work intended for publication which I would hand over to them in draft form, or (weather permitting) continuing with astronomical observations likely to improve the geography of the hinterland, the perfecting of our charts, and the importance of linking our longitudes in the Pacific with those which serve as the basis of the Atlantic charts. This point appeared to me of the greatest importance for the harmonization of the national tasks in both oceans. I therefore instructed Galiano to carry out a series of longitude observations from Mexico [City] to Vera Cruz and the mouth of the Guazahualcos [Río Coatzacoalcos] which had to link up with the port of Tecoantepeque [Tehuantepec] in the Pacific, just as we linked Acapulco with Vera Cruz, Panama [City] with Chagres, and possibly the region of Realejo with Omoa.[1] At the same time Don Arcadio Pineda, who has the necessary learning and skills, would study the documents of the past and present administrations of Nueva España,[2] while Don Martín de Olavide would either demonstrate his thoroughness in revising our drafts, or would join the excursions of Galiano who, with some of our instruments on board, or those which he had from Mexico belonging to the Cádiz Royal Astronomical Observatory, had managed to provide himself with a set adequate for his purposes.

Apart from these advantages our commission would also benefit from the assurance that there would not be any risk to the completion of the programme on these coasts, even if some chance, either very fortunate or very unlucky,[3] prevented the return of the corvettes to Acapulco next October as planned. Thus Galiano's instructions provided that if our return had not taken place by the beginning of November, he should give top priority to sailing with a schooner[4] from San Blas to Cerro de Soconusco,[5] where our detailed observations had ended.

It was no less important to take full advantage of the activities of the natural history team and above all to make a useful scientific comparison of the lithology, zoology, botany and mineral exploitation in South America with those of this area. Don Antonio Pineda, Don Luis Neé, the artist Guio and the clerk Villar[6] consequently had orders to look after this important matter, and even to go ahead of us in the galleon to the Philippines,[7] while Don Antonio [Tadeo] Haenke stayed with the corvettes to continue the study of the shores which we were to visit very shortly.

Finally, if our return to these shores were to take place next October it was our plan to assign two other officers to the San Blas schooner. They, equipped with a

---

[1] On the north coast of Honduras about twelve miles east of the Guatamala/Honduras border.
[2] The imperial administrative regime developed under the Habsburgs was overhauled and eventually replaced under the Bourbons by a more centralized system of *intendentes*, although elements of both regimes co-existed for a long time. For literature on the 'intendancy system' see Charles R. Cutter, *The Legal Culture of Northern New Spain 1700–1810*, Albuquerque, 1995, p. 168, n. 58.
[3] The first reference is to the chance, however remote, that a passage might be found; the second to the possibility of a mishap in unfamiliar waters.
[4] The *Mexicana*, which had recently been built at San Blas.
[5] Paredones de Soconusco is a group of hills 85 miles ESE of Salina Cruz.
[6] For Julián del Villar y Pardo see p. 69, n. 3 above.
[7] A reference to the annual *nao* or galleon from Acapulco to Manila, which usually left the Mexican coast in March on its westbound voyage. See p. 15, n. 1 above.

chronometer, a theodolite, and sextants, after filling in the stretches of coast as yet unsurveyed, would work with precision on the soundings and the description of Golfo de Nicaragua and Río San Juan, places that I considered to be of the greatest importance both for trade and for national defence. The command of this schooner and its operations would have been given to Don Juan [Gutiérrez] de la Concha if his poor state of health and incorrigible appetite for work had not dissuaded me. Naturally it will be entrusted to Don Juan Vernacci who, once his work is completed, will begin to make his way back to Europe, where eventually I intend to send back from the Philippines Don Felipe Bauzá and another officer so that matters can go forward with the greatest possible speed and despatch.

Having dictated the relevant orders for this purpose, and everything now having been arranged for them to be carried out, let me be allowed, Sire, to inform Your Excellency not so much of the personal merit of each of these individuals, since that has already or will very soon be made obvious, but rather the mutual regard of the entire officer complement of both corvettes, which makes the separation of some of them very painful to all. It has only been put into effect because the best service of His Majesty requires it, and because we flatter ourselves that the King in his goodness will regard us, whether we are in the corvettes or on subsequent missions, as working as one until we have the satisfaction of laying at his royal feet the fruit of our labours. Still more must we be saddened by the departure of Don Manuel Novales, who may be compelled to return to Spain by the dire state of his health, harassed by tropical disease, and aggravated, to my distress, by the launch expeditions in Panamá and Realejo, in which this officer displayed with excessive zeal his will to succeed.[1]

Before concluding this dispatch, although it is already too long, I also wish to remind Your Excellency of the efficiency with which His Excellency the Viceroy has assisted the expedition. It is not possible to summarize it in a few lines, but the log books will describe it at much greater length. For now I shall confine myself to telling Your Excellency that the illustrator, Don Tomás de Suria, so sensibly chosen by the Viceroy himself, will continue with us for this next cruise, though classified as an artist, so that neither he nor the Royal Exchequer will suffer serious harm if he has to accompany us to the various places which we still have to visit.

Other discharges from service and the current muster book of both complements will be seen by Your Excellency in the attached official return.[2]

The corvette *Descubierta* at anchor in the port of Acapulco, 28 April 1791.

4. Malaspina to Valdés. San Blas, 12 October 1791.[3]
Excellency.
In compliance with the orders of His Majesty which Your Excellency was good enough to communicate to me under date of 23 December of the year just past, the corvettes *Descubierta* and *Atrevida* of the royal navy sailed from the port of Acapulco

---

[1] Having been put ashore at this point, Novales rejoined the *Descubierta* on her return to Acapulco from Alaska with his health much restored after treatment by Dr O'Sullivan of Mexico City.
[2] See p. 73 above.
[3] AMN, MS 583, ff. 88v–89v.

on 1 May with the aim of investigating at the 60th parallel whether the passage from the Pacific to the Atlantic which the navigator Ferrer Maldonado recorded does exist. Having compared the speculations of M. de Buache with Maldonado's original account, and with our own and the English voyages, the existence of the passage appeared, in truth, highly improbable. Consequently, it was somewhat difficult to direct the operations of the two corvettes so as on the one hand not to leave the least doubt on the matter, and on the other not to waste six months of time and effort. But as various stretches of the coast of Northwest America still lacked topographical precision, and our present-day navigation calls for a more exact survey of the coasts of California, as well as those which extend north of Cabo Mendocino, I finally decided that even if the original purpose of the voyage might be frustrated, I would not fail to use the time on other matters of equal importance.

I shall pass over for the moment scholarly speculation concerning the authenticity of the account in question, the possibility of a passage, and the reflections on both presented by M. Buache to the Royal Academy of Sciences, all matters which require more extensive treatment, and I shall deal with them in a separate paper.[1] I shall only say to Your Excellency, to justify the steps I am taking, that it did not seem possible to accept the assumption of the French geographer that the latitude of 60° calculated by Ferrer Maldonado was accurate. The most recent voyages of Captain Dixon[2] and of our vessels from San Blas[3] have greatly changed the aspect of the question from that which M. de Buache had proposed after studying only the voyage of Captain Cook.

After considering these points, and in agreement with Don José Bustamante, I decided to examine with great care the coast which from Cabo Buen Tiempo [Cape Fairweather] continues (on Captain Cook's chart) by Bahía de Behring, Monte de San Elías and Isla de Kaye as far as Cabo Hinchinbrook at the Entrada del Principe Guillermo [Prince William Sound]. This gulf has been carefully explored last year by Don Salvador Fidalgo.[4] The Russians, now established at the Río de Cook [Cook Inlet], could not fail to know of nor hide the existence of a communicating channel. Therefore it seemed pointless to sail farther west since it would be more useful to survey the above-mentioned coasts – the more so because Captain Cook's sighting of them had been at a great distance. Referring to Bahía de Behring, he suspected that at a little distance within it there might be either low-lying land or water.

Navigation to the coast was easy. On 24 June we sighted it a long way off at about 57°, and on the 27th, favoured with exceptional luck, we had not only dispelled our doubts about Bahía de Behring but had also approached the vicinity of Puerto Mulgrave and Monte de San Elías. The sight of a substantial inlet to the east of that mountain in approximately 59°45' appeared at the time to confirm more and more the success of our search. We at once altered course to survey it, but as its steep shores

---

[1] As he did in his 'Disertación' of the following summer, printed on pp. 468–80 below.
[2] In 1787 George Dixon in the trading vessel *King George* had explored along the Northwest Coast, and had entered and named Port Mulgrave (today's Yakutat Bay) just north of latitude 59°N.
[3] A reference to the Spanish voyages to Alaska of Juan Pérez (1774), Bodega y Quadra (1775), Ignacio de Artega (1779), Esteban José Martínez (1788), and Salvador Fidalgo (1790).
[4] See Cook, *Flood Tide of Empire*, pp. 277–8, and p. 54, n. 4 above.

made it risky to look for an anchorage inside it, nearby Puerto Mulgrave was preferred instead. This enabled the corvettes to take on wood and water, and to make the usual observations, while our armed launches could enter the inlet to follow if possible the tracks of Ferrer Maldonado. The launches surveyed the inlet on the 2nd and 3rd. I decided to command them myself so as to extend our navigation as far inland as possible; and so their crews, provisions, arms and navigational instruments were allocated with that end in view. But the end of the inlet extended only a few leagues from its mouth, and even then a part of that channel was obstructed by a mass of ice floes which finally joined the permanent ice near Isla Haenke.[1] The expedition was consequently very brief, and since by now all the essential objectives for our call at Puerto Mulgrave had been met, by the evening of the 5th the corvettes set sail again to continue their investigations.

On the following passage it was now our main objective to take advantage of the winds from NW to explore the coast. Although infrequent, they are the only ones which completely clear the inland mountains. Revealing everything clearly and distinctly, they avoid those optical illusions resulting either from the ice which covers the whole cordillera down to its base or from the fog which obscures the coast down to the shoreline. Many incidents, arising partly from the weather conditions and partly from the nature of the coast, slowed up this survey much more than I had expected, and even compelled us to anchor off Monte San Elias. Nevertheless, by 28 July when we found ourselves once more off Monte Buen Tiempo we could consider the orders of His Majesty as having been complied with since we knew that between that mountain and the Entrada del Principe Guillermo there is no intervening river along the shore nor does the unbroken line of the coastal cordillera leave the least hope of the existence of an inlet.

The chart which I enclose[2] will clarify still further the voyage and surveys which, although unsuccessful in the main objective, will nevertheless not appear useless when it is considered that the position of the coast has now been laid down with much greater accuracy, deleting from Captain Cook's chart Bahía de Behring and the passage between the mainland and Isla de Kaye,[3] and adding to it the islands of Galiano and Triste[4] at the Entrada del Principe Guillermo. Furthermore, Puerto Mulgrave and the nearby islands and Puerto del Desengaño can now be used with greater knowledge and safety. Finally the botanical and lithological excursions of Don Tadeo Haenke, as well as the experiments with the pendulum in latitude 59°34', will contribute to the progress of science which His Majesty so greatly fosters and desires. The names used on this chart have been in part adopted from those of Captains Cook and Dixon, but they have been changed either when names have been given at the same time by our seamen, or when the anchorage to which they had been attached could not be recognized.

[1] Named in honour of the naturalist. For the survey of the inlet see Plate 14, p. 129 above.
[2] Possibly 'Carta esférica de los reconocimientos hechos en la costa NO. de América entre los paralelos 57° y 60°30', lat. N., por las corbetas *Descubierta* y *Atrevida* de la Marina Real, año de 1791' in AMN, Sig. II. B (7). See p. 96, n. 1 above.
[3] Here Malaspina is wrong and Cook right since there is in fact a channel between the two.
[4] Middleton Island and Seal Rocks; Malaspina's names have not survived.

Although we could still count on a month of good weather, winds from the NW carried us by 31 July within sight of the Archipielago de Bucareli.[1] After carefully surveying the intermediate coast we flattered ourselves that there was nothing to prevent our sailing through Estrecho de Dixon [Dixon Entrance] or the Canal de Reina Carlota [Queen Charlotte Sound] to arrive conveniently at Nutka. But a succession of severe storms from the SE and south, which did not die down until 7 August, forced us to change plans and to set course directly for Cabo Frondoso[2] in latitude 50°N, from where we sailed close to the coast to the said port of Nutka.

We did not waste the fifteen days which we spent at that port. The experiments with the pendulum were continued, and all the inner channels explored. We were also able to cultivate friendly relations between the natives and our settlement there, helping the latter with whatever might ensure its well-being in the coming winter. Finally, we were able to gain some knowledge about the religion, laws and customs of those natives, and about a part of the inland geography, such impressions of course adding much interest to the scientific account.

We departed from that port on 28 August, and without leaving the coast, which we surveyed and worked along almost daily, we were able to anchor at Monterey on 11 September, not without running an obvious risk of shipwreck, from which we were saved by abandoning two anchors from the *Atrevida* and one from the *Descubierta*.

Finally, having continued our hydrographic work by the same method as far as Cabo San Lucas, and having compared our longitudes at the mission of San José with the observations of Don Vicente Doz, and of the Abbé Chappe, the two corvettes parted company, the *Atrevida* steering for Cabo Corrientes to perfect our charts as far as Acapulco, the *Descubierta* to this Department to take on board all the effects which will be needed in case I collaborate with Capitán de Navío Don Juan de la Bodega in those measures which are most appropriate to the royal service and to the greater perfection of the charts.

During this whole time the officers and crews have enjoyed the best of health, and our contacts with the natives have been completely peaceful, although in Port Mulgrave there could twice have been trouble, on one occasion when we were in superior numbers, and on another with some disadvantage to us and not without serious risk to the commanding officer of the *Atrevida*.[3] Finally our acquisitions for the royal collection have been numerous and very interesting, while Don Tomás Suria has recorded with the greatest accuracy everything which the skill of the artist could supply to make the narrative of the events of this expedition more easily understood.[4]

May God &c.

From the corvette *Descubierta* at anchor in the roads of San Blas, 12 October 1791.

---

[1] Probably the coast of Prince of Wales Island.

[2] A further Spanish rendering of Cabo Woody (Woody Point) which Malaspina used in his journal (p. 165 above); it was renamed Cape Cook in 1860 by Captain G. H. Richards in HMS *Plumper*.

[3] See pp. 129-31, 132-4 above.

[4] A copy of this letter seems to have been sent by Valdés to Martín Fernández de Navarrete (1765–1844) on 28 February 1792 with a request that he should add its findings to his forthcoming work on the Spanish voyages. Oregon Historical Society, Malaspina Papers, MS 2814/222 (contains

only the covering letter from Valdés). In 1800 Fernández de Navarrete presented his examination of Ferrer Maldonado's voyage to the Real Academia de Historia, and two years later his (anonymous) Introduction to *Relación del viage hecho por las goletas Sutil y Mexicana en el año 1792 para reconocer el Estrecho de Fuca*, Madrid, 1802 included a few pages (pp. XLIX–LII) on Ferrer's voyage. For his authorship of the Introduction see María Dolores Higueras Rodríguez and María Luisa Martín-Méras, trans. John Kendrick, 'The Malaspina Expedition on the Northwest Coast of North America in 1791 [and 1792]', in Inglis, *Spain and the North Pacific Coast*, especially pp. 914-15. Fernández de Navarrete's full investigation into the apocryphal voyage of Ferrer Maldonado was not published until after his death as 'Examen de la relación de Lorenzo Ferrer Maldonado sobre el descubrimiento del estrecho de Anián', in Salvá and Sainz de Baranda, *Documentos inéditos*, pp. 71–101.

APPENDIX 2

The Ferrer Maldonado Fantasy

INTRODUCTION

From its inception the aims and objectives of the Malaspina expedition were intended to reflect the new rationalism of the European Enlightenment. It would not be a voyage of discovery in the traditional sense, for as Malaspina explained, 'The safest and shortest routes between the most distant corners of the earth had been pieced together. Any attempt at a further voyage of discovery would have invited scorn … .'[1] It was ironic, then, that less than two years into the voyage Malaspina was diverted from his chosen course to investigate a fictitious report that two hundred years earlier a Spanish seaman had discovered a navigable northern passage between the Atlantic and Pacific Oceans.

In March 1791 Malaspina in the *Descubierta* had reached Acapulco, while Bustamante in the *Atrevida* was farther north at San Blas. After visiting the Viceroy of New Spain in Mexico City, Malaspina intended to rejoin Bustamante, and sail to the Hawaiian Islands. At that point instructions reached Malaspina from Antonio Valdés, Ministro de Marina, to sail instead north to latitude 60°N on the Alaskan coast, and search there for the entrance to a passage into the Atlantic Ocean reportedly discovered by Lorenzo Ferrer Maldonado in 1588.[2] Much remains unclear about the chain of events that led to these new orders. In the original plan for the voyage drawn up by Malaspina and Bustamante in 1788, the Northwest Coast of America was mentioned only in the vaguest terms: 'After following the coast of California, the voyage will continue to the north between Asia and America as far as the snows will allow … .'[3] There was no mention of exploration in any general way, though on a coast still not fully charted this could be assumed, nor of a specific search for a Northwest Passage.

Malaspina's interest in the region was shown by the fact that he took pains to collect all available journals and reports about the Russian voyages to Alaska which had intrigued and alarmed successive Viceroys of New Spain, and had led to a series of reconnaissance voyages north from San Blas since the mid-1770s.[4] Then in June 1789, only weeks before the corvettes were due to leave Cádiz, José Espinosa y Tello, a young naval officer who was searching Spanish archives for journals that might

---

[1] See Vol. I of this edition, p. lxxix.
[2] See p. 417 above.
[3] See Vol. I of this edition, p. 314.
[4] See Cook, *Flood Tide of Empire*, chaps 3, 4.

prove useful to the expedition, found a curious document in the Archivo de Indias in Madrid[1] that he drew to Malaspina's attention.[2] It took the form of a 'Relación' or 'Relation' by a Spanish navigator, Lorenzo Ferrer Maldonado, in which he described a voyage he claimed to have made in 1588 through a passage linking the Atlantic and Pacific oceans.[3] The provenance of this particular document is far from certain, but it seems to have been one of several copies of the 'Relation' that Ferrer Maldonado had presented to the Spanish Crown in 1609, more than twenty years after his supposed voyage. One version had already come to light, in 1781, when the historian Juan Bautista Muñoz discovered it in the collection of the Duque del Infantado and made a copy now at the Real Academia de la Historia in Madrid.[4]

For almost three hundred years the search for the Northwest Passage had been encouraged by accounts of voyages that had allegedly been made through the long sought-for strait; but Ferrer Maldonado's story was the most extraordinary of them all. He himself was a navigator and cosmographer, whose best-known work, *Imagen del Mundo*, was published in 1626, a year after his death.[5] In his 'Relation' of 1609 Ferrer Maldonado claimed that in 1588 he had sailed from Spain on a voyage during which he entered 'the Strait of Labrador' or Davis Strait. This was 290 leagues long, and took his vessel almost as far north as latitude 75°N. Although this part of the voyage was made in February, and the ship was coated with ice, the sea itself never froze. From this farthest point north the vessel sailed SW and WSW for 790 leagues. There in latitude 60°N Ferrer Maldonado reached the fabled Strait of Anian, the name given since the mid-sixteenth century to the waterway which was thought to separate Asia and America, and which some maps showed as providing a navigable route between the Pacific and Atlantic oceans. The strait was fifteen leagues long, with mountainous sides. Near its opening into the Pacific was a harbour capable of holding five hundred ships, and while his ship was at anchor there Ferrer Maldonado encountered a large vessel entering the strait with a rich cargo of pearls, golds, brocades, silks and porcelain. Its crew were Lutherans from the Hanseatic ports with whom Ferrer was able to converse in Latin. In June his ship left the harbour on its return voyage, finding temperatures north of the Arctic Circle warmer than those in the hottest parts of Spain. The Strait of Anian, with its narrow entrances and high sides, could easily be defended, he thought, and he drew sketch maps showing how it could be fortified.

The lack of interest in Spain of Ferrer Maldonado's presentation of his 'Relation' in 1609, more than twenty years after the event, is entirely understandable. Why he waited so long to disclose his sensational discovery was not explained, although his reference to the discoveries of Quiros might hold the key. It was in 1609 that Pedro Fernández de Quiros, a Portuguese-born navigator in the service of Spain, published his celebrated 'Eighth Memorial' in which he inflated his discovery in 1606 of the island of Espiritu Santo (Vanuatu in the SW Pacific) to epic and mystical proportions. It covered, he told Felipe III, 'the fifth part of the Terrestrial Globe', and was double

[1] See p. 141, n. 3 above.
[2] See Vol. I of this edition, p. 318.
[3] See Document 1, pp. 437-52 below for the text of Ferrer Maldonado's 'Relación'.
[4] See p. 437, n. 4 below.
[5] For a biographical sketch of Ferrer Maldonado see pp. 435-7 below.

the size of Spain's existing empire.¹ Ferrer's 'Relation' can perhaps be seen as the northern counterpart of Quiros's 'Memorial', a rival bid to attract attention and patronage. What is more difficult to understand is its re-emergence in the late eighteenth century, in a climate of opinion generally regarded as altogether more critical and less credulous; and after the failure of repeated attempts to find a navigable passage from both the Atlantic and Pacific sides of the North American continent.

The sequence of events as Malaspina prepared to sail is puzzling. On 24 April 1789 Malaspina asked Valdés whether when on the coast north of California he should look for the Northwest Passage 'according to the well-known but very imprecise manuscript of Ferrer Maldonado'.² This was presumably a reference to a summary of the 'Relation' that had appeared the year before in the fourth volume of the monumental work by E. Malo de Luque (the pseudonym of the Duke de Almodóvar), *Historia política de los establecimientos ultramarinos de las naciones europeas*, although to describe it as 'well-known' at this time is surprising. This volume also contained a short but favourable report on Malaspina's recent voyage round the world in the *Astrea* in 1786-88, a note that would have brought the work to Malaspina's notice, and presumably made him well disposed towards Almodóvar. On 9 June 1789 Malaspina wrote to Valdés again.³ Among 'the valuable documents' Espinosa's search had turned up was a copy of Ferrer Maldonado's 'Relation' which, Malaspina wrote, bore 'all the hallmarks of authenticity'.

This last phrase was one used by Almodóvar in his examination of the account, although Malaspina did not go on to quote the historian's further comments that there were some 'prodigious' differences between Ferrer Maldonado's observations and those of Cook, and that such discrepancies left the whole matter 'immersed in doubts'. A major problem was that if, as Almodóvar supposed, the Strait of Anian was in fact Bering Strait, then it was difficult to see how this could be the passage that Ferrer Maldonado had sailed through. In his investigation of Bering Strait in 1778 Cook had shown that it led only to fields of impenetrable pack-ice, and that it was located between latitudes 66°N. and 67°N, whereas Ferrer Maldonado's strait was in latitude 60°N. Faced with these difficulties, Almodóvar wondered whether the mysterious strait was perhaps Cook's River or Norton Sound, or alternatively whether:

> in the course of two centuries sands may have closed an entrance or a river; that the low-lying beaches on an extraordinarily rainy year may have opened a passage which only remained open momentarily and by chance, that volcanoes with their eruptions and some earthquakes or other phenomena produced by nature, about which our understanding is inadequate, may have varied the position of the terrain or lakes or rivers in those little-known lands; that some comet or other extraordinary event or meteor could have temporarily broken a good portion of ice and allowed the odd channel to become passable, allowing that voyager to make his way through ... .⁴

---

¹ There is a useful collection of facsimile reprints of the various versions of the Eighth Memorial of Quiros printed between 1609 and 1625 in Carlos Sanz, ed., *Australia: su descubrimiento y denominación*, Madrid, 1973. See also the appearance of Quiros's discoveries on Ferrer Maldonado's map of 1609, p. 443 below.
² See Vol. I of this edition, p. 318.
³ See ibid., pp. 318–19.
⁴ Eduardo Malo de Luque [Duque de Almodóvar], *Historia política de los establecimientos ultramarinos de la naciones europeas*, IV, Madrid, 1788, pp. 588–9.

Malaspina considered that a close search of the American coast between latitudes 60°N and 65°N was called for, and thought that despite the failures of Cook and La Pérouse to find a strait in that locality there was now 'scope for a new exploration'. He finished by asking whether he should send copies of Ferrer Maldonado's 'Relation' to the learned societies of Paris and London. In a reply that reached Malaspina the day he sailed, Valdés authorized him to search for the passage 'according to circumstances', but ordered that nothing about the voyage of 1588 should be communicated to foreign nations until Malaspina returned.[1]

Like most other objectives of the expedition, the matter was left to Malaspina's discretion. When he reported the results of the first year of the expedition's surveys to Valdés in September 1790, he anticipated that his priority the following summer would be a 'thorough' examination of the Alaskan coast to confirm or otherwise the authenticity of Ferrer Maldonado 'Relation' '(which on mature reflection I do not find wholly absurd)'.[2] In a private letter of this time to Gherardo Rangoni he expressed much the same sentiment when he referred to Ferrer Maldonado's discovery as not 'altogether improbable'.[3] However, when the lateness of his arrival at Acapulco at the end of March 1791 made it impossible to carry out his planned visits to both the Northwest Coast and the Hawaiian Islands that year, Malaspina decided that the survey of Hawaii should have priority, and that he would abandon the Alaskan part of his voyage.[4]

This decision was overturned when Malaspina found on his arrival in Mexico City new orders from Madrid which had been forwarded by Bustamante from San Blas.[5] The letter of 22 December 1790 from Valdés was short and to the point. Malaspina was to sail north to search for Ferrer Maldonado's strait, using as guide a report just issued in France. This latter turned out to be a memoir investigating Ferrer Maldonado's 'Relation' which had been presented to the Académie Royale des Sciences of Paris on 13 November 1790 by Jean-Nicolas Buache de la Neuville, who held the prestigious position of *Géographe du roi*. Forty years earlier his uncle, the celebrated geographer Philippe Buache, had in collaboration with Joseph Nicolas Delisle, offered the same learned society a controversial memoir and map based on the alleged discoveries of Juan de Fuca in 1592 and of Admiral Bartholomew de Fonte in 1640.[6] Both the admiral and his voyage were fictitious, but this was not conclusively proved until Captain George Vancouver's investigations along the Northwest Coast in 1792-4. Buache de la Neuville had already shown signs of following in his uncle's footsteps

---

[1] See Vol. I of this edition, p. 319. Dario Manfredi has argued that it was it was this prohibition, coming too late to prevent a copy of Ferrer Maldonado's account from reaching France (see p. 454 below), that accounts for some of the variations in Malaspina's attitude towards the account in the following months. See Dario Manfredi, 'An Unknown Episode behind the Northwest Coast Campaign of Malaspina's Expedition', in Inglis, *Spain and the North Pacific Coast*, pp. 119–24.

[2] See Vol. I of this edition, p. 320.

[3] See Manfredi, *Lettere*, pp. 241–2.

[4] See pp. 54-5 above.

[5] See pp. 63, 417 above.

[6] For more on this see Numa Broc, *La Géographie des Philosophes: Géographes et voyageurs français au XVIIIe siècle*, Paris, 1974; Glyn Williams, *Voyages of Delusion: the Northwest Passage in the Age of Reason*, London, 2002, ch. 8, 'Maps, Hoaxes and Projects'.

with a map and memoir published in 1781 which tried to reconcile Fonte's discoveries with Captain Cook's explorations of 1778 along the Northwest Coast. The map identified Cook's Sandwich Sound (later Prince William Sound) with the Río de los Reyes that had supposedly led Fonte deep into the continent in 1640, and it showed Cook's River (later Cook Inlet) running from a series of Fonte-style waterways to the north.[1] In 1785 the geographer had been responsible, at least in part, for the instructions to La Pérouse which ordered him to explore the northwest coast of America for signs of a passage to Hudson Bay. Undaunted by the failure of the La Pérouse expedition to find any such strait, and by the commander's conclusion that the idea of a Northwest Passage was as 'absurd' as those 'pious frauds' of a more credulous age which all good rationalists had rejected,[2] in 1790 Buache de la Neuville introduced for the first time to a wider public the voyage of Ferrer Maldonado. He had obtained a copy of Ferrer's 'Relation' from José de Mendoza y Ríos, a naval officer who travelled to Paris soon after Espinosa's retrieval of the document in the summer of 1789, and who may have been unaware that a few weeks afterwards Valdés had expressly prohibited its showing to foreigners. Who exactly in Spain was impressed by Buache's attempts to prove the authenticity of the Ferrer Maldonado narrative is not clear, although the very recent dispute with Britain over the future of the Northwest Coast (the Nootka Sound Convention between the two nations was concluded in October 1790) had made the area a particularly sensitive one, whose importance would be vastly increased if by chance a navigable passage were to be found. Buache's memoir of November 1790 consisted of an abbreviated account of the voyage of 1588, supported by specious arguments and a list of outdated references. Of the recent surveys by navigators – Spanish, British and French – who had followed Cook to the Northwest Coast Buache made no mention.[3]

Malaspina's reaction to his new instructions confirms the impression given by his decision of a few weeks earlier to abandon the Alaskan leg of his voyage, that his doubts about the Ferrer Maldonado account had increased during the voyage and that Buache's paper had done nothing to lessen them. In his letter to Valdés of 28 April 1791 Malaspina referred to some of the 'difficulties' in the account which he felt Buache had not dealt with, and it was in a mood of resignation rather than enthusiasm that he seems to have followed the new orders to sail north from Acapulco.[4] In private letters of the same time to Azzo Giacinto, Malaspina referred to the 'Relation' as 'apocryphal' and 'false',[5] though as we have seen this differed from the rather more favourable opinion he held before the expedition's departure, and indeed during the earlier stages of the voyage. In 1792 Malaspina was to compose a lengthy 'Disertación' which criticized the account, Buache's support of it, and speculative geography in general;[6] but his fellow commander, José de Bustamante, was prepared to state his

---

[1] See Jean-Nicolas Buache de la Neuville, 'Nouvelle Carte de la Partie Septentrionale du Globe', Paris, 1781, and *Considérations géographiques et physiques sur les nouvelles découvertes au Nord-Est de l'Asie et au Nord-ouest de l'Amérique*, Paris, 1781.

[2] See John Dunmore, ed., *The Journal of Jean-François de Galaup de la Pérouse 1785–1788*, 2 vols, London, 1994, I, p. 165.

[3] See Document 2, pp. 453–60 below for a copy of his 'Memoir'.

[4] See p 420 above.

[5] Manfredi, *Lettere*, pp. 252, 263.

[6] See Document 4, pp. 468–80 below for Malaspina's 'Disertación'.

objections in advance. In a closely-reasoned set of 'Reflexiones' written before the corvettes sailed for Alaska he dismissed Ferrer Maldonado's 'Relation' as fictitious.[1] Whatever their reservations, Malaspina and Bustamante joined forces once more at Acapulco, and prepared for their unexpected voyage to the north. They had gathered much valuable information, not least from the admirable Bodega y Quadra, now in command at San Blas, about the Spanish exploring ventures that had followed his voyage to Alaska in 1775. The most recent of these were the expeditions of Esteban José Martínez in 1788 (who at Unalaska became the first Spanish officer to encounter Russian traders), and Salvador Fidalgo in 1790 (who entered Prince William Sound and Cook Inlet, and surveyed much of the intervening coast). In addition to the reports, journals and charts of his Spanish predecessors on the Northwest Coast, Malaspina also had on board a remarkably up-to-date collection of accounts published in England, some of them forwarded to him from Spain after his departure. These included William Coxe's *Account of the Russian Discoveries Between Asia and America* (1780), the official account of James Cook's *Voyage to the Pacific Ocean* (1784), George Dixon's *Voyage round the World 1785–1788* (1789), Nathaniel Portlock's *Voyage Round the World; but More Particularly to the North West Coast of America* (1789), and John Meares, *Voyages Made in the Years 1788 and 1789, From China to the North West Coast of America* (1790).

Malaspina followed Bodega's advice on the best course to follow north from the Mexican coast, and took his ships on a long curving track well out to sea before heading in towards the Alaskan coast in about latitude 56°N which he reached in late June near Cook's Cape Edgecumbe.[2] The cold was so intense that the artist Suria was unable to sketch on deck, and had to retreat below to complete his drawings. From this landfall the vessels sailed north towards the location of Ferrer Maldonado's supposed strait in latitude 60°N, and on 27 June were off Yakutat Bay, visited by the British trader George Dixon four years earlier, and named by him Port Mulgrave. Although Dixon had stayed there ten days he had not made a complete survey, and admitted in his journal that 'How extensive the sound is, I cannot say'.[3] Despite earlier doubts, excitement grew among the officers as the *Descubierta* and *Atrevida* steered towards a great cleft in the coastal range in latitude 59°15′N. We saw, Malaspina wrote, 'an inlet whose mouth and course seemed to tally with the coast described by Ferrer Maldonado. At once imagination soon supplied a thousand reasons in support of hope'. The appearance of the opening, Teniente Tova Arredondo wrote, 'had the most exact conformity' with the strait described by Ferrer Maldonado. Suria took up the story in his journal: 'Great was the joy of the commander and of all the officers because they believed, and with some foundation, that this might be the so much desired and sought-for strait ... Transported with joy our commander steered towards the opening.' Even the sceptical

---

[1] See Document 3, pp. 461–7 below for Bustamante's 'Reflexiones'. At least one other member of the Malaspina expedition, Ciriaco Cevallos, drew up a refutation of the Ferrer Maldonado account. This was published as a pamphlet, *Disertación del Teniente de Navío D. Ciriaco Cevallos, embarcado en la corbeta Atrevida sobre la navegación al Asia por el NE* (Cádiz, 1797), but we have been unable to trace a copy.

[2] For the events of the Alaskan part of the voyage see pp. 96–163 above, and Donald C. Cutter, *Malaspina and Galiano: Spanish Voyages to the Northwest Coast, 1791 and 1792*, Vancouver, 1991, pp. 22–70.

[3] [Beresford], *Voyage ... by Captain George Dixon*, p. 170.

Bustamante was caught up in the enthusiasm of the moment, and entered in his journal that, in the imagination at least, the inlet coming into view matched the description and sketch in Ferrer Maldonado's account – 'there was hardly anyone among us who was not ready to believe in the probable existence of the longed for passage'.[1] By nightfall the corvettes were at anchor inside the bay, close to a beach and a Tlingit village. Here the expedition's portable observatory was set up, the artists made their drawings of people and places, wood and water were taken on board, and a trade in sea-otter pelts took place.

By 2 July Malaspina was ready to explore in person the inner reaches of the inlet in search of the Strait of Anian. He took two launches and fifteen days' provisions, and left Bustamante in charge of the ships. It took only a few hours in the boats to dispel all hopes, for soon after mid-day the water shoaled and the thunderous sound of large chunks of ice calving from a glacier could be heard. Then the end of the inlet came in sight, its low shore blocked by a glacier behind which rose the steep walls of the coastal range. A disheartened Malaspina named the spot Puerto del Desengaño, and the outer entrance Ferrer, 'after the ancient mariner'. The juxtaposition of the two names was probably not accidental. After taking possession of the area, Malaspina prepared to head out to sea. Much had been accomplished in the week's stay. The scientists on board had gathered a rich harvest of ethnographic and natural history material, and the artists had made some superb sketches and paintings; but the over-riding fact was that there was no strait leading deep into the interior.

The disappointment showed in the following weeks, as the corvettes first headed for Prince William Sound, more to satisfy officialdom in Madrid that the expedition had reached as far as the latitude of Ferrer Maldonado's supposed strait than to carry out any serious survey work. In the event, strong winds kept the ships from entering the sound, and without attempting to reach Cook Inlet they bore away back down the coast on their way to Nootka. Several inlets were sighted, but none was investigated. Suria claimed that some officers regretted this reluctance to search further, but that Malaspina was 'whimsical and had formed the opinion that there was not and could not be any such strait.'[2] Certainly, Malaspina had lost whatever belief he might have had in the authenticity of Ferrer Maldonado's account. He later reflected that Buache's interpretation of that account was an example of the damage done by the division of geography between academic scholars and practical navigators, and the 'great readiness by geographers to continue to espouse outdated opinions whatever their foundation'. A reader in the twentieth-first century, he concluded, would be amazed to see how seriously the stories of Fuca, Fonte and Maldonado had been taken in an age that called itself scientific and enlightened.[3]

Perhaps the last word should be left with Juan Bautista Muñoz, the discoverer or rather rediscoverer of Ferrer Maldonado's 'Relation'. Writing in late July 1791, and not knowing that a few weeks earlier in distant Alaskan waters Malaspina's expedition

---

[1] For these reactions see pp. 103–4 above (Malaspina); Cutter, *Malaspina and Galiano*, p. 23 (Tova Arredondo); Cutter, *Journal of Suria*, p. 35 (Suria); Higueras, *Diario de Bustamante*, p. 241 (Bustamante).

[2] Cutter, *Journal of Suria*, p. 58.

[3] See p. 477 below.

had failed to find a strait where Ferrer Maldonado had described one, Muñoz made no attempt to hide his contempt for the account and its author. He had been uneasy, he wrote, about the document since he had first set eyes on it ten years earlier, and had been unable to find any supporting evidence for it in the archives. There was only one conclusion he could draw: the account was 'a fiction … a straightforward lie', written by one who 'had shown clear signs of being a greedy and vainglorious charlatan'.[1]

---

[1] His letter is printed below as Document 5, pp. 481–4.

DOCUMENT 1

The 'Relation' of Lorenzo Ferrer Maldonado

Lorenzo Ferrer Maldonado was born c.1550 in Guadix, about fifty miles from Granada as the crow flies, behind the Sierra Nevada.[1] There is a street named after him, or perhaps after one of his brothers, a clergyman who had also lived there. However, part of Lorenzo's family hailed from the small town of Adra, in the lower Alpujarra region near Almería, on the Mediterranean shore, which may explain why a landsman would one day be drawn to the sea. His parents, like so many at the time, probably moved inland to Guadix from the Alpujarra region in search of safety from the Barbary pirates. As a youth Lorenzo fought alongside the people of Guadix in the Granada Morisco War (1568–70), the last armed struggle on Spanish soil between Christianity and Islam.[2] If this left a mark on the young man, the news of the naval victory of Don John of Austria against the Turks at Lepanto in 1571 would also have left a strong impression, as might also the first-hand accounts of Don Pedro de Mendoza, the Governor of Río de la Plata and founder of Buenos Aires, whose family had a close friendship with the Ferrers and Maldonados.

So there was no lack of inspiration for a young man who was, apparently, prone to hallucinations, and eventually gained a reputation for being as imaginative as he was ambitious, but a clear account of what he did after the war has yet to be found. To shed some light on this period one has only indirect reports. Carlo Amoretti, librarian of the Biblioteca Ambrosiana in Milan provided some clues from the researches of the Hispanic bibliographers Antonio de León and Nicolás Antonio. The latter wrote that Ferrer Maldonado chose the army as a career, 'undertook military studies, and became proficient in the nautical arts and geography'.[3] Amoretti claimed that the evidence provided by Nicolás Antonio showed that the 'Relation' of 1609 was the genuine work of Ferrer Maldonado, and that the author was 'well versed in geography and the art of navigation'. Whether his presumed military career was also genuine is open to doubt, for Ambassador García de Silva y Figueroa, who met Ferrer at court years later, derided him for using the military rank of 'captain' before his name.[4]

---

[1] Much of the detail in this introduction comes from Carlos Asenjo Sedano, 'El misterioso navegante descubridor Lorenzo Ferrer Maldonado, siglos XVI–XVII', in *Revista de historia naval*, Madrid, 1988, VI, pp. 17–25. We are indebted to the Instituto de Historia y Cultural Naval, Armada Española, for permission to use material from Dr Asenjo's article. His contribution is especially valuable since it contains recent research in the archives of the Public Notary Protocols at Guadix. Other biographical details come from Martín Fernández de Navarette, *Biblioteca marítima española*, Madrid, 1851, II, pp. 347–8, and 'Carácter y circunstancias de Lorenzo Ferrer Maldonado', in Salvá and Sainz de Baranda, *Documentos inéditos*, pp. 76–85.

[2] For this brutal conflict see Diego Hurtado de Mendoza, *The War in Granada*, translated with an introduction by Martin Shuttleworth, London, 1982.

[3] Nicolás Antonio, *Bibliotheca hispana nova*, 2 vols, Madrid 1783, 1788.

[4] Salvá and Sainz de Baranda, *Documentos inéditos*, p. 79.

Oddly, in 1581 he signed a deed using the honorific title of 'Micer Lorenzo Ferrer',[1] and this he did several times until 1583. Shifts from relative opulence to financial difficulties are a recurrent theme in Ferrer's life. After the death of his father his relations with his mother, brothers and sisters were tense, and he was involved in several law suits with them. From 1584 Ferrer held the post of *jurado*, a municipal officer, at the Guadix town hall. In 1587, now married, he was still in Guadix, but there is no further mention of him there until 1589.

It is in 1588, the 'missing' year in Ferrer's life at Guadix, that the mysterious voyage described in his 'Relation' is supposed to have taken place. It may well be that he was at sea in 1588, for maritime references to him now begin to appear in the legal records. It is quite possible that he made the first part of the voyage he later described, sailing out of Lisbon, the Hispanic pivot between the Indies and the northern ports of Flanders and the Hanseatic League. Such a voyage would explain how in later years he described himself as a mariner who had spent time in Flanders and the Baltic. It could also explain the upturn in his fortune, for on their return to Guadix in 1589 he and his wife spent money freely. They had slave servants, and visited Granada to buy quality furnishings for a house which they rented in the best part of Guadix. Yet by January 1590 their resources had dwindled to a point where Lorenzo had to sell his slaves, and sue a certain Capitán Bartolomé de Velasco for the return of a loan of twenty ducats. He and his brothers also sold the family chapel they owned in Berja. More intriguingly, also in 1590 Ferrer granted Don Luis Serrano powers of attorney to obtain satisfaction for unpaid salaries due to him as *capitán* of the two ships *La Esperanza*, master Juan de Llanos, and *Santa Ana*, master Miguel de Alvear, both of Seville. As Carlos Asenjo asks, where had these two vessels been, and what was the precise connection between their two masters and Ferrer Maldonado?[2] Like much else in his life, these questions remain unanswered.

If we are to believe his brother-in-law, in 1600 Lorenzo Ferrer tried to involve in a new venture the Marquis of Estepa, who was dazzled by certain accounts supported by documents and deeds written in an ancient script (Ferrer was known for his skill in calligraphy). At this point the Granada magistrates intervened, and Ferrer was charged with forgery and counterfeiting. His defence counsel described him as 'a man of genius, author of curious books, who knew many languages, was a Latin scholar and an astrologer', but the magistrates were not impressed. His brother-in-law went to prison, but Ferrer could not be found, and so begins another obscure period of his life, at least as far as the written record is concerned.

We owe to García de Silva a first-hand account of Ferrer Maldonado's next known appearance, in the glittering world of the Spanish court in 1609. There he was greeted as an experienced navigator who knew Flanders and the Hanseatic ports. He distributed memorials to ministers, claiming that in 1588 he had discovered the fabulous Strait of Anian, and that within three months of leaving Spain he could reach the Philippines. De Silva was not deceived; he saw Ferrer Maldonado as a rogue whose 'designs he had drawn on half a sheet of paper'.[3] It was also at this time that Ferrer

---

[1] A curious choice, for 'Micer' was a form of address equivalent to Señor used in the States of the Crown of Aragon.
[2] Asenjo, 'El misterioso navegante', p. 22.
[3] Salvá and Sainz de Baranda, *Documentos inéditos*, pp. 78–9.

competed for the prize offered by Felipe III for an effective solution to the problem of finding longitude at sea, but, says de Silva, his sharp practices were uncovered.[1]

Ferrer Maldonado died in Madrid on 12 January 1625.[2] At the time he was living in Calle de Silva, in the ancient district of San Martín in the heart of the city. In accordance with his last wishes he was buried near his home in the Chapel of Our Lady in San Martín.[3] A year later his learned treatise, *Imagen del mundo sobre la esfera, cosmografía, y geografía teórica de planetas y arte de navegar*, dedicated to the Bishop of Mexico, was published in Alcalá. In the dedication he threw a posthumous dart at his critics – envious slanderers who endeavoured through their denigration of his work to rescue their names from oblivion. This was not quite Ferrer Maldonado's last word, for two hundred years after the event, his supposed voyage of 1588 reappeared to cause more stir and controversy than it ever did in his lifetime.

Text of the 'Relation'

A Relation of the Discovery of the Strait of Anian; made by me, Captain Lorenzo Ferrer Maldonado, in the Year 1588; in which is given the Course of the Voyage, the Situation of the Strait, the Manner in which it ought to be fortified, the Advantages of this Navigation, and the Loss which will arise from not prosecuting it.[4]

Sire

It will be necessary, in the first place, to state the advantages which may result from the navigation of the Strait of Anian into the South Sea. Having well considered the route which has hitherto been taken to the Philippines, China, Japan, and other parts of that sea, it appears from the best charts that almost half the length of the voyage will be saved by sailing through this strait. This will easily be seen on inspecting a terrestrial globe, or a map having the pole at its centre, though it will not be apparent on a plain chart, which exhibits the meridian at the very pole as large and expanded as it were the equinoctial line, and therefore in such charts one route will not seem shorter

---

[1] Ibid., p. 83; for the prize see pp. 482-3 below.
[2] Martín Fernández de Navarrete, *Biblioteca marítima española*, 2 vols, Madrid, 1851, II, p. 348. The death was registered in the Parish 'Libro de óbitos' with the number 462.
[3] The chapel was destroyed during the Napoleonic invasion of Madrid. Eventually, any remains found in its tombs were placed in a common grave.
[4] The 'Relación' found by Juan Bautista Muñoz in 1781 in the library of the Duque del Infantado has so far not been traced, although enquiries have been made at the Real Academia de Historia, Madrid; the Archivo Histórico Nacional, Sección Nobleza, Toledo; and the Archivo des Indias, Seville. What seems to be the master copy of the document, dated 24 March 1781, written in a neat clerical hand, and signed by the amanuensis with Muñoz's own scroll (a 'B' and an intricate spiral flourish), is now in the Real Academia de la Historia: Colección Muñoz (Doc. 9/4802, ff. 1–17). Other contemporary copies, both bearing Muñoz's name, are in AMN, MS 1777, ff. 1–22 and MS 331, ff. 293–314. Two further contemporary copies are in the Real Biblioteca, Madrid: Colección Ayala, vol. XXXI (II/2845), doc. 1, ff. 1–20, and vol. XLVIII (II/2861), doc. 3, ff. 29–46. Both of these last give the full text of the 'Relation' as copied by Muñoz, but not the maps and sketches of the Strait of Anian. Two other copies were acquired by the British Museum in the mid-nineteenth century; they are in British Library: Add. MS. 17,622, ff. 158v–174; Add. MS. 17,624, ff. 91–115. The translation printed above is of the document in the Real Academia de la Historia; it was first published in English in John Barrow, *A Chronological History of Voyages into the Arctic Regions ...*, London, 1818, pp. 29–50, but with a considerable number of errors and omissions in the text which the present translation has corrected.

than another. This theory may perhaps require demonstration, yet it is unnecessary to treat of it here. Suffice it to say, by navigating this strait almost half the voyage is abated. Besides this advantage, it is productive of another much greater, namely that after one embarkation a ship may proceed directly from Spain to the Philippines, something not possible with the present route which requires one to disembark in New Spain and proceed 150 leagues overland. Hence it happens that most people who are sent to those parts to serve in the presidios and provide support, remain in New Spain, either exhausted by the fatigues of the voyage, or attracted by the delights of that country. Besides this it has another great advantage, namely that Your Majesty (trading with all the spiceries of the Moluccas, the archipelago, and other parts) by means of this strait might have sole possession of that trade with the greatest ease; and storing its produce in the magazines of Seville, it would yield more than five millions[1] a year, obliging many nations to come to Spain for that commodity. In return, they would bring an abundance of all things necessary for these kingdoms, making it unnecessary to export the silver which comes every year from the Indies, by which Spain is left in such great want of specie. Let it be remembered also, that by opening this strait to navigation it is in our power to prevent the trade between China and the Indies, and to transfer it to Spain, which will also extend to the Philippines and the countries in those parts; for the trade of China with the Indies has been most disadvantageous to Spain, since it has obstructed the greater part of the trade Spain used to carry. This proved to be the cause why Your Majesty's commerce is so much diminished, while China and the Philippines carry on this trade with the Indies to such an extent that it becomes impossible for us to maintain our position in those parts as we should, in order to resist our many enemies. In consequence of which, these kingdoms' strength will suffer and they might not be able to survive. However, with possession of that passage and navigation they could grow in such numbers and opportunities (because of their wealth) that they would bring to this sea merchant fleets as large as those which go to the Indies, producing for Spain great abundance of the valuable products of China and Tartary, and from other lands at a very cheap rate; for of gold alone we may obtain two millions every year, from which we may derive great profit, since gold in China is less than half the value it is here. Added to which, many other commodities may be acquired, which now these kingdoms are supplied with by our enemies, who thereby enrich themselves, and gather enough strength to make war against us.

It is of great consequence also to supply those parts with soldiers for the defence of those kingdoms; and this we might do with great facility by means of this strait, thereby preventing our enemies from becoming masters of them, as might be the case for want of soldiers and assistance. And God being willing, by means of this navigation we should have an opportunity of converting the inhabitants of those parts, for whose souls it pleased God to suffer – which would be, if not the greatest of all advantages, certainly not the least.

Many other things might be offered in favour of this navigation – the most essential, however, is obviously how to prevent the great disadvantages which would result

---

[1] There is no indication of the currency, but presumably *ducados* (ducats).

from not investigating and fortifying the Strait of Anian; for since it is no longer a matter of doubt that such a place exists, as I can testify to have seen it myself, it is very evident how great a misfortune it would be were it discovered and fortified by our enemies, who are endeavouring to find it with great earnestness, as we know that last year, 1608, several ships left England to look for it.[1] The Strait of Anian being occupied by our enemies would occasion serious injury to us on account of their proximity to it. They might easily send through it a fleet which, divided into squadrons of thirty ships, might make themselves masters of the lands of New Spain and Peru where, by offering the natives of the Indies freedom and liberty of conscience, it is probable that many, if not all, would go over to them. Thus they might strengthen themselves in those seas to such a degree that we, having no place from whence we might quickly send succour, might be irrecoverably deprived of our territories. This danger is so much to be feared that even if we were not assured by our own eyes that the strait exists in the South Sea, we ought to be anxious to seek it in order to fortify it, or to reassure ourselves if there be no such place, and satisfy our minds that no such danger was to be apprehended. And let me remark, that if our enemies have not occasioned us any very great losses in the South Sea, it is because they do not possess a port of such consequence as that of the Strait of Anian, as will be explained further. Since it now appears that by command of Your Majesty and the Council of State it is proper to consider the proposed navigation and the method of fortifying the strait, it will be opportune to give some account of the courses to be steered, and of the site and harbour of that place, with all the circumstances of my voyage, beginning with the navigation. By attending to the following instructions, any good seaman will readily discover the strait.

Departing from Spain, suppose from Lisbon,[2] the course is NW for a distance of 450 leagues, when the ship will have arrived at latitude 60 degrees, where the island of Friesland will be seen, anciently called Tyle or Tule.[3] It is an island somewhat smaller than Ireland. From thence the course must be followed to the westward, running along the parallel of 60 degrees for 180 leagues, which will bring the navigator to the land of Labrador, where the strait of that name or Davis's Strait begins, the entrance of which is very wide, somewhat more than thirty leagues. The land on the coast of Labrador which is to the west is low, but the opposite side of the mouth of the strait is composed of very high mountains. Here two openings will appear, between which are these high mountains. One of these openings runs ENE and the other NW; that which runs ENE should be ignored, which is the one on the right hand looking towards the north, because it leads to Grutlandia,[4] and ultimately to the sea of Frieslandia. Taking therefore the other opening, and turning the bow NW, by proceeding in this direction eighty leagues, the ship will reach latitude 64 degrees. Here the strait takes another turn to the north, continuing 120 leagues, and as far as latitude 70 degrees, when it again turns to the NW and continues in that direction ninety leagues, which will bring the ship almost to latitude 75 degrees, at which point it will

---

[1] There is no record of any English voyage in search of the Northwest Passage in 1608.
[2] This was the period when the crowns of Spain and Portugal were united.
[3] Thule of classical times, later Iceland.
[4] Greenland.

have passed through the whole Strait of Labrador. That is to say, it begins at 60 degrees and ends at 75 degrees, being 290 leagues in length, and having three turns or reaches, the first and last of which run NW – SE, and the middle one north-south, being sometimes narrower than twenty leagues, and sometimes wider than forty, and containing many ports, bays and sheltering places, which might be of service in case of necessity. As far as 73 degrees the shores appear to be inhabited, for in many places we observed smoke. To some thoughtless people it has seemed impossible to navigate at so high an altitude to the pole. In answer to this, it may be observed that the Hanseatics live in latitude 72 degrees, into whose harbour, namely that of San Miguel and in all the Bay of San Nicolás, nearly a thousand merchant ships enter each year, and to pass into the Sea of Flanders they must ascend to latitude 75 degrees in order to round Finamarca.[1]

Having cleared the Strait of Labrador we began to descend from that latitude, steering West by South for 350 leagues until we arrived in latitude 71 degrees, when we perceived a high coast without being able to discover whether it was part of the continent or an island, but we remarked that if it was the continent it must be opposite the coast of New Spain. From this land, seen at 71 degrees, we directed our course WSW for 440 leagues, until we came down to 60 degrees, in which parallel the Strait of Anian was discovered. Thus the same course must be followed as mine, at least as far as Friesland; for I set sail from the Baccallaos[2] in search of that island to procure provisions and other necessaries, which we obtained from some nearby islands called Zelandillas.[3] They are three in number, only one of which is inhabited, and the other two serve as pastures for the cattle of those natives, who are rather wild although they seem to be Catholic Christians. Returning to our voyage I say that in my opinion it would be more prudent when you clear the Strait of Labrador to follow the opposite coast to New Spain, for two reasons: first, to discover what population it contains, and secondly to seek provisions and necessaries for the ships which have to sail along this route.

According to the above relation, it appears that the distance from Spain to Friesland is 450 leagues, and from there to Labrador 130, and to the termination of that strait 290 – which make in all 920 leagues [sic]. These added to 790, which we found to be the distance from the north part of the Strait of Labrador to the Strait of Anian, makes it altogether 1,710 leagues from Spain to the Strait of Anian.

The season in which we cleared the Strait of Labrador was very hard, being only the beginning of March, and as we were navigating the strait during the latter part of February, we suffered great hardships on account of the darkness, the cold and the storms. The days during that time were short, and the cold so great that the waves of the sea, which beat against the ship's side, froze in such a manner that the vessel seemed to be made of crystal, and we were obliged to chip off the ice, for it grew so thick that in some places we found it more than a hand's span in thickness. It is a great mistake to suppose that this sea can freeze all over; for as it is wide, and rapid currents are always running through the strait, these and the great waves occasioned by its continual motion will not allow it to freeze. However, along the shores of the sea, and

---

[1] Finmark, at the northern tip of Norway/Finland.
[2] The cod fishery of the Grand Banks of Newfoundland.
[3] Unidentified.

the parts where the sea is calm, I think it may freeze, and we noticed that the water which splashed against the shore froze. This only I know, and we were told it in the Zelandillas, that a strait between Friesland and Grutlandia was frozen for most of the year because it was in the midst of mountains and high land on the Friesland side, by which the rays of the sun were prevented from falling upon it. And being thus surrounded by high hills, it was not affected by the winds, which might have set its waves in motion; and therefore the continual calm had allowed it to be frozen and rendered it unnavigable, and the same thing occurs in the large bay mentioned above.

But when we returned through the Strait of Labrador, which was in June and part of July, we enjoyed continual daylight, so that when we arrived at the Arctic Circle, or latitude 66½ degrees, we did not lose sight of the Sun, nor did it sink below the horizon until we reached midpoint in the Strait of Labrador, and thus, from the Sun always continuing above the horizon, the air was so warm that we felt more heat than even in central Spain. Yet when we exposed ourselves to the rays of the Sun they did not much bother us, and because there are always strong currents and winds coming from the north, the Strait of Labrador is easily and quickly cleared. The rapid currents, occasioned by the flux and reflux, are of great assistance in entering and leaving the strait, even when the winds are contrary; and as they blow incessantly from the north it is necessary, on leaving Spain for Anian, to take advantage of the tides. We shall now conclude this relation with the course of the ship and the events of the voyage.

The strait we discovered in 60 degrees, at the distance of 1,710 leagues from Spain, appears by ancient tradition to be the one which geographers name on their maps the Strait of Anian.[1] If this be so, it must be a strait with Asia on one side and America on the other, which seems to be the case according to the following narrative.

As soon as we emerged in the great [South] Sea we coasted along the shores of America for more than one hundred leagues, the head of the ship being turned SW until we reached 55 degrees, on which coast there were no inhabitants, nor any opening to indicate the vicinity of another strait through which the South Sea flowing into the North Sea [Atlantic] might separate that part. From hence we concluded that all the coasts belonged to America, and that continuing along it we might shortly arrive at Quivira[2] and Cape Mendocino. We left this coast (which, as was said before, we knew continued further), and standing to the west sailed four days with so strong a wind that we made thirty leagues a day. Having sailed by dead reckoning 120 leagues to the point pricked on the chart (although we did not possess any of this sea), we discovered an extensive land with high mountain ranges and a long continuous coast, from which we kept a convenient distance to fulfil our object of always sailing in the open sea – sailing at one time to the NE, at another towards NNE, and again to the N, from whence it appeared to most of us that the coast trended NE-SW. We could not mark any particular points because, as I have said, we were sailing in the open sea; and therefore can only affirm that the land is inhabited very nearly to the strait's entrance, since we saw smoke rising up in many places. This country, according to our

---

[1] Not very ancient, at least from the standpoint of 1588/1609, for a named Strait of Anian appeared on the maps of Gastaldi, Ortelius and Mercator only from the 1560s onwards.
[2] A rumoured land rich in gold thought to lie somewhere north of New Spain.

cosmographers, must belong to Tartary or Cathay; and a few miles from the coast must be situated the great city of Cambalu, the capital of Tartary. Finally, having followed the said coast, we found ourselves at the entrance of the same Strait of Anian which, fifteen days before, we had passed through into the great sea, which we knew to be the South Sea, where Japan, China, the Moluccas, India, New Guinea and the land discovered by Captain Quiros[1] are situated, with all the coasts of New Spain and Peru.

At the mouth of the strait, through which we passed to the South Sea, there is a harbour situated on the American side, capable of holding 500 ships, though in some parts it is rough with a bad roadstead, on account of the currents which, with the tide flowing from north to south, enter the harbour, and beat violently against one part of it not far from the mouth as you enter on the right-hand side. It must be understood that the mouth of the harbour is open to the north, and runs in forming a spiral or winding turn. The shores of this harbour seem never to have been touched by human footsteps, but in one part of it there is a backwater on whose edges we found an immense quantity of the egg shells of sea birds, which generally lay them on the sea shore. These appeared to have been brought there by the currents from the north, and were so many in number that they formed a wall one *vara*[2] high and eight paces wide. We found in this harbour a large river of fresh water, so deep that we were able to enter with our ship to procure water, and I think that a ship of 500 tons burden might enter it. The greater part of this harbour has a sandy bottom, particularly near the place where the river flows into it, and where the currents beat upon it. Farther north there is a sheltered spot formed by some rocks more than two *picas*[3] high in places, on which is a flat surface having a narrow neck surrounded by the sea, leaving land jutting out on the east side, where an extensive settlement might be established, and for the present a fortress raised, which would be of great service. The mainland adjoining this harbour is very pleasant, containing extensive plains on the SE side which end at the harbour, and these are bounded in places by thickets in which we found rosemary. These plains once cleared might serve for neat farms or gardens, and on account of the situation most of them might be well watered. Although this land is situated in latitude 59 degrees, it is of a very pleasant temperature because the mountains, which are to the north, shelter and protect all the land which is lying to the south. The climate is very good, for the cold of the winter is not excessive, but on the contrary very moderate, because the country is always open to the rays of the Sun, and is unaffected by the north winds, being open only to those which blow from the south, which are always mild, and especially so there, because they come directly off the sea. The proof of this was evident from the species of fruit which we found there. Although this land is in so high a latitude, it is not on that account less fit to be inhabited, since many other countries are on the same parallel: Edinburgh in Scotland, the principal cities of Sweden, Haapsalu [in Estonia] and Riga, cities in Livonia [Latvia], Dublin in Ireland, Nidrosia [Trondheim], a city in Norway, many parts of Muscovy, and many other very pleasant countries which are inhabited, traded with, and well

---

[1] Espiritu Santo (Vanuatu); see pp. 428-9 above.
[2] A Spanish yard, approximately three feet.
[3] *Pica*, approximately 14 feet.

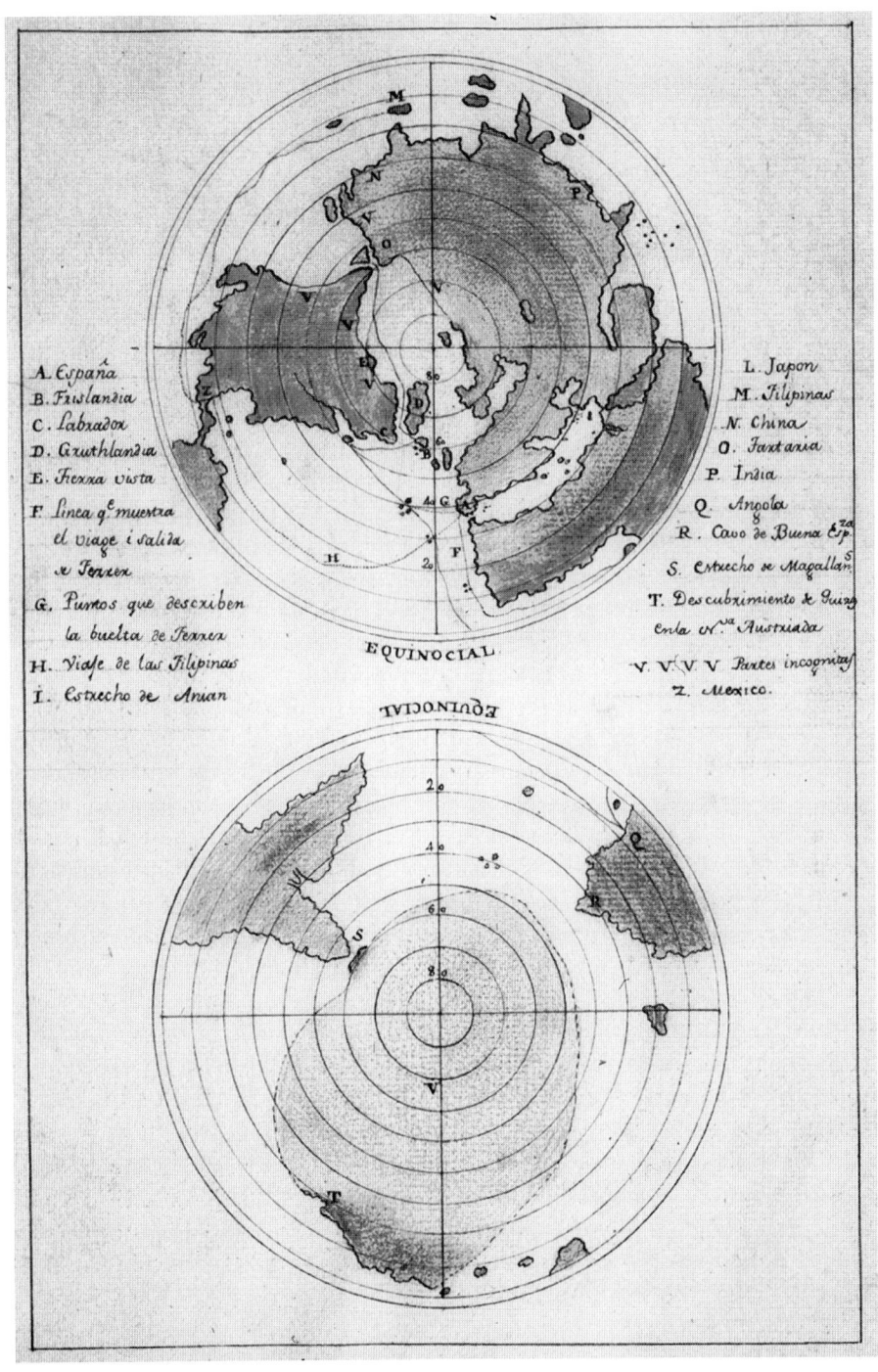

Plate 42. Map of the world showing in the northern hemisphere Ferrer Maldonado's voyage, and in the southern hemisphere the shadowy outlines (T) of Quiros's discoveries of 1606. [1609/1781]

known, and although they are a long way from the warmth of the coast the cold is tolerable. The longest day of summer in this land is eighteen and a half hours, and the longest night in winter the same, therefore the summer nights are five and a half hours long, and the day in winter about the same. Upon the banks of the river which flows into the harbour, and on those of another which is farther down on the SE side, grow many enormous trees, most of them fruit-bearing. Some are similar to those of Spain, such as apple, pear and wild plum; and others quite unknown, of various types. Therefore, that we might fall into no danger (as might possibly have happened) I ordered my people not to eat any fruit that had not been pecked at by the birds, and by this means we avoided eating any harmful fruit. Most of these were fruits of last year remaining upon the trees, for in that season there was no ripe fruit, being the latter part of April, all May, and part of June. As the fruit was preserved on the trees from one year to another we knew that the winter could not have been very severe. We found in a low and apparently very temperate valley bounded by the river wild grapes and lychees, which is a delicious fruit from India, always found in temperate climates. At the head of the harbour, looking between north and east, and all over within these two points of the compass, there are low and accessible mountains, abounding in all kinds of game, where we found partridges, rabbits (somewhat different from those in Spain), deer marked with black and white spots upon a dun skin, and with long branching antlers, but some had none. We saw two species of swine, one similar to those of the Indies which have the navel in the spine [sic], but larger, and others resembling the wild boars of Spain, but very big. We also found buffaloes and many other animals, but no beasts of prey. The sea produces abundance of fish, and all kinds of shell-fish, very good and savoury, larger than any we know, for we caught crabs half a *vara* across, while those of our own coasts are not larger than the palm of a hand.

The coast on the side of Asia or Tartary has very high mountains, so high that at their greatest altitude they are covered with snow all the year, particularly those which look to the north. These are so rugged and craggy that they are unaccessible; most of the trees growing on them are very lofty pines, which grow down to the shores of the sea. On the Asian side, opposite the entrance of the harbour, there is a backwater with a large patch of reeds, which we found to be an admirable fishing place. There we caught many large fish, some familiar to us such as conger-eels and sole, and others all much larger than those which are found here. We saw numbers of large fish swimming past us on their way from the South to the North Sea [Atlantic]. Among them were whales, porpoises, and other great monsters. It appeared that they were making this journey in order to leave the warm waters of the South Sea, as it was now early summer, to enjoy the cool waters of the North Sea.

The Strait of Anian is fifteen leagues in length, and can easily be passed with a tide lasting six hours, as those tides are very rapid. There are six bends in its length, and two entrances which lie from north to south, I mean the bearing of the two is north and south. The entrance on the north side (through which we passed) is less than a quarter of a league in width, and on both sides there are two rocky ridges, but that on the Asian side is higher and steeper than the other, receding underneath in such a manner that nothing which falls from the upper part of the mountain can strike its base. The entrance into the South Sea near the harbour is more than a quarter of a

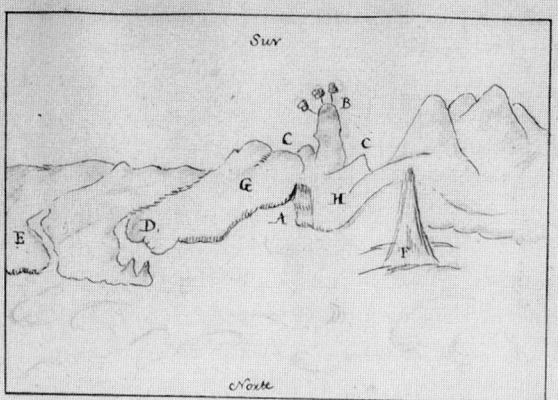

PRESPECTIVA DEL ESTRECHO POR LA VANDA D.^l NORTE

A. Boca del Estrecho por la vanda del Norte. B. Peñón muy alto blanco, con tres arboles. CC. Sillares. D. Rio donde hicimos agua y tiene un abrigo. E. Otro Rio. F. Peñon pelado, aislado. G. Parte d. America, d. montes bajos. H. P.^te d. Asia, d. montes m, a. y pinares.

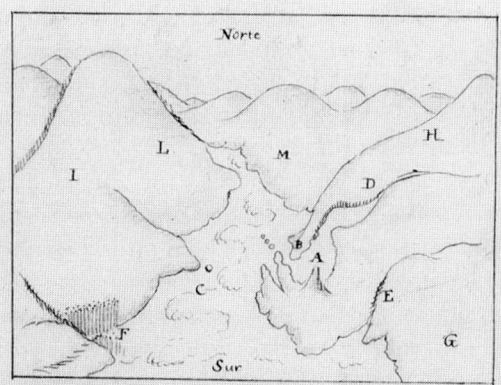

PRRSPECTIVA DEL ESTRECHO POR LA VANDA DEL SUR

A. Puerto que pueden surgir quinientas naves. B. Sitio para hacer fuerte ó poblacion. C. Boca del Puerto por la vanda del sur. D. Rio fondable de buena agua E. Rio bueno con muchos frutales. F. Cañaveral junto á el qual hai buena pesquera. G. Llanos de monte bajo para hacer siembra H. Montes de mucha caça. I. Montes m. a. de grand. pinares. L. P.^te d. l Asia. M. P.^te d' America.

Plate 43. (a) Perspective view of the Strait of Anian from the north. [1609/1781]
(b) Perspective view of the Strait of Anian from the south. [1609/1781]

league wide, and from thence the passage runs in a slanting direction, increasing the distance between the two coasts. In the middle of the strait, at the end of the third bend, there is a great crag or steep rocky islet about three *estados*[1] in height, and as its form is round, its diameter must be 200 paces. It is near the mainland of Asia, but the sea on that side is full of shoals and rocks, and can only be navigated with boats. The distance between this islet and the mainland of America is less than half a quarter of a league in width, and although its channel is so deep that two or even three ships might sail through together, it is near the shelving places of the banks upon which two bastions might be built with little trouble, narrowing the channel to a musket shot. Upon this island, or upon the shoals and the opposite coast, there might be raised, as was said earlier, two bastions which with the assistance of artillery might guard and defend the strait in great safety. And if the currents were not so strong, a chain might be placed across which would be of great service, and even now we might make one with such diligence as to resist the currents. The situation of the strait is such that with three watch-towers within sight of each other we might see out into the North Sea for thirty leagues, and by means of smoke signals give notice to the bastions and fortresses of the harbour of the approach of any ships, and prevent them from sailing through the strait if they are enemy ships by keeping continually in the harbour two ships prepared for such an eventuality. These should lie across the course of the vessel endeavouring to pass between the two bastions, and if she had to wait for the tide they might delay and embarrass her while the fortresses are cannonading and sinking her, for it must be mentioned that although many ships might come together, no more than two or three at once could pass through the channel. If we wish to have a lookout on the South Sea (though I do not think that is necessary at present), the strait has two high mountains, one on the Asian coast, the other on the American, which face each other; and since both of them adjoin the fortress and watch-towers, and command a view over the two coasts in opposite directions, each might give notice of all vessels sailing in the South Sea. By this means the strait might be well defended, and the Spaniards alone navigate it; for in truth I know of no place yet discovered which thus holds communication with almost all the countries of the world. From this strait we may sail to all of them, and thus we may presume that in course of time it will prove a powerful and rich settlement.[2]

The northern entrance to the strait is the most difficult to recognize because its coast runs east and west, and the two sides formed by the strait close over on each other; and as the entrance and the bends it makes run north-south and south-west it cannot be seen from the open sea, and it is therefore not surprising that it has escaped the notice of those who sought it. When we arrived there we did not discover it for some days, during which we wandered up and down the coast, under the direction of my *piloto*,[3] Juan Martínez, a Portuguese and a native of Algarve, an old man of great experience. I found, however, that he was ignorant of the landmarks of these mountains (which I sketched for a further voyage, if I should undertake it, which I thought

[1] *Estado*, a measurement based on the average height of a man.
[2] The suggested system of bastions, forts and watch-towers is shown on Ferrer Maldonado's 'Plan', opposite. Likewise, his comments on the location of the Strait of Anian in relation to world commerce is illustrated by his polar projection map, p. 443 above.
[3] Not a pilot, but the equivalent of a master on a British vessel.

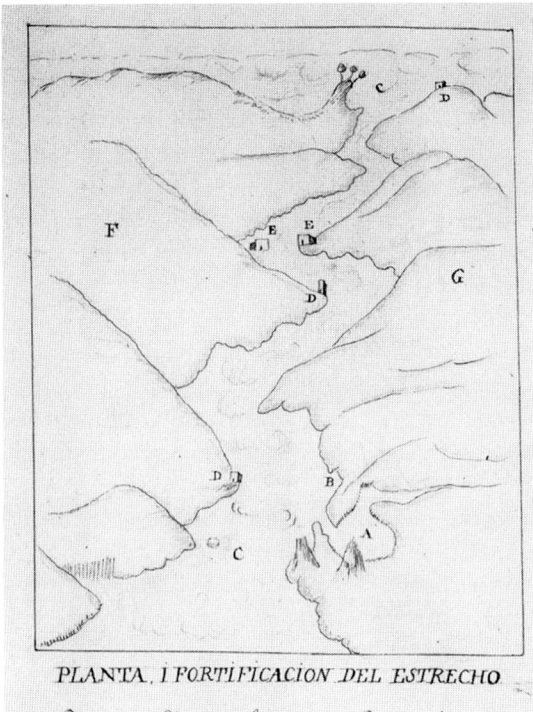

Plate 44. Plan for fortifying the Strait of Anian. [1609/1781]

I might); for although we knew that the strait was to be found in 60 degrees of latitude along an extensive coast running east and west, it occasioned us great doubt. The *piloto* thought that we had not arrived within a hundred leagues of the strait according to his reckoning of the ship's course. To me it seemed that we were already near it; and as it happened going in a boat to coast along the shore the current carried me into the strait, so that it was discovered. The reason of my thinking that we had arrived at the strait, or were close upon it, was occasioned by the strong currents we found there, running from the land and returning to it. They were so strong that at times, when our ship was well offshore, with the sea on the beam, we found her near it; and at other times, being near the land, we found her well offshore.[1]

On the land close to the strait is a very high peak, white in colour, of a lofty mountain on the Asian shore. This peak is rugged and inaccessible; on its highest point are three very large trees which, when viewed from north to south, are seen very

---

[1] The assumption here is that the ship was at anchor and that the observers ('we') were in the boat; even so, it is difficult to follow the argument.

distinctly from one another, and on each side of this high peak the mountains present the familiar appearance of two large saddles. One league from the mouth of the strait on the west side there is a high and steep rock, which is surrounded by the sea, and when the tide is low I think it may be four *picas* from the shore. At the eastern side of the entrance to the strait there is a large and beautiful river of fresh water with many trees on its banks, where we watered our ship, for there is a good shelter between two great rocks, which form a point. There is another river one league before reaching this one, with good water but without trees. The mountains visible on the coast of Asia from the north side are very high indeed when seen from the North Sea, having some very high trees growing on them, which when approached seem to be mostly pines. The mountains on the coast of America are lower and with fewer trees, but on neither side do they appear to bear fruit.

In the harbour where our ship anchored, namely the one mentioned as being at the entrance of the strait on the south side, we remained from the beginning of April to the middle of June, when a large vessel of 800 tons burden came from the South Sea in order to pass through the strait, wherefore we put ourselves on our guard. But having come to an understanding with one another, I found them willing to give up some of the merchandise they carried, most of which evidently consisted of articles similar to those of China, such as brocades, silks, porcelain, feathers, chests, precious stones, pearls and gold. These people seemed to be Hanseatics from the Bay of San Nicolás or the Port of San Miguel. In order to understand each other we were forced to speak Latin, those of our party who knew that language speaking with those on board the ship who understood it. They did not seem to be Catholics, but Lutherans. They said that they had come from a very large city little more than a hundred leagues from the strait, and although I cannot well remember its name, I think they called it Roba or some such name, which they said had a good harbour and a navigable river, and was subject to the Great Khan, as it belonged to Tartary, and that in that port they had left another ship belonging to their country. We could not learn more from them, for they acted with great caution and little confidence, being fearful of our party, wherefore we separated from them, and having left them near the strait in the North Sea, we set sail for Spain. We had reason to think these people Hanseatics because, as they live in latitude 72 degrees, it is easy and very advantageous to them to use this strait.

Having thus given a full relation of the particulars of this voyage, and of the disadvantages which will be the consequence of not following it up, it may be proper to give some account of the things needful to be provided for any person undertaking the voyage, and of the expenses which would be incurred by the necessary preparations, so that the intention of Your Majesty and the royal service be brought into effect.

The necessaries and expenses of the voyage

In the first place three ships must be provided: the flagship of 150 tons burden, and the other two each of a hundred tons. These must be built with caissons below the waterline, according to a plan which shall be given in due course. By this contrivance a vessel may be preserved from sinking even though a leak should open in her bottom, because only the compartment in which the damage occurred would be flooded and not any of the others, as all the bulkheads would be caulked. Even supposing that the vessel should receive damage between wind and water, the water will run out again at the same place that it entered, as I am convinced by the experience of the ship in which I made this voyage. These ships should be cross-ribbed, and lined with lead, having many knees and bolts, the heads of which must be closely let into the wood. The lower part of these vessels should be flat and well ballasted. Being built in this way, any one of the vessels will sail close to the wind and will be safe though situated near a lee shore, which is the greatest danger in which a ship can be placed; for these ships are very weatherly and will lie within five points of the compass, and if by mischance they should run aground on a sand-bank, which might happen in sailing through unknown seas, they would be got off with more ease than ordinary vessels. Having flat bottoms they would not capsize, and might hope for help from their companions in the open sea.

It would likewise be proper to carry two launches, one of them completely assembled, and the other [in frame] capable of being assembled in the event of the first being lost. These must carry oars, that they may better come up to their ships in all weathers, or perform other services that may be required. This boat must sail near the coast within sight of the three ships, which must always be four leagues apart while at sea, and alert them to any remarkable features noticed on the coast. Therefore it is advisable that its commander should be a skilled person, intelligent, courageous, cautious, and trustworthy. The launch must be large enough to contain twenty butts of water in case of necessity, which together with the three ships and the launch in frame, all of them fit for sea and well equipped, will cost 8,000 ducats.

It would also be advisable to carry in these ships six pieces of cannon, for as these ships must be very strong they can well bear their weight, and also twelve lesser pieces. These eighteen pieces of cannon must be divided between the three ships, and will cost 1,500 ducats. Also 200 muskets, at three ducats each, will cost 600. Moreover 150 arquebuses, to be taken on shore when necessary (as is often the case in these voyages of discovery) at two ducats each would cost 300 ducats. Pikes, gunpowder, lead, rope, pumps, fireworks, cannon balls and other ammunition, would come to 700 ducats.

There must be three *pilotos*, prudent, active men, and Spanish, with their mates, and twenty-four good mariners, who should be divided between the three ships. They will return expert from the voyage, and may become pilots for this route. Finally, 200 men should be employed, if possible most of them seamen, because when necessary a sailor can serve as a soldier, but a soldier can never perform the duties of a sailor. These should be divided as follows: eighty men in the *capitana*'s ship, and in each of the other ships fifty men; and the remaining twenty in the launch, so if there should be occasion to make use of the oars there may be people ready for that occasion. These may be paid by the year, giving each *piloto* 1,000 ducats, and each of the 200 men forty-eight ducats at the rate of four ducats a month, which will amount to 9600 ducats a year. And because among these 200 men there must be experienced officers and petty officers, these, attended with *pilotos*, would bring their earnings for a year to 3,000 ducats.

There should also be sufficient supplies of cables, anchors, wood, pitch, hemp and sails; tools, nails and lengths of timber to repair any damage inflicted by the enemy's cannon, which will amount to 1,500 ducats.

Also 200 ducats worth of wax tapers for the lanterns of the *capitana* and *almiranta*; for as the days on this route are very long and the nights short, there will be no necessity for any more, for without doubt the Sun will for many days not descend out of sight.[1]

There must be divided among the ships 200 ducats worth of medicines. And, as all maritime affairs are uncertain, it would be well to carry provisions for two years, for the wine at least may serve on the return voyage. Reckoning on the usual rations, the three ships will need 2,200 *quintales* of biscuit which, at four ducats a *quintal*, will amount to 8,800 ducats. And as the biscuit might spoil, in which case the people would suffer great inconveniences, it would be well to take 400 *quintales* of flour, which purchased at two ducats a *quintal*, will cost 800 ducats. The rations of wine for two years will amount to 9,125 measures of thirty-two *arrobas*, which at the rate of six *reals*, would cost 4,977 ducats.

Hung beef, pork, bacon, and hens for the sick, 2,500 ducats, 400 ducats worth of dried fish, 600 ducats worth of oil, vinegar and pulse, 300 ducats worth of cheese, one hundred ducats worth of salt – for it will be of much importance to carry out a good quantity, as it will be of use when there is plenty of fish, or when arriving at a place where meat can be procured they can be preserved during the entire voyage by means of the salt.

All which expenses will amount to 47,077 ducats; and this is the most that the fitting out of the ships will cost, though there will be other lesser items which are absolutely necessary. On careful reflection it will be seen how cheaply so great an advantage may be purchased, which indeed is one of the greatest that can now offer itself, for by this means we may prevent the great misfortunes which could befall Your Majesty's kingdoms if the navigation of this strait is neglected. Finally, it will be advisable to take possession of whatever others might seize, to our prejudice; for I know not how one would suffer foreigners to take possession of that which has been discovered by a Spaniard, particularly when it is in their power to injure us by so doing, and to make war on us. Not only this, but should they acquire possession of the strait, they will without doubt give to the devil the best fruits of this kingdom – the souls of the natives – disseminating among them their wicked and perverted doctrines; for we run all these risks by neglecting the navigation of this strait and leaving it open for our enemies, by which they may get possession of all those kingdoms. And they may do so with the greater ease by means of the recent discovery of Terra Australis;[2] for it is so large and extensive a region (according to their account of it) that whoever has possession of it will also be masters of the entire South Sea; for if notwithstanding the distance of the route they have to pass round the Cape of Good

---

[1] It is items such as this (and still more the note in the next sentence which specifies that only the same amount should be spent on medicines for a voyage expected to last two years as on wax tapers) that might arouse suspicions that the 'Relation' was written tongue-in-cheek. In a rather later period the document might have been construed as a Swiftian satire on foolish projectors and their even more foolish schemes.

[2] A reference to the claims of Quiros; see pp. 428-9 above.

Hope, the enemy[1] has now found the means to establish in the Indies and those parts six factories together with, as reported, eight forts on the island of Ternate, to the great prejudice of Your Majesty. It is easy to see that if they discover this short passage and convenient harbour, they might annoy us much more. On which account it is much more reasonable to consider the losses which may follow from not taking and fortifying this strait, than the expenses which would accrue from making the voyage, for whoever wishes to perform and enjoy great achievements must suffer great expenses, and experience many anxieties. Finally, if Your Majesty gains the sovereignty of the sea, you will also obtain that of the land, and if not it will be difficult to preserve what we already possess. I speak as a man who has much experience of sea affairs, and well knows the great value of the sovereignty of the sea, without which it is impossible to enjoy the empire of the land. These last reasons will be sufficient for those who understand matters of state, and if there are any who are negligent in their duty, let them be vigilant and put themselves on their guard, for I suspect that we have numerous open and secret enemies who have many motives for wishing ill to Spain.

Let no one say, as I think has been said, that there is not enough money for such enterprises because Your Majesty is necessitous, and if there are any who alleges this, and perceives the King to be in want, let him assist with some of his riches, and not forget that it will be better to dispose of them in this way than be deprived of all his possessions by the enemy at some future time. Much as he may expend in this way, the man who undertakes to carry into execution so arduous an enterprise will lay out much more, for I, as a seaman, am not ignorant of how many dangers attend it. He alone will bear witness to it who shall experience the violence of the North Sea, the storms and its turbulent waters. Certainly, sailing in company, and with good ships as will be found for this voyage, there is no reason to dread the sea, however rough it may be; but they must coast along the shore for reasons mentioned elsewhere, and coasting along in such rough seas is dangerous above all things, so much so that there is no sailor whose courage would not fail him at the very thought of it. I think therefore that if there is anyone willing to undertake it, it is advisable not to lose sight of him, for there may be found one who will do it, but I doubt whether there will be two. And let it be remembered that such voyages cannot be of the least profit to the person who performs them, but on the contrary will be attended with many inconveniences and troubles. As to its profits, I know not whether it will be productive of any the first time. We have no reason to be assured that our enemies may not have discovered this passage or some other which leads to the South Sea because we know that they are great seamen, and as enterprising as myself, ready to rush forward impetuously as I have done. I repeat, Sire, that their desire is to discover this strait, as I learn from the account of Capitan Balthazar de Just, residing in Fontarabia,[2] who was corresponding with me about this affair on 7 July this year, 1609, that the French have put a garrison on the banks of the River of Canada three hundred leagues inland,

---

[1] In this case the Dutch.
[2] The captain has not been identified, but Funeterrabía, harbour town in the Gulf of Biscay near the French border, was a favoured place for retired mariners.

and were confident of discovering a passage from thence of the South Sea.[1] I mention this, not because I believe that a passage will be found, for it is impossible that this river could run another thousand leagues or more; furthermore, I myself sailed along most of the stretch left to be discovered of the American coast of the South Sea without finding any entrance or river of importance. But I mention it, Sire, so that Your Majesty can see how diligently our enemies are in making use of every means to discover a passage.

Also let me advise Your Majesty that if you should send an expedition on another voyage of discovery, let it be done secretly, and organized in such a manner that the captains must be commanded not to open their instructions until they have sailed forty leagues from the land; because by means of this precaution we may deceive the spies, supposing them prepared to observe us. If it please God that we should again discover this strait, we should fortify it the very next year, because it is utterly impossible that the many people who will be necessary for this expedition will also be so silent and prudent as not to make public this voyage and its directions, for if they are heard of by our enemies they themselves may seek, find and fortify it in such a manner that many men and very great expense will be necessary to regain it from them. Therefore it would be advisable to be very circumspect from the moment the expedition departs on the discovery.

Copied from the original quarto manuscript, probably of the author himself, in the possession of His Excellency the Duque del Infantado. The tables and sketches were copied from the same manuscript. All of which I have carefully checked. Madrid, 24 March 1781.

Juan Bautista Muñoz

---

[1] A reference to Samuel de Champlain's establishment of a settlement at Quebec on the St Lawrence River in 1608.

DOCUMENT 2

The Memoir of Jean-Nicolas Buache de la Neuville

Memoir[1] on the ancient discovery of the Northwest Passage from the North Sea to the South Sea through the northern part of America

Read at the Académie Royale des Sciences of Paris [on 13 November 1790]
by
M. Buache,[2] Principal Geographer of His Most Christian Majesty

The importance of the NW Passage to America has been recognized for nearly three hundred years. It is still the object of frequent investigations by the trading nations of Europe, and a prize of twenty thousand pounds sterling is on offer by the English Parliament to her navigators if they discover it.[3]

Considering the many unsuccessful attempts that have been made to this end, and, recently, the voyage undertaken by the celebrated Cook to survey the Northwest Coast of America where one of the entrances of the passage was thought to lie[4]; by Mr Young to examine again Hudson Bay,[5] where the other [eastern] entrance was thought to be; and by Mr Hearne[6] and Mr Pond[7] travelling from Hudson Bay to the limits of the Frozen Sea through lands where a strait had been imagined, anyone could be led to doubt the existence of a communication between the two seas, and this is probably the general opinion to this day. Notwithstanding this, reassured by the weight of

---

[1] A Spanish translation of the French original of the memoir was sent to Malaspina by Valdés on 22 December 1790 (see pp. 417-19 above), and formed the basis for the comments of Malaspina and Bustamante (Documents 3 and 4 below). The copy translated here from the Spanish is in Real Academia de la Historia, Colección Muñoz (Doc. 9/4802, ff. 27-37).

[2] Jean-Nicolas Buache de la Neuville; see pp. 430-31 above.

[3] The Act offering a £20,000 reward was passed in 1775, shortly before Cook sailed on his final voyage, and was a revised version of the original Act of 1745 in that it opened the award to naval vessels as well as to those privately owned.

[4] In 1778 Cook explored the Northwest Coast from Vancouver Island to Bering Strait without finding a passage.

[5] It is not clear which 'Mr Young' this is. In 1777 (in the same period as the other voyages mentioned here) Lieut. Walter Young commanded a discovery expedition, but to Baffin Bay, not Hudson Bay. Alternatively, the reference may be (as Bustamante clearly assumed it to be in his mention of it on p. 464 below) to the voyage of James Young, a Hudson's Bay Company captain, who in 1689 took a ship north along the west coast of Hudson Bay from Churchill River, but was forced back by ice after sixty miles. For both voyages see Alan Cooke and Clive Holland, *The Exploration of Northern Canada 500 to 1920: A Chronology*, Toronto, 1978, pp. 43, 97.

[6] In 1771-2 Samuel Hearne made a prodigious overland journey across the NE shoulder of the North American continent from Churchill, Hudson Bay, to the shores of the Arctic Ocean at the mouth of the Coppermine River, without crossing any sizeable waterway.

[7] Peter Pond was an employee of the Northwest Company in the 1770s and 1780s and was never in Hudson Bay, but he was the first non-native fur-trader to cross the Athabasca portage and to reach Great Slave Lake.

evidence I am now commending to the Academy the relation written by a navigator who at the very time when its existence began to be questioned found the NW Passage. The account of the discovery is authentic. The facts mentioned in it in no way contradict the details contained in the accounts of other navigators; furthermore they confirm the truth of many other incidents told by different authors which had until now been regarded as fictitious or doubtful because they could not be checked.

A Spanish navigator called Lorenzo Ferrer Maldonado discovered in the year 1588 the NW Passage that I am about to describe, and his relation of this discovery is contained in a manuscript memoir that he presented in person to the King of Spain in 1609 to persuade him that the navigation leading to the passage should be repeated in order to secure its possession. An officer of the Spanish navy, Sr Mendoza,[1] known to this Academy for his learning and industry, has been commissioned by the court at Madrid with the task of forming an establishment to produce nautical charts similar to our own here in France.[2] It is he who delivered to me a true copy of this manuscript. After I had read it and discussed it with him, he kindly let me have it to be used as I saw fit. While Sr Mendoza is busy among us assembling the material required for his establishment, his government has issued instructions for all the archives in Spain to be searched, and for any original accounts of ancient Spanish voyagers and navigators to be collected. As a result of this, I dare say that presently we may expect great benefits will accrue to geography from his knowledge and endeavours.

The memoir of the said Spanish navigator is entitled 'A Relation of the Discovery of the Strait of Anian, made by me, Captain Lorenzo Ferrer Maldonado, in the Year 1588; in which is given the Course of the Voyage, the Situation of the Strait, the Manner in which it ought to be fortified, the Advantages of this Navigation, and the Loss which will arise from not prosecuting it.'

In this memoir the author has plotted the track and drawn up a separate plan of the Strait of Anian with two views, one showing its entrance, the other its outlet, which he also drew up to facilitate their surveying. The plan and the views are those which I now have the privilege of presenting in more detail to this body. As today I am only able to offer a general idea of this discovery, I shall limit myself to a description of the route followed by the navigator in 1588 and thereby give evidence of the existence of the NW Passage.

Here is the relation of the navigator ...[3]

This is a summary of the voyage and of the discovery which the Spanish navigator said he made in 1588. In the details I have omitted, which I intend to relate during our sessions or in private meetings, enough evidence will be found concerning both the

[1] José de Mendoza y Ríos; see p. 431 above.
[2] Less ambitiously, Mendoza's mission in various European countries was to put together a collection of books and scientific instruments to form the basis of the library of the marine department in Cádiz. See Palau et al., *Diario del viaje de Malaspina*, p. 635.
[3] Buache's summary of Ferrer Maldonado's account (which is given in full in Document 1) is here omitted.

existence of the passage and of the navigator's learning. For the moment, though, my purpose is to examine the route that he has plotted for us, and to make some remarks about the major occurrences of his discovery.

The navigator's route from Lisbon to the island of Friesland, and from Friesland to the Strait of Labrador, is that laid down by modern navigators from Lisbon to Cape Farewell at the entrance of Hudson Strait,[1] where the same latitudes and distances are found.

The route that he describes henceforth from the [Atlantic] ocean to the South Sea falls, as we have seen, into three parts: 1st the passage of the Strait of Labrador, from the ocean to the Frozen Sea [Arctic Ocean]; 2nd the 700 leagues navigation or run within the Frozen Sea; 3rd the passage of the Strait of Anian which leads from the Frozen Sea to the South Sea.

The Strait of Labrador, for which the navigator gives a distance or length of 290 leagues, is divided into three parts, as is easily understood: the first part which he says is eighty leagues long to the the NW is really Hudson Strait from its entrance to Hudson Bay, with the same bearings and distance. In the year 1588 Hudson Bay was not yet known, nor could the navigator have sighted it since he followed the northern coast of the strait, which is always freer from, or less obstructed by, ice. In the second part he sailed north for a distance given as 120 leagues; we must point out that the strait runs north of Hudson Bay, and that in the English charts it is described as the Nameless Strait or Undiscovered Strait,[2] that is a strait to which no name has yet been given, or a strait not yet discovered. This is a part where only the south side has been sighted; by Baffin in 1616, Foxe in 1631, and Thomas James in 1632. These navigators attempted to penetrate [the area] in the hope of finding the passage they were looking for, but retreated fearful of the ice they saw coming from the north. It is worth noting that Baffin, finding himself south of the entrance and seeing that the tides were setting north, inferred from this that there was a passage; consequently he gave the name Cape Comfort to a point of land near where he had noticed this phenomenon.[3] In the same way, Foxe inferred from the high number of whales seen in the NW part of Hudson Bay that there should be in some part or locality a passage to the South Sea, and he held this belief until he died.[4] The English charts that have been published in the last forty years show a communication between Nameless Strait and Baffin Bay; but as this is based on conjecture it is conceivable that it discouraged further searches, particularly since navigators who have reached Baffin Bay in search of the passage have found nothing but ice in its SW part where the outlet of Nameless Strait was supposed to be. Ancient charts give Baffin Bay less width than the modern ones; they do not place it as far west, and they do not show it so near Hudson

---

[1] A curious slip – Cape Resolution marks the entrance of Hudson Strait; Cape Farewell is at the southern tip of Greenland.

[2] As in, for example [Thomas Jefferys], 'Chart comprising Greenland with the Countries and Islands about Baffins Bay and part of Hudsons Bay', London, 1775.

[3] On the NE coast of Baffin Island.

[4] See Miller Christy, ed., *The Voyages of Captain Luke Foxe and Captain Thomas James of Bristol*, 2 vols, London, 1894, II, pp. 371, where Luke Foxe in 1631 wrote that he thought there might be a passage near Roe's Welcome in the northwest of Hudson Bay, 'being moved by the high flowing of the Tyde and the *Whales*'.

Bay. I believe, with de Lisle and d'Anville, who adopted them, that they should be preferred.[1]

The third part of the Labrador Strait, which ends at the Frozen Sea, is in a region which we do not yet know; therefore it does not contradict any of the notions that we have been given. Rather, I believe that it confirms what has been seen without [arousing] much interest in a chart included in *The American Traveller*,[2] and in a large Japanese chart brought from Japan by Kaempfer[3] and deposited in the collection of Hans Sloane. The chart from *The American Traveller* shows a strait joining the Frozen Sea and Hudson Bay, where the names of Spurrell and Fowler are given to two capes that form the entrance of this strait at the Frozen Sea end.[4] The Japanese chart, which still shows as unknown the coasts of northern America, also indicates a strait through with the Frozen Sea communicates with the ocean, and it places this strait in the same place where the Spanish navigator has taken us. Thanks to the wise researches of M. Guignes we know that the Chinese navigated in ancient times to the Northwest Coasts of America.[5] It is also known from Benjamín of Tudela,[6] an Indian [*sic*] author of the twelfth century, that the Chinese knew the Frozen Sea, which they named Nikpha. They used to say that those who enter that sea cannot leave it, and that they die when their provisions are exhausted. Seixas in his *Theatro naval*[7] says that hulls of Chinese

---

[1] Probably a reference to Guillaume Delisle, whose 'Carte du Canada ou de la Nouvelle France', Paris, 1703, shows a shrunken Baffin Bay, and J. B. Bourguignon d'Anville, who produced numerous maps of North America in the middle decades of the eighteenth century.

[2] *The American Traveller*, London, 1769, written by 'an Old and Experienced Trader' (Alexander Cluny), with a chart which, as the next sentence states, showed a strait connecting Hudson Bay with the Arctic Ocean. There is no evidence that Cluny ever went north of Hudson Bay.

[3] Engelbert Kaempfer (1654–1716), physician and traveller, who spent much time in Japan in the late seventeenth century. His history of Japan was published under the direction of Hans Sloane in London in 1727. After Sloane's death Kaempfer's manuscripts passed with other items in Sloane's collection to the new British Museum A version of Kaempfer's chart was published by Philippe Buache, uncle of the memoir's author, Buache de la Neuville, in his *Considérations géographiques*, Carte VI.

[4] George Spurrell and John Fowler were ship captains serving the Hudson's Bay Company in the mid-eighteenth century, and their names were presumably added to Cluny's fictitious strait to give it some appearance of authenticity.

[5] Joseph de Guignes (1721–1800) was a leading French orientalist, and the author of numerous books on China, its history, trade and language. He also propounded the thesis that in the fifth century BC a Chinese junk sailed east until it reached Fou Sang, the name its crew gave to part of the Northwest Coast of America, where they found civilized peoples. He gave an advance copy of his essay on this subject, printed in the December 1752 issue of the *Journal des savants*, to Philippe Buache before publication, and the geographer's 'Carte des nouvelle découvertes au nord de la Mer du Sud' of August 1752 not only shows 'Fou-Sang' on the Pacific coast of North America between latitudes 54°N. and 58°N., but marks the route that the Chinese vessel was supposed to have followed in 458 BC.

[6] Benjamin of Tudela (c.1130–c.1175). In his native Tudela, the chief city of Navarre, Rabbi Benjamin was recognized as a learned man for his knowledge of the Torah and the teachings of Talmudic law. But it is his book of travels, first published in 1543, that ensured him lasting fame. He is thought to have set out on his travels in 1165, returning to Tudela seven or eight years later. He visited France, Italy, Greece, Sicily, Syria, Palestine, Egypt and the Persian Gulf, but it is improbable that he went farther east although he describes India and China. Buache would have had Latin, French and English versions of Benjamin's *Itinerary* available to him. See José Ramón Magdelena, ed., *Libro de Viajes de Benjamín de Tudela*, Barcelona, 1989; and for commentary see Sandra Benjamin, *The World of Benjamin of Tudela: A Medieval Mediterranean Travelogue*, Madison, Calif. and London, 1995.

[7] Francisco de Seixas y Lovera, *Theatro naval hydrographico* ..., Madrid, 1688, f. 46.

vessels have been found in Hudson Bay; this allows us to understand where the Japanese obtained the information they include in their charts.

The *American Traveller* does not make the slightest reference to the information shown in the chart included in this book. M. Vaugondy, who in the year 1774 did some research on this matter,[1] informs us that the author was an English captain named Cluny, and that he had sailed along part of the coast of the Frozen Sea north of America. Since then this information has not been made use of because no one has been capable of appreciating it, but today one can believe that it is not without foundation. Let me cite here an article from the *London Gazette* that will deserve more credence in our day. On 4 April 1769 it reported that an officer who had served in the ships of the Hudson's Bay Company had found the wished-for Northwest Passage to the East Indies, that he had successfully passed a strait from Repulse Bay to another [strait] through which he had entered the Tartarian Ocean. It adds that at the instance of the East India Company and Hudson's Bay Company his log and charts had suddenly disappeared when they were about to be published.[2]

In the *Journal des savants* for the month of November 1773 there is also a letter from M. de la Lande[3] where he says that in 1769 a Danish ship named the *Crown of the North*, commanded by Baron de Ulfeld, passed from the [Atlantic] Ocean to the Frozen Sea, then into the South Sea, whence it returned to Europe by way of the Strait of Le Maire.[4]

The whole of the Spanish navigator's relation and his own testimony leave us in no doubt, I think, about the communication from Hudson Bay to the Frozen Sea, and consequently about the Northwest Passage, which is the main subject of this paper.

The navigation of the Frozen Sea from the Strait of Labrador to the entrance of the Strait of Anian perhaps will be considered difficult, but not impossible as would have been assumed from the voyages of Phipps and Cook.[5] From the Spanish navigator's track we can see that the coast trends south from the outlet of the Strait of Labrador, and that the halfway point between the two straits lies at latitude 74°N. Mr Hearne found the mouth of the Coppermine River near 71°40′N,[6] and Mr Pond, in a map of

---

[1] A leading French geographer, Didier Robert de Vaugondy, whose *Mémoire sur les pays de l'Asie et de l'Amérique*, Paris, 1774, examined the route into the Arctic Ocean supposedly followed by Cluny. See Mary Sponberg Pedley, *Bel et Utile: the Work of the Robert de Vaugondy Family of Mapmakers*, Tring, 1992, pp. 70, 86, 89.

[2] Buache's summary of the item in the *London Gazette* (and other newspapers) is accurate, but the original, fanciful article has all the appearance of a 'puff' to publicize Cluny's forthcoming book rather than a factual report. See Williams, *Voyages of Delusion*, pp. 228–30.

[3] Joseph-Jérôme Lefrançais de Lalande, a distinguished astronomer much involved in questions of geography and navigation.

[4] Yet another in the long line of apocryphal voyages that were supposed to have discovered a Northwest Passage.

[5] A reference to the voyage of Captain John Constantine Phipps, whose expedition of 1773 towards the North Pole was forced back by sea ice north of Spitsbergen in latitude 80°N; and to the final voyage of Captain James Cook, who in 1778 sailed through Bering Strait but encountered pack ice not far north of 70°N.

[6] Hearne gave the latitude as 71°54′N, although this was in fact almost four degrees too far north.

his discoveries, presented to the Academy in 1786 by M. de la Rochefoucauld,[1] shows the mouth of the Arobosca River close to 65 degrees.[2] The latter [Pond] did not reach the Frozen Sea, but he tells us that near Lake Arobosca he spoke with forty natives who lived near the coast.[3] These confirmed that in that sea the water flowed and ebbed; they assured him that they did not know of any land to the north, and that although they had often seen ice floes there, the navigation of the rivers discharging there was free from the beginning of summer. Mr Pond also questioned many of the natives who had accompanied Mr Hearne on his journey, but says that they were silent about its principal circumstances, and that to this day travelling west is prohibited to all. Surely the same happened in the voyage of Mr Young,[4] about which no information has ever been obtained, and in that of Captain Cluny; but however little from Mr Pond reaches us it is enough to show that the Frozen Sea off America is not unnavigable.

It only remains for me to discuss the strait through which the Spanish navigator passed from the Frozen Sea to the South Sea which he called the Strait of Anian, in conformity with the charts of his time. It can be seen that this strait, which he places in 60 degrees latitude, and which is no more than a quarter of a league in width, cannot be Bering's strait found by Cook in sixty-six degrees latitude, and nineteen leagues wide. Therefore there is another strait that we do not know in that part of Northwest America, between the islands and the stretches of land that we consider to be part of the continent. Indeed, this is what many of the Russian charts show, particularly that which Mr Staehlin published about his discoveries. In it a large island may be seen near many smaller ones situated to the east of Bering's strait, and separated from the American continent by another strait.[5]

The navigator's relation here poses a great difficulty that I cannot leave unmentioned. His dead reckoning on emerging from the Strait of Labrador puts the Strait of Anian west of Bering's, and on the NE part of Asia, where we know that there is no strait. It is therefore necessary to suppose that there is a considerable error in his dead

---

[1] Vicomte Jean-François Rochefoucauld (1735–1789), a leading figure in French intellectual and political life of the period.

[2] Peter Pond made a series of maps of the Canadian Northwest in the mid-1780s to present to influential persons and organizations; they invariably showed Great Slave Lake six or seven hundred miles nearer the Pacific than it is, and so encouraged hopes of a transcontinental water route.

[3] Pond's 'Lake Arobosca' was not Lake Athabasca, as might be assumed, but Great Slave Lake, from which Alexander Mackenzie in 1789 travelled north to the Arctic Ocean down the river which now bears his name.

[4] See p.453, n .5 above.

[5] J. von Stählin's 'Map of the New Northern Archipelago discover'd by the Russians in the Seas of Kamtschatka and Anadir', London, 1774, showed 'Alaschka' or Alaska as a huge island rather than as a peninsula. Between it and the American continent, shown ending in longitude 140°W, lay a wide strait in latitude 65°N which led into the Arctic Ocean. Cook took the chart with him on his third voyage, and denounced its inaccuracy in the strongest terms. The relevant passage in his published journal, which Buache had seen, ran: 'If Mr Staehlin was not grossly imposed upon, what could induce him to publish a map, so singularly erroneous; and in which many of these islands are jumbled together in regular confusion, without the least regard to truth?...It is a map to which the most illiterate of his illiterate sea-faring countrymen would have been ashamed to set his name.' Cook and King, *Voyage to the Pacific Ocean*, II, p. 506.

reckoning. So I do not dare trust my ability to determine in any satisfactory manner the position of this strait, and I only suggest the following as possible.

The latitude of the Strait of Anian, established or fixed at 60 degrees, must be almost certain since it was given in the *piloto*'s account, and was found correct by the navigator who stayed there long enough to confirm it. This being supposed, the strait should be either towards Shoal Ness[1] west of Cook's River, or towards Mount St Elias east of the same river, for these are the only parts of America situated in that latitude. The Russians have surveyed all the area around Shoal Ness, as may be seen in the latest chart of their discoveries,[2] without finding a strait; consequently we need to examine the vicinity of Mount St Elias. On the other hand, we shall adopt the following position as far as the route of the navigator is concerned when he came out of the strait to enter the South Sea. It should be noted that he sailed on a SE course and that as far as 55 degrees of latitude the coast situated SE of Mount St Elias must be that of America. Likewise, the coast that he found 120 leagues west of the American coast, which he followed in the NE direction up to the port, can only be understood as the coast of Alaska and lands near Cook's River. The navigator has assumed that this coast was part of Tartary, but this is on the basis of what he himself says, trusting the charts of his time, and because he had assumed that his strait was the one shown on those charts with the name of Anian.

I would even be inclined to accept the position of this strait when considering the claims made by Spain as to her rights over this part of the coast of America. There is no doubt that the Spaniards have had knowledge about the presumed strait, considering that independently of our navigator's relation, one can read in Purchas how when Drake entered the South Sea the Viceroy of Mexico wanted to build a fort at the southern entrance of the strait, and that by chance in the year 1609 a ship from Acapulco sailed in those parts and came to Lisbon.[3] This is how one recognizes the date of our navigator's memoir and his project of fortifying the strait. Ancient charts showed a continuous coastline 1700 leagues long stretching from the southern point of California to Japan, and it is conceivable that this was the result of the first discoveries that were made, and that later this was removed through lack of supporting evidence. The extension by the Spaniards of their rights up to the entrance of Prince William Sound has no doubt been done with good reason, and it is to be presumed that they wish to include the strait within the limits of their claims.

As for the new establishments that are being formed in these parts we shall soon have precise details. It is known that the Russians have advanced beyond Cook's River,[4] and perhaps they will attempt again their ancient navigation through the strait

---

[1] Cook's 'Shoal Ness' is now Cape Avinof.

[2] It is not clear which chart this, but it is possibly Alexander Wilbrecht, 'Carte des decouvertes faites par les Russes et par le Capitain Anglois Jacques Cook dans la Mer du Sud', St Petersburg(?), 1787, which combined Cook's charts with Russian ones and showed the area near Shoal Ness as unbroken coastline. The map is reproduced in Derek Hayes, *Historical Atlas of the Pacific Northwest*, Seattle, 1999, p. 63.

[3] Scrutiny of Samuel Purchas, *Hakluytus Posthumus or Purchas His Pilgrimes*, London, 1625 (repr. 20 vols, Glasgow, 1905–7), has failed to reveal this information.

[4] Although their most easterly settlement, Fort St George on the Kenai Peninsula, established in 1787, was only just east of the entrance of Cook Inlet.

where they were first seen by our navigator in 1588. It is also conceivable that the English are only waiting for the moment they feel sure of their possession of this part of America which they are disputing with the Spaniards to make public the knowledge that they now have about the Northwest Passage.[1]

We have seen in the Spanish navigator's memoir that his *piloto* had a precise description of the Northwest Passage; from this one should infer that such a passage was already known, or at least discovered, before 1588, the time of his voyage. He tells us that his *piloto* was Portuguese, a man old and very experienced; but we know from Purchas that a Portuguese named Martin Chaeke had discovered a passage from the Indies to the North Sea in 1555, that he had written an account of his voyage, and that the said passage was found in 59 degrees latitude which, as may be seen, is that of the strait discovered by our navigator.[2] An English pilot named Thomas Cowles testified in writing in 1579 that he had read the printed account in 1567, although he had not been able to see it after that time, because it had been banned and all copies collected by order of the King of Portugal who feared that such a discovery might harm his trade. Also in Purchas one reads that this passage from the South Sea to the North Sea was confirmed by a Portuguese that the English took prisoner at the time of Queen Elizabeth; and that another Portuguese had talked to Frobisher as if he had sailed through it.[3] In sum, it was well known to the Lisbon pilots.

After all these considerations I believe that we may accept as a constant fact the discovery, which I have just described, of that Northwest Passage which has been sought for such a long time. To preserve the memory of the man, and to ensure the glory he deserves, I believe that I should give the name Ferrer to the strait he discovered, all the more so since it is quite improbable that the true Strait of Anian is in this locality. I shall thus name the strait joining Hudson Bay with the Frozen Sea, until now known as Nameless Strait.

Bringing this discovery to light, I have provided a solution to a great number of difficulties that, while being interesting truths, had declined to the category of fables. This will now encourage reading the history of ancient navigation with greater interest. I may also have destroyed preoccupations which have probably hindered the progress of navigation in the northern seas for a long time. I dare hope that at the close of the eighteenth century the study of lands near the Pole, and even the Pole itself, will be added to all those other studies which, thanks to this century of enlightenment, have enriched geography.

---

[1] The mentions in this and the preceding paragraph of rival Spanish and British claims are references to the respective positions of the Spanish and British governments in the Nootka Sound dispute, provisionally settled by the Nootka Convention of 28 October 1790, little more than two weeks before Buache de la Neuville read his memoir in Paris.

[2] Cowles's account of the voyage of Martin Chaeke or Chacke was published by Purchas in 1625. It is most easily accessible in the 1905–7 Glasgow reprint of Samuel Purchas, *Hakluytus Posthumus, or Purchas His Pilgrimes*, XIV, Glasgow, 1907, pp. 414–15.

[3] Ibid., XIX, p. 254.

DOCUMENT 3

The 'Reflections' of José Bustamante y Guerra

José Bustamante y Guerra: 'Reflections on the Memoir by Monsieur de Buache, member of the Académie Royale des Sciences of Paris, read on 13 November 1790, on the Northwest Passage from the Ocean Sea to the Pacific by the northern part of America.' [April 1791][1]

Before beginning the next campaign to the north where, at His Majesty's orders, we are to undertake the age-old objective of searching for a passage between the Atlantic and the South Sea, it will be in order to set out the objections to M. Buache's report, the basis of which is the account of a voyage made by a Spanish navigator, Lorenzo Ferrer Maldonado, which Don Alejandro Malaspina brought from Spain. It will also be useful to draw attention to the frequent and well-organized expeditions made by the English in search of the same passage, in the course of which, their fond hopes having being disappointed, they confirmed that it was unlikely to exist.

Before adducing the reasons which seem to argue against its existence I must declare my feelings of respect and appreciation for those who have supported the said memoir. Capitán de Fragata José de Mendoza y Ríos, who was on a mission to Paris, presented to M. Buache, who acknowledges the fact, all the material for drawing it up. To those ties which bind together members of a single corps, and this officer is well known in the navy, I must add our long friendship as an important reason to hold him in esteem. However, today's circumstances do not permit us to hide our opinions on a matter of such importance, and for the sake of authenticity these should be recorded in our journals before we obtain the factual evidence that we are about to seek.

Capitán Lorenzo Ferrer Maldonado presented his report to King Felipe II[2] in 1609, having sailed through the strait in 1588, as he specifically asserts, and he goes on to state in the third line that in the previous year, 1608, several ships sailed from England in search of that strait.

Certain omissions or differences are noticeable between the sailing directions relating to that voyage which we have received from the court,[3] and those outlined by M. Buache in his report. For example, he omits in the third line, after [blank in original] that the island of Frislandia will be sighted, in ancient times named Tile or Thule, fabled in antiquity.

---

[1] Translated from the Spanish 'Reflexiones' as printed in María Dolores Higueras Rodríguez, ed., *La expedición Malaspina 1789–1794. Tomo VIII: Diario general del viaje corbeta Atrevida por José Bustamante y Guerra*, Madrid, 1999, pp. 223–30. Its first sentence indicates that Bustamante wrote his 'Reflections', which in places show signs of hasty composition, during the month of April 1791. The corvettes left Acapulco for Alaska on 1 May 1791.

[2] A mistake for Felipe III.

[3] That is, the 'Relation' of Ferrer Maldonado.

The entrance which should be to the right when looking north, and which M. Buache supposes to run NE, must run ENE according to the original.

M. Buache does not seem to notice that in a channel no less than twenty or forty leagues wide our mariner sees fires, coves and shelter on both shores. It is impossible to see that far by day, nor is it to be supposed that there is stubble being burnt off in these latitudes; furthermore, mists and heavy cloud are almost inevitable in high latitudes in both hemispheres. It was these that caused the separation of Captain Furneaux during Cook's second voyage, and accounts for the fact that Mr Forster's boat lost both vessels from view and heard the bell of the *Discovery* before seeing either of them.[1]

The courses followed by Ferrer Maldonado imply that the winds were always well aft, and M. de Buache copies these to the letter. Why does not a good geographer find out which is 'the port of San Miguel or the Bay of San Nicolás, where every year almost a thousand trading vessels enter, which to pass into the Sea of Flanders, must go up to latitude 75° to get round Finmark'. This is what M. Buache fails to mention although this discovery is of the highest importance in the history of European nations and commerce. The northernmost point seems at present to be Archangel, from where they only have to reach latitude 71°30' on the North Cape to sail into the Baltic.

M. de Buache clearly states that the sea water which was thrown onto the ship froze instantly, so that the sails had to be furled, having become more than a palm's width thick [with ice].[2] The belief that the sea of which he speaks can freeze is wrong, since it is a very broad strait with violent currents, these and the rough seas not allowing it to freeze because of the continuous movement; and so Ferrer Maldonado is convinced that it can only freeze on shore, and where the water is calm, to judge by what was happening around his ship.

These three points are all impossible to determine when studied by the mariner and compared with what is definitely known to take place in the very high latitudes of both hemispheres. Consider, apart from the second and third voyages of Cook, that of Phipps,[3] that of Pagès,[4] our own to Cape Horn, and, among others, that of the King's frigate *Cabeza* in the year '89,[5] which encountered icebergs on the return, but with no greater degree of cold. He also states that the prevailing winds are unfavourable northerlies, and that it is necessary to make use of the tides, a good practice for the months of February and March. Furthermore, supposing that there are

---

[1] The *Resolution* and *Adventure*, Cook's ships on his second voyage, were separated several times. Here Bustamante seems to be referring to the separation of 8 February 1773 in 'thick Fogg'. Beaglehole, *Voyage of Resolution and Endeavour*, p. 90. The incident involving Johann Reinhold Forster, naturalist on the voyage, happened on 14 December 1772, and is described in Nicholas Thomas and Oliver Berghof, eds., *A Voyage round the World* by George Forster, 2 vols, Honolulu, 2000, I, p. 67. The ship's bell was that of the *Adventure*, not the *Discovery*, which was Cook's consort vessel on his third voyage.

[2] This is misleading; Ferrer Maldonado's 'Relation' referred to ice of this thickness on the sides of the ship, not, as is implied here, on the sails. The same error is made in the final sentence of the next paragraph.

[3] See p. 457, n. 5 above.

[4] Captain Vicomte de Pierre Marie François Pagès (1748–93), who sailed from Holland in 1776 in a whaling vessel which made for Spitsbergen. It reached latitude 80°30'N where it was beset by ice. See his *Voyage auteur du monde et vers les deux pôles, par terre et par mer*, Paris, 1782.

[5] For the *Cabeza* see Vol. I of this edition, pp. 23, 112 and n.

currents so rapid that they prevent the formation of ice, or set always in one direction, or are periodical because of the effect of the tides – if the first is the case, how did he find them favourable both going and returning; if the second, how did he counter the contrary currents in an immense ocean when he could not drop anchor? Our sailors on the Lima route should be asked if they can furl sails which are a palm thick [with ice].

The southeasterly passage to 55° can only be made to the east of Alaska; after Shoal Ness and Cape Newenham the coast trends very much to the west.[1] Why then does M. de Buache not remark upon this, wavering between one place and the other?

The voyage of Quiros, cited by Ferrer, had not been completed by October 1706 [1606], the approximate date of his arrival at Punta Salagua,[2] near the port of Navidad on the Californian coast. Our author gives the year 1609 for it, and although the date is later the month was very close.

M. Buache also omits to mention the nature of the terrain surveyed by Ferrer, that is to say, its excellence at about 59°, although only sheltered from the northerly winds by the mountains, where Ferrer finds rosemary and orchards, and says that there are many trees of great size, most of them fruit trees bearing good fruit, and some looking similar to those of Spain, such as apples, pears, wild plums (especially from small trees), almost all of them left over from the previous year, those of this year not having yet ripened since it was only April or May. There are vines of wild grapes and lychees, a fruit from China, and a great quantity of game, partridges and rabbits, somewhat different from those of Spain, and deer mottled black and white on a dun background, with large spreads of antlers, although not all had these. Two kinds of pigs were seen, some like those of the Indies, and others very large and like the wild boar of Spain.

Nor does M. Buache give a satisfactory account of the meeting with the Asian vessel of 800 tons from the bay or harbour of San Nicolás, returning of course to its own country in the 75th parallel, laden with brocades, silks, porcelain, feathers, chests, precious stones, pearls and gold. Its crew spoke Latin, were Lutherans, had come from another large city called Roba, subject to the great Khan of Tartary, and, what is more, another vessel was to follow them along the same route.

It then became clear that not only was this passage known, but that it was also safe enough to be used by Asian and Lutheran and other vessels of 800 tons with precious cargoes. Where, then, are the documents which vouch for these voyages? Or have these records been lost as well as the authentic Spanish ones? For one cannot term as such as paper which having been presented to the King, turns up in the archives of the Duke of Infantado, but cannot be found in the archives of Simancas, or in any of the other places belonging to the Crown, and is not mentioned by any contemporary author. Would it not have been usual to send it to Mexico, particularly as in the year 1602 of the same reign sailing directions for Sebastián Vizcaíno were drawn up, covering Acapulco to Cape Mendocino, which are to be found in Simancas, in Mexico, and in other places?[3]

---

[1] Bustamante is wrong; the coast trends almost due north, although after Norton Sound it turns due west.

[2] On the coast of Mexico, about 105 miles SE of Cabo Corrientes.

[3] The Vizcaíno expedition of 1602–3 reached latitude 43°N, near Cape Blanco, the farthest north on the coast of any Spanish expedition until 1774.

If the existence of the strait is confirmed, and gives a free passage to Asian ships, why bother to discover it and take possession, if it is already sailed by ships of 800 tons (which have an enormous interest in it) without strengthened hulls or any of the other special precautions that we have to take. And why bother with vessels of 150 or 100 tons? If the Lutherans have already been there, why express an anxiety that unless we act quickly, infidels and heretics will step in and divert the natives to hell? If it was only the need for provisions that distracted him [Ferrer Maldonado] from the cod fishery to go north through the ice floes, how did he forget in a moment all his ideas about finding the entrance, spending many days in doing so, when all the time he had on board his *piloto*, the Portuguese Martínez, who was the repository of all this information?

Finally, why are the launches in their passage four leagues offshore, if the middle of the track runs along a channel from twenty to forty leagues wide, the second part is a broad inlet, and the third part is very short and narrow? Where did Ferrer make the hull strengthenings for his vessels – in a remarkably short time at that – when he had to spend winter in the course of his projected passage? And why was it not until nineteen years later [sic] that he presented his account, for in that respect he mentions no earlier submissions as having been rejected or ill-received? What secret intentions did he have for the opposite or Asian coast, when he did not approach it at the time; how will the ships whose construction he proposed turn out to be so weatherly? How did he manage to hit directly on the northern entrance of the Strait of Anian in winter without going astray to either east or west, and how could he imagine that this was the only passage, with no other channel from the Frozen Sea to the Pacific other than this stretch of fifteen leagues easily passed through in a single tide?

But let us leave, not a moment too soon, geographical distances, particularly that of the port of Tartary, a hundred leagues from the Strait of Anian, which not even the indulgent judgement of M. Buache's can allow. How can this geographer admit the following two premises? Firstly, that the navigators Baffin, Fox, Thomas Smith, and James Young,[1] who had set forth at about the same time resolved to make the attempt, and with rewards in mind, were alarmed at the sight of ice in summer, when our own Ferrer had no fear of them in winter, without any particular purpose or rewards etc. Secondly, that the Hudson's Bay Company might conceal any knowledge of this sort acquired in 1769[2] or later, when the British government dispatched two expeditions in 1778 and 1779[3] for the same purpose, and certainly not with any intention of tarnishing their honour or risking excessive costs. As for the latitude given by the *piloto* at the southern entrance of the strait, I cannot imagine how he could take it as

---

[1] A reference to the northern voyages of William Baffin (1616) and Luke Foxe (1631). Thomas Smith was not a navigator but a promoter of Arctic voyages, and Baffin named Smith Sound in the far north of Baffin Bay after him. For James Young see p. 453, n. 5 above.

[2] A reference to London newspaper reports in the spring of 1769 to the supposed Arctic voyage of Alexander Cluny, a former employee of the Hudson's Bay Company. See p. 456, n. 2 and p. 457, n. 2 above.

[3] This is not at all clear: it could be a misdated reference to the expeditions to Davis Strait of Richard Pickersgill (1776) and Walter Young (1777), or a reference to the attempts to sail north of Bering Strait by James Cook (1778) and by his successor Charles Clerke (1779).

the base point for his calculations, since it is precisely one of the parallels most carefully surveyed by Captain Cook, more recently by our own navigators, and is already occupied by the Russians, who if they have reached higher latitudes will surely have seen the Frozen Sea if it is only eighteen leagues away.

To have chosen old charts rather than modern ones for the width of Baffin Bay is another unpardonable fault on M. Buache's part; so is the use nowadays of Japanese charts,[1] or the vague reports of Purchas and Seixas,[2] or finally the English gazettes of 1769[3] and the *Journal des savants* of 1773,[4] in order to suggest that voyages which at present could not for a moment be concealed from the keen curiosity of Europe – as also having recourse to an obscure instruction from the Conde de Monterrey to fortify the strait at the time of the English mariner Drake, or to the rights which Spain now claims, when these were well known to extend to the north of all parts of the Pacific Ocean both discovered and still to be discovered, as confirmed by our claims and concerns regarding the first moves of the Russians from Siberia towards these western coasts of America.

The same chart by Mr Staehlin, mentioned by M. Buache, is shown to be an absurdity by Cook's voyage, since it separates the island of Alaska from the mainland and makes the limits of America retreat considerably to the north in this area.[5]

Now M. Buache considers as authentic the account of such a discovery, as shown by the statements in his memoir: 'The account of the discovery is authentic. The facts mentioned in it in no way contradict the details contained in the accounts of other navigators; furthermore they confirm the truth of many other incidents told by different authors which had until now been regarded as fictitious or doubtful because they could not be checked.' Here M. Buache's argument becomes a vicious circle, whose purpose is as difficult to make out as its results are easy to refute.

Consider also the present location of the Russian establishments on Cook's River and our recent voyages, which still seem to be ignored in Europe, especially that of Teniente Salvador Fidalgo,[6] and it will be seen without prejudice that M. Buache's memoir is a very poorly-researched work, intended in fact to mesmerize Europe, to disparage the English, and to promote new voyages, rather than to serve that love of truth which should be the principal role of an Academy of Sciences.

I am still inclined to believe that M. Buache has another objective in persuading the public to believe in the existence of a passage. The history on which it is founded, and with which he attempts to achieve this, is very much like that which allowed the voyage and discoveries by Admiral Fonte along the same coasts to be considered true. Among those who most strongly supported the existence of the passage which bears the admiral's name was another Buache, an academician and geographer who, with

---

[1] As reproduced by Kaempfer; see p. 456 above.
[2] A reference to Samuel Purchas, compiler of *Hakluytus Posthumus or Purchas his Pilgrimes*, London, 1625, and Francisco de Seixas y Lovera, *Theatro naval hydrographico* ..., Madrid, 1688.
[3] See p. 457 above.
[4] A reference to Baron Ulfeld's supposed voyage through the Northwest Passage; see p. 457, n. 4 above.
[5] See p. 458, n. 5 above.
[6] In 1790 Fidalgo commanded the *San Carlos* which surveyed stretches of the Alaskan coast including Cook Inlet and Prince William Sound. See p. 54, n. 4 above.

M. De L'Isle, presented to His Most Christian Majesty [Louis XV of France] in 1750 a map which extended and justified the results of Fonte's voyage, supported by another map by the Englishman Mr Ellis.[1] The foregoing makes me suspect that our M. Buache, being the son of the other,[2] is now seeking to imitate with better prospects the ideas of his father, and to exonerate him of the superficiality with which, from weak and unlikely principles, he had attributed the hallmark of authenticity to that discovery so as to postulate without hesitation the existence of the Fonte passage.

If this were his intention, however, I believe he should expect from the public the same legitimate criticism aimed at making him more circumspect in his opinions in future, and ready to examine with greater care matters which not only serve to give fame to an Academy of Sciences, but which also determine the credit and reputation of whoever promotes them.

Having set forth all the arguments against the accuracy of M. Buache's memoir as presented by its author, we shall now give a brief account of the various attempts made to search for the desired passage to the NE of America and the Pole. Despite the fact that self-interest and glory have been the principles guiding these dangerous expeditions, it will be seen that all efforts were in vain, and that the brightest hopes were dashed ... .[3]

In this series of voyages I have omitted that of Admiral Fonte, assumed to have been made in 1640, during the reign of Felipe IV, because his ambiguous and implausible account has earned the scorn of all who have consulted it. The Jesuit Venegas deals with it at length in his history of California,[4] finally classing it as hypothetical or apocryphal. M. Buache and M. De Lisle are somewhat more indulgent, considering it to be true, as shown in the letter which they presented to His Most Christian Majesty on 18 April 1750, which included the discoveries of that admiral. The truth is that however thorough the inquiries entrusted from Paris to such men of good character as Capitans Jorge Juan, Don Antonio Ulloa[5] and others to look for the original report of this voyage, it could not be found in Spain, and therefore the copy which Buache presented to the Academy of Sciences was translated from the English original, a sufficient circumstance to stamp it as suspect.[6]

[1] In 1750 Joseph Nicolas Delisle read a paper to the Academy of Sciences which argued that the recent Russian explorations confirmed the discoveries of Admiral de Fonte, and accompanied it with a map by Philippe Buache, 'Carte des nouvelles découvertes au nord de la Mer du Sud', which was published in Paris in 1752. Henry Ellis, in *A Voyage to Hudson's Bay by the* Dobbs Galley *and* California, *In the Years 1746 and 1747, For Discovering a North West Passage*, London, 1748, supported the case for a Northwest Passage with several charts showing unexplored inlets on the west coast of Hudson Bay.

[2] Jean-Nicolas Buache de la Neuville was in fact the nephew of Philippe Buache.

[3] There follows a list, which is omitted here, of voyages from John Cabot's in 1497 to John Constantine Phipps's in 1773.

[4] Miguel Venegas was the work's nominal author. The correct reference is to Andrés Marcos Burriel, *Noticia de la California*, 3 vols, Madrid, 1757. Vol. III, appendix VII, contained a 150-page critical analysis of the Fonte account, which was not included in the English edition of 1759. On this see Glyndwr Williams, 'An Eighteenth Century Spanish Investigation into the Apocryphal Voyage of Admiral Fonte', *Pacific Historical Review*, 30, 1961, pp. 319–27.

[5] For Antonio Ulloa and Jorge Juan see Vol. I of this edition, p. xciv, n. 1.

[6] There is no evidence to support Bustamante's assertion of a French-inspired search for the Fonte account in Spanish archives before 1750. For more on the circumstances in which Delisle and Buache claimed to have found the account see Williams, *Voyages of Delusion*, pp. 248–55.

In view of so many efforts to resolve the question of the passage or communication between the two seas, it will not seem rash to decide that belief in its existence is as false as the memorial of Ferrer Maldonado's voyage. However, geography owes to this lengthy controversy the great progress that it has made in this part of the globe, without which it would have been much slower and less accurate.

DOCUMENT 4

The 'Dissertation' of Alejandro Malaspina

Dissertation regarding the authenticity of the voyage made in 1588 by Ferrer Maldonado from a port near Newfoundland to the Pacific Ocean and his return in the opposite direction. M. de Buache's considerations, as presented to the Académie Royale des Sciences on 13 November 1790, the misleading trails of similar voyages, and the real benefits of any through way between the two seas for a passage to Asia, are here examined. [Summer, 1792][1]

It is a truly unfortunate circumstance for geography and for its benefits to society that the natural division of the pursuits from which it springs and expands should be prejudicial to it, when in most other sciences this very division has enormously helped their progress. Thus, with similar advantages, navigation, physics, mechanics, and medicine, which at present are divided into many subsidiary branches, have followed each other closely, providing many objects of study for the learned, and inventions for the benefit of society. And as for commerce – society's original bond, the true measure of balance between nations, and the sole motivator of peace, civilization and plenty – had it been contained within its proper limits, by now it would have reached the full extent which the Supreme Creator of Nature intended, if only geography had been perfected and directly assisted this end. The whole of Europe quickly set out to perfect it, and would certainly have succeeded, if only her scientific system or her less than full recognition of the qualities of geography had not led her to confuse it with other sciences.

This mistake should not seem strange. Progress in geography, as in the other sciences, was dependent on reasoning and experiment. The rough education of mariners, to whom experience must necessarily be entrusted, makes them in the eyes of the public seem bound to misunderstand matters of reasoning, so that in this science more than in any other a natural division between the thinkers and the men of action seems necessary. This, nevertheless, is the source of all errors. The former have no part in experience, and the latter are allowed to contradict matters of reasoning. Mariners therefore exaggerate their accounts at will, while the learned sometimes accept with equal readiness the reliability of seamen. In the end this chaos of misunderstanding hinders rather than encourages the progress we desire. Unfortunately, a correct knowledge of geography is closely linked to Europe's political system. Since

---

[1] Translated from the 'Disertación' in Cerezo, *Diario de Malaspina*, I, pp. 279–85, which was taken from AMN, MS 92, ff. 246–251v. The present translation includes the final seven paragraphs of the 'Disertación' which are missing in MS 92, and are taken here from the printed version in Salvá and Sainz de Baranda, eds, *Documentos inéditos*, pp. 247–50. Internal evidence (p. 471, l. 7 below) indicates that the 'Disertación' was written by Malaspina during the summer of 1792, a year or so after his voyage to Alaska.

this is currently a favourite occupation of most scholars, particularly in our capital cities, there are more likely to be misunderstandings, or rather a lack of communication, between mariners and geographers. Whether magnetism directly affects the nerves; whether Atlantis ever existed; whether the population of America came from the north, east, or west; and whether the condition of the Moon is in fact that described to us by Herschel,[1] an account which received as much credence as when, not long ago, we read in the epochs of nature indications of its absolute coldness – all these are isolated facts of interest to a few, and their acceptance or rejection have no influence on the well-being of society. But the existence of a southern continent whose inhabitants and products could either enrich or destroy Europe; the authenticity of Captain Carver's report of the Shining Mountains;[2] the conviction that there is an easy waterway between the Pacific and the Atlantic, and so no need to sail to the southern hemisphere – these are matters in which all nations will readily intervene, either to augment their own power, or to weaken that of others who aim to maintain a much-desired equilibrium.

The development of geography in this area is still more problematical. Practical experience is costly, and fraught with danger for those involved, and is a doubtful benefit for the body of physical evidence which relies on the perceptions of each individual. Unavoidably, the fatal consequences of many difficulties has either been that the fundamental principles of science should be treated with slavish respect since they come from the mouths of a few mariners who reveal them like oracles; or that the confusion of ideas continues, particularly at this time when the amount of information contributing to it is so much greater.

England was the first to recognize the need to decide on one or the other of these two possibilities; and quite rightly preferring the first, placed all their trust in Captain James Cook. The useful results of such a sensible decision were shown within a few years. The southern continent of President de Brosses disappeared;[3] the waterway between the two oceans so persistently advocated by Mr Dobbs closed up;[4] the limits of permanent ice towards the North Pole, which Captain Phipps and Russian seamen had previously explored, were established;[5] and the same nation was able to send ships to Botany Bay and the Northwest Coast of America with the same confidence as it sent them to the Mediterranean or the Antilles.

The expedition of the Comte de la Pérouse seemed to confirm that this same

---

[1] Sir William Herschel (1738–1822), first President of the Astronomical Society, and one of the most distinguished astronomers of his age.

[2] Jonathan Carver, in his *Travels through the Interior Parts of North America*, London, 1778, postulated the existence of a great range of mountains running from north to south down the middle of the continent which he named the Shining Mountains.

[3] James Cook's first two voyages (1768–71 and 1772–5) demolished the theory of a great southern continent advanced by, among others, Charles de Brosses in his *Histoire des navigations aux Terres Australes*, Paris, 1756.

[4] Arthur Dobbs (1689–1765) was a passionate advocate of a navigable Northwest Passage, and in the 1740s organized two unsuccessful expeditions to search for it.

[5] Captain Constantine John Phipps attempted in 1773 to reach what he hoped might be an open polar sea, but was forced back in latitude 80°N. Since Bering's first voyage in 1728 the Russians had mounted a series of expeditions from Kamchatka towards Bering Strait and Alaska.

system had been accepted by the French.¹ The sole objective of that voyage was to complete the work of the English navigator [Cook] on those coasts that either he had not explored, or had been forced to leave poorly charted. Once knowledge of the habitable globe had been established geography could rely on the discoveries of those two expeditions as complete and free from outside reasoning since they had been carried out by the navigators themselves. Spain then accepted and even strengthened this system with the expedition of the corvettes *Descubierta* and *Atrevida*, which were to carry out a comprehensive survey of the coasts of America and Asia.

In fact, with so many investigations, either already published or soon to be published, with all the accuracy made possible by astronomy, with the truthfulness dictated by philosophy, and with a clarity of approach that should no longer be regarded as irreconcilable with a seaman's education, and finally with the excellence that the engraver's perfection and the generosity of the monarchs now made possible, geography should already be considered as having been restored to good health. It represents without the slightest error the rights of nations, and with complete certainty guides those entrusted with the public good through the various plans for routes and trade. The geographer's profession would accordingly become useless, and those least instructed in this type of work would be able, with the simple aid of callipers, to follow closely future navigators and the useful progress they might make for society. However, this has not come about. Reason has once again come into direct conflict with navigation, and while it has not been possible to reverse the existence of the southern continent, nevertheless M. de Monnier has defended in four memoirs the existence of Captain Bouvet's Cap de la Circoncision;² D. Barrington has established, perhaps with some preconceptions, a series of voyages towards the North Pole which have crossed latitude 82°N;³ Dalrymple has supported, and almost the whole English nation has subscribed to, the plans of Captain Meares who, not content with denigrating Captain Cook's report on the searches which he carried out in the river named after him, has revived the almost forgotten routes of Admirals Fonte and de Fuca.⁴ Finally, M. de Buache has read a memoir at the Académie des Sciences in Paris in which he not only asserts the veracity of the voyage made in 1588

---

¹ A reference to the French naval expedition to the Pacific of 1785–88 commanded by Jean François de la Pérouse.

² In 1739 the French navigator Jean Baptiste Charles Bouvet de Lozier sighted land in the South Atlantic that he named Cap de la Circoncision, which he – and some geographers – hoped might be part of the great southern continent. In reality it was an isolated island, next sighted in 1808 by Captain James Lindsay in the *Swan*. The position of Bouvet Island was finally established by modern methods in 1898. See David, *Charts and Views*, II, p. xliii.

³ Daines Barrington (1727–1800) had published details of a number of northern voyages by whalers and others that, he argued, showed that the polar sea was ice-free. See, for example, *The Probability of Reaching the North Pole Discussed*, London, 1775.

⁴ Alexander Dalrymple (1737–1808), a noted geographer whose *Memoir of a Map of the Lands around the North-Pole*, London, 1789, held out fresh hopes that a Northwest Passage might be found between Hudson Bay and the Pacific. John Meares (1756?–1809) was a half-pay British naval officer who commanded vessels in the sea-otter trade of the North Pacific. See p. 53, n. 2 above. In his *Voyages made in the Years 1788 and 1789, from China to the North West Coast of America*, London, 1790, he argued that there might yet be a Northwest Passage, and he used as evidence the supposed voyages of Bartholomew de Fonte in 1640 and Juan de Fuca in 1592.

by Ferrer Maldonado, in which he discovered a passage between the two seas – the Atlantic and the Pacific – but also goes on to deduce from that discovery the validity of many other facts recounted by different authors which since it has not previously been possible to understand them, have been regarded as fabulous or debatable.

Mr Wales responded to the first of these accusations immediately,[1] while the second cannot have found many supporters since no further attempts have been made to reach the Pole. At this very moment the schooners *Mexicana* and *Sutil* will be determining the inner limits of the Estrecho de Fuca described by Captain Meares.[2] Finally, the fourth point, the verification of which was entrusted to the corvettes *Descubierta* and *Atrevida* by His Majesty's order last year, 1791, would need no further proof other than the journal of that voyage, and the different views and descriptions of the coast which was then surveyed with that objective in mind.

A detailed analysis of the circumstances of Ferrer Maldonado's voyage was therefore futile, and we would certainly have omitted one had it not been at the same time clear that there was such a great readiness by geographers to continue to espouse outdated notions whatever their foundation; and if we had not good reason to believe that it was not only Ferrer Maldonado but some other individual who had hurried to claim either the honour of an already accepted discovery or the profits from a difficult and distant commission, likely to bring with it the use of a considerable sum of money. Around the year 1602 the Governor of Manila was sent the following royal command...[3]

The real benefit of a passage between one sea and another is also an objective which is of prime importance to link with considerations of social consequence, for it is one thing to put forward in isolation the proposition that a passage exists, and another to make the common inference that the search for it must be made at any cost and whatever the risks. Many have been misled precisely by this confusion of ideas; and it should have been dispelled by a comparison between this and the urgent question in the southern hemisphere as to whether the Canal de Santa Bárbara in Tierra del Fuego exists, and whether it is navigable.[4] The useful benefits arising from a survey of this sort would be considerable; and in future ancient accounts should be

---

[1] William Wales (1734?–98), the astronomer on Cook's second voyage. This is probably a reference to Wales's brief comment in 1778 that 'M. Bouvet's land was nothing else [than an island of ice]'. William Wales, *Remarks on Mr. Forster's Account of Captain Cook's last Voyage round the World ...*, London, 1778.

[2] A reference to the 1792 expedition of two of Malaspina's officers, Dionisio Alcalá Galiano and Cayetano Valdés, which completed the survey of the Strait of Juan de Fuca. See John Kendrick, ed. and trans., *The Voyage of the Sutil and Mexicana 1792: The Last Spanish Exploration of the Northwest Coast of America*, Spokane, 1991.

[3] Sentence unfinished, but Malaspina is referring to a *real cédula* or royal command signed in Zamora, 16 February 1602 in which Felipe III ordered Don Pedro de Acuña, Governor of the Philippines, to consult Hernando de los Ríos Coronel, explorer of the coasts of China and Formosa, who had made representations about 'the discovery of two straits ... one that is called Anian which separates the land of China and the coast of Asia from that of America and New Spain, and another strait through New Mexico ...' He was presumably the 'other individual' of Malaspina's previous sentence. See Salvá and Sainz de Baranda, *Documentos inéditos*, XV, pp. 234n–235n. Seven years later Ferrer Maldonado presented *his* memorial at Court.

[4] The Canal de Santa Bárbara connects the western end of Estrecho de Magallanes to the sea, running south through a maze of islands.

examined with greater care, or even if they are found to be authentic, dismissed where the facts have no bearing on the well-being of society.

At court at the beginning of the seventeenth century there was in fact a Lorenzo Ferrer Maldonado, Principal Cosmographer of the Indies, but there is nothing in the archives at Simancas to support the notion that he was the author of the memorial presented; nor for that matter is the memorial to be found anywhere but in the archive of His Excellency the Duque del Infantado. It is also a fact that in the years immediately preceding, His Majesty's Council discussed the Northwest Passage, not only because this is mentioned in the above-mentioned command, but because it was precisely at this time that the efforts of the English navigators, Davis, Lancaster, Hudson, Button and Gibbons would have aroused most interest on the part of the Spanish government.[1]

However, in Madrid these facts were not sufficient for Maldonado's voyage to be accepted as real. Malo de Luque considered that the differences between the 'authenticity' of the memorial and the 'evidence' of proof to the contrary reached such a point that he could not accept it;[2] and in the plan for a voyage by the corvettes *Descubierta* and *Atrevida* His Majesty's orders merely indicated that verification of this [memorial] should be sought only if information acquired during the course of the voyage should support it.[3]

Meanwhile, an examination of the account of the [Ferrer Maldonado] voyage, which became increasingly thorough as the time drew nearer when it would be shown before the eyes of the nation either true and glorious or apocryphal and unfounded, uncovered a large number of inconsistencies, which will be described here with all possible brevity. We do not know how they escaped the attention of M. Buache.

1. It was very strange that news of a discovery of such importance to the monarchy should only have been presented to His Majesty in 1609 when it had been made in 1588, so that it must have remained unmentioned for the long period of twenty-one years, precisely at the time when the desire for such a discovery was most intense.

2. If the tracks are expressed in courses and distances, they give a latitude of only 68°39′ at the end of Estrecho de Labrador, which Maldonado estimated at 75°.

3. It is hard to reconcile the situation of a mariner collecting food supplies in the Zelandillas, having been engaged in the cod fishery, with his sudden decision, or rather inspiration, to sail to the Pacific Ocean, at the cost of immense labour, and during the hard winter season – a decision his crew would not easily accept unless some practical benefit was put to them.

4. Nor was it easy to ascertain which was Puerto de San Miguel or Bahía de San Nicolás, where according to our voyager 'nearly one thousand trading vessels enter each year, which in order to go to the Sea of Flanders must ascend to latitude 75 degrees to round Finmark'.

---

[1] A reference to the northern voyages of John Davis (1585–7), Henry Hudson (1610–11), Thomas Button (1612–13) and William Gibbons (1614). Sir James Lancaster of the East India Company never sailed to the Arctic, but in a letter in 1603 from the East Indies made the cryptic and unexplained statement that there was a Northwest Passage in latitude 62½°N. See Purchas, *Pilgrimes*, XIV, p. 435.

[2] Not quite the conclusion reached by Malo de Luque (the Duque de Almodóvar); see p. 429 above.

[3] For the text of this instruction see Vol. I of this edition, p. 319.

5. In a channel forty to twenty leagues wide, fires, towns, coves and harbours could be seen, and at the same time our navigator did not know whether the sea along the shores froze or not, even though the water that sprayed around the vessel was freezing and the sails were a span thick with ice.[1]

6. Since during the voyage towards the Pacific 'the prevailing winds were contrary from the north, and it was necessary to take advantage of the tides', one would assume that the custom of anchoring and weighing anchor at the beginning and end of each tide would be observed; this would have been made difficult not just by the manoeuvre itself, but also by the need to sail in the middle of the channel and by the need to keep both shores in sight.

7. A very clear contradiction is noticeable between the Portuguese *piloto*'s local knowledge and his ignorance of the only place where he had need of it; also between the coincidence of the favourable tides that enabled them to keep the ship within sight of Estrecho de Anian for several days, and the quick embaying in the creek of the boat the moment it was launched; and Ferrer Maldonado's conclusion that there was no other strait.

8. We also marvelled at the good fortune with which this navigator always enjoyed extremely favourable winds. Voyaging westward from the coast of America he reached that of Asia after only five days, and although they must obviously have been in need of food, having left a harbour that as he himself says 'seemed never to have been touched by human footsteps', this was ignored for reasons that are not revealed.

9. It was not possible to reconcile this passage into the Pacific with the coasts surveyed by Captain Cook, the exact position of which nobody can doubt.

10. It was not easy to understand Maldonado's lack of good sense in claiming as his own the discovery of a strait easily navigated not only by 'an 800-ton Hanseatic vessel with a cargo of brocades, silks, porcelains, feathers, chests, precious stones, pearls and gold, whose crew were Lutheran and spoke Latin, but also another that was to follow very shortly, both of them having come from a very large city apparently called Roba, ruled by the Great Khan of Tartary'.[2]

11. Under these circumstances, it was even more to be wondered at that our navigator should have repeatedly advised secrecy and speed in the project he proposed, and especially that he should have visualized the robust construction and small size of the exploring ships, given that such discoveries were unnecessary since he had already surveyed it all – nor could there be the slightest risk in a place he had navigated in winter, and where the Hanseatic ships passed through so richly laden.

12. We have left to one side the improbability of the topography, the fruit, animals and birds he described, the heat he experienced on his return voyage which was greater than that of Spain in the summer, and finally the close proximity of the coasts of America and Asia throughout the whole region he surveyed, so that for the 300 leagues that he coasted over a period of eleven days, now to the SE, now to the north, there was no opening other than the mouth of the strait.

---

[1] See p. 462, n. 2 above.
[2] Here, as elsewhere, and despite the quotation marks, Malaspina is paraphrasing rather than directly quoting Ferrer Maldonado's 'Relation' (cp. p. 448 above).

These many considerations were soon strengthened by our own survey of the coast from Prince William Sound to Cape Fairweather, and Teniente de Navío Salvador Fidalgo's explorations the previous year towards the inner reaches of Prince William Sound.[1] Everything combined to show the utter improbability of such a passage, and greatly undermined M. Buache's arguments, of which we will now only examine those concerned with the Pacific Sea, for our considerations cannot venture as far as the other sea [the Atlantic] without becoming involved in another hypothesis which would probably divert us from the truth.

We shall not therefore inquire as to why M. de Buache left the names of the fabulous Thule, used by Ferrer for Frislandia, in the summary of the route, why he changes to NE the direction ENE which Maldonado attributes to the false mouth to be passed when sailing to the Labrador Strait; why, in contradiction to the definite facts stated by the Hudson's Bay Company and the latest steps taken by the British government, from whom the former surely would not have concealed their information, he only gives information from Purchas and Seixas, the English gazettes of 1769, the *Journal des savants* of 1773,[2] and a confused order from the Conde de Monterrey who surely had no such knowledge since at 43° one of General Vizcaíno's ships believed that it had reached Estrecho de Anian;[3] and finally why does he suppose that our navigator was not driven back in winter by the dangers and trials that forced all the English navigators to retreat in summer, as various accounts show.

However, even if we do not delve further into these problematical details, and continue with our consideration of the coasts of the Pacific Sea, we would try in vain to believe that either the 60th parallel is the one that marks the position of the southern entrance [of the Strait of Anian] or that there exists in that area a locality to the north of which which lies all the high and mountainous ground, and to the south the land he describes as quiet and gently rolling. In the first place, it is the north end of the strait which must be supposed to lie in 60° and the southern end must therefore lie in 59°15′. This confirms not only the descriptions which Ferrer gives of the fine southerly port but also the account of the voyage, since this makes it lie on a course from the SE of more than a hundred leagues, at 55°. In that case it would be Mount Fairweather that lay to the right, or to the right of the passage, rather than Mount St Elias as M. de Buache supposes, and this in fact would be more favourable to those who defend the voyage since the land from that mountain onwards is actually rather lower, even if it is snowbound in August and although Cape Cross and Mount Fairweather itself are of no mean height.

But the source of the most serious geographical inconsistencies is undoubtedly the east-west direction which Ferrer gives to the north coast. How is it that it does not pass Mount St Elias, the Cape Suckling area, and Prince William Sound, even if we concede an error of half a degree in his favour in Piloto Martínez's observations? I

---

[1] See p. 54, n. 4 above.

[2] For details on the sources listed by Malaspina in this sentence see pp. 456-7 above.

[3] In 1603 the *Tres Reyes* commanded by Martín de Aguilar, part of the Sebastián Vizcaíno expedition which sailed north from Acapulco the previous year, reached latitude 43°N near Cape Blanco. Aguilar died before this point, but his *piloto* reported that there, as the coast turned NE, a large river flowed down to the sea. See p. 195, n. 5 above.

confess that even if the account were accepted as true, an equal or greater difficulty would still remain for geographers since they would have to regard all the latest voyages made since 1774 as fabulous.[1]

Captain Cook's casual comment while identifying Bahía de Behring that between the extremities of the two mountain ranges which lay towards Mount Fairweather and Mount St Elias a gap of some leagues could be seen that he could not say with certainty was low land or water, went far to preserve hopes regarding the problem in question.[2] But we were fortunate enough to be able to dispel this doubt as well, seeing that snow alone had caused that illusion, and that the whole mountain range was solidly joined.

But even though convincing reasons have been given us as to why Ferrer Maldonado's voyage should not be accepted as authentic, one essential piece of information is still missing from the evidence, and that is to find the source of a memorial, written in a style befitting the time at which it was composed, and with a disinterestedness that allows no suspicion to be cast upon its author, containing mention of the voyage of Quiros which had just been completed in 1606,[3] and finally with a most authentic seal which shows it to be from a reputable archive. It is not easy to resolve these doubts satisfactorily, nor will we attempt to do so directly. We will therefore content ourselves with merely setting out a few accepted points regarding national history which may have given rise either to this project or to other similar ones, as the current thorough examination of the archives will demonstrate.

The fact that by about the year 1524 news of the Northwest Passage was already widespread in Spain, or at least an understandable interpretation had been given to Cabot's mysterious expeditions,[4] can be doubted by no one, bearing in mind the letter written with the [blank] by the celebrated Hernán Cortés to [the Emperor] Charles V. That illustrious leader not only had not been idle in this regard, guided, as he himself says, by a constant wish and determination to think of every way in which he might put into execution and realize his desire to be of use to His Majesty's royal service, but had also, with that fine judgment that he unfailingly displayed until the very end of his life, prepared two expeditions for the same purpose: one would follow the coast of Florida in the North Sea [Atlantic] and the other, in the Pacific, would either look for a passage to the east, to the north of California, or should the coast oblige them to sail west, ultimately find the Philippines. Here is his plan, which deserves to be compared with the one put forward by the British government in this present happy age for navigation. '*Because if it exists* (these are his words)[5] it cannot be

---

[1] It was in 1774, with the voyage of Juan Pérez, that the Spaniards (followed by the British and other nations) began serious exploration along the Northwest Coast from the south.

[2] For Cook's comments in 1778 when he was off Bering's Bay (now Yakutat Bay) see Cook and King, *Voyage to the Pacific Ocean*, 2, pp. 347-8.

[3] Another reference to the controversial voyage of Pedro de Quiros in 1605–6 during which he discovered Espiritu Santo in the New Hebrides (Vanuatu).

[4] Probably a reference to Sebastian Cabot, who spent much of his life in the service of Spain, rather than to his father John Cabot, though possibly to both. John Cabot made two voyages in 1497 and 1498; these were followed by the shadowy voyage of Sebastian Cabot in 1508 or 1509 which may have reached Hudson Strait, and which formed the basis for later claims that he had discovered the Northwest Passage.

[5] From here until the end of the paragraph Malaspina is quoting or paraphrasing Cortés' letter of 1524 to the Court; see Anthony Pagden, ed. and trans., *Hernán Cortés: Letters from México*, New Haven, 1986, pp. 326–8.

hidden from the latter [expedition] in the South Sea nor from the former [expedition] in the North Sea, because those in the South [Sea] will take the coast until they find the aforementioned strait or until they reach the land discovered by Magallanes, while the others in the North [Sea] will sail north, as I have said, until they reach the Bacallaos.[1] So, one way or another, the secret cannot fail to be uncovered. Because (I mentioned the Tierra de los Bacallaos) it is believed to be the case that there is a passage on that coast that crosses to the South Sea; and if it found to lie, as shown in a certain drawing that I have of the locality, in the same place as the archipelago that Magallanes discovered, by Your Majesty's command, it would apparently come out very near, and if God our Lord should see fit for the aforementioned strait to be found there, navigation from the spice countries to Your Majesty's realms would be very favourable and short – two-thirds less than the route now sailed and without risks or danger to ships coming and going because they would always come and go through Your Majesty's kingdoms and domains, and any need they might have could be met anywhere they could wish to make harbour without the slightest danger, since they would be within Your Majesty's lands'.

It deserves to be said with equal emphasis that before the end of the sixteenth century these same voices had grown louder, something that was quite natural among us since we presumed that the English must have felt a similar anxiety to conceal their discoveries. And as the terrible period of the Monarchy's decline had begun, there was no lack of plotters hoping to destroy it. Around the year 1615 Padre Fr Juan de Torquemada, referring to Sebastián Vizcaíno's voyage to the coasts of California, and confirming Felipe III's motives for his decision to give the order for the said voyage to be undertaken, adds the following:[2] 'His Majesty also learned how other Viceroys had attempted to make the same discovery at his father's command and that they had not succeeded (as will be shown further on). His Majesty had also found, among other papers, a report which certain foreigners had given to his father in which they spoke of notable things which they had seen in that country, having been carried there forcibly by the weather in a ship from Costa de Bacallaos, which lies in Terranova [Newfoundland], and in which they described how they passed from the North Sea to the South Sea through an Estrecho de Anian which is beyond Cape Mendocino, and that they had seen a populous and rich city, well fortified and walled, and full of refined, courtly and well-mannered people, and other things worth discovering and seeing'.

Torquemada, continuing this account and describing Martín de Aguilar's voyage,[3] again commented that this passage was probably the river that led to a great city discovered by the Netherlanders while driven off-course on a return voyage, and that it was the Estrecho de Anian, through which the ship that discovered it had passed, crossing from the North Sea into the South Sea; and that no doubt it was in the region or vicinity of the city called Quivira,[4] and that this was indeed the place

---

[1] The region of cod, or the Newfoundland Banks.
[2] Fr Juan de Torquemada wrote his *Monarquía indiana* between 1603 and 1613; it was published in three volumes in Seville in 1615.
[3] See p. 474, n. 3 above.
[4] See p. 441, n. 2 above.

referred to in the account that His Majesty read and which aroused his interest, and moved him to order that the greatest care be taken to make this discovery and to properly inform him of everything.

Now there is no doubt that many projects were presented at the Spanish Court from the time of Felipe II onwards; and that all of them, or at least most of them, were based on a voyage made by a Dutch ship, and that our Ferrer Maldonado was influenced by these same ideas.

In which case, why would it be absurd to suppose one of three things? That Maldonado, moved by a worthy national zeal, at a time when making discoveries was the object of European aspirations, tried to claim as his own what others had accomplished; or that he was thinking of other undertakings to be funded by the Treasury, and said that he had not found the mysterious entrance, since it had already been concealed from Piloto Martínez in his presence; or finally that this was a draft that friends had later advised him it would be better to hide rather than producing it before the King.

But why occupy so much time with this sort of inquiry? Or why should we believe Ferrer Maldonado's account could be true while no positive evidence is found of its origin, when we ourselves see, in an age which we call scientific and enlightened that accounts such as those of Ferrer Maldonado and Coronel Ríos[1] are not only written but published. The voyages of Admiral Fonte and of Fuca have already been resuscitated as though the hope of finding a passage at 48° and 55° had necessarily to be associated with some absurdity; and surely, even if the extremely costly searches intended to settle this hydrographic question were to cease at this moment, how great would be the confusion of a reader in the twenty-first century on reading first the Appendixes of the learned Padre Venegas,[2] the Introduction to Captain Cook's third voyage,[3] and afterwards the reflections of Captain Meares. Finally, how great would be his state of confusion if he were to believe that the voyage of the American brig, the *Lady Washington*, which is described in them, was true,[4] thereby dismissing the surveys by the Spanish officers Quimper and Eliza,[5] while relying for differences in longitude on a journal in which a chronometer is used, lunar distances are given at every stage, and to the publication of which the British nation's most learned persons have contributed?[6]

Happily, Captain Dixon, stung by various accusations which he felt touched on

---

[1] A reference to Hernando de los Ríos Coronel (see p.471, n. 3 above), whose *Memorial* was published in 1621 in Madrid.

[2] See p. 466, n. 4 above.

[3] Dr John Douglas wrote a long Introduction, much of it critical of speculative geography, to the authorized account of Cook's third voyage, published in 1784 as Cook and King, *Voyage to the Pacific Ocean*.

[4] In his *Voyages* of 1790 John Meares asserted that the *Lady Washington* of Boston, commanded by Robert Gray, had sailed through the strait of Fuca into an inland sea, and back into the Pacific farther north through the strait discovered by Fonte. See p. 86, n. 4 above.

[5] Manuel Quimper carried out the first partial survey of the Strait of Juan de Fuca in 1790; Francisco Eliza resumed the task the following year.

[6] The sense of this passage is far from clear; but Malaspina seems to be picturing the lot of the unfortunate reader who tries to follow the contradictory interpretations contained in Meares' reflections and in Cook's journal.

him in the eyes of the public as a result of that journal, has undertaken to reply in a tome inspired by his resentment of the book against which he argued.[1] Happily also, the judicious instructions given to Captain Cook for his third voyage will always set out the question clearly and in terms that cannot be altered either by the existence of islands instead of a continuous coast, or by a few ships sailing inland to the east. Last, happily, Capitanes de Fragata Galiano and Valdés, in sailing up the whole of the Estrecho de Fuca this year, will decide the question in such a way that no room is left for further arguments.[2] These had led us little by little to assume that the Northern Continent of America was divided into different pieces allowing many communications from one sea to the other, and consequently to assess present-day navigation as poor and timid. For even though this was its sole purpose, it had nevertheless been unable to discover what our forbears had found without looking, and without the assistance either of other voyages or of the precision of our geographical calculations.

Here I must conclude this somewhat discursive dissertation. If the widespread eagerness in Europe to discover the Northwest Passage had generally caused the true benefits of such a discovery to be lost from sight, I would not be compelled to regard this examination as pertinent to the national interest. Our ships are excessively costly to fit out, our assessment of what goes on in the whole of the continent of America is still hesitant, unspoken and poorly analysed; but in the end we cannot defer considering any project that may lead to the complete restoration of the Monarchy's former splendour and power.[3]

The question of the Northwest Passage was from the beginning placed by geographers in such a high latitude that all possibility of it being useful was excluded, and in all probability it would have suffered the same fate as that of the navigation through Estrecho de Magellanes, compared with the deep sea passage around Cabo de Hornos, if the strong bias, almost infatuation, with which it was regarded by Mr Dobbs had not, as usual, changed the nature of the proposition. Originally the question asked was whether there was a passage in the northern hemisphere *useful* for a communication between Europe and Asia; this was soon replaced by another question, whether there was any communication between the Pacific and Atlantic oceans in the northern hemisphere.

The confusion of ideas, quite reprehensible even in Mr Dobbs's day, is much more so at present when the navigation of the globe is known to an unsurpassed degree. Obviously, the object of navigation is trade. When considering a voyage one should never lose sight of factors such as its shortness, safety, ease and economy. So what are the advantages of any new routes when compared to those already used by Europeans when they sail to China by way of the Cape of Good Hope? Are we always going to count on the good fortune of Admiral de Fonte who not only sailed the 866 leagues from Port Abel to Río los Reyes in twenty days,[4] but sailed 260 of them wandering

---

[1] George Dixon, who had been on the Northwest Coast in the late 1780s, vigorously criticized Meares' conduct and claims in his *Remarks on the Voyages of John Meares*, London, 1790.
[2] See p. 238 above.
[3] The paragraphs which follow (in AMN, MS 92) are missing in the transcription in Cerezo, *Diario de Malaspina*, I, pp. 279–85. See p.468, n. 1 above.
[4] Malaspina added a note here to the effect that this figure treated departure and arrival dates as complete days.

through the channels between the islands of the San Lázaro archipelago while his longboats and pinnaces were running one mile ahead to sound the depth of water and to survey shoals, reefs and sunken rocks?[1]

And let no one imagine that the usefulness of this passage, at least for foreigners, is limited to voyages to China, for it could also include among its advantages a shorter route to the Pacific Ocean, a destination that will become as frequent and remunerative in coming centuries as it is useless, unrewarding and hazardous in our time. The present experience of the English in Botany Bay, and the repeated surveys undertaken by all the maritime nations of an increasing number of Pacific islands, are sure evidence that the whole political constitution of the globe will have to change before the inhabitants or products of those islands are of the slightest interest to Europeans.

Regarding the project of Señor de la Bastide presented not so long ago to the Count of Fernán Nuñez in Paris,[2] whose purpose was to outline the operations required to achieve such a communication by way of Lago de Nicaragua,[3] with all costs to be recovered by reciprocal taxes on Spanish shipping, the volume of such shipping has not been assessed, and it ought to be enough to declare his memorandum as untimely, even if we ignore the many errors it contains in mechanical, hydrographic and political terms.

A regular voyage to China from European ports may be considered as lasting five months if it undertaken by a well-found vessel with a good captain; the length of time is much shorter to the coasts of Coromandel and Malabar. It is practical in all seasons, the temperatures are not unpleasant, the ports of call are healthy, pleasing and useful for trading purposes, the winds are seasonal and well-known, and the route is so economical and quiet that little damage to the sails needs to be taken into account. So, will it be possible for us to transpose all these advantages to the only area on which geographers' eyes are cast with unbending attention, that between 60 and 80 degrees of northern latitude, where the sea is permanently frozen, and where inaccessible and farflung groups of horrid and barren islands offer only hazard and danger to navigators?

The question posed in our day with such passion by geographers can therefore be reduced to the following presumption, devoid now of those pleasing touches that have so far coloured its appearance in the eyes of politicians. Which is the nation whose navigators by excessive luck rather than ability will manage to sail northwards beyond the limits of navigation fixed by Captains Cook and Clerke, and sail, if there is a passage, from the northern extremity of America until they reach European seas?

---

[1] A further note by Malaspina commented that he had omitted altogether the eighty-six leagues reputedly covered on 11 August, as well as the details of how Captain Bernardo had reached latitude 80°N, was able to carry out surveys, and had found a native messenger ready to take charge of his correspondence with the Admiral.

[2] Count Carlos José Fernán Nuñez was a distinguished diplomat who espoused the ideals of the Enlightenment under Carlos III, and who wrote a biography of the King. He was at this time Spanish ambassador in France, where his tact and fine judgement helped Spain at a time of great tension between Paris and Madrid.

[3] Lago de Nicaragua, in present-day Nicaragua, is separated from Golfo de Papagayo by a strip of land eleven miles wide. Malaspina considered that communication from the gulf to the lake, and from there by way of Río San Juan to the Atlantic was an issue of major importance, as much for the general geography of the globe as for Spanish interests. See p. 20 above.

Unless this proposition is considered, it is inconceivable that the clamour of geographers concerning such a discovery will finally die down, and their insults in the name of science to modern navigation will cease. Any monarch who is a lover of human kind, and any navigator who scorns to pursue a useless project, will together direct their efforts to perfect the survey of the few points useful to navigators that have not yet been settled, or to the prosperous benefit and encouragement of the fruitful links that society brings to commerce.

DOCUMENT 5

The Response of Juan Bautista Muñoz

Juan Bautista Muñoz y Ferrándiz was born in Museros, Valencia, on 12 January 1745. After obtaining his BA and MA (in theology, Greek and mathematics) he moved to Madrid with other *valencianos* who shared his sceptical attitude towards traditional Spanish scholasticism. His main claim to fame followed his appointment by Carlos III as Cosmógrafo Mayor de Indias, when he moved to create a general archive for documents relating to Spain's overseas empire – the Archivo General de Indias housed at Seville.[1] This project was associated with a commission to Muñoz for a history of the New World, which would rebut and correct such critical works on Spain's overseas activities as William Robertson's *A History of America* (London, 1777) and the Abbé Raynal's *Histoire philosophique et politique des deux Indes* (Paris, 1770). As Muñoz explained the link:

> In 1779 I represented to the King the need of writing a General History of the Indies authorized by reliable and incontestable documents. I began then to survey several archives in this court belonging to the Department of the Indies. Very early on I felt the lack of ancient documents, and saw that it was necessary to look for them mainly at Simancas, Seville and Cadiz. I discussed the matter with the Marquis of Sonora and thereby understood how little we knew concerning the documents deposited in other places, the scant interest or curiosity paid in the last two centuries to their inventory and conservation, and the great benefit that would arise from the establishment of a general archive where one would find, together and classified, so many documents that had been dispersed and unused in a great number of offices.[2]

With officials at the Secretaría del Despacho de Indias watching him with suspicion, Muñoz began a systematic search and survey of the nation's archives. He soon discovered that much of what was needed was not in Madrid, and his search moved to Simancas, Seville and Cadiz. In 1781 he found in the archive of the Duque del Infantado in Madrid the manuscript of Lorenzo Ferrer Maldonado's 'Relation' of 1609 and had it copied. Ten years later he commented on it in the letter printed below. Muñoz managed to complete only one volume of what had been planned as a multi-volume history of the New World. At the end of Book I of this first and only volume he wrote that 'The ways and means by which glorious Spain has made possible such rare transformations in both hemispheres will be the subject of my story.'[3] Little is known of

---

[1] See p. 141, n. 3 above.
[2] Spanish from Pedro González García *et al.*, *Archivo General de Indias – Los archivos españoles*, Madrid, 1995.
[3] J. B. Muñoz, *Historia del Nuevo Mundo*, I, Madrid, 1793, p. 25.

Muñoz's private life except that he was married and had a daughter. He died on 11 July 1799.[1]

Text

Juan Bautista Muñoz to unknown correspondent, 31 July 1791[2]

… the text by Ferrer about which you wish to have my opinion truly does not deserve much attention. I found it myself when I began my archival investigations in the archive of the Sr Duque del Infantado, and from that very moment felt uneasy about the author's veracity. As I wanted to overcome my doubts I took a copy to Simancas to see whether I might find in that general archive any documents relating to the voyage and its discoveries. I found absolutely nothing. On the contrary, what I saw there were later papers, dated as much as ten years after the time of the pretended navigation, mentioning efforts made by the English to find a strait between the Atlantic and Pacific through the northern regions, and certain rumours about a discovery of the kind that ought to have caused some concern to the Ministry.[3] Similar efforts and rumours continued in the following years, and greatly increased with the voyages of the Dutch to both Indies which were likely to damage the interests and reputation of Spain. The trade with China and Japan, and the wish to shorten the route to those parts, gave considerable importance to the discovery of such a strait. We in particular longed for it in order to facilitate the voyage to the western coasts of America, the Philippines and the Moluccas. With such feelings spread all over Europe, would Ferrer have concealed his own successful expedition for more than twenty years? For the time which lapsed ran all the way from 1588, when he claims to have completed it, to 1609 when he produced the account of it, indirectly and without mentioning that before that time he never uttered a word about the matter. It is incredible that any man should have kept silent for so long, particularly on the part of someone who had shown clear signs of being a greedy and vainglorious charlatan.

This is the impression I formed of Ferrer after reading at Simancas about his proposals and promises on the subject of the fixed point, as they used to say, to determine longitude at sea – a problem that he and the Portuguese Fonseca offered to

---

[1] These details come from the work of two biographers of Muñoz: Justo Pastor Fuster, who included a study of Muñoz's life in his more extensive *Biblioteca Valenciana*, Valencia, 1830; and Antonio Ballesteros Beretta, who wrote a bibliographical essay issued in the *Revista de Indias* in 1941 and 1942. Part of this essay was reproduced as a homage to Muñoz in the three-volume *Catálogo de la colección de Don Juan Bautista Muñoz* published in 1954 by the Real Academia de la Historia, the main keeper of Muñoz's papers.

[2] This is a draft of a letter from Muñoz to a correspondent he calls 'Amigo y Señor mio'. It forms part of the Colleción Muñoz in the Library of the Real Academia de la Historia, Madrid (RAH Doc.9/4802, ff. 18–19).

[3] It is not easy to identify these English voyages within the time span indicated by Muñoz. The three voyages of John Davis to Baffin Island and Davis Strait took place in 1585–7, before Ferrer Maldonado's claimed voyage of 1588; while the next significant northern exploration by the English, Henry Hudson's entering of Hudson Strait and Hudson Bay, was not until 1610, the year after Ferrer Maldonado presented his memorial to the Spanish court. One possibility is that the reference was to Thomas Cavendish's attempted Pacific voyage of 1591, on which Davis sailed with an agreement that once the squadron reached California he would be allowed to sail north with two ships to find the Pacific entrance of the Northwest Passage. The voyage was a failure, and no such attempt was made.

solve, in the hope of obtaining the prize offered by Felipe III,[1] and in doing so demonstrated their frivolity, vanity and poor intellect. How poor this was in Ferrer's case I could judge for myself by reading his work on cosmography and navigation printed in 1626 under the title *Imagen del universo* [sic],[2] whose merits are quite inferior to those of Céspedes[3] and other authors who preceded him. I was further convinced about his pedantic character after reading what the learned and wise D. García de Silva had to say in his *Comentarios*[4] about the embassy he had led to [the court of] the King of Persia in 1618. He calls him ignorant, an imposter and a gossip. He rebuts him on the discovery of a new strait. He also ridicules him as an unraveller of enigmas who boasted that he could decipher Solomon's clavicle,[5] as a miserable alchemist who would use artful cunning to exploit the greed of fools, mesmerizing them with promises of making the philosopher's stone. Silva is a beautiful place.[6] Our friend Navarrete[7] to whom I have transmitted all my thoughts must have sent them on to you. Just reading it is sufficient to pay no notice whatsoever to the voyage in question. But the account itself, when read at leisure, offers evidence enough of being a fiction, as are also the island of Friesland where he claims to have sailed from Lisbon, the encounter with a 800-ton ship from the Hanseatic cities on her way from the South Sea to pass the strait, and the allegedly exact account of the Portuguese *piloto* Juan Martínez.

M. Buache took pains to give it publicity, and used the wealth of his talent and geographical erudition to add a glimmer of probability to a straightforward lie. He knows that the passage from the South Sea to the Frozen Sea as described by Ferrer cannot be that which is known and acknowledged,[8] and he breaks into conjectures about the existence of another one unknown in our days. He considers it as proof of the reality of the voyage made in 1588 the fact that there are details in the account

---

[1] Luis de Fonseca, a contemporary of Ferrer Maldonado, was a Portuguese at the court of Felipe III. At the time Maldonado was in Madrid and presented his account of the discovery of the Strait of Anian, Fonseca submitted to the Consejo Real de Indias a proposal on the fixed point and on what he described as 'vertical and regular East to West and North to South compass needles' to work out longitude at sea. On condition that his methods were tested and found valid, he was offered a perpetual income of 6,000 ducats. During a voyage from Acapulco to the Philippines in 1611, such tests were carried out, but with disappointing results. See Salvá and Sainz de Baranda, *Documentos inéditos*, pp. 81–3.

[2] *Imagen del mundo sobre la esfera, cosmografía, y geografía teórica de planetas y arte de navegar*, Alcalá, 1626.

[3] Andrés García de Céspedes was a Spanish sixteenth-century astronomer who wrote books on mathematics, navigation and astronomy. In 1596 he was appointed, with Antonio de Herrera, cosmographer and 'Cronista de Indias', which post he held until 1606. He was the author of eleven works, of which three were published.

[4] García de Silva y Figueroa, *Comentarios de d. García de Silva y Figueroa de la embajada que de parte del rey de España don Felipe III hizo al rey xa Abas de Persia*, Sociedad de bibliófilos españoles, 36, 2 vols, Madrid, 1903–5.

[5] I.e. the notorious *Clavicula Salomonis*, or 'Key of Solomon', a *grimoire* or manual of black magic, possibly medieval but attributed, like some other magic texts, to the biblical Solomon. In Ferrer Maldonado's time it would have existed only in manuscript.

[6] This needs explanation. Writing informally to a close friend Muñoz has interjected here, unexpectedly, a thought that has nothing to do with Ferrer Maldonado. The link is the man he is quoting, de Silva, which seems to have triggered the recollection that Silva, the geographic place in Galicia, is beautiful.

[7] Martín Fernández de Navarrete; see p. 425, n. 4 above.

[8] That is, the passage through Bering Strait.

applicable to Hudson Bay which were not known at that time. But he does not realize that they could have been known in 1609, the date of the deception.[1] This information, new at the time, added to that which had been given much earlier by Spanish navigators about a strait separating Asia from America, were the foundations on which our imposter erected the fabric of his invention ... .[2]

---

[1] A doubtful proposition; see p. 482, n. 3 above.
[2] The remainder of the letter is personal, as are the first fifteen lines, and both sections are omitted here.

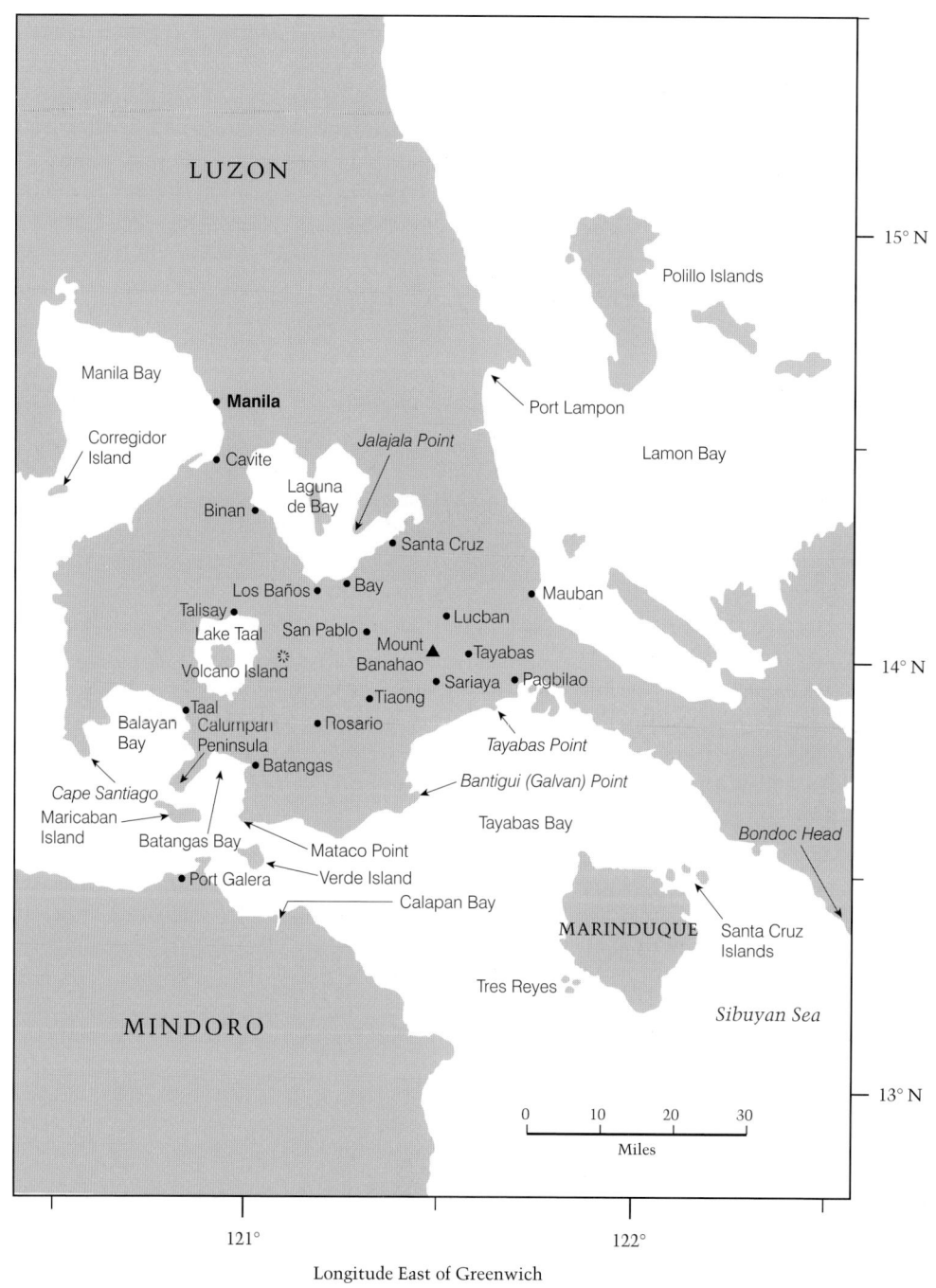

Fig. 7. Central Luzon, March to November 1792

APPENDIX 3

Tova's Account of his Survey of the South Coast of Luzon[1]

The work of the expedition's *comandante* and Don Juan Maqueda on the opposite [i.e. the east] coast, that of Don Francisco Viana from Cape Engaño to Manila, and that carried out by the corvettes since entering San Bernardino Strait, almost completed a circle around the island of Luzon leaving, however, an interesting stretch of coast to be surveyed between Bondoc Head and Cape Santiago. I was made responsible for this task wherever the terrain permitted, as set out in the instructions.[2] In order to carry out these aims, as the expedition *comandante* had laid down, the most direct route naturally seemed to be by way of Laguna de Bay to Santa Cruz, then across to the Tayabas coast by land, getting as far to the east as possible. From there travel either by land or sea as far as Bondoc Head, then working along the rest of the coast to Cape Santiago, finally returning by way of Lake Taal to Binan[3] and Manila. To this end the *comandante* had asked Fray Juan de Herenas, the minister at Pililla,[4] to lend us his eighteen-oar *guilalo* to use on the lagoon, which arrived in Manila on the afternoon of 14 September.

15 September 1792
Having received the *comandante*'s final orders on the 15th, Pilotin Don Juan Inciarte of the *Atrevida* and a seaman from the same corvette were now under my command and, when we had requested a passport from the Captain-General and letters of introduction to the friars who administer the towns on our route from the provincial brothers of San Francisco and San Agustín, we were entirely ready to set out on the following day.

16 September
Therefore at seven o'clock in the morning, having put chronometer number 11, theodolite number 3, my sextant, compass and lead-line on board the *guilalo*, we left the fort of Manila. The sea-keeping qualities of our craft, its numerous and skilful crew, constantly urged on by a most agreeable shanty from the *arráez* or coxswain,

---

[1] Held in the Biblioteca Menéndez Pelayo de Santander, AMs 1.040.
[2] AMN, MS 427, ff. 139-139v.
[3] On the western shore of the lagoon.
[4] Not identified.

keeping the beat for the oarsmen, had us moving rapidly and pleasantly along the river banks, almost all beautifully forested and adorned by nature. The slower current from around the mouth of the Pasig allowed greater speed to the entrance to the lagoon, where we arrived at half past eleven, this being surrounded by several fish weirs and therefore very shallow, in parts only half a fathom, and in others with so little depth that the *guilalo* touched bottom. A moderate breeze which then set in from NW allowed us to use the sail, and brought us to Binan at two in the afternoon. As I had only come here to arrange for a boat to take me back to Manila on my return, a somewhat difficult matter, I decided at once to ask this favour of Padre Herenas, and soon afterwards we left to spend the night at Santa Rosa.[1]

17 September
The crossing from here to Santa Cruz took us very close to Jalajala Point[2] and, as I did not know if bearings had been taken there, we took the opportunity to do so while the men had their meal and rested,[3] finally reaching Santa Cruz at eleven o'clock in the morning. The poor state of the roads to Majaijay[4] and Lucban[5] made it necessary to use *jamacas*[6] and we were delayed until it would no longer have been possible to reach Majaijay in daylight, because of the difficulties of the *gobernadorcillo* or alcalde in gathering together enough Indians to carry them and the instruments, to which was added the fact that Father Fray Miguel Persiva, the *doctrinero*[7] who would have supplied them, was not in the town at the time. Such a delay could not but be highly annoying for me in a season when the periods of good weather are so valuable, but as we were now resigned to spending the night there the time was not entirely wasted. A base was measured on the western bank of the [Lumban] river and, although only 442 feet long, was all that could be managed on the extremely marshy and waterlogged ground. It at least gave us the position of the church tower from which, when the bearings were taken again, we could link a number of points on the lagoon to the heights of Tayabas[8] and Los Baños,[9] which fortunately had just become visible. The *guilalo* was sent off that afternoon and I dispatched a letter to Father Herena asking him to send it back to Binan by the 30th of this month. By nightfall we already had all the assistance needed to set off very early. Two *jamacas* with twenty-four Indians to provide replacements, walking almost constantly up to their knees in mud and carrying the instruments hung from poles, brought us to Majaijay by ten o'clock.

[1] On the SW shore of the lagoon.
[2] The extremity of a promontory extending from the NE side of the lagoon.
[3] Malaspina measured a base and observed for longitude at the point; see p. 376 above.
[4] The village of Maja-ya north of Mount Banahao.
[5] A village on the NE side of .Mount Banahao.
[6] For a full description of *jamacas* see p. 378 above.
[7] A missionary whose principal task was to explain the Christian doctrine to the natives.
[8] The 2165-metre high Mount Banahao, which Malaspina and Maqueda referred to as Mount Lucban or Majaijay (p. 374 above), Mte de Tayabas on 'Carta general del archipiélago de Filipinas (northern sheet)'.
[9] The 1113-metre high Mount Maquiling, 3 miles SW of Los Baños on the southern shore of Laguna de Bay, Alto de Viñan on 'Carta general del archipiélago de Filipinas (northern sheet)'.

18 September

It would scarcely be possible to travel this route by horse in this season. Only the natives, accustomed to carry the *jamacas* with total assurance, and who are naturally strong, can provide the traveller with a degree of comfort hard to find with any other type of conveyance. This was already well known among us and is described by the *comandante* [in his account of] his journey to the opposite coast through these same towns.[1] His observations regarding their beautiful situation, neatness and economy relieve me of the need to deal with a subject about which, in truth, I would have to give but the briefest description, since my time among them was so short in all the places I passed through. Our departure from Majaijay was only delayed by the need to arrange the change-over of the porters. By two in the afternoon, after having had our meal with the friar, we were making good time for Lucban, although the track was just as muddy as that we had taken the day before. It was no later than five in the afternoon when we reached Lucban. By using what was left of the day to walk around the village with its kind friar Father Fray Domingo de la Soledad, being informed by his knowledge and equally being pleased by the cleanliness, good order and solid construction of its streets and houses, I was able to form an opinion just as favourable as that I had found in the *comandante*'s journal. All arrangements were made that afternoon to leave for Tayabas at five the following morning, but they did not allow for the inconstancy of the weather as during the night the wind blew violently from SW. The rain that fell unceasingly until twelve the next day would have detained us there for a second night if we had not been able to take advantage of some clearing of the sky which came when the weather changed abruptly to the east at about that time. The hill of the same name,[2] from the foot of which this town lies about two miles, brings rain to it more frequently than in the rest of the province. It bore S45°30′W from the monastery, which in this direction was in transit with Mount Tayabas, a mountain of larger size and greater height with which it is perfectly aligned. On the other side lies Mount San Pablo,[3] of about the same height as that of Lucban. This uniformity gives a truly majestic appearance to Mount Tayabas, which is undoubtedly the largest and highest in the surrounding provinces. At two in the afternoon, although the rain had not entirely ceased, we could make our way in *jamacas* towards Tayabas. As a result of the rains the track was very bad, but having at last overcome this difficulty and that posed by the streams, full and running continuously, at five we reached that town, the principal one of the district, no less satisfied with the diligence of our bearers and warmly welcomed by the friars at the monastery.

This town lies about four leagues from the sea on the eastern slope of the mountain of the same name.[4] The nearby strait and coast have very convenient points on which to take useful bearings, but as the sky was still not completely clear and the horizon was somewhat overcast, we could only sight with confidence from the church tower the northern end of Marinduque bearing S37°19′E, the westernmost

---

[1] See pp. 378-9 above.
[2] Tova refers to a separate peak, about 1800 metres in height on the NE slopes of Mount Banahao about 2 miles SW of Lucban.
[3] The 1300-metre high Mount San Cristobal, a distinctive peak, about 4 miles west of Mount Banahao.
[4] Tayabas is situated about 7 miles ESE of the summit of Mount Banahao.

point of that island S18°57'E, the most SW of the Tres Reyes¹ S17°48'E and a few other islands off the nearby coast.

It was among my first tasks to question people knowledgeable about the country and get reliable information from the friars about the route which I should take towards Bondoc Head, then to make the necessary arrangements to leave very early, and lastly to find out as much as possible about the economic state of this principal town, the population of which is about 8,000, according to the last census. It occupies a fertile situation, dominating all the beautiful coastal plains, while its gentle slope, providing an incline to take advantage of rainfall, makes it both clean and attractive from various points of view. Its houses, generally built of timber on streets set out in straight lines, are spaced so as to provide the necessary room around each one for a good sized kitchen garden, fenced in with canes, where each family grows the vegetables they need, a few fruit trees and many pepper-bearing trees. Outwardly it appears to be very neat and well ordered and administered. The traveller sees nothing that does not weigh in the inhabitants' favour.

Indeed, a town where farming produces more than 100,000 *cavanes*² or 50,000 *fanegas*³ of rice annually, the value of which is no more than eight *reales*, which annually produces a large quantity for Mambulao,⁴ where it sells for six *pesos* a *caván*, which breeds in its rich and productive pastures considerable numbers of cattle, horses and *carabao*,⁵ making good profits from these herds, which produce oil, vinegar and other goods and, finally, which has expanded its limits by means of the recent appropriation of a large area of highly fertile land which had been wrongfully claimed by the town of Sariaya,⁶ seems set for progress towards a real affluence, of which the rising population is already a good sign. The pepper cultivated at present willingly and profitably by the inhabitants in their small market gardens, with very little work and no waste, is another of the products which must enrich them in time. Their harvest would have been more than usual here and in the other villages of the province, if the hurricane or *baguío*, as it is called locally, of the previous year had not destroyed much of the plantations. Despite this misfortune a harvest of fifty *cavanes* is still expected in Tayabas alone, and the product of the present planting will not be less than 150 within three years. This is the usual time which these trees take to bear fruit and is a considerable drawback, given the natives' character, for their progress. However, they are constantly encouraged by the enthusiasm of the alcalde and the friars who have managed to bring about an interest in its cultivation. The alcalde has drawn up a contract with the company for the purchase of pepper from the inhabitants of this town, and from those of Lucban and other villages, at a price of twelve and a half *pesos* per *caván*.

The information we obtained corresponded exactly with that given to me on my departure from Manila by Don José Gómez, commanding officer of the *vintas del*

---

¹ A group of three densely wooded islands, a short distance from the SW side of Marinduque Island.
² The *caván* is a Filipino dry capacity unit of measurement for grains, pulses or seeds equal to 75 kilogrammes.
³ A Castilian dry capacity unit of measurement equal to 55½ litres.
⁴ Now Port José Panganiban, 55 miles east of Mauban.
⁵ Water buffalo.
⁶ Situated 6 miles SSE of the summit of Mount Banahao.

corso.¹ They all agreed that the trip [to Bondoc Head] could only be made along the opposite coast, in some twelve to fifteen days,² and that by staying on this side it would not be easy to get further than Pagbilao, about four leagues to the SE. I therefore had no reason to delay in setting out for that town so as not to waste a day of clear skies which allowed us good observations for latitude and longitude on the beach nearby. Indeed, accompanied by Father Fray Baltasar López, the warden of this monastery, who took the trouble to come with us for no other reasons than his zeal for the King's service and his obliging nature, we reached Pagbilao at nine in the morning by horse, riding in these parts being the best way to travel over this terrain, which is generally flat but fairly muddy.

At ten we had descended the river³ in small fishing canoes to the beach at its mouth, about two miles south of the town and, having taken hour angles for which there was no horizon during the afternoon, we had a view of a bay of some size.⁴ This terminated to the south in a point we named *punta primera* [first point],⁵ which hid from us the continuation of the bay to Galvan Point,⁶ and to the north by a large indentation in the coast, extending ESE which, together with the NE headland of an island,⁷ thus concealing from view its prolongation towards Bondoc Head. This island, extending from NE to SW and possibly two and a half to three leagues long, is high and thickly forested, with a peak on its NE headland shaped exactly like a saddle,⁸ a sharper one towards the centre and a third near the SW end. On its western, or landward, side there is another smaller island.⁹ The bay, almost enclosing both of them, would give excellent shelter in both monsoons were it not for the lack of depth almost throughout. The fish weirs which extended as far as the middle of the bay and the depth of one fathom between them and the river mouth convinced us that it was unusable. In these parts there were few vessels to be found other than small fishing canoes, which we could not have used to extend our soundings to seaward. The breeze, then blowing fresh from the east, was enough to prevent such a manoeuvre, but by assuming as reliable some of the local knowledge from the fishermen it could be concluded that the depth between the fish weirs and the landward island was two and a half and three fathoms, increasing to three and a half along the extension of the island towards the channel between the NE headland of the larger island and the coast. The depth of the river, which is no wider than two-thirds of a cable at its broadest point, continues at one fathom until it nears the town, while its shores, thickly forested with mangroves, present only an impenetrable wall of roots. A base of only 350 feet, which was all that was possible in this terrain, measured to the south of

---

¹ A fleet of launch-like craft used to drive off the pirates; see p. 379, n. 3.
² I.e. by sailing east from Mauban, south past Catanduanes Island and then NW through the Strait of San Bernardino.
³ Tayabas River, which enters Tayabas Bay 15 miles NE of Bantigui Point.
⁴ Pagbilao Bay.
⁵ Bocboc Point, the western entrance point of Pagbilao Bay.
⁶ Now Bantigui Point, a wooded headland 109 metres in height, forming the western entrance point of Tayabas Bay.
⁷ Pagbilao Grande Island.
⁸ Mount Mitra, the summit of the island.
⁹ Pagbilao Chica Island

the river mouth and near the watch tower, was enough to plot the bay and the islands, and from whose extremities we could even take bearings to the NE point of Marinduque. The *punta primera*, lying one mile to the south, prevented us from taking an observation for latitude from the base on which we observed hour angles, but another [point] bearing WSW at the same distance allowed us to make out a good horizon. Having obtained a latitude of 13°56′25″N and calculating the northern end of the base to be 13°56′45″, its longitude was determined as 42′17″ east of Manila.

When we had returned to the monastery with Father López and the friar from this town, both of whom had accompanied us all morning, I intended to take advantage of the calm of the following morning to make our way in the small canoes, already prepared with their outriggers, to the east side of the large island, to measure a good base and to join it, as far as we could reach, to the prolongation of the coast towards Bondoc Head and then to return, sounding the NE channel and other adjacent parts of the bay. We did not lose a moment in putting this plan into execution and making the necessary preparations, but the warnings of the friars on the one hand and, on the other, those of the native pilots, kept me from carrying it out without a certain degree of imprudence. They unanimously declared that the pirates rarely left these islands and coastal rivers in peace, that some remained even during the season of *vendavales*, and that with the arrival of the light easterly breezes, which were now beginning, they definitely infested these parts with their *pancos*. These considerations, supported by fairly recent examples, and the complete lack of armaments for their canoes and their small size, even making light of the risk they posed because of their weakness at sea, very soon made me give up the idea of a plan which I could no longer attempt without directly contravening my orders. However, a subsequent report of a small galley belonging to the *alcalde mayor* of Tayabas now lying in the Cota River[1] ready to set out for Catanduanes [Island][2] with merchandise, renewed my desire not to leave unexplored that stretch of coast. I therefore undertook to survey it and sent off that night a messenger who assured me that he would wait for my arrival, which took place no later than nine the following day.

21 September

This small vessel crewed by twelve men, with two falconets and some muskets, still needed the rest of the day to finish taking on its load of rice. Father López, our extremely energetic agent, took charge of getting it ready to set out very early the next morning. For our part we only arranged to proceed downstream to the beach, where we observed a latitude of 13°51′45″, calculating the longitude according to number 11 as 35′ east of Manila and measuring a base of 920 feet near the watchtower. This allowed us to link by bearings from its extremities not only the rest of the bay as far as Galvan Point, where it ends, but also other points on Marinduque, the Santa Cruz Islets[3] and Mount Tayabas [Banahao], as well as the whole of the coast that we had not seen from the base at Pagbilao. For this, however, it was necessary to repeat

[1] Tayabas River.
[2] A large island 40 miles north of the eastern entrance to San Bernardino Strait.
[3] A group of three islands off the NE side of Marinduque Island, consisting of Santa Cruz, Maniuayan and Mompog Islands.

some bearings and estimated distances from Camalabaman Point,¹ lying SEbyE of us and concealing a stretch of the coast consisting of small points and tiny bays.

We would have mistaken Galvan Point, which bore S32°15′W from the base, for an island if the natives' information had not assured us that this was the effect of the extremely flat ground between it and the point which they named as Bujanji,² with a small indentation which increases the distance and gives that appearance to Galvan Point, which is high and forested. The coast included so far in our work from Pagbilao to Galvan Point is bare, with beaches running down to the sea, except for a number of points that are thickly wooded, like the river mouths. Several rivers drain into this bay, and among these the Pagbilao and the Cota are the largest, although no more than one fathom deep. The latter, distributing its waters by a branch running eastward which is augmented by another smaller one that joins it, also flows out behind Camalabaman Point, leaving it cut off, with all the stretch of coast from here as far as the watch tower at its principal mouth. The Mayao, Nayin and Siriaya Rivers are smaller, but their shoals extend offshore for one and a half to two miles (and these sandbanks must be kept in mind along the entire length of the bay).

The town of Pagbilao, being the nearest and lying only two miles from the banks of its river, as we have said, is therefore the most exposed to the pirates' raids. Having been destroyed more than once by them on other sites closer to the sea and withdrawn to its present position, it has taken precautions for its own safety by means of a cane enclosure, whose trunks and foliage interwoven by nature itself form a rectangular area which would be difficult to penetrate at a first onslaught. Its four corners are defended by *bantays* or wooden turrets, and from these the local inhabitants take turns to keep watch at night. Some falconets and muskets, not in the best condition, form all the defence of this town, whose small resources are inadequate for the decent maintenance of the friar and the monastery without help from Tayabas.

The *Casa Real*³ of Tayabas, as it is called in these parts, dates almost to the time of the conquest of these islands, according to Father López. Constructed to defend this principal town and its surroundings from the raids of the Moros,⁴ who took shelter in the river and came up it to the crop fields, it has the appearance of being better fortified. It is contained within an equilateral triangle formed of a stockade and ditch, if it may be called such, with a wooden tower or small bastion at each corner, the one facing the river being defended by a calibre six cannon in poor condition, and the others by two falconets. A rampart or narrow bank inside the stockade is arranged for musket fire, of which weapons there are only eighteen which, together with a certain number of pikes and large piles of stones, constitute the entire defence to be mounted by eighteen Indians who take guard duty in turns at the orders of another Indian whom they call the *castellano*. The *Casa Real* and two storerooms, all built of cane, are within the triangle, and the *alcalde mayor* of Tayabas uses them for storage of trading merchandise, consisting principally of rice.

---

¹ Tayabas Point, the eastern entrance point of Tayabas River.
² Subuquin Point, 2¼ miles NW of Bantigui Point.
³ I.e the town hall.
⁴ I.e. Joloanos or Mindanaon pirates: see p. 275, n. 5 above.

The great abundance of this product and cattle in the province of Tayabas allows the *vintas del corso* to replace the stores consumed during their first sortie from Manila. They enter this river and, after taking on board the necessary salt meat and rice in only a few days, then continue on their way. The establishment of the *vintas*, although certainly useful, has had little or no effect on the pirates, if the inhabitants are to be believed, but this does not apply to the towers recently built at all the river mouths and even on stretches of the coast where there are none of these. The feeble defence provided, at the most, by the occasional small cannon of minor calibre, or two or three falconets, perhaps an old musket, a few pikes and plenty of stones, with three or four men and their *castellano*, to whom they refer as the *bantay* sentinel, has done more by its presence than by any real strength to lessen the landings and incursions of the Moros on the villages and fields. Their alarms given by a bugle or conch, which can be heard at a great distance, warn the farmers and fishermen of the enemy's approach so that they may avoid capture.

22 September

Having thus spent the night in the Cota River, with dawn promising very good weather, we set out in the little galley at five in the morning. The ebb tide, flowing at its fastest as we approached the bar, impeded the steering of this little craft, which had no other means except her six oars. These were not particularly well handled and so we soon ran aground on one of the rocky ledges scarcely known to the *arráez* or coxswain. It was not without difficulty that we were able to pull her out into the channel by means of a warp passed to us from the small canoe, although the depth was scarcely one fathom. It was far from easy to get clear of this channel, narrow and winding as it was, until the turn of the tide. Such a waste of time, combined with the considerable ignorance and clumsiness of the crew, began to incline me to leave them behind, hoping to avoid further delays in the future arising from similar circumstances and ignorance of the language. A moderate breeze that set in from east persuaded me to take this step, now all the more necessary as I could anticipate the loss of at least the rest of the day, and perhaps longer, before reaching a place where I could work to some effect. I thought it likely that the light easterlies or calms would continue, yet I had to guard against a SW wind, not unusual in this season, that might prevent me from returning in time to continue my work as far as Cape Santiago, even if my purposes had been achieved by the date given in my orders, that is, 5 October. Since, on the other hand, I believed this stretch of coast to be much more important than that of Bondoc, these considerations did not delay me for a moment in carrying out this plan. Having put our instruments ashore, therefore, and provided ourselves with horses in Cota, we were able to reach Sariaya by nine in the morning. This town is the last administered by Franciscan friars in these parts. It consists of 2,400 inhabitants and, being only two leagues from the sea, they are obliged to keep constant watch for the Moros. A cane fence, similar to that of Pagbilao, and a square of lime and stonework in front of the church, with a few loopholes, shelter it from their attacks and allow them to enjoy freely the same advantages as Tayabas, derived from the fertility of the soil and cattle breeding, to which the inhabitants apply themselves equally to the cultivation of pepper.

The zeal and energy of the friar was no less than we had experienced until now in those of the same order. This, however, was not enough to prevent the *gobernadorcillo*'s indolence from detaining me until two in the afternoon, through his dilatory assistance in providing Indians and horses. These finally came and we could take the road for Tiaong, which we did not reach until eight o'clock that night, having been constantly held up by deep gullies.

23 September

Next day, Sunday Mass kept us in this small village until nine that morning. The Sun was hard to bear and, during the afternoon on horseback, we had to put up with a sudden heavy storm, when we were already close to Rosario, which we reached at five o'clock, completely soaked. This mishap and information about the bad condition of the roads leading to Batangas persuaded me to use the *jamaca* again, although I regretted this later as these natives were very different from those of Majaijay and Lucban, walking so slowly and unwillingly that I soon lost hope of reaching Batangas by noon to enable me to make a latitude observation. It was already one in the afternoon when we arrived in this town, where the *alcalde mayor* and Augustine friars did everything to show themselves prepared to give us all necessary assistance. The former allowed us the use of a small *panco* that had been given him by the commanding officer of the *vintas del corso* and, armed with his falconet, forty muskets, some pikes and eight men, it was left ready for work in the bay the next morning.

This town, lying no more than a quarter of a league from the sea, has more than once felt the need to make preparations against the pirates' brazen attacks. It is equipped with twelve small cannon of calibre from two to half a pound, some falconets or swivel-guns and a considerable number of muskets and pikes for its defence. A kind of square fortification surrounding the church, solidly built of lime and stone with a bastion at each corner, is big enough to receive most of the local population, if attacked, and from it the village opposite can be defended with fire. This consists largely of timber and cane houses and, although its site is level and attractive, it is not as tidy as Tayabas. Its inhabitants, numbering 8,800, make a number of women's waistbands, striped cotton cloth, and tablecloths, from which goods they realize a certain amount. There are few families without a loom in the house. Cotton, cacao, indigo and pepper are profitably cultivated in the district as well, although so far not in great quantity. Although also produced in small amounts, the *sibucao*[1] is said to be of excellent quality. Apart from a very large rice harvest, wheat is grown as well, the product of the whole province being not less than 8,000 *picos*.[2] Stockbreeding is another valuable and widely practised occupation of this province. At the same time it is one of the areas most troubled by the Moros, who never leave this coast in peace. The bay of Maricaban,[3] Balete [Point],[4] Port Galera, Verde Island and all the rivers

---

[1] A small thorny tree, whose wood is so hard that it is used to make nails and tenons, and is therefore useful in boat building. It is also used for dying cloth, as the trunk produces a red dye when boiled.

[2] A Filipino measure of weight equivalent to 63 kilogrammes.

[3] Possibly Port Maricaban, formed by the narrow strait between Maricaban Island and Caban Island off its NW extremity.

[4] The western entrance point of Calapan Bay on the north coast of Mindoro opposite Verde Island.

and points from Marinduque to Mariveles[1] are also havens for these pirates, from whom nothing near the sea is safe.

25 September
Gripped by terror, these inhabitants take anything they see on the water for Moros or their *pancos*. We set out at dawn on the 25th in the *alcalde mayor's* small *panco* for Motocob Point, the eastern entrance point of the bay,[2] Three leagues from the river[3] mouth, already well offshore, two large tree trunks, drifting with the current, were believed to be pirates, until coming closer I could satisfy myself through the glass. We therefore continued towards the point, which we closed at nine o'clock, not without difficulty because of the strong westerly current. Its rocky terrain, almost circular in shape and thickly wooded down to the shore, made it impossible for us to measure a base, but facing us only three to four miles offshore was Verde Island, whose western extremity bore S4°30′W, while the eastern point of Maricaban [Island] bore N86°W, Calumpan Point[4] at the western end of the bay bore N70°45′ while other points on Mindoro and the coast of Luzon offered themselves for this purpose. Arenas Point, on the continuation of this headland towards Galvan [Point] was also in sight, bearing E3°N distant two miles. Although its position in between did not allow us to fix the position of Galvan Point, this had already been well placed by the previous base and accordingly these stretches of coast were fairly well linked. At noon, after we had observed a latitude of 13°37′30″, we calculated the longitude to be 1°34′ west of Manila. Having completed the [round of] bearings, we returned, taking soundings along the coast, postponing the measurement of the base later at a suitable spot. When we were a cable off Motocob Point the depth was twenty-five fathoms, but when we approached to half a cable offshore it dropped to eighteen. Keeping this distance offshore the depth continued to decrease to fourteen, thirteen, eight and six fathoms until we were abreast the small point of Sigueian.[5] Here the coast recedes further, forming a sizeable indentation as far as the river mouth with the same depth of six and five fathoms, sandy ooze, half a cable offshore, but there are frequently depths of thirty, thirty-five and forty fathoms, a cable or more offshore. Close to the river, which has two mouths, there is a large sandbank stretching for more than three cables, which is almost uncovered at low water. The anchorage, which must be on the inner side of Sigueian Point, in the indentation mentioned above, although entirely sheltered from the easterly monsoon, has a considerable disadvantage in that the depth increases rapidly with distance offshore, which probably means that anchors drag in a fresh breeze. However, as one is able to come close inshore an anchor may be placed on the beach, thus avoiding this problem. Having measured a base of 1,008 feet on the beach beside the river mouth, we were able to fix the position of Mocotab Point from it and by repeating the bearings that had already been taken there, we could rely on the accurate placing of those points and the entire bay, linking them also to Mount

---

[1] On the south coast of Bataan Peninsula opposite Corregidor Island.
[2] Mataco Point.
[3] Calumpan River.
[4] Cazador Point, the southern extremity of Calumpan Peninsula.
[5] Pinamucan Point, 5 miles north of Mataco Point.

Tayabas and that of [Mount] Taal or Macolot,[1] to which we took satisfactory bearings from the base.

26 September
Father Fray Melchor Fernández, not content with all the kindness that he had already shown us, decided to accompany us very early, and thus, having set out at six in the morning, we arrived easily at Bauan by ten. In this town, which lies at the head of the same [Batangas] bay, very close to the beach, we had another opportunity to make a latitude observation, when I went to the beach at noon, the result of which was 13°46′52″. As its situation was even more suitable for measuring a base we did so using the same points as on the previous day. After our meal we continued on our way towards Taal[2] and, after arriving there at nightfall, we wished only to rest and make the necessary preparations for the following day's work.

27 September
The very strong westerly breeze blowing at dawn on the 27th did not allow any work at sea. Even without this obstacle it would not have been easy to find any suitable vessels for that purpose. A base of 1,230 feet, measured on the beach of this bay, was enough to ratify the position of Cape Santiago and confirm that of Maricaban Island and its islets to the east and, finally, to link all the bay with the work of the day before, which reached as far as Calumpan Point. My mission was to conclude here and it only remained for me to observe the latitude and calculate the longitude with the chronometer. The fast moving heavy scud obliged me to keep it in my hand. Close to noon, when I was standing on a log to make the observation, I found that it had stopped. When I looked at it again it had still some hours to run. I was quite sure that I had not knocked it in any way and it was only necessary to give it a slight shake to set it going again. This calmed my fears of some breakdown, which would hardly have been surprising after twelve days of continuous movement on horseback, although I had tried to avoid this by carrying it carefully in my hand at all times.[3] At last, having made a reliable latitude observation of 13°52′50″ and having taken hour angles at two o'clock, it was then necessary to remain there until the following day to repeat these altitudes, which would serve not only to determine longitude, but later in Manila the chronometer's rate and error.

28 September
On the morning of the 28th, having sent the theodolite and chain [upstream] by river,[4] we set out by land for Lake Taal or Bongbong Lagoon, where we measured a base of 330 feet on its SW shore which sufficed to plot all the areas not concealed from our view by Volcano Island, lying approximately in the middle [of the lagoon].

---

[1] A 957-metre height on the SE shore of Lake Taal: see p. 498. Present-day Mount Taal is the active volcano on Volcano Island in the centre of Lake Taal.
[2] In the NE corner of Balayan Bay on the eastern bank of the Pansipit River.
[3] The fact than Arnold number 11 stopped is hardly surprising since it was probably a box chronometer (see p. 341, n. 3 above) and so not suitable for transporting long distances over rugged countryside.
[4] Pansipit River, which connects Balayan Bay with Lake Taal.

This amounted to no less than the entire northern part of the lagoon, which is almost circular in appearance, with a diameter of four leagues. Furthermore it is so deep that barely beyond its shores no bottom could be obtained with our twenty-five fathom lead-line, according to the fishermen who work there. Mount Taal or Mocotab, which rises from the very SE shore of the lagoon, is so steep that it only presents a magnificent sheer wall. With the intention of sounding the river that flows into the [Balayan] bay we went back along it in the *banquillas*.[1] Its depth, remaining almost constant at one and one and a half fathoms from the mouth of the lagoon, diminishes towards the end so that during the dry season the natives can cross it on foot near the Casaisai sanctuary on its eastern bank. Its greatest width is no more than one-third of a cable today, but the old bed, that is before the eruption of the year '54, was not less than one and a half to two cables wide and is now thickly scattered with small houses and adorned by fertile rice fields. We did not fail to establish its shape as we went along by means of compass headings and estimated distances and, as its mouths have been plotted from both bases, there will be no doubt as to the direction of these and the length of the river, which would be approximately one league.

After returning to the town [Taal] we took altitudes at the same time as on the previous day, in the same place, and thus we were able to start on our return to Manila by way of the lagoon itself, having acquired some information about the Taal anchorage, as the breeze, still strong from the west, prevented us from examining it ourselves.[2] The entire area or indentation between Lipo Point[3] and the river mouth seems as if specially designed to anchor in during easterlies, as do the Visayan vessels that visit [this anchorage]. The depth appears to be nine, ten and twelve fathoms. The need for vigilance and precautions against the Moros raids, imposed on this town, is no less than for the others, although its position on an elevated site which dominates the beach and river mouth gives it a certain degree of protection, as it is defended by two little forts, now in fairly poor condition, a few small calibre cannon and a watch-tower constructed at the expense of the town, although at present this is more or less abandoned on the beach. Not long ago Taal was the principal town of the province, but Batangas now holds this position. Its population is still larger, being not less than 10,000 people, but these, as in the other towns of which we have spoken, are not all inhabitants of the town, as many live among the fields. Their industry in weaving and agriculture is no less than that of Batangas, and the climate is much cooler, with better air.

We left the town at two in the afternoon and, with some difficulty because of the rapid current in the river, were able to get out into the lagoon. The breeze, still strong from the west, carried us by five o'clock to the shore of the island which, lying not far away in the middle of the lagoon, stretches from east to west with a length of about two leagues. [On the island] stands the famous Taal or Bongbong volcano, which I proposed to climb. Indeed, despite the short time remaining of the day, the slope on this southern side being fairly gentle and of no great height, it was easy to reach the crater in little over twenty minutes. It could even have taken less had it not been for

---

[1] A dugout Filipino canoe, fitted with outriggers, propelled by oars, paddles or a quadrangular sail.
[2] The anchorage for small craft off the mouth of the Pansipit River.
[3] A point about halfway between Cazador Point and Taal.

the fissures and crevices running vertically to be found at every step. A sight as interesting as it was horrifying met our eyes and although the lack of time and knowledge of the subject did not allow us to reap any great benefit from it, our fatigue was at least rewarded by the satisfaction of our curiosity.

A large crater, roughly triangular in shape, the longest side of which would be at least 600 feet, a sulphur coloured lake at the bottom where we could see the seething and boiling of the water, of which the steam and unbearable smell of sulphur were sufficient evidence, were other matters requiring the attentive examination of an intelligent observer. We found ourselves with no way to measure the depth. We tried to achieve this by throwing stones and seeing how long they took to fall, but they disappeared in the steam and therefore the sound as they struck bottom could not be heard. A rough calculation led us to estimate the depth as 800 *varas* and I believe this to be not far from the truth. It was difficult to guess how far the other two arms of the lagoon ran, but they extended one westward and the other to the SE, but as there is at the western head of the island another small pyramidal hill which has erupted, according to information, on the same occasions as this one, it may be inferred that the arm extending in that direction communicates with it. It seems equally likely, or necessary, that the inner lagoon has the same level as the outer one. We spent no longer than ten minutes at the crater and, having collected some pieces of lava and other specimens to be found there, we descended to the beach at dusk and continued on our way to Tanaguan,[1] which we reached at ten o'clock at night.

As we had not yet finished the survey of the lagoon, it was necessary to return to the beach at dawn where, having taken some bearings and transits and estimated some distances, we had to content ourselves with these figures, because of the lack of space for a base, to plot the part that we had not seen since measuring the previous base. Before the eruption of the volcano in '54, the town of Tanaguan stood right on the shore of the lagoon but having been destroyed by the ash, as were Sala, Lipa and Taal, they were all moved to the sites they now occupy one and one and a half leagues from it. This prodigious eruption is notorious in the islands. Its deafening roar was heard and cinders fell even in the remotest provinces. In the nearer ones it caused great destruction and, contaminating the air with the putrefaction of the almost boiled fish, which were thrown from the Taal lagoon onto its beaches, there followed epidemics which ravaged the surrounding parts. These and other circumstances are recorded in the Taal archives, from which I have extracted them, but the need for brevity does not allow me to linger on the subject, nor to speak of two earlier eruptions, one having taken place in the year '16.

29 September
We left Tanaguan at nine in the morning and passed through San Pablo to Calauan[2] and Bay, where we measured a short base, the waterlogged state of the terrain allowing no room to extend it. Here we were also able to comply with our *comandante*'s orders and repeat some bearings and transits at Los Baños[3] and on the intermediate

---

[1] Talisay on the north shore of Lake Taal.
[2] About midway between San Pablo and Bay.
[3] Near the southern shore of Laguna de Bay, 3 miles WNW of Calauan.

coast, spending the night at the latter town. Our botanist, Don Tadeo Haenke, had just arrived here the day before and, after carrying out some experiments with the thermal waters, he was preparing to set out for the cinnamon plantation at Calaguá[1] and from there to the volcano at Taal. From him I had the pleasure of hearing of the health of all our companions in Manila. With this double satisfaction I left for Binan in the morning, where I found ready the *guilalo* of Padre Herenas and, after resting all day, was able to reach Manila at seven in the evening of the 2nd, having taken some bearings from the Guadalupe tower[2] on the way.

3 October

Having then calculated the altitudes observed on the 27th and 28th, the chronometer showed a daily loss of 16″ over a period of two days, the same as found in Manila on arrival by comparison with the other chronometers. Consequently we may consider correct the meridian difference of 11′19″ and 11′22″ [east of Manila] given by the said altitudes observed on those days on the beach at Taal.

---

[1] A transcription error for Calauan, which was visited by Pineda in April: see p. 403 above. Malaspina makes no mention of this further expedition by Haenke.

[2] Not identified.

WORKS CITED IN VOLUME II

Antón Solé, Pablo, 'Los padrones de cumplimiento pascual de la expedición Malaspina: 1790-1794', in *La expedición Malaspina (1789–1794): bicentario de la salida de Cádiz*, Cádiz, 1991, pp. 173-238.

Antonio, Nicolás, *Bibliotheca hispana nova*, 2 vols, Madrid, 1788.

Archer, Christon, 'Esteban José Martínez', *Dictionary of Canadian Biography*, IV, Toronto, 1979, pp. 519-21.

Archer, Christon, 'Pedro Alberni', *Dictionary of Canadian Biography*, V, Toronto, 1983, pp. 10-11.

Archer, Christon I., 'Seduction before Sovereignty: Spanish Efforts to Manipulate the Natives in their Claims to the Northwest Coast', in Robin Fisher and Hugh Johnston, eds, *From Maps to Metaphors: the Pacific World of George Vancouver*, Vancouver, 1993, pp. 127-59.

Archer, Christon, 'The Transient Presence: a Re-appraisal of Spanish Attitudes towards the Northwest Coast in the Eighteenth Century', *BC Studies*, #18, Summer 1973, pp. 3-32.

Arias Divito, Juan Carlos, *Las expediciones científicas durante el siglo XVIII: Expedición botánica de Nueva España*, Madrid, 1968.

Asenjo Sedano, Carlos, 'El misterioso navegante descubridor Lorenzo Ferrer Maldonado, siglos XVI-XVII', *Revista de historia naval*, Madrid, 1988, VI, pp. 17-25.

Ballesteros Beretta, Antonio, *Catálogo de la colección de Don Juan Bautista Muñoz*, Madrid, 1954.

Barreiro-Meiro, Roberto, ed., *Colección de diarios y relaciones para la historia de los viajes y descubrimientos. VI: Esteban José Martínez (1742–1789)*, Madrid, 1964.

Barrington, Daines, *The Probability of Reaching the North Pole Discussed*, London, 1775.

Barrow, John, *A Chronological History of Voyages into the Arctic Regions ...* , London, 1818.

Bayly, William, *The Original Astronomical Observations made in the course of a Voyage to the Northern Pacific Ocean ... in His Majesty's Ships the Resolution and Discovery*, London, 1782.

Beaglehole, J. C., ed., *The Journals of Captain James Cook on His Voyages of Discovery. II. The Voyage of the* Resolution *and* Adventure, *1772–1775*, Hakluyt Society, extra ser. 35, Cambridge, 1961 (repr. 1969).

Beaglehole, J. C., ed., *The Journals of Captain James Cook on His Voyages of Discovery. III. The Voyage of the* Resolution *and* Discovery, *1776–1780*, 2 vols, Hakluyt Society, extra ser. 36a-36b, Cambridge, 1967 (repr. 1969).

Beals, Herbert K., ed. and transl., *For Honor and Country: The Diary of Bruno De Hezeta*, Oregon Historical Society, Portland, Oreg., 1985.

Beals, Herbert K., ed. and transl., *Juan Pérez on the Northwest Coast*, Oregon Historical Society, Portland, Oreg., 1989.

Beechey, F. W., *Narrative of a Voyage to the Pacific and Beering's Strait ... in the Years 1825, 26, 27, 28*, London, 1831.

Benjamin, Sandra, *The World of Benjamin of Tudela: A Medieval Mediterranean Travelogue*, Madison, Calif. and London, 1995.

[Beresford, William], *A Voyage round the World 1785–1788 by Captain George Dixon*, London, 1789.

Blair, E. H., and Robertson, J. A., *The Philippine Islands, 1493–1898*, 55 vols, Cleveland, Ohio, 1903-9.

Blanco, Manuel, *Flora de Filipinas, según el sistema sexual linneo*, 2 vols, Manila, 1837 (enlarged into 4 vols, Manila, 1877-83; repr. 1944).

Bolton, Herbert E., *Rim of Christendom: A Biography of Eusebio Francisco Kino*, New York, 1936.

Boturini Benaduci, Lorenzo, *Idea de una nueva historia de América*, Madrid, 1746.

Boxer, C. R., *Fidalgos in the Far East, 1550–1770*, London, 1969.

Boxer, C. R., 'Piracy in the South China Sea, 1550-1950', *History Today*, December, 1980, pp. 40-44.

Boxer, C. R., *South China in the Sixteenth Century*, Hakluyt Society, 2nd ser. 106, London, 1953.

Braga, J. M., *The Western Pioneers and their Discovery of Macao*, Macau, 1949.

British Columbia Pilot, 9th edn, vol. I, Taunton, 1979.

Broc, Numa, *La Géographie des philosophes: géographes et voyageurs français au XVIIIe siècle*, Paris, 1974.

Brosses, Charles de, *Histoire des navigations aux Terres Australes*, Paris, 1756.

Brunal-Perry, Omaira, *Architectural Sketches of the Spanish Era Forts of Guam*, Guam, 1994.

Buache, Philippe, 'Carte des nouvelles découvertes au nord de la Mer du Sud', Paris, 1752.

Buache, Philippe, *Considérations géographiques et physiques sur les nouvelles découvertes au nord de la Grande Mer*, Paris, 1753.

Buache de la Neuville, Jean-Nicolas, *Considérations géographiques et physiques sur les nouvelles découvertes au nord-est de l'Asie et au nord-ouest de l'Amérique*, Paris, 1781.

Buache de la Neuville, Jean-Nicolas, 'Nouvelle Carte de la partie septentrionale du globe', Paris, 1781.

Burriel Marcos, Andrés, *Noticia de la California*, 3 vols, Madrid, 1757.

Buzeta, Manuel, OSA, *Diccionario geográfico, estadístico, histórico de las islas Filipinas*, 2 vols, Madrid, 1850.

Cabello, Paz, 'The Ethnographic Collections: A Special Legacy of the Spanish Presence on the Northwest Coast, 1774-1792', in Inglis, *Spain and the North Pacific Coast*, pp. 137-54.

Carano, P., and Sánchez, P. C., *A Complete History of Guam*, Rutland, Vt., and Tokyo, 1964.

Carver, Jonathan, *Travels through the Interior Parts of North America*, London, 1778.
Castro, Agustín María de, *Osario venerable*, Manila, 1780.
Cerezo Martínez, Ricardo, *La expedición Malaspina 1789–1794*. Tomo II: *Diario general del viaje por Alejandro Malaspina*, 2 parts, Madrid, 1990.
Cevallos, Ciriaco, *Disertación del Teniente de Navío D. Ciriaco Cevallos, embarcado en la corbeta Atrevida sobre la navegación al Asia por el NE*, Cádiz, 1797.
Chapman, Allan, 'The Achievement of Jesse Ramsden', in R. G. W. Anderson *et al.*, eds, *Making Instruments Count,* Aldershot, 1993, pp. 418-30.
Chappe d'Auteroche, Jean Baptiste, *Voyage en Californie pour l'observation de Vénus sur le disque du soleil*, Paris, 1972.
Chapuis, Olivier, *A la mer comme au ciel*, Paris, 1999.
Chinese Repository, The, VII, October, 1828.
Christy, Miller, ed., *The Voyages of Captain Luke Foxe and Captain Thomas James of Bristol*, Hakluyt Society, 1st ser. 88, 89, 2 vols, London, 1894.
[Cluny, Alexander] *The American Traveller*, London, 1769.
Coates, Austin, *A Macao Narrative*, London, 1978.
Coates, Austin, *Prelude to Hong Kong*, London, 1966. [Rpt. as *Macao and the British 1637–1842: Prelude to Hong Kong*, Hong Kong, 1988.]
Cock, Randolph, 'Precursors of Cook: The Voyages of the *Dolphin,* 1764-68', *The Mariner's Mirror*, 85, 1999, pp. 30-52.
Cook, James, *A Voyage towards the South Pole and round the World*, 2 vols, London, 1777.
Cook, James, and King, James, *A Voyage to the Pacific Ocean … for making Discoveries in the Northern Hemisphere*, 3 vols, London, 1784.
Cook, Warren, *Flood Tide of Empire: Spain and the Pacific Northwest*, New Haven and London, 1973.
Cooke, Alan, and Holland, Clive, *The Exploration of Northern Canada 500 to 1920: A Chronology*, Toronto, 1978.
Cortés, Hernán, *Cartas de relación*, Sevilla, 1522.
Coxe, William, *Account of the Russian Discoveries between Asia and America*, London, 1780.
Coxe, William, *A Comparative View of the Russian Discoveries with those made by Captains Cook and Clerke*, London, 1787.
Crozet, Julien Marie, *Crozet's Voyage to Tasmania, New Zealand, the Ladrone Islands, and the Philippines in the Years 1771–1772*, trans. H. L. Roth, London, 1891.
Cruikshank, Bruce, *Filipiniana in Madrid,* Honolulu, 1984.
Cummins, J. S., ed., *Christianity and Missions 1450–1800,* Aldershot, 1997.
Cummins, J. S., 'Pox and Paranoia in Renaissance Europe', *History Today*, August, 1988, pp. 28-35.
Cummins, J. S., ed., *Sucesos de las Islas Filipinas by Antonio de Morga*, Hakluyt Society, 2nd ser. 140, Cambridge, 1971.
Cutter, Charles R., *The Legal Culture of Northern New Spain 1700–1810*, Albuquerque, 1995.
Cutter, Donald C., *California in 1792: A Spanish Naval Visit*, Norman, Okla., and London, 1990.
Cutter, Donald C., 'California, Training Ground for Spanish Naval Heroes', *California Historical Society Quarterly*, 40, June 1961, pp. 109-22.

Cutter, Donald, 'José Cardero: Proto artist of the Pacific Coast', paper given at the Vancouver Conference on Exploration and Discovery, Simon Fraser University, 1992, in Special Collections, The Library, University of British Columbia, Spam 22863.

Cutter, Donald, ed., *Journal of Tomás de Suria of his Voyage with Malaspina to the North-West Coast of America*, Fairfield, Wash., 1980.

Cutter, Donald C., *Malaspina and Galiano: Spanish Voyages to the Northwest Coast, 1791 and 1792*, Vancouver, 1991.

Cutter, Donald C., 'Pedro Alberni y los primeros experimentos de agricultura científica en la costa Noroeste del Pacífico', *Revista de historia naval*, V, 18, 1987, pp. 41–55.

Cutter, Donald C., 'Spain and the Oregon Coast', in Thomas Vaughan, ed., *The Western Shore: Oregon Country Essays Honoring the American Revolution*, Portland, Oreg., 1976, pp. 28–46.

Dahlgren, E. W., *Were the Hawaiian Islands Visited by the Spaniards before their Discovery by Captain Cook in 1778?*, Stockholm, 1916.

Dalrymple, Alexander, *Memoir of a Map of the Lands around the North-Pole*, London, 1789.

Dampier, William, *A New Voyage Round the World*, London, 1697.

David, Andrew C. F., 'John McCluer', *Oxford Dictionary of National Biography* (forthcoming).

David, Andrew, et al., eds, *Charts and Coastal Views of Captain Cook's Voyages. III. The Voyage of the* Resolution *and* Discovery*, 1776–1780*, Hakluyt Society, extra ser. 46, London, 1997.

Dawson, Warren R., ed., *The Banks Letters*, London, 1958.

de Beer, Gavin, *The Sciences were never at War*, London, 1960.

de Laguna, Frederica, 'Tligit', in *Handbook of North American Indians*, 7, Smithsonian Institution, Washington, D.C., 1990, pp. 203–28.

de Laguna, Frederica, 'Tlingit: People of the Wolf and Raven', in William Fitzhugh and Aron Crowell, *Crossroads of Continents: Cultures of Siberia and Alaska*, Washington, D.C., 1988, pp. 58–63.

de Laguna, Frederica, *Under Mount Saint Elias: The History and Culture of the Yakutat Tlingit*, Smithsonian Contributions to Anthropology, 7, pt 1, Washington, D.C., 1972.

Delisle, Guillaume, 'Carte du Canada ou de la Nouvelle France', Paris, 1703.

Dermigny, Louis, *La Chine et l'occident: le commerce à Canton au XVIIIe siècle, 1719–1833*, 4 vols, Paris, 1964.

Díaz-Trechuelo, M. L., *La Real Compañía de Filipinas, 1785–1834*, Sevilla, 1965.

Didier Robert de Vaugondy, *Mémoire sur les pays de l'Asie et de l'Amérique*, Paris, 1774.

Dixon, George, *Remarks on the Voyages of John Meares*, London, 1790.

Dolan, Ronald E., ed., *The Philippines: A Country Study*, Washington, D.C., 1993.

Driver, Marjorie G., ed., *The Guam Diary of Naturalist Antonio de Pineda*, Guam, 1990.

Dunmore, John, ed., *The Journal of Jean-François del Galaup de la Pérouse, 1785–1788*, 2 vols, Hakluyt Society, 2nd ser. 179-180, London, 1994.

Earnshaw, Thomas, *Longitude: An Appeal to the Public*, London, 1808.

Ellis, Henry, *A Voyage to Hudson's Bay by the* Dobbs Galley *and* California*, In the Years 1746 and 1747, For Discovering a North West Passage*, London, 1748.

Engstrand, Iris H. W., 'Antonio Pineda and his Environmental Impact Survey of 1791', in *Colonial Latin American Historical Review,* 9, 2000, pp. 487-508.
Engstrand, Iris H. W., ed. and trans., *Noticias de Nutka: An Account of Nootka Sound in 1792 by José Mariano Moziño,* Seattle, 1991.
Engstrand, Iris Wilson, *Royal Officer in Baja California: Joaquín Velázquez Cárdenas de León,* Los Angeles, 1976.
Engstrand, Iris H. W., *Spanish Scientists in the New World,* Seattle and London, 1981.
Espinosa y Tello, José, *Memorias sobre las observaciones astronómicas, hechas por los navegantes españoles en distintos lugares del globo,* 2 vols, Madrid, 1809.
Espinosa y Tello, José, *Memoria sobre las observaciones astronómicos, que han servido de fundamento á las cartas de la costa NO de América,* Madrid, 1805.
Fernández, Pablo, *Dominicos donde nace el sol,* Barcelona, 1958.
Fernández de Navarette, Martín, *Biblioteca marítima española,* 2 vols, Madrid, 1851.
Fernández de Navarette, Martín, 'Examen de la relación de Lorenzo Ferrer Maldonado sobre el descubrimiento del estrecho de Anián', in Miguel Salvá and Pedro Sainz de Baranda, eds., *Colección de documents inéditos para la historia de España,* XV, Madrid, 1849, pp. 71-101.
[Fernández de Navarrete, Martín], Introduction to *Relación del viage hecho por las goletas Sutil y Mexicana en el año 1792 para reconocer el Estrecho de Fuca,* Madrid, 1802.
Fireman, Janet R., *The Spanish Royal Corps of Engineers in the Western Borderlands.* Glendale, Calif., 1977, pp. 93-136.
Ferrer Maldonado, Lorenzo, *Imagen del mundo sobre la esfera, cosmografía, y geografía teórica de planetas y arte de navegar,* Alcalá, 1626 (posthumous).
Findlay, Alexander G., *A Directory for the Navigation of the Pacific Ocean,* 2 vols, London, 1851.
Fisher, Robin, and Johnston, Hugh, eds, *From Maps to Metaphors: the Pacific World of George Vancouver,* Vancouver, 1993.
Foust, Clifford, *Rhubarb: The Wonder Drug,* Princeton, 1992.
Fry, Howard T., *Alexander Dalrymple and the Expansion of British Trade,* London, 1970.
Furber, Holden, *Rival Empires of Trade in the Orient, 1600–1800,* Minneapolis and Oxford, 1976.
Fuster, Justo Pastor, *Biblioteca Valenciana,* Valencia, 1830.
Gibson, James, 'Nootka and Nutria: Spain and the Maritime Fur Trade of the NW coast', in Mercedes Palau Baquero and Antonio Orozco Acuaviva, eds, *Malaspina '92: Primeras jornadas internacionales,* Cádiz, 1994, pp. 137-160
Gibson, James R., *Otter Skins, Boston Ships, and China Goods,* Montreal and London, 1992.
Gillispie, Charles C., ed., *Dictionary of Scientific Biography,* New York, 1970-.
González, Pedro María, *Tratado de las enfermedades de la gente de mar, en que se exponen sus causas y los medios de precaverlas,* Madrid, 1805.
González Cabrera Bueno, José, *Navegación especulativa y práctica,* Manila, 1734 (facsimile edition ed. W. M. Mathes, Madrid, 1970).
González Claverán, Virginia, 'Antonio Pineda: Naturalist and Pre-Archaeologist', in Inglis, *Spain and the North Pacific Coast,* pp. 60-68.

González Claverán, Virginia, *La expedición científica de Malaspina en Nueva España (1789–1794)*, Mexico City, 1988.
González Claverán, Virginia, *Malaspina en Acapulco*, Madrid, 1989.
González García, Pedro, et al., *Archivo General de Indias – Los archivos españoles*, Madrid, 1995.
Gough, Barry, 'George Dixon', *Dictionary of Canadian Biography*, IV, Toronto, 1979, pp. 217-19.
Gough, Barry, 'Nathaniel Portlock', *Dictionary of Canadian Biography*, V, Toronto, 1983, p. 686.
Gould, R. T., *The Marine Chronometer*, London, 1923.
Guillermo, Artemio R. and May Kyi Win, *Historical Dictionary of the Philippines*, London, 1987.
Haenke, Tadeo, *Reliquiae Haenkeanae seu descriptiones et icones plantarum, quas ... in insulis Phillipinis [sic] et Marianis collegit Thaddeus Haenke*, Prague, 1827.
Harland, John, *Seamanship in the Age of Sail*, London, 1984.
Hart, Catherine Poupeney, 'A Personal View of the Northwest Coast: the Journal of Tomás de Suria', in *To the Totem Shore: The Spanish Presence on the Northwest Coast*, Madrid, 1986, pp. 176-89.
Hart, Catherine Poupeney, *Relations de l'expédition Malaspina aux confins de l'empire espagnol*, Longueil, Québec, 1987.
Hayes, Derek, *Historical Atlas of the Pacific Northwest*, Seattle, 1999.
Hawkesworth, John, ed., *An Account of the Voyages undertaken by the Order of His Present Majesty for Making Discoveries in the Southern Hemisphere*, 3 vols, London, 1773.
Henry, John Frazier, *Early Maritime Artists of the Pacific Northwest Coast, 1741–1841*, Seattle, 1984.
Higueras Rodríguez, María Dolores, *Catálogo crítico de los documentos de la expedición Malaspina (1789–1794) del Museo Naval*, 3 vols, Madrid, 1985-94.
Higueras Rodríguez, María Dolores, ed., *La expedición Malaspina 1789–1794. Tomo IX: Diario general del viaje de la corbeta Atrevida por José Bustamante y Guerra*, Madrid, 1999.
Higueras Rodríguez, María Dolores, and Martín-Merás, María Luisa, transl. John Kendrick, 'The Malaspina Expedition on the Northwest Coast of North America in 1791 [and 1792]', in Inglis, *Spain and the North Pacific Coast*, pp. 181-97.
Higueras Rodríguez, María Dolores, and Pimentel Igea, Juan, eds, *La expedición Malaspina, 1789–94. Tomo V: Antropología y noticias etnográficas*, Madrid, 1993.
Holm, Bill, 'Cultural Exchange across the Gulf of Alaska: Eighteenth Century Tlingit and Pacific Eskimo Art in Spain', in José Luis Peset, ed., *Culturas de la costa noroeste de América*, Madrid, 1989, pp. 105-13.
Home, R. W., *Electricity and Experimental Physics in 18th-century Europe*, Aldershot, 1992.
Horsburgh, James, *India Directory*, 3rd edn, London, 1827.
Howay, Frederic W., ed., *Voyages of the Columbia to the Northwest Coast 1787–1790 and 1790–1793*, Massachusetts Historical Society, Boston, 1941.
Howse, Derek, and Hutchinson, Beresford, *The Clocks and Watches of Captain James Cook*. Antiquarian Horological Society, London, 1969.
Hurtado de Mendoza, Diego, *The War in Granada*, translated with an introduction by Martin Shuttleworth, London, 1982.

Ibáñez y García, Luis, *History of the Marianas, Caroline and Palau Islands,* trans. Marjorie G. Driver, Guam, 1992.

Ibáñez Montoya, María Victoria, *La expedición Malaspina, 1789–1794.* Tomo IV: *Trabajos científicos y correspondencia de Tadeo Haenke,* Madrid, 1992.

Inglis, Robin, 'Lapérouse 1786: A French Naval Visit to Alaska', in Stephen Haycox, James K. Barnett and Caedmon Liburd, eds, *Enlightenment and Exploration in the North Pacific, 1741–1805,* Seattle, 1997, pp. 49–64

Inglis, Robin, 'Maquinna of Nootka: Portrait of an Indian Chief on the Edge of the Empire', in Alejandro R. Díez Torre, Tomás Mallo, Daniel Pacheco Fernández, eds, *De la ciencia ilustrada a la ciencia romántica: Actas de las II Jornadas sobre España y las expediciones científicas en América y Filipinas,* Madrid, 1995, pp. 32–52.

Inglis, Robin, ed., *Spain and the North Pacific Coast: Essays in Recognition of the Bicentennial of the Malaspina Expedition 1791–1792,* Vancouver, 1992.

[Jefferys, Thomas], 'Chart comprising Greenland with the Countries and Islands about Baffins Bay and part of Hudsons Bay', London, 1775.

Jones, Oakah L., 'The Spanish Occupation of Nookah Sound, 1790–1795', MA thesis, University of Oklahoma, 1960.

Joppien, Rüdiger, and Smith, Bernard, *The Art of Captain Cook's Voyages,* 3 vols, New Haven and London, 1985–8.

Kandert, Joseph, 'Catalogue of Ethnographic Collections of Tadéus Haenke', *Annals of the Náprstek Museum 13,* Prague, 1985, pp. 201–15.

Keaton, G. W., 'International Status of Macao before 1887', in *Chinese Social and Political Science Review,* XI, Peking, 1927, pp. 404–13.

Kendrick, John, *Alejandro Malaspina – Portrait of a Visionary,* Montreal and Kingston, 1991.

Kendrick, John, 'End of the Northern Mystery: the Spanish in Juan de Fuca and Beyond, 1790–1792', in Inglis, *Spain and the North Pacific Coast,* pp. 100–110.

Kendrick, John, trans. and ed., *The Voyage of the Sutil and Mexicana 1792: The Last Spanish Exploration of the Northwest Coast of America,* Spokane, 1991.

Lamb, W. Kaye, *George Vancouver, A Voyage of Discovery to the North Pacific Ocean,* 4 vols, Hakluyt Society, 2nd ser. 163–6, London, 1984.

Lamb, W. Kaye, 'The Mystery of Mrs Barkley's Diary', *British Columbia Historical Quarterly,* 6, 1942, pp. 31–59.

Lamb, W. Kaye, and Bartroli, Tomás, 'James Hanna and John Henry Cox; the first Maritime Trader and his Sponsor', in *B.C. Studies,* #84, Winter 1989–90, pp. 3–36.

Landín Carrasco, Amancio, 'Mourelle de la Rúa in the South Sea', in *Spanish Pacific from Magellan to Malaspina,* Madrid, 1988, pp. 133–44.

Langdon, Steve J., *The Native People of Alaska,* Anchorage, 1993.

Las Barras y de Aragón, Francisco de, 'Noticia de la vida y obras de D. José Antonio Alzate y Ramírez', *Boletín de la Real Sociedad Española de la Historia Natural,* sección biológica 48, 1950, pp. 339–53.

Le Gentil de la Galaisière, Guillaume-Joseph, *Voyage dans les mers de l'Inde,* Paris, 1779–81.

Lim, Hilario, *Memorial to Pius XII,* Manila, 1957

Ljungstedt, Anders, *A Historic Sketch of the Portuguese in China*, Boston, 1836; Hong Kong, 1992.

Lloyd, C. C., 'The Conquest of Scurvy', *British Journal of the History of Science,* 1, 1963, pp. 357-63.

Lo-shu Fu, *A Documentary Chronicle of Sino-Western Relations (1644–1820),* Tucson, 1966.

López Piñero, J. M., 'Los comienzos de las ciencias modernas en España', in *Actas del segundo congreso de historia de la medicina*, 2 vols, Madrid, 1965, I, p. 287.

Magdalena, José Ramón, ed., *Libro de Viajes de Benjamín de Tudela*, Barcelona, 1989.

McDowell, Jim, *Hamatsa: the Enigma of Cannibalism on the Pacific Northwest Coast,* Vancouver, 1997.

Malo de Luque, Eduardo [Duque de Almodóvar], *Historia política de los establecimientos ultramarinos de la naciones europeas,* IV, Madrid, 1788.

Manfredi, Dario, 'An Unknown Episode behind the Northwest Coast Campaign of Malaspina's Expedition', in Inglis, *Spain and the North Pacific Coast,* pp. 119-24.

Marat, Jean-Paul, *Mémoire sur l'électricité médicale*, Paris, 1784.

The Mariner's Handbook, Taunton, 1979.

Martín-Meras, Luisa, 'The Evolution of Spanish Cartography on the Northwest Coast of America', in Inglis, *Spain and the North Pacific Coast,* pp. 18-28.

Martins do Vale, M., *Os portugueses em Macau, 1750–1780,* Macau, 1997.

Masefield, John, ed., *The Voyages of Captain William Dampier,* 2 vols, New York, 1906.

Meares, John, *Voyages made in the Years 1788 and 1789, from China to the North West Coast of America*, London, 1790.

Montero y Vidal, José, *Historia de la piratería muslim-mahometana en Mindanao, Jolo y Borneo,* 2 vols, Madrid, 1880.

Morse, H. B., *Chronicles of the East India Company Trading to China, 1635–1834,* 5 vols, Oxford, 1926.

Mortimer, George, *Observations and Remarks made during a Voyage ... in the brig Mercury commanded by John Cox, Esq,* London, 1791.

Mourelle de la Rúa, Francisco Antonio, 'Journal of a Voyage in 1775', in Daines Barrington, *Miscellanies,* London, 1781, pp. 469-534.

Müller, Gerhard Friedrich, *Voyages from Asia to America for Completing the Discoveries of the North West Coast of America,* London, 1761.

Muñoz Garmendia, Félix, ed., *La expedición Malaspina, 1789–94.* Tomo III: *Diarios y trabajos botánicos de Luis Neé,* Madrid, 1992.

Muñoz, J. B., *Historia del Nuevo Mundo,* I, Madrid, 1793.

Murphy, Robert C., *Oceanic Birds of South America,* 2 vols, New York, 1936.

Murray, Dian H., *Pirates of the South China Coast, 1790–1810,* Stanford, 1987.

Navarro García, Luis, *Don José Gálvez y la Comandancia General de las Provincias Internas del norte de Nueva España,* Sevilla, 1964.

New Catholic Encyclopedia, 17 vols, New York, 1967-79.

Nichelson, William, *Sundry Remarks and Observations made on a Voyage to the East Indies,* 2nd edn, London, 1773.

Nokes, J. Richard, *Almost a Hero: The Voyages of John Meares R.N., to China, Hawaii and the Northwest Coast,* Pullman, Wash., 1998.

Novo y Colson, Pedro, ed., *Viaje político-científico alrededor del mundo por las Corbetas Descubierta y Atrevida, al mando de los capitanes de navío D. Alejandro Malaspina y D. José Bustamante y Guerra desde 1789 a 1794*, Madrid, 1885.

Nunes, Doyce, ed., *The Transit of Venus*, Los Angeles, 1982.

O'Donnell, Hugo, *España en el descubrimiento, conquista y defensa del Mar del Sur*, Madrid, 1992.

Olson, Wallace M., *Through Spanish Eyes: Spanish Voyages to Alaska, 1774–1792*, Auke Bay, Alaska, 2002.

Orth, Donald J., *Dictionary of Alaska Place Names*, Geological Professional Paper 567, Department of the Interior, Washington, D.C., 1967.

Pacific Coasts of Central America and United States Pilot, 9th edition, Taunton, 1995.

Pagden, Anthony, ed. and trans., *Hernán Cortés: Letters from México*, New Haven, 1986.

Pagès, Pierre Marie François, Vicomte de, *Voyage auteur du monde et vers les deux pôles, par terre et par mer*, Paris, 1782.

Palau, Mercedes; Zabala, Aránzazu; Sáiz, Blanca, eds, *Viaje científico y político … Diario del viaje de Malaspina*, Madrid, 1984.

Patrick, Elizabeth Nelson , 'The Salvador Fidalgo Expedition, 1790: the last Spanish Exploration of the Far North Pacific Ocean', unpublished PhD dissertation, University of New Mexico, 1981.

Pedley, Mary Sponberg, *Bel et Utile: the Work of the Robert de Vaugondy Family of Mapmakers*, Tring, 1992.

Phelan, J. L., *Hispanization of the Philippines*, Madison, 1959.

Pierce, Richard, 'John Kendrick', *Dictionary of Canadian Biography*, IV, Toronto, 1979, pp. 410-12.

Pierce, Richard A., *Russian America: A Biographical Dictionary*, Kingston, Ontario and Fairbanks, Alaska, 1990.

Porrúa, Enrique J., ed., *The Diary of Antonio de Tova on the Malaspina Expedition (1789–1794)*, Lewiston, Queenston and Lampeter, 2001.

Portlock, Nathaniel, *A Voyage round the World; and more particularly to the North-West Coast of America*, London, 1789.

Purchas, Samuel, *Hakluytus Posthumus, or Purchas His Pilgrimes*, 20 vols, Glasgow, 1905-7 (reprint of 1625 edn).

Relación del viage hecho por las goletas Sutil y Mexicana en el año 1792 para reconocer el Estrecho de Fuca, Madrid, 1802.

Remarks on the Philippine Islands, and the capital Manila (1819–1822), by an Englishman, Calcutta, 1828.

Rey Tejerina, Arsenio, ed., *Tomàs de Suria a l'expedició Malaspina Alaska 1791*, Valencia, 1995.

Richards, E. G., *Mapping Time: The Calendar and its History*, Oxford, 1998.

Ritzler, R., and Sefrin, P., *Hierarchia catholica medii et recentioris aevi*, VI (1730-1799), Padua, 1958.

Salvá, D. Miguel, and Sainz de Baranda, D. Pedro, eds., *Colección de documentos inéditos para la historia de España*, XV, Madrid, 1849.

Sánchez, Joseph P., *Spanish Bluecoats: The Catalonian Volunteers in Northwestern New Spain, 1767–1810*, Albuquerque, 1990.

Sánchez Carrido, Araceli, *Indios de América del Norte*, Madrid, 1991
Sanz, Carlos, ed., *Australia: su descubrimiento y denominación*, Madrid, 1973.
Sarrailh, Jean, 'La Notion de l'utile dans la culture espagnole à la fin du XVIIIe siècle',
  Bulletin hispanique, 50, 1948, pp. 495-510.
Sayer, Robert, and Bennett, John, *The American Atlas ... by the Late Thomas Jefferys*,
  London, 1776.
Schurz, W. L., *The Manila Galleon*, New York, [1939] 1959.
Seixas y Lovera, Francisco de, *Theatro naval hydrographico ...*, Madrid, 1688.
Sharp, Andrew, *The Discovery of the Pacific Islands*, Oxford, 1960.
Silva y Figueroa, García de, *Comentarios de d. García de Silva y Figueroa de la embajada
  que de parte del rey de España don Felipe III hizo al rey xa Abas de Persia*, Sociedad de
  bibliófilos españoles, 36, 2 vols, Madrid, 1903-5.
Sloane, Hans, *Voyage to Jamaica*, London, 1707.
Sotheby's, *Natural History, Atlases and Travel*, Catalogue 93607, 7 December 1993.
Sotos Serrano, Carmen, *Los pintores de la expedición de Alejandro Malaspina*, 2 vols,
  Madrid, 1982.
Spate, O. H. K., *The Spanish Lake*, Canberra, 1979.
Stählin, J. von, 'Map of the New Northern Archipelago discover'd by the Russians in
  the Seas of Kamtschatka and Anadir', London, 1774
[Strange, James] *James Strange's Journal and Narrative of the Commercial Expedition from
  Bombay to the Northwest Coast of America*, Fairfield, Wash., 1982.
Stix, Hugh, *The Shell*, London, 1978.
Stommel, Henry, *Lost Islands: the Story of Islands that have Vanished from Nautical Charts*,
  Vancouver, 1984.
Streit, Robert, ed., *Bibliotheca missionum*, Aachen, 1916-.
Suttles, Wayne, ed., 'Nootkans of Vancouver Island', *Handbook of North American Indians*,
  7, 'Northwest Coast', Smithsonian Institution, Washington, D.C., 1990, pp.
  391-411.
*Tables Requisite to be used with the Astronomical and Nautical Ephemeris for Finding the
  Latitude and Longitude at Sea*, 2nd rev. edn, London, 1781.
Teixeira, Manuel, *Macau no séc. XVIII*, Macau, 1984.
Thomas, Nicholas, and Berghof, Oliver, eds, *A Voyage round the World* by George
  Forster, 2 vols, Honolulu, 2000.
Thornton, Walter, 'An Account of a Voyage made by Fr. John Riobo as Chaplain of
  His Majesty's Frigates the *Princesa* and *Favorita*', *Catholic Historical Review*, 4, 1918.
Thurman, Michael E., *The Naval Department of San Blas*, Glendale, Calif., 1967.
Torquemada, Fr Juan de, *Monarquía Indiana*, 3 vols, Sevilla, 1615.
Tovell, Freeman, 'Manuel Quimper and the Exploration of the Strait of Juan de Fuca',
  in *Resolution* (Maritime Museum of British Columbia), #14, 1990, pp. 14-21.
Tuck, Gerald, *A Guide to Seabirds on the Ocean Routes*, London, 1980.
Verdun de la Crenne, Jean-René-Antoine de; Borda, Jean-Charles de; Pingré,
  Alexandre-Gui, *Voyage fait par ordre du Roi en 1771 et 1772 en diverses parties de l'Europe,
  de l'Afrique et de l'Amérique, pour vérifier l'utilité de plusieurs méthodes et instrumens
  servant à déterminer la Latitude et la Longitude, ... suivi de recherches pour rectifier les
  cartes hydrographiques, par De Verdun de la Crenne, de Borda, et Pingré*, 2 vols, Paris, 1778.

Viana, Francisco Xavier de, *Diario de viaje,* ed. H. Martínez Montero, 2 vols, Montevideo, 1958.
Vilar, Pierre, *A History of Gold and Money, 1450–1920,* London, 1976.
Vreeland, Nena, *et al.,* eds, *Area Handbook for the Philippines,* Washington, D.C., 1976.
Wagner, Henry R., 'Apocryphal Voyages to the Northwest Coast of America', *Proceedings of the American Antiquarian Society,* n.s., 61, 1931, pp. 179-234.
Wagner, Henry R., *The Cartography of the Northwest Coast of America to the Year 1800,* 2 vols, Berkeley, 1937.
Wagner, Henry R., *Spanish Explorations in the Strait of Juan de Fuca,* Santa Ana, Calif., 1933.
Wagner, Henry R., *Spanish Voyages to the Northwest coast of America in the Sixteenth Century,* San Francisco, 1929.
Waife, S. O., *Notable Medical Books,* Indianapolis, 1976.
Walbran, John T., *British Columbia Coast Names,* Vancouver, 1909.
Wales, William, *Remarks on Mr. Forster's Account of Captain Cook's last Voyage round the World ...,* London, 1778.
Whinnom, K., 'Spanish in the Philippines', *Journal of Oriental Studies,* 1, 1954, pp. 129-94.
Whitehead, Peter J. P., 'Emmanuel Mendes da Costa (1717-91), and the Natural History of Shells (1778)', *Bulletin of the British Museum (Natural History),* 6, 1977, pp. 1-24.
Wilbrecht, Alexander, 'Carte des découvertes faites par les russes et par le capitain anglois Jacques Cook dans la Mer du Sud', St Petersburg(?), 1787.
Williams, Glyndwr, 'An Eighteenth Century Spanish Investigation into the Apocryphal Voyage of Admiral Fonte', *Pacific Historical Review,* 30 (1961), pp. 319-27.
Williams, Glyndwr, *A Voyage round the World in the Years MDCCXL, I, II, II, IV by George Anson,* Oxford, 1974.
Williams, Glyn[dwr], *Voyages of Delusion: the Northwest Passage in the Age of Reason,* London, 2002.
Winter, Alison, *Mesmerism: Powers of Mind in Victorian Britain,* Chicago, 1998.

TRACKS OF THE MALASPINA EXPEDITION – PROPOSED AND ACTUAL 1789–1794